Fifth Edition

Bridges Not Walls

A Book About Interpersonal Communication

Edited by

JOHN STEWART

University of Washington

McGraw-Hill Publishing Company

New York   St. Louis   San Francisco   Auckland   Bogotá   Caracas
Hamburg   Lisbon   London   Madrid   Mexico   Milan   Montreal
New Delhi   Oklahoma City   Paris   San Juan   São Paulo   Singapore
Sidney   Tokyo   Toronto

Bridges Not Walls:
A Book About Interpersonal Communication

1 2 3 4 5 6 7 8 9 0   DOC DOC   8 9 4 3 2 1 0 9

ISBN 0-07-061537-3

This book was set in Goudy Oldstyle and Souvenir Light by University Graphics, Inc.

The editors were Hilary Jackson and Fred Burns;
the designer was Leon Bolognese;
the production supervisor was Valerie A. Sawyer.

R. R. Donnelley & Sons Company was printer and binder.

Library of Congress Cataloging-in-Publication Data

Bridges not walls: a book about interpersonal communication / edited
by John Stewart.—5th ed.
   p.   cm.
  Includes bibliographical references.
  ISBN 0-07-061537-3
  1. Interpersonal communication.   I. Stewart, John Robert, (date).
BF637.C45B74   1990
158′.2—dc20
                        89-36896

COVER PHOTO

Promenade, August Macke, 1913. Städische Galerie Im Lenbachhaus, Munich. Photograph Artothek.

CHAPTER OPENING PHOTO CREDITS
Chapter 1: Christopher of Kirkland; *Chapter 2*: Gale Zucker/Stock, Boston; *Chapter 3*: John Stewart; *Chapter 4*: Phyllis Graber Jensen/Stock, Boston; *Chapter 5*: Ulrike Welsch; *Chapter 6*: Ellis Herwig/The Picture Cube; *Chapter 7*: Richard Wood/The Picture Cube; *Chapter 8*: John Stewart; *Chapter 9*: Hazel Hankin; *Chapter 10*: Ulrike Welsch; *Chapter 11*: Pamela Price/The Picture Cube; *Chapter 12*: Eli Reed/Magnum; *Chapter 13*: Ulrike Welsch; *Chapter 14*: Photo by C. Steven Short, Courtesy of Fawcett; *Chapter 15*: John T. Wood; *Chapter 16*: UPI/Bettmann Newsphotos.

Page 48: Dana Fineman/Sygma

About the Author

John Stewart has been teaching interpersonal communication at the University of Washington since 1969. He attended Centralia (Junior) College and Pacific Lutheran University, then got his M.A. at Northwestern University and completed his Ph.D. at the University of Southern California in 1970. John coordinates the basic interpersonal communication course at the University of Washington and also teaches upper-division and graduate courses. He is currently editor of the *Western Journal of Speech Communication* and provides communication consulting services for engineering and architectural firms. John is married to Kris Chrey, a Seattle attorney, and has two children and two grandchildren.

Books and Men

Imagine yourself in a situation where you are alone, wholly alone on earth, and you are offered one of the two, books or men. I often hear men prizing their solitude, but that is only because there are still men somewhere on earth, even though in the far distance. I knew nothing of books when I came forth from the womb of my mother, and I shall die without books, with another human hand in my own. I do, indeed, close my door at times and surrender myself to a book, but only because I can open the door again and see a human being looking at me.

Martin Buber

About the Author

John Stewart has been teaching interpersonal communication at the University of Washington since 1969. He attended Centralia (Junior) College and Pacific Lutheran University, then got his M.A. at Northwestern University and completed his Ph.D. at the University of Southern California in 1970. John coordinates the basic interpersonal communication course at the University of Washington and also teaches upper-division and graduate courses. He is currently editor of the *Western Journal of Speech Communication* and provides communication consulting services for engineering and architectural firms. John is married to Kris Chrey, a Seattle attorney, and has two children and two grandchildren.

Books and Men

Imagine yourself in a situation where you are alone, wholly alone on earth, and you are offered one of the two, books or men. I often hear men prizing their solitude, but that is only because there are still men somewhere on earth, even though in the far distance. I knew nothing of books when I came forth from the womb of my mother, and I shall die without books, with another human hand in my own. I do, indeed, close my door at times and surrender myself to a book, but only because I can open the door again and see a human being looking at me.

Martin Buber

Contents

Preface

This edition of *Bridges Not Walls* maintains the approach and basic format that have characterized the previous four editions. It also offers a new chapter on relationships and twenty other readings that either replace or supplement materials used before. The book continues to be designed primarily for college students enrolled in interpersonal communication classes. Much of the material is also suitable for off-campus communication workshops and seminars. Chapters address all the topics typically included in an interpersonal communication course, and readings are drawn from a wide range of disciplines, including communication, clinical and social psychology, philosophy, and organizational behavior.

The book retains its humanistic perspective, which means that its editor and most of its contributors are convinced that human beings differ from nonhumans, and that the differences are significant. The communication theory presented here is a relational or transactional one. Communication is treated as an inherently mutual process, one that is not reducible to "sending and receiving" or "codes and messages." We emphasize how communicators co-create or negotiate understanding-in-context.

This is a book for persons who want practical ideas and skills that will help them communicate more effectively with their spouses, friends, family, and coworkers. But unlike most self-help literature, it resists the tendency to ignore conceptual issues and to reduce interpersonal effectiveness to techniques or formulas. The authors represented here recognize that there is much more to good communication than simply being "open and honest." For example, there are thought-provoking discussions of the nature of interpersonal contact, self-awareness, person perception, listening, disclosure, and confirmation in Chapters 1, 2, 5, 6, 7, 8, and 9, and three well-developed philosophies of communication in Part 5. The book also includes systematic treatments of verbal and nonverbal communicating, conflict, male-female communication and intercultural contacts, but no reading claims to offer the definitive "six steps" or "twelve easy techniques" for guaranteed success. The editor and the authors emphasize that the unique situation, the constancy of change, and especially the element of human choice all make it impossible to design and execute a purely technical approach to *human* relationships.

This point is rooted in the book's definition of its subject matter. *Bridges Not Walls* does not define interpersonal communication as something that only happens in face-to-face settings, during discussions of weighty topics, or in long-term intimate relationships. Instead, the term "interpersonal" designates a quality, type, or kind of communication that emerges between people whenever they are able to highlight in their speaking and listening aspects of what makes them human. The editor's introduction in Chapter 1 explains this definition and clarifies how subsequent readings extend and develop it.

Throughout the book the point is made that different qualities or levels of interpersonal contact are possible or appropriate in different situations. "More" interpersonal communication is *not* always "better." We do argue, though, that in most cases our personal, educational, and professional lives could profit from increased interpersonal contact.

Readings in Chapters 1, 2, 3, 5, 6, 9, and 16 also emphasize that communication is more than just a way to get things done: Who we are as persons emerges in our contacts with others. I discuss this as the "person building" function of communication, and I clarify how it complements the "instrumental" and "expressive" functions. New readings by James J. Lynch, Stephen Greenblatt, and William W. Wilmot develop and extend the treatments of this idea that are introduced in Chapter 1 and the confirmation chapter. It's discussed in detail by Martin Buber in Part 5.

These conceptual commitments are complemented by my commitment to readability. As in all earlier editions, I have selected materials that develop this humanistic, transactional, person-building approach *and* that speak directly to the student reader. I continue to look especially for authors who "write with their ears," or *talk* with their readers. Selections from past editions by Virginia Satir, Carl Rogers, Hugh Prather, Neil Postman, and Leo Buscaglia continue to be in this edition partly because they do this so well. I have also discovered some new authors who bring this same degree of access-ability and readability to *Bridges Not Walls,* including Robert Fulghum, John and Kris Amodeo, Dolores Curran, and Deborah Tannen.

New Features

As I mentioned above, there is a new chapter on relationships made up of five new readings. The overview essay is coauthored by Roger Fisher of *Getting to Yes* fame and focuses on how to build a relationship. Then Alice G. Sargent discusses some findings from her research into superior-subordinate relationships, Mara Adelman and her coauthors outline the nature of friendship and its development, and Dolores Curran discusses "Traits of a Healthy Family" and "The Couple Relationship."

In addition, several chapters have been significantly updated. For example, I've added a selection by James J. Lynch to Chapter 2 to develop the "person-building" idea. Three of the four readings on verbal codes are new, including a brief story about "Language and Self-Fashioning," and an extended treatment of the "most popular piece of language," *questions*. Three of the four selections in the self-awareness chapter are new. Bill Wilmot overviews the process, Robert Fulghum delightfully summarizes it in his "All I Need to Know I Learned in Kindergarten," and a selection from Gregory Stock's *Book of Questions* encourages some self-reflection by the reader. Wilmot's introduction to Chapter 6 "Being Aware of Others," is also new, and I have shortened Russell A. Jones' discussion of stereotyping as a process of social cognition.

There is a new discussion of listening and the rhetorical process in Chapter 7, and Bolton's discussion of listening has been shortened. Elaine Hatfield begins the self-disclosure chapter with a temperate discussion of "The Dangers of Intimacy," and John and Kris Amodeo contribute a new treatment of disclosure in intimate relationships. John (Sam) Keltner wrote an essay on "The Struggle Spectrum" especially for this edition of *Bridges Not Walls,* and it now begins the conflict chapter. This chapter also includes two other new readings to supplement Jack Gibb's classic on defensiveness. One is called "Working With Anger" and the other, a coauthored essay by Hugh Prather and his wife Gayle, suggests "How to Resolve Issues Unmemorably."

Chapter 12, "Communication Between Women and Men," includes a new reading from Deborah Tannen's best-selling book, *That's Not What I Meant.* The intercultural communication chapter also adds two new readings, one by Larry A. Samovar and his colleagues and the other by Letty Cottin Pogrebin, author of a major national study on friendship. Pogrebin's selection is an especially interesting discussion of communication across the cultural boundaries separating different races, sexual preferences, ages, and levels of physical disability.

Erich Fromm's approach to interpersonal communication has been deleted from Part 5, partly in response to readers who found it "too heavy," and partly to make room for some of the new materials. The Carl Rogers selection in this chapter is also new and is easier to read than the selection included in earlier editions. In short, this edition really is "new," but the approach and structure will be very familiar to readers of earlier editions.

Plan of the Book

This edition maintains the five-part division of the last one, starting with "basic ingredients," treating "input" or listening dimensions separately from the "output" or speaking dimensions, discussing "bridging differences" in a four-chapter section, and closing with three synthesizing "approaches" at the end. This structure makes the mateials easy to adapt to each instructor's approach to the course. It makes sense to me to assign the chapters in the order they are presented, but both the sections and the chapters within each section are self-contained enough to be read in whatever sequence fits an individual's course structure and teaching preferences.

Part 1 is made up of chapters on each of four "basic ingredients." The first chapter introduces the editor and the primary assumptions behind the book. I include this material in the text itself in order to emphasize the potential for, and the limits of, interpersonal quality communication between writer and reader. I also want readers to remember that a book is always some*body's* point of view; I'd like them to respond to what's here not as "true because it's printed in black and white" but as the thoughtful speech of a person addressing them.

Chapter 2 includes three readings that introduce the book's humanistic and transactional approach. My essay describes how I think about interpersonal communication and why the book approaches the topic as it does. Then James J. Lynch discusses the link between quality of communication and quality of life, and Dean Barnlund's classic essay outlines a meaning-centered philosophy of communication.

Chapters 3 and 4 round out Part 1 with discussions of verbal codes and nonverbal cues. Each begins with an overview essay and then offers two or three additional readings to develop central ideas. Chapter 3 develops the link between language and self-identity, sensitizes the reader to a dozen problematic words, and analyzes the impact of various kinds of questions on interpersonal contact. Chapter 4 includes treatments of silence and touch. Space limitations force this chapter to be selective; teachers may well want to supplement what's here with their own favorite treatments of, for example, eye contact, posture, or paralinguistics.

Part 2 is called "Openness as 'Inhaling'" and focuses on the receiving dimensions of interpersonal contact. My introduction includes a discussion of why I've chosen the terms "openness," "inhaling," and "exhaling." On the one hand, a book can only treat one topic at a time, while on the other hand, "sending" or "speaking" and "receiving" or "listening" sound like vestiges of a linear view of communication, not a relational or transactional one. My compromise is to use the profitably ambiguous term "openness" in both Part 2 and Part 3 and to highlight its "inhaling" meaning in Part 2 and its "exhaling" meaning in Part 3. The allusions to breathing also emphasize the indivisibility of these two parts of the whole.

Chapter 5 begins with William W. Wilmot's overview of "The Social Self." This analytic reading is followed immediately by Robert Fulghum's popular and poignant summary of "All I Need to Know," about getting along in the world. Then the reader encounters another suggestive, open-ended list of questions for reflection, and the chapter closes with William S. Howell's discussion in "Coping with Internal Monologue." A similar structure characterizes the person perception chapter. Wilmot again provides the overview of social scientific literature. Russell A. Jones's substantive analysis of stereotyping fleshes out the theoretical discussion. This is followed by Paul Tournier's decidedly humanistic discussion of "The World of Things and the World of Persons."

There are three treatments of listening in Chapter 7. Links between listening and rhetorical processes are discussed in the first selection from the book by Carol A. Roach and Nancy J. Wyatt. Then a selection from communication consultant Robert Bolton's popular book *People Skills* lays out some basic processes. These approaches are affirmed in the final reading in this chapter, but Milt Thomas and I also argue that they are limited, and we propose a new "dialogic" approach to listening based on the metaphor, "sculpting mutual meanings." This reading translates the relational, transactional perspective introduced in Chapters 1 and 2 into an approach to listening.

Part 3 is called "Openness as 'Exhaling'" and consists of chapters on self-disclosure and confirmation. As I mentioned above, the disclosure chapter begins with a discussion of "The Dangers of Intimacy" and ends with Neil Postman's critique of "The Communication Panacea." In between, John and Kris Amodeo argue for the vital importance of self-revealing communication, especially in intimate relationships. Chapter 9 is unchanged from the fourth edition. It begins with Cissna and Sieburg's excellent overview of confirmation, uses Maurice Friedman's essay to develop and apply the construct, and closes with an extended story of confirmation as it is communicated in a Moroccan culture.

Part 4, "Bridging Differences," begins with the new chapter on relationships, which I have already described. Chapter 11 focuses on conflict, and includes John (Sam) Keltner's informative and useful discussion of "The Struggle Spectrum," Jack Gibb's classic "Defensive Communication," a treatment of how to work with anger, and a series of fruitful suggestions for keeping intimate conflicts "unmemorable."

Chapter 12 analyzes differences between women and men by presenting Judy Pearson's overview of female-male language choices and Deborah Tannen's discussion of "his and hers" intimate talk. Chapter 13 presents cross-cultural differences. L. E.

Sarbaugh provides the overview discussion, Larry A. Samovar, Richard E. Porter, and Nemi C. Jain analyze intercultural problems and guidelines, and then Letty Cottin Progrebin offers her analysis of "crossing boundaries" that I described above.

As in earlier editions, Part 5 collects some "Approaches to Interpersonal Communication," statements by noted writers that summarize their views of and ways of being-in-relation. Leo Buscaglia's irrepressible humor and conversational style make his essay at least as much fun as it is informative. Carl Rogers has always appeared in this section, but this edition includes an essay from his 1980 book, *A Way of Being.* This version of Rogers's approach is definitely familiar, but it is updated and more clear than in earlier editions. I conclude again with Martin Buber's "Elements of the Interhuman" the selection that continues to draw the most complaints from both students and teachers. I hear that Buber is "too confusing," "too hard to read," and "too heavy," but I also hear what happens when students in my classes—and in those taught by teaching assistants in our department—actually begin to connect with him. When readers connect with Buber, they begin to appreciate the depth and importance of interpersonal communication in a new way, and they are motivated to apply these ideas, even in the face of hardships and challenges. All this makes teaching Buber rewarding for me and many people I work with. I agree that it's difficult to make Buber accessible to the basic course student, but I keep rediscovering that it can be done. So I include Buber for those who agree; those who don't can leave this selection unread.

Other Features

In earlier editions, discussion questions called "Probes" followed each reading. Reviewers suggested that these be supplemented with questions that encourage students to review the main points each selection makes. I agree completely with the wisdom of this suggestion, so now there are two sets of questions for most readings. The first set, "Review Questions," focuses on recall and directs the reader to key ideas in the selection. Then "Probes" encourage students to reflect on or challenge points the author has made, and to link ideas in the reading with those expressed in earlier essays.

Many of the readings also include extensive bibliographies. There are lengthy reference lists, for example, of sources discussing verbal and nonverbal communication, self-perception, person-perception, listening, disclosure, confirmation, relationships, and male-female communication. Finally, a detailed index locates and provides cross references to authors and key ideas.

As before, I want to emphasize that this book *about* interpersonal communication cannot substitute for the real thing—for direct contact between vital human beings in the concrete, everyday world. That's why I've again begun the book with Buber's comment about "Books and Men" and ended with Hugh Prather's reflections on the world of ideas and the world of persons. (The title of Buber's comment raises the issue of sexist language. Both he and Tournier wrote the selections included in this book before we were aware of the overwhelming male-dominance of pre-1975 Standard American English. I hope readers who are offended by Buber's and Tournier's usage can listen behind what I believe in this case is a surface feature for the commitment to *human* respect that characterizes both authors.)

Acknowledgments

Authors and publishers of material reprinted here have again been very cooperative. This book would not have been possible without their help.

I am also grateful to reviewers of earlier editions. Seven persons offered insightful and helpful comments that guided the revision process: Marcanne Andersen, University of Wisconsin, Stout; Rob Anderson, Southern Illinois University, Edwardsville; Timothy Edgar, University of Maryland; George Kline, Spring Arbor College; Joyce Kuhn, University of Missouri, Kansas City; James Norwig, Luther College; and Judy Ringle, Oregon State University. In addition, seven persons responded to questionnaires about the previous edition, providing useful suggestions for this revision: Buford Crites, College of the Desert; Ann. L. Gardner, Clark College; Mary Hale, University of Colorado; Navita Cummings James, University of South Florida; Ann Burnett Pettus, Vanderbilt University; Kimberly Walters, DeAnza College; and Ethel Wilcox, University of Toledo.

Many people I'm fortunate enough to contact regularly have contributed in direct and indirect ways to what's here. I especially appreciate current and former interpersonal communication teachers in our program like Milt Thomas, Jeff Kerssen, Daena Goldsmith, and Carole Logan, and other graduate students like Karen Barnes, Judy Heinrich, and Ken White, who continually prompt me to learn and grow. As my primary graduate assistant for the past two years, Karen has been especially supportive and helpful. I'm also lucky to have colleagues who encourage and challenge my ideas like John Angus Campbell, Mac Parks, Teri Albrecht, Susan Kline, and Jody Nyquist; and important friends like Walt Fisher, Sam Bradley, and Gary D'Angelo who do the same. Thanks also to Jane Suchan Held who spent a long afternoon at Sinclair Island preparing the manuscript for revision. My most important living relationships—with Kris, Lisa and Corey, Marcia and Mark and Jamie and Joshua, and other immediate family members—are still the central reasons for and the ultimate tests of the ideas in this book.

Two things that have not changed through all five editions are my awareness of the difficulty and the necessity of interpersonal communication and my excitement about the challenge of working toward achieving it. I hope that some of this excitement will rub off on you.

John Stewart

Part 1

The Basic Ingredients

Chapter 1

Introduction to the Editor and to the Assumptions Behind This Book

"riting about interpersonal communication, especially in a context like this one, is extremely difficult, primarily because it's almost impossible to practice what you preach." In 1972, I began the introduction to the first edition of *Bridges Not Walls* with that sentence, and it is as true for me now—in 1989—as it was sixteen years ago. Now, as then, the problem is that I could simply think of you as "reader" or "student" and of myself as "author," "editor," or "teacher" and then proceed to "tell you what I want you to know." But the result of that kind of thinking would be a lot closer to superficial role-relating than to interpersonal communication.

The reason that such an approach doesn't work is that, although I am obviously writing this, I am *not* simply "author," "editor," or "teacher," and you are not just "reader" or "student." Each of us is a unique person. My name is John Stewart, I have been teaching college for about twenty-two years, and I like almost everything about my job—the constant contact with young, growing persons; the excitement of keeping up with changes in my field; the satisfaction that comes from experiencing a good class session or finishing a good paragraph; and the freedom to work at my own pace. I also like to sail on salt water, to watch what sunsets do to mountains, to smell the wet freshness of Pacific Northwest winters, to feel the exhilaration of making it up a steep hill on a bike or down a moguled hill on skis, to celebrate Christmas with a crowd of family, and to hug friends. I don't like phony smiles, smug, pretentious academicians, rules that are vaguely stated but rigidly enforced, unfulfilled commitments, or clam chowder. I was raised in a small town in Washington state and live with Kris, the woman I'm married to, in a house in Seattle that overlooks the Cascade Mountains and Lake Washington. Kris and I are in the twelfth year of our marriage, and things just keep getting better! My daughters, Marcia and Lisa, who were eleven and twelve when I edited the first edition of this book, are now both married, and their husbands, Mark and Corey, and children, Jamie and Joshua, are all very special additions to our family. I continue to feel challenged as I teach courses I've never taught before and research aspects of interpersonal communication that are new to me. I recently resigned from an eight-year stint of balancing a part-time interpersonal communication consulting practice with my academic and family life. I'm editor of a scholarly journal now, and my days and years continue to be filled and productive.

The longer I work with the subject matter of interpersonal communication, the more I'm struck by the extent to which who I am today is a function of the experiences of genuine contact I've had with others. Some of those persons are no longer alive— my first real "boss," Marc Burdick; my closest friend, Allen Clark, who died while I was finishing the second edition of this book; and my dad and father-in-law, who died nine and seven years ago. I also recall especially important teachers, Alice Atkinson, Robert Harris, Peter Ristuben, and Walter Fisher; close colleagues like Frank Bussone, Gary D'Angelo, Helen Felton, and John Campbell; and several important authors who have made themselves available for contact in their writing—I'm thinking especially of Martin Buber, Carl Rogers, Gregory Bateson, and Hans-Georg Gadamer. Contacts with all those persons have helped shape me. At the same time, I sense the presence of an unchanging, central me, a core self that's never static but that's firmly anchored in values, understandings, goals, and blind spots that make me who I am.

If I were just "writer" or "author" I could also conceal the fact that I am still excited about doing this fifth edition of *Bridges* and that I'm pleased and a little amazed that the book continues to speak to so many different people. I am also still grateful that I get to share some ideas and feelings about interpersonal communication that have helped me grow. I'm pleased that readers allow me to talk with them directly and personally instead of in the safe, sterile, distant style of most "educational materials."

The role-restricted attitudes I mentioned will also get in the way of our communicating, because *you* are not simply "reader" or "student." Where were you born and raised, and how has that affected you? Are you reading this book because you want to or because somebody told you to? If you're reading this as part of a college course, how do you expect the course to turn out? Challenging? Boring? Threatening? Useful? Exciting? Inhibiting? How do you generally feel about required texts? About administrative regulations? About going to school? What groups have you chosen to join? A sorority or fraternity? Student government? An honor society? Alateen? Young Life? What other important choices have you made recently? To move? Change majors? End a relationship? Quit work? Make a new commitment?

I'm not trying to say that you have to pry into the intimate details of somebody's life before you can communicate with him or her, but I am trying to say that interpersonal communication happens between *persons,* not between roles or masks or stereotypes. Interpersonal communication can happen between you and me only when each of us makes available some of what makes us a person *and* when each is aware of some of what makes the other a person too.

One way to conceptualize what I'm saying is to think about what I call your Contact Quotient, or CQ. Your CQ is a measure of how well you *connect* with another person or persons. It's the quotient that expresses the ratio between the quality of contact you accomplish and the quality of contact that's possible. In other words:

$$CQ = \frac{\text{Richness or quality of contact achieved}}{\text{Richness or quality of contact possible}}$$

A husband and wife who've been married for forty years have a huge CQ denominator. When one is giving the other the silent treatment, his or her numerator is painfully small, as is the CQ. When they're making languorous love, their numerator is very high and their CQ approaches unity. You and I, on the other hand, have a pretty small denominator. The quality of contact we can achieve is relatively low. But we can still strive toward a CQ of 1/1, and that's my primary goal in this introduction.

It's going to be difficult, however, to maximize the CQ between you and me. I can continue to share with you some of who I am, but I don't know whether what I write is what you need to know me as me. In addition, I know almost nothing about what makes you a person—nothing about your choices, your feelings, your individuality. That's why *writing* about interpersonal communication is sometimes frustrating for me; interpersonal communication can be discussed in print, but not much of it can happen here.

More can happen, though, than usually happens with a "textbook." The relationship can be closer to interpersonal-quality communication than it often is. I will work toward that by continuing to share some of what I'm actually thinking and feeling in my introductions to the readings, the probes at the end of each selection, and the three essays I've authored or coauthored. I hope you'll be willing to share yourself by becoming honestly involved enough in this book to see clearly which of the ideas are worthwhile for you and which are not. I also hope you'll be able to make yourself available to other persons reading this book, so they can benefit from your insights and you can benefit from theirs.

Two Basic Assumptions

Before we begin breaking human communication down into some manageable parts, I want to discuss a couple of assumptions that guided my selection and organization of the materials in this book. I believe that when you know something of this book's rationale, it'll be easier for you to understand what's being said about each topic, and you'll be in a better position to accept or adopt what works for you while leaving aside the rest.

One of my basic assumptions is that the *quality of each person's life is directly linked to the quality of the communication he or she experiences.* One way to clarify and explain this assumption is to talk about "quality of life" from a medical point of view. In two recent books, James J. Lynch, who is codirector of the Psychophysiological Clinic and Laboratories at the University of Maryland School of Medicine, discusses the connection between physical health and interpersonal communication. I've reprinted a selection from Lynch's most recent book[1] in chapter 1, so I'll just outline what he says here.

One of Lynch's important discoveries is that blood pressure changes much more rapidly and consistently than we used to believe, and that some of the most radical blood pressure changes occur when we speak and listen. Lynch was led to this discovery by his interest in hypertension, or sustained high blood pressure, a disease that afflicts an estimated 40 million people in the United States and that killed over a million of us in 1980.[2] Computerized instruments permit Lynch and other medical researchers to monitor blood pressure constantly and to map the effects of a person entering the room, nonverbal contact, reading aloud, and conversation. Speech appears to affect blood pressure directly; in one study the mean arterial pressure of healthy nurses went from 92 when they were quiet to 100 when they "talked calmly."[3] In another study using graduate students, vocalization raised their mean arterial pressure from 87 to 94, and as Lynch emphasizes, "Surprisingly, talking about feelings did not increase a student's pressure more than simply reading a book aloud: that is, all verbal activities elicited statistically equal rises in blood pressure and heart rate, while all quiet periods were accompanied by significantly lower blood-pressure readings."[4]

Listening has the opposite effect. Rather than just returning to baseline when a person stops speaking, blood pressure actually drops below baseline when we concentrate on the other person.[5] And this only happens when we talk with people; "conversation" with pets does not produce the same result.[6]

Lynch's 1977 book discusses some of the more global effects of essentially the same phenomenon. There he reports the results of literally hundreds of studies that correlate loneliness and poor health. For example, people with few interpersonal relationships tend to die before their counterparts who enjoy a network of family and friends.[7] And a 1970 study by two Swedish doctors of identical twins found that smoking habits, obesity, and cholesterol levels of the twins who had heart attacks were *not* significantly different from the twins with healthier hearts. But there were some other important differences, one of which was what the doctors called "poor childhood and adult interpersonal relationships." The twins with heart disease were the ones who had experienced more unresolved conflict, more arguments at work and home, and less emotional support.[8] After thirty years of work with heart disease patients in this country, two other doctors reached some similar conclusions. They found that although there are some relationships between heart problems and such factors as heredity, weight, and smoking, there is a much stronger link with one's pattern of interpersonal behavior. The person who is most likely to suffer a heart attack is the one who is "aggressively involved in a *chronic, incessant* struggle to achieve more and more in less and less time . . . against the opposing efforts of other things or other persons."[9] These doctors believe that continuous competitive and aggressive communication can increase your chances of heart disease.

What conclusions can we draw from evidence like this? In 1977 Lynch put it this way:

> Human companionship does affect our hearts, and . . . there is reflected in our hearts a biological basis for our need for loving human relationships, which we fail to fulfill at our peril. . . . The ultimate decision is simple: we must either learn to live together or increase our chances of prematurely dying alone.[10]

In other words, quality of life is not just a matter of ample food, warm clothing, education, and modern conveniences. *The quality of your life is directly linked to the quality of your communication.* I believe that learning to communicate can not only help you to develop trust, clarify an idea, obtain a job, make a sale, get an 'A,' or make the right group decision. Communication *can* help with these things, but even more fundamentally, it affects your growth, your health, and your development as a person.

Interestingly, philosophers make this point as strongly as medical researchers do. For example, Reuel Howe writes,

> To say that communication is important to human life is to be trite, but that bit of triteness witnesses to an invariable truth: communication means life or death to persons. . . . Both the individual and society derive their basic meaning from the relations that exist between [persons]. It is through dialogue that man accomplishes the miracle of personhood and community.[11]

The Jewish philosopher Martin Buber's entire approach to communication is based on the idea that you and I discover and build our humanness in relationships with other persons. To paraphrase Buber,

> The fundamental fact of human existence is person with person. The unique thing about the human world is that something is continually happening between one person and another, something that never happens in the animal or plant world. . . . *Humans are made human by this happening.* . . . This special event begins by one human turning to another, seeing him or her as this particular other being, and offering to communicate with the other in a mutual way, building from the individual world each person experiences to a world they share together.[12]

Jesuit psychologist John Powell puts the same idea in simpler terms: "What I am, at any given moment in the process of my becoming a person, will be determined by my relationships with those who love me or refuse to love me, with those I love or refuse to love."[13]

I am not saying that you have to be a theologian—or even that you have to be religious—in order to communicate well. I am also not saying that the quality of your communication is the be-all and end-all of your life, but I do believe that it is very important. I am not saying that if you fail to experience what I call interpersonal-quality communication *all* the time, you will become impoverished, inhumane, or antisocial. But I am saying that communicating is not just one of the many trivial and mundane things you do—along with combing your hair, washing the dishes, and earning a living. My basic belief is this: The quality of your life is directly related to the quality of your communication.

My other basic assumption is that *there is a basic movement in the human world, and it is toward relation not toward division.* This may also sound a little vague, but I think it'll get clearer if you bear with me for a couple of paragraphs. First, I believe that human life is a process or activity and that the general kind of process we humans are engaged in is the activity of becoming who we are, growing into fully developed persons. So far, no big deal, right?

Second, persons are relational, not solitary, beings. To be a person is to experience relationships with other persons. If you could create a human organism in a completely impersonal environment—an artificial uterus, machine-assisted birth, mechanical feeding and changing, and so on—what you'd end up with would *not* be a person. That's because in order to become a person you have to experience relationships with other persons. That's one point made by various accounts of "feral," or "wild," children. For example, in *The Forbidden Experiment: The Story of the Wild Boy of Aveyron,* Roger Shattuck tells about a "remarkable creature" who came out of the woods near a small village in southern France on January 9, 1800, and was captured while digging for vegetables in a village garden. The "creature"

> was human in bodily form and walked erect. Everything else about him suggested an animal. He was naked except for the tatters of a shirt and showed no modesty, no awareness of himself as a human person related in any way to the people who had captured him. He could not speak and made only weird, meaningless cries. Though very short, he appeared to be a boy of about eleven or twelve. . . .[14]

The creature was taken for treatment to a distinguished physician named Dr. Pinel. Dr. Pinel, one of the founders of psychiatry, was unable to help him, partly because, as Shattuck puts it, "the boy had no human sense of being in the world. He had no sense of himself as a person related to other persons."[15] The "savage of Aveyron" made progress toward becoming human only after he was taken on as a project by another medical doctor named Jean-Marc Gaspard Itard. Itard's first move was to give the boy a foster family and to put him in the care of a mature, loving mother, Madame Guérin. In that context they were able to teach the boy to "use his own chamberpot," dress himself, come when he was called, and even associate some letters of the alphabet with some pictures.

Itard's first report about his year of efforts to train and socialize the wild boy emphasizes the importance of human contact in becoming a person. Itard describes in detail events that demonstrate the significance of "the feeling of friendship" between the boy and Itard and especially between the boy and Mme. Guérin: "Perhaps I shall be understood if people remember the major influence on a child of those endless cooings and caresses, those kindly nothings which come naturally from a mother's heart and which bring forth the first smiles and joys in a human life."[16] Without that contact, this young human organism was a "creature," a "savage"; with them, he began to develop into a person.

If it's true that what we're doing as persons is becoming who we are, and that we are relational beings, then you can say that the basic movement in the human world is toward relating, not away from it. Another way to put it is to say that the underlying, fundamental force in the human world is centripetal, not centrifugal. (Remember that when you whirl a weight on a string, centrifugal force is what forces the weight *out,* away from the center, and centripetal force is what holds it *in.*)

So what about all this? Well, to say that humans are fundamentally "relaters" is to say that we are fundamentally "communicators," since relating happens by means of communication. That's another way of saying what I said already—that communication is not just one of the mundane things we do as we trip through life; it is the defining thing; communication is what makes us who we are. But it also means something else. If humans are *fundamentally* communicators, then whenever we are freed from ignorance and fear, we *will* move toward others, not away from them. So my approach as an interpersonal communication teacher is not to say, "You *should* establish person-to-person relations," or, "You had *better* communicate more effectively or you'll be a bad person," but to recognize that if we can work together to increase your knowledge and diminish your fear, you *will* establish more person-to-person relations. So will I. *Naturally.* That will happen not because we're "being good" or buying into a certain value system but because we're being who we are: persons.

Again I'm not saying that if everybody just relaxes, holds hands, smiles, and stares at the sunset, all conflict will disappear and the world will be a happy place. Sometimes the fear that prohibits interpersonal communication is legitimate; we are often acutely vulnerable to another person's gossip, lies, or manipulation. Our ignorance can also be devastating. If I don't know how to listen, how to tell you my feelings, or how to clarify an abstract idea, that fact alone can inhibit our contact.

But the point is, the kind of communicating outlined in this book is not just a trendy, pop psychology exercise in narcissism. It's grounded in some basic beliefs about who we are and what communication means in human life. In the first selection of Chapter 2 I say more about this point by distinguishing between the instrumental and the ontological functions of communication (pp. 22–24). When you read those pages, you might want to refer back to these two assumptions.

So far I've tried to say that for me, interpersonal communication differs from non-interpersonal communication in that it consists of *contact between* (inter) *persons.* That means that for interpersonal communication to happen, each participant has to be willing and able to make available some of what makes him or her a person and to be aware of some of what makes the other a person. This willingness and ability will happen only when the people involved (1) are familiar with the basic ingredients of the human communication process, (2) are willing and able accurately to perceive and listen to others, (3) are willing and able to make themselves and their ideas available to others, (4) have some resources to deal with differences, and (5) can put the whole complex of attitudes and skills together into a human synthesis that works for them.

That's why I've organized this book into five sections. This chapter introduces me and a couple of my basic assumptions. The second chapter explores some of what it means to say that interpersonal communication means contact between persons. I feel strongly that it's vital to understand both concepts—"contact between" and "persons"—so I've discussed them in some detail in Chapter 2, and I've included two additional articles that speak to some of the same ideas in different ways. The third and fourth chapters complete the outline of the basic ingredients of human communication. Chapter 3 discusses verbal codes—how words can help people understand you and help bring people together. In Chapter 4, several authors talk about how nonverbal codes work in human communication, and specifically how silence and touch affect our relationships with others.

In Part Two the focus shifts to one aspect or dimension of communication that I label "openness as 'inhaling.'" I explain why I chose that label at the end of my article in Chapter 2. In the first chapter of Part Two, several readings explore self-perception, and in Chapter 6 there are three treatments of how we perceive others. Chapter 7 concentrates on effective listening and includes three readings.

Part Three looks at the other dimension of communicating, which you might think of as "sending" or "output." I call it "openness as 'exhaling.'" In Part Three, Chapter 8 deals with self-disclosure, the process of making yourself available. Chapter 9 includes three articles that discuss confirmation, which I think is the most important kind or function of "exhaling."

Part Four focuses on bridging differences. Chapter 10 discusses relationships and includes essays about the superior—subordinate relationship, friendship, the family, and the couple relationship. More and more communication scholars and teachers are studying conflict, and we now have some understanding of defensiveness and the potential values of conflict. These are the topics of Chapter 11. Communicating across differences between women and men and communicating across cultures are the topics of Chapters 12 and 13. You've probably experienced some or all of those potentially difficult phenomena in your daily living, and each reading in these three chapters offers insights and practical suggestions.

In the final part of the book I've collected three statements, each of which integrates, synthesizes, and pulls together the ideas in the other readings. The authors in Part Five are important in the development of the ideas in this book; you will find their names scattered throughout the writings in other chapters. Leo Buscaglia has been famous for several years for his university courses on love and his insightful and inspirational speeches and books about improving communication. Carl Rogers was a well-known humanistic psychotherapist who was an important figure in the human potential movement. Finally, Martin Buber was a philosopher and the person who is most responsible for originally explaining the basic ideas everyone else in this book developed.

Before each essay or article there are some introductory comments that pinpoint what I think are the key ideas that appear there. At the end of each reading I've included two kinds of questions. "Review questions" prompt your recall of key ideas from the readings. "Probes" are questions intended to provoke your thinking, especially your thinking about how the ideas in that reading relate (1) to your own life experience and (2) to ideas in the other readings. I've omitted Review Questions from two or three of the shortest readings. I've also included several of Hugh Prather's comments as connecting thoughts. As you may have discovered already by reading his books *Notes to*

Myself and *I Touch the Earth the Earth Touches Me,* Hugh is uniquely able to capture in a few lines insights that it takes most of us pages to explain.

So that's what's coming. I hope it will be helpful *and* fun.

References

1. James J. Lynch, *The Language of the Heart: The Body's Response to Human Dialogue* (New York: Basic Books, 1985).
2. Lynch, p. 33, citing *Cardiovascular Primer for the Workplace,* Health Education Branch, Office of Prevention, Education, and Control. National Heart, Lung, and Blood Institute. U.S. Department of Health and Human Services. Public Health Service. National Institutes of Health. NIH Publication no. 81–2210 (January 1981).
3. Lynch, pp. 123–124.
4. Lynch, p. 127.
5. Lynch, pp. 160ff.
6. Lynch, pp. 150–155.
7. James J. Lynch, *The Broken Heart: The Medical Consequences of Loneliness* (New York: Basic Books, 1977), pp. 42–51.
8. E. A. Liljefors and R. H. Rahe, "Psychosocial Characteristics of Subjects with Myocardial Infarction in Stockholm," in *Life Stress Illness.* ed. E. K. Gunderson and Richard H. Rahe (Springfield, Ill.: Charles C Thomas, 1974), pp. 90–104.
9. Myer Friedman and Ray H. Rosenman, *Type A Behavior and Your Heart* (New York: Knopf, 1974), p. 67.
10. Lynch, *The Broken Heart,* p. 14.
11. From *The Miracle of Dialogue* by Reuel L. Howe, copyright 1963 by the Seabury Press, Inc. Used by permission of the publisher. Cited in *The Human Dialogue,* ed. F. W. Matson and A. Montagu (New York: The Free Press, 1968), pp. 148–149.
12. This is a paraphrase of what Buber says in *Between Man and Man* (New York: Macmillan, 1965), p. 203. Italics added.
13. John Powell, *Why Am I Afraid to Tell You Who I Am?* (Chicago: Argus Communications, 1969), p. 43.
14. Roger Shattuck, *The Forbidden Experiment: The Story of the Wild Boy of Aveyron* (New York: Farrar Straus Giroux, 1980), p. 5.
15. Shattuck, p. 37.
16. Shattuck, p. 119.

Chapter 2

Introduction to Interpersonal Communication

Perceptions are not of things but of relationships. Nothing, including me, exists by itself—this is an illusion of words. I <u>am</u> a relationship, ever-changing.

HUGH PRATHER

ne of the best courses I took during my first year of college was "Intro-duction to Philosophy." Part of the appeal was the teacher; he knew his stuff, and he loved to teach it. But as I discovered a few years later, I also enjoyed the course because I was comfortable with the kind of thinking that was going on in the materials we read and the discussions we had. It seemed as though I usually thought that way myself. As I continued through college, I supple-mented my speech communication courses with other work in philosophy. The topics I talk about in this essay reflect that dual interest.

Originally, the Greek words for "philosophy" meant the love of wisdom, where "wisdom" was contrasted with the kind of knowledge it takes to do art, politics, or science. That meant that *philo-sophia* was concerned with "eternal truths" and such general questions as "What does it mean to be a 'good' person?" or, "How do you know that you really *know* something?" Later, philosophy was defined as the "system-atic critique of presuppositions," which is another way of saying that it's concerned with first principles, basic understandings, underlying assumptions. If you've read much phi-losophy you may have the impression that it can be stuffy or even nit-picking to the point of irrelevance. But frequently it's exciting and important, because the philosopher says, "Hold it! Before you go off to spin a complicated web of explanations about human communication, or an economic system, or the history of culture, or the operation of a political system, or whatever, try to get clear about some *basic* things: When you're talking about human communication, what are you assuming, for example, about what actually gets passed between people when they communicate?" The philosopher might say, "If each human perceives the world in his or her own way, then I can only com-municate with *my perception* of you; I can *never* really get in touch with you. All I can do, when it comes right down to it, is communicate with myself!"

Such basic issues intrigue me. I know that many potentially exciting conversations have been squelched by someone's dogmatic insistence that everybody "define the terms." But I also know that a great deal of fuzziness can be cleared up when a con-versation starts with some shared understandings about what's being discussed.

In the following essay I describe my understanding of the topic of this book — interpersonal communication. I talk mostly about what's meant by the two halves of the word "interpersonal," *contact between* (inter) and *person*. My main goal is to clarify how the approach to interpersonal communication taken in this book is a little different from what you might be expecting. Basically, it's different because it acknowledges and emphasizes the fact that communication is not only important for getting things done; it also affects *who we are as persons*.

Interpersonal Communication: Contact Between Persons

John Stewart

The fact that you're reading this indicates that you've decided to think and hopefully to talk about the topic of interpersonal communication. You could have made many different choices. You could have decided to study public speaking, television production, or organizational communication. You could also have decided to read, think, and talk about geology, mathematics, English literature, or religion—in fact, you may be doing some of that now too. But what is this "interpersonal communication"? What does it mean to study *this* topic?

Does it just mean "two-person" communication? Or perhaps two- to five-person communication (but after five people it becomes "group discussion" or "small group decision making")? Or does the term mean informal, face-to-face communication? Or warm, supportive communication? Or therapeutic communication? What *are* you using this book to study?

I don't want to make too big a deal out of "defining our terms," but I believe that interpersonal communication is more than any of the things I've mentioned so far. For me, when the term "interpersonal" is used to modify the word "communication," it means something more than just "two-person," "face-to-face," "informal," or "warm and supportive." The term "interpersonal" designates a type or quality of human contact that can characterize many different communication events, including a telephone conversation (which obviously isn't face to face), an intense argument (which is hardly ever warm and supportive), a ten-person committee meeting, or even a public speech. This definition or approach grows out of the two assumptions I discussed in this book's introduction, and it expands the study of interpersonal communication from just an instrumental enterprise to one with ontological implications. For me *interpersonal communication is the type or quality or kind of contact that occurs when each person involved talks and listens in ways that highlight the individual's and the other person's humanness.*

So what does all *that* mean? "Ontological not instrumental"? "Type or quality or kind"? "Contact"? "Highlight humanness"? Well, I mean all these terms to do more than just confuse or to generate jargon. My purpose in this first reading is to unpack this definition and to explain how this approach to interpersonal communication underlies everything that's in this book.

Persons

Let's start with "highlight humanness." It seems to me that as you and I move through our daily family, work, social, and school lives, we tend to relate with others in two different ways: We treat others and are treated by them as objects or as humans. I don't mean that there is a sharp dichotomy; sometimes we treat others and are treated by them more as persons than as objects, and sometimes it's the other way around. But "personifying" (or "humanifying") and "objectifying" seem to be two ends of a continuum that describes how we relate with others. Communication with bank tellers, receptionists, registration clerks, and most other institutional representatives tends to be objectifying, and much of the time that's completely expected and legitimate; in fact, it's almost impossible to do anything else. Communication with family members, lovers, and spouses tends at least part of the time to be personifying. One central theme of this book is that although all our communicating cannot highlight humanness or personness (i.e., it cannot all be interpersonal-quality communication), *more of it could be.* If it were, things would be greatly improved both for us and for the people we contact.

In order to move in this direction, it's important to recognize what an object–person communication continuum or relationship scale looks like. Early in this century a man named Martin Buber described this sliding scale in a little book that became a classic. The name of the book is *I and Thou,* and since its publication in 1922, it's been translated into more than twenty languages, sold millions of copies all over the world, and continues to be read, discussed, and cited by communication scholars and teachers, philosophers, psychologists, educators, sociologists, anthropologists, and theologians. You might think from its title that Buber's book is a religious work, but it's not just that. The "Thou" in the title is the English translation of the German word for the familiar form of the pronoun "you." Buber originally wrote the book in German and called it *Ich und Du,* which became *Je et Tu* in French, and since English used to include "thee" and "thou," it was translated into English as *I and Thou.* The most recent translation, as you will see in a minute, keeps that title but renders *Du* as "You" in the text of the book itself.

In his book and in virtually all the writings he did between 1922 and his death in 1965, Buber focused in one way or another on the relationship scale or communication continuum between objects and persons. In a three-paragraph section near the end of the first part of *I and Thou,* Buber summarized the distinctions between objects and persons that were the foundation of his entire approach to interpersonal communication. Here's my paraphrase of what he says with some marginal notes I'll explain in a minute:

> The world is twofold for humans in accordance with their twofold perspective. {This, by the way, is the same sentence as the first one in his book. Buber's signaling that these paragraphs are a summary of his main point.}
>
> On the one hand, a human perceives the surrounding world, plain things and beings as things; he or she perceives what happens in the world, plain processes and actions as processes, things that consist of qualities and processes that consist of moments, things recorded in terms of spatial coordinates and processes recorded in ⟨space–time⟩ terms of temporal coordinates, things and processes that are ⟨measurable⟩ bounded by other things and processes and capable of being measured against and compared with those others—an ordered world, a detached world. This world is somewhat reliable; it has density ⟨reliable⟩ and duration, its structure can be surveyed; one can get it out again and again: one recounts it with one's eyes closed and then checks with one's eyes open. There it stands—right next to your skin if you think of it that way, or nestled in your soul if you prefer that: it is your object and remains that, according to your pleasure—and remains primally alien both outside and inside you. You perceive

it and take it for your "truth"; it permits itself to be taken by you, but it does not give itself to you. It is only *about* it that you can come to an understanding with others: although it takes a some- what different form for everybody, it is prepared to be a common object for you; but you cannot encounter others in it. Without it you cannot remain alive; its reliability preserves you; but if you were to die into it, then you would be buried in nothingness. 〈**talk** *about* **not** *to*〉

Or the human encounters being and becoming as what confronts him or her—always only *one* being and everything only as a being. What is there reveals itself in occurrence, and what occurs there happens to one as being. Nothing else is present but this one.... Measure and comparison have fled. It is up to you how much of the immeasurable becomes reality for you.... The world that appears to you in this way is unreliable, for it appears always new to you, and you cannot take it by its word. It lacks density, for everything in it permeates everything else. It lacks duration, for it comes even when not called and vanishes even when you cling to it. It cannot be surveyed: if you try to make it surveyable, you lose it. It comes—comes to fetch you—and if it does not reach you or encounter you it vanishes—but it comes again, transformed. It does not stand outside you, it touches your ground.... Between you and it there is a reciprocity of giving: you say You to it and give your- self to it; it says You to you and gives itself to you. You cannot come to an understanding *about* it with others; you are lonely with it; but it teaches you to encounter others and to stand your ground in such encounters.... 〈**unique**〉 〈**unmeasurable**〉 〈**unreliable**〉 〈**not space–time**〉 〈**addressable**〉 〈**talk** *to* **not just** *about*〉

The It-world hangs together in space and time.

The You-world does not hang together in space and time.[1]

As you can see, Buber's words for objects and persons are "It" and "You." His point is that as humans we have the twofold ability to relate to what's around us as either an "it" or as a "you." And the difference between these two modes of relating is very significant.

Unique

Consider for a minute the characteristics of Its and Yous (objects and per- sons) that I've highlighted in the margins of the preceding quotation. Perhaps most important, persons are unique, and objects aren't. Although a microscopic exami- nation of the pencil I'm writing with right now might reveal some nicks, coloration, or erasure contours that are different from any other pencil, for all practical pur- poses, this pencil is the same as any other no. 2 pencil. The same can be said for all the other objects around me now—my typewriter, chair, lamp, paperweight, coffee cup, pocket calculator, and so on. There might be some minute distinctions, but for all practical purposes this typewriter is interchangeable with others of the same model, and so are the other objects here.

Persons aren't that way. We can be treated as if we're interchangeable parts, but for *many* practical purposes it's important to remember that we are not; each of us is unique. I remember hearing of a geneticist who said that given the com- plexity of each individual's makeup of genes and chromosomes, the probability of two persons other than identical twins having the same genetic materials was one in ten to the ten-thousandth power. That's less than one chance in a billion trillion! In other words, each of us is virtually a genetic one of a kind. But even if we weren't—even when identical twins have the same biological raw material—each is still unique, because each experiences the world differently. If you doubt it, recall the differences between any twins you've known. Or you might check the uniqueness of others with a little experiment. After you finish this chapter, ask a friend who's also read it how he or she is experiencing this book, or this paragraph, or this sentence. Superficially, your experiences may be similar, but if you probe them even a little, it will be clear that they're unique. There's only one you.

Unmeasurable

A second difference that Buber notes is that the object world is completely measurable, it's a space-and-time (spatiotemporal) world, and the human world is not. Part of what he means is that even extremely complex objects, such as giant computers, well-equipped automobiles, and fifty-story buildings, can be described completely in terms of space and time. That's what blueprints do; they record all the measurements necessary to re-create the object—length, width, height, velocity, amperage, voltage, specific gravity, circumference, hardness, and so on. Although it's difficult to measure some things directly—the velocity of a photon, the temperature of a kiss, the duration of an explosion—the parts of all objects are measurable, at least in theory.

The same can't be said for persons. Even if I accurately identify your height, weight, temperature, specific gravity, velocity, and electric potential, I will not have exhaustively accounted for the person who's you. Some psychologists acknowledge this point by including in their model of the person the notion of a "black box," an unmeasurable, uniquely human something that is continuously affecting human behavior and that escapes all the rigorously scientific measurement that can be applied to it. Less scientifically inclined people call this unmeasurable part the human "spirit," "soul," "psyche," or "personality." But whatever you call it, it's there.

The clearest manifestations of this unmeasurable part of us are those phenomena we call "emotions" or "feelings." Although we can measure things related to feelings—brainwaves, sweaty palms, heart rate, paper and pencil responses—what the measurements record is a long way from the feelings themselves. "Pulse 110, respiration 72, Likert rating 5.39, palmar conductivity .036 ohms" might be accurate, but it doesn't quite capture all of what's going on in me when I greet somebody I love.

Another thing, these unmeasurable emotions or feelings can't be turned off or on at will; they're always part of what we are experiencing. Contemporary educators pretty much agree now that it's unrealistic to try to focus a class exclusively on the "intellectual," "objective" aspect of some subject matter, because people are always thinking *and* feeling. As one writer put it, "it should be apparent that there is no intellectual learning without some sort of feeling, and there are no feelings without the mind's being somehow involved."[2] Sometimes what we are experiencing is more thinking than feeling and sometimes vice-versa, but neither function is ever entirely missing. We're always feeling something, or perhaps more accurately "feeling somehow."

In short, there is more to persons than just what's observable and measurable.

Although the human "spirit" and human "feelings" are concretely *real* in the sense that we are experiencing them all the time, these elements of us cannot be exhaustively accounted for in space-and-time terms. Commmunication that is responsive to these unmeasurable, uniquely human parts is more interpersonal than communication that isn't.

Choice

A third distinction Buber identifies is that the It world is "reliable" and the You world is unreliable. That means that things and processes occur in predictable patterns. If I leave my hammer on the dock next to the boat, it will rust, because unprotected metal with a given iron content always oxidizes in a saltwater environment. *Always.* It can't choose not to. The difference between the reliability of the object world and the unreliability of the human world is choice. My typewriter can't choose to start typing, this pencil can't choose to start writing, and my pocket calculator can't choose to start balancing my checkbook. Automatic pilots, photoelectric switches, and thermostats sometimes seem to "operate on their own" or "turn themselves off and on," but they too are dependent on actions initiated outside them. The pilot has to be programmed; the thermostat reacts to the temperature, which reacts to the sun rays, which react to the earth's rotation, and so on. Similarly, a ball can only react to the force of a foot that kicks it, and if you're good enough at physics calculations, you can pretty much pinpoint how far and where it will go, based on weight, velocity, the shape of your shoe, atmospheric conditions, and so on.

But you can't predict what will happen very accurately if you kick your roommate, your teacher, or the grocery clerk. The reason you can't is that when persons are involved, human choice intervenes between cause and effect, stimulus and response. If you tap my knee, you may cause a reflex jerk, but the behavior that accompanies my reflex might be anything from giggles to a lawsuit, and there is no way that you can predict for sure which it will be. Like objects, persons sometimes react, but we can also *choose, decide, act.*

The importance of choice is a key point of several approaches to studying persons that go under the general heading "existential." You've probably heard that term before in reference to plays, novels, philosophy, or psychology. One of the existentialists' main insights is that persons are subjects, not objects. Part of what they mean is that human subjects, like grammatical subjects, "define themselves through their own activities while objects are defined by the activities of subjects; subjects modify [choose]; objects are modified [get chosen upon]."[3] Nobody argues that humans are *completely* free to choose to do anything they want to. I can't fly, return to my childhood, or run faster than a speeding bullet. But my future is not determined by my past or present, and neither is yours. We can choose to respond to conditions that confront us.

The more we're aware of our ability to choose, the more human we are. When I feel like, "I *had* to shout back; he was making me look silly!" or "I just *couldn't* say anything!" or "Sure I *withdrew,* but she made me—she was always on my back about something!" I'm out of touch with part of what it means to be a person. Persons can act, not just react; persons can choose. And interpersonal communication is in part communication that maximizes our ability to do those uniquely personlike things.

Addressable

The fourth distinction Buber identifies is that persons are addressable and objects aren't; you can only talk *about* objects but you can talk *to* persons, or better yet, *with* them. Notice how he makes this point. An It, he says, "permits itself to be taken by you, but it does not give itself to you." A You, on the other hand, "comes to fetch you. . . . Between you and it there is a reciprocity of giving: you say You to it and give yourself to it; it says You to you and gives itself to you."

Addressability is the clearest difference between the kind of contact you can have with a person and the kind you can have with the "almost human" pet cat, dog, or horse. For example, you may have looked into the eyes of a pet animal and noticed what seemed to be a real glance of reciprocity—almost as if you were being addressed. Buber describes an experience like that which he often had with a house cat.

> Undeniably, this cat began its glance by asking me with a glance that was ignited by the breath of my glance: "Can it be that you mean me? Do you actually want that I should not merely do tricks for you? Do I concern you? Am I there for you? Am I there? What is coming from you? What is that around me? What is that?!" . . . There the glance of the animal, the language of anxiety, had risen hugely—and set almost at once.[4]

Later he explains that animals are not "twofold," like humans; they cannot perceive both the it-world and the you-world. Especially tame animals can step up to the threshold of mutuality, but they cannot cross it. All the unasked "cat" questions that Buber paraphrases dissolved in a twitch of feline ears and tail, and the cat stayed an "it." Experiments with chimpanzees, dolphins, and whales have raised some questions about this phenomenon. But so far the evidence supports the point that animals are not addressable in the sense that persons are.

In short, addressability also characterizes the human world. We certainly treat each other as objects and as animals—for example, in crowds, bureaucracies, and wars. But we also engage in fully mutual address-and-response. As you sit in an audience of several hundred, the speaker can say your name and single you out for immediate contact: "Jeff Peterson? Are you here? Your question is about apartheid, and I want to try to answer it now." Or even more commonly and more directly, you may sit across from a friend and know from the touch of the friend's eyes, her hand, and her voice that she means *you;* she "comes to fetch you" and "touches your ground."

In summary, when I say that interpersonal communication maximizes the humanness of the persons involved, the word "persons" means more than just "thinking quadriped" or the "animal who laughs." Persons are different from objects or Its in four special ways, and it's impossible to communicate with them as persons unless you keep these differences in mind.

1. Each person is a unique, noninterchangeable part of the communication situation.
2. A person is more than just an amalgamation of observable, measurable elements; he or she is always experiencing feelings or emotions.
3. Persons are "unreliable" because they are choosers who are free to act, not just react to the condition they're in.

4. Persons are addressable; they can be talked *to* not just *about* and they can respond in kind with mutuality.

The first step toward communicating interpersonally, then, is to contact others in ways that affirm your and their "personness." This means doing several things, and each chapter that follows is about one or more of these things. For example, it means looking for the uniqueness in each person (Chapter 6) instead of being satisfied with what makes this person "just like every other _____ (jock, company man, sorority Sally, farm kid, etc.)." It also means remembering that even in a conflict situation, both you and the other person are *choosing* to feel as you do, so you both need to own your feelings, to be responsible for them (Chapter 11). Sharing some of your feelings (Chapter 8) and listening to the feelings of the other (Chapter 7) are also important, as is the process of using addressability to sculpt mutual meanings (Chapter 7). The key is to be aware of your own and the other's personness and to communicate in ways that demonstrate your awareness.

Contact

When I say that interpersonal communication is a type or quality or kind of contact, I mean to emphasize that it's something that happens *between* people, not something one person does to someone else. Just as your ability to communicate interpersonally is affected by your recognition of what it is to be a *person,* it will also be affected by your recognition of what it means to say that communication occurs *between* persons.

There are several practical reasons why it's important to develop your ability to see the betweenness, or relational nature, of human communication. For one thing, until you do, it's hard to keep from getting mad at the person who criticizes you or to keep from feeling defensive whenever you're being evaluated or controlled. Until you see the betweenness, it's also hard to keep track of the complex, continually changing myriad of things that affect your communication with a person you are close to. Without a relational perspective that focuses on contact, it's also difficult not to let the past determine what's going on in the present. In fact, all the communication behaviors discussed in later chapters—touch, tone of voice, self-disclosure, confirmation, interpretive listening, and so on—make real sense only when you see them relationally, as part of what's going on *between* persons.

The problem is, most people don't actually see communicating that way. If you were to ask the person on the street what communication means, he or she would probably say something like "getting your ideas across" or "making yourself understood." This is a common view of the communication process, a view that's operating every time someone says, "How did you screw that up? I *told* you what to do!" or "I'm sure they understood; I *explained* it three times." In these cases the conception that is operating is that communication is something I do. From this point of view, communication doesn't occur "between," but rather "in" the communicator. When things don't work out, it's because I didn't communicate well or because you didn't, the company didn't, the supervisor didn't, or whatever. From this point of view, in other words, communication is an *action*, something determined entirely by the communicator's choices. As the diagram below indicates, this point of view says that communication is like giving or getting an inoculation;

ideas and feelings are prepackaged in a mental and physical syringe and then forced under pressure in a straight line into the receiver.

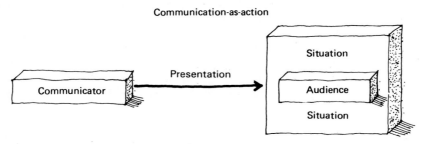

If you think about it for a minute, it becomes pretty clear why this view is inaccurate. When you see communication as just an action, you're ignoring feedback, something that's present whenever people communicate. Even on the phone, we make noises to indicate we're listening to a long comment or story. If you doubt the importance of this feedback, try being completely silent and see how soon the person on the other end asks, "Are you still there?"

The model of communication as action is also oversimplified in another way. It suggests that when you speak, there can be "an audience"; that is, a group of persons who are homogeneous—whose backgrounds, thoughts, feelings, and attitudes toward the topic and communicator are more similar than different. It also implies that the communicator's identity is not greatly affected by what goes into, or goes on during, the communication experience. In other words, it implies that regardless of any changes in the situation, the communicator is, for example, always "teacher" and never "learner," always "boss" and never "friend."

The point is, the common view that communication is an *action,* something one person *does* to somebody else, is drastically oversimplified. All of our communication behavior is affected by not only our own expectations, needs, attitudes, and goals, but also the responses we are getting from the other person involved. So it's more accurate to view communication as an *interaction,* as a process of *reciprocal* influence.

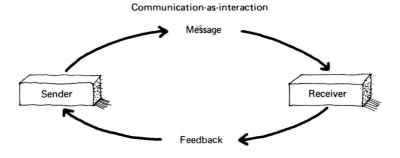

The interactional point of view can account for quite a bit of complexity. Communicologist David Berlo, for example, includes in an interaction the expectations, hypotheses, or guesses that you sometimes make about how the person will respond.[5] This point of view emphasizes that communication involves not just action, but rather action and reaction; not just stimulus, but also stimulus and response. According to this perspective, a "good" communicator not only skillfully prepares and delivers messages, but also watches for significant reactions to his or her communication. The study of human communication becomes a study of how people "talk" and how they "respond."

Although the interactional viewpoint is an improvement over communication-as-action, it still has some weaknesses. The most serious one, it seems to me, is that although it's not as oversimplified as the action view, the interactional view still distorts human communication by treating it as a series of causes and effects, stimuli and responses. For example, think about the last time you had a conversation with someone you know. What was the stimulus that caused you to greet the other person? His or her greeting? His or her look? Your expectations about the other's eagerness to talk with you? Was your greeting a response, or was it a stimulus to his or her next utterance? Or was it both? What caused you to say what you said? What the other person said? What you thought the other's words *meant?* What you *felt* because of those words? What you felt because of *how* the other person said what she or he said? What you felt because of how the other *looked* when speaking? Are you able to distinguish clearly between the stimuli and responses in this conversation or between the actions, the hypotheses about the reactions, and the reactions?

Psychologist George Kelly reported that he had "pretty well given up trying to figure out" the relationship between stimuli and responses. He wrote, "Some of my friends have tried to explain to me that the world is filled with 'S's' and 'R's' and it is unrealistic of me to refuse to recognize them. But before they have talked themselves out they become pretty vague about which is which."[6]

What I'm saying is that it's more accurate to see communication as an interaction than to see it as just an action one person performs. But if you stick to an interactional view, you will still miss an important part of what it means to focus on the *contact* or the "between," and the part you will miss is the one part that makes the most difference, the part that can make interpersonal-quality communication happen.

Over the last thirteen years I've found that helping students see this "part," helping them to see communication from this relational point of view, is one of the most important and most difficult things I do as a teacher. In my own life I am also continually reminded of how important it is to see communication relationally or to focus on the contact—every time I try to explain a concept in class, discuss a disagreement over a grade, pursue an idea with a colleague or student, or divide housekeeping responsibilities or plan a weekend with Kris. Every time my communication is really important, in other words, I rediscover how necessary it is to view what's happening relationally, to see that it's occurring *between* persons. Since this perspective is so vital, I want to talk about it in different ways using three different terms: "transaction," "relationship," and "spiritual child."

Transaction

One way to say what I mean is to use the term "transaction" and to contrast it with the *action* and *interaction* points of view.* As I said, if you see communication

---

*John Dewey and Arthur Bentley originally made this three-part distinction in their book *Knowing and the Known* (Boston: Beacon Press, 1949).

as an *action*, you're likely to be most concerned with each individual's performance. But human communication is much more than just independent message-sending. If you view communication as an interaction, you'll begin to see *some* of this "much more." The most obvious additional element you will see is feedback—how one's communication behavior is in part a response to the other person's, how human communication continually involves mutual and reciprocal influences.

It is important to see beyond performance to feedback, but there is another element that you will still miss if you stick within the interactional perspective. That element is this: *Every time persons communicate, they are continually offering definitions of themselves and responding to definitions of the other(s) which they perceive.* This process goes on all the time. Your clothes are part of your "this is how I define myself" message, just as mine are. Your tone of voice also reveals how you define yourself in relation to the situation and the person you're talking with. Recall in your mind's ear the sound of your voice when you're talking with a young person whom you define yourself as superior to. Contrast this with your tone of voice when you see yourself as an inferior talking with your supervisor or your parent. Touch, distance, eye contact, and choice of words all contribute to self-definition too. Look at the ways I've defined myself in relation to you in this book—the words I have chosen, the examples I have used, and so on. I have also assumed how you're defining yourself, and part of what I'm doing is responding to what I think is your self-definition. *And I could not not do these things.* This process of self-definition and response to the definition of the other is going on whenever people communicate.

The term "transaction" has been used to talk about this process. When it's used this way, it means more than it does in the phrase "business transaction." A dictionary of psychological terms defines a transaction as "a psychological event in which all parts or aspects of the concrete event derive their existence and nature from active participation in the event."[7] In other words, a transaction is an event in which *who we are* (our "existence and nature") emerges out of the event itself. Human communication is this kind of event. Human communication is transactional. Whenever humans communicate, part of what's going on is that each is defining himself or herself in relation to the other persons involved.

Here's where the "instrumental" and "ontological" terms become important. "Ontology" is the philosopher's word for the study of being, especially human being. What is it to be a person? How is a human being different from other kinds of being? These are some of the questions of ontology. "Instrumental" means used as an instrument to accomplish a goal, to produce a product or effect. If you think about it, when you recognize that all communication is transactional, because it's where the "existence and nature" of the persons happens, you've noticed something ontological about communication. As I said in this book's introduction, communication is more than just instrumental. We do use communication to "do" things, but it's also the way we become who we are. The quality of each person's life is directly linked to the quality of communication he or she experiences. Our human being happens or comes-to-be in the contacts we experience. Whenever humans communicate, part of what's going on is that each is defining himself or herself in relation to the other persons involved.

Obviously, this defining process has some limits. I am male, forty-eight, and brown-eyed; I can't define myself as female, ten, and blue-eyed. But I *can* offer a definition of myself that says I see myself as more masculine—or more feminine—than you and in some ways as younger or older than you. Then it's up to you to

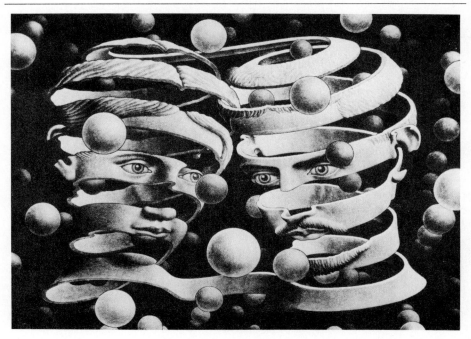

From *M. C. Escher: His Life and Work* by F. H. Boul, J. R. Kist, J. C. Loder, and F. Wjerda, ed. J. L. Loder (New York: Abrams, 1981). The print is #409, "Bond of Union," April 1956, Lithograph, 253 × 339 (10 × 13⅜").

respond to the definition of self I offer. You may accept, partly accept, or reject it altogether. The point is, at a given moment, neither of us can change our identity absolutely, but we do change in relation to each other.

The only even nearly adequate "model" of this transactional perspective that I've ever seen is the "Bond of Union" print shown here by M. C. Escher. It graphically illustrates two persons whose "existence and nature" are intertwined. Each one is a "function," in the mathematical sense, of the other, so much so that not only are the bands that constitute each head joined at the top and bottom, but they also intersect at one additional point. This image does not highlight how communication accomplishes our relational be-ing, but it does clearly illustrate many of the "transactional" and "ontological" points I've been making.

To review, then, you can see human communication as an action if you want to, but if you do you will miss a lot of what's happening. You can look at human communication as an interaction too, but you will still miss an important part of what's going on. The part you will miss is the ongoing process of self-definition-and-response-to-definition-of-the-other—the ontological part—and you won't see this clearly until you recognize that communication is a transaction, an event defined by this very process. All human communication is transactional. We're always engaged in the definition-and-response-to-definition process. Sometimes we see our communication as transactional and sometimes we don't. I'm convinced that when we don't, it's a lot harder to help interpersonal-quality communication happen.

The main reason is that when you see communication as an action you aren't focusing on the *contact between* the persons involved. All you're seeing is one person's choices, one person's behavior. When you see communication as an interaction, you still aren't seeing the contact between person A and person B. You see each person functioning something like a sophisticated billiard ball—reacting to forces from the other billiard balls, the table surface, cue stick, pads, and so on. From an interactional point of view, one's actions are affected by the others, but *who one is* doesn't change.

When you adopt a transactional point of view, though, you can't help but look at the contact *between* the persons involved. If you focus your attention on just person A, for example, you realize that since person A is who he or she is only in relation to person B, you have to look immediately at what's happening *between* them. The same goes for person B. Since *who the persons are*—their "existence and nature"—emerges out of their meeting with each other, you can't help but focus on the meeting itself rather than on the individual meeters.

Relationship

I want to shift vocabularies now and make the same point in slightly different terms. The authors of one of the two or three most influential communication books written in the last twenty years earned their well-justified fame in part by distinguishing between the *content* aspect of communication and the *relationship* aspect.[8] The authors' names are Paul Watzlawick, Janet Beavin, and Don Jackson. As they explain, the content aspect of communication is the information, the "facts," the data in the message. The difference between "I'll meet you here in twenty minutes" and "I'll meet you at the post office in an hour" is a difference in communication *content*. Up to the publication of their book, most communication studies focused on content. People concentrated on creating and researching ideas, organizing information systematically, and building persuasive arguments. If attention was paid to style or delivery, it was mainly to insure that the message had vitality, smoothness, or the right amount of ornamentation.

Watzlawick, Beavin, and Jackson argued persuasively that there's also another aspect of communication that most communication scholars and teachers have overlooked, the *relationship* aspect. They called it that because it has to do with the way the people communicating are relating with each other. The difference between "I'll meet you here in twenty minutes" and "Why the hell didn't you call before now? Get over here in twenty minutes or you're in deep trouble!" is a difference in *relationship* communication: How I perceive myself, how I see you, how I see you seeing me, and vice versa—how you perceive yourself, your perception of me, and how you see me seeing you. So whereas the information makes up the content aspect, the relationship aspect refers to the quality of type or kind of *contact* that's occurring *between* the communicators.

Watzlawick, Beavin, and Jackson point out that the relationship aspect is a part of *all* human communicating. You cannot write or say or respond to anything without at least implicitly offering a definition of the relationship between yourself and the other(s) involved. In addition, any response from the other will include his or her own definition-and-response-to-yours. For example, if you begin a letter with "Dear Professor Nichols:" the "Professor" title and the colon help define the relationship as more formal than a letter to the same person which begins, "Dear Marie." You decide which to use by noticing how the other person defines herself in relation to you. I've already mentioned in my discussion of basic assumptions how, in face-to-face contacts, the communicators' tone of voice, touch, distance, and eye contact also contribute to this process of relationship defining.

Another way we define the relationships we're in is by organizing—or what Watzlawick, Beavin, and Jackson call "punctuating"—the sequence of communication events we experience. For example, let's assume that a couple you are friends with has heard that you're studying interpersonal communication, so they ask you to help them out. Jill tells you that Jack withdraws all the time; he won't talk with her and it's driving her nuts. Jack tells you that Jill consistently nags him. "Sure I withdraw," he says, "You would too if she nagged you like she does me."

If you were going to apply this insight about relationship communication, you might diagram the couple's relationship as has been done this way:[9]

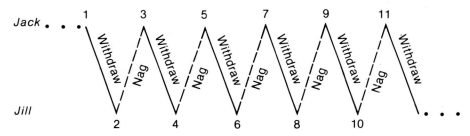

The diagram allows you to see that, for Jill, the sequence goes 1-2-3, 3-4-5, 5-6-7, and so on. She believes that Jack "starts" the pattern; it's his fault because he won't talk to her. As Jill says to you, "I'm just responding to him—like any normal person would."

Jacks sees it differently; for him the sequence goes 2-3-4, 4-5-6, 6-7-8, and so on. He thinks it starts with Jill's nagging, and he's just reponding the way any normal person would—by withdrawing. For our purposes, the point is that Jack and Jill each define the relationship differently, depending on how they organize, or "punctuate," it—specifically, where each believes it "starts." The ellipses at the left and right of the diagram indicate that both Jack and Jill are "right" *and* "wrong." Things actually started before this nag–withdraw sequence got going, and they will continue beyond it. The definition of the *between*, the quality of the *contact*, or the *relationship* depends on how each person punctuates the ongoing flow of events.

I want to emphasize that both the relationship aspect of communication and the "punctuation" notion focus your attention not on the individual communicators but on their *contact*, what's between them, the *transaction* in which they're involved. It's like the "bridges" in the title of this book. The metaphor of *Bridges Not Walls* is meant to highlight not only the difference between separation and connection but also the importance of the *between*. Think of a bridge that spans a deep canyon. The structure of the bridge is that-which-connects the two sides. When you're focusing on the bridge itself, your attention is not on the forest on one side or the rocks on the other, but on the contact, the relationship, the between.

This is exactly where your attention needs to be if you're going to promote and enhance what this book means by interpersonal-quality communication. As

I've already indicated, our inability—or unwillingness—to see communication relationally has the most impact when we're in the middle of a conflict. When you're really arguing with someone, it *seems* obvious that he or she is "making you mad," that the argument is the other person's "fault," because he or she "started" it, that you're "right" about important points and that the other person is "wrong." But all these conclusions that *seem* so obvious come from seeing what's happening not as a relationship, but as a cause–effect, stimulus–response thing. For example, as Chapter 10 points out, nobody *makes* you feel angry; your anger emerges in the relationship, and it's partly *your* choice to feel angry. Similarly, you won't get anywhere trying to figure out whose "fault" an argument is. You will probably get something like this: "I clam up because you keep nagging me; it's your fault!" "But I only nag you because you won't say anything; it's your fault!" In a sense, neither person is "right" or "wrong," and both are. The conflict emerges in the relationship. As long as you're looking at just one side, you'll stay stuck in the blaming game and communication won't improve much.

Spiritual Child

Let me briefly put this point one more way, then we'll go on to something else. I was discussing this transactional, relational idea with John Keltner several years ago. John is an interpersonal communication teacher who wrote the first widely used interpersonal speech communication textbook. He said that the idea reminded him of an interesting concept that he and Loraine Halfen Zephyr had talked about. John and Zephyr suggested that it's easier to see human communication transactionally or relationally if you think in terms of a "spiritual child" that is the inevitable offspring of every human meeting.

In other words, whenever you encounter someone, the two of you together create a spiritual child—your *relationship*. Unlike the creation of physical children, there are no contraceptives available for spiritual children; when two people meet, they always create a relationship of some sort. Also unlike physical children, the spiritual child lives as long as at least one person lives. If two persons once have a relationship, their relationship endures, even though years and continents may separate them. The spiritual child can change drastically, but it can't be killed. That's one of the reasons why it's so hard to deal with the breakup of a long-term, intimate relationship. Since the spiritual child won't die, the relationship won't cease to exist, and each person has to learn to live with a radically, maybe even tragically different "child."

Zephyr describes the creation of this "third being" in these words:

> In human interaction, a natural spiritual child is conceived, and there is no available contraceptive.... When you and I interact, something new is present, a new organism, we. Yet you or I are not lost. The bits and pieces of the relating come together in a holographic process, and an entity emerges which embodies all the qualities of the actors and the process of the interacting.... If we come together in care, authenticity, honesty, and positive regard, our child will be healthy, vibrant, winsome, and beautiful. We will love it. We will receive much joy in the nurturing of it and we will be nourished in return.

> If our child is created in dishonesty, exploitation, contempt, disregard, our child will be sickly, crippled, distorted, toxic, frustrated. It will be ugly. We will fly from it, abandon it, but its influence will linger.[10]

At first it probably feels a little strange to think of your relationship with someone as a "spiritual child." But try letting the metaphor work for you. Many people today are rediscovering the power of "right brain" or metaphoric thinking.[11] They emphasize that metaphors are one of the best ways to "make the strange familiar." Metaphors do that by linking something unknown with something we know very well. So a complex ethical idea gets labeled "moral bankruptcy" and it immediately becomes clearer. Or we can say, "That's just part of the game of life," "They want to rape the earth," or "This office is a zoo." Each metaphor economically illuminates a complex idea by linking something strange with something familiar.

The spiritual child metaphor can work that way too. Here are two examples of how it helped Zephyr respond to communication problems she experienced:

I had not "seen" a spiritual child for some time. A situation developed in which a friend, with whom I had a very strong and healthy, delightful, nurturing child, became angry and afraid and felt invaded when a third person began living in our apartment. I found myself becoming more and more disgusted with the whole scene; I was very anxious and didn't know what to do to change what was happening.

One day, I thought of the spiritual child concept. I realized I had never consciously attempted to evoke an image. I had never asked or told my subconscious mind to produce one for me. I decided to do it, but I really didn't know how.

I sat in a rocking chair alone and said aloud, "I am experiencing our child as stubborn, balky, angry, afraid." Then I realized I was talking about the way I was experiencing my friend. So I closed my eyes, cleared my mind, and became very still and calm. Bingo! There it was, so clear—the child was about a year old, perfectly formed, but very very delicate. It was in a crawling position with a long white garment on. As soon as it recognized that it had my attention, it put its thumb in its mouth and turned over in a fetal position. In my mind was the question, "What are you telling me?" The answer came back in a plaintive tone, "What's going to happen to me?"

Immediately I recognized how close I was to walking out of that relationship. I was fed up, but I had not been aware of it. As soon as I got that understanding, the image left.

Now, I had a choice. Did I really want to end our interaction? No, I valued this relationship. Yet, it was also clear that it wasn't only my decision. We had often spoken of our "child" and how healthy it was and how its influence was such a comfort to us.

When my friend came home from work, I told her of my experience. Out of the discussion that followed came two conclusions. We both wanted that child, but what we had to nourish it with right now was poisonous. So we decided to withdraw all nourishment for a time. I was moving into a house for the summer. We had no contact for two months. At the end of that time, I invited her to dinner, and we very tentatively, carefully, and gently resumed interaction. Today, five years later, our child is robust, stable, mature and truly a delight.

Another incident made it clear to me that the child can be represented in the mind's eye in the form of a symbol. I had had a wounding experience with my secretary at the end of a long hard day. We were both very weary and irritable. I was rather ruthlessly pressing her for information, and she was responding to that pressure with a lot of expressed anger. I didn't know how to approach her to heal that wound, and again decided to evoke an image of the child.

I put myself in a quiet place and cleared my mind. What I got was an onion! I couldn't believe it, and tried to make it go away so I could get the "real" image. It wouldn't go, so I said to myself, "How is this onion like our relationship? What are the qualities of an onion?" I thought of how an onion is layered and the core is very deep inside. One has to probe very deeply to get to (understand) the core. "Ah, that's it. Our child is very deep; we have to take off a lot of layers to understand it." Although there was some relief, it was not complete, and the image remained. I knew I hadn't gotten it yet, so I just watched. As I did, I noticed the golden brown skin of the onion began to separate like it was peeling itself away from the top of the onion. As I watched I noticed how very thin that skin was—thin skin. We had a very thin-skinned child! Immediately the image vanished. What does one do with a very thin-skinned child? Treat it very very carefully and gently.

I was very consciously careful and gentle in all my interactions. At the end of the second day, my secretary told me she was embarrassed about her outburst. Now that she had selected the time, I told her of my evoking our child and what had happened. As we discussed it, we learned a lot about our relationship and came to a new level of trust. The visualization of the onion was a holographic process in which the activities of the left brain were sufficiently quieted so that material from the unconscious could emerge through the right brain activity of imaging. When the left brain began to dominate, to "figure it out," the insight was momentarily blocked. So, when we need some information, we contact the storehouse. In the beginning, relaxation of the body and attending to the breathing will help to "clear the mind." When you feel suffi-ciently relaxed and quiet, ask for a picture and calmly and patiently and confidently wait. Make no effort. Efforting delays or completely frustrates the process.... It is sim-ilar to a meditative state, and one way of beginning to experience this method of "seeing" is to block the left brain messages by concentration on the breath. Once the picture appears, an interpersonal dialogue can take place. Sometimes just watching tells everything.[12]

I hope that the spiritual child metaphor is useful for you. It gives me another way to look at the contact, the relationship, the transaction, what's between the persons. As a child, you are neither of your parents, but the result of their meeting, their contact. Similarly, the spiritual child who is born whenever two persons com-municate is an entity that emerges *between* them.

I also hope that you will keep this "contact," "transaction," "relationship" point in mind when you read the titles of Part Two and Part Three of this book. On the one hand, I want these parts of the book's organization to acknowledge that communication contact is made up of two parts or "moves": "input and out-put," "receiving and sending." On the other hand, those labels won't work because they're not relational; they highlight the sides of the canyon rather than the bridge. So I've chosen two other language strategies.

The first is to use the word "openness," because it has both meanings. "Being open" can mean being both receptive to others' ideas and feelings *and* willing to disclose. A person can be open in the sense that he or she is tolerant, broadminded, and willing to listen (open to "input") and open in the sense that he or she does not hesitate to share ideas and feelings with others (open with "output"). So I use "open" in the titles of both Part Two and Part Three.

My second language move is to use "exhaling" and "inhaling" to identify which sense of "openness" each part deals with. I chose those words because each of us has firsthand experience with how inseparable they are. Try inhaling without exhaling or vice versa. I'd like you to think of "output and input" or "sending and receiving" that way too—as inseparable, *always* occurring together. The one disadvantage is that inhaling and exhaling can't happen simultaneously, but both senses of openness can and do. So my choice of labels is a bit of a compromise. But I hope that the titles for Parts Two and Three help reinforce the transactional, relational point I've been making.

The communicative challenge here is to use terms that clarify without distorting. Milt Thomas, a friend who's contributed a great deal to this book, suggests the metaphor of velcro. That fabric fastener or zipper substitute is made up of the hook side and the loop side, but neither is worth anything without the other. Velcro works because of the *between*, the *contact*.

Summary

All of this can be summarized by saying that when I use the term *interpersonal communication* I mean "contact between persons." Both key concepts—*contact between* and *persons*—carry a lot of meaning in that statement. But if you keep in mind what it is to be a person and what's meant by contact, you can come up with a fairly straightforward definition of interpersonal communication:

> Interpersonal communication is the kind, type, or quality of transaction, relationship, or spiritual child that happens when two or more humans are willing and able to meet as persons by making available some of their personness—their uniqueness, unmeasurable aspects, active choosing, and addressability—and by being sensitive to or aware of some of the other's personness. Or more briefly, interpersonal communication is the quality of contact that occurs when each person involved talks and listens in ways that maximize their own and the other person's humanness.

As I've already said, this book is organized around this definition, and each chapter further explains and gives examples of one aspect of interpersonal-quality communication. Part One (Chapters 1–4) explores the basic ingredients—the assumptions, the transactional perspective, the function of words, and the working of nonverbal cues. Part Two (Chapters 5–7) deals with the "inhaling" dimensions—self-awareness, awareness of others, and listening. In Part Three (Chapters 8–9) the readings explore the "exhaling" dimensions of communication—self-disclosure and confirmation. The readings in Part Four (Chapters 10–13) suggest how the approach to interpersonal communication outlined in the rest of the book can apply to communication across differences—in relationships, in conflict, in male-female contacts, and across cultures. Part Five (Chapters 14–16) includes essays by three people who have been able to put all of these ideas together.

I hope the ideas and suggestions here work for you. They make a real difference to me!

References

1. Paraphrased from Martin Buber, *I and Thou*, trans. Walter Kaufmann (New York: Scribner, 1970), pp. 82–84.
2. George Isaac Brown, *Human Teaching for Human Learning: An Introduction to Confluent Education* (New York: Viking, 1971), p. 4.
3. Ervin Singer, *Key Concepts in Psychotherapy,* 2nd ed. (New York: Basic, 1970), p. 17.
4. Buber, *I and Thou,* p. 145.

5. David Berlo, "Interaction: The Goal of Interpersonal Communication," in *The Process of Communication* (New York: Holt, Rinehart and Winston, 1960), pp. 106–131.
6. George A. Kelly, "The Autobiography of a Theory," *Clinical Psychology and Personality: The Selected Papers of George Kelly,* ed. Brendan Maher (New York: Wiley, 1969), p. 47.
7. Horace B. English and Ava Champney English, *A Comprehensive Dictionary of Psychological and Psychoanalytical Terms* (New York: Longmans, Green, 1958), p. 561.
8. Paul Watzlawick, Janet Helmick Beavin, and Don D. Jackson, *Pragmatics of Human Communication* (New York: Norton, 1968), see especially Chapter 2.
9. Watzlawick, Beavin, and Jackson, pp. 54–59.
10. Loraine Halfen Zephyr, "Creating Your Spiritual Child," in *Bridges Not Walls: A Book About Interpersonal Communication,* 3rd ed., ed. John Stewart (Reading, Mass.: Addison-Wesley, 1982), p. 34.
11. See, e.g., Paul Watzlawick, *The Language of Change: Elements of Therapeutic Communication* (New York: Basic Books, 1978); and Roger von Oech, *A Whack on the Side of the Head: How to Unlock Your Mind for Innovation* (Menlo Park, Calif.: Creative Think, 1982).
12. Zephyr, pp. 37–38.

Review Questions

1. True or False: "According to my definition, interpersonal communication can't happen between two people who are talking to each other on the telephone." Explain.
2. What does Buber mean when he says that humans have a "twofold perspective"?
3. Which statement best characterizes what I mean by a transactional view of communication?
   a. "Let me make myself perfectly clear."
   b. "You'd understand me if you'd only listen!"
   c. "I can sell anything to anyone."
   d. "I'm not sure we mean the same thing."
   e. "You make me so mad I could scream!"
4. Biology is the study ("ology") of life ("bios"). Ontology is the study of
   a. truth
   b. knowledge
   c. being
   d. reality
5. My approach to interpersonal communication focuses on
   a. What goes on in people's heads more than what goes on between them.
   b. What goes on between people more than what goes in inside their heads.
6. According to Paul Watzlawick and his colleagues, "punctuating" a communication sequence means
   a. evaluating its parts by identifying what's "better" and "worse."
   b. organizing its parts into "causes" and "effects."
   c. organizing its parts into what occurred chronologically "first," "second," "third," and so on.
   d. None of the above.
7. The term "spiritual child" is a metaphor for a _____.
8. Why do I use the terms "openness," "inhaling," and "exhaling" as I do in the divisions of this book?

Probes

1. Does this essay say that people who experience a certain kind or quality of communication are actually "more human" than those who don't? How can that be? What does it mean to be "more" or "less" *human*?

2. What's the relationship between the "unmeasurable" characteristics of objects and persons and their "spatiotemporal" characteristics?
3. What's the relationship between the human characteristics of "choice" and "predictability"?
4. Give your own description of addressability. What does it mean to be able to talk *to* and *with* someone as contrasted with only being able to talk *at* or *about* objects?
5. Squeeze together the thumb and index finger of your left hand. Now describe their *contact*—not what the thumb is doing or what the index finger is doing, but their *contact*. (You'll probably find that it's difficult to describe contact. This is why I use the three different terms: "transaction," "relationship," and "spiritual child.")
6. The next time you watch your favorite television program, take five minutes to notice the "relationship messages" of the central character. Specifically what does the character say and do to define him- or herself in relation to the others in the program? Notice dress, posture, tone of voice, word choice, eye contact, timing, and touching behavior.

The following pages come from one of the books I quoted in the introductory essay. As I mentioned there, James Lynch is a professor and clinic director at the University of Maryland School of Medicine. Since the early 1980s, he's written extensively about the impact of dialogue on our physical health. His books contain a great deal of detailed evidence about how the quality of the communication we experience affects the quality of our lives.

This is the introduction to his most recent book, *The Language of the Heart*. He argues here that "human dialogue not only affects our hearts significantly but can even alter the biochemistry of individual tissues at the farthest extremities of the body." To some people, that probably sounds like eastern mysticism or New Age pseudoscience. But Lynch's documentation is impressive; in his book, he cites literally hundreds of medical studies that support his claims. He also points out that it is difficult for some people to accept the link between dialogue and physical health, because we've been taught for years that the human body is essentially a complex machine. We know that talk, human conversation, or dialogue is not reducible without remainder to the programmable, cause-and-effect elements of mechanics. And yet this nonmechanical phenomenon significantly affects our allegedly mechanical bodies. How can that be?

Without trying to provide an easy answer to this question, Lynch briefly describes what he believes are the historical ideas and attitudes that have led us to our current picture of the human body. And he tells how the discoveries he and his colleagues are making are beginning to provide the foundation for a new type of clinic that integrates medicine and speech communication.

I include this essay in order to encourage you to think about how the communication *you* experience is more than just a way to accomplish tasks, negotiate deals, and get your needs met. There's an important link between how you talk and *who you are*. No complete study of speech communication in any of its forms—public speaking, argumentation, organizational communication, media, or interpersonal relationships—should overlook this link.

The Language of the Heart

James J. Lynch

It is obvious that we human beings are distinguished from all other living creatures by the fact that we speak. Whether man or woman or child, we can share our desires, thoughts, plans, and—above all—feelings with each other through dialogue. Coupled to this is another simple yet sublime truth: that while we speak with words, we speak also with our flesh and blood. As we shall see, study after study reveals that human dialogue not only affects our hearts significantly but can even alter the biochemistry of individual tissues at the furthest extremities of the body. Since blood flows through every human tissue, the entire body is influenced by human dialogue. Thus, it is true that when we speak we do so with every fiber of our being.

This "language of the heart" is integral to the health and emotional life of every one of us. Yet this vital truth has been largely obscured by a scientific-philosophical perspective we all share and that leads us to think about the human body solely in terms of its mechanical functions. In an age dominated by dramatic images of heart transplants, artificial heart machines, and even the implantation of a baboon's heart into a human baby, it is all too easy to look on the human body solely as a machine incapable of either listening or speaking to others. Nonetheless, the essence of the human being is the body's involvement in dialogue—a process in which no machine can ever engage. For the human heart speaks a language that not only is vital to our well-being but makes possible human feelings and binds human beings together. . . .

To appreciate why we tend to think about the body as a machine, we need only recall an outstanding event of late 1982 and early 1983. For the first time ever, at the University of Utah's Medical Center in Salt Lake City, the life of a human being was sustained by an artificial heart machine. The public's response to this endeavor was electric, perhaps equaled only by the excitement over the first heart transplant operation performed by Christiaan Barnard in Capetown, South Africa, in 1969. And, as in that earlier operation, hourly news bulletins told the world of Dr. Clark's progress, as relentlessly and efficiently pulsating with the timed sighs of its own air compressors, a machine outside of his body kept the life-sustaining fluid—blood—flowing through it. For 112 days, the machine kept beating, pumping blood through his body, until with the failure of other organs, his circulatory system collapsed, and he died. Thirteen hundred mourners, including a personal representative of the President of the United States, attended his funeral in the town of Federal Way in the state of Washington.

Clearly, not only Dr. Clark but the medical profession had attempted, and accomplished, a heroic and extraordinary feat. Moreover, this feat, heralded all over the world, was the culmination of a belief on which medical scientists have acted for over three centuries: that is, that the human body is made up of a group of

From *The Language of the Heart: The Human Body in Dialogue* by James J. Lynch. Reprinted by permission of Basic Books, Inc., Publishers.

essentially mechanical organs that, when not running properly, can be tinkered with, like any mechanism, in the hope of setting it right again.

At about the same time, my colleagues and I at the Psychophysiological Clinic at the University of Maryland Medical School, were seeing, also for the first time, quite a different aspect of the human cardiovascular system that would lead us to develop an entirely new type of clinic, one based on an understanding of the connection between human communication and the cardiovascular system. For computer technology allowed us to see that as soon as one begins to speak, one's blood pressure increases significantly, one's heart beats faster and harder, and microscopic blood vessels in distant parts of the body change as well. Conversely, when one listens to others speak or truly attends to the external environment in a relaxed manner, then blood pressure usually falls and heart rate slows, frequently below its normal resting levels.

Initially, this discovery seemed more a curiosity than a conceptual breakthrough, especially when contrasted with the human and technical drama in Utah. Yet the data were so clear and so predictably consistent that we could not ignore them. They showed us that centuries of religious, philosophical, literary, and poetic wisdom that had suggested links between words and the human heart contained the core of an astonishingly fertile truth, and one central to medicine. Once aware of this truth, we tested for it in a variety of cases and research studies. We examined thousands of individuals, from newborn babies crying in their cribs; to preschool children reciting their ABCs; to grade-school children reading aloud from textbooks; to nursing and medical students describing their daily work routine; to hypertensive patients in our clinic, and those waiting anxiously for cardiac by-pass surgery; to schizophrenics in psychiatric wards; to elderly patients in nursing homes describing their loneliness, and in patients close to death. In each and every one, the link between language and the heart was clear and undeniable.

Yet, as I shall discuss, there was a powerful force that made it initially difficult for us to appreciate fully that we were indeed creating a new type of clinic. That force had to do, as I have said, with an unexamined philosophical perspective we brought to our own research. It included a vision of the human body shared by virtually everyone in our society, and first formulated by the French philosopher René Descartes in the seventeenth century. Living in an era that witnessed the beginnings of modern science, Descartes harnessed the discoveries of scientists like Galileo, Copernicus, Kepler, Harvey, and Pascal and cast their findings into a new and comprehensive philosophical system. As Descartes himself stated, he intended to create a totally new medicine, one based on the idea that the human body is a machine. He accomplished his goal so brilliantly that his influence, though pervasive, is scarcely understood today. Rather, like the air we breathe, his perspective is simply taken for granted.

Descartes promulgated and defended the idea that the human body functions like all other bodies in nature, according to mechanical principles. He separated mental functioning from bodily mechanics, arguing that the capacity to think has to be the result of the existence of the human soul. While ostensibly innocent, it was an extraordinary vision, one that permeates the way we in the Western world came to understand the nature of human beings, the human body, human health, and the links between our individual bodies and our social existence. After Descartes, issues of health and illness were relegated strictly to medical science; while spiritual and social concerns came to be seen as having little in common with physical health.* Physicians would come to be trained much as were the highly skilled technicians who maintained the French water gardens where statues were cleverly designed to move by means of water pressure, and that helped to inspire Descartes's concept. Three centuries after him, it would make "perfect sense" to think about a heart transplant in a human being much as a mechanic thinks about replacing a faulty water pump in an automobile: heart disease had become a mechanical problem in a faulty hydraulic system. Indeed, as the doctor treating the baby girl with the transplated baboon heart said, "The heart ... 'is a muscular pump and is not the seat of the soul.'"[1]

The stage, thus, was set with Descartes. From then on, thinker after thinker, scientist after scientist—including, as we shall see, those seminal masters of modern times, Marx, Darwin, Freud, and Pavlov—thought about the human body in mechanical terms. Whether in social evolution or in social revolution, the body was uncritically accepted to be an isolated, self-contained group of organs functioning strictly according to mechanical principles. In the process, the emotional life of human beings came to be seen as a reflection of mechanical functions inside a well-regulated machine. Unique aspects of human emotional life and the unique nature of human speech were obscured by a scientific perspective that accepted the human body as mechanically similar to other animal bodies, and human emotional life as comparable to the emotional life of animals.

Our thinking about these issues has developed over two decades of research. When we originally began our journey, we sought to understand how human relationships and human loneliness affect cardiovascular health. In 1977, I summarized our findings in *The Broken Heart.*[2] That book was based on the fact that human loneliness is among the most important causes of premature death in modern America. In our studies, for virtually every cause of death—whether suicide, cancer, cirrhosis of the liver, automobile accident, or heart disease—the incidence of premature death was far higher among people who lived alone than among those who were married. While in certain cases—such as suicide, cirrhosis of the liver, or lung cancer—we could easily detect the factors that caused premature death, in others the mechanisms were far less clearcut, especially for heart disease, the leading cause of death in the United States. It was far from obvious why the single, the widowed, and the divorced were two to four times more likely than married people to die prematurely from hypertension, stroke, and coronary heart disease.

While human loneliness appeared to be the single most important and compelling emotional factor in these premature deaths, we were at a loss to explain how this feeling state influenced the heart. Though the statistics were unambigu-

---

*Descartes's influence was every bit as pronounced in religious circles as in medicine. Thus, today no theological school—be it Catholic, Protestant, or Rabbinical—deems it necessary to teach its students elementary anatomy and physiology. The body is considered utterly irrelevant to religious questions, even though the Bible was rooted in such concerns (for example, Talmudic dietary regulations, or Christian and Judaic notions about blood and the heart). Hospital chaplains are today trained so as to feel no need to understand even the most rudimentary aspects of physical disease; instead, they see their job as caring for the soul. Likewise, psychologists can go through college and graduate school without any training in anatomy and physiology. And even the most elementary introductory courses in psychology or philosophy are not required to gain entrance to medical schools, though such schools do require advanced training in calculus, physics, and chemistry.

ous, we did not understand how a human experience such as loss or bereavement could lead to premature death from hypertension, stroke, or heart attack any more than we understood how loneliness caused elevations in blood pressure. While pondering this question, we were equally troubled about how to counteract this problem effectively, since many of the patients who appeared in the coronary-care unit recapitulated the very statistics we had uncovered linking loneliness to increased risk of heart disease.

These questions led us to explore loneliness in hypertensive patients. Since hypertension was, and still is, the single most important medical problem in modern America (it has been estimated that anywhere between forty million to sixty million Americans are hypertensive), we assumed that loneliness played an important role in the problem in at least a significant percentage of these cases.

Yet our efforts to examine the interlocking problem of human loneliness and hypertension quickly confronted us with a whole series of paradoxes. While it seemed intuitively obvious that human dialogue ought to be the best antidote to human loneliness, a large and well-documented literature had amply warned that certain types of social interaction can cause marked increases in the blood pressure of hypertensive patients. Even more to the point, the type of psychotherapeutic dialogue that seemed best suited to delve into issues surrounding the loneliness of hypertensive patients had already been shown to be precisely the type of encounter that would cause their blood pressure to rise to dangerous levels. This problem was compounded further when we discovered a striking relationship between speaking and blood pressure. While the blood pressure of almost everyone we tested rose during speech, that of hypertensive patients increased far more than that of any other group. Sometimes a hypertensive person's blood pressure would surge 50 percent above the resting baseline level as soon as he or she began to speak. Thus, we were forced to recognize that our psychotherapeutic "cure" could make hypertension worse. We began to wonder whether hypertensive patients were trapped inside their own bodies, damned if they withdrew from their fellow human beings and damned if they tried to relate to them.

Through our efforts to reconcile this dilemma, we uncovered a new dimension of the cardiovascular system which allowed us to develop an entirely new way to approach the treatment of vascular disorders, such as hypertension and migraine headaches. And we came finally to recognize that the human cardiovascular system does far more than change in response to internal and external demands: it also communicates. Since our hearts can speak a language that no one hears or sees and therefore cannot understand, we can get sick at heart. . . .

In machines created by humans, it is perfectly clear who and what controls the internal mechanisms and why a particular machine, such as the pump that replaced Barney Clark's heart, was created. That pump was designed to fill a particular purpose, and it was absolutely regulated by its creators. Yet who is in charge of, and what controls, the machinery of the human heart is another matter. Control is exercised from both inside and outside. This idea, though simple when it first occurred to us, gradually led us to understand that internal bodily mechanisms, such as blood pressure, long thought to be primarily regulated by the internal machinery of the human body, are also powerfully influenced by the force of human dialogue. Once this force was recognized, we came to understand that dialogue gives the body its very humanity.

Since human dialogue, and its relationship to our hearts and feelings, is the central issue of this book, let me define it as I did in *The Broken Heart*:

> In its most general meaning, dialogue consists of reciprocal communication between two or more living creatures. It involves the sharing of thoughts, physical sensations, ideas, ideals, hopes, and feelings. In sum, dialogue involves the reciprocal sharing of any and all life experiences....
>
> Other characteristics of the process of dialogue are that it is reciprocal, spontaneous, often nonverbal, *and* alive.[3]

At the core of this book is the idea that we human beings are biologically interrelated—and that any attempt to maintain or restore health must be based on that reality. Scientific attempts to understand the human body apart from the most basic of all human traits—the fact that we speak—is all too likely to produce a medicine that brilliantly treats isolated parts of the human body, while it seriously neglects the individual as a whole and as a part of nature. We can understand and cope with illness only when we are able to view ourselves as part of a complex world beyond the confines of our own individual skin. The response of our hearts, blood vessels, and muscles when we communicate with spouse, children, friends, colleagues, and the larger community has as much to do with our cardiovascular health as do factors such as exercise or diet.

So vital to human health is the language of our hearts that—if ignored, unheard, or misunderstood—it can produce terrible physical suffering, even premature death. For the language of our hearts cries out to be heard. It demands to be understood. And it must not be denied. Our hearts speak with an eloquence that poets have always, and truly, sensed. It is for us to learn to listen and to understand.

Notes

1. *The New York Times*, October 31, 1984, p. A18.
2. James J. Lynch, *The Broken Heart: The Medical Consequences of Loneliness* (New York: Basic Books, 1977).
3. Lynch, pp. 217, 218.

Review Questions

1. Lynch claims that a "vital truth" has been "largely obscured" by our mechanistic scientific-philosophical perspective. What is that "vital truth"?
2. What is the primary distinctive feature of the approach to cardiovascular health that Dr. Lynch and his colleagues are taking in their clinic at the University of Maryland?
3. Lynch claims that a seventeenth-century philosopher named _____ is primarily responsible for our current mechanical view of the human body.
4. Our mechanical view of the human body begins from the belief that there is a fundamental separation between what and what?
5. What has Dr. Lynch's research shown about the relationships between loneliness, heart disease, and dialogue?
6. Lynch believes that, if our efforts to understand the human body don't pay attention to speech, what will occur? What problem will the neglect of speech create?

Probes

1. Based on your own experience with the medical profession, how do you think most medical doctors might be responding to Lynch's belief that doctors can learn from "centuries of religious, philosophical, literary, and poetic wisdom"?
2. Is Lynch arguing that Descartes single-handedly established our modern view of the human body? What's his point here?
3. Lynch implies that Descartes' scientific-philosophical perspective especially affected the way we view *speech*. What does he say about this topic?
4. What does Lynch mean when he says that control of the human heart is exercised from both inside and outside"?
5. What's the relationship between Lynch's definition of dialogue and my definition of interpersonal communication?

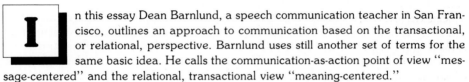

In this essay Dean Barnlund, a speech communication teacher in San Francisco, outlines an approach to communication based on the transactional, or relational, perspective. Barnlund uses still another set of terms for the same basic idea. He calls the communication-as-action point of view "message-centered" and the relational, transactional view "meaning-centered."

Barnlund shows how theories that are not meaning-centered can't adequately explain human communication, a process he describes as being complex, circular, irreversible, unrepeatable, and involving the total personality of all the participants. He also explains that a meaning-centered philosophy focuses on "the state of mind, the assumptive world and the needs of the listener or observer." At the end of this piece, Barnlund talks about some of the ethical implications of this viewpoint.

Persons in my classes have often been able to use this message-centered/meaning-centered distinction to summarize and clarify the whole action–interaction–transaction analysis I talked about before. If you view human communication as a process of message-creating, message-sending, and message-receiving, you're looking at it as an action or interaction. Only when you see how our communicating is a process of *meaning*-sharing do you begin to view it transactionally, or relationally.

Toward a Meaning-Centered Philosophy of Communication

Dean C. Barnlund

... To be acceptable, a philosophy of communication should fulfill the following criteria: (1) It should provide a satisfactory explanation of the aim of com-

This is an abridgment of an article originally appearing in the *Journal of Communication* 12 (1962): 197–211. Reprinted by permission of the *Journal of Communication* and the author.

munication. (2) It should provide a technically adequate description of the process of communication. (3) It should provide a moral standard that will protect and promote that healthiest communicative behavior. Once this process is defined and its nature exposed, the way should be clear for facing the practical decisions involved in giving effective instruction.

Aim of Communication

We begin by asking why men communicate? What human need does it, or should it, satisfy? While there is almost universal agreement that communication is tied to the manipulation of symbols, there is widespread disagreement as to what constitutes effectiveness in this endeavor. A brief review of some abortive explanations of communication is essential because, in spite of repeated criticism, these conceptions continue to influence current training in speech.

One of these theories is that the aim of communication is to transmit information. Success hinges on mastery of the facts, effective arrangement of materials, and strength of expression. It is a message-centered philosophy of communication. And it is largely amoral. Critical standards for determining the effectiveness of communication, as in the critical evaluation of literature, are internal; they are found within the message itself. When a writer or speaker or critic asks, "Was it well said?" he is usually viewing communication as a mode of expression. The training in communication that follows from this premise and perspective is destined to be truncated and unrealistic. Talk is not a guarantee of communication. Facts and ideas are not shared because they are articulated loudly or even well. Messages do not influence automatically because of being broadcast on the mass media. The inadequacy of this approach lies in its neglect of the listener as terminus of the communicative act, in its failure to provide an explanation of how meaning arises through communication, and in its disregard for all but public and continuous discourse.

A second theory is that the aim of communication is to transfer ideas from one person to another. Here the listener is admitted as part of the communicative situation. The focus, however, in research and training, is upon the message formulator. Effectiveness in communication is thought to turn not only on the content and phrasing of the message, but on the intelligence and credibility of the source. Relatively little attention is paid to the listener other than to note that messages should be adapted to his interests. It ends by becoming a speaker-centered philosophy. Communicative events are explained largely in terms of the experiential milieu that shaped the mind of the speaker and find expression in his messages.

As an explanation of communication it, too, fails in several important respects. First, the listener tends to be regarded as a passive object, rather than an active force in communication. Unfortunately, it is not that simple to deposit ideas in another mind. Teachers of great intelligence and high purpose often find their lessons disregarded or misapplied. Messages flowing through an industrial complex are not received undistorted like images in a hall of mirrors. Second, this approach also fails to provide a satisfactory theory of meaning, and of how messages from highly credible sources can provoke so many and such contradictory meanings. Finally, it is too parochial. It neglects man's communication with himself—an area that is fast becoming one of the most vital in communication research—and it fails to account for the fact that communication is as often a matter of hiding or protecting what is in men's minds as it is a matter of revealing their thoughts and intentions.

Neither of these schools of thought, of course, omits the constituent elements in communication altogether. It is, rather, a question of emphasis. Questions of emphasis, however, are not irrelevant or inconsequential in establishing a productive orientation for a discipline. The pedagogical consequences of both of these approaches is to place a disproportionate emphasis on the source and message elements in communication. Both schools of thought tend, also, to minimize or overlook completely the interactive and dynamic nature of the communicative process.

Communication, as I conceive it, is a word that describes the process of creating a meaning. Two words in this sentence are critical. They are "create" and "meaning." Messages may be generated from the outside—by a speaker, a television screen, a scolding parent—but meanings are generated from within. This position parallels that of Berlo when he writes, "Communication does not consist of the transmission of meaning. Meanings are not transmitted, nor transferable. Only messages are transmittable, and meanings are not in the message, they are in the message-user."[1] Communication is man's attempt to cope with his experience, his current mood, his emerging needs. For every person it is a unique act of creation involving dissimilar materials. But it is, within broad limits, assumed to be predictable or there could be no theory of communication.

The second, and more troublesome, word is "meaning." Meaning is not apparent in the ordinary flow of sensation. We are born into, and inhabit a world without "meaning." That life becomes intelligible to us—full of beauty or ugliness, hope or dispair—is because it is assigned that significance by the experiencing being. As Karl Britton put it, "A world without minds is a world without structure, without relations, without facts."[2] Sensations do not come to us, sorted and labeled, as if we were visitors in a vast, but ordered, museum. Each of us, instead, is his own curator. We learn to look with a selective eye, to classify, to assign significance.

Communication arises out of the need to reduce uncertainty, to act effectively, to defend or strengthen the ego. On some occasions words are used to ward off anxiety. On other occasions they are means of evolving more deeply satisfying ways of expressing ourselves. *The aim of communication is to increase the number and consistency of our meanings within the limits set by patterns of evaluation that have proven successful in the past, our emerging needs and drives, and the demands of the physical and social setting of the moment.* Communication ceases when meanings are adequate; it is initiated as soon as new meanings are required. However, since man is a homeostatic, rather than static, organism, it is impossible for him to discover any permanently satisfying way of relating all his needs; each temporary adjustment is both relieving and disturbing, leading to successively novel ways of relating himself to his environment.

... Communication, in this sense, may occur while a man waits alone outside a hospital operating room, or watches the New York skyline disappear at dusk. It can take place in the privacy of his study as he introspects about some internal doubt, or contemplates the fading images of a frightening dream. When man discovers meaning in nature, or in insight in his own reflections, he is a communication system unto himself. Festinger refers to this as "consummatory communication." The creation of meanings, however, also goes on in countless social situations where men talk with those who share or dispute their purposes. Messages are exchanged in the hope of altering the attitudes or actions of those around us. This can be characterized as "instrumental communication," as long as we remember that these two purposes are not mutually exclusive.

What I am describing is a meaning-centered philosophy of communication. It admits that meaning in the sender, and the words of the messages, are important, but regards as most critical the state of mind, the assumptive world and the needs of the listener or observer. The impact of any message from "See me after class" to "What's good for General Motors is good for the country" is determined by the physical, personal, and social context, the most critical ingredient of which is the mind of the interpreter. Communication, so defined, does not require a speaker, a message, or a listener in the restricted sense in which these terms are used in the field of speech. All may be combined in a single person, and often are.

A theory that leaves out man's communication with himself, his communication with the world about him and a large proportion of his interactions with his fellow man, is not a theory of communication at all, but a theory of speech-making. Indeed, it seems applicable to speechmaking only in the most formal and restricted sense of that word. There is little in the traditional view of speech that is helpful in the analysis of conversation, interviewing, conflict negotiations, or in the diagnosis of the whole span of communicative disorders and breakdowns that are receiving so much attention currently. Upon so limited a view of communication it is unlikely that there can develop theories of sufficient scope and stature to command the respect of other disciplines or of the larger public that ultimately decides our role in the solution of man's problems. The field of speech seems to be fast approaching what the airlines call a "checkpoint" where one loses the freedom to choose between alternative flight plans, between a limited interest in speechmaking, and a broad concern with the total communicative behavior of man. By defining communication operationally, by examining a wider range of communicative acts, the way might be prepared for making the startling theoretical advances that have, so far, not characterized our field.

The Communication Process

A satisfactory philosophy should also provide a starting point for the technical analysis of communication. One way of accomplishing this is to ask what characteristics would have to be built into a scientific model that would represent, at the same time and equally well, the entire spectrum from intrapersonal to mass communication. It should not be a model that is mechanically or structurally faithful, but one that is symbolically and functionally similar. Space is too limited here to more than suggest a few of the principles that would have to be reflected in such a model.

1. Communication is not a thing, it is a process. Sender, message, and receiver do not remain constant throughout an act of communication. To treat these as static entities, as they often are in our research, is questionable when applied to the most extreme form of continuous discourse, is misleading when used to analyze the episodic verbal exchanges that characterize face-to-face communication, and is totally useless in probing man's

communication with himself. Changes in any of these forces, and few forces remain constant very long, reverberate throughout the entire system. Students of communication are not dissecting a cadaver, but are probing the pulsing evolution of meaning in a living organism.

2. Communication is not linear, it is circular. There are many situations in life where a simple, linear, causal analysis is useful. One thing leads to another. A, then B, then C. I push over the first domino and the rest, in turn, topple over. But this sort of thinking is not very helpful, though quite appealing in its simplicity, in studying communication. There is not first a sender, then a message, and finally an interpreter. There is, instead, what Henderson calls "mutual dependence" or what I have termed "interdependent functionalism." The words "sender" and "receiver" no longer name the elements in a communicative act, but indicate the point of view of the critic at the moment.

3. Communication is complex. Someone once said that whenever there is communication there are at least six "people" involved: The person you think yourself to be; the man your partner thinks you are; the person you believe your partner thinks you are; plus the three equivalent "persons" at the other end of the circuit. If, with as few as four constants, mathematicians must cope with approximately fifty possible relations, then we, in studying communication, where an even greater number of variables is concerned, ought to expound with considerable humility. In this age of Freudian and non-Freudian analysts, of information theory specialists, of structural linguists, and so on, we are just beginning to unravel the mysteries of this terribly involved, and therefore fascinating, puzzle.

4. Communication is irreversible and unrepeatable. The distinction being suggested here is between systems that are deterministic and mechanical, and those that are spontaneous and evolutionary. One can start a motor, beat a rug, or return a book. But you cannot start a man thinking, beat your son, or return a compliment with the same consequences. The words of a teacher, even when faithfully repeated, do not produce the same effect, but may lead to new insight, increased tension, or complete boredom. A moment of indifference or interest, a disarming or tangential remark, leave indelible traces.

5. Communication involves the total personality. Despite all efforts to divide body and mind, reason and emotion, thought and action, meanings continue to be generated by the whole organism. This is not to say that some messages do not produce greater or lesser dissonance, or shallower or deeper effects on the personality; it is only to hold that eventually every fact, conclusion, guilt, or enthusiasm must somehow be accommodated by the entire personality. The deeper the involvement produced by any communication, the sooner and more pervasive its effects upon behavior.

Research or instruction that disregards these characteristics of the communicative act would appear both unsound and of dubious value.

The Moral Dimension

The perennial and legitimate concern with ethics in the field of speech arises out of the inherent moral aspect of every interpersonal communication. As was noted earlier, the aim of communication is to transform chaotic sense impressions into some sort of coherent, intelligible, and useful relationship. When men do this privately, either in confronting nature or in assessing their own impulses, they are free to invent whatever meaning they can. But when men encounter each other, a moral issue invades every exchange because the manipulation of symbols always involves a purpose that is external to, and in some degree manipulative of, the interpreter of the message. The complexity of communication makes it difficult to know in advance, and with certainty, the impact of any bundle of words upon the receiver of them. The irreversibility of communication means that whatever means is provoked by a message cannot be annulled. A teacher may erase a blackboard, a colleague apologize, or an employer change his mind, but there is no way of erasing the effect of a threatening ultimatum, a bitter remark, or a crushing personal evaluation.

Meaning, in my opinion, is a private preserve and trespassers always run a risk. To speak of personal integrity at all is to acknowledge this. Any exchange of words is an invasion of the privacy of the listener which is aimed at preventing, restricting, or stimulating the cultivation of meaning. Briefly, three types of interference may be distinguished. First, there are messages whose intent is to coerce. Meaning is controlled by choosing symbols that so threaten the interpreter that he becomes capable of, and blind to, alternative meanings; second, there are messages of an exploitative sort in which words are arranged to filter the information, narrow the choices, obscure the consequences, so that only one meaning becomes attractive or appropriate; third, there is facilitative communication in which words are used to inform, to enlarge perspective, to deepen sensitivity, to remove external threat, to encourage independence of meaning. The values of the listener are, in the first case, ignored, in the second, subverted, in the third respected. While some qualification of this principle is needed, it appears that only facilitative communication is entirely consistent with the protection and improvement of man's symbolic experience. Unless a teacher is aware of these possibilities and appreciates the differences in these kinds of communication, it is unlikely that he will communicate responsibly in the classroom....

Alfred North Whitehead once said that any discipline deserving a place in the curriculum must have a philosophy, a method, and a technique. The statement is undoubtedly true, but somewhat incomplete if philosophy, method, and technique exist as isolated units of instruction. Too often what results is that the technical and moral aspects remain separate, lacking any vital connection in the classroom, and more importantly, in the personality of the student. The result is schizophrenic communication. Men learn to blot out all but technical considerations when communicating in a coercive or prejudicial way, but turn around and attack someone else's communication on moral grounds when it proves technically superior to their own. It is this sort of inconsistency that fosters pathological communication and pathological personalities.

Integrative instruction in communication encourages the student to work out better meanings concerning his own communication with himself and his fellowmen. By "better" I refer to meanings that permit more consistency in his personality between what he assumes, what he sees, and what he does. By "better" I refer to meanings that will increase his openness, curiosity, and flexibility. By "better" I refer to meanings that will make him more independent, and more confident of his own judgment....

References

1. David Berlo, *The Process of Communication* (New York: Holt, Rinehart and Winston, 1960), p. 175.
2. Karl Britton, *Communication: A Philosophical Study of Language* (New York: Harcourt, Brace, 1939), p. 206.

Review Questions

1. According to Barnlund, what is "inadequate" about the views that (a) the aim of communication is to transmit information and (b) the aim of communication is to transfer ideas from one person to another?
2. What is a "meaning"?
3. What is "consummatory communication"?
4. What does it mean to say that communication is "not linear but circular"?
5. Why does Barnlund even talk about a "moral" dimension of communication? Do you believe communication has a "moral" dimension? How so?

Probes

1. Barnlund argues that some definitions of communication are "inadequate." What difference does it make if they are? What kinds of real-world problems—if any—are created by inadequate definitions?
2. How do you respond when Barnlund defines communication as the "process of creating a meaning"? Does that describe what you're doing when you communicate?
3. What are some examples from your own experience of the irreversibility and unrepeatability of communication?
4. Barnlund says that communication is "meaning-centered" and that meanings are "within" persons. How are these ideas similar to and different from what I say at the beginning of this chapter about communication happening *between* persons? Are meanings "inside" or "between"?

Chapter 3

Verbal Codes

He wished to be crowned
robed in language
and seated on a verb

JOHN ANGUS CAMPBELL

The basic ingredients or raws materials of human communication are usually divided into two large categories—verbal cues and nonverbal cues. As Mark Knapp mentions in the next chapter, there are some problems with that division; it's sort of a "words" and "other" categorization. But the division is popular because these two kinds of cues tend to work differently. They perform somewhat different communicative functions.

I say "tend to" and "somewhat" because the differences between words and nonwords are often differences of degree. Words generally carry most of the information load in human communication. We use words to describe, explain, outline, detail, compare and contrast, and so on. Nonverbal cues, on the other hand, generally carry the metamessages or the metacommunicative part of the transaction—how the people involved define themselves, what the feeling or emotional content is, and so on.

It's important, though, to develop an awareness of both sets of cues. Consequently, the purpose of the next three selections is to introduce how words work in communication, and the three articles in Chapter 4 will do the same for nonverbal cues.

I wrote this next section for a book that Gary D'Angelo and I authored. My purposes here are to introduce language as a topic of study and then to discuss the six main ways words function in human communication. First I talk about the primary differences between verbal and nonverbal cues. Then I try to respond to the question, "What is language?" As you probably know, that question has been addressed by many different linguists, semanticists, philosophers, anthropologists, communication scholars, and teachers. I briefly review the four main responses they've made: (1) language is a system of symbols, (2) language is an activity, (3) language and perception are interrelated, and (4) the limits of my language are the limits of my world. This review is meant to demonstrate that the study of language is a little complex and to suggest how your view of language affects the ways you communicate verbally.

The final section of this reading discusses how words function to refer or stand for things, to perform actions, to evoke emotions, to reduce uncertainty, to express complex and abstract ideas, and to promote human contact. I hope that when you recognize how flexible and multifaceted language is, you'll be able to use more of its resources in your own communicating.

Verbal Communication

John Stewart and Gary D'Angelo

Recently one of John's students completed an internship project working for the sales manager at a large mobile home dealership. Barbara planned to work part-time as a mobile home salesperson, and she wanted to explore how her speech communication training might help her. Early in her project she was struck by how important it seemed to be to use the right words as she talked with prospective customers. When Barbara asked her supervisor about this part of her job, he gave her the following lists.

Common Expressions	Improved Expressions
House	Home
Buy	Invest
Cost	Investment
Down payment	Initial investment
Deal	Offer or opportunity
Contract	Agreement
Lot	Homesite or location
Second mortgage	Additional financing
Small	Cozy
Large	Expansive
Sound barriers	Acoustically engineered
Layout	Design concept
No, it's not included	Personal, optional feature
Sales lot	Display center
Dealer	Retailer
Salesperson	Consultant

Obviously Barbara's supervisor had given a lot of thought to the impact words have on the relationship between customer—or should we say "client"—and the mobile home "consultant." And you don't have to be hypersensitive or a communication genius to hear the obvious differences. Which of the following sounds less threatening and more inviting to you?

> "With the offer we've outlined, your initial investment will require only a minimum of additional financing, depending on the optional features you decide to include in the design."

or

> "With the deal we've outlined, your down payment will require only a small second mortgage, depending on how much you add to what's not included in the layout."

In this project Barbara learned firsthand about the impact of a part of our communication that we often take for granted: verbal cues—the words we use. We talk and write words every day, and the struggle of learning our first language happened before we knew enough to worry about it. When we study a second language, we learn how difficult the process can be, but even then we already have at least one language to "do it in." As a result, we don't have to give much thought to the complexities of verbal language; the words we use have become second nature to most of us.

Preview

As the preceding lists suggest, however, there's more to our use of words than meets the eye. Our goal in this chapter is to increase your awareness of the verbal parts of your communicating. We'll do that by (1) describing what verbal cues are, (2) identifying some important characteristics of language, and (3) describing the six ways words function.

What Are "Verbal Cues"?

By "cue" we mean the smallest identifiable unit of communication. The term "verbal" comes from the Latin word for "word." So a "verbal cue" is a single word. Pretty simple, right? But just to make sure that we're using these words the same way you are, think about how you would fill in the empty spaces in this chart.

	ORAL	NON-ORAL
VERBAL		
NONVERBAL		

Remember that the word "oral" means "by mouth" and the word "verbal" means "words." Given those definitions, what would you put in the upper left box? What kind of communication is oral and verbal? When you've got that one filled in, move to what is verbal but non-oral, that is, words *not* spoken by mouth. Then fill in the lower left box—examples of cues that come out of your mouth but are not made up of words. And finally, you can probably come up with many examples of non-oral, nonverbal communication cues. When you've finished, the chart should look something like this:

	ORAL	NON-ORAL
VERBAL	Spoken words	Written words
NONVERBAL	Tone of voice, sigh, scream, vocal quality, pitch, loudness, and so on	Gesture, movement, appearance, facial expression, touch, and so on

The point the chart makes for this chapter seems simple enough. Everybody knows what a word is, right? Well, yes and no. Scholars have been studying language since about 400 B.C., when an ancient named Panini wrote a lengthy commentary on the Vedas, the sacred books of India. But they have not agreed on the defining characteristics of the basic unit of their study, the word. What's the problem? Well, if you define language as what people write, then you can define a word as a group of letters set off by space. But linguists generally agree that written language is a secondary reflection of what people *say*, that the spoken word is primary. And that creates difficulties. Would you say that your "Howareya?" to somebody you meet on the street is one spoken word or three? Is "loves" a different word from "love"? What about the "words" Don Martin creates? Is "FWAK" a word? How about "SWAP" and SPOP"?

Obviously, we aren't going to be able to answer a question that's stumped linguists for more than two thousand years. For our purposes it'll be good enough

© 1975 by Don Martin.

to avoid the problem by agreeing that things like "cat," "spinnaker," and "dialogue" are words and things like

are not. This approach won't handle the borderline cases, but they're fairly uncommon, anyway. The main point we want to make is that studying words is not as simple as it might first appear to be.

What Is Language?

"Language" is a term that is even harder to define than "word." One respected scholar named Charles Osgood lists and discusses sixteen "defining characteristics" of language and twelve more that are "nondefining" but nonetheless important characteristics.[1] Rather than laboring through a list like that, we want to identify just four primary features. One comes from the historical study of language, and the other three have been highlighted fairly recently. All four of these characteristics of language relate directly to the ways we can use words to encourage or discourage interpersonal-quality communicating.

Language Is a System of Symbols

About twenty-five hundred years ago a Greek philosopher named Aristotle began one of his major works on language this way: "Spoken words are the symbols of mental experience and written words are the symbols of spoken words."[2] Almost every scholar and teacher who's written about or taught language since then has repeated and applied Aristotle's point. For example, Osgood explains this feature by saying that all language follows "rules of reference to events in other channels." As he explains, "This criterion implies that for anything to be a language it must function so as to *symbolize* (represent for the organism) the not-necessarily-*here* and not-necessarily-*now*."[3] The behavior of honeybees is said to satisfy this criterion. When some species of bees locate a nectar source, they return to the hive and do an elaborate dance that symbolizes the not-here—the source of the nectar—and the not-now—it can be found at some flying time in the near future. So if you rely only on this "symbolic" feature, you can say that honeybees "have a language."

It also seems obvious that not only honeybee dances but also human words symbolize or represent their meanings. The word "dog" refers to a certain kind of animal, "tree" symbolizes a certain kind of botanical life, and so on. In 1923 two writers spent a good part of a book called *The Meaning of Meaning* elaborating just this point. C. K. Ogden and I. A. Richards diagrammed this insight with their famous triangle of meaning. It looks like this:

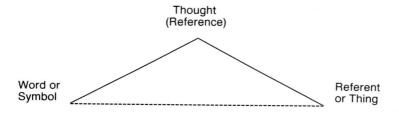

Thought
(Reference)

Word or
Symbol

Referent
or Thing

The triangle is meant to illustrate how words are related to both thoughts and things. The word-thought relationship is direct—that's why that line is solid. As Aristotle put it, words stand for thoughts. But the word-thing relationship is different. The dotted line across the bottom of the triangle emphasizes that there is only an *arbitrary,* indirect relationship between the word and its referent—the thing it refers to. For example, in English the word "three" is used to talk about this many units: * * * and the word "four" is used to talk about this many: * * * *. But the word "three" itself has more letters than the word "four." It's "bigger" even though "what it means" is *smaller.* That's because there is no necessary relationship between the size of the word itself and the size of the quantity it designates. In that sense, it's arbitrary. Different cultures also agree that "chien," "perro," "hund," or "dog" will be used to talk about the same animal. In each case, there is an arbitrary rather than a necessary relationship between the word and how it's used or interpreted.

Ogden and Richards' triangle makes this point by using a dotted line across the bottom. That line illustrates the main point of the triangle—that **"the word is not the thing."** Words, Ogden and Richards emphasized, are arbitrary symbols that members of a culture agree to use to represent or symbolize things they sense and experience. But there's no necessary connection between word and thing.

About thirty years ago some people who called themselves general semanticists wrote a number of books that described the communication problems we get into when we *forget* that "the word is not the thing." They also offered several suggestions about how to use language to prevent or solve these problems. For example, they pointed out that we sometimes give concrete labels to abstract entities or processes and then forget that we're dealing with the label and not the abstraction or process itself. "Charisma" and "leadership" are two examples. Once we've attributed someone's success to her "charisma," we start trying to figure out why she "has it," how she can get more of "it," and how she might pass "it" on to others. We make "charisma" into a thing and then treat it as if it were one. This process is called **reification,** from the Latin word *res,* which means "thing." To "reify" something is to "thingafy" it.

One form of reification occurs when we forget that we're using the same, unchanging word to talk about a reality that's constantly changing. "Mother" or "my mom" is the same label you've been using ever since you can remember to symbolize or refer to an important person in your life. Yet that person has been constantly changing; she obviously isn't the same today as she was when you were ten years old. The fact that the label hasn't changed, even though she has, can sometimes create problems. For example, you might expect her to clean up after you or always to be sympathetic when you screw things up, just because she's "mom." But *she* may have decided that adults—especially her own children—can clean up after themselves and should be allowed to experience the consequences of their own foulups. When you treat her like an unchanging label instead of a changing person, you're committing what general semanticists called **static evaluation.** This type of reification occurs because the label we use—the word—is static. We forget, though, that the word is *not* the thing, so we treat the thing or person as if it were static, too.

Another problem that's highlighted by the point that "the word is not the thing" is what's called **bypassing.** Bypassing means using different words with the same meaning or the same words with different meanings. It's called "bypassing" because, when it occurs, communicators pass by each other rather than making contact. For example, in their campaign ads two state politicians hammered away at each other because one wanted to "radically readjust the state budget" while the other wanted to "significantly increase the salaries of state employees." When they met face to face in a televised debate, they discovered that they were both talking about the same thing. That's one kind of bypassing—different words for the same meaning. The other kind occurred when a high-school basketball team from a small town in Idaho went on a special trip to Australia. The team members were asked to speak to the student bodies of the Australian high schools they visited, and one team member named Randy kept wondering why everyone laughed so much when he walked up to the microphone and said "Hi! I'm Randy." It took him awhile to learn that in Australia, the word "randy" means "horny," wanting to have sex.

Labeling is the fourth problem general semanticists identified. Labeling occurs when we respond to the word instead of the thing the word symbolizes or represents. The main reason we don't want to read "dead cow" on a restaurant menu is that, even though we "know" that we're not going to eat the words on the menu, we still have a tendency to respond to the words as if they were "the thing" we've ordered for dinner. There's also the story of the menswear retailer who divided a shipment of handkerchiefs into two identical piles and then labeled one "Genuine Irish Linen Handkerchiefs—$1.50" and the other "Noserags—$.50." The "handkerchiefs" were sold in two days, but nobody bought the "noserags." This same phenomenon of labeling is also operating when people get angry because they're stereotyped as "jock," "nigger," "sorority sally," "shyster lawyer," or "bitchy feminist." We're definitely not saying that stereotyping or name calling is acceptable, but it is helpful to remember that all those labels are *words* and not the realities they're used to talk about. When we get angry, it's because we're forgetting that the word is not the thing.

Euphemisms are very similar to labels. They are neutral, vaguely positive, or ambiguous words used to talk about negative things. For example, your hairdresser may insist that he or she doesn't ever "dye" hair but that you can get a "tint" or "rinse." Or consider the fate of a course that was introduced fairly recently into high schools and junior highs across the country. The course covered such things as the biology of human reproduction, causes and dangers of venereal disease, and, in some cases, methods of contraception. When school authorities labeled the courses "Sex Education," they were frequently attacked for allowing such material to be taught. But when they changed the labels to "Social Hygiene" or "Family Health," community members were much less worried, even though the content of the courses remained unchanged. That kind of thing happens because people respond to the words as if they were the things they symbolize. Euphemisms can help avoid that problem.

There are also two more "cures" for problems created by our tendency to forget that "the word is not the thing." The first is called **dating,** and it means that you put a date or time frame around some of the statements you make. So you move from "Mom'll lend me the money" to "The last time I needed money, Mom lent it to me, but I don't know about this time." Or you replace "You can't drink in Salt Lake City" with "When we were in Salt Lake City two years ago, it was really inconvenient to find a bar." When you use "dating" you also add to statements like "Professor Crowell is really enthusiastic" something like "—or at least she was last quarter in the group discussion class." Similarly, "Michelle seemed phony the other night" is a statement that's dated, in this sense, and "Michelle's a phony" isn't. You can use language to highlight rather than to obscure the fact that the words you're using are different from and only *indirectly* or *arbitrarily* related to the realities they symbolize.

A second cure is what the general semanticists called **indexing.** The term comes from mathematics, where subscript or superscript numbers are used to distinguish one variable from other, similar ones—x_1, x_2, x_3, and so on. You index verbally when you use words to highlight individual differences. So, for example, the overgeneralization might be "Since Seattle's supposed to be one of the most 'livable' cities, it's got to have lots of theater," and the indexed statement could be "Since Seattle's rated as one of the most 'livable' cities, it should have lots of good theater, but it may not—it's a long way from New York and Los Angeles." In this example, indexing highlights some possibly *unique* features of Seattle. Or you'd replace the statement "You'll get 70,000 miles out of those radials" with "I've gotten as high as 70,000 miles out of those radials, and if you do the kind of driving I do, you should get that, too." Two interpersonal communication teachers summarize their advice about indexing this way.

1. Before you make a statement about an object, person, or place, consider whether your statement is about that specific object, person, or place or whether it is a generalization about a class to which the object, person, or place belongs.
2. If your statement is a generalization, inform your listener that it is not necessarily accurate.[4]

So the view of language that's been popular in the past emphasizes that words are symbols which stand for or represent various realities, and that problems arise when we forget that "the word is not the thing it symbolizes." When you look at language from this point of view, you can identify several kinds of language trouble we often get into: static evaluation, bypassing, and labeling, for example. Euphemisms can be either part of the problem or part of the solution; sometimes we use them because we forget that the word is not the thing, and sometimes they can help avoid that problem—as they did in the Sex Education example. Dating and indexing are two additional ways we can help cope with problems created by people forgetting that the word is not the thing.

Language Is an Activity

It can be helpful to view language as a system of symbols, because it alerts us to several problems we create by the ways we use words. But that view is also drastically oversimplified. The triangle of meaning assumes that language is essentially made up of nouns, labels for things in the world. And it doesn't take much reflection to realize that it's much more complicated than that. As we directly experience it, language isn't simply a list of nouns but an *activity*, a living process that's happening all around us, literally from before we are born to the day we die.

As we mentioned before, research on unborn infants suggests that they can hear, and an important part of what they hear is talk, spoken language. Then at birth, the first sounds the newborn hears are the exclamations of the people present when he or she's delivered. From that instant on, each of us lives in a "sea" of language that is as all-encompassing as the water fish are born into. Even when we "get away from it all" to a seashore or mountaintop, we use language to help get there and reflect in language while we're there.

When you view language as an all-encompassing activity, it leads you toward different explanatory metaphors than the triangle of meaning or the symbol metaphor. For example, you can see how the activity of language is like a "game" or a series of games that we "play." Especially in the last ten or twelve years, a number of thinkers and teachers have emphasized how much we can learn about language when we think of it in terms of "language games" we "play."

For example, we now recognize that we follow at least two different kinds of rules when playing language games. One set of rules defines the game itself—like the rules that determine whether you're playing baseball or football. These are called constitutive rules, because they constitute or make up what the game is. One rule of football, for example, is that you need a field roughly twice as long as it is wide and as close to 100 yards long as you can find. If you have a roughly square space and you're focusing on one corner of the square so the space looks like a diamond, it's likely you'll be playing baseball instead of football. Football also takes a certain kind of ball, and no bats or mitts. So the rules governing the playing field and basic equipment are constitutive rules. Similarly, certain rules define when the language game you're playing is a "greeting" or a "request" and not an "apology" or an "attempted seduction." If, when you're introduced to a stranger, the first words out of your mouth are "Can I borrow a hundred dollars?" you're violating a constitutive rule, because that request isn't part of what counts as "a greeting." "Can I borrow a hundred dollars?" is not a bad or awkward greeting; it isn't a greeting at all!

On the other hand, "regulative" rules are those that govern not what the game is but how it is played. The rule that you have to tag a baserunner to make the out is an example of a regulative rule in baseball. You know it's regulative and not constitutive, because "crossout" is still considered baseball—that's a form of the game where you make the out by throwing the ball across the basepath in front of the runner. The infield fly rule and the rules governing penalties in football are other examples of regulative rather than constitutive rules. In language games, regulative rules define, for example, various ways you can greet someone. A handshake, a smile and head nod, and a hug all count as "greetings," depending on the context and your relationship with the person. There are also rules governing how to make an apology, ask someone out, borrow money, and so on.

The distinction between constitutive and regulative rules helps identify the seriousness of a rule infraction. Simply put, it's usually easier to break a regulative rule and get away with it than it is to break a constitutive rule with impunity. That's because, if you violate a regulative rule you simply "aren't doing it right," but when you break a constitutive rule you aren't even in the ballpark; you're playing the wrong game!

A second insight the game metaphor provides is that we are "played by the game" as much as we play it. When you're playing a game, whether it's Monopoly, bridge, chess, poker, tennis, or baseball, you get caught up into it. You still have some free choice, but your choices are limited by the structure of the game itself. There are many things you can't do if you want to continue to play the game. In that sense you are *being played by it*: the game itself is partly determining what you do next. Games have that quality; they "play us" almost as much as "we play them." Individually, or even as a group, we don't fully control them; they have some control over us. Of course, we can always quit, but then we're out of the game.

Language has that quality, too. It is larger than any individual or group of speakers or writers. We join it much more than we form it. Our choices and our behaviors are constrained by the language we're born into and the languages we learn. Language is a cultural phenomenon, and it constantly "plays" us by directing and limiting our thinking, feeling, and acting. This point leads directly to a third important characteristic of language.

Language and Perception Are Interrelated

One of the most important lessons learned from the twentieth-century study of language concerns the links between language and perception. The basic insight is usually called the Sapir-Whorf hypothesis after the two people who originally wrote about it, Edward Sapir and Benjamin Lee Whorf. It has been summarized by Whorf in these words: "The background linguistic system (in other words the grammar) of each language is not merely a reproducing instrument for voicing ideas but rather is itself the shaper of ideas, the program and guide for the individual's mental activity, for his analysis of impressions. ... We dissect nature along lines laid down by our native language."[5]

So if your native language is an Eskimo dialect which includes well over a dozen words for "snow," you will perceive snow differently from the native English speaker, who only knows "sleet," "slush," "powder," and "corn." Your language affects what you perceive. Similarly, if you've spent enough time on boats and around the water to learn a dozen different words for water conditions, you will perceive more differences in the water than will the person who was born and raised in Cheyenne, Oklahoma City, or Calgary. That person might distinguish between "waves" and "smooth water," but you will see and feel differences between cats' paws, ripples, chop, and swells that he or she won't even notice.

As we try to write about communication experiences, we notice one particular way our native language limits our perceptions. Unlike some languages, English maintains clear distinctions between subjects and predicates, causes and effects, beginnings and ends. The word system of the Navaho doesn't do that. According to Harry Hoijer, Navaho speakers characteristically talk in terms of processes—uncaused, ongoing, incomplete, dynamic happenings. The word the Navaho use for "wagon," for example, translates roughly as "wood rolls about hooplike."[6] As Hoijer explains, the Navaho words that we would translate "He begins to carry a stone" mean not that the actor produces an action, but that the person is simply linked with a given round object and with an already existing, continuous movement of all round objects in the universe. The English language, on the other hand, requires us to talk in terms of present, past, future, cause and effect, beginning and end. But some things English speakers would like to discuss just can't be expressed in these terms. We would like to be able to talk more clearly about the ever-changing, processlike, ongoing nature of communication and about the "betweenness" of the quality of communication we've labeled "interpersonal." But the English language makes it difficult to do that.

Our language also affects the ways we perceive females and males. One accomplishment of the feminist movement of the 1960s and 70s is that we now recognize how the male bias of standard American English has contributed to the ways English-speaking cultures perceive women and men. The fact that, until recently, there were no female firefighters was not "caused" simply by the existence of the word "fire*man*." It's not that simple. But changes in job titles have helped open several occupations to more equal male/female participation. Consider, for example, "parking checker" instead of "meter maid," "chair" or "chairperson" instead of "chairman," "salesperson" instead of "salesman," and "server" instead of "waiter" or "waitress." We have also just about stopped referring to some physicians as "woman doctors" and some attorneys as "lady lawyers," and it is more than a coincidence that these changes have been accompanied by significant increases in the numbers of women in those two professions....

Our primary point, is that language both *reflects* and *affects* the ways we perceive both women and men. That's one important implication of the Sapir-Whorf hypothesis. There is an interdependence, a reciprocal relationship between language and perception: language affects what we perceive, and our perceptions are reflected in our speaking and writing.

The Limits of My Language Are the Limits of My World

This fourth feature of language summarizes, in a sense, all the other three. Especially in the last thirty years, language researchers and teachers have become increasingly aware of how language is not simply a tool we use, but that it is the way we *be* who we are. A philosopher of language named Ludwig Wittgenstein first wrote "The limits of my language are the limits of my world" in a book published in 1953.[7] Wittgenstein was also one of the thinkers who wrote about "language games." But one of the clearest expressions of what that sentence *means* appears in a book called *Hunger of Memory* by Richard Rodriguez, a Mexican-American who grew up in Sacramento in the 1950s and 60s. When Rodriguez talks about his childhood, you understand just how "the limits of my language are the limits of my world."

The first chapter of Rodriguez's book describes how he lived as a young boy in the Spanish-speaking world of his home and how he was then moved into the world of *los gringos* as his parents, brothers, and sisters obeyed the request of his schoolteachers to speak English at home rather than Spanish. Rodriguez tells the following story to illustrate how his father was at home in Spanish and a stranger in the world of English, and to suggest the impact his homelessness had on his son, Richard.

> There were many times like the night at a brightly lit gasoline station (a blaring white memory) when I stood uneasily, hearing my father. He was talking to a teenaged attendant. I do not recall what they were saying, but I cannot forget the sounds my father made as he spoke. At one point his words slid together to form one word—sounds as confused as the threads of blue and green oil in the puddle next to my shoes. His voice rushed through what he had left to say. And, toward the end, reached falsetto notes, appealing to his listener's understanding. I looked away to the lights of passing automobiles. I tried not to hear anymore. But I heard only too well the calm, easy tones in the attendant's reply. Shortly afterward, walking toward home with my father, I shivered when he put his hand on my shoulder. The very first chance that I got, I evaded his grasp and ran on ahead into the dark, skipping with feigned boyish exuberance.[8]

Later Rodriguez contrasts that feeling of alienation with the warm comfort he felt when being spoken to in Spanish.

> A family member would say something to me and I would feel myself specially recognized. My parents would say something to me and I would feel embraced by the

sounds of their words. Those sounds said: *I am speaking with ease in Spanish. I am addressing you in words I never use with los gringos. I recognize you as someone special, close, like no one outside. You belong with us. In the family.*

... Walking down the sidewalk, under the canopy of tall trees, I'd warily notice the—suddenly—silent neighborhood kids who stood warily watching me. Nervously, I'd arrive at the grocery store to hear the sounds of the gringo—foreign to me—reminding me that in this world so big, I was a foreigner. But then I'd return. Walking back toward our house, climbing the steps from the sidewalk, when the front door was open in summer, I'd hear voices beyond the screen door talking in Spanish. For a second or two, I'd stay, linger there, listening. Smiling, I'd hear my mother call out, saying in Spanish (words): "Is that you, Richard?" All the while her sounds would assure me: *You are home now; come closer; inside. With us.*[9]

Rodriguez's story poignantly illustrates that, although there's definitely some truth to the idea that "language is a system of symbols" and "the word is not the thing," there is much more to language than that description includes. Language is not simply a tool we use to represent or symbolize "things" in the world. It is an all-encompassing activity that we are born into and that constantly affects all we perceive. All that is what it means to say that "the limits of my language are the limits of my world." Perhaps the most important feature that marks us as humans is that we are born into a linguistic "soup" in which we simmer throughout our lives. As one author summarizes,

in all our knowledge of ourselves and in all knowledge of the world, we are always already encompassed by the language that is our own. We grow up, and we become acquainted with {people} and in the last analysis with ourselves when we learn to speak. Learning to speak does not mean learning to use a preexistent tool for designating a world already somehow familiar to us; it means acquiring a familiarity and acquaintance with the world itself and how it confronts us.[10]

How Does Language Function? What Do Words Do?

Words Refer to or Stand for Things

One way we use words is to refer to the not-here and the not-now. That's the function highlighted by the triangle of meaning and the symbol metaphor. But what we've said about language being an activity, affecting perception, and making up our "world" suggests that there are also some other important functions of language.

Words Perform Actions

Sometimes we use words not to talk about things but to perform an action. The words "I do" or "I will" in a marriage ceremony do not refer to any things; they make up part of the act of getting married. "I christen thee" at a ship launching works the same way, as does "I promise" or "I'll bet you...." When you make a serious bet or an important bargain with someone, the words you use to seal the agreement don't symbolize or refer to objects or events or even states of mind. They constitute, for example, the act of betting itself. When you sing in the shower or curse your smashed finger, these words are also functioning as actions; they don't "stand for" or "refer to" actions. Cursing *is* a part of being angry; singing *is* part of being happy, romantic, melancholy, or whatever. In short, performing actions is one of the things we often use words for.

Sometimes people try to sharply divide words and actions, as with "Let's stop talking and start *doing* something!" But that kind of thinking can both cheapen your view of language and distort what's happening as you communicate. Saying "I love you" is a significant action; it's more significant to some people than to others, but it is always part of some kind of commitment. If you remember that many words do perform actions, you'll be less likely to contribute to misunderstandings that are revealed by such comments as "I do feel that way; did you hear what I said?" or "Look, when I said I'd do it, I meant it. Don't you trust me?"

Words Evoke Emotions

Have you ever had the experience of being so caught up in a book, short story, or magazine article that you began to get angry, nervous, or excited? Recently several newspaper articles about a four-year-old child-abuse victim named Eli Creekmore have affected people in the Pacific Northwest that way. Eli was apparently beaten to death by his father, and it's clear that the words reporters used to describe the tragedy elicited strong emotions in their readers. Letters to the editor and television news interviews reported those experiences, and the angry public outcry apparently affected the prosecuting attorney's decision to charge Eli's father with manslaughter.

You've probably had a similar experience with words, maybe while reading an exciting adventure, science fiction, or a love story. You might even feel a little silly when you realize how emotional you've gotten over nothing more than a bunch of black marks on a page. But words have that power. They can evoke strong emotions.

Spoken words can, too. Certain terms that are applied to people of your race or religion, or to people who live where you do, can trigger immediate emotional responses. In high school it might be "socie," "stoner," "head," "Jock," "crack freak," "zipper head," or "FOB—Fresh Off the Boat." College labels might include "airhead," "dormie," and "frat rat." If you're black, being called "nigger" can be positive or negative, but the term is never neutral; it always elicits some emotion. In one sense all these examples are nothing more than sounds—just as written words are nothing more than marks on a page. But we know that they have power. Language can and often does evoke all kinds of emotions.

Words Can Reduce Uncertainty

Words can reduce your uncertainty by limiting the possible conclusions you can draw about something or someone. When you see a large, rectangular, green-and-white freeway sign in the distance, you know that it could possibly indicate many different things, including an approaching exit, a lane change, and so on. When you get close enough to read the first words, the number of possibilities is reduced significantly, and when you can read all the words, your original uncertainty about the sign is reduced even more. The goal of sign writers is to use words that reduce your uncertainty to zero. They try to avoid ambiguously worded signs

> SAN FRANCISCO TRUCKS PROCEED
> RIGHT LANE MERGE LEFT
> ONE MILE

in favor of those whose meaning is unmistakable

> LAST EXIT BEFORE
> TOLL BRIDGE

Words can also reduce your uncertainty about people. When a friend you're used to seeing every day suddenly disappears for several days, you know that the absence could indicate many different things. Your friend might be ill, in trouble, angry at something you've done, tired of being around you, moving, or a dozen other things. Your uncertainty about why your friend is absent can be reduced when he or she explains verbally that "I took a few days off to collect my thoughts."

Not all words *do* function to reduce uncertainty, but the point is they *can*. They can categorize, point, specify, distinguish, and clarify much more efficiently than can nonverbal cues, and that's one reason why they're so important for interpersonal communication. That's why we suggest that you use words to check out inferences you and others are making about who means what, who's in what mood, and who wants to do X but doesn't want to do Y. When misunderstanding is the problem between people, it can often be solved simply by using more words to reduce the people's uncertainty.

Words Can Expess Complex and Abstract Ideas

If you're standing in the kitchen and you want to tell your spouse or roommate where the coffee is, you can point. If you just want to express your anger or delight, you can shriek or chuckle. But if you want to find out why the person who interviewed you didn't think your four years on the job was "relevant work experience," if you want to analyze the effects of terrorism on American foreign policy, or if you want to clarify the reasons behind your position on abortion, you will need to use words. Language is the only means we have of developing complex or abstract ideas, solving problems, exploring relationships, or expressing anything beyond the simplest logical functions. You can say "Yes" or "No" without words, but try "It all depends," or "Give me a chance to talk with Allen and the people in London, and then either I'll write you or my secretary will call by Friday." Those ideas cannot be communicated clearly without using written, spoken, or signed words.

Although you may understand, at some level of awareness, that only words have this power to express abstract ideas, you may still sometimes communicate as if you didn't know it. For example, have you ever said "If you really cared about me, you'd *know* how I feel"? Often that is our way of saying something like this: "I'm nonverbally expressing myself, and you should understand those complex and abstract thoughts and feelings just from my tone of voice and facial expression. *Without* words!" When we talk about the situation that way, you can see how unreasonable it often is. Complexities and abstractions require words. As the next chapter notes, nonverbal cues are powerful ways of expressing emotions, but they are inherently imprecise and ambiguous. If you want to clarify feelings, judgments, opinions, or positions, you have to use words.

Words Can Promote Human Contact

The final function of words we want to mention is the contact function. Words, especially spoken ones, can promote human contact, can bring people together. Martin Buber describes the unifying function of words this way: "The importance of the spoken word, I think, is grounded in the fact that it does not want to remain with the speaker. It reaches out toward a hearer, it lays hold of {the hearer}, it even makes the hearer into a speaker, if perhaps only a soundless one."[11]

Buber's point is that your words are both intensely private, personal, individual things *and* public, available to others. Consequently, thoughtful speaking can make some parts of you present to others. Gerard Egan calls this kind of speaking *Logos,* or "language filled with the person who is speaking. . . . Logos here means translating oneself or handing oneself over to others, through the medium of speech."[12]

If Ellen were really angry at Jamie, for example, she could punch her out, avoid her, or shout her down with obscenities. None of these responses would promote much contact. If Ellen wanted to do something with Jamie about her anger, she might say something like this: "Look, Jamie, I'm really pissed at you. I could try to swallow it or I could blow up, but I don't think either of those would solve anything, because I think that in a way my anger is really *our* problem—yours and mine. I'd like to talk with you about it. Are you willing?" If you can overlook the artificial sound that comes from these words being in print, perhaps you can see that this language could work to help Ellen and Jamie meet each other. It would be risky and difficult, but it might also be very satisfying and productive.

Summary

Words, in short, are a flexible and richly varied part of many communication contexts. They can *refer* the persons involved to nonverbal things or events. Sometimes we use words to *perform actions.* Words can also *evoke emotions,* and the language you use can *reduce uncertainty.* Words are necessary whenever you want to *express complex or abstract ideas.* Finally, and perhaps most important for us, words can *unify* persons, can bring humans together.

Notes

1. Charles E. Osgood, "What Is a Language?" *Psycholinguistic Research: Implications and Applications,* ed. Doris Aaronson and Robert W. Rieber (New York: Lawrence Erlbaum Assoc., 1979), reprinted in *The Signifying Animal,* ed. I. Rauch and G. F. Carr (Bloomington, IN: Indiana Univ. Press, 1980), pp. 9–50.

2. Aristotle, *De Interpretatione*, trans. E. M. Edghill, *The Basic Works of Aristotle*, ed. R. McKeon (New York: Random House, 1941), p. 40.
3. Osgood, "What Is a Language?" p. 12.
4. Kathleen S. Verderber and Rudolf F. Verderber, *Inter-Act: Using Interpersonal Skills*, 4th ed. (Belmont, CA: Wadsworth, 1986), p. 89.
5. John B. Carroll, ed., *Language Thought and Reality: Selected Writings of Benjamin Lee Whorf* (New York: Wiley, 1956), pp. 212–213.
6. Harry Hoijer, "Cultural Implications of Some Navaho Linguistic Categories," *Language* 27 (1951): 117.
7. Ludwig Wittgenstein, *Philosophical Investigations* (Oxford: Basil Blackwell, 1963).
8. Richard Rodriguez, *Hunger of Memory: The Education of Richard Rodriguez* (New York: Bantam Books, 1982), p. 15.
9. Judy Cornelia Pearson, "Language Usage of Women and Men," in *Gender and Communication* (Dubuque, IA: Wm. C. Brown, 1985), pp. 16–17.
10. Hans-Georg Gadamer, "Man and Language," in *Philosophical Hermeneutics*, trans. and ed. David E. Linge (Berkeley: University of California Press, 1976), pp. 62–63.
11. Martin Buber, "The Word That Is Spoken," in *The Knowledge of Man*, ed. Maurice Friedman, trans. M. Friedman and R. G. Smith (New York: Macmillan, 1965), p. 112.
12. Gerard Egan, "The Elements of Human Dialogue: Pathos, Logos, Poiesis," *Encounter: Group Process for Interpersonal Growth* (Monterey, CA: Brooks-Cole, 1970).

Review Questions

1. Use the verbal/nonverbal–oral/nonoral distinctions to classify the following cues: a wave of greeting, technical jargon, a burp, perfume, **this kind of typeface,** a hug.
2. Explain the meaning of the two solid lines in Ogden and Richards' "triangle of meaning." Explain the meaning of the dotted line.
3. Give an example from your own communication experience in the last forty-eight hours of reification, static evaluation, euphemism.
4. Dating and indexing are designed to apply what insight about the nature of language?
5. In the poker game called seven-card stud, there's a rule that each player is dealt seven cards. Is that a constitutive rule or a regulative one? What about the rule in five-card draw that you should never discard a pair?
6. Does the Whorf-Sapir hypothesis say that language affects perception or that perception affects language?
7. According to the reading, Rodriguez's story illustrates that language is much more than a system of symbols. Specifically what "more" does language include?
8. What action is performed by the words "I do" in a marriage ceremony?
9. Make a list of five words that evoke emotions in you.
10. Which functions of words overlap with which other functions? In other words, do words that promote human contact also often perform actions? Do words that reduce uncertainty also refer or stand for? And so on.

Probes

1. Pick a sport or game that you're familiar with. Give an example of "being played by" that sport or game. Now give an example of "being played by" the rules of the communication "game" between you and your mother or father.
2. When English-speakers experience a conflict, we tend to ask, "Whose fault is it?" How might a Navajo speaker respond differently to interpersonal conflict?
3. When we first learn geography, the "world" is a planet, a sphere three-fourths covered with water, on which we can locate countries and cities. What is the meaning of the term "world" in the sentence "The limits of my language are the limits of my world"?

4. How do words function most often in your communication experience? To refer or stand for? To perform an action? Evoke emotion? Affect perception? Reduce uncertainty? Express abstract ideas? Bring people together?
5. Without jumping forward to the next chapter, can you identify some ways that the *non-verbal* parts of communication affect how the *verbal* parts function?
6. Do you agree that the English language promotes sexism? Why or why not?
7. What's your most recent experience when *words* (not touch, tone of voice, or other non-verbal cues) made it possible for you to make contact with another person?

This brief story illustrates an important function of language that Gary D'Angelo and I don't discuss in our essay. Stephen Greenblatt, a professor at the University of California, tells how he experienced the link between the words we speak and who we are. His term for this function is "self-fashioning," and the book that includes this excerpt describes in detail how many different historical figures used their language to "fashion" themselves.

Language and Self-Fashioning

Stephen Greenblatt

A few years ago, at the start of a plane flight from Baltimore to Boston, I settled down next to a middle-aged man who was staring pensively out of the window. There was no assigned seating, and I had chosen this neighbor as the least likely to disturb me, since I wanted to finish rereading Geertz's *Interpretation of Cultures*, which I was due to teach on my return to Berkeley the following week. But no sooner had I fastened my seat belt and turned my mind to Balinese cock-fighting than the man suddenly began to speak to me. He was traveling to Boston, he said, to visit his grown son who was in the hospital. A disease had, among other consequences, impaired the son's speech, so that he could only mouth words soundlessly; still more seriously, as a result of the illness, he had lost his will to live. The father was going, he told me, to try to restore that will, but he was troubled by the thought that he would be incapable of understanding the son's attempts at speech. He had therefore a favor to ask me: would I mime a few sentences so that he could practice reading my lips? Would I say, soundlessly, "I want to die. I want to die"?

Taken aback, I began to form the words, with the man staring intently at my mouth: "I want to ..." But I was incapable of finishing the sentence. "Couldn't I say, 'I want to live'?" Or better still (since the seat belt sign had by this time flashed off), he might go into the bathroom, I suggested lamely, and practice on himself in front of a mirror. "It's not the same," the man replied in a shaky voice, then turned back to the window. "I'm sorry," I said, and we sat in silence for the rest of the flight.

I could not do what the man had asked in part because I was afraid that he was, quite simply, a maniac and that once I had expressed the will to die, he would draw a hidden knife and stab me to death or, alternatively, activate some device secreted on board the plane that would blow us all to pieces (it's not for nothing that I have been living in California for the past ten years).

But if paranoia tinged my whole response, there were reasons for my resistance more complex than the fear of physical attack. I felt superstitiously that if I mimed the man's terrible sentence, it would have the force, as it were, of a legal sentence, that the words would stick like a burr upon me. And beyond superstition, I was aware, in a manner more forceful than anything my academic research had brought home to me, of the extent to which my identity and the words I utter coincide, the extent to which I want to form my own sentences or to choose for myself those moments in which I will recite someone else's. To be asked, even by an isolated, needy individual to perform lines that were not my own, that violated my sense of my own desires, was intolerable. . . .

Probes

1. Why do *you* believe the man wanted Greenblatt to mouth the words "I want to die"?
2. This story recounts what is certainly an extreme example of how verbal cues work in communication. Sometimes extreme examples are good because they vividly illustrate important points. Sometimes they are bad because they distort. Which do you think is happening here? Does the story make an important point? Or does it distort how language works?

 irginia Satir was a family counselor who spent over forty years helping parents and children communicate. Her small book *Making Contact* is her response to the many persons who asked her to write down the ideas and suggestions that she shared in workshops and seminars. As she says in the introduction, "The framework of this book is the BARE BONES of the possible, which I believe applies to *all* human beings. You, the reader, can flesh out the framework to fit you."

I like the simple, straightforward, no-nonsense way she talks about words, and I think she's pinpointed several insights that can help all of us communicate better. If we did, as she suggests, pay more attention to the ways we use the ten key words she discusses, I'm convinced that we'd experience considerably less conflict, misunderstanding, and frustration. See if you don't agree.

Paying Attention to Words

Virginia Satir

Words are important tools for contact. They are used more consciously than any other form of contact. I think it is important to learn how to use words well in the service of our communication.

Words cannot be separated from sights, sounds, movements, and touch of the person using them. They are one package.

However, for the moment, let's consider only words. Using words is literally the outcome of a whole lot of processes that go on in the body. All the senses, the nervous system, brain, vocal chords, throat, lungs, and all parts of the mouth are involved. This means that, physiologically, talking is a very complicated process....

If you think of your brain as a computer, storing all your experiences on tapes, then the words you pick will have to come from those tapes. Those tapes represent all our past experiences, accumulated knowledge, rules, and guides. There is nothing else there until new tapes are added. I hope that what you are reading will help you to add new tapes out of getting new experiences.

The words we use have an effect on our health. They definitely influence emotional relationships between people and how people can work together.

Words Have Power

Listen to what you say and see if you are really saying what you mean. Nine people out of ten can't remember what they said sixty seconds ago, others remember.

There are ten English words that it is well to pay close attention to, to use with caution and with loving care: *I, You, They, It, But, Yes, No, Always, Never, Should.*

If you were able to use these special words carefully it would already solve many contact problems created by misunderstanding.

I

Many people avoid the use of the word *I* because they feel they are trying to bring attention to themselves. They think they are being selfish. Shades of childhood, when you shouldn't show off, and who wants to be selfish? The most important thing is that using "I" clearly means that you are taking responsibility for what you say. Many people mix this up by starting off with saying "you." I have heard people say "You can't do that." This is often heard as a "put-down," whereas "I think you can't do that" makes a more equal relationship between the two. It gives the same information without the put-down.

From Virginia Satir, *Making Contact* (Millbrae, Calif.: Celestial Arts, 1976). The excerpt covers twelve pages in the text of Satir's book. Courtesy of Celestial Arts Pub. Co., 231 Adrian Rd., Millbrae, Calif. 94030.

"I" is the pronoun that clearly states "me" when I am talking so it is important to say it. If you want to be clear when you are talking, no matter what you say, it is important to state clearly your ownership of *your* statement.

"I am saying that the moon is made of red cheese."
(This is clearly your picture)

instead of saying ...

"The moon is made of red cheese."
(This is a new law)

Being aware of your clear use of "I" is particularly crucial when people are already in crisis. It is more clear to say "It is my picture that ..." (which is an ownership statement). Whoever has the presence of mind to do this can begin to alter an escalating situation. When "I" is not clear, it is easy for the hearer to get a "you" message, which very often is interpreted as a "put-down."

You

The use of the word *you* is also tricky. It can be felt as an accusation when only reporting or sharing is intended.

"You are making things worse" can sound quite different if the words "I think" are added. "I think you are making things worse...."

When used in clear commands or directions, it is not so easily misunderstood. For example, "I want you to ..." or "You are the one I wanted to speak to."

They

The use of *they* is often an indirect way of talking about "you." It is also often a loose way of spreading gossip.

"They say ..."

"They" can also be some kind of smorgasbord that refers to our negative fantasies. This is especially true in a situation where people are assessing blame. If we know who "they" are we can say so.

How many times do we hear "They won't let me." "They will be upset." "They don't like what I am doing." "They say ..."

If someone else uses it, we can ask "Who is your *they?*"

The important part of this is to have clear who "they" are so that inaccurate information is not passed on and it is clear exactly who is being referred to. Being clear in this way seems to add to everyone's security. Information becomes concrete which one can get hold of, instead of being nebulous and perhaps posing some kind of threat.

It

It is a word that can easily be misunderstood because it often isn't clear what "it" refers to. "It" is a word that has to be used with care.

The more clear your "it" is, the less the hearer fills it in with his own meaning. Sometimes "it" is related to a hidden "I" message. One way to better understand your "it" is to substitute "I" and see what happens. "It isn't clear" changed to "I am not clear" could make things more accurate and therefore easier to respond to.

"It often happens to people" is a statement that when said straight could be a comfort message that says, "The thing you are talking about has happened to me. I know how feeling humiliated feels."

To be more sure that we are understood, it might be wiser to fill in the details.

But

Next is the word *but*.
"But" is often a way of saying "yes" and "no" in the same sentence.

"I love you *but* I wish you would change your underwear more often."

This kind of use can easily end up with the other person feeling very uncomfortable, uneasy, and frequently confused.

Try substituting the word "and" for "but," which will clarify the situation. Your body will even feel different.

By using "but" the speaker is often linking two different thoughts together, which is what causes the difficulty.

Thus "I love you, but I wish you would change your underwear more often" could be two expressions.

"I love you" and "I wish you would change your underwear more often."

It could also represent someone's best, although fearful, attempt to make an uncomfortable demand by couching the demand in a love context, hoping the other person would not feel hurt.

If this is the case, what would happen if the person were to say "I want to ask something of you that I feel very uncomfortable about. I would like you to change your underwear more often."

Yes, No

A clear "yes" and "no" are important. Too many people say "yes, but" or "yes, maybe" or "no" just to be on the safe side, especially if they are in a position of power.

When "yes" or "no" are said clearly, and they mean NOW and not forever, and it is further clear "yes" and "no" relate to an issue rather than a person's value, then "yes" and "no" are very helpful words in making contact.

People can get away with much misuse of words when trust and good feeling have been established and when the freedom to comment is around. However, so often people feel so unsure about themselves that the lack of clarity leaves a lot of room for misunderstanding and consequent bad feelings. It is easy to build up these bad feelings once they are started.

"No" is a word that we all need and need to be able to use when it fits. So often when people feel "no," they say "maybe" or "yes" to avoid meeting the issue. This is justified on the basis of sparing the other's feelings. It is a form of lying and usually invites distrust, which, of course, is death to making contact.

When the "no" isn't clear, the "yes" can also be mistrusted. Have you ever heard "He said yes, but he doesn't really mean it."

Always, Never

Always is the positive form of a global word. *Never* is the negative form. For example:

Always clean up your plate.
Never leave anything on your plate.

The literal meaning of these words is seldom accurate and the directions seldom applicable to life situations. There are few cases in life where something is always *or* never. Therefore to try to follow these demands in all situations will surely end up in failure like the rules I described earlier.

Often the use of these words is a way to make emotional emphasis, like ...

"You *always* make me mad."

meaning really ...

"I am NOW very mad at you."

If the situation were as the speaker states, the adrenals would wear out.

Sometimes the words *always* and *never* hide ignorance. For example, someone has spent just five minutes with a person and announces,

"He is always bright."

In most cases the literal use of these two words could not be followed in all times, places and situations. Furthermore, they are frequently untrue. For the most part they become emotionally laden words that harm rather than nurture or enlighten the situation.

I find that these words are often used without any meaning in any literal sense.

These words are related to the inhuman rules I talked about earlier, so they have the potential for the same unnecessary guilt and inadequacy feelings because they are almost impossible to apply.

Should

"Ought" and "should" are other trap words from which it is easy to imply that there is something wrong with you—you have failed somehow to measure up.

Often the use of these words implies stupidity on someone's part ...

"You should have known better."

This is frequently heard as an accusation. Sometimes it merely represents some friendly advice. When people use the words "ought" and "should," often they are trying to indicate a dilemma in which they have more than one direction to go at a time—one may be pulling harder than the rest although the others are equally important ...

"I like this, but I should get that."

When your words are these, your body often feels tight. There are no easy answers to the pulls which "ought" and "should" represent. Biologically we really can go in only one direction at a time.

When your body feels tight your brain often freezes right along with your tight body, and so your thinking becomes limited as well.

Hearing yourself use the words *ought* and *should* can be a tip-off to you that you are engaged in a struggle. Perhaps instead of trying to deal with these opposing parts as one, you can separate them and make two parts.

"I like this ..." (one part)
"But I should get that"

translated into ...

"I also need that ..." (a second part).

Such a separation may be helpful in considering each piece separately and then considering them together.

When you do this your body has a chance to become a little looser, thus freeing some energy to negotiate a bit better.

When I am in this spot, I can help myself by asking whether I will literally die in either situation. If the answer is *no*, then I have a different perspective, and I can more easily play around with alternatives, since I am now out of a win-loss feeling in myself. I won't die. I may be only a little deprived or inconvenienced at most.

Start paying attention to the words you use.

Who is your *they?*
What is your *it?*
What does your *no* mean?
What does your *yes* mean?
Is your *I* clear?

Are you saying *never* and *always* when you mean sometimes and when you want to make emotional emphasis?

How are you using *ought* and *should?*

Review Questions

1. What reasons do people give for *not* using the word "I"?
2. What is similar about the problems Satir finds with the words "they" and "it"?
3. Does Satir suggest that we should not use the words "but," "yes," and "no"? What is she saying about these words?
4. How does a person's use of the words "ought" and "should" reflect that person's value system?

Probes

1. When you're in a conversation, can you recall what you said sixty seconds earlier? Try it. What do you notice?

2. Notice how, as Virginia Satir says, "it" and "they" both often work to hide the fact that some *I* is actually talking. When do you hear yourself using "it" and "they" that way?
3. What happens when you substitute "and" for "but"?
4. Do you experience your body responding as Satir describes to the words "ought" and "should"?

s the title to this next selection indicates, questions are probably the most often-used pieces of language. In fact, these authors estimate that "about 25 percent of everything we utter is followed by a question mark." Not only is that fact a surprise to most of us, but we also are not usually aware of how many different *kinds* of questions there are. This reading is particularly useful because of the way it distinguishes "loaded" and "semi-innocent" questions from "open" and "closed" ones and shows how "multiple-choice" and "disclosing" questions function in interpersonal relationships.

Earlier in their book, Goodman and Esterly distinguish among four main functions of interpersonal messages: "disclosure," "reflection," "interpretation," and "advisement." Disclosure offers some personal history that enables another to know more about who you are. Reflection "mirrors back the heart of another's message." An interpretation starts with the other's message, but then it remanufactures it, classifies it, and delivers it as a piece of news. Interpretations involve speculations and inferences, and they are one of the main ways we make sense out of and add meaning to conversations. Advisements basically offer advice, although the authors claim that they are more complicated than the simple term "advice" suggests. Part of the authors' point in this next reading is that questions can perform all four of these important conversational functions. Sometimes questions disclose, sometimes they reflect, sometimes they interpret, and sometimes they advise.

The reading also points out how "loaded" questions can contribute in important ways to a conversation, and that multiple choice questions can be both helpful and manipulative. Their discussion of disclosing questions is a useful addition to what some other authors say about disclosure in Chapter 8 of *Bridges Not Walls*. In short, Goodman and Esterly do a good job of showing how the apparently simple category of talk called "questions" is really impressively complex. After you read these next pages, I suspect you'll be much more aware of all the questions you ask and all the different ways you use them.

Questions—The Most Popular Piece of Language

Gerald Goodman and Glenn Esterly

We use questions all over the place. We use them for reasons that are plain and veiled, innocent and wicked, protective and generous, loving and spiteful ... and for other reasons known only to a few super-specialized linguists. The spoken question is used for a wider range of motives than any other talk tool. That's why it's the most popular piece of language for adults, and by far the favorite with kids.

I estimate about 25 percent of everything we utter is followed by a question mark. My students accuse me of exaggerating when I mention that figure. They find it hard to imagine people trying to find out something during every fourth utterance.

It *is* hard to believe that such a huge amount of our talk is motivated by curiosity. The typical person in a typical conversation doesn't seem *that* eager to gather information.

But gathering information isn't the issue here. The issue is question use— and questions are used for much more than gathering information. Many of our questions aren't the least bit aimed at "finding out." I'm not just referring to those colloquial questions like, "How ya doin?" (a friendly, familiar way to say, "Hello"), but to an entire family of talk tools that are loaded with the potential to perform dozens of important psychological functions. The biggest news about questions is that much of the "asking" in our lives is, in fact, "telling."

Loaded Questions

"Loaded" questions are typically described as somewhat sinister things, with hidden agendas. They're viewed as questions that require much thought about the motives behind them or that are scheming in a way that won't let you win, no matter how you might answer. People I've questioned over the years feel these talk tools range all the way from slightly sneaky to down right menacing. Dictionaries agree to the extent of labeling loaded questions as being worded "unfairly." Still ...

I think loaded questions are unappreciated, misunderstood, underestimated, and simply not recognized as bits of language that allow us to be bolder and more verbally involved with each other without sacrificing respect. Of course, they can be indirect, threatening, demanding, and even carry the answer to the alleged question they ask. But they also carry—and often enhance—important advisements, interpretations, and self-disclosures. I'm saying these mischievous talk tools that "tell" have their good points, too. And spotting them in action expands our conversational perspective because loaded questions both carry and attenuate messages. They serve a surprising variety of our daily needs, particularly controlling the degree of directness in our conversation.

My best reckless guess is that about half of our questions are loaded with extra meaning. Their messages are more important than the questions they ostensibly ask. We maneuver verbally every day with them—for better or worse. Getting to know what they are and what they can do is useful for spotting subtle coercion, noticing signs of respect, diagnosing some discomfort, and even watching how early signs of personal attraction are veiled.

Here's an example of how questions become loaded with advisements and interpretations (disclosing questions are in a later section).

Two women are finishing lunch and talking. June, eating an ample slice of cheesecake, says to Stacy, her sister: "If Ted {her skinny husband} walked in and saw me eating this, I'd crawl under the table."

Stacy asks, "Isn't it about time you gave up that dumb cheesecake habit?"

If humans were equipped with a reflex for detecting any loaded question, it would go off at this point: advisement alert!

Stacy uses a question loaded with advice—an "advising question" that carries a rather insistent, commanding piece of advice. June can't answer because her mouth is full, but even if she could, a yes or no would not be forthcoming. The formal grammar of Stacy's loaded question calls for simple agreement or disagreement. But the embedded rules of the talk game say, "Change your reading of this question into a piece of commanding advice: 'Cease and desist with the cheesecake.'" So Stacy's question isn't really motivated by curiosity or an urge to find out. She's irritated or frustrated or worried, and she's advising June to change her habit. There's no need to answer.

As June chews, Stacy speaks again with a question mark in her voice: "Why don't you try counting to ten while you picture a fresh, low calorie, juicy orange?"

Advisement alert!

That talk tool is loaded with a prescription for performing self-care in the area of cheesecake addiction. Stacy has delivered an explicit diagnosis, a command for action, and a therapy treatment plan with two quick advising questions. If June seriously attempted to answer her sister's second advising question as if it were a genuine inquiry, she'd be performing sarcasm: "Because I believe a cheesecake a day keeps the doctor away." Or if she habitually went around answering all loaded questions as if they were innocent inquiries, she'd be diagnosed as nothing less than mentally disturbed. Inability to follow all of the implicit rules for using questions is an emblem for pathology in thinking. Most of us just obey this language law automatically. Even nursery school children know how to play a few subtle games with questions. Some three- and four-year-olds use loaded questions, observes Professor Mathilda Holvman, who found that "at this early period in language development, children already use the interrogative form {questions} analogously to their mothers for making suggestions {a form of advisement}...." These kids used advising questions such as "Where my tapioca?" to commandingly advise, "Get me some tapioca." There's no doubt—literally "no question"—in the kids' minds that the tapioca will be delivered.

As children grow into adults, they use social commands with less insistence. When they begin to learn that others have wills of their own, the advising question serves to soften the presumptuousness of hard advisements that directly suggest or command. As kids mature, the self-absorbed "Where's my tapioca?" will eventually become, "Could you bring me some tapioca?" And later, when adult decorum arrives, "If it's not too much trouble, could you bring me some tapioca next time you're at the fridge."

The ability of questions to soften advisement, to make us sound less presumptuous and more deferent, explains why they're so popular. It's the main reason one out of four utterances has a question mark at the end. The almost ritualistic "asking" that's performed by couching advice in the question format offers a moment of respect, or some attenuation for our pushy commands. At minimum, our use of questions for *telling* offers some recognition of the other person's will. That fact is worth remembering. Loaded questions often soften telling—"Don't you think it might be useful to remember the previous five words?"

The same kind of recognition occurs with "interpretive" questions. I'll illustrate by having June defend her diet: "Stacy, aren't you being a hypocrite about my cheesecake when you always eat three eggs for breakfast?"

Interpretation alert!

Here's a loaded question that classifies Stacy as a hypocrite. June's diagnosis is nothing more than grown up name-calling, made more presentable—and less hostile—because it's cradled in a loaded question. Drop the question and you have, "Stacy, you're a hypocrite."

Now let's have Stacy resist the interpretation: "Well, that's not fair. I haven't had a three-egg breakfast all month. I cut down; I only eat two now."

June replies, "Only two! But doesn't 14 eggs a week dump enough cholesterol into your system to harden arteries on the spot?"

Interpretation alert!

This time, instead of classifying Stacy, June uses the interpretative question to explain a cause (14 eggs' worth of cholesterol) for an effect (heart disease candidate).

Loaded questions aren't difficult to spot in conversations. They often start with a mild opposition and words like wouldn't, couldn't, aren't, doesn't, and shouldn't. "Wouldn't it be better if? ..." "Why don't you? ..." "Shouldn't we try to? ..." "Aren't you being? ..." "Doesn't that make you? ..."

They render us incapable of responding with a simple rejection. You can easily find one by remaining quiet while people within earshot engage in earnest discourse....

Semi-Innocent Questions

... There are questions that *do* want to find out and willingly accept answers—decent, straightforward, simple questions like, "Can I have some ice cream after dinner, Mommy?" I put these in a category called "semi-innocent" as a reminder that they aren't always perfectly innocent questions. Even though semi-innocents differ significantly from loaded questions—because they can be appropriately answered—they can serve some scheming purposes....

Sometimes kids use questions to resist demands: "Why do I have to do the dishes?" Or in calling for justice: "Is Shirley gonna stay up later than me again?"

Semi-innocents in the hands of adults serve a panoply of daily needs, from getting a bit of approval ("What do ya think of this new sweater?") to a trite pickup gambit ("Haven't I seen you around here before?"). For both adults and kids, these semi-innocent questions—with their motives and ability to extract answers—are major managers in social exchange....

Closed Questions for Short Answers

... Closed questions want brief answers like yes or no or maybe. Brief doesn't always mean trivial. Answers to closed questions can be vital. We recognize these oft-demanding talk tools by their context—and especially by their music: an upward inflection at the end. They often slide to a higher note on the last syllable. We sing closed questions with a voice that sounds eager or impatient, wanting a speedy, cogent, short answer: "Can I use your *phone?*" "Will you marry *me?*" "Are you *ready?*" "Do you under*stand?*" "Did ya know what *to do?*" ...

Open Questions for Longer Answers

... Open questions don't perch at the end of a high note like most impatiently eager closed innocents. Open-ended questions invite long, unrushed, rambling answers. ("What did ya do in the war, Daddy?") In the hands of a skilled talker, leisurely open questions get to the heart of things faster than those fast-paced, closed inquiries. That's why open questions are illegal in 20 Questions. The distinct shapes and sounds associated with open and closed questions signal the listener as to the type of answer wanted....

Errors in asking open questions for closed questions and vice versa are one significant source of frustration in conversation. The errors consistently waste time and truncate information. These tiny communication breakdowns where people need to know more than their closed questions can find out, or find themselves swamped with unwanted long answers from open questions, produce minor irritations, little stresses at having to try again. For some, it may happen dozens of times a week, or thousands of times a year. Using open and closed questions with some awareness is basic to effective information-gathering—not only in social exchange but in the workplace (especially in the workplace). These talk tools are so easy to learn that we could teach them in third grade. Learning and using them as adults won't guarantee results, but getting accustomed to using the right tool can make stunning improvements in effective information-gathering.

Multiple-Choice Questions for Multiple-Choice Feelings

... Multiple-choice questions—a series of closely connected closed questions—can help sort out confusion and choose the "correct" answer. They tend to control information: "Did she say anything about liking it? Did she smile? Or couldn't you tell?" ...

The way we all fall victim to the multiple-choice as a rhetorical device amazes me. In the fast flow of conversation, we rerely stop the process to address the half-masked, fully loaded piece of persuasion carried by the question.... But when the conversation becomes uneasy *and* polite at the same time, and you're feeling subtly coerced by some indirect aggression, look around for one of those loaded multiple-choice questions as the culprit.

Now for an example of a generous, sensitive multiple-choice to counter any thoughts that this talk tool only sells opinion.

During an intense conversation within a self-help group for recently divorced older women, one woman discloses a confused message about her emotional hurt and psychological numbness. One of her peers carefully responds: "Are you saying it's hurting a little bit less, or that you were just getting used to the pain, or that you can't tell the difference anymore?" Those choices disentangled a confusion of feelings into three likely possibilities. The empathic question helped the woman sort out her condition, showed that someone was listening seriously, and set the stage for moving out of her doldrums. So the multiple-choice can also be a sensitive caretaker. Even more than some other omnibus talk tools, multiple-choices have multiple personalities.

Disclosing Questions

Still another side of multiple-choice questions is that they can disclose. One way the multiple choice does that is to display knowledge, even to brag.

A teenage boy talks to a mechanic about a problem with his car. The boy says: "Ya think the carburetor's too lean, or does the fuel pump sound weak, or could it be a clogged gas line?" Pretty smart. The boy's disclosing his sophistication about engines and demonstrating he's not just a know-nothing. That can be self-protective if the message to the mechanic is also, "Don't try to sell me parts I don't need." More often, multiple choices that disclose knowledge are simply semi-innocent ways to show off and enhance self-esteem.

But self-disclosing questions, of any type, are less common than advising or interpreting questions. Maybe it's because we do less disclosing in general than advising or interpreting. In any case, disclosing questions work well for diluting embarrassment when they're used to reveal our imperfections, to blunt the directness of a negative emotion, or to veil the nakedness of a tender feeling.

They can be loaded with high-risk confessions or minor revelations. Disclosures invite immediate feedback. The difference between disclosing with loaded or semi-innocent questions isn't as important as the fact they both *intentionally* reveal private thoughts or feelings. Innocent questions frequently disclose *unintentionally*. They give away privacy when a perceptive listener interprets varied meaning. Please don't confuse the "taking" of meaning behind the innocent question with the deliberate, intentional giving of disclosure done by loaded questions and semi-innocents. Many talk tools inadvertently reveal the talker's motives, but loaded and semi-innocent questions are spoken *precisely* to disclose.

Grandma on the phone to her four-year-old grandson can get away with, "Do you know how much I missed getting a good-bye kiss yesterday?" But the same loaded message won't work for a young man communicating with an elegant woman he's recently met (unless it's done with a great sense of humor).

Out of context, disclosing questions can look like advising or interpreting questions. For example, I watched my neighbor's nine-year-old waiting for one of her two teenage brothers to break away from a TV football game and drive her to the local video rental store. She plaintively, sincerely asked: "Are you guys gonna be watching *all* afternoon?" Translation: "I'm so bored, but I don't dare try to push you guys around now 'cause Mom isn't home and if I complain harder, you'll pretend to be more annoyed than you are as an excuse for not driving me, which will get you uninterrupted viewing. So please have mercy on your nice little sister." I'm not kidding. Ordinary nine-year-olds can think and feel that way. The girl in this case leveled with me when I asked about it. (Unfortunately, her disclosing question didn't work; her brothers sat glued to the set through the game. But since she gave me a fine talk specimen, *I* drove her to the video store.)

Imagine now the girl's question being asked by a strong, no-nonsense mother, annoyed at waiting for her boys to help with a task: "Are *you* guys gonna be watching all *afternoon?*" Some disclosure of frustration is carried, of course, but the force of the question is mostly a command. And, unlike the previous example, these guys aren't given an invitation to answer. In no uncertain terms, the loaded question advises the boys to comply—soon. Her question uses the same words as the girl's disclosing question, but the different contexts create separate meanings. Asking someone "Shouldn't your poison ivy be healed already?" can disclose different emotions when asked by a caring mother (worry), a formal colleague (courteous concern), and a dermatologist (bewilderment).

Some disclosing questions disguise negative emotions, such as disbelief, semicleverly: "You mean you finished reading the entire chapter in 20 minutes?" Here's one that is partly effective in describing childish braggadocio: "Have you any idea what that car cost me?"—as if asking about a serious fact instead of boasting about conspicuous consumption.

The melodic Yiddish language, which specializes in loaded questions, brings the disclosing question to the level of art. I can demystify some of that subtlety with a classic Yiddish question that discloses nine different messages, from surprise to insult, depending on which word is emphasized. Try it first with a slightly mocking (tongue-in-cheek) feeling and overemphasized first word. "*You* want me to buy two tickets for your daughter's recital?"

Now try it with the same tone overemphasizing the second word: "You *want* me to buy two tickets for your daughter's recital?"

See how the quality of disclosure changes?

You can create seven more messages by emphasizing the words "me," "buy," "two," "tickets," "your," "daughter's," or "recital." Emphasizing "me" adds the meaning: "Of all people, you chose *me?*" Or perhaps: "You have the nerve to ask *me* after you failed to show up at my son's Bar Mitzvah?" Emphasizing "buy" could connote that the tickets should be given as a gift ... and so on, as each emphasized word loads the question with a newly revealed feeling until the final outrageous insult from accentuating "recital." I can almost hear a Yiddish father from a past generation affectionately roughhousing with another that his beloved daughter's piano performance wasn't even worth the prestigeful word "recital"—both men then dissolving in laughter.

Ordinary disclosing questions don't demand that the listener answer. The Yiddish variety tries to leave the listener speechless.

The Big Question About Questions

On her deathbed, a whimsical Gertrude Stein asked her intimates, "What's the answer?" Getting no response, she characteristically flipped her meaning upside-down to reveal something essential. Laughing, she asked, "In that case, what's the question?"

Her cryptic playfulness symbolized a profound search, both in her life and over the history of civilized arts and sciences—the search for important questions. Even before Socrates used the Socratic question, wise teachers struggled to steer students away from easy answers and toward the discovery of capable questions. Ironically, capable questions about the ways humans use everyday verbal questions are rather rare. We academics haven't come up with a strong set of questions for illuminating the spoken question's essential character. As a result, we know little about the psycholinguistic laws governing one of our most frequently used talk tools.

I believe our failure to capture a clear picture of the question's character is a result of its chameleon-like quality—its penchant for quick change allows it to perform dozens of psychological tasks, from flirting to rejecting. And it's not only those message-carrying members of the loaded question family that advise, interpret and disclose; it's also those semi-innocent creatures that work as quick-change artists instantly ready to serve our momentary motives. More than any member of the question family, semi-innocents illustrate why it's so hard to establish a simple picture for these pieces of language.... Here are some representative, everyday motives, along with the semi-innocents that do their work.

Complaining   "Isn't it hot in here?" "Have you any idea how long it's been since we went to a movie?"

These questions disclose a complaint and leave room for the listener to add his or her opinion—to "correct" the complaint: "It's actually not very hot in here right now. Maybe your heavy sweater ..." Or: "You're right, it's been six months since we've been out to a movie; seems we've fallen into the tube." ...

Requesting Approval   "Do you like my haircut?" "Did I do all right?" "Did I do it faster than you even hoped?"

These press for positive confirmation while watering down the message: "Please agree that I'm good."

Resisting Demands   "Why do I hafta do everything?" "Are ya sure you need it?" "Could you write me a memo so I can see if it's feasible?"

These devices help say an indirect "no." They resist advising; they're great for stalling: "Why do ya wanna know?"

Softening Surprise   "And you did that all by yourself?" "Are you trying to tell me we're washed up?" "Are you kidding?" "Would you believe he ate the whole thing?"

Initiating Flirtation   (The pickup question) "Haven't we met someplace before?" "Do people come and tell you that you look like Linda Gray?" "Would you happen to know if this store carries chutney?" "Is that a good book you're reading?"

Pickup lines are so loaded with trepidation, humor, posing, and straining for originality that they must be placed in context. "Haven't we met someplace before?" is such an archaic cliche that it makes occasional comebacks on campus as a satirical, yet serious, gambit. A semi-innocent about a specific item, like chutney in a store, usually comes from a semisincere, semihelpless male. If the woman takes his bait, he may push his luck with something like, "Do you live in the neighborhood?" ...

Bragging   (The show-off question) "Do you think it's fair for me to play chess with him?" "Did I ever show you the snapshots of me and Kenny Rogers?" "Will we see your team at the championships?"

They can become ridiculous mockeries of leisure-class/jet-set conspicuous consumption. "Did you see that garish display at Gucci's last week?" "What colors are your Mercedes this season?" "Don't you love the Riviera in spring?"

This type of semi-innocent (actually 95 percent guilty) question may look fictional in print, but reasonable facsimiles appear in real life with regularity—especially when the real life is preoccupied with status or wealth.

Demonstrating a Common Bond   "Don't we make a great team?" "Isn't it strange we both crave Chicago-style pizza?" "Can ya believe the coincidence—both of us having been in Marvin Diskin's communications course?" "So you're involved in saving whales, too?"

These semi-innocents take some of the bluntness from the intention to become more attached, to "share," to be similar, symmetrical. They're employed frequently (and frequently tritely) by novelists and screenwriters.

Reducing Anxiety   (The ice-breaker question) Two strangers alone, moving slowly to the 37th floor: "Isn't this the slowest elevator?" Two strangers alone in a classroom: "Do you think we're the only ones enrolled in this course?"

Awkward silences are broken by semi-innocents. They usually ask the listener to say *something.... anything.* They even work on painful pauses between friends: "Do you think we should finish this some other time?"

Semi-innocents are frequently used, with blatant insincerity, for melting interpersonal tension by changing uncomfortable topics: "Hey, by the way, who won the game?" "How 'bout us getting some coffee?" They also break painful silences: "Hot enough for ya?" "Think it's gonna rain?" (I think Mickey Rooney said that last one to Judy Garland when the scene called for a nervous moment.)

Softening Persuasion   "Does the idea of working a year before starting college sound appealing to you?"

A gentle inquiry with a mild suggestion and room for an answer. Say the reply were, "Mom, please don't worry about me being ready for college now. I can make it." Then Mom could get away with saying, "I was just asking a question, Son." She lamely claims her innocence, but anyone within earshot knows she's only semi-innocent.

All of these semi-innocent questions that water down persuasion, reduce anxiety, show a common bond, mask flirtation, seek approval, resist demands, attenuate surprise, and declaw complaints make face-to-face relationships more comfortable. We customize them to fit each situation. Linguists would call them contextualized.

They also soften the often bumpy ride of conversation by blunting the impact of insults, sales pitches, early affection (infatuation), intense personal needs for connection, excitement, anger, rejection, depression, joy—almost any emotion that can hurt, confuse or embarrass. They're shock absorbers. In that sense, they dilute the raw exchange of feelings. The moment we drop an innocent question in a context that allows it to attract extra meaning and serve our psychological needs to be less than direct, it becomes a sophisticated semi-innocent talk tool. It becomes a marvelous manager of detours, deflections, and even double-talk. It melts the potency of language, often for good reason. It helps create interpersonal rituals where deep feelings aren't so intense and opinions are merely inquiries. That's why adults get hooked on questions. As these devices move beyond the simple open-and-closed innocence of pure information-gathering, they take on a new identity as heavy-duty, multipurpose, always-ready talk tools that both carry and regulate the power of our meaning. We're starting to understand some of the ways they work, but there's a long way to go before the picture is complete—Gertrude Stein's last words are still appropriate.

Review Questions

1. True or False: Goodman and Esterly believe that most questions are used not to "ask" but to "tell." Explain.
2. What's the difference between a question that's "loaded with advisement" and one that's "loaded with interpretation"?
3. What kind of question frequently begins with words like, "Wouldn't it be better if? ..." "Shouldn't we try to? ..." or "Aren't you being? ..."?
4. What is the primary difference between "closed" and "open" questions?
5. Goodman and Esterly use the term "multiple-choice question" to label a series of closely connected _____ questions.
6. What kind of question is the following inquiry by a mother-in-law: "Are you guys really not going to stop and see us when you drive through town next weekend?"

Probes

1. If it's true that one out of every four utterances is a question, and that most questions actually do "tell" rather than "ask," shouldn't we stop using such indirect means of communicating and be more straightforward with our talk? Wouldn't it be better to reform our conversation choices rather than to spend all this time learning about how we use questions to mask and distort what we mean? Explain.
2. Goodman and Esterly note that questions can often *soften* criticism, advice, or persuasion. Can they also *harden* communication? Can you think of examples of questions that make one's message more direct and blunt?
3. The authors briefly mention how children use "semi-innocent" questions to resist demands or call for fairness. What other ways have you noticed children using questions? How does the child's use of questions differ from the adult's?
4. Goodman and Esterly do not mention many differences between the ways males and females use questions. Do you hear differences in your own communication experience? What are they?
5. In the final section of the reading the authors discuss nine types of "semi-innocent" questions that people use to complain, request approval, brag, and so on. Which of the nine do you hear others asking most often? Which do you use most frequently?

Chapter 4

Nonverbal Cues

It is not necessary to always think words. Words often keep me from acting in a fully intuitive way. Fears, indecision, and frustration feed on words. Without words they usually stop. When I am trying to figure out how I should relate to someone, especially a stranger, if I will stop thinking words, and listen to the situation, and just be open, I find I act in a more appropriate, more spontaneous, often original, sometimes even courageous way. Words are at times good for looking back, but they are confining when I need to act in the present.

HUGH PRATHER

D id you ever stop to think how your communication is affected by breath and body odors? Furniture placement and window location? Dilation of the pupils of your and other people's eyes? Angle of pelvic tilt or thrust? Visible cigarette butts? Audibility of breathing? It's not always obvious, but we are affected by the meanings we give these and a multitude of other nonverbal cues. Some nonverbal cues are more obvious—tone of voice, rate of speaking, amount and type of gesture, proximity, facial expression, touch, and so on. But whether they're obvious or subtle, nonverbal cues strongly affect communication. In fact, Knapp indicates that some researchers believe that about 65 percent of social meaning of most human communication events is carried by nonverbal cues. Sixty-five percent! If you want to promote interpersonal quality communication, it is obviously crucially important to become aware of what nonverbal cues are and how they work.

This chapter moves toward that end by presenting an overview of nonverbal cues and a discussion of two important and frequently overlooked cues, silence and touch. The purpose of this first article is, frankly, to increase your awareness of how many types of nonverbal cues there are and how many different ways they function in our day-to-day contact. If you count both main and subcategories, Knapp identifies thirteen types of nonverbal cues, each of which can operate in six different ways. That adds up to a mind-boggling set of possible combinations, more than anybody could keep absolute track of.

The point, though, is not to overwhelm you with categories, but to emphasize that what we do nonverbally and how we do it makes a difference in our communicating. People sensitive to nonverbal cues are much more able to listen effectively and empathically, to distinguish appropriate from inappropriate self-disclosure, to reduce others' defensiveness, to provide meaningful support, and to handle conflict interpersonally. So the sensitivity you can pick up from this article and the information and skills available in the next three selections can help you apply much of what is in the rest of the book.

Nonverbal Communication: Basic Perspectives

Mark L. Knapp

Those of us who keep our eyes open can read volumes into what we see going on around us.
—E. T. HALL

Herr von Osten purchased a horse in Berlin, Germany, in 1900. When von Osten began training his horse, Hans, to count by tapping his front hoof, he had no idea that Hans was soon to become one of the most celebrated horses in history. Hans was a rapid learner and soon progressed from counting to addition, multiplication, division, subtraction, and eventually the solution of problems involving factors and fractions. As if this were not enough, von Osten exhibited Hans to public audiences, where the horse counted the number of people in the audience or simply the number who were wearing eyeglasses. Still responding only with taps, Hans could tell time, use a calendar, display an ability to recall musical pitch, and perform numerous other seemingly fantastic feats. After von Osten taught Hans an alphabet that could be coded into hoofbeats, the horse could answer virtually any question—oral or written. It seemed that Hans, a common horse, had a complete comprehension of the German language, the ability to produce the equivalent of words and numerals, and an intelligence beyond that of many human beings.

Even without the promotion of Madison Avenue, the word spread quickly, and soon Hans was known throughout the world. He was soon dubbed Clever Hans. Because of the obviously profound implications for several scientific fields and because some skeptics thought there was a gimmick involved, an investigating committee was established to decide, once and for all, whether there was any deceit involved in Hans's performances. A professor of psychology and physiology, the director of the Berlin Zoological Garden, a director of a circus, veterinarians, and cavalry officers were appointed to this commission of horse experts. An experiment with Hans from which von Osten was excluded demonstrated no change in the apparent intelligence of Hans. This was sufficient proof for the commission to announce that there was no trickery involved.

The appointment of a second commission was the beginning of the end for Clever Hans. Von Osten was asked to whisper a number into the horse's left ear while another experimenter whispered a number into the horse's right ear. Hans was told to add the two numbers—an answer none of the onlookers, von Osten, or the experimenter knew. Hans failed, and with further tests he continued to fail. The experimenter, Pfungst, discovered on further experimentation that Hans could only answer a question if someone in his visual field knew the answer.[1] When Hans was given the question, the onlookers assumed an expectant posture and increased their body tension. When Hans reached the correct number of taps, the onlookers would relax and make a slight movement of the head—which was Hans' cue to stop tapping.

The story of Clever Hans is frequently used in discussions concerning the capacity of an animal to learn verbal language. It also seems well suited to an introduction to the field of nonverbal communication. Hans's cleverness was not in his ability to verbalize or understand verbal commands, but in his ability to respond to almost imperceptible and unconscious movements on the part of those surrounding him. It is not unlike that perceptiveness or sensitivity to nonverbal cues exhibited by a Clever Carl, Chris, Frank, or Harriet when they are closing a business deal, giving an intelligent and industrious image to a professor, impressing a date, knowing when to leave a party, and in a multitude of other common situations . . .

Perspectives on Defining Nonverbal Communication

Conceptually, the term *nonverbal* is subject to a variety of interpretations— just like the term *communication*. The basic issue seems to be whether the events that are traditionally studied under the heading *nonverbal* are literally nonverbal. Ray Birdwhistell, a pioneer in nonverbal research, is reported to have said that studying *nonverbal* communication is like studying *noncardiac* physiology. His point is well taken. It is not easy to dissect human interaction and make one diagnosis that concerns only verbal behavior and another that concerns only nonverbal behavior. The verbal dimension is so intimately woven and so subtly represented in so much of what we have previously labeled nonverbal that the term does not always adequately describe the behavior under study. Some of the most noteworthy scholars associated with nonverbal study refuse to segregate words from gestures and hence work under the broader terms *communication* or *face-to-face interaction*.

Another possible source of confusion in defining nonverbal communication is whether we are talking about the signal *produced* (nonverbal) or the internal code for *interpreting* the signal (frequently verbal). Generally, when people refer to nonverbal behavior they are talking about the signal(s) to which meaning will be attributed—not the process of attributing meaning.

The fuzzy line between verbal and nonverbal communication is augmented by an equally difficult distinction between vocal and nonvocal phenomena. Consider the following: (1) Not all acoustic phenomena are vocal—for example, knuckle-cracking; a gurgling stomach; farting; slapping one's thigh, another's back, or a desk top; snapping one's fingers; and clapping. (2) Not all nonacoustic phenomena are nonverbal—for example, some of the gestures used in American Sign Language used by many deaf people. (3) Not all vocal phenomena are the same— some are respiratory and some are not. A sigh or prespeaking inspiration of breath may be considered vocal and respiratory; a click or "tch, tch!" might be classified as vocal but nonrespiratory. (4) Not all words or "apparent" word strings are clearly or singularly verbal—for example, onomatopoetic words such as *buzz* or *murmur* and nonpropositional speech used by auctioneers and some aphasics. Neat categorization for each behavior under consideration is often difficult. Realistically, we should expect that there will be points of overlap—behaviors that fit some aspects of one category and some aspects of another.

Instead of trying to classify behavior as either nonverbal or verbal, Mehrabian chose instead to use an "explicit-implicit" dichotomy.[2] In other words, Mehrabian believed that it was the subtlety of a signal that brought it into the nonverbal realm—and subtlety seemed to be directly linked to a lack of explicit rules for coding. Mehrabian's work has focused primarily on the referents people have for various configurations of nonverbal and/or implicit behavior—that is, the meaning you attach to these behaviors. The results of extensive testing reveal a threefold perspective.[3] (1) Immediacy. Sometimes we react to things by evaluating them— positive or negative, good or bad, like or dislike. (2) Status. Sometimes we enact or perceive behaviors that indicate various aspects of status to us—strong or weak, superior or subordinate. (3) Responsiveness. This third category refers to our perceptions of activity—slow or fast, active or passive.

Perspectives on Classifying Nonverbal Behavior

The following classification schema was derived from an examination of writing and research currently being conducted in which the authors either explicitly or implicitly categorized their own work as being subsumable under the label *nonverbal*.

Body Motion or Kinesic Behavior

Body motion, or kinesic behavior, typically includes gestures, movements of the body, limbs, hands, head, feet and legs, facial expressions (smiles), eye behavior (blinking, direction and length of gaze, and pupil dilation), and posture. The furrow of the brow, the slump of a shoulder, and the tilt of a head—all are within the purview of kinesics. Obviously, there are different types of nonverbal behavior just as there are different types of verbal behavior. Some nonverbal cues are very specific, and some are more general. Some are intended to communicate, and some are expressive only. Some provide information about emotions, and others carry information about personality traits or attitudes. In an effort to sort through the relatively unknown world of nonverbal behavior, Ekman and Friesen[4] developed a system for classifying nonverbal behavior acts. These categories include:

Emblems These are nonverbal acts that have a direct verbal translation or dictionary definition, usually consisting of a word or two or a phrase.[5] There is high agreement among members of a culture or subculture on the verbal "translation" of these signals. The gestures used to represent "A-OK" or "Peace" (also known as the victory sign) are examples of emblems for a large part of our culture. Mostly, these emblems are culture specific. For example, Fig. 1 shows variations in suicide emblems depending on the popularity of a method (hanging, shooting, or stabbing) for a particular culture. However, some emblems portray actions that are common to the human species and seem to transcend a given culture. Eating (bringing hand up to mouth) and sleeping (tilting head in lateral position, almost perpendicular to the body, accompanied sometimes with eye closing and/or a hand or

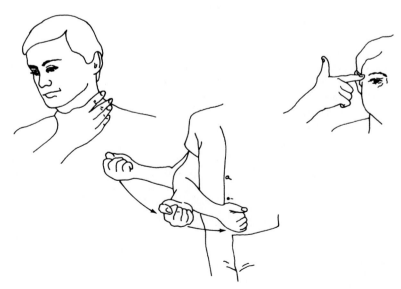

Figure 1
Emblems for suicide. Top left, the South Fore, Papua, New Guinea; top right, the United States; bottom, Japan.

hands below the head like a pillow) are two examples of emblems that Ekman and his colleagues have observed in several cultures. Ekman also found that different cultures also seem to have emblems for similar classes of messages, regardless of the gesture used to portray it, for example, insults, directions (come, go, stop), greetings, departures, certain types of responses (yes, no, I don't know), physical state, and emotion. The number of emblems used within a given culture may vary considerably, from less than 100 (United States) to more than 250 (Israeli students).

Emblems are often produced with the hands—but not exclusively. A nose wrinkle may say "I'm disgusted!" or "Phew! It stinks!" To say "I don't know" or "I'm helpless" or "I'm uncertain" one might turn both palms up, shrug shoulders, or do both simultaneously. Ekman believes that facial emblems probably differ from other facial expressions by being more stylized and being presented for longer or shorter durations. Facial emblems may also emphasize particular parts of the face; for example, the smile may be used to indicate happiness or surprise by mechanically dropping the jaw or dramatically raising the eyebrows.

Emblems are frequently used when verbal channels are blocked (or fail) and are usually used to communicate. Some of the sign language of the deaf, nonverbal gestures used by television production personnel, signs used by two underwater swimmers, or motions made by two people who are too far apart to make audible signals practical are all situations ripe for emblem production.

Our own awareness of emblem usage is about the same as our awareness of word choice. Also, like verbal behavior, context can sometimes change the interpretation of the signal; that is, giving someone "the finger" can be either humorous or insulting, depending on the other cues accompanying it. Ekman has also observed "emblematic slips," analogous to slips of the tongue. He gives an example of a woman who was subjected to a stress interview by a person whose status forbade free expressions of dislike. The woman, unknown to herself or the interviewer, displayed "the finger" on the arm of her chair for several minutes during the interview.

Unlike verbal behavior, emblems are not generally strung together like words, although there are exceptions. You may be talking on the phone when a visitor enters and you have to indicate "wait a minute," "come in," and "sit down" in succession. Finally, some emblems seem to be specifically adapted to particular subgroups within a given culture. For instance, Fig. 2 shows two gestures, one which

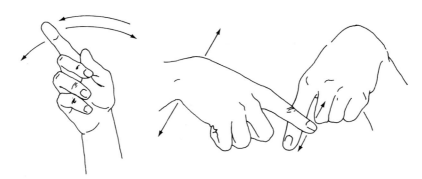

Figure 2
Finger emblems (United States). "No" (left) and "Shame on you" (right).

seems to be used primarily when adults are talking to children ("no-no") and one which seems primarily limited to usage by children ("shame on you").

Illustrators   These are nonverbal acts that are directly tied to, or accompany, speech and serve to illustrate what is being said verbally. These may be movements that accent or emphasize a word or phrase, sketch a path of thought, point to present objects, depict a spatial relationship, depict the rhythm or pacing of an event, draw a picture of the referent, or depict a bodily action. They may also be emblems used to illustrate verbal statements, either repeating or substituting for a word or phrase. Illustrators seem to be within our awareness, but not as explicitly as emblems. They are used intentionally to help communication, but not as deliberately as emblems. Many factors can alter the frequency with which illustrators are displayed. We would expect to find more illustrators in face-to-face communication than when communicating over an intercom;[6] we would expect people who are excited and enthusiastic to display more illustrators than those who are not; and we would expect more illustrators during "difficult" communication situations; for example, not being able to find the right words to express a thought or being confronted by a receiver who either isn't paying attention or isn't comprehending what you're trying to say. Illustrators are probably learned by watching others.

Affect Displays   These are primarily facial configurations that display affective states. Although the face is the primary source of affect, the body can also be read for global judgments of affect; for example, a drooping, sad body. Affect displays can repeat, augment, contradict, or be unrelated to, verbal affective statements. Once the display has occurred, there is usually a high degree of awareness, but it can occur without any awareness. Affect displays are often not intended to communicate, but they can be intentional.

Regulators   These are nonverbal acts that maintain and regulate the back and forth nature of speaking and listening between two or more interactants. They tell the speaker to continue, repeat, elaborate, hurry up, become more interesting, give the other a chance to talk, and so forth. Some of the behavior associated with greetings and good-byes may be regulators to the extent that they indicate the initiation or termination of face-to-face communication.

In recent years the various nonverbal behaviors associated with turn-taking are the regulators that have been given the most attention.[7] Turn-taking refers to the cues we use: to tell another person we want to talk, to keep another person from getting the floor away from us, to give up a speaking turn and ask the other person to continue, and to show we are finished speaking and the other person can take a turn. Generally we don't say these things verbally; they are communicated by many nonverbal behaviors. Probably the most familiar regulators are head nods and eye behavior. If head nods occur frequently in rapid succession, the message may be "hurry up and finish," but if the nods follow points made by the speaker and appear slow, deliberate, and thoughtful they may signal "keep talking" or "I like what you're saying." We found people who were trying to terminate a conversation severely decreased the amount of eye contact with the other person.[8]

Regulators seem to be on the periphery of our awareness and are generally difficult to inhibit. They are like overlearned habits and are almost involuntary, but we are very much aware of these signals when they are sent by others.

Adaptors These nonverbal behaviors are perhaps the most difficult to define and involve the most speculation. They are labeled adaptors because they are thought to develop in childhood as adaptive efforts to satisfy needs, perform actions, manage emotions, develop social contacts, or perform a host of other functions. Ekman and Friesen have identified three types of adaptors: self-, object-, and alter-directed.

Self-adaptors, as the term implies, refer to manipulations of one's own body, such as holding, rubbing, squeezing, scratching, pinching, or picking oneself. These self-adaptors will often increase as a person's anxiety level increases. Picking one's nose can be a self-adaptor; an adult who wipes the corner of his or her eye during times of sadness (as if to brush away tears) may be showing a response that reflects that person's early experiences with sadness. Ekman and his colleagues have found the "eye cover act" to be associated with shame and guilt, and the "scratch-pick act" to be associated with hostility—aggression toward oneself or toward another displaced onto oneself.

Alter-adaptors are learned in conjunction with our early experiences with interpersonal relations—giving and taking from another, attacking or protecting, establishing closeness or withdrawing, and the like. Leg movements may be adaptors, showing residues of kicking aggression, sexual invitation, or flight. Ekman believes that many of the restless movements of the hands and feet, which have typically been considered indicators of anxiety, may be residues of adaptors necessary for flight from the interaction. An example from the interaction behavior of baboons will help illustrate the nature of these alter-adaptors. When a young baboon is learning the fundamentals of attack and aggression, the mother baboon will watch from close by. The young baboon will enact aggressive behavior, but will also turn the head laterally to check whether the mother is still there. As an adult, the baboon may still perform this lateral head movement during threatening conditions even though the mother is no longer there and no functional purpose seems to be served by this movement.

Object-adaptors involve the manipulation of objects and may be derived from the performance of some instrumental task—such as smoking, writing with a pencil, and so on. Although we are typically unaware of performing these adaptor behaviors, we are probably most aware of the object-adaptors. These behaviors are often learned later in life, and there seem to be fewer social taboos associated with them.

Since there seem to be social constraints on displaying these adaptive behaviors, they are more often seen when a person is alone. At least, we would expect that we would see the full act rather than just a fragment of it. Alone you might pick your nose without inhibition; when other people are around you may just touch your nose or rub it "casually." Adaptors are not intended for use in communication, but they may be triggered by verbal behavior in a given situation associated with conditions occurring when the adaptive habit was first learned.

Physical Characteristics

Whereas the previous section was concerned with movement and motion, this category covers things that remain relatively unchanged during the period of interaction. They are influential nonverbal cues that are not movement bound. Included are such things as physique or body shape, general attractiveness, body or breath odors, height, weight, hair, and skin color or tone.

Touching Behavior

For some, kinesic study includes touch behavior; for others, however, actual physical contact constitutes a separate class of events. Some researchers are concerned with touching behavior as an important factor in the child's early development, and others are concerned with adult touching behavior. Subcategories of touch behavior may include stroking, hitting, holding, guiding another's movements, and other, more specific instances.

Paralanguage

Simply put, paralanguage deals with how something is said and not what is said. It deals with the range of nonverbal vocal cues surrounding common speech behavior. Trager believed that paralanguage had the following components.[9]

Voice Qualities   This includes such things as pitch range, pitch control, rhythm control, tempo, articulation control, resonance, glottis control, and vocal lip control.

Vocalizations   (1) *Vocal characterizers.* This includes such things as laughing, crying, sighing, yawning, belching, swallowing, heavily marked inhaling or exhaling, coughing, clearing of the throat, hiccuping, moaning, groaning, whining, yelling, whispering, sneezing, snoring, stretching, and the like. (2) *Vocal qualifiers.* This includes intensity (overloud to oversoft), pitch height (overhigh to overlow), and extent (extreme drawl to extreme clipping). (3) *Vocal segregates.* These are such things as "uh-huh," "um," "ah," and variants thereof.

Related work on such topics as silent pauses (beyond junctures), intruding sounds, speech errors, and latency would probably be included in this category.

Proxemics

Proxemics is generally considered to be the study of our use and perception of social and personal space. Under this heading, we find a body of work called small group ecology, which is concerned with how people use and respond to spatial relationships in formal and informal group settings. Such studies deal with seating arrangements and spatial arrangements as related to leadership, communication flow, and the task at hand. The influence of architectural features on residential living units and even on communities is also of concern to those who study human proxemic behavior. On an even broader level, some attention has been given to spatial relationships in crowds and densely populated situations. Our personal space orientation is sometimes studied in the context of conversational distance, and how it varies according to sex, status, roles, cultural orientation, and so forth. The term *territoriality* is also frequently used in the study of proxemics to denote the human tendency to stake out personal territory—or untouchable space—much as wild animals and birds do.

Artifacts

Artifacts include the manipulation of objects with the interacting persons that may act as nonverbal stimuli. These artifacts include perfume, clothes, lipstick, eyeglasses, wigs and other hairpieces, false eyelashes, eyeliners, and the whole repertoire of falsies and "beauty" aids.

Environmental Factors

Thus far we have been concerned with the appearance and behavior of the persons involved in communicating. This category concerns those elements that impinge on the human relationship, but are not directly a part of it. Environmental factors include the furniture, architectural style, interior decorating, lighting conditions, smells, colors, temperature, additional noises or music, and the like, within which the interaction occurs. Variations in arrangements, materials, shapes, or surfaces of objects in the interacting environment can be extremely influential on the outcome of an interpersonal relationship. This category also includes what might be called traces of action. For instance, as you observe cigarette butts, orange peels, and wastepaper left by the person with whom you will soon interact, you are forming an impression that will eventually influence your meeting.

Perspectives on Nonverbal Communication in the Total Communication Process

There is a danger that the reader may forget that nonverbal communication cannot be studied in isolation from the total communication process. Verbal and nonverbal communication should be treated as a total and inseparable unit. Argyle states, "Some of the most important findings in the field of social interaction are about the ways that verbal interaction needs the support of nonverbal communications."[10] What are some of the ways in which verbal and nonverbal systems interrelate?

Before outlining some of the verbal/nonverbal interrelationships, we should recall that there may be nonverbal interrelationships as well—that is, nonverbal channels interacting others. An example of a nonverbal interrelationship is a loud "Well!" preceding a handshake, which makes you anticipate a firm handshake. Odors can shorten or lengthen distance, interaction distance can affect vocal loudness, and so on. Argyle has identified the primary uses of nonverbal behavior in human communication as: (1) expressing emotion, (2) conveying interpersonal attitudes (like/dislike, dominance/submission, and the like), (3) presenting one's personality to others, and (4) accompanying speech for the purposes of managing turn-taking, feedback, attention, and the like.[11] None of these functions of nonverbal behavior is limited to nonverbal behavior alone—that is, emotions and attitudes can be expressed and interaction can be managed verbally, as well. In some cases, however, we rely more heavily on verbal behavior for some purposes and on nonverbal behavior for others. Like words and phrases, nonverbal signals can have multiple meanings and multiple uses—for example, a smile can be part of an emotional expression, an attitudinal message, part of a self-presentation, or a listener response to manage the interaction. Nonverbal behavior can repeat, contradict, substitute for, complement, accent, or regulate verbal behavior.[12]

Repeating   Nonverbal communication can simply repeat what was said verbally. For instance, if you told someone that he or she had to go north to find a newspaper stand and then pointed in the proper direction, this would be considered repetition.

Contradicting   Nonverbal behavior can contradict verbal behavior.[13] A classic example is the parent who yells to his or her child in an angry voice, "Of course I love you!" Or the not-so-confident person about to make a public speech who, despite trembling hands and knees and beads of perspiration on the brow, says, "I'm not nervous." If there is no reason to suspect that conflicting cues might be present, we probably rely mainly on verbal messages. It has been said that when we receive contradictory messages on the verbal and nonverbal levels, we are more likely to trust and believe in the nonverbal message.[14] It is assumed that nonverbal signals are more spontaneous, harder to fake, and less apt to be manipulated. It is probably more accurate to say, however, that some nonverbal behaviors are more spontaneous and harder to fake than others, and that some people are more proficient than others at nonverbal deception.[15] With two contradictory cues, both of which are nonverbal, we predictably place our reliance on the cues we consider harder to fake. Sometimes we choose to be more direct with nonverbal cues because we know that they will be perceived as being less direct.

Young children seem to give less credence to certain nonverbal cues than do adults when they are confronted with conflicting verbal and nonverbal messages.[16] Conflicting messages in which the speaker smiled while making a critical statement were interpreted more negatively by children than by adults. This was particularly true when the speaker was a woman. Other work casts a further shadow on the "reliance on nonverbal cues in contradictory situations" theory.[17] Shapiro found student judges to be extremely consistent in their reliance on either linguistic or facial cues when they were asked to select the affect being communicated from a list of incongruent faces (sketched) and written messages. Vande Creek and Watkins extended Shapiro's work by using real voices and moving pictures. The stimulus persons were portraying inconsistencies in the degree of stress in verbal and nonverbal channels. Again they found that some respondents tended to rely primarily on verbal cues, some on nonverbal cues, and some responded to the degree of stress in general—regardless of the channels manifesting it. The cross-cultural research of Solomon and Ali suggests that familiarity with the verbal language may affect the reliance that one has on verbal or nonverbal cues. They found, for instance, that persons who were not as familiar with the language used to construct the contradictory message would rely on the content for judgments of affective meaning. Those who knew the language well were more apt to rely on the vocal intonation for the affective meaning. It thus appears that some people will rely more on the verbal message whereas others will rely on the nonverbal. We do not know all the conditions that would affect these preferences. Although one source of our preferences for verbal or nonverbal cues may be learned experiences, others believe that there may also be an even more basic genesis—such as right-left brain dominance.

Although there are times when inconsistent messages are produced to achieve a particular effect, such as sarcasm, there are some who believe that a constant barrage of inconsistent messages can contribute to a psychopathology for the receiver. This may be particularly true when people have a close relationship and the receiver has no other people to whom he or she can turn for discussion and possible clarification of the confusion. Some research finds that parents of disturbed children produce more messages with conflicting cues,[18] whereas other work suggests that the differences are not in conflicting cues, but in negative messages;

that is, parents with disturbed children sent more negative messages.[19] Either situation is undesirable and the combination of negativity, confusion, and punishment can be very harmful.

Substituting   Nonverbal behavior can substitute for verbal messages. When a dejected and downtrodden executive (or janitor) walks into his or her house after work, a facial expression substitutes for the statement, "I've had a rotten day." With a little practice, people soon learn to identify a wide range of these substitute nonverbal displays—all the way from "It's been a fantastic, great day!" to "Oh God, am I miserable!" We do not need to ask for verbal confirmation of our perception. Sometimes, when substitute nonverbal behavior fails, the communicator resorts back to the verbal level. Consider the woman who wants her date to stop "making out" with her. She may stiffen, stare straight ahead, or act unresponsive and cool. If the suitor persists, she is apt to say something like, "Look Larry, please don't ruin a nice friendship," and so on.

Complementing   Nonverbal behavior can modify, or elaborate on, verbal messages. An employee may nonverbally reflect an attitude of embarrassment when talking to his or her supervisor about a poor performance. Further, nonverbal behavior may reflect changes in the relationship between the employee and the supervisor. When the employee's slow, quiet verbalizations and relaxed posture change—when posture stiffens and the emotional level of the verbalized statement increases—this may signal changes in the overall relationship between the interactants. Complementary functions of nonverbal communication serve to signal one's attitudes and intentions toward another person.

Accenting   Nonverbal behavior may accent parts of the verbal message much as underlining written words or *italicizing* them serves to emphasize them. Movements of the head and hands are frequently used to accent the verbal message. When a father scolds his son about staying out too late at night, he may accent a particular phrase with a firm grip on the son's shoulder and an accompanying frown on his face. In some instances, one set of nonverbal cues can accent other nonverbal cues. Ekman found that emotions are primarily exhibited by facial expressions, but that the body carries the most accurate indicators regarding the level of arousal.[20]

Regulating   Nonverbal behaviors are also used to regulate the communicative flow between the interactants. The way one person stops talking and another starts in a smooth, synchronized manner may be as important to a satisfactory interaction as the verbal content that is exchanged. After all, we do make judgments about people based on their regulatory skills—for example, "talking to him is like talking to a wall" or "you can't get a word in edgewise with her." When another person frequently interrupts or is inattentive we may feel that this is a statement about the relationship—perhaps one of disrespect. There are rules for regulating conversations, but they are generally implicit. It isn't written down, but we seem to "know" that two people shouldn't talk at the same time, that each person should get an equal number of turns at talking if he or she desires it, that a question should be answered, and so forth. Wiemann's research found that relatively minute changes in these regulatory behaviors (interruptions, pauses longer than three seconds, unilateral topic changes, and the like) resulted in sizable variations in how competent a communicator was perceived.[21] As listeners, we are apparently attending to, and evaluating a host of, fleeting, subtle, and habitual features of another's conversational behavior. There are probably differences in the actual behaviors used to manage conversational flow across cultures or with certain subcultural groups. We know that as children are first learning these rules they use less subtle cues—for example, tugging on clothing, raising a hand, and the like. Some of the behaviors used to facilitate this conversational regulation follow.[22]

When we want to indicate that we are finished speaking and the other person can start, we may increase our eye contact with the other person. This is often accompanied by the vocal cues associated with ending declarative or interrogative statements. If the other person still doesn't pick up the conversational "ball," we might extend silence or interject a "trailer," for example, "you know ..." or "so, ah...." Keeping another from getting in the conversation requires us to keep long pauses from occurring, decrease eye contact, and perhaps raise our volume if the other person tries to "get in." When we do not want to take a speaking turn we might give the other person some reinforcing head nods and maintain attentive eye contact, and, of course, keep from speaking when the other begins to yield. When we do want the floor we might raise our index finger or enact an audible inspiration of breath with a straightening of the posture as if we were "ready" to take over. Rapid nodding may also signal the other person to hurry up and finish, but if we have trouble getting in we may have to talk simultaneously for a few words or engage in "stutter starts" that, hopefully, will be more easily observed cues to exemplify our desire to speak.

Conversational beginnings and endings also act as regulatory points. When greeting others, our eye contact signals that the channels of conversation are open. A slight head movement and an "eyebrow flash" (a barely detectable but distinct up-and-down movement of the eyebrows) may be present. The hands are also used in greetings for salutes, waves, handshakes, hand slaps, emblematic signals like the peace or victory sign, a raised fist, or thumbs up. Hands may also perform grooming activities (putting fingers through one's hair) or be involved in various touching activities like kissing, embracing, or hitting another on the arm. The mouth may form a smile or an oval shape as if one were ready to start talking.[23]

Saying good-bye in semiformal interviews brought forth many nonverbal behaviors, but the most common included the frequent breaking of eye contact and for increasingly longer periods of time, positioning one's body toward an exit, leaning forward, and rapidly nodding. Less frequent, but also very noticeable were accenting behaviors; for example, "This is the termination of our conversation and I don't want you to miss it!" These accenters included what we called *explosive* hand and foot movements—raising the hands and/or feet and bringing them down with enough force to make an audible slap while simultaneously using the hands and feet as leverage to catapult out of the seat. A less direct manifestation of this is to place your hands on your thighs or knees in a "leveraging" position (as if you were soon to catapult) and hope that the other person picks up the good-bye cue.[24]

It should be clear from the preceding that verbal and nonverbal behavior work together in many ways. In order to fully understand a communicative transaction we must analyze both types of behavior as an inseparable unit.

Perspectives on Nonverbal Communication in American Society

The importance of nonverbal communication would be undeniable if sheer quantity were the only measure. Birdwhistell, who is generally considered as a noted authority on nonverbal behavior, makes some rather astounding estimates of the amount of nonverbal communication that takes place. He estimates that the average person actually speaks words for a total of only 10 to 11 minutes daily—the standard spoken sentence taking only about 2.5 seconds. He goes on to say that in a normal two-person conversation, the verbal components carry less than 35 percent of the social meaning of the situation; more than 65 percent of the social meaning is carried on the nonverbal band.

Another way of looking at the quantity of nonverbal messages is to note the various systems that humans use to communicate. Hall outlines ten separate kinds of human activity that he calls "primary message systems."[25] He suggests that only one involves language. Ruesch and Kees discuss at least seven different systems—personal appearance and dress, gestures or deliberate movements, random action, traces of action, vocal sounds, spoken words, and written words. Only two of the seven systems involve the overt use of words.[26]

It is not my purpose here to argue the importance of the various human message systems, but to put the nonverbal world in perspective. It is safe to say that the study of human communication has for too long ignored a significant part of the process.

Further testimony to the prevalence and importance of nonverbal communication is available if we scrutinize specific facets of our society. For example, consider the role of nonverbal signals in therapeutic situations; an understanding of "disturbed" nonverbal behavior would certainly help in diagnosis and treatment. Nonverbal cues are also important in certain situations in which verbal communication is constrained—for example, doctor-nurse interaction during an operation. The significance of nonverbal cues in the arts is obvious—dancing, theatrical performances, music, pictures, and so on. It is the nonverbal symbolism of various ceremonies and rituals that creates important and necessary responses in the participants—for example, the trappings of the marriage ceremony, the Christmas decorations, religious rituals, funerals, and the like. We can also see how an understanding of nonverbal cues would better prepare us for communicating across cultures, classes, or age groups—and with different ethnic groups within our culture. Teaching and understanding the blind and deaf is largely a matter of developing a sophistication with nonverbal signals. Everyday matters like forming impressions of people you meet, getting through a job interview, understanding advertising or the audience/speaker relationship in a public speech are all heavily laden with nonverbal behavior. Nonverbal cues are also being analyzed in the hope of predicting future behavior of people.[27] One expert claims to have analyzed hand gestures of prospective jurors in eleven major trials in 1975, hoping to predict how they would vote on the defendant....

Classroom Behavior   The classroom is a veritable gold mine of nonverbal behavior, which has been nearly untapped by scientific probes. Acceptance and understanding of ideas and feelings on the part of both teacher and student, encouraging and criticizing, silence, questioning, and the like—all involve nonverbal elements. Consider the following instances as representative of the variety of classroom nonverbal cues: (1) the frantic hand waver who is sure that he or she had the correct answer; (2) the student who is sure that he or she does not know the answer and tries to avoid any eye contact with the teacher; (3) the effects of student dress and hair length on teacher-student interaction; (4) facial expressions—threatening gestures, and tone of voice are frequently used for discipline in elementary schools; (5) the teacher who requests student questioning and criticism, but whose nonverbal actions make it clear that he or she will not be receptive; (6) a student's absence from class communicates; (7) a teacher's trust of students is sometimes indicated by the arrangement of seating and monitoring behavior during examinations; (8) the variety of techniques used by students to make sleeping appear to be studying or listening; (9) the professor who announces that he or she has plenty of time for student conferences, but whose fidgeting and glancing at a watch suggest otherwise; (10) teachers who try to assess visual feedback to determine student comprehension;[28] (11) even classroom design (wall colors, space between seats, windows) has an influence on student participation in the classroom.

> To summarize our speculations, we may say that by what she said, by how and when she said it, by her facial expressions, postures, and perhaps by her touch, the teacher may have communicated to the children of the experimental group that she expected improved intellectual performance. Such communications together with possible changes in teaching techniques may have helped the child learn by changing his self-concept, his expectations of his own behavior, and his motivation, as well as his cognitive style and skills.[29]

Courtship Behavior   We know there is "something" that is highly influential in our nonverbal courtship behavior. Like other areas of nonverbal study, however, we are still at a very early stage in quantifying these patterns of behavior. On a purely intuitive level, we know that there are some men and some women who can exude such messages as "I'm available," "I'm knowledgeable," or "I want you" without saying a word. For the male, it may be such things as his clothes, sideburns, length of hair, an arrogant grace, a thrust of his hips, touch gestures, extra long eye contact, carefully looking at the woman's figure, open gestures and movements to offset closed ones exhibited by the woman, gaining close proximity, a subtleness that will allow both parties to deny that either had committed themselves to a courtship ritual, making the woman feel secure and wanted, "like a woman," or showing excitement and desire in fleeting facial expressions. For the woman, it may be such things as sitting with her legs symbolically open, crossing her legs to expose a thigh, engaging in flirtatious glances, stroking her thighs, protruding her breasts, using an appealing perfume, showing the "pouting mouth" in her facial expressions, opening her palm to the male, using a tone of voice that has an "invitation behind the words," or any of a multitude of other cues and rituals—some of which vary with status, subculture, region of the country, and the like. A study by some students in Milwaukee of a number of singles' bars suggested that smoking a cigar was taboo for any male who wished to pick up a female in these places. Other particularly important behaviors for males operating in this context seemed to be looking the female in the eyes often; dressing slightly on the "mod" side, but generally avoiding extremes in dress; and staying with one woman for the entire evening.

Another group of Milwaukee undergraduate students focused on the non-verbal courtship behavior of homosexuals and found many similarities to hetero-sexual courtship rituals. Homosexuals were found to lavishly decorate their living quarters to impress their partners, to use clothing for attraction and identification, and to use eye behavior to communicate their intentions. Scheflen has outlined four categories of heterosexual nonverbal courtship behavior—courtship readi-ness, preening behavior, positional cues, and actions of appeal or invitation.[30] The Milwaukee students found these to be useful categories in analyzing homosexual nonverbal courtship behavior, as well. Contrary to a popular stereotype, most homosexuals do not have effeminate and lisping characteristics. This raises the question of what nonverbal cues are used for identification purposes between two homosexuals. Certainly the environmental context may be influential (gay bars), but other cues are also used. For instance, brief bodily contact (leg to leg) and other body movements, such as certain tilts of the head or hands, have been reported. In public places, however, the most common and effective signals used by homosex-uals are extended eye glances. Uninterested males will most likely avoid these long, lingering glances whereas those males who maintain such eye contact suggest that they are open for further interaction.

Nielsen, citing Birdwhistell, described the "courtship dance" of the North American adolescent.[31] He claims to have identified twenty-four steps between the "initial contact between the young male and female and the coitional act." He explains that these steps have an order to them. By this he means that when a male begins holding a female's hand, he must wait until she presses his hand (signaling a go-ahead) before he can take the next step of allowing his fingers to intertwine with hers. Females and males are labeled "fast" or "slow" according to whether they follow the order of the steps. If a step is skipped or reversed in the order, the person who does so is labeled "fast." If a person ignores the signal to move on to the next step, or takes actions to prevent the next step, he or she is considered "slow." This ordering would suggest that only after the initial kiss may the male attempt to approach the female's breasts. She will probably block his approach with her upper arm against her side since protocol forbids approaching the breast from the front. The male really does not expect to reach the breast until after a considerable amount of additional kissing.

We have thus far concentrated on nonverbal courtship behavior of unmar-ried men and women. Certainly additional volumes can be written on marital non-verbal courtship behavior patterns, as the whole repertoire of messages for inviting or avoiding sexual intercourse is largely nonverbal. For example, some observers have noted that "staying up to watch the late show" is a common method of saying "not tonight."

Summary

The term *nonverbal* is commonly used to describe all human communication events that transcend spoken or written words. At the same time we should realize that these nonverbal events and behaviors can be interpreted through verbal symbols. When we consider a classification schema of vocal/nonvocal, verbal/nonverbal, acoustic/nonacoustic, respiratory/nonrespiratory we learn to expect something less than discrete category placement. Instead we might more appropriately put these behaviors on continua with some behaviors overlapping two continua.

The theoretical writings and research on nonverbal communication can be broken down into the following seven areas: (a) body motion or kinesics (emblems, illustrators, affect displays, regulators, and adaptors), (2) physical characteristics, (3) touching behavior, (4) paralanguage (vocal qualities and vocalizations), (5) proxemics, (6) artifacts, (7) environment. Nonverbal communication should not be studied as an isolated unit, but as an inseparable part of the total communication process. Nonverbal communication may serve to repeat, contradict, substitute, complement, accent, or regulate verbal communication. Nonverbal communication is important because of the role it plays in the total communication system, the tremendous quantity of informational cues it gives in any particular situation, and because of its use in fundamental areas of our daily life.

References

1. O. Pfungst, *Clever Hans, The Horse of Mr. Von Osten* (New York: Holt. Rinehart and Winston, 1911).
2. A. Mehrabian, *Nonverbal Communication* (Chicago: Aldine-Atherton, 1972), p. 2.
3. In various verbal and nonverbal studies over the last three decades, dimensions similar to Mehrabian's have been consistently reported by investigators from diverse fields studying diverse phenomena. It is reasonable to conclude, therefore, that these three dimensions seem to be basic responses to our environment and are reflected in the way we assign meaning to both verbal and nonverbal behavior. Cf. A. Mehrabian, "A Semantic Space for Nonverbal Behavior," *Journal of Consulting and Clinical Psychology* 35 (1970): 248–257; and A. Mehrabian, *Silent Messages* (Belmont, Calif.: Wadsworth, 1971).
4. P. Ekman and W. V. Friesen, "The Repertoire of Nonverbal Behavior: Categories, Origins, Usage and Coding," *Semiotica* 1 (1969): 49–98. Also see the following for updated reports with specific research foci: P. Ekman and W. V. Friesen, "Hand Movements," *Journal of Communication* 22 (1972): 353–374 and P. Ekman and W. V. Friesen, "Nonverbal Behavior and Psychopathology," in *The Psychology of Depression: Contemporary Theory and Research*, ed. R. J. Friedman and M. M. Katz (Washington, D. C.: Winston, 1974).
5. One treatment of emblems per se can be found in P. Ekman, "Movements with Precise Meanings," *Journal of Communication* 26 (1976): 14–26. Figures 1.1, 1.2, and the research reported in this section are drawn primarily from this work. Additional information on American emblems can be found in Chapter 6.
6. A. A. Cohen and R. Harrison, "Intentionality in the Use of Hand Illustrators in Face-to-Face Communication Situations," *Journal of Personality and Social Psychology* 28 (1973): 276–279. See also A. A. Cohen, "The Communicative Functions of Hand Illustrators," *Journal of Communication* 27 (1977): 54–63.
7. For a summary of these efforts, see J. M. Wiemann and M. L. Knapp, "Turn-Taking in Conversations," *Journal of Communication* 25 (1975): 75–92.
8. M. L. Knapp, R. P. Hart, G. W. Friedrich, and G. M. Shulman, "The Rhetoric of Goodbye: Verbal and Nonverbal Correlates of Human Leave-Taking," *Speech Monographs* 40 (1973): 182–198.
9. G. L. Trager, "Paralanguage: A First Approximation," *Studies in Linguistics* 13 (1958):1–12.
10. M. Argyle, *Social Interaction* (New York: Atherton Press, 1969), pp. 70–71.
11. M. Argyle, *Bodily Communication* (New York: International Universities Press, 1975).

12. See P. Ekman, "Communication Through Nonverbal Behavior: A Source of Information About an Interpersonal Relationship," in *Affect, Cognition and Personality,* ed. S.S. Tomkins and C. E. Izard (New York: Springer, 1965).

13. A sometimes subtle inconsistency can also be perceived within verbal communications. When you are trying to express an idea with which you basically disagree, the linguistic choices may reflect differences in directness—for example, "John has done good work" is less direct than "John does good work." See M. Wiener and A. Mehrabian, *Language Within Language* (New York: Appleton-Century-Crofts, 1968).

14. Some evidence to support this notion is found in the following two sources: E. Tabor, "Decoding of Consistent and Inconsistent Attitudes in Communication" (Ph.D. diss., Illinois Institute of Technology, 1970); and A. Mehrabian, "Inconsistent Messages and Sarcasm," in A. Mehrabian, *Nonverbal Communication* (Chicago: Aldine-Atherton, 1972), pp. 104–132. For an understanding of the cognitive processes used in interpreting inconsistent messages, see: D. E. Bugental, "Interpretations of Naturally Occurring Discrepancies Between Words and Intonation: Modes of Inconsistency Resolution," *Journal of Personality and Social Psychology* 30 (1974): 125–133.

15. See pages 81–87 for a discussion of our level of awareness of various nonverbal behaviors.

16. D. E. Bugental, J. W. Kaswan, L. R. Love, and M. N. Fox, "Child Versus Adult Perception of Evaluative Messages in Verbal, Vocal and Visual Channels," *Developmental Psychology* 2 (1970): 367–375. Also see D. E. Bugental, L. R. Love, and R. M. Gianette, "Perfidious Feminine Faces," *Journal of Personality and Social Psychology* 17 (1971): 314–318.

17. J. G. Shapiro, "Responsivity to Facial and Linguistic Cues," *Journal of Communication* 18 (1968): 11–17; L. Vande Creek and J. T. Watkins, "Responses to Incongruent Verbal and Nonverbal Emotional Cues," *Journal of Communication* 22 (1972): 311–316; and D. Solomon and F. A. Ali, "Influence of Verbal Content and Intonation on Meaning Attributions of First-And-Second-Language Speakers," *Journal of Social Psychology* 95 (1975): 3–8.

18. D. E. Bugental, L. R. Love, J. W. Kaswan, and C. April, "Verbal-Nonverbal Conflict in Parental Messages to Normal and Disturbed Children," *Journal of Abnormal Psychology* 77 (1971): 6–10.

19. N. G. Beakel and A. Mehrabian, "Inconsistent Communications and Psychopathology," *Journal of Abnormal Psychology* 74 (1969): 126–130.

20. P. Ekman, "Body Position, Facial Expression and Verbal Behavior During Interviews," *Journal of Abnormal and Social Psychology* 68 (1964): 194–301. Also P. Ekman and W. V. Friesen, "Head and Body Cues in the Judgment of Emotion: A Reformulation," *Perceptual and Motor Skills* 24 (1967): 711–724.

21. J. M. Wiemann, "An Exploration of Communicative Competence in Initial Interactions: An Experimental Study" (Ph.D. diss., Purdue University, 1975).

22. Vocal cues involved in the turn-taking mechanism are treated in Chapter 10 and kinesic signals are listed in Chapter 6. For further reading in this area, see S. Duncan, "Some Signals and Rules for Taking Turns in Conversations," *Journal of Personality and Social Psychology* 23 (1972): 283–292; S. Duncan, "Toward a Grammar for Dyadic Conversation," *Semiotica* 9 (1973): 29–46; and J. M. Wiemann, "An Exploratory Study of Turn-Taking in Conversations: Verbal and Nonverbal Behavior," (M.S. thesis, Purdue University, 1973).

23. P. D. Krivonos and M. L. Knapp, "Initiating Communication: What Do You Say When You Say Hello?" *Central States Speech Journal* 26 (1975): 115–125.

24. Knapp, Hart, Friedrich, and Shulman, "The Rhetoric of Goodbye: Verbal and Nonverbal Correlates of Human Leave-Taking."

25. E. T. Hall, *The Silent Language* (Garden City, N.Y.: Doubleday, 1959).

26. J. Ruesch and W. Kees, *Nonverbal Communication: Notes on the Visual Perception of Human Relations* (Berkeley and Los Angeles, Calif.: University of California Press, 1956).

27. M. J. Saks, "Social Scientists Can't Rig Juries," *Psychology Today* 9 (1976): 48–50, 55–57. Also see R. T. Stein, "Identifying Emergent Leaders from Verbal and Nonverbal Communications," *Journal of Personality and Social Psychology* 32 (1975): 125–135; and P. Ekman, R. M. Liebert, W. V. Friesen, R. Harrison, C. Zlatchin, E. J. Malmstrom, and R. A. Baron, "Facial Expressions of Emotion While Watching Televised Violence as Predictors of Subsequent Aggression" (report to the Surgeon General's Scientific Advisory Committee on Television and Social Behavior, June, 1971).

28. At least one study suggests that even experienced teachers are not very successful at this. Cf. J. Jecker, N. Maccoby, M. Breitrose, and E. Rose, "Teacher Accuracy in Assessing Cognitive Visual Feedback from Students," *Journal of Applied Psychology* 48 (1964): 393–397.

29. R. Rosenthal and L. Jacobson, *Pygmalion in the Classroom* (New York: Holt, Rinehart and Winston, 1968).

30. A. E. Scheflen, "Quasi-Courtship Behavior in Psychotherapy," *Psychiatry* 28 (1965): 245–257.

31. G. Nielsen, *Studies in Self-Confrontation* (Copenhagen: Munksgaard; Cleveland: Howard Allen, 1962), pp. 70–71.

Review Questions

1. According to Knapp, what problems can be created by defining the topic of this chapter as *not* something (nonverbal) rather than something affirmative or positive?
2. To what extent does the verbal/nonverbal–vocal/nonvocal chart Gary D'Angelo and I offer in Chapter 3 respond to Knapp's concerns about the definition of "nonverbal" communication?
3. What are emblems? Give an example of an emblem you use.
4. Name two communication contexts or settings where regulators are especially important.
5. Give one example of each of the subcategories of paralanguage that Knapp mentions.
6. What's the difference between the functions of complementing and accenting? Give a clear example of each.
7. What is a "courtship dance"?

Probes

1. Give an example from your own experience of the cultural differences among one of the categories of cues Knapp discusses. For example, how do emblems, illustrators, or regulators differ from one culture to another?
2. Pay attention during your next conversation to your own use of regulators. How do you indicate that it's your conversational partner's turn to talk? When you're in a group, how do you nonverbally "ask" to speak?
3. What do you notice about your own use of adaptors? When do you tend to use them most? Least?
4. What messages about "territory" do you get from the furniture placement in your employer's office? If you were in the position your boss is in, would you change the furniture placement? Why?
5. Give an example from your own communication experience of verbal and nonverbal cues contradicting each other. Which did you believe?
6. In addition to waving, how do you "say" goodbye nonverbally?

s I mentioned in Chapter 1, we frequently think of communicating as something we do "to" someone else. In this essay Rollo May reminds us of the communicative importance of *not* doing, of pausing. May is a well-known counselor who has written several influential and insightful books about communication and human growth. I've found a great deal of wisdom in his books, and if you hear some of that here, I'd encourage you to read *Freedom and Destiny*—the book this comes from—or *Love and Will* or *Power and Innocence,* two of his other works.

This essay is in this chapter to underscore the importance of silence as a kind of nonverbal communication. Knapp mentioned silence in his first essay in this chapter, but we don't usually recognize how significant it can be. If you doubt its importance, remember how it can actually reverse your meaning, as in the old joke punchline, "Don't . . . stop!" versus "Don't stop!"

May points toward some parts of Eastern cultures as helpful reminders to those of us in the West about the significance of the pause. His quotations from Lao Tzu illustrate how negation can become affirmation, "the void can be where most happens." He also illustrates how aspects of the native North American culture affirmed this same insight—that silence can be rich and full.

May's discussion connects with a theme that's important to me when he notes that, "there seems to be no pause in technology. Or when there is it is called a 'depression' and is denied and feared," and that, "The significance of the pause is that the rigid chain of cause and effect is broken." My way of making this point is to say that we often "technologize" much of what's human out of our human communicating, and we do that in part by failing to realize that linear causality simply doesn't apply to *human* systems and processes.

May also makes the point that even infinitesimally small pauses can be packed with significance. Again, if you doubt this, reflect on your own experience. How important is a pause of even a few milliseconds when you ask someone, "Do you really mean that?" "How good *are* my chances?" or "Are you sure that's everything?"

May argues that the pause, even for only a moment, is the "locus of the speaker's freedom." By that he means that pauses help shape the unique dimensions of each individual speaker's comments. When it is the pause before a response to a thoughtful question, it can also be the locus of the speaker's creativity.

You may or may not agree with everything May says here, but I hope that his words will provoke you to think about silence as part of your nonverbal communication. May is clearly not a social scientist; he's not quantifying silence or subjecting it to a rigorously causal analysis. But there's wisdom of a different kind here, if you'll pause and listen for it.

The Significance of the Pause

Rollo May

I don't think I handle the notes much differently from other pianists. But the pauses between the notes—ah, there is where the artistry lies!
—ARTUR SCHNABEL'S answer to reporters who inquired about the secret of his genius.

The goal of fasting is inner unity. This means hearing but not with the ear; hearing, but not with the understanding; it is hearing with the spirit, with your whole being. The hearing that is only in the ears is one thing. The hearing of the understanding is another. But the hearing of the spirit is not limited to any one faculty, to the ear, or to the mind. Hence, it demands the emptiness of all the faculties. And when the faculties are empty, then the whole being listens. There is then a direct grasp of what is right before you that can never be heard with the ear or understood with the mind. Fasting of the heart empties the faculties, frees you from limitations and from preoccupations.
—THOMAS MERTON, *The Living Bread*

. . . We {have} defined freedom as the capacity to pause in the midst of stimuli from all directions, and in this pause to throw our weight toward this response rather than that one. The crucial term, and in some ways the most interesting, is that little word *pause*. It may seem strange that this word is the important one rather than terms like *liberty, independence, spontaneity*. And it seems especially strange that a word merely signifying a lack of something, an absence, a hiatus, a vacancy, should carry so much weight. In America especially, the word pause refers to a gap, a space yet unfilled, a nothing—or, better yet, a "no thing."

The pause is especially important for the freedom of being, what I have called essential freedom. For it is in the pause that we experience the context out of which freedom comes. In the pause we wonder, reflect, sense awe, and conceive of eternity. The pause is when we open ourselves for the moment to the concepts of both freedom and destiny.

The word *pause*, like the word *freedom*, seems essentially to signify what something is *not* rather than what it is. We have seen that freedom is defined almost universally by what it is not—or, in a sentence definition, "Freedom is when you are anchored to nobody or nothing." Similarly, the pause is a time when no thing is happening. Can the word *pause* give us an answer not only as to why *freedom* is a negative word, but is also loved as the most affirmative term in our language? It was, notes the anthropologist Dorothy Lee, "this conception of *nothingness* as *something-ness* that enabled the philosophers of India to perceive the integrity of non-being, to name the free space and give us the zero."

One version of a famous question is "How many Zen Buddhists does it take to screw in a light bulb?" The answer is two: one to screw it in and one *not* to screw it in. And the latter is as important as the former, for emptiness is something in Eastern thought.

It should not surprise us that this contribution to our thinking and experience comes mainly from the East, especially from India, China, and Japan. In our crisis of thought and religion in the West, the wisdom of the East emerges as a corrective. This wisdom recalls us to truths in our own mystic tradition that we had forgotten, such as contemplation, meditation, and especially the significance of the pause.

Freedom is experienced in our world in an infinite number of pauses, which turn out not to be negative but to be the most affirmative condition possible. *The ultimate paradox is that negation becomes affirmation.* Thus, *freedom* remains the most loved word, the word that thrills us most readily, the condition most desired because it calls forth continuous, unrealized possibilities. And it is so with the "pause." The "no thing" turns out to bespeak a reality that is most clearly something. It is paradoxical that in our lives empty can be full, negative can be affirmative, the void can be where most happens. In the *Tao Teh Ching*, for example, Lao Tzu says,

> We put thirty spokes to make a wheel:
> But it is on the hole in the center that the use of the cart hinges.
>
> We make a vessel from a lump of clay;
> But it is the empty space within the vessel that makes it useful.
>
> We make doors and windows for a room;
> But it is the empty spaces that make the room livable.
>
> Thus, while existence has advantages,
> It is the emptiness that makes it useful.

The Language of Silence

This conception of the pause gives us a whole new world. It is in the pause that people learn to *listen to silence*. We can hear an infinite number of sounds that we normally never hear at all—the unending hum and buzz of insects in a quiet summer field, a breeze blowing lightly through the golden hay, a thrush singing in the low bushes beyond the meadow. And we suddenly realize that this is *something*—the world of "silence" is populated by a myriad of creatures and a myriad of sounds.

Luther Standing Bear, describing his childhood as an Oglala Dakotan in the 1870s, wrote that children "were taught to sit still and enjoy {the silence}. They were taught to use their organs of smell, to look when apparently there was nothing to see, and to listen intently when all seemingly was quiet." And Modupe, writing of his so-so childhood in French Guinea, says, "We learned that silences as well as sounds are significant in the forest, and {we learned} how to listen to the silences.... Deeply felt silences might be said to be the core of our Kofon religion. During these times, *the nature within ourselves found unity with the nature of the earth.*"

In Japan, free time and space—what we call pauses—are perceived as *ma*, the valid interval or meaningful pause. Such perception is basic to all experience and specifically to what constitutes creativity and freedom. This perception persists in spite of the adoption of Western culture and science. Even in 1958, Misako Miyamoto wrote of the Nō plays, "The audience watches the play and catches the feeling through not only the action and words but also the *intervals of the period of pauses....* There is a free creation in each person's mind ... ; and the audience relates to this situation with free thinking." Of silent intervals in speech, she says, "Especially {in} the pauses in a tone of voice, I can feel the person's unique personality and his joy, sorrow or other complicated feelings." On listening to a robin in early spring, "It sang with pauses, ... I could have time to think about the bird {in} the silent moment between one voice and others, ... The pauses produced the effect of the relation between the bird and me."

Lest these examples seduce us into assuming that this valuing of the pause is chiefly in Oriental and esoteric cultures, let me point out that the phenomenon is just as clear, though not as frequent, in our own modern culture. John Cage, a composer noted for his originality, gave a concert in New York which consisted of his coming out on the stage, sitting down at the keyboard for a period of time, and not playing a note. His aim, as he explained to a less-than-pleased audience, was to give them an opportunity to listen to the silence. His recorded music shows precisely this—many pauses are interspersed with heterogeneous notes. Cage sharpens our awareness, makes our senses keener, and renders us alive to ourselves and our surroundings. Listening is our most neglected sense.

The very essence of jazz is in the space between notes, called the afterbeat. The leader of a band in which I once played used to sing out "um-BAH," the "Bah"—or the note—coming always between the beats. This syncopation is a basis of jazz. Duke Ellington, for example, keeps the audience tantalized, on edge, expectant—we *have* to dance to work out the emotion building up within us. On an immediate level this expectancy has a similarity to the exquisite levels of feeling before orgasm. Hence, some musicians can simulate the process of sexual intercourse in the tantalizing beat of their songs. In the ever-changing jazz group at Preservation Hall in New Orleans, this infinite variety, with each person improvising, produces each time a piece of music never before played and never to be played again. This is freedom *par excellence.*

There seems to be no pause in technology. Or when there is, it is called a "depression" and is denied and feared. But pure science is a different matter. We find Einstein remarking that "the intervals between the events are more significant than the events themselves."

The significance of the pause is that the rigid chain of cause and effect is broken. The pause momentarily suspends the billiard-ball system of Pavlov. In the person's life response no longer blindly follows stimulus. There intervenes between the two our human imaginings, reflections, considerations, ponderings. Pause is the prerequisite for wonder. When we don't pause, when we are perpetually hurrying from one appointment to another, from one "planned activity" to another, we sacrifice the richness of wonder. And we lose communication with our destiny.

Time and the Pause

The length of time of the pause is, in principle, irrelevant. When we look at what actually happens in people's experience, we note that some pauses can be infinitesimally small. When I am giving a lecture, for example, I select one word rather than another in a pause that lasts for only a millisecond. In this pause a number of possible terms flash before my mind's eye. If I want to say the noise was "loud," I may consider in this fraction of second such words as "deafening," "startling," or "overwhelming." Out of these I select one. All this happens so rapidly—strictly speaking, on the preconscious level—that I am aware of it only when I stop to think about it afterward.

Note in this last sentence I say "stop to think." This habitual phrase is another proof of the importance of the pause. Hannah Arendt remarks in *Thinking* (volume 2 of *The Life of the Mind*) on the necessity of "stopping" to think—i.e., pausing as essential to the process of reflection.

But something else, even more interesting, occurs in those small, multitudinous pauses as one speaks. This is the time when I "listen" to the audience, when the audience influences me, when I "hear" its reaction and ask silently, What connotations are they taking from my words? For any experienced lecturer the blank spaces that constitute the pauses between the words and sentences is the time of openness to the audience. At such times I find myself noting: There someone seems puzzled; here someone listens by tipping his head to one side so as not to miss any word; there in the back row—what every speaker dreads to see—is someone nodding in sleep. Every experienced speaker that I know is greatly helped by the cultivation of his awareness of facial expressions and other subtle aspects of unspoken communication from the audience.

Walt Whitman once remarked that "the audience writes the poetry," and in an even clearer sense the audience gives the lecture. Hence, a lecture delivered from the same notes, say once to a social club and then again to graduate students at a large university, will often seem to be two entirely different speeches.

The pause for milliseconds while one speaks is *the locus of the speaker's freedom*. The speaker may mold his speech this way or that, he may tell a joke to relax the audience, or—in a thrilling moment of which there cannot be too many in a lecturer's career—he may even be aware of a brand new idea coming to him from heaven knows where in the audience.

Cassandra, we are told in Aeschylus' drama, foretold the doom of Mycenae. A prophetess, she was sensitive to communications on many different levels of which the average person is unaware. This sensitivity caused her much pain, and she would gladly have given up her role if she could have. She was "doomed," or destined to listen on these different levels; she could not escape hearing the messages coming in her pauses. Quite apart from the roles of prophetess or mystic—which we see also in Tiresias and Jeremiah and Isaiah—it would seem that multitudes of us have such capacities, but we train ourselves (a process abetted by much contemporary education) to suppress this sensitivity to the pauses. And we may do this in the hope of avoiding the pain. The difference between the charlatan and the genuine prophet may well be the sense of pain the latter experiences in his or her prophecies.

The pauses may be longer, for instance, when one is answering questions after a lecture. In response to a question, I may silently hem and haw for a moment while different possible answers flash through my mind. At that time I do not usually think of Kierkegaard's proclamation "Freedom is possibility," but that is what I am living out in those moments of pause. The thrilling thing is that at such a time a new answer that I have never thought of may suddenly emerge. It is often said that intellectually creative people—like John Dewey, for example—are a strain to listen to and are not good public speakers, because the time they pause to consider different possibilities requires a capacity to wait that most people find tedious.

One's freedom may involve still larger pauses. "Let me sleep on it" is a not infrequent remark when one is making an important decision like buying a house. These are the situations in which a longer interval between stimuli is desired; there may be many different houses available, or one can decide not to buy any at all. The decision then requires complex consideration, pondering, setting up possibilities for choice, and playing "as if" games with oneself to assess various factors like view and design and so on. My point is simply that freedom consists of these possibilities. The pauses are the exercise of one's freedom to choose among them.

We recall that Jesus and Buddha, each following his own inner guidance, went off into his separate wilderness to engage in his quest. Both "paused" for forty days, if the records are to be believed. These were assumedly times for each of intense concentration, times of considering possibilities, of listening to whatever voices were available on deeper levels within themselves, voices from nature, voices from what we now term archetypal experiences, voices from what Jesus called God and Buddha called Atman and I would call Being. These assumedly were periods in which they experienced their visions and integrated themselves around their messages.

But students tell me that they have professors who *pause permanently*. These teachers make a career out of pausing. The pause is then not a preparation for action but an excuse for never acting at all. It has been remarked that the academic profession is the only one in which you can make your living by questioning things. How much it is still true in academia that persons substitute talking for decision or rationalize lack of commitment by calling it "judicious pausing" I do not know. Nevertheless this is a tendency that confronts us all: to use pausing as a substitute for committed action. In our action-oriented life in America this misuse of pausing is a not infrequently found neurotic reaction. But this dilemma is not overcome by acting blindly, without consciousness and without reason. To be free obviously requires the courage to act when it is necessary to act if one's freedom is to be actualized at all.

A person may ponder for months and years or all life long, never finding satisfactory answers. This occurs particularly with the question of death. Hamlet spoke for many of us when he stated his concern with what might happen beyond death,

> When we have shuffled off this mortal coil,
> {It} must give us pause.

But our personal freedom can be actualized regardless of whether we find satisfactory answers or not, or even if there are no answers at all. We can exercise our freedom even against destiny. Indeed, in the long run to "know that he dies," as Pascal said, is the most essential and triumphant experience of freedom possible for a human being.

Review Questions

1. How is May's "definition" of the pause similar to Knapp's definition of his topic?
2. What does May mean when he says that "The significance of the pause is that the rigid chain of cause and effect is broken"?

3. According to May, what is the relationship between the pause and "freedom"?
4. List three different messages that might be inferred from a short pause in the middle of a conversation.

Probes

1. The introductory quotation by Thomas Merton includes the idea that "the hearing of the spirit ... demands the emptiness of all the faculties." What does Merton mean? How does this point relate to silence as nonverbal communication? How does his idea relate to what Robert Bolton says about hearing and listening in Chapter 7?
2. Do you agree with May that both the pause and freedom are "positive negatives," that is, phenomena defined by absence instead of the presence of something?
3. Briefly describe an event in your own experience that makes the same point Lao Tzu makes with his examples of the cart wheel, the vase, and the room.
4. What is the most vivid example you can recall of a pause or silence being significant? What's the most meaningful pause or silence you can remember?
5. Can May's point about the significance of the pause in jazz be made about any other kind of music? Explain.
6. How much of your personal schedule of this week's activities seems to reinforce May's point that in a technological society pauses are rare and often viewed as negative? In other words, how technologically frenetic is your schedule this week?
7. Give an example from your own experience of a significant pause of just a few milliseconds.

 s Mark Knapp's first essay in this chapter indicates, there are many forms or types of nonverbal communication, including appearance and dress, tone of voice, facial expression, gestures, posture and movement, distance and space relationships, and even architecture and decoration. All have potential message value; each can contribute to or detract from interpersonal-quality communication. So why do I omit them all and include one essay on silence and another on touch? Because, as I've mentioned in reference to May's piece, these are two modes of nonverbal communication that are both powerful and often overlooked.

This is especially true of touch. Partly because of the views toward sex and sexuality that are prevalent in the United States and some other Western cultures, touch and talk about it have become almost taboo. We know that touch is important in greeting, giving support, and conflict, but its sexual meanings all but overshadow everything else. Young persons learn very clearly where and when they can legitimately touch their parents, their friends, and themselves without being branded as "effeminate" or "aggressive" if they are male or as "masculine" or "easy" if they are female. When you read Leo Buscaglia's remarks about hugging in Chapter 14, some of you will smile or grimace with disbelief or discomfort. Touch, in brief, is the one mode of nonverbal communication with which most of us are the least comfortable.

James Hardison tries to remedy this in the next reading. He notes that our genuine desires to express warmth and caring are often frustrated by our awkwardness and inability to use touch to communicate. His goal is to suggest how we can, in small ways, use touch to build more gestures of caring into our day-to-day relationships.

Hardison emphasizes how touch can build trust, even in a completely nonsexual context. Doctors, dentists, and beauty operators, for example, can enhance or reduce trust by the ways they touch their patients or clients. Trust is also obviously important in intimate relationships, and a great deal of it—or its opposite—is communicated by touch.

Touch is also an important part of our contact with strangers and with persons from other cultures. In both contexts we can profit from the recognition of (1) the reality of legitimate differences, (2) the desirability of adding appropriate touch to our repertoire of communication skills, and (3) the effectiveness of a "progressive, slowly developing, step-by-step pattern of touching behavior for specific purposes. . . ."

Hardison suggests that we begin our efforts to change with those closest to us. It's easiest to control the level of risk in these relationships and to make progress toward more effectively communicating the genuine feelings of warmth, support, and caring that we experience.

I hope this essay will at least prompt you to consider your touching attitudes and behaviors. There is no need for all of us to turn into exuberant huggers, especially if that kind of behavior violates cultural norms we've been taught. But even a little more touch could humanize our communication contacts substantially.

Touching for Improving Interpersonal Relationships

James Hardison

Interpersonal relationships form the bases of what we perceive as our state of being. Yet a common complaint today is the alienation workers feel for management, students express about teachers, youth experience with parents, and spouses sense with each other. It seems that despite our efforts to the contrary, our interactions often result in conflict and misunderstanding. On the other hand, our good intentions abound. We wish to give and receive warmth through physical affection. We desire to aid one another in emotional development and self-actualization. We try to maintain an atmosphere in which one individual cares about another's needs and welfare. In short, we care about one another and wish to convey the warmth we feel.

Warmth is a measurable physical quality; however, the type of warmth we are talking about has an internal dimension. How do we derive the concept of "warmth"? In our earliest years, particularly in that period before we developed verbal skills, we depended on tactual senses for a large portion of our learning,

Excerpted from *Let's Touch: How and Why to Do It* by James Hardison. © 1980. Used by permission of the publisher, Prentice-Hall, Inc., Englewood Cliffs, N.J.

coping, and experiencing. We were touched by our parents for consolation, companionship, and protection. Their warm bodies provided us with a feeling of security allowing us to move about with less fear and more emotional strength. Our behavior and adjustment in later life were fundamentally influenced by the degree of emotional warmth we received through our parents' touching. In feeding, bathing, clothing, comforting, and entertaining us, our parents gave us our first concept of love and affection—warmth.

Each of us has the potential for giving physical affection and communicating warmth as we truly seek to improve our interpersonal relations. Our associates, colleagues, and friends also have the need to be touched. They subconsciously have the desire to make human contact, but they may be held back because many of them feel that "it's not nice to touch," or that touching will imply or lead to "something sexual." As individuals in search of a better way to relate to others, we must take the initiative, be slightly daring, and transcend the taboos and unreasonable social restrictions placed on us. We must turn to one of our most natural instincts, the tendency to touch in a caringly human way.

Touching in Times of Crisis

Have you ever noticed how interpersonal relationships take on more importance in times of crisis? Little children might feel independent as they play outside with their buddies, but an injury will quickly bring them to their parents in search of reassurance and care. Even the momentary crisis experienced by young lovers descending the steepest drop on a roller coaster is enough to trigger the need (or at least the pretext of it) to hold each other securely until the danger passes. Other minor crises include fender-bender auto accidents, final exams, and major business transactions. In any one of these crises, significant persons frequently give us verbal consolation as well as tactual reassurances.

Accordingly, interpersonal relationships are intensified in times of severe crisis, as in interactions between survivors after a death or even between distraught individuals who are separated by long-term physical barriers or divorce. Our friends seek us out more readily when they know we have experienced a crisis. They want us to know that they are close by to help, and they often signal this through touch. Through loving and supportive touches, a person can help to heal a friend's deepest wounds. Touching in such circumstances is something most of us do naturally. Why should we reserve our capability to use touch effectively only for times of crisis? Why not try, in small ways, to build such caring gestures into our day-to-day relationships?

Touch in Everyday Relationships

If we consider everyday activities in interpersonal relationships, we may see that we have friends and associates with whom we feel more comfortable in communication and touching exchanges. We may not even be aware of the exchanges we engage in; moreover, we may be unconscious of the messages we send out through touch. A case of unconscious touching occurred in the lounge outside a board of trustees' meeting room in a community college in Southern California.

Two large lounge chairs were situated side by side, with high armrests close together. A close personal colleague and I sat in the adjoining chairs, placing our hands, parallel and palms down, on the front of each armrest. An active observer, I counted twenty-two contacts from my colleague as we conversed. He would emphasize a point in conversation or assure himself that he had my full attention by reaching over and patting the back of my hand, my forearm, or wrist. During a brief recess in our conversation, I asked him if he had been aware of any touching exchanges while we had been talking. He was surprised to learn that he, a forceful and very masculine character, had been touching the hand of another male. When I explained that I had accepted his touching as a catalyst to communication, he became aware that he could touch another male's hand to improve communication and interpersonal relationships. He later admitted that he had heretofore locked himself (as most Americans do) into the stereotyped role in which touching is generally taboo—especially between males—because of the "sexual overtones" or "sexual connotations." I have a high regard for my colleague because of his ability to accept his natural tendency to touch as a wholesome and useful behavior pattern.

Many of us have similar unconscious habits. If we become more aware of our touching practice, we can learn to use our natural inclinations in a deliberate way to improve interpersonal relationships.

Touch Can Build Trust

Touching can facilitate a sense of trust and empathy. From early childhood, we begin learning how much we can trust people by the way they touch us. We affix a supreme trust to our parents as we feel their tender and caring touch in feeding, bathing, clothing, and rocking us. Our trust in them stabilizes in proportion to how often they touch us and how often their contact satisfies our needs. Basically, the same commitment to touch is carried forward throughout life; we tend to trust those people whose touching either satisfies our needs or brings us pleasure. The greater the satisfaction received, the greater interest we have in maintaining the touching.

The same dynamics of trust come into play in adult touching experiences. This is particularly true in the helping professions. If we examine very closely why we go to a certain doctor, dentist, or chiropractor, we may find that we are highly influenced by the way these people have touched us and by how much trust they inspired.

Consider your dentist. When you are in the office, seated in the dental chair, you must at least be able to trust that the hands about to treat you will be clean and gentle.

I believe that dentists are acutely aware of the need to communicate trust through touch. They know that patients don't return to dentists who squeeze the inside of their lips to their teeth. Nor do they return to dentists whose novocaine needle hurts more than they imagine the treatment would.

I experienced two contrasting examples of dentists' touching activities. One dentist entered the examinination room, shook hands with me warmly, and proceeded to wash his hands in front of me before touching my mouth. Both tactually and visually, his behavior inspired trust. Another dentist neglected both these steps and cleaned my teeth so brusquely that he cut my gum tissues unnecessarily;

they bled considerably. Touch and the trust it fosters accounted for the distinctly different impressions these dentists made.

Making a similar point, a woman told me of her experience at a beauty salon over a period of three years. The owner combed and set her hair each week with great care. While the owner washed the woman's hair, she took special interest to see that the strands did not become entangled; she made sure that the roots were not being pulled, nor the ends split, as she combed her hair, and she used a light touch in setting her hair. Mainly in response to the owner's touch, the patron had complete trust in her abilities. Then the owner sold the salon and moved away. The new owner, less cautious, showed little regard for the patron's comfort as she handled her hair. She failed to communicate trustworthiness to her customer and soon lost her.

The effective use of touch to improve relationships requires sensitivity and discretion. As we have seen, though touch has the potential to convey warmth and build trust, it can just as easily produce a tremendous "turn-off."

Trust in Opposite-Sex Friendships

Clearly, the trustworthiness we communicate can alter our relationships. Our trust in ourselves with regard to touch can also alter relationships. When establishing a new friendship, can you trust yourself to be just friendly and not to expect sexual intimacy with a member of the opposite sex? That's a difficult task for a lot of us. We are so bound by cultural mores that many of us are locked into believing that persons of the opposite sex are not capable of being just good friends; we assume they must eventually become intimate if they maintain a close relationship. In actuality, many people form relationships with members of the opposite sex that do not lead to sexual relations.

A woman account executive of my acquaintance in San Francisco had an experience of this type. She and her friend did not follow the "expected" pattern between men and women. She had attended a business cocktail party where she met a charming man with a lot to say; he startled her with his witty comments, unusual thoughts, and sensitivity. The two later found themselves in her apartment. It was six-thirty in the morning, the sun rising, before they both realized that they had spent the whole night talking, occasionally touching and hugging, experiencing a profound interchange of conversation. They also realized and reflected on the fact that they had not performed the standard antics of a brief conversation followed by a jump into bed, not an uncommon routine for either of them. They agreed to maintain a relationship characterized by the meaningful combination of talking and touching they had enjoyed on their first meeting. Such a relationship requires a high degree of mutual trust and respect. Seven years later, these two people are still enjoying what they consider a most rewarding friendship....

Touch in Other Cultures

Tactual expressions are a component of interpersonal relations in all cultures. Every group exhibits some form of touching to express feelings of friendship and love. North and South Americans kiss on the lips, touch cheek to cheek, kiss each other on the cheek, and round it off with hugs. Eskimos, on the other hand, hug rarely and touch noses to express their love. They lightly tap nose to nose, or one partner moves his or her nose in a circular motion around that of the mate, touching it lightly.

Samoans express their most profound love, not by prolonged kissing or touching noses, but by one partner pressing his or her flattened cheek to the cheek of the other party and taking impassioned staccato breaths that cause airjet sounds to emanate from the nose. The staccato pattern also characterizes their sexual relations. Samoans copulate in an abrupt, rapid manner, involving direct contact only between the genitals and almost never including a hug. . . .

Some African tribes use an arm grasp in greetings. Participant A extends both forearms, with the hands in a palm-up position and the elbows slightly bent. Meanwhile, participant B places an arm over each of the forearms of A. B's hands then grasp A's forearms at the inside elbow joint. This African arm clasp might well be considered as an alternative to the standard Western handshake to avoid some of its disadvantages. The standard handshake appears to have little meaning other than a cursory recognition of the individual. We might bring about a benevolent revolution by examining the various ways of revealing warmth, determining the effects of passivity in the exchange, measuring the relationship between the pressure applied and the meanings given (or received), and determining the significance of varying types of grasps and embraces. Such a study could give us some new insights and a refreshing perspective on how to use touch to express friendship and love. . . .

Difficulties in Touching Strangers

Touching to improve interpersonal relations cannot occur so easily between strangers. Most of us are not very open to touch as part of our communicating, a limitation that is even more pronounced among strangers. Basically, we are not a touching society, and we tend to feel discomfort in most touching interactions. Factors that contribute to this are (1) our basic lack of trust in strangers and (2) our resistance to being observed in touching interactions. We frequently have unverified suspicions about strangers, so we tend to proceed very cautiously with them, especially when it comes to touching. Although the handshake is generally an acceptable opening gesture in meeting a stranger, some people are reluctant to extend a hand to someone they do not know. This reluctance can be seen in churches where a handshake is part of the ritual; resistance is sometimes expressed as an actual refusal. Whatever the reasons for this resistance, it is clear that interpersonal relating must be entered into willingly; moreover, the imposition of a touching exchange can have an adverse effect. In some areas, congregational resistance to shaking hands has brought about a compromise from the pulpit. Religious leaders are asking their congregations to recognize their fellow church members by alternate modes: smiling or simply verbalizing a greeting.

We resist being observed in touching actions, perhaps mostly because we envision a sexual link to touching. Our cultural mores prohibit us from observing the most intimate form of touching—sexual intercourse. We extend our reluctance to being observed to many signs of affection, whether or not they are sexual in intent. As mature adults, we shy away from hugging or embracing in public, even for expressing friendship.

Modern psychologists have sought out ways through encounter group sessions to modify our behavior to allow us to feel more open to nonverbal touching behavior. Conflicting views have been presented. Some psychologists tell us that most touching techniques used in encounter groups are of little benefit, perhaps even harmful, since they foster defensiveness, produce stress, and have a potential for being psychologically disturbing. Their position underscores our cultural trait of little openness to touching strangers. It also points to a reluctance to have touching activities observed. I strongly recommend, however, that we consider a progressive, slowly developing, step-by-step pattern of touching behavior for specific purposes that would allow us to transcend the discomfort associated with touching strangers in general, while enabling us to relax just a bit about our touching behavior.

Understandably, most of us are not ready to embrace a complete stranger on the first meeting. If we are interested in developing a relationship, we want more information to go on. The information can generally be gained through verbal exchanges, which are more distant, less threatening, and more easily controlled than tactual contact. We can generally determine, through conversation, if we wish to move closer to others, and we can slowly assess their trustworthiness as they simultaneously determine ours.

If we are consistent in the meanings of our touching behavior, and others are similarly consistent with us, an unthreatening progression will follow. We will know, as will they, that a light touch by a hand on the arm is an act of friendliness and an expression of interest, not one of hostility or aggression. We can progressively work out understandings, such as whether a pat on the knee is used to show playfulness, to emphasize a point, or even to express a greeting. We can communicate that a hug or a full embrace means a warm greeting (a commitment of the entire self to it, so to speak), not sexual aggression. All touching transactions, in order not to threaten the relationship, must proceed with moderation and clearly expressed intentions.

Begin with Those Closest to You

A healthy improvement in the ability to be comfortable about touching might be brought about through slow, progressive, deliberate acts. This certainly doesn't mean that we become touching exhibitionists, ready to show everybody that we are the world's greatest touchers. A good place to begin could be in our homes. How many friends have confided that they never saw their parents hold hands, hug, or kiss each other? This state of affairs obviously encourages the children's future reticence to express themselves through touch. I suggest that couples begin to express their caring through touch in their homes freely, regardless of who is watching. Children or others who observe might be surprised or possibly ill at ease about what they see, viewing it as a departure from "dignified" behavior; but after several observations, they will probably be able to regard it as the honest expression of affection and caring it is. Don't hesitate on this; it is worth the risk. It can gradually make your life richer with meaning and expressed feelings.

Let's start with those people who are very significant in our lives. If they are a part of the family, very close friends, or loving mates, they will be more accepting of this new idea.... Without giving notice, take your mate's hand. Say nothing. Just hold the hand as unobtrusively as possible for a few minutes; then go back to doing whatever you were doing before. Or take your child lightly in your arms at intervals during the day. Let the child return to play or study without entering into verbal exchanges. The next time you are with a colleague you admire, dare to go over and give the associate a light pat on the back, saying, "You know, I really enjoy working with you" or "It's really great to be here with you." All these recommendations are designed to aid in improving interpersonal relationships. If our honest intent is to improve, we will do so. To gauge our progress, we might make "before" and "after" assessments of our relationships during a six-month period; a greater trust will surely emerge.

Touching behavior can have a significant impact on interpersonal relationships. Our touches and tactual expressions, when applied appropriately and tactfully, can carry with them a sense of warmth and companionship. Touches tend to improve interactions and communications. They cement our social and personal bonding with those people who are special to us.

Review Questions

1. How does Hardison suggest we try to counter the automatic link that tends to be made between touching and "inappropriateness" or "something sexual"?
2. Hardison argues that touch is more common in everyday relationships than we sometimes think. What evidence does he give to support his claim?
3. Hardison tells a story about a San Francisco couple who spent a night together in "profound . . . conversation" without having sex. What point does this story make about touch and communication?
4. What does Hardison say we should do about the difficulties we have touching strangers?

Probes

1. On a 10-point scale where 1 means "painfully awkward" and 10 means "utterly confident," where would you rank yourself on the following: (a) Your use of touch in your communication with family members? (b) Your use of touch in your job? (c) Your use of touch in your intimate relationships?
2. In a group of five to seven persons, discuss specific times when genuine feelings of caring or warmth were not communicated because of the person's inability to use touch appropriately and effectively.
3. What is your memory of touching in your family as you were growing up? What touch norms did you learn there?
4. Give an example from your own experience of the touch communication of a dentist, doctor, hair stylist, or other professional.
5. What are some specific differences that you've observed between white and nonwhite members of your community?
6. What is the most embarrassing experience involving touch that you can recall? (You don't need to share it with anyone, just recall it privately.) What did that experience reveal about the touch norms or values for touching that are most important to you?
7. How *consistent* is your touching? How might you increase its consistency?

Be Still

The wise leader speaks rarely and briefly. After all, no other natural outpouring goes on and on. It rains and then it stops. It thunders and then it stops.

The leader teaches more through being than through doing. The quality of one's silence conveys more than long speeches.

Be still. Follow your inner wisdom. In order to know your inner wisdom, you have to be still.

The leader who knows how to be still and feel deeply will probably be effective. But the leader who chatters and boasts and tries to impress the group has no center and carries little weight. . . .

Remember that the method is awareness-of-process. Reflect. Be still. What do you deeply feel?

JOHN HEIDER,
The Tao of Leadership

Part

2

Openness as "Inhaling"

Chapter 5

Being Aware of Yourself

To know how other people behave takes intelligence, but to know myself takes wisdom.

To manage other people's lives takes strength, but to manage my own life takes true power.

If I am content with what I have, I can live simply and enjoy both prosperity and free time.

If my goals are clear, I can achieve them without fuss.

If I am at peace with myself, I will not spend my life force in conflicts.

If I have learned to let go, I do not need to fear dying.

—JOHN HEIDER
The Tao of Leadership

his is an excerpt from the third edition of a book called *Dyadic Communication,* written by Bill Wilmot, a speech communication teacher at the University of Montana. As an aside, Bill was finishing his Ph.D. at the University of Washington just when I first came to Seattle to teach. We've been friends ever since.

This excerpt corrects two distorted ideas about "the self" that many people believe. The first is that our "self" is fundamentally an *internal* thing—a composite of personality characteristics, attitudes, values, beliefs, and habits that make us unique. One of Bill's major points here is that the self is not internal but *social.* This means that it grows out of contacts with others and functions primarily to guide our communication. The eight short quotations Bill reprints in the first segment of the article all make this central point.

If you've always considered your self to be an internal thing, I encourage you to read this essay as thoughtfully as you can. Why? Because your belief about this issue can affect your whole view of communication. If you believe that selves are internal and that communication functions to divulge or to hide parts of these internal selves, then communication becomes a basically *reproductive* process. What "comes out" more or less effectively reproduces what's "inside." But if you recognize the truly *social* nature of selves, then you see how communication itself affects *who we are.* In that sense it is *productive* not just reproductive. That's the central idea behind the definition of interpersonal communication that grounds *Bridges Not Walls.*

The second "commonsense" idea Bill challenges is the notion that we each have one real self that we can hide or reveal. Sometimes this is referred to as the "artichoke" model of the self—there are many layers of leaves on the outside, but there's also a solid "heart" at the center. Bill seriously questions the artichoke model of the self. As he notes, each of us does have habits and patterns that we carry from situation to situation, but we also change as we adapt to the circumstances we experience. In that sense our self is a fluid thing; important aspects of it are different in different situations.

You may or may not accept these commonsense views of the self. But I encourage you to listen carefully to what Bill has to say about the connections between selves and communication.

The Social Self

William W. Wilmot

Each to each a looking glass
Reflects the other that doth pass. {2}
— CHARLES HORTON COOLEY

Cooley's famous two-line poem expresses the fact that self-concepts are essentially social. Although the material and spiritual selves contribute to the self-concept {10}, social life is the beginning and sustenance for all the components of the self-concept. The material and spiritual selves have meanings for us because of others around us. Why be concerned with clothes (part of the material self) if others are not around to see them? The meanings one attaches to herself or himself (the spiritual self) are likewise molded in society. Frankl {4} goes so far as to say that the "true meaning of life" is to be found in the world rather than in one's psyche or spiritual self. In any event, *our communication transactions with others* mold our self-concept. In fact, our self-identity is carved within our relationships {1}.

Many social scientists agree in principle with Cooley's notion of the "looking-glass" self. Following are some short statements that emphasize that our communicative transactions are the cornerstone of the self-concept.

... the sense of identity requires the existence of another by whom one is known.

— R. D. LAING

The self may be said to be made up of reflected appraisals.

— H. S. SULLIVAN

It is well to remember that all the information a person possesses about himself is derived from others. His impression of the impact he had upon others is what makes up the picture of himself.

— J. RUESCH

... will conceive of himself as he believes significant others conceive of him.

— C. GORDON AND K. GERGEN

The becoming of a person is always a social becoming: I become a person as I progress through social situations.

— TIRYAKIAN

... we maintain our natural level of self-esteem so long as we do not lose the approval, affection, and warmth of those around us.

— L. WOODMAN

We are who we are only in relationship to the other person(s) we're communicating with.

—J. STEWART

I am not what I think I am. I am not what you think I am. I am what I think you think I am.

—BLEIBERG AND LEUBLING

This vitally important social self is built primarily in three ways: (1) by the reflected appraisals of others or the "looking glass" self, (2) by the comparison of the self with others, and (3) by the playing of social roles.

The Looking-Glass Self

That the appraisals of others affect us has been demonstrated time and time again. Rosenthal {14}, for example, showed that if teachers expected students to be intelligent, the latter performed better in school. Tell someone he is untalented enough times and he will begin to perceive himself that way. Guthrie {8} and Kinch {11} both relate similar stories that demonstrate the impact that the evaluations of others can have. In the Kinch example, five males in a graduate-level class wanted to see if the notion of the "looking-glass" self could be put to use. Their subject was the woman in the class who could be described at best as "plain." They planned to respond to her as if she were the best-looking girl on campus and to watch the effects of the treatment. Here is how it went:

> They agreed to work into it naturally so that she would not be aware of what they were up to. They drew lots to see who would be the first to date her. The loser, under the pressure of the others, asked her to go out. Although he found the situation quite unpleasant, he was a good actor and by continually saying to himself "she's beautiful, she's beautiful ..." he got through the evening. According to the agreement, it was now the second man's turn and so it went. The dates were reinforced by the similar responses in all contacts the men had with the girl. In a matter of a few short weeks the results began to show. At first it was simply a matter of more care in her appearance; her hair was combed more often and her dresses were more neatly pressed, but before long she had been to the beauty parlor to have her hair styled, and was spending her hard-earned money on the latest fashions in women's campus wear. By the time the fourth man was taking his turn dating the young lady, the job that had once been undesirable was now quite a pleasant task. And when the last man in the conspiracy asked her out, he was informed that she was pretty well booked up for some time in the future. It seems that there were more desirable males around than those "plain" graduate students {11}.

Besides the poetic justice involved, the impact of others' views is clear. The girl perceived the actual response of the men such that she had to change her self-concept, which in turn changed her behavior. While this example is one of the best to illustrate how the views of others can affect one's self-concept, I do not endorse it as a *modus operandi*. Clearly, there are some sexist implications in it that cause one to doubt the wisdom in performing the experiment. However, the point is clear—the way we see others seeing us greatly influences how we see ourselves. It is so important that "no more fiendish punishment could be devised" than to be "turned loose on society and remain absolutely unnoticed by all the members thereof" {11}.

The Self by Social Comparison

The second subcategory of the social self is the image we build of ourselves by comparison with others. More often than not, the comparison is made with peers. Sally, a young woman who is concerned about her attractiveness, wants to be invited to an upcoming party. If Sue gets an invitation and Sally doesn't, Sally is painfully aware of how she compares. Similarly, Joan knows she is an excellent student only if she can compare herself with other students for some idea of her relative standing.

A formal theory of social comparison processes has been offered by Festinger {3}. The aspects of the theory that are relevant to our discussion follow. We all have a basic drive to have correct opinions about the world and for accurate self-appraisals. When objective, nonsocial means of evaluation are not available or are ambiguous, we evaluate our opinions and abilities by comparison with others. We often choose peers for comparison because they closely approximate our ability and opinions.

By recalling James's formula for self-esteem, the impact of social comparison on our self-concepts can be made evident. If self-esteem equals success divided by pretentions, determination of degree of success is crucial. How does one arrive at some estimate of his or her success? By comparison with others. In addition, how does one establish goals or pretentions? By comparison with others. The entire process of establishing self-esteem is dependent upon our comparison with others.* This process takes place in every activity from school, to skiing, to selling life insurance. In fact, when "objective" standards are established for performance (every tenderfoot Boy Scout has to be able to tie a square knot), these standards arise from the past performance of others.

As a side comment, a person's level of pretentions or goals is affected by past performance in trying to attain a goal. Furthermore, a person's criteria for degree of success will be modified if he is told of someone else's performance. If he finds that his performance is below that of someone he considers to have little ability, he will raise his expectations. Conversely, if one is performing above another who is thought to have a great deal of ability, aspirations will be lowered. Whichever is the case, the social comparison with others is another social aspect central to the self-concept.

The Playing of Social Roles

... a man has as many social selves as there are individuals who recognize him.
—W. JAMES {10}

The complexity of modern society places us in situations that demand widely different behaviors. When our society was more agrarian, an individual's niche in the

---

*Obviously, a large part of the comparison with others is based on their reactions, their evaluation of our performance. Even here the "looking-glass" nature of self-concept plays a part.

social order was rather firmly established. The family was the basis of one's identity, and job and home were closely meshed. Now, however, it is not unusual that our family members do not even know the people we work with. We are expected to be effective people in the hustle and bustle of city life and then, as if by magic, transform ourselves into fully functioning family members. To our parents we are one person, to our co-workers or fellow students another, and to our closest loved ones still a third.

An alarm bell has been sounded. Many people perceive our social lives as tearing us apart, as making us into social chameleons who change personality with every new situation. Goffman {7}, for example, perceives a person as running around trying to "convey an impression to others which is in his interests to convey." From this point of view, we conduct our social relationships as types of calculated performances. We are always playing roles in order to make the proper impressions. As a result, there is little left in the way of an identifiable self-concept. The person wears masks and plays his socialized role "so well that he forgets who he is or what he looks like when the staged performance is over" {6}. According to this view, we have an "other-directed" culture where we conform to others' expectations rather than to any inner sense of values {13}. We become "yes-men" in the organization by adopting the correct lifestyle and adopt "Yes, J.B., you're right!" behaviors just to please our superiors {15}. We sell ourselves out to the social order.

However, we do have to adjust to the presence of others to lead successful social lives. Can you imagine a marriage, for instance, in which the husband wears a tuxedo to breakfast every morning? We have different relationships with different people—we rarely kiss the boss good morning. The question is whether one's degree of adaptation is so far-ranging as to cause psychological trauma. Our behavioral change in the presence of another is not necessarily calculated like a stage play; it can be an honest adjustment to the other's style. In a very honest sense, we are not the same to all people. Different relationships conceal and reveal different aspects of our personality {12}.

We all have different roles or role identities that are prominent at different times. Your adjustment to the demands of being a student requires different behaviors than those expected during a long holiday at home. Based on a number of factors, the role identities are called into prominence {12}. Based on the importance to you on a given role, you do develop some consistency in your communication behavior. Within a particular relationship, some consistency must exist or else no trust or enduring relationship can result. In fact, when your actual behavior is consistent with your self-perception, then those communicating with you are also perceiving you in that role. But when your behavior seems out of line with the role others ascribe to you, they regard you as playing a game. A student who has attended college and undergone dramatic changes in interests and lifestyle is often accused of "putting on airs" or being a "smart college kid" upon returning home. His behavior is no longer consistent with their images of him, and that is disrupting to them.

Hart and Burks {9} have extended the notion of successful role playing. They term someone who can adapt to the complexities of modern life as a *rhetorically sensitive* person. The rhetorically sensitive person tries to accept the necessary demands of different roles as a natural part of human existence. The choices facing us are not whether to play a role, but in which role to play. We literally "select those aspects of ourselves which will best meet the social conditions we face," in order to be socially competent. As we noted earlier, "each new relationship requires a unique form of adaptation" {5}, and as a result, to become rhetorically sensitive means that one is capable of adaptation to those demands. This is *not* to say that people should be chameleons—changing complete colors at the alteration of the surroundings. Rather, we each select and adapt the parts of ourselves that are appropriate to a given situation. The parts of your "self" that you reveal to your best friend are not the same parts that you reveal in a class of thirty people—yet both are parts of you that you select for the circumstances.

Often our self-concept is so discrepant from how others see us that we must convince them that our view of ourselves is accurate. People who are successful in convincing others that how they perceive themselves is accurate have been called self-confident, autonomous, strongwilled, or persuasive. All of us have degrees of conviction and strong will, yet we are affected by others' views....

In a sense, it is inaccurate to talk about "hiding the self" or "staging a presentation." We do not have some *real self* that we can hide or reveal. We don't have some entity that we dress up and dress down for display. In a given situation, we have a set of behaviors that we consider to be (1) appropriate to the situation and (2) consistent, to some degree, with the self-concept we have. If we violate our expectations or personal desires too much, then we feel that we have played a game in that situation. Take the student, for example, who feels that he has received an unjust grade on an essay test. He sits up late at night outlining his arguments and rehearsing the defense he will make to the instructor. Just before entering the instructor's office, he wipes his sweaty brow, takes a deep breath, and then marches in. Once in the presence of the instructor, he is about one-fourth as self-assured, logical, and bombastic as he wanted to be. He is self-conscious, awed by the instructor's knowledge, and unable to hit hard verbally. The instructor, regrettably, cannot be budged from her evaluation and the student returns home with the same grade. Was the student untrue to himself? Was he playing a game? No—he was simply adjusting to the presence of the instructor and setting forth appropriate behaviors. Even in more extreme cases, such as job interviews, when individuals are consciously planning to present only their best aspects, they are not violating any real self. They are simply selecting an appropriate repertoire of their possible behaviors.

The "looking-glass" self, the self built by social comparison, and the demands of our social roles are all interrelated. They are variations on the same theme—our self-concept is formed by our social relationships with others.

References

1. Bernal, G., and J. Baker, "Toward a Metacommunicational Framework of Couple Interactions," *Family Process 18*, no. 3 (1979): 293–302.
2. Cooley, Charles Horton, "The Social Self: On the Meanings of 'I' " in *The Self in Social Interactions*, Vol. I: *Classic and Contemporary Perspectives*, Chad Gordon and Kenneth J. Gergen (eds.). New York: Wiley, 1968, pp. 87–91.
3. Festinger, Leon, "A Theory of Social Comparison Processes." *Human Relations 2*, no. 2 (May 1954): 117–140.
4. Frankl, Viktor E., *Man's Search for Meaning: An Introduction to Logotherapy.* New York: Simon and Schuster (Pocket Books), 1972.
5. Gergen, Kenneth J., *The Concept of Self.* New York: Holt, Rinehart and Winston, 1971.
6. Glasser, William, *Reality Therapy.* New York: Harper & Row, 1965.

7. Goffman, Erving, *The Presentation of Self in Everyday Life*. Garden City, N.Y.: Doubleday, Anchor Books, 1959.
8. Guthrie, E. R., *The Psychology of Human Conflict*. New York: Harper & Row, 1938.
9. Hart, Roderick P., and Don M. Burks, "Rhetorical Sensitivity and Social Interaction," *Speech Monographs* 39, no. 2 (June 1972): 75–91.
10. James, William, *The Principles of Psychology*, I. New York: Holt, 1890.
11. Kinch, John W., "A Formalized Theory of the Self-Concept," in *Symbolic Interaction*, 2d ed., Jerome Manis and Bernard N. Meltzer (eds.). Boston: Allyn and Bacon, 1972, pp. 245–252.
12. McCall, George J., and J. L. Simmons, *Identities and Interactions*. New York: Free Press, 1966.
13. Riesman, David, *The Lonely Crowd*. New Haven, Conn.: Yale University Press, 1950.
14. Rosenthal, Robert, "The Pygmalion Effect Lives." *Psychology Today*, September 1973.
15. Whyte, William H., Jr., *The Organizational Man*. Garden City, N.Y.: Doubleday, Anchor Books, 1957.

Review Questions

1. What does it mean to say that "self concepts are essentially social"?
2. Give an example from your own experience of a person's self being affected by other people's impressions of him or her—in other words, of the looking-glass self.
3. What does Bill mean when he says that "self-esteem equals success divided by pretentions"?
4. According to Bill, what's the relationship between a social role and a self?
5. What does it mean to be a "rhetorically sensitive" person?
6. Bill argues that instead of having a "real self," we have a set of behaviors that are (a) consistent, and (b) _____.

Probes

1. In order to change from the belief that your self is an internal thing to the recognition that it is a social phenomenon, you have to be willing and able to give up certainty and predictability. What forces make this a difficult move to make?
2. Do you agree that the five male graduate students' treatment of the "plain" looking woman was sexist? If not, why not? If so, specifically how was it sexist?
3. In his discussion of social comparison theory, Bill writes, "When objective, nonsocial means of evaluation are not available or are ambiguous, we evaluate our opinions and abilities by comparison with others." Do you believe this only happens when nonsocial evaluations are unavailable or ambiguous? Or does it happen all the time?
4. Bill mentions the "alarm" some people feel about social pressures turning us into chameleons who "change personality with every new situation." Do you notice this happening? What can you do to keep yourself from falling into this pattern?
5. What's the difference between being "rhetorically sensitive" and being a "social chameleon"?

This simple personal credo is the centerpiece of a book that's currently a national best-seller. Robert Fulghum shared this statement of belief with his Seattle church congregation, then read it at a primary school celebration. Washington State Senator Dan Evans heard it, was impressed, and eventually read it into the *Congressional Record*. I include it here because I believe we can learn about ourselves by listening to these reflections of a man who is very self-aware.

All I Really Need to Know I Learned in Kindergarten

Robert Fulghum

Each spring, for many years, I have set myself the task of writing a personal statement of belief: a Credo. When I was younger, the statement ran for many pages, trying to cover every base, with no loose ends. It sounded like a Supreme Court brief, as if words could resolve all conflicts about the meaning of existence.

The Credo has grown shorter in recent years—sometimes cynical, sometimes comical, sometimes bland—but I keep working at it. Recently I set out to get the statement of personal belief down to one page in simple terms, fully understanding the naïve idealism that implied.

The inspiration for brevity came to me at a gasoline station. I managed to fill an old car's tank with super-deluxe high-octane go-juice. My old hoopy couldn't handle it and got the willies—kept sputtering out at intersections and belching going downhill. I understood. My mind and my spirit get like that from time to time. Too much high-content information, and *I* get the existential willies—keep sputtering out at intersections where life choices must be made and I either know too much or not enough. The examined life is no picnic.

I realized then that I already know most of what's necessary to live a meaningful life—that it isn't all that complicated. *I know it.* And have known it for a long, long time. Living it—well, that's another matter, yes? Here's my Credo:

ALL I REALLY NEED TO KNOW about how to live and what to do and how to be I learned in kindergarten. Wisdom was not at the top of the graduate-school mountain, but there in the sandpile at Sunday School. These are the things I learned:

> Share everything.
> Play fair.
> Don't hit people.
> Put things back where you found them.
> Clean up your own mess.
> Don't take things that aren't yours.
> Say you're sorry when you hurt somebody.
> Wash your hands before you eat.
> Flush.
> Warm cookies and cold milk are good for you.

Live a balanced life—learn some and think some and draw and paint and sing and dance and play and work every day some.

Take a nap every afternoon.

When you go out into the world, watch out for traffic, hold hands, and stick together.

Be aware of wonder. Remember the little seed in the Styrofoam cup: The roots go down and the plant goes up and nobody really knows how or why, but we are all like that.

Goldfish and hamsters and white mice and even the little seed in the Styrofoam cup—they all die. So do we.

And then remember the Dick-and-Jane books and the first word you learned—the biggest word of all—LOOK.

Everything you need to know is in there somewhere. The Golden Rule and love and basic sanitation. Ecology and politics and equality and sane living.

Take any one of those items and extrapolate it into sophisticated adult terms and apply it to your family life or your work or your government or your world and it holds true and clear and firm. Think what a better world it would be if we all—the whole world—had cookies and milk about three o'clock every afternoon and then lay down with our blankies for a nap. Or if all governments had as a basic policy to always put things back where they found them and to clean up their own mess.

And it is still true, no matter how old you are—when you go out into the world, it is best to hold hands and stick together.

Probe

1. For just one day, try literally applying Fulghum's Credo in your own life. What do you notice? What happens?

 ere are 20 of the 267 questions included in an unusual and interesting work by Gregory Stock called *The Book of Questions*. The author points out that these are not "trivia" questions but questions about your values, beliefs, and life, about money, sex, integrity, generosity, pride, and death. One purpose of the questions is to develop your own self-awareness. As Stock says,

> Here is an enjoyable way to find out more about yourself and others, and to confront ethical dilemmas in a concrete rather than an abstract form. To respond to these questions, you will need to examine and interpret your past, project yourself into hypothetical situations, face difficult dilemmas, and make painful choices. These questions can be an avenue for individual growth. . . .

The questions are not presented in any particular order. In fact, one goal of this arrangement is to confront you with successively different challenges as you move through the questions.

Stock argues that we often pull back from questions like these, even though they are "the very ones that will open paths to understanding and intimacy." If you respond to the questions alone, you'll develop your self-awareness. You can also learn something about yourself by noticing which questions you tend to skip over and which really intrigue you. If you discuss them with others, you'll grow closer.

As you move through these questions, try to remember probably the most important point of all about them: there are no correct or incorrect answers. Only honest or dishonest ones.

Twenty Questions

Gregory Stock

1

If you were to die this evening with no opportunity to communicate with anyone, what would you most regret not having told someone? Why haven't you told them yet?

2

If you were able to live to the age of 90 and retain either the body or the mind of a 30-year-old for the last 60 years of your life, which would you want?

3

You are offered $1,000,000 for the following act: Before you are ten pistols— only one of which is loaded. You must pick up one of the pistols, point it at your forehead, and pull the trigger. If you can walk away you do so a millionaire. Would you accept the risk?

4

Without your kidney as a transplant, someone close to you will die within one month. The odds that you will survive the operation are only 50 percent, but should you survive you would be certain of a normal life expectancy. Would you consent to the operation?

5

Would you be willing to become extremely ugly physically if it meant you would live for 1,000 years at any physical age you chose?

6

At a meal, your friends start belittling a common acquaintance. If you felt their criticisms were unjustified, would you defend the person?

7

If you were happily married and then met someone you felt was certain to always bring you deeply passionate, intoxicating love, would you leave your spouse? What if you had kids?

8

If you knew that in one year you would die suddenly, would you change anything about the way you are now living?

9

If you could increase your I.Q. by forty points by having an ugly scar stretching from your mouth to your eye, would you do so?

10

When you are with your friends, do your interactions include much touching—for example, hugging, kissing, roughhousing, or rubbing backs? Would you like to have more of this?

11

In love, is intensity or permanence more important to you? How much do you expect from someone who loves you? What would make you feel betrayed by your mate—indifference? dishonesty? infidelity?

12

Would you accept twenty years of extraordinary happiness and fulfillment if it meant you would die at the end of the period?

13

What do you seek in a friend yet neither expect nor want in a lover? Are you attracted to people who are healthy for you to be around?

14

How forgiving are you when your friends let you down?

15

What do you value most in a relationship?

16

If you saw someone cheating on a test, what would you do? What if you had signed an honor code?

17

When you make a big sacrifice, do you tell people about it or keep it to yourself? Do you feel annoyed when your sacrifices aren't acknowledged by others? What would you never willingly sacrifice? your life? your health? your integrity? your dreams?

18

How would you react if you were to learn that your mate had had a lover of the same sex before you knew each other?

19

What are you looking for when you converse with people? What kinds of things do you usually discuss? Are there other things that would be more interesting to you?

20

If you were guaranteed honest responses to any three questions, whom would you question and what would you ask?

Probes

1. As you moved through the questions, what did you notice about the ones you skipped and the ones you lingered over? Do you avoid questions about death? Sex? Money? What primary values surfaced? Physical attractiveness? Loyalty? Integrity? Security?
2. Often the process of responding to these questions leads people to write similar questions of their own. What questions would you add to this list?
3. Did you notice any inconsistencies between your responses to different questions? Do some values surface in some situations and different values in other situations? What does this say about what Bill Wilmot (in the previous reading) called the *social* aspects of your self?

 've included this reading because students in my interpersonal communication classes have told me that William Howell's notion of "internal monologue" is one of the most helpful ideas they encounter all term. This reading comes from Howell's book *The Empathic Communicator,* which I often use as a text.

Howell is an interpersonal communication and intercultural communication teacher at the University of Minnesota; his book is based on his many years of experience with both these topics. By "internal monologue" he means the internal or "covert" self-talk that's often going on. The central point of this excerpt is that your "covert" communicating is always affecting your "overt" communicating, and that those effects can be damaging unless you learn to manage your internal monologue. Your internal monologue also affects the other person's communicating as he or she generates additional IM in response. This interactive, reciprocal feature of internal monologue is the point of the final model on page 130.

Howell also emphasizes that IM can act like a "power disc brake on internal and external adjustment to changing events." Our abilities to be flexible and to cope with change can be seriously undermined by internal monologue.

Whether internal monologue occurs in dyads, groups, or organizations, it is generally stressful, and it almost always reduces communication effectiveness. Howell discusses nine typical causes of this phenomenon and offers three suggestions for controlling it. In my experience, what Howell calls ego involvement, habit, and rationality are three of the most common causes. My internal monologue often peaks when I'm embarrassed because I've made what others might view as a simple mistake. I also engage in IM when some habitual expectations aren't met and when I can't make fully rational sense out of what's happening.

Howell points out that personal and social roles can contribute to IM. He also broadens this point beyond male–female roles to those of parent–offspring, student–professor, boss–employee, and so on.

The first suggestion for controlling or managing your IM is to become aware of it and to recognize how it can work against you. The second is to learn to manage stress more effectively—for example, by maintaining physical relaxation. The third is potentially the most helpful; it is to refocus your attention from "inside" to "the between." This is a point Milt Thomas and I discuss in detail in Chapter 7, and it is crucial. The more you are actually concentrating on what's going on *between* you and the other person(s), the less you will be able to get tied up in your internal monologue.

The final section of the essay lists almost fifty questions you can ask yourself in order to begin controlling your IM. My students report that it's been worth the time they've invested in responding to these questions.

I hope that Howell's discussion will clarify how your *self*-awareness affects your *interpersonal* communicating. After you've read this discussion, you should be ready to think seriously about your awareness of others (Chapter 6) and your listening (Chapter 7).

Coping with Internal Monologue

William S. Howell

The basic element in simple or complex relationships seems to be two people, a unit we term a *dyad*.... Since the basic human unit of interpersonal communication is the dyad, we can proceed to construct a dyadic model. This model should portray intrapersonal events as well as the interpersonal process.

Let us assume that the circles that follow represent two persons: A, a supervisor, and B, an employee supervised by A. As the interaction begins, A is approaching B, her purpose being to offer B a suggestion to improve the way he does his job.

A rushes up to B full of good intentions. She initiates the interaction by saying, "Hey, B, I want to talk to you about how you are doing your job."

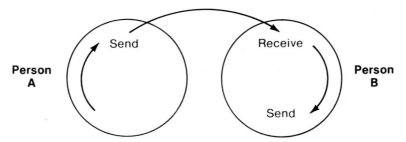

It happens that B, in addition to being A's subordinate, is also a timid soul, chronically insecure and apprehensive. When the boss hurries up with the abruptly expressed intent of discussing B's working methods, B is alarmed. He sends back a nonverbal message through a stiffened body, raised eyebrows, and compressed lips.

Fortunately, A is a sensitive communicator, and she picks up the nonverbal message. Many of us would pay no attention to B's reaction. We would simply go ahead and say what we had planned to say. A, however, not only interprets the cue as a sign that B is disturbed, but knows she must adapt to this reaction immediately. So, instead of continuing with her planned message, she changes her next verbal comment to "Hey, relax! It's not important, just a minor detail!"

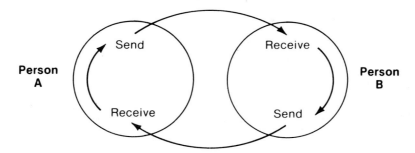

As the developing model shows, important events are happening intrapersonally. When B becomes alarmed and sends off the nonverbal cue of apprehension, this influences his reception of the next bit of communication from A. B at this point has only one interest, to find out how much threat there is in A's visit. And when A attempts reassurance, this conditions her reception of the next message from B. A's concern at this moment is to determine whether B has calmed down enough to go to work on the job suggestion, or whether she must provide more reassurance. When we represent these internal dynamics of A and B, the dyadic model is complete.

We should relieve suspense concerning the A and B episode. After A's reassurance, B responds by saying, "Well, you can't blame me for getting uptight! You came on real strong!" A must then either provide more reassurance or continue with her original message. She decides that B has indeed been reassured, and they proceed to interact about details of job modification.

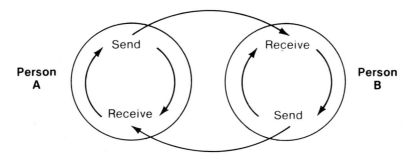

The model suggests that everything A does or says changes B's behavior. Further, whatever A receives modifies what she sends, and everything A sends changes the way she receives the next bit of communication. The same is true of B. Here is a dyadic interaction model of communication showing continuing intrapersonal and interpersonal feedback, and complete interdependence. This ongoing adjustment may be viewed as the process of *coping*. In John Keltner's words, "Coping with others is the essence of social interaction. Our ability to cope with others can develop only as we interact with each other in *our here and now*." ... In this case, only when A was convinced that B was no longer upset did she mention her ideas and invite B to react to them. A made a wise decision in this instance. To see why, let us look more closely at B's internal state.

When B became apprehensive, a stream of uncontrolled thoughts raced through his mind. "Is A about to fire me?" "I must have been doing very poorly." "Perhaps I'll be transferred to something I don't like." "Probably I'll be demoted." "I'm really in danger," and so on. It is easy to see how sudden fear can generate compelling notions that displace or inhibit normal thinking. What was going on in B's head was the extraneous and obstructive conscious thinking known as *internal monologue (IM)*.

What happened to B happens frequently to everyone. People want to concentrate fully on a topic, but their minds wander. If they happen to be in an emotional state, the power of irrelevant thoughts is multiplied. Their attention is divided between what they should be doing and a stream of distractions. The more intense and constant the internal monologue, the lower a person's ability to pick up cues from the environment and respond sensibly to them. Apparently, A recognized this fact. Since she wanted B to consider her message thoughtfully, with a minimum of distraction, she made the relaxing of B's tension her top priority.

Completing the Model for Interactive Communication

The whirling circle model can now be seen to be incomplete, simply because it assumes that people are capable of uniformly thoughtful, task-oriented communication. Actually, of course, two people interacting in a dyad are often distracted and inhibited by internal monologue. To be complete, the dyadic model must show the presence of internal monologue whenever it becomes sufficiently intense to interfere with an ongoing interaction.

The following model represents the communication between A and B immediately after A's opening comment, when B becomes emotional.

The appearance of "IM" suggests that normal effects of receiving or of sending are distorted wherever internal monologue is present. Not only is information processing affected in a person experiencing the disturbance, but the second indi-

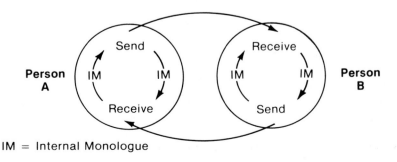

IM = Internal Monologue

vidual generates internal monologue in adjusting to the effects of the first's internal monologue. A's efforts to calm B are "extraneous and obstructive" to her intended purpose. Thus, a combination of B's internal monologue and A's countermonologue inhibits their working productively together. Until this extraneous and obstructive communication runs its course, the "IM" remains in the model. When it subsides to the point of insignificance, the "IM" is effectively removed and the circles of interaction and internal information processing can once again whirl freely.

To carry the whirling circle metaphor a step further, we can say that internal monologue acts like a power disc brake on external and internal adjustment to changing events. A sudden strong IM hits the brake pedal hard. Often the wheels lock, and adjustment to the other person and to events stops. Conversely, an interaction free of IM normally keeps the wheels rolling along at a good clip. In fact, speed of rotation becomes a measure of effectiveness. The faster the circles whirl, the more the resources of the persons involved are being combined in a joint venture. There seems to be no upper limit. In highly productive spoken interactions, greater speed of rotation is obtained by fragmentary verbalizing and increased reliance upon nonverbal codes.

A first step in controlling IM is to be aware of it and recognize its inhibiting effects. You can reduce the probability that IM will become a problem by avoiding topics likely to precipitate compelling, distracting thoughts. A mark of the highly proficient interpersonal communicator is the ability to "turn off" IM, or to not allow it to begin. This is an act of will that calls not only for self-discipline but lots of practice. It requires sufficient mastery of the mind that you can direct *all* your attention to the other person and stop being aware of self. A person who is "selfless" in this sense is unlikely to generate internal monologue—unless you choose to do so to avoid continuing an interaction!

To appreciate the impact IM has upon person-to-person communication, we need to look at it more closely. Specifically, we need to consider kinds of internal monologue and then probable causes.

Kinds of Internal Monologue

Extraneous and obstructive mental activity in interpersonal communication occurs in two markedly different forms—relaxing and stressful. Daydreaming while listening to a lecture is usually relaxing, for example. Worrying about the outcome of a job application interview, however, is normally stressful.

Relaxing IM often provides welcome relief. Recall a time you were trapped in conversation with a person who insisted on telling you, in seemingly endless detail, about happenings in which you were not interested. For you, IM was an escape hatch that permitted you to explore the fantasy of your choice or plan some coming event. But even though it eased your pain, this recreational IM did interfere with your listening. Thus, pleasant internal monologue can be just as extraneous and disruptive as the more stressful, less enjoyable forms.

Stressful IM is a somewhat frantic effort of the conscious mind to cope with the perplexing or with the unknown. In the example given earlier, Employee B was precipitated into an interaction with his boss that he did not understand. A flood of possible interpretations "took over" his conscious mind in an attempt to make sense out of a perplexing situation. The content of B's IM reveals why such monologue is usually stressful. Every question he asked himself and every possibility he considered pointed toward punishment for him. His IM could be said to be "disaster oriented."

The gloomy nature of B's internal monologue in this instance is entirely typical. Only a dedicated positive thinker can react to the unexpected appearance of a boss who says, "I want to talk with you about how you're doing your job," and infer that praise and a promotion are coming! Most people tend to think negatively in such circumstances, a tendency that is not only normal but necessary.

When people are placed in an enigmatic situation, one in which the outcome is unclear, why do they characteristically become concerned about what could go wrong rather than about what could go right? The answer is surprising: Because negative IM protects them from the unknown more efficiently than positive thinking. If you predict favorable consequences and they are in fact disastrous, you feel foolish and incompetent as well as sad. If you anticipate gloom and doom and disaster indeed strikes, however, you have softened the blow. You can say, "I knew it!" Being right is some small comfort. If events come to a happy conclusion, the fact that your prediction was wrong is quickly forgotten. Thus, uncertainty almost invariably produces an IM that is upsetting, depressing, and stressful.

What happens in individuals often occurs in groups. The tendency to assume the worst when in doubt is par for the course in organizations. The standard script for this scenario in a working organization develops when everyone knows that significant changes are on the way but no one has information about what the changes will be. Immediately, predicting the future becomes a major conversational pastime. Rumors quickly fill the gap of missing information. The most popular rumors, of course, are vivid descriptions of bad times ahead. Just as an individual becomes tense and emotional by contemplating unpleasant consequences, groups within an organization can become upset. Two results are loss of morale and lowered productivity.

In dyads, groups, and organizations, much stressful internal monologue can be avoided by supplying abundant information on plans, goals, purposes, and directions. People who know what is coming tend not to waste time and energy speculating about it and accordingly view the future less emotionally. Their time and energy become more available to do useful work.

The extent to which people are susceptible to internal monologue varies tremendously. Some persons produce IM whenever a situation becomes uncomfortable or unpleasant. Others have a greater ability to concentrate and focus their mental faculties upon the topic at hand. Usually they can keep IM from starting; if it does start, they can control it or "turn it off" at will. Because extraneous and obstructive thoughts are managed better by persons who control their IM, these people are able to get more done and be more creative than the rest of us.

Assorted Causes of Internal Monologue

An enormous number of distractions interfere with person-to-person communication. By now, you can call to mind dozens of situations in which IM generates spontaneously. To control compelling IM, however, you ought to be able to identify and classify its source. Here, then, are a few sources of internal monologue and, finally, a basic conflict in people's thinking that makes them vulnerable to IM.

Unexpected, Disturbing Events   One major source of IM is any surprising development. For example, you make a statement to a friend expecting automatic, total agreement and get vigorous dissent instead. "How can this be? What does he know I don't know? Does this mean I've offended this person?" Your IM is off and running. Very seldom does such a situation provide opportunity to explore the causes of your friend's unexpected behavior directly, so your internal monologue keeps speculating and getting in the way.

Often, unexpected happenings can change a familiar, predictable interaction into one clouded with uncertainty. The instructor of your class in nonverbal communication asks you to help him with his lecture on the ways familiar gestures are interpreted in various cultures. Your planned—and rehearsed—role is to make the illustrative gestures. When you come to class, you find that the instructor is ill and has requested that you conduct the class. For some time at the beginning of the class period, your internal monologue about what your friends are thinking, how well you are doing, whether you will be able to remember the most important points, and so on will probably interfere with your performance. As your attention shifts from concern with self to interaction with members of the class, the IM typically reduces and disappears.

Covert Forces   Everyone possesses **covert forces** that are powerful sources of internal monologue. These are consequences of being human. They are said to be covert because they operate out of awareness; that is, people feel their effects without knowing the cause. Many could be mentioned, but we will examine six covert forces and typical instances of the IM they generate.

1. *Ego involvement* is the tendency to feel that what one does is a projection of one's inner self. After the spring banquet, you are introducing the speaker of the evening and forget her name. You feel ashamed, humiliated. The IM resulting from this insignificant mistake is energized by ego involvement. A sensible reaction would be to laugh at "goofing up," enjoy being kidded by members of the audience, and forget it. Many people, however, would suffer for days. They would be distracted by internal monologue, nagging thoughts of their public failure.

    Ego involvement makes it difficult to be venturesome. Internal monologue plays the role of censor: "Will this cause people to admire me? If I say this, will I be criticized? This should be said, but it will not be approved of. Let someone else do it." When you withhold your resources because of what people will think or say, your ego involvement IM is at work. Ego involvement constantly frets over what other people think. The IM it produces attempts to protect your self-image.

2. *Emotion...* [is] a major component of the motivational complex.... When any emotion is active, people behave differently than when they are unemotional. The emotion of fear produced the internal monologue in Employee B. Any threatening situation makes people develop highly distracting thoughts. Fright changes perception of an interaction. Anger exaggerates and distorts. An angry IM will cause people to say and do things they later regret. The emotion of love, however, is associated with

a different kind of monologue, one that makes us less critical of and more receptive to the loved person or object. These strong emotions fill the conscious mind with compelling fantasies, making it unlikely that rationality can prevail.

3. *Anxiety*, a third covert force, resembles the emotion of fear. People can be "anxious about" something without being "afraid of" it. Anxiety is a state of tension which causes people to try to make something happen instead of letting it happen. A salesperson may be unable to resist pressuring a customer to buy. A parent becomes anxious when a child is slow to talk. The youngster who has missed school because of illness is returned to classes too soon by an anxious mother. A guest shows up for dinner a half hour early. A batter swings early at a changeup pitch. Anxious IM says "Hurry up," "Do it now," "Don't think or talk it over," "Settle this once and for all." In group work, anxious IM increases tension, produces compulsive decision making, and reduces thoughtful deliberation.

4. Another covert force that increases internal monologue in person-to-person communication is *habit*, the internal pressure to complete processes in routine ways. When habitual expectations are not met, the owner of the habit tends to generate IM. When a meeting starts late or runs long overtime, some less flexible and adaptable members of the group are sure to be irritated. Their IM often centers upon the persons responsible for violating customary boundaries. Habit governs most people more than they like to admit. A significant amount of extraneous and obstructive fantasizing may well result from being forced into deviant patterns of speaking or acting. These patterns are uncomfortable simply because they are not habitual.

5. The next covert force is *sexuality*. Often members of a male–female dyad will combine discussion of a topic with distracting thoughts of their sexual relationship. In mixed groups, men and women relate to each other quite differently than in same-sex groups. This is not intentional and hence the behavior is influenced by a force that is truly covert.

6. Completing this arbitrary list is a covert force that may surprise the reader. It is *rationality*. How can rationality, which enables people to be logical, methodical, and accurate, be a covert force? Answer: It becomes covert and a source of internal monologue when it produces a compulsion to fit everything into an orderly arrangement.

   Rationality urges people to make sense of everything they participate in. Yet many worthwhile experiences *don't* make sense in any demonstrable and logical way. They have value in and of themselves, but it is a value that can't be articulated. Appreciation of a beautiful picture or of an exceptional musical performance are examples of worthwhile nonrational experiences. Yet people often feel compelled to explain—be logical about—such an experience. People in the Western world tend to believe that they should have a reason for every opinion. This conviction promotes much rationality-based internal monologue.

   One IM that comes from the compulsion to be sensible about everything is rationalization. People enjoy a play and later, when they talk about it, make up "good reasons" why it was enjoyable. They feel pleasure, so they say, "The lighting was well done," "Stage movements were balanced," and "Costumes were colorful." These are interesting observations but amount to a completely inadequate description of the feelings of aesthetic experience. In fact, they are extraneous and disruptive and function as typical internal monologue.

Personal Relationships   The final general cause of IM we will examine is the nature of personal relationships. Two factors that are *not* mutually exclusive are involved: (1) feelings people have about each other, and (2) roles emerging from position or status.

Think about yourself communicating with four sorts of associates: strangers, lovers, friends, and enemies. The relationship you have with any one of these will add to whatever you do together a "qualifying" IM. The monologue tends to be qualifying because it is used to interpret and evaluate whatever your partner does. Lovers and friends benefit from your enhancement of their contributions; strangers and enemies are made objects of suspicion and their comments are scrutinized critically, if not outright rejected. Your monologue rationalizes by manufacturing reasons for assigning credibility to one and mistrusting the other.

Position and status roles generate internal monologue that structures both the style and content of an interaction. On a social occasion, a plumber converses with a physician. Typically, their interaction is free and open until they mention their work. Then the conversation becomes relatively stiff, guarded, and limited to "safe" general topics. Each person's internal monologue is trying to instruct its owner about what to say and how to behave to meet the expectations of the other. This is certainly a good intention, but it removes from the conversation any sparkle that might have developed.

IM changes behavior whenever the roles that intersect differ in position or status. Here are some examples of role dyads that pose expectation-meeting problems: parent–offspring, student–professor, boss–employee, nurse–doctor, minister–member of the congregation, you and the President of the United States. Much of the position and status IM is triggered by a conscious or out-of-awareness realization that each role has boundaries that must not be crossed. The President has to act and sound like a president. Many of his habitual pre-Presidential ways of communicating are out of bounds. He can "stretch the presidential stereotype" slightly (thereby demonstrating a strong individualism), but if he goes too far, he will be punished by adverse reactions in the media and by slumps in opinion polls. A President probably is pressured by internal monologue as much as anyone in our society.

Similarity in position and status contributes to reduction of IM. When you and a close friend of the same sex talk over a problem that is important to both of you, there may indeed be few if any extraneous and obstructive thoughts to interfere with your sharing of ideas.

Controlling Internal Monologue

IM, which represents unnecessary scripting that reduces effectiveness, seems to be a problem for everyone. We have examined assorted specific examples of IM in action. Now let us turn our attention to what we can do about it.

Two general classifications of internal monologue were discussed, the relaxing and the stressful. Relaxing IM is indeed a problem, but a minor one compared to the stressful kind with its deep roots in covert forces. Woolgathering and fantasizing to avoid less pleasant concentration upon a task show inability to control attention. People who daydream when they should be paying attention can do something about it, if motivated sufficiently. Training in listening comprehension and exercises to improve reading speed are useful. Practicing attention control by listening to difficult material on educational radio, identifying your internal monologue as soon as it begins and "turning it off" is a self-help method of gaining mastery of recreational relaxing IM. Regular practice of this simple exercise helps to reduce unwanted daydreaming and fantasizing.

Stressful internal monologue differs from the recreational variety by being based upon a feeling of discomfort, dis-ease, a sensation that something is about to go wrong or has already done so. This sensation creates mental and physical tensions that cause the conscious mind to become active. But since the resulting thoughts are extraneous and obstructive to the main flow of events, tension is usually increased rather than relieved. Left to run its course, IM often increases in a vicious spiral rather than slowing down to quiet extinction.

The sequence, then, is *stress-tension-accelerated* IM. Breaking the sequence is the best means of control. How is this accomplished?

Competent communicators break the chain by doing something to reduce tension. When they feel stress, they may talk about it. By refusing to become ego involved, they can remain relaxed. They can share their feeling with other persons, find out if it is mutual, and defuse it by analyzing it together.

Another technique is learning to maintain physical relaxation. It is a fact that mental tension cannot develop in a relaxed body. Mental and physical tension are closely connected; they grow and decline together. It is possible to learn to reverse the "natural" tendency to become tense under stress. Some athletes learn to be most relaxed when competition is keenest. Biofeedback sessions over a period of time are useful in developing ability to break the sequence by refusing to become tense.

A third way to slow the vicious spiral of IM under stress is the simplest and most difficult. You can turn off internal monologue by directing your attention away from it. Then it will die of malnourishment. When extraneous thoughts intrude, ignore them. Voluntarily devote all your energy to what is going on *between* yourself and another person. This is the natural method by which internal monologue is contained and conquered. In an earlier hypothetical example, you unexpectedly found yourself teaching a class. Your IM ran rampant until you found yourself highly involved in interaction with the students. IM then extinguished itself. You were too busy with more interesting matters to pay any attention to it.

Coping successfully with stressful IM eliminates most unnecessary and harmful scripting. Consequently, it is a "must" for the development of competence in interactive person-to-person communication ...

Self-Analysis: You and Your Internal Monologue

Internal monologue (IM) is extraneous and obstructive conscious thinking. In the past few days, when has IM interfered with your person-to-person communication? Did you conquer it, or did it conquer you? Could it have been avoided by better management of the interaction? Did something within you start the IM, or did a happening outside yourself precipitate it? Did other persons in the interaction show effects of their internal monologue? If so, what were the symptoms? If not, why were the others free of IM when you were handicapped by it?

Explain to yourself precisely the consequences of your IM as it changed both your ability to adjust to changing circumstances and what you did—or did not—say. If you were to repeat this interaction, could you restrict or control your internal monologue? How would you go about preventing it? Once your IM has started, what techniques could you use to reduce or minimize it?

Why is it desirable that the circles in the whirling circle model rotate freely? Is it true that there is no upper limit to the speed of rotation, that faster is indeed better?

What is a greater problem for you, relaxing or stressful internal monologue? Think of a time you used IM as an escape mechanism. What are the favorite fantasies of your recreational internal monologue? Does your relaxing IM pretend to do useful work, like planning the future, or does it simply try to have fun?

Think of a time when a stressful, uncomfortable situation started your IM. Was your internal monologue script disaster oriented or optimistic? Did your IM predict an actual outcome? Can you recall being in a group under stress when the group monologue filled an information gap? Describe the incident. What, if anything, put a stop to the rumors that circulated? When one group monologue ended, did another begin?

Which of the six covert forces mentioned in this chapter energizes your internal monologue the most? Are you addicted to novelty or are you a creature of habit? Does this characteristic start an IM under certain circumstances?

What, if any, monologue tends to begin when you work with members of the opposite sex? Are your expectations of a woman conversationalist different from your expectations of a man? Is your style of speaking with a person of the other sex different from your manner of speaking with a person of the same sex? If so, list detailed differences.

How strong is your covert rationality? Do you feel a compulsion to put things in order, or do you enjoy disarray and impulsive decisions? Can you remember rationalizing a hasty conclusion? Was the rationalization for yourself, or for the benefit of others?

Think of an acquaintance with whom you communicate stiffly and with whom you rely upon scripting. Then think of another with whom you are relaxed and spontaneous. Decide which produces more IM for you and explain why that is the case.

Select three persons you know well, one of high status, one of your own status, and one well below yourself in status. What characterizes the role you play in communicating with each? Are any of these persons the same individuals you selected while reading the previous paragraph? Do you relate scripting to status differential?

What is your level of tension while talking to a group? What circumstances reduce this tension and what increases it? Are you less tense or more tense in talking to a group of strangers instead of people you know? Why?

Think of a time when you were ill at ease when talking with another person. Did you mention your discomfort and talk about it? Why or why not? Do you usually feel free to discuss feelings when interacting with friends? With strangers? Do you often reveal your feelings to your conversational partner? Would doing this reduce or increase internal monologue?

How much do you monitor your conversation? If you monitor a lot, why do you do so? Do you trust your out-of-awareness critical thinking to tell you what to say at moments of crisis?

When you are engaged in task-oriented activities with several other people, is your predominant style acting out or working through? Can you give examples of situations from work, family, or recreation where acting out is your preferred style? Can you cite other situations where working through would clearly be preferable?

Have you experienced one-to-one communication that approached Buber's ideal of dialogue? What requirements must two people meet if they are to attain a high level of working through?

Are the anticipated risks that hold people back from working through real or imaginary? Think about it.

Review Questions

1. How is the model of communication that Howell develops in this reading similar to and different from the view of communication offered in Chapter 1?
2. Give an example from your own experience of two persons' IM affecting each other. How is this phenomenon "like a power disc brake"?
3. What two different kinds of internal monologue does Howell describe?
4. What is "ego involvement"? Give an example of its operation in your communication.
5. Why does Howell call "rationality" a covert force that can cause internal monologue?
6. What is Howell's third suggestion for controlling internal monologue? Is it similar to or different from the advice, "Don't think of a pink elephant"?

Probes

1. In what situation do you experience the most ego involvement? Are there any communication *advantages* of this phenomenon?
2. Sexuality is a common and influential cause of IM, especially for adolescents. Can you recall a time from that period of your life when IM significantly affected your communication? What was the outcome?
3. Do you agree or disagree with Howell when he says, "Many worthwhile experiences *don't* make sense in any demonstrable and logical way"? Explain.
4. Based on your own observation, how does IM function at a typical party? Does it produce any positive effects? How do you cope with IM in a party context?
5. What are some concrete ways to follow Howell's third suggestion to "devote all your energy to what is going on *between* yourself and another person"?

Chapter 6

Being Aware of Others

When I'm critical of another person, when I see his behavior as a "fault," my attitude includes these feelings: I think of him as one thing (instead of having many parts). I dislike him. I "just can't understand" his action. He seems unjustified. And I think he "knows better." If I feel this way I am in reality seeing my own self-condemnation. "Fault" means failure to meet a standard. Whose? Mine. Another person's behavior is "bad" or "understandable" according to my experience with myself. My criticism of him amounts to: If I had said that or acted that way I would think of myself as selfish, opinionated, immature, etc. A part of me wants to act that way or thinks of myself as acting that way and condemns this. If I understood why I act like that, or want to, and had forgiven myself for it, I wouldn't be condemning this person now. I'm getting upset with him because there is something in me I don't understand and haven't yet accepted.

HUGH PRATHER

I n the previous chapter I noted that the excerpt from Bill Wilmot's book challenged two commonsense ideas about selves. This excerpt challenges another commonsense belief, this time about perception. The belief is outlined in the first sentence of the essay; it's the conviction that we perceive and observe other people "in a correct, factual, unbiased way." In other words, many people believe that perception is fundamentally a process of soaking up sense data. There's a "real world" out there waiting to be sensed, and we see, hear, smell, taste, and touch it in more or less "objective" ways.

The problem with this commonsense belief is that it is not supported by the psychological and communication research that's been designed to test it. Even more importantly, it's not supported by everyday experience. Consider, for example, the widely recognized problems with eyewitnesses in the courtroom. Two people who both witness an auto accident or a mugging can perceive it in significantly different ways. And even when lawyers and juries compare eyewitness accounts with photographs and videotapes, they find that "what happened" and "what that meant" depend on whom you ask. Except perhaps for the simplest of events, what we call "reality" and the lawyer calls "the facts" is a transaction between perceiver and perceived. That's why Bill labels this excerpt "The Transactional Nature of Person Perception."

First Bill introduces what he means by "transactional." The basic idea is that perception is a *mutual* process, it happens *between* perceiver and perceived, it is a *two-way* phenomenon. This is true basically because human beings live not in a world of things but in a world of *meanings*. We don't respond to objects and persons but to what they *mean* to us. So even in the case of nonhumans, as Bill puts it, "The meaning attached to an object is a function of (1) the perceiver, (2) the object, and (3) the situation."

When we move from the perception of objects to the perception of persons, four elements are added to the process. The first is the-perception-of-being-perceived. When you smell a rose, your smelling is not affected by any thoughts about the how the rose feels about being smelled. But when you smell a person, it is. Person perception is significantly affected by the perception-of-being-perceived. We know that people can or do see us seeing them, feel us touching them, notice us smelling them. Our recognition of this fact affects how we perceive them. Bill discusses this phenomenon.

The second feature person perception adds to object perception is what Bill calls "the imposition of structure." We don't just perceive isolated aspects of persons; we notice some features and then we put other features with them. So if we perceive a person to be warm and approachable rather than cold and aloof, we are also likely to perceive him or her as intelligent and competent. This is how we operate with what are called "implicit personality theories." Interestingly, Bill notes, our imposition of structure leads us to see not only "more than what's there" but also "less than what's there." If we label someone, for example, we can stop noticing what's unique about him or her and perceive the person simply as a representative of that label—"professor," "jock," "nurse," and so on.

Third, we assume consistency on the part of the others we're perceiving. Thus, although we might accept in theory the idea that people change, we are often shocked when people we know do things we don't expect. Bill relates some interesting stories about how this tendency to assume consistency can produce humorous results.

The fourth feature of person perception that Bill discusses is the attribution of causality and responsibility. When we see a rock roll down a slope, we don't believe that the rock "meant" to move that way. But we do make that assumption about people. Whatever we perceive them to be doing, we assume that some choice-making process prompted the action. Sometimes we attribute the action primarily to causes "inside" the individual, and sometimes we attribute it to "outside" causes. But in both cases we are viewing human activity as purposeful.

There are obviously several important ideas in this reading. I've put it at the beginning of this chapter because it overviews most of what it is vital to know about person perception. The other readings in the chapter will develop, elaborate, and illustrate several of the points Bill Wilmot makes here.

The Transactional Nature of Person Perception

William W. Wilmot

The psychologically naive individual operates under the assumption that he or she "perceives and observes other people in a correct, factual, unbiased way" [14]. If Charlie perceives Sam as dishonest, that means for him that Sam *is* dishonest. Such an approach, although it makes "reality" easy to deal with, ignores the transactional nature of perception. There is no objective world of persons. We each interpret others in different ways. To be sure, there is much agreement over evaluations. Two women may both agree, after each had to fight her way home, that Sam is "handy with the hands." But what does it mean? Sam needs affection? Sam is a male chauvinist? Sam's mother rejected him? Sam is overreacting because he's afraid of women? Sam would make a bad husband? Sam would make a good husband? Just as we can never know the real or ultimate self, we cannot know what Sam is really like. We can say, however, that "This was my experience and this is how I reacted," recognizing that others experience a different aspect of Sam and attach their own meanings. The following anecdote illustrates the point that our meaning for another's behavior is subject to error.

The small son of upper-class parents worried them considerably. In the presence of strangers, the boy stammered, withdrew, and became quiet. When around other children he became afraid and nervous. The parents felt the need to secure some professional help for the boy but wanted to do it so that the boy would not be embarrassed or feel singled out. Finally they hit upon an idea. An old college friend of the father was a clinical psychologist, so they invited him to dinner. After

Excerpts from William W. Wilmot, "Perception of the Other," in *Dyadic Communication*, 3d ed., pp. 77–86. Copyright © 1987 by McGraw-Hill, Inc. Reprinted with permission.

Figure 1
Disappearing dot.

the meal, they revealed the real reason they had asked him over—to diagnose the son's problem. He accepted the task of observing the boy the next day (after, of course, collecting appropriate information on history and behavior).

> He watched, unseen, from a balcony above the garden where the boy played by himself. The boy sat pensively in the sun, listening to neighboring children shout. He frowned, rolled over on his stomach, kicked the toes of his white shoes against the grass, sat up and looked at the stains. Then he saw an earthworm. He stretched it out on the flagstone, found a sharp-edged chip, and began to saw the worm in half. At this point, impressions were forming in the psychologist's mind, and he made some tentative notes to the effect: "Seems isolated and angry, perhaps overaggressive, or sadistic, should be watched carefully when playing with other children, not have knives or pets." Then he noticed that the boy was talking to himself. He leaned forward and strained to catch the words. The boy finished the separation of the worm. His frown disappeared, and he said, "There. Now you have a friend." {23}.

The transactional nature of perception occurs in both the perception of objects and perceptions of people. You might think that objects, since they are "real" and objective facts, can be observed without interference of our own views. However, as Bateson says, "objects are my creation, and my experience of them is subjective, not objective" {3}. The meaning attached to an object is a function of (1) the perceiver, (2) the object, and (3) the situation. For an illustration of this, look at Figure 1.

Hold the book level with your eyes and close your left eye. With your right eye look directly at the asterisk and then move the book back and forth slowly about 12 inches away. You will notice that the spot, which you can first see, disappears at a certain point. The "disappearance" of the spot on the right occurs because we have an absence of photo receptors (rods and cones) at that point on the retina {30}. But this physical "blind spot" makes an important point as well. We all have "blind spots" in our perceptions of both objects and people, and even if we had all the physical equipment, we could not "objectively" perceive objects. For purposes of illustration, look at Figure 2 {29}. What do you see?

•   •   •

•   •   •   •

Figure 2
Arrangement of dots.

Probably dots arranged in the forms of a triangle and a square. Look again! On the left are three dots and on the right are four dots. Why did they not produce the following shapes in your mind?

Or why were they not seen as totally unrelated to one another? Clearly, what you perceived was as much a function of you as of the arrangement of dots.

If the perception of objects is a "transaction between the brain and the environment" {22}, the process of person perception is certainly no less a transaction. As a *minimum* in person perception, there is (1) the perceiver, (2) the person, and (3) the situation. In addition, some important elements are added in a dyadic relationship that are not present in the perception of objects. To begin with, there is a *mutually shared field* {28}. You see him and he sees you. The person you are perceiving is engaging in the same process you are. The complexity of the situation is described by Tagiuri {27}:

> The perceiver, in some sense aware of many of the general properties of the other person (consciousness, mind) or his specific attributes (for example, generosity), has to allow for the fact that he himself, with similar properties, is also the object of perception and thought and that, as such, he influences his own object of perception. Observer and observed are simultaneously observed and observer. Their reciprocal perceptions, in a continuous recycling but varying process during which each person uses the variations in himself and the other person as a means of validating his hypothesis about the other.

Your own behavior in a dyadic transaction produces reactions in the other, which you then use as the basis of your perception. And the same process is occurring for the other participant. The process of person perception is obviously more complex than is object perception because the object is not adjusting to our presence. Often the conclusion that another person's behavior is consistent simply means that we provide a "self-picture which remains relatively stable and coherent," which has consistent effects on the other's behavior {11}. The personality characteristics you perceive in a person may depend in part on the characteristics he or she perceives in you {18}.

We can never perceive the "real" person because the concept of the "real" person is a myth. The other person's behavior is just as relationship-bound as ours is. For example, if you perceive a person to be acting in a hostile manner, her perception of your behavior as hostile could have triggered her response. Furthermore, we often project onto others. We see things in them that are not in them, but in us {14}. For instance, if you are feeling alone and bitter because of the recent loss of a romantic partner, you may tend to perceive other people as being lonely. And conversely, "when you're smiling, the whole world smiles with you."

At the very least, person perception is a transactional process because what we see *is as much a function of us* as it is of the qualities of the other person. For example, when you are really angry at someone, your reaction may say more about you than it does him. There is no "immutable reality" {9} of the other person awaiting our discovery. We attribute qualities to the other based on the cues we have available, and the unique way that we interpret them. Our perception of the other, while seeming certain, is grounded in permanent uncertainty.

Research dealing with person perception is beginning to recognize more fully the transactional nature of the process. For instance, Delia's work argues that the communicative transactions influence perceptions of others {7}. At this point, we can specify that there are some general principles about the process of attaching meaning to another's behavior, and they will be discussed under the topic of perceptual regularities. Two of the most important perceptual regularities occurring in dyadic contexts are (1) the imposition of structure and (2) the attribution of causality and responsibility.

Perceptual Patterns

Perceptual Sets

There are certain patterns that regularly occur in our perceptions of others. These "perceptual sets" arise because of our desire to "make sense" out of others' behavior—to place it in a category with a label. Perceptual sets are the result of these regularities: (1) imposing structure, (2) assuming consistency on the part of the other.

Just as we impose structure upon objects, such as seeing the dots of Figure 3.2 in a pattern, we impose a structure upon a person's behavior. We always have to act on the basis of incomplete information, and we make sense of the incomplete information *by going beyond it* {5}. We take the initial and incomplete information and use it to define the person, to place her in a particular category. We do this because our world of experience has (1) structure, (2) some stability, and therefore (3) meaning {12}. The Asch {1} study is one of the best examples of how we structure impressions of others based on partial information. Subjects were given a list of traits of an individual and were asked to write a paragraph describing the person. They also chose from a list of opposing traits those they felt characterized the person. Subjects formed overall impressions of persons based on such terse descriptions as *intelligent, skillful, industrious, warm, determined, practical,* and *cautious.* And furthermore, when the word *warm* was replaced by the word *cold,* impressions were considerably altered. Overall impressions of others are based on partial evidence; we translate the partial evidence, whether it comes from a list of words or from a short transaction with the other, into a meaningful structure. Once we construct this model of the other, we guide our responses appropriately {19}. For instance, if you interpret a new acquaintance's acts as generally morose, you will use this overall structure as the basis for your reactions.

The structure that we impose upon situations is uniquely ours. As Kelly {16} noted, we interpret information within the realm of our personal constructs. We "make sense" out of the other through our own personal experiences and ways of viewing the world {8}. In fact, the person's behavior is understandable to *us only to the extent that we can tie it back to our own experience* {31}—only to the extent that we have a construct for it. While the way each of us construes events is personal, there is enough commonality between two peoples' constructs to allow overlap in constructs {10}. Therefore, if you and Sharon both observe Bob in the same situation, your interpretations of his behavior may have enough commonality that you "agree" on what you perceive to be his personality.

The meaning that we impose on the behaviors of others has been termed the "implicit personality theory" that each of us has {6}. We each have an intuitive notion about which traits are likely to go together and use those ideas as a basis for judgment of others. If a car salesperson misrepresents some of the information about a car to you, you may well refer to him as a "shyster," imputing a definite personality trait. But some other person may say, "Hey, the person isn't a shyster. He is just required to turn the best profit possible. It's all part of the job." Each of you is imposing a different implicit personality theory on the behavior of the other. One research study in communication demonstrates that implicit personality judgments are made early in the course of our interactions with others. Berger {4} found that if people act somewhat consistently both early and late in their interactions with others, they are judged to have traits that carry on through the other interactions. If you meet your college roommate and she acts "warm and outgoing" toward you, you will probably conclude that she is a "friendly person." This early attribution will carry forth until there is compelling evidence to cause you to alter your attribution—such as her moving all your belongings out into the hall and changing the lock on the door.

As noted earlier, our perceptual sets about others involve imposing structure and "going beyond" the information about another. Paradoxically, not only do we "see more than is there," but we also "see less than is there." Once we impose a perceptual structure on another, it blocks us from seeing other attributes of the person. For instance, one man when asked what his ex-wife's name is says "FANG!" Such a label short-circuits our thinking about her, blocking us from seeing her other qualities as a mother, friend, or co-worker. I once had an experience of being stranded on a lonely Montana back road, about 20 miles from the nearest town. There was almost no traffic, it was dark, and the car engine had just had a major seizure. One car finally came over the horizon, and I managed to stand in the middle of the road and get the man to stop. As I sat in the back of the car, the driver said, "Hi—what do you do?" I said, "I'm a professor at the university." There was a silence, an "Oh," and then the conversation ended. The rest of the ride to Townsend was filled with the sounds of silence while I wondered what his perceptual set was for college professors.

One fascinating study with mental health workers also illustrates perceptual sets in action—blocking people from seeing other information. Over 100 mental health workers were shown a videotape of a therapy session with a female client. Half of the professionals was told that the client was lesbian and the other half was told that she was heterosexual. When the professionals were asked to assess her psychological adjustment, those who thought she was lesbian saw her as being more defensive, less nurturant, and less confident and having less self-control and more negative attitudes toward men. On the other hand, those who believed her to be heterosexual reacted to her in a totally positive way and even wondered why she was in therapy {17}. The label of *lesbian* activated a perceptual set that did not allow the mental health workers to see the behavior they could see in the case of someone else.

Perceptual sets permeate perceptions of others, and the imposed structure both adds and misses important information. These processes are so pervasive that you can be assured that someone's description of another person will not be accurate. The perceiver's imposed structure will not present an accurate picture to you of the other person no matter how hard they try. Our language gives us shortcuts for explanations, but unfortunately, it also guarantees misrepresentation of another.

A related aspect of our imposition of structure is that we assume personal consistency on the part of others. Because we attribute a "definiteness of attitudes, sentiments, and views" to others {14} when it is not there, we are often surprised. The young woman who had been a serious student shocks her parents by quitting her job and traveling alone around the world. The boy who had been a juvenile delinquent suddenly breaks his habits and spends his next few years helping others. And the freewheeling, loose bachelor joins the monastery. Research evidence does not support the notion that people are consistent in their behavior, yet we are often dismayed when they act inconsistently. As Mischel {20, 21} has pointed out, our behavior is a product of the unique combination of the people we are around and our adjustment to them and is not due to any inherent personality trait.

Often our expectation for consistency in others' behavior can produce humor. Joe was a semiserious student in one of my classes (he attended and participated, but did not study very hard). He was older than the other students, about thirty, and was the father of four children. All in all, I saw him as a responsible, hard-working student. One day during a rather rigorous final examination, he was sitting in the back of the room and like the other students, was intensely involved in the test. All of a sudden, when I looked his way his hand shot into the air with a huge middle finger extended—and a grin on his face. His gesture was so unexpected and so disruptive to my view of him that all I could do was laugh in front of a very puzzled class.

We often punish people who violate our conceptions of what they are. When we label someone's behavior as insincere or label her as a fake, we are only saying that she violated how we expect to perceive her. One study demonstrated that predictable people tend to be liked more than unpredictable ones {11}. Because (1) we want consistency in the other, (2) our behavior often produces consistency in the other's response, and (3) we construct a consistent view of the other, we have a tendency to evaluate him in terms of particular personality traits {14}. If someone always acts intelligently around us, we tend to ascribe it as a personality trait, when in fact it as well as all his other behaviors are situationally determined. The total mix of (1) your meaning and behavior and (2) his meaning and behavior produces the "personality" you perceive. There may be certain tendencies for response—he may wish to be a happy person—but the situation has to be appropriate in order to observe that quality in him.

Attribution of Causality and Responsibility

The second perceptual regularity characteristic of person perception is the attribution of causality. As human beings, we want to come to grips with our environment; we want to make sense out of the world. One of the techniques we utilize to this end is the attribution of causality. From the general view that events are caused, we view human behavior as being caused. Most of us feel we are in part responsible for our actions, and we impose this same perspective on others. We see them as at least partly responsible for their actions {27}.

When we mentally attach causes to the behaviors of others, we essentially have two choices: attribution to *external* causes or attribution to *internal* causes; that is, we ascribe the behavior of another either to the actor (internal locus) or to the circumstances surrounding him or her (external locus) {24}. We tend to attribute the person's actions to external causality under the following conditions {2}:

1. *High consensus.* Other people also act in this manner in this kind of situation. For instance, if we think that most people will suffer depression when they lose a loved one, then person A's depression is seen as being caused by the loss of a loved one.
2. *High consistency.* If the person acts similarly to the way she is acting in this situation on other occasions, then we assume that the situational constraints produce the behavior.
3. *High distinctiveness.* If this person acts differently in other situations, then we assume that her depression has been produced by circumstances of this situation. For instance, if someone lies when interviewed by the police for a drug charge but does not lie in other situations, we would tend to see the lying as produced by the strong arm of the law, and not by some personality trait.

The conditions leading to an attribution of internal causality are the opposite of those cited earlier. If there is low consensus (others in this situation do not act this way), then we attribute the behavior to a personality, or internal state of the person. Suppose that an out-of-work, recently divorced friend of yours has been evicted by his landlord. During the process of moving, he physically harms his ex-wife because she had come over to claim some of the furniture. You will see your friend as "aggressive" or "hostile," because most people would not act violently in such a situation. Therefore, whenever attributing causes to the other, the more unique or bizarre the behavior, the more likely we are to attribute it to some internal state. If there is low consistency (the person is in the situation often, but acts differently), we tend to attribute the behavior to internal states that are unpredictable. Take the evicted friend again. If he has been with his former mate many times before in dealing with the property, but this one time he assaults her, we are likely to conclude that he "has gone off the deep end," or some similar situation. Finally, if there is low distinctiveness (the person acts similarly in a number of situations), then we assume it is a function of personality not of the situation. If our friend has been in many physical spats with others before, we would see him as an aggressive person and would see his assault on his ex-wife as just fitting a firmly established pattern.

The key to attribution of causality is, as Kelley {16} notes, the amount of covariation. If the behavior occurs with the presence of the person and not when the person is not present, then we conclude that the person has caused it. With the man who assaulted his former mate, if the woman has been physically assaulted many times by many former romantic partners, we would conclude that something in her behavior toward men contributes to the responses that they have toward her {16}.

When attributing causality, the judgment centers on whether we think the other has the power to create the effects. In most situations, we also attribute responsibility—where we impose an emotional or moral judgment along with the notion of causality. Researchers in attribution theory separate the two processes, but the preceding examples combine the notions of causality and responsibility because in most reactions to others, the two are intertwined.

The degree of responsibility we place on others for events depends on a number of factors. If external forces are not very strong or if the ability to withstand those forces is regarded as high, we tend to place causality and responsibility in the lap of the other. If the person has the ability to create effects, he is typically held responsible for those effects {26}. When observing a disintegrating marriage, for example, if we feel that one of the partners had it in his power to cause the demise of the marriage by having an outside relationship, we place the responsibility on him. Furthermore, if we see the person intending to gain the desired goal, we are more likely to assign responsibility to him. In sum, people are held responsible for the effects they intend to create and for effects they have the ability to create {13}.

The crux of the matter is that in analyzing social situations, we usually have two choices. We can ascribe the effects either to the person or to the environment. If we see another fail at a task, we can attribute it to a lack of ability, "a personal characteristic, or to the difficult task, an environmental factor" {13}. Whichever path we choose has consequences for our transactions. If, in the preceding case, we see the person as failing because of a lack of ability, we may concomitantly perceive him as a weak-willed, nonpowerful person. Our tendency will be to blame him and to take the "he-had-it-coming" attitude toward his misfortunes. This attribution often follows the "belief in a just world" notion that many people have {25}. If a person is fired, has children in trouble with the law, or is experiencing any other difficulty, this belief allows people to conclude that if bad things happen to a person, he or she somehow deserves it. This attribution pins the effects of behaviors solely upon the person.

If, on the other hand, we ascribe his failure to environmental causes ("Anyone would have failed at that."), then we will see him in a friendlier light and be sympathetic to his plight. A special form of attributing causes to environmental forces occurs in the case of unconscious motivation. If you see someone's behavior as caused by circumstances beyond his understanding and control ("He had a bad childhood and that is why he is insane."), you will absolve him of blame. Our courts of law recognize that environmental forces may be so overwhelming in some cases that the individual should not be tried.

The attribution process is central to the ongoing communication transactions we have with others. If we see someone as "trustworthy" and "having to slightly bend the truth," our communication behavior toward her will be markedly different than if we view her as a "liar who cannot be trusted in any situation." In our communicative transactions with others, we make attributions, attach meanings to their communicative behaviors, and take action based on them. The process of attribution, therefore, occurs constantly in our communication with others.

References

1. Asch, Solomon E., "Forming Impressions of Personality." *Journal of Abnormal and Social Psychology* 41 (1946): 258–290.
2. Baron, Robert A., and Donn Byrne, *Social Psychology: Understanding Human Interaction*, 2d ed. Boston: Allyn and Bacon, 1977.
3. Baxter, Leslie A., Personal correspondence, March 22, 1978. Department of Communications, Lewis and Clark College, Portland, OR.

4. Berger, Charles R., "Proactive and Retroactive Attribution Processes in Interpersonal Communications." *Human Communication Research 2*, no. 1 (Fall 1975): 33–50.
5. Bruner, Jerome S., David Shapiro, and Renato Tagiuri, "The Meaning of Traits in Isolation and in Combination," in *Personal Perception and Interpersonal Behavior*, Renato Tagiuri and Luigi Petrullo (eds.). Stanford, Calif.: Stanford University Press, 1958, pp. 277–288.
6. Cronbach, Lee J., "Processes Affecting Scores on 'Understanding of Other,' and 'Assumed Similarity.'" *Psychological Bulletin 52* (2955): 177–193.
7. Delia, Jesse G., "Change of Meaning Processes in Impression Formation," *Communication Monographs 43* (June 1976): 142–157.
8. Delia, Jesse G., Andrew H. Gonyea, and Walter H. Crockett, "Individual Personality Constructs in the Formation of Impressions," Paper presented to Speech Communication Association Convention, Chicago, 1970.
9. Dettering, Richard, "The Syntax of Personality." *ETC: A Review of General Semantics 26* (June 1969): 139–156.
10. Duck, Steven, *Personal Relationships and Personal Constructs*. New York: Wiley, 1973.
11. Gergen, Kenneth J., "Personal Consistency and the Presentation of Self," in *The Self in Social Interaction*, vol I: *Classic and Contemporary Perspectives*, Chad Gordon and Kenneth J. Gergen (eds.). New York: Wiley, 1968, pp. 299–308.
12. Hastorf, Albert H., David J. Schneider, and Judith Polefka, *Person Perception*. Reading, Mass.: Addison-Wesley, 1970.
13. Heider, Fritz, *The Psychology of Interpersonal Relations*. New York: Wiley, 1958.
14. Ichheiser, Gustav, *Appearances and Realities: Misunderstanding in Human Relations*. San Francisco: Jossey-Bass, 1970.
15. Jacobson, N. S., "A Component Analysis of Behavioral Marital Therapy: The Relative Effectiveness of Behavior Change and Communication/Problem-Solving Training." *Journal of Consulting and Clinical Psychology 52* (1984), 295–305.
16. Kelley, Harold H., "Attribution in Social Interaction," in *Attribution: Perceiving the Causes of Behavior*, Edward E. Jones et al. Morristown, N.J.: General Learning Corporation, 1972.
17. Lewis, Robert A. (ed.), *Men in Difficult Times*. Englewood Cliffs, N.J.: Prentice-Hall, 1981.
18. Marlowe, David, and Kenneth J. Gergen, "Personality and Social Interaction," in *The Handbook of Social Psychology*, vol. III: *The Individual in a Social Context*, Garner Lindzey and Elliot Aronson (eds.). Reading, Mass.: Addison-Wesley, 1969, pp. 590–665.
19. McGuire, Michael T., "Dyadic Communication, Verbal Behavior, Thinking, and Understanding, vol I: Background Problems and Theory," *Journal of Nervous and Mental Disease 152* (April 1971): 223–241.
20. Mischel, T., *Personality and Assessment*. New York: Wiley, 1968.
21. Morton, Teru L., and Mary Ann Douglas, "Growth of Relationships," in *Personal Relationships*, vol. II, Steve Duck and Robin Gilmour (eds.). New York: Academic Press, 1981, pp. 3–26.
22. Parry, John, *The Psychology of Human Communication*. New York: American Elsevier, 1967.
23. Schlien, John M., "Phenomenology and Personality," in *Concepts of Personality*, Joseph W. Wepman and Ralph W. Heine (eds.). Chicago: Aldine-Atherton, 1963, pp. 291–330.
24. Schopler, John, and John C. Compere, "Effects of Being Kind or Harsh to Another on Liking," *Journal of Personality and Social Psychology 20*, no. 2 (1971): 155–159.
25. Shaver, Kelly G., *An Introduction to Attribution Processes*. Cambridge, Mass.: Winthrop Publishers, 1975.
26. Taguiri, Renato, "Social Preference and Its Perception," in *Person Perception and Interpersonal Behavior*, Renato Taguiri and Luigi Petrullo (eds.). Stanford, Calif.: Stanford University Press, 1958, pp. 316–336.
27. Taguiri, Renato, "Person Perception," in *The Handbook of Social Psychology*, vol. III: *The*

Individual in a Social Context, Gardner Lindzey and Elliot Aronson (eds.). Reading, Mass.: Addison-Wesley, 1969, pp. 395–449.

28. Taguiri, Renato, and Luigi Petrullo (eds.), *Person Perception and Interpersonal Behavior.* Stanford, Calif.: Stanford University Press, 1958.
29. Vernon, Glen M., *Human Interaction: An Introduction to Sociology,* 2d ed. New York: Ronald Press, 1972.
30. Von Foerster, Heinz, *Observing Systems.* Seaside, Calif.: Intersystems Publications, 1981.
31. Walster, Elaine, "The Effect of Self-Esteem on Liking for Dates of Various Social Desirabilities," *Journal of Experimental Social Psychology* 6 (1970): 248–253.

Review Questions

1. What does Bill Wilmot mean by the term "transactional"? How does it relate to what I wrote about this process in Chapter 1?
2. In this article Bill claims that "We can never perceive the 'real' person because the concept of the 'real' person is a myth." What does he mean?
3. What does Bill mean when he says that we make sense of the incomplete information we sense by "going beyond it"?
4. Define the term "implicit personality theory."
5. How does the example of the mental health workers perceiving the heterosexual/lesbian woman illustrate the idea that we sometimes perceive "less than what's there"?
6. Give an example from your own experience of a problem you had making sense of an inconsistent action of a friend.
7. We can attribute choices to _____ causes or _____ causes.
8. Explain the operation in the attribution process of "high consensus," "high consistency," and "high distinctiveness."

Probes

1. If you were to keep walking across the room you're in, eventually you'd run into a piece of furniture, window, door, or wall. If someone stomped on your bare toes, it would hurt. What's "transactional" about these perception processes? Don't they involve perceiving a "real" obstacle and "real" pain?
2. Give an example from your own experience where your perception of a person said as much about you as it did about that person.
3. Bill claims that we make sense of incomplete information by "going beyond it." Don't we sometimes make sense of something by going more deeply *into* it rather than beyond it? Give an example of this phenomenon.
4. If perception is as transactional as Bill claims, how can he account for perceptual similarities and regularities? For example, everybody agrees that ex-President Reagan is male, a conservative Republican, and an effective public speaker. What's transactional about our perception of Reagan?
5. In your own communicating, how do attribution processes affect your communication success?

 lthough this next author's treatment of perception is a little too "social scientific" for my taste, this is a very authoritative, up-to-date, and quite readable account of the crucially important topic of person perception. Jones adds important dimensions to Wilmot's discussion and develops some points Wilmot just mentions.

Jones's first main point is that the processes we call "stereotyping" are normal and unavoidable. As he puts it, there are "certain flaws in the way in which we process information about other people" that are not deficiencies or errors but are frequently shortcuts that simplify our perceiving.

In the section called "Perception of Other People," the author explains how person perception is really sense-making. At the most basic level, "taking in" information is really trying to understand, as he puts it, "what another person is up to." We do this in part by segmenting the stream of behavior we observe, and the ways we choose to segment it significantly affect what it means to us.

In the next section, Jones discusses how it can appear that situations we experience control our perception by choosing *for* us what to attend to and what to treat as significant. This phenomenon affects the self-perception of minority persons who are "tokens" and the ways we perceive people directly in our line of sight as contrasted with those on the periphery of our vision.

Under the heading of "Categorization," Jones reviews how categories induce us to exaggerate similarities—for example, among racial or same-sex groups. As he summarizes, the problem is that once we have made a distinction between "us" and "them" on the basis of a single characteristic, "we may infer that 'they' possess additional characteristics for which we have no evidence."

In the following section, Jones lays the foundation for and then explains what he sees as the single most significant characteristic of our processes of deciding what people are up to. He calls it the "fundamental attribution error," and it is our tendency to overemphasize personal factors and underemphasize situational ones. We tend, in other words, to make sense out of what we observe people doing by attributing their actions to their attitudes or personalities instead of recognizing the significance of the situation they're in.

You may want to read this selection more than once in order to get all of what's here. If you choose to do that, I think it will be worth the effort, because the ways you perceive the people you contact *significantly* affect how you communicate with them.

Perceiving Other People: Stereotyping as a Process of Social Cognition

Russell A. Jones

Stereotypes and Information Processing

Stereotypes are often claimed to be the result of illogical or faulty reasoning processes. It is seldom made clear exactly what and where the faults are, but the

From "Perceiving Other People ..." in *In the Eye of the Beholder: Contemporary Issues in Stereotyping*, Arthur G. Miller, ed. (Praeger Publishers, New York, 1982), p. 41–85. Copyright © 1982 by Praeger Publishers. Abridged and reprinted with permission.

usual implication is that people who hold stereotypes are intellectually deficient. Archie Bunker, for example, with his myriad stereotypes of blacks, Jews, southerners, Californians, and almost every other group imaginable is clearly not too bright, and the revelations of his convoluted reasoning are filled with half-truths, inappropriate generalizations, malapropisms, and superstitions. Unfortunately, the Archie Bunkers of the world are not the only ones with stereotypes. We all have them, and it is very unlikely that increasing everyone's IQ by 20 or 30 points would change that fact. But is there any truth to the claim that stereotypes can result from faulty reasoning processes?

The purpose of this chapter is to examine some of the evidence bearing on that claim. In particular, we shall concern ourselves with evidence suggesting that stereotypes are in fact the normal result of certain flaws in the way in which we process information about other people. As we shall see, there are a number of imperfections in the ways in which we take in, manipulate, and try to make sense of the information about those we see and hear and interact with. However, far from being indications of abnormal or deficient functioning, these "imperfections" are in many cases information-processing shortcuts and procedures that usually serve us well and make our tasks easier.

For example, because of the tremendous amounts of information impinging on our eyes and ears in any given situation, we usually have to be quite selective about what we attend to. We simply cannot take it all in, so we pick out what we think are the most important aspects of a situation. But situations change, and our normal habits of attention may retard perception of those changes because we are looking elsewhere, at what we think is important. Similarly, once we have categorized another person in a particular way, we are likely to ignore the differences between that person and others who have been so categorized simply because categorization is, by definition, based on the perception of similarities. We tend to overgeneralize the bases of our categorizations and to act as if people categorized on the basis of similarity in one characteristic are likely to be similar in other respects, even when these "other respects" had no part in our initial categorization.

We shall explore these and a number of other information-processing biases in the pages to come. We begin with some basic issues in the perception of other people: how we go about attending to the behaviors of others, what sorts of things we are most likely to notice, and what is likely to happen once we make the leap from observation to categorization. We are seldom content with the simple perception of differences in behavior of different categories of people, however. We feel a need to explain those differences, to understand why they occurred. As we shall see, there is a fundamental error that we are likely to make in trying to explain why someone behaved as he or she did. We are likely to underestimate the extent to which that person's behavior was constrained by the situation, and to overestimate the extent to which it was due to his or her personal characteristics, to the sort of person he or she is.

Our explanations for behavior are also biased by several motivational forces. There is some evidence, for example, that we tend to blame victims for their misfortunes, even when the misfortune was entirely unpreventable. Such apparently irrational explanations serve to protect our sense of security. If we can convince ourselves that the victim failed to take certain precautions against disaster, all we have to do to prevent a similar disaster from occurring to us is to take those precautions. Once we have fleshed out our perceptual distinctions among people and groups with explanations for those differences, we are often in deep trouble, because we tend to rely on these internal representations. What we remember about a person or group becomes for us what they are, and what we can remember is often unrepresentative and distorted. We shall look at some of the reasons why this is so....

Perception of Other People

Perception has to do with the "taking in" of information. As Erdelyi (1974, pp. 13–14) puts it, "Broadly conceived, perceptual processes may be best thought of as spanning the full sequence of events associated with information intake and consolidation, beginning just after stimulus input and ending prior to permanent storage in long-term memory." Thus, perception includes a number of different processes: attention, the encoding or interpretation of what we have just seen or heard or felt or tasted, short-term memory, and rehearsal of what we have encoded. Our encodings or interpretations, as well as what we choose to attend to and all other aspects of perception, are, of course, partially determined by what we have previously stored in long-term memory. Someone with an extensive knowledge of herbs and spices, for example, may get a great deal more enjoyment out of a gourmet meal because he or she will be more likely to be able to distinguish and name and remember the various tastes than someone without such knowledge....

Segmenting the Stream of Behavior

If we want to find out what another person is like, one of the best ways to start is by simply observing that person: watching, listening, smelling, comparing what he or she does with what others do, and comparing what he or she does with what we would have done in the same situation. Our purpose in observing another's behavior is, first of all, to make sense of what the person appears to be doing. An intriguing line of research by Newtson and his colleagues (1973, 1977) has focused attention on the perceptual processes involved when we try to understand what another person is up to. The basic assumption behind Newtson's research is that the perceiver does not passively take in information about the behavior observed. Rather, the perceiver actively participates in the perceptual process by organizing the ongoing observed behavior into meaningful segments or actions. Thus, to a large extent the perceiver controls the amount and kind of information obtained when observing another's behavior, and may literally generate more or less information from a given behavioral sequence, depending on such factors as expectations and attentiveness....

We attend most closely to the unusual in behavior, and we do so, apparently, in order to learn, to gain sufficient information about the person performing this unusual behavior so that we may anticipate how he or she is going to behave in the future. Further, one consequence of our focused attention is that we are more likely to see the behavior as being personally caused, as being due to some quality of the person we are observing, at least when the behavior is not constrained by a particular task. It should follow, then, that if there are certain situations in which particular people are unusual or salient, we are more likely to pay closer attention to them than to those around them and, perhaps, more likely to attribute their behaviors to their personality dispositions.

Tokens and Other Distinctive People

As noted above, in most situations there is simply more information available than we can handle. We are overwhelmed with sights, sounds, and smells, and have to select small portions of what is available to attend to and encode. The aspects of a situation that we choose to attend to are, of course, a function of many things, such as our interests and experience. There is some evidence, however, that in many situations we do not "choose" at all, at least not in a conscious, rational manner. Sometimes it seems as if situations "choose" for us by drawing our attention to certain of their features.

Consider the question of self-perception. There are literally thousands of things that each of us could tell another person if we were asked to describe ourselves. McGuire, McGuire, Child, and Fujioka (1978), however, suggest that what we notice about ourselves and what we choose to tell another person about ourselves are often those characteristics that are unusual in our customary environments. It follows that the only son of a couple who also have three daughters should be more conscious of his maleness than the son of a couple who also have one daughter. Similarly, a black child in a classroom with 29 white children should be more conscious of his or her identity as a black than would the same child in a classroom with 15 white and 14 other black children. Further, McGuire et al. argue that distinctiveness influences our conceptions of ourselves in two major ways: directly, in that we may define ourselves in terms of our distinctive or unusual features, and indirectly, in that others may perceive us and respond to us in terms of our distinctive attributes.

In support of the hypothesis that we define ourselves in terms of our distinctive attributes, McGuire et al. (1978) and McGuire, McGuire, and Winton (1979) report a study in which students in a predominantly white school system were interviewed and asked to describe themselves. Only 1 percent of the predominant white group spontaneously mentioned their ethnic group membership, while 17 percent of the black and 14 percent of the Hispanic students did so. Similarly, males were significantly more likely to mention being male when they came from households in which females were in the majority, and females were significantly more likely to mention being female when they came from households in which males were in the majority. Further, boys who came from homes where the father was absent were significantly more likely to mention being male than were boys who came from homes in which the father was present. Thus, there is some evidence that those characteristics we possess that are unusual in our normal environments are particularly salient in our self-perceptions.

It also seems to be the case that in perceiving other people, as in self-perception, we attend most closely to the unusual and the distinctive. Further, this focusing of attention on the distinctive has consequences for how we interpret what we have seen. "Distinctive" may, in fact, be too strong a word. In observing other people, we often seem to attend merely to whatever or whoever is easiest to attend to—the closest person, the person with the loudest (clearest) voice, the person we can see most easily. Taylor and Fiske (1975; 1978) prefer the term "salient" to "distinctive," and argue that, all too often, we unthinkingly devote the lion's share of our attention to whatever or whomever happens to be the most salient stimulus in our environment....

Kanter (1977) defines a "token" as someone identified by ascribed characteristics such as race or sex, who carries with him or her a set of assumptions about status or likely behavior, and who is a member of a group in which all of the other members differ from the token on one such ascribed characteristic. Thus, a white in a group of blacks or a male in a group of females would be a token. In order to study the experiences of token women in ongoing social interaction, Kanter gained access to the sales division of a large industrial corporation, a division consisting of over 300 men and only 20 women. Further, since the sales division was geographically decentralized into a number of field offices, the skewed ratio of men to women in the sales force meant that each field office had only one female, or at most two, on the sales staff. Kanter spent hundreds of hours interviewing both male and female members of the sales division, observing their interactions in training groups, sitting in on their sales meetings, and participating in their informal social gatherings.

On the basis of her observations, Kanter argues that the proportional rarity of tokens in such groups is associated with three perceptual phenomena: (1) visibility—because of their differentness, tokens capture a larger share of attention; (2) polarization—the presence of the token, who has characteristics different from those of the other group members, makes the others more aware of their similarities to each other and their differentness from the token; and (3) assimilation—the token's attributes tend to be distorted to fit preexisting beliefs about the token's "social type." Each of these perceptual phenomena has consequences for the token. Visibility, for example, creates demanding performance pressures, because everything the token says or does is closely attended to. He or she cannot just slip into the shadows and relax. Polarization leads to an exaggeration of the dominant majority culture within the group and isolation of the token. Assimilation results in the token's being forced into limited roles within the group.

According to Kanter, the interaction dynamics accompanying the presence of a token in a group are heightened and dramatized when the token's social category is physically obvious. While it is true that such physically obvious stimuli as another's age, sex, or race do influence much of our social interaction, it seems to be the case that most of the discriminations we make among people are not based on physically obvious stimuli. We group people in many different ways—in terms of their intelligence, or friendliness, or arrogance, or modesty. We make such categorizations for our own convenience, of course, since they lessen the volume of information we have to retain. Once we categorize another person as, say, intelligent, we anticipate how he or she will react in certain future situations, even though we may never have seen him or her perform in similar situations. However, the very act of categorization may induce distortions in what we think we know about another person, distortions that may underlie what Kanter refers to as the polarization and assimilation processes that occur in groups with a token member of a race or sex different from that of the majority.

Categorization

The number of ways in which people are perceived to differ is enormous and, with the possible exception of sex, each of these individual differences varies along a continuous dimension. People are not, for example, simply intelligent or unintelligent, but vary in their degree of intelligence. We all know that. For convenience, however, we often break up these individual-difference dimensions into categories—such as "dumb," "average," and "smart." Transforming the gradual and continuous variations in intelligence into these three clear-cut categories makes life easier for us, in that it simplifies a tremendous amount of information and, for most everyday uses, such gross distinctions may suffice. The danger is that once we have classified two people or two groups into different categories, we may exaggerate the differences between them and ignore their similarities—or, conversely, once we have classified two people or two groups into the same category, we may exaggerate their similarities and ignore their differences....

One way to look at this question of whether categorization induces us to exaggerate intracategory similarities is in terms of confusion. That is, if we have categorized people on the basis of attribute A—say, sex or skin color—are we more likely to confuse their standings on some other characteristic or on some behavior? If we observe a group of three males and three females interacting, for example, and are later asked to recall who said what during the interaction, what sorts of errors are we likely to make? If we do not categorize people by sex, we should be as likely to err by attributing something that a female said to a male as to another female, and vice versa. However, if we do categorize by sex, then we should be more likely to err by attributing something that a female said to another female than to a male, and something that a male said to another male than to a female.

Taylor, Fiske, Etcoff, and Ruderman (1978) provide some evidence on this point. Harvard undergraduates were asked to listen to tape-recorded discussions in which either six men or three men and three women took part. A picture of each speaker was projected onto a wall as he or she spoke, and subjects who listened to the six men found that three were white and three were black. Following the tape-slide presentation, subjects were asked to identify the participants who had made each of a number of suggestions during the discussion. Subjects who had heard the six-man discussion were more likely to err by attributing suggestions made by blacks to other blacks and by attributing suggestions made by whites to other whites than they were to err by attributing suggestions made by blacks to whites or vice versa. That is, the errors in attribution were more often intraracial than interracial. Similarly, errors made by subjects who listened to the discussion carried on by three males and three females were more often intrasex than intersex. As Taylor et al. (1978, pp. 790–791) note, subjects do "indeed process information about social groups using race and sex as ways of categorizing the group members and organizing information about them.... As a result of the categorization process, within-group differences tended to be minimized, whereas between-group differences remained clearer."

To avoid this sort of intracategory confusion, Hayakawa (1963) suggests that we should develop the habit of indexing our ideas, particularly our abstractions and categorizations. That is, we should constantly remind ourselves that two items or people or events that we have placed in the same category are not, thereby, the same. When dealing with people, we may categorize two people as similar with respect to one or even a dozen attributes, but they may differ with respect to thousands of attributes and items of personal history, interests, attitudes, values, and plans for the future. The problem is that once we have categorized or labeled someone, we tend to reify the label, to treat the word as if it captures the true essence of all that person is, when in fact the label at best designates the person's standing on one of thousands of personal attributes. ...

The problem is that we know so much more about ourselves and others than the mere fact(s) of group membership. During the course of our experience with others, we learn to expect certain characteristics to co-occur. Having made a distinction between "us" and "them" on the basis of one characteristic, we may infer that "they" possess additional characteristics for which we have no evidence....

Explanations of Behavior

In perceiving another's behavior, we tend to simplify as time passes. We start out observing discrete actions marked off by noticeable changes in the features we happen to be monitoring, and gradually organize these discrete actions into larger units. Zadny and Gerard (1974) have found that attributing a purpose or intent to an actor allows us to organize a behavioral sequence into larger units, and that, having done so, we tend to pay attention only to those aspects of the other's behavior that are relevant to the attributed purpose. If we are correct about our attributed intention, the accuracy of perception of the other's behavior will, of course, be enhanced. If we make a mistake, however, and attribute the wrong intention, the selectivity of our subsequent perceptions will make it quite difficult for us to realize the error. Even when we are correct about what the person is trying to do, we are rarely satisfied to stop at this point. We usually want to know why the person has a particular intention, why he or she is doing whatever we have observerd.

Seeking the Causes of Behavior

Much of the research and theory on how we go about trying to pin down the cause of someone's behavior stems from the work of Heider (1958). The basic premise of Heider's work is that in order to understand the interpersonal world around us, we attempt to link the fleeting and variable interpersonal behaviors and events in which we find ourselves immersed to relatively unchanging underlying conditions or dispositional properties. According to Heider, any given behavior is dependent upon a combination of personal and situational forces. Further, the personal component can be broken down into ability and motivation. Heider's claim is that we tend to invoke these three general types of explanations (situation, ability, motivation), in varying degrees, whenever we want to understand why someone behaved in a particular way.

Building on Heider's basic premise, E. E. Jones and Davis (1965; also Jones, 1978) have developed a theory to explain some of the processes mediating the gap between observing someone perform a particular behavior and attributing a particular disposition to that person. The key to their conception is the idea that any given behavior represents a choice from among several that could have been performed, and that any effects of the behavior that are common to all of the alternatives could not be used to explain why the person behaved as he or she did. On the other hand, any consequences that are unique to a given behavior may provide some evidence on why the behavior was performed or why that particular course of action was chosen. Jones and Davis assume, as does Heider, that the more an act appears to be caused, or "called for," by the environment or situation, the less informative that act is about the person who performs it. Specifically, behaviors that are high in general social desirability, such as being polite, do not tell us much about a specific person because nearly everyone does these things....

Thus, attribution theory, as formulated by Heider, Jones and Davis, and Kelley, assumes that we behave in a fairly rational, scientific manner when we try to understand or explain why a person behaved as he or she did. There is evidence, as we have seen, that under certain conditions we are as rational as attribution theory postulates. In spite of such findings, it is one of the ironies of modern social psychology that the overwhelming message of research on attribution processes is that in seeking to understand and predict behavior, we often, even usually, do not behave in the rational, analytic manner postulated by attribution theory. For example, consider the distinction between an outcome that is determined by skill and one that is determined by chance. In principle, this distinction can be easily made. In skill situations one presumably can influence the outcome; in chance situations one cannot. This distinction is basic to attribution theory, because if we are going to explain why someone behaved in a particular way, we must be able to separate those outcomes that are due to the person's ability and motivation and those outcomes that are due to situational factors such as luck. According to Langer (1975), however, in our day-to-day experience this distinction is often blurred, if not totally ignored. People often act as if things that can influence only skill-related outcomes can also influence chance outcomes....

The Fundamental Attribution Error

When we observe someone's behavior, we observe that behavior in a context. Only in science fiction movies are we ever likely to see people behaving in a featureless environment, and then only for very brief periods—until they climb back into the spacecraft. Behavior usually occurs in complex, many-faceted situations, and quite often it is constrained by the situation in which it occurs. But, as noted before, we simply cannot take in and process all of the information available to us at any given time, and so we are likely to focus on the most salient aspects. When observing another person in a particular setting, the most salient aspect is likely to be the behavior of that person. Heider (1958) referred to this phenomenon as "behavior engulfing the field." Subsequent research has documented the fact that in making attributions about the causes of behavior, we often do give undue weight to what a person says or does, and too little attention to the conditions surrounding the person's behavior. The result is that we tend to see others' behavior as being due to their personal characteristics, to the sort of person they are; this is what L. Ross (1977) has termed the fundamental attribution error—that is, the tendency to underestimate the impact of situational factors in producing another's behavior and to overestimate the role of dispositional or personality factors.

The fundamental attribution error has been well documented in various areas. For example, E. E. Jones and Harris (1967) found that after having heard an unpopular attitude position being defended by another person, observers attributed belief in that position to the person, even when they knew the person had been assigned to defend the position by the debating team adviser. But the fundamental attribution error is not a mere laboratory phenomenon. It apparently plays a major role in our understanding of history, for example. As children we are told of the exploits of heroes and heroines. We learn of Caesar, Columbus, Florence Nightingale, and Robin Hood, but seldom are we told of the complex social circumstances surrounding these figures. As Carr (1961) puts it:

> It is easier to call Communism "the brainchild of Karl Marx" ... than to analyze its origin and character, to attribute the Bolshevik revolution to the stupidity of Nicholas II ... than to study its profound social causes, and to see in the two world wars of this century the result of the individual wickedness of Wilhelm II and Hitler rather than of some deep-seated breakdown in the system of international relations. [p. 57]

This does not mean, of course, that there are not great men and women who play crucial roles in various settings. It does mean that the perception of history is biased by what Boring (1963) referred to as the principle of "focus and margin." We focus on the most prominent and easily identifiable features, which are usually individual men and women, and we relegate to marginal status the elaborate and complex web of events surrounding those people. In short, we commit the fundamental attribution error.

In a similar manner the roles that we play in our day-to-day life may make us appear to have qualities and characteristics that we do not really possess. Interpersonal encounters are typically constrained by roles such as teacher–student, policeman–traffic offender, lecturer–audience. And, as L. D. Ross, Amabile, and Steinmetz (1977) point out:

> Roles confer unequal control over the style, content, and conduct of an encounter; such social control, in turn, generally facilitates displays of knowledge, skill, insight, wit, or sensitivity, while permitting the concealment of deficiencies. Accurate social judgment, accordingly, depends upon the perceiver's ability to make adequate allowance for such role-conferred advantages and disadvantages in self-presentation. [p. 485]

Again the point is that in forming an impression of another, we may not give sufficient weight to the situation in which we observe the other's behavior....

There are also motivational sources of bias in our perceptions of others— that is, sources of bias that stem from our needs to protect and enhance our self-esteem. The false consensus effect seems to be on the border between motivational and nonmotivational biases. It may be a function of the vested interest we have in preserving our view of what is appropriate, or it may be a selective exposure effect due to the fact most of our friends and associates are basically similar to us and, hence, are likely to respond as we do in any given situation....

Summary

We began this chapter by calling attention to the possibility that the existence of stereotypes may be in part a function of imperfections in the way we process information about others. In exploring that possibility we started by examining some data on how we perceive others' behaviors, and found that we do not passively take in information about behavior. Rather, we organize the observed behavior into meaningful segments. We also noted that the smaller the units we use, the more differentiated our impressions are likely to be, and under some conditions, the more likely we are to make dispositional attributions about the person we are observing. We also seem to attend more closely to the unusual, to that which is different.

This, of course, has implications for what we notice about ourselves and others. We saw that in groups, those members who are in the minority ("tokens") by virtue of some irrelevant, but highly visible, difference from the other group members are more constantly "visible" and, hence, under greater performance pressure. They also seem to produce polarization within the group and an exaggeration of the dominant majority culture. The token's own characteristics are likely to be distorted to fit preexisting beliefs about his or her "social type." The latter was seen to be an example of certain basic perceptual processes that accompany categorization—that is, we tend to exaggerate the similarities between objects or people placed in the same category, and to exaggerate the differences between objects or people placed in different categories.

Once we have categorized someone in a particular way, we often infer additional characteristics for which we have no evidence. Such inferences stem from our preexisting implicit theories of personality—the categories we employ to encode the various features and behaviors of others and the beliefs we hold concerning which of these categories tend to go together and which do not. We saw that our implicit theories influence how we encode another's behavior, and introduce a systematic distortion into what we remember about another's behavior. We are likely to "remember" that categories of behavior we believe to be associated both occurred, when in fact only one of them may have.

We usually are not satisfied with simple observation, however. We want to know why someone behaved as he or she did. We seek to explain behavior and, according to attribution theories, we do so in a relatively logical, rational manner. We seem to understand that behavior can be a function of ability, effort, situational factors, or any combination of these. We employ a covariation principle in our search for explanations—that is, we look for things that are present when the behavior is present and absent when the behavior is absent. Research on attribution processes, however, has found that we are not quite so rational as the theorists paint us. We confuse chance-determined and skill-determined outcomes. Once we know which of several possible outcomes did occur, we see it as being more inevitable than it really was. We are subject to the fundamental attribution error—that is, we tend to underestimate the power of situational constraints on behavior and to overestimate the role of dispositional factors. We are subject to a false consensus effect of seeing our own responses as typical and different responses as more revealing of the actor's personality quirks. We are also subject to egotism in explaining behavior. We give ourselves more credit for success and less blame for failure than we accord others. We apparently have a need to convince ourselves that we understand others when we anticipate having to interact with them, a need for effective control that again leads us to infer that we know more about them than we really do. . . .

References

Asch, S. E. "Forming Impressions of Personality," *Journal of Abnormal and Social Psychology* 41 (1946): 258–290.

Benedetti, D. T., and J. G. Hill. "A Determiner of the Centrality of a Trait in Impression Formation," *Journal of Abnormal and Social Psychology* 60 (1960): 278–280.

Boring, E. G. *History, Psychology, and Science.* New York: Wiley, 1963.

Briscoe, M. E., H. D. Woodyard, and M. E. Shaw. "Personality Impression Change as a Function of the Favorableness of First Impressions," *Journal of Personality* 35 (1967): 343–357.

Cantor, N. and W. Mischel. "Traits as Prototypes: Effects on Recognition Memory," *Journal of Personality and Social Psychology* 35 (1977): 38–48.

Carr, E. H. *What Is History?* New York: Vintage, 1961.

Cohen, C. E. "Cognitive Basis of Stereotyping." Paper presented at the 85th annual convention of the American Psychological Association, San Francisco, 1977.

Cohen, C. E. "Person Categories and Social Perception: Testing Some Boundaries of the Processing Effects of Prior Knowledge," *Journal of Personality and Social Psychology* 40 (1981): 441–452.

Dailey, C. A. "The Effects of Premature Conclusions upon the Acquisition of Understanding of a Person," *Journal of Psychology* 33 (1952): 133–152.

Darley, J. M., and R. H. Fazio. "Expectancy Confirmation Processes Arising in the Social Interaction Sequence," *American Psychologist* 35 (1980): 867–881.

Dion, K. K., E. Berscheid, and E. Walster. "What Is Beautiful Is Good," *Journal of Personality and Social Psychology* 24 (1972): 285–290.

Erdelyi, M. H. "A New Look at the New Look: Perceptual Defense and Vigilance," *Psychological Review* 81 (1974): 1–25.

Fischoff, B. "Hindsight/Foresight: The Effect of Outcome Knowledge on Judgment under Uncertainty," *Journal of Experimental Psychology: Human Perception and Performance* 1 (1975): 288–299.

Fishbein, M., and I. Ajzen. *Belief, Attitude, Intention and Behavior: An Introduction to Theory and Research*. Reading, Mass.: Addison-Wesley, 1975.

Hayakawa, S. I. *Symbol, Status, and Personality*. New York: Harcourt, Brace, & World, 1963.

Heider, F. *The Psychology of Interpersonal Relations*. New York: Wiley, 1958.

Jones, E. E. "Update of 'From Acts to Dispositions: The Attribution Process in Person Perception,'" in *Cognitive Theories in Social Psychology*, ed. L. Berkowitz. New York: Academic Press, 1978.

Jones, E. E., and K. E. Davis. "From Acts to Dispositions: The Attribution Process in Person Perception," in *Advances in Experimental Social Psychology*, vol. 2, ed. L. Berkowitz. New York: Academic Press, 1965.

Jones, E. E., and V. A. Harris "The Attribution of Attitudes," *Journal of Experimental Psychology* 63 (1966): 244–256.

Kanter, R. M. "Some Effects of Proportion on Group Life: Skewed Sex Ratios and Responses to Token Women," *American Journal of Sociology* 82 (1977): 965–990.

Kelley, H. H. "Attribution Theory in Social Psychology," in *Nebraska Symposium on Motivation*, vol. 15, ed. D. Levine. Lincoln: University of Nebraska Press, 1967.

Kelley, H. H. "The Processes of Causal Attribution," *American Psychologist* 28 (1973): 107–128.

Langer, E. J. "The Illusion of Control," *Journal of Personality and Social Psychology*, 32 (1975): 311–328.

McGuire, W. J., C. V. McGuire, P. Child, and T. Fujioka. "Salience of Ethnicity in the Spontaneous Self-Concept as a Function of One's Ethnic Distinctiveness in the Social Environment," *Journal of Personality and Social Psychology* 36 (1978): 511–520.

McGuire, W. J., C. V. McGuire, and W. Winton. "Effects of Household Sex Composition on the Salience of One's Gender in the Spontaneous Self-Concept," *Journal of Experimental Social Psychology* 15 (1979): 77–90.

Malpass, R. S., and J. Kravitz. "Recognition for Faces of Own and Other Race," *Journal of Personality and Social Psychology* 13 (1969): 330–334.

Newtson, D. "Attribution and the Unit of Perception of Ongoing Behavior," *Journal of Personality and Social Psychology* 28 (1973): 28–38.

Newtson, D. "Foundations of Attribution: The Perception of Ongoing Behavior," in *New Directions in Attribution Research*, vol. 1, ed. J. H. Harvey, W. J. Ickes, and R. F. Kidd. Hilsdale, N.J.: Erlbaum, 1976.

Newtson, D., G. Engquist, and J. Bois. "The Objective Basis of Behavior Units," *Journal of Personality and Social Psychology* 35 (1977): 847–863.

Nisbett, R., and L. Ross. *Human Inference: Strategies and Shortcomings of Social Judgment*. Englewood Cliffs, N.J.: Prentice-Hall, 1980.

Pyszczynski, T. A., and J. Greenberg. "Role of Disconfirmed Expectancies in the Instigation of Attributional Processing," *Journal of Personality and Social Psychology* 40 (1981): 31–38.

Rosenberg, S., and R. A. Jones. "A Method of Investigating and Representing a Person's Implicit Theory of Personality: Theodore Dreiser's View of People," *Journal of Personality and Social Psychology* 22 (1972): 372–386.

Ross, L. "The Intuitive Psychologist and His Shortcomings: Distortions in the Attribution

Process," in *Advances in Experimental Social Psychology*, vol. 10, ed. L. Berkowitz. New York: Academic Press, 1977.

Ross, L. D., T. M. Amabile, and J. L. Steinmetz. "Social Roles, Social Control, and Biases in Social-Perception Processes," *Journal of Personality and Social Psychology* 35 (1977): 485–494.

Rubin, J., F. Provenzano, and Z. Luria. "The Eye of the Beholder: Parent's Views on Sex of Newborns," *American Journal of Orthopsychiatry* 44 (1974): 512–519.

Rubovits, P. C., and M. L. Maehr. "Pygmalion Black and White," *Journal of Personality and Social Psychology*, 25 (1973): 210–218.

Snyder, M., E. D. Tanke, and E. Berscheid. "Social Perception and Interpersonal Behavior: On the Self-Fulfilling Nature of Social Stereotypes," *Journal of Personality and Social Psychology*, 35 (1977): 656–666.

Taylor, S. E., and S. T. Fiske. "Point of View and Perceptions of Causality," *Journal of Personality and Social Psychology*, 32 (1975): 439–445.

Taylor, S. E., and S. T. Fiske. "Salience, Attention, and Attribution: Top of the Head Phenomena," in *Advances in Experimental Social Psychology*, vol. 11, ed. L. Berkowitz, New York: Academic Press, 1978.

Taylor, S. E., S. T. Fiske, N. L. Etcoff, and A. J. Ruderman. "Categorical and Contextual Bases of Person Memory and Stereotyping," *Journal of Personality and Social Psychology* 36 (1978): 778–793.

Zadny, J., and H. B. Gerard. "Attributed Intentions and Informational Selectivity," *Journal of Experimental Social Psychology* 10 (1974): 34–52.

Review Questions

1. What's a stereotype?
2. If stereotyping is, as Jones suggests, part of the "normal" process of person perception, why should we try to control or avoid it?
3. What does it mean to say that we define *ourselves* in terms of our distinctive attributes?
4. Jones suggests that we learn to limit "intracategory confusion" by, in Hayakawa words, "indexing our ideas." What does it mean to "index our ideas"?
5. Attribution theory is based on the observation that one of the first things we normally do when we notice someone else is try to identify the _____ of their behavior.
6. What is the fundamental attribution error?

Probes

1. Without thinking about it, we often talk and act as if perception were a passive rather than an active process. For example, we may say—and believe—"I *couldn't* understand that teacher; he was too confusing." Give an example from your own experience where you or someone else has done this. In the example you cite, what active processes were being overlooked?
2. How do you respond to Jones's point that stereotyping is not a "disease" we can get over but is an inherent part of everyone's perceptual processes?
3. Recall a recent conflict you've experienced with a friend or family member. What role did your "segmenting" of the other person's behavior play in your perception of the conflict?
4. When have you been a "token"? Did the experience affect you as it did the people Jones discusses? How so?
5. Compare and contrast what Jones says about female "tokens" with Judy Pearson's discussion of gender differences in communication in Chapter 12.
6. The research Jones discusses by Taylor, Fiske, Etcoff, and Ruderman provides some evidence for part of what I say about uniqueness in Chapter 1. Discuss the link between these two points.
7. One of the basic differences between our perception of objects and our perception of people is that we perceive people as choosing to do what they do. Jones argues that we

overdo that process, that is, we underestimate the impact of situational factors on human behavior. Do you agree with Jones? Discuss.

8. How might you resist the tendency to "ignore new information" by relying on your categorizations? Be as specific as you can.

This article also discusses how we perceive others, but Paul Tournier's approach is significantly different from Russell Jones's. Tournier does not speak as a social scientist but as a psychiatrist. He emphasizes our tendency to perceive people as if they were mechanisms or objects which can, as he says, "be confined within concepts, formulae, and definitions."

You and I depersonalize people whenever we treat them as if they could adequately be described by our stereotypes or generalizations. Tournier explains how seeing others as persons instead of as things can mean a "complete revolution" for some. Although he takes examples from his experience as a counselor and doctor, his ideas apply to your communication and to mine too. When we stop seeing only what Tournier calls "personages," or objectified others, and start seeing "persons," all kinds of changes are likely to take place. We can see teacher-student communication differently. Communication with family members can change. As Tournier puts it, "the atmosphere of office, workshop, or laboratory" can be "rapidly transformed when personal fellowship is established."

It goes without saying that we can't communicate person to person *all* of the time. Sometimes external factors—time, rigid roles, ignorance, fear—prevent it. Some situations call for idea-centered more than person-centered contacts. But, Tournier says, we should learn to "answer idea with idea but answer the person with the person." That is, we should know the difference between communicating interpersonally and noninterpersonally so we can strive for the former whenever it is possible.

I apologize for the sexist sound of Tournier's language. He wrote this before we had been sensitized to the inappropriateness of using "his" and "he" to mean "persons."

The World of Things and the World of Persons

Paul Tournier

There are two worlds, or ways of looking at the world, of entering into relationship with it, depending on the spirit in which we approach it. We may see in it nothing but things, mechanisms, from those of physics to those of biology and even of psychology. Art, philosophy, religion can also become things, collections of concepts, formulae, definitions. On the other hand, one can lay oneself open to the world of persons, awaken to the sense of the person. By becoming oneself a person one discovers other persons round about, and one seeks to establish a personal bond with them.

The person always eludes our grasp; it is never static. It refuses to be confined within concepts, formulae, and definitions. It is not a thing to be encompassed, but a point of attraction, a guiding force, a direction, an attitude, which demands from us a corresponding attitude, which moves us to action and commits us. The world of things does not commit us. It is neutral, and leaves us neutral. We are cold, objective, impersonal observers, watching the operation of blind and inexorable mechanisms.

I am not claiming that we must shut our eyes to things, nor that we should cut ourselves off from intellectual objectivity, from the fascinating study of the ordinances and mechanisms of things. But I ask that we should not limit ourselves to the study of things, for they are only one half of the world, the static, impassible, unfeeling half. Even the heavenly bodies, moving with their unimaginable velocities, return in their orbits to the same position; this is the universal cycle of things, eternally starting again.

It is the person that has meaning, a birth and an end. The God of the philosophers is immutable; only the personal God has a purpose for history and for each being. To the scientist, man is but an episode in the universal dance of the atoms and the electrons. As the old French song says of the marionettes, "Three little turns, and off they go!" Off they go to dance elsewhere in a purposeless round.

From infant school to university we are taught to know things, to isolate them, identify them, count them, measure them and classify them. There is no need for me to dwell on the enormous development that has taken place over the centuries in this field, so that now specialization within the narrowest limits is the order of the day. This has not been without its effect on our minds. They are becoming incapable of perceiving what is not objective.

In this depersonalized state of mind man himself becomes a thing. Anatomy and physiology study his body as a thing, and psychology his mind as a thing, a mechanism. Economics studies him as a thing, an instrument of production and consumption, while sociology studies him as an element of society. He is a pawn on the chess-board of politics, a cog in industry, a learning-machine, everywhere a fraction of the mass.

... What I want to show now is how this unilateral view of the world and of man is completely upset by the awakening of the sense of the person.... When I turned from ecclesiastical activity to spiritual ministry, from technical to humane medicine, I was discovering the world of persons; I was discovering persons everywhere. Since that time, though I have not stopped being interested in things, I am much more passionately interested in persons.

I remember a visit paid to me by one of my former colleagues on the executive authority of the Church. I had fought him tooth and nail—that is to say, I had treated him as a thing, an adversary. The only thing about him that had mattered to me was his opinions, and the weight they might carry in the balance of our arguments. Ideas by themselves, detached from the person, are but things, abstractions, counters in the give and take of discussion.

And now here he was opening his heart to me. I too opened mine to him. He had come to talk to me about his personal life and his sufferings. I was making the discovery of his person, which I had never looked for before. I was so busy combating his ideas. I was discovering his person, his secrets, his solitude, his feelings. I even discovered that his ideas were not abstractions, but that they arose out of the sort of person he was, and protected his suffering like a shield. I talked with him about my own personal experiences, and realized that this former adversary had the same needs and the same difficulties as I, the same longing to find life and fellowship again. . . .

A man may spend years in an office, seeing in his employees only their work, their good qualities and their failings, and then, when personal contact is established, suddenly discover what lies behind the façade: the secret sufferings, the sequels of unhappy childhood, disappointed hopes, struggles to remain faithful to ideals. Then, too, he may understand the profound significance of the qualities and failings he has seen, and the meaning that work can have when it is no longer a thing but the activity of a community of persons.

It is as if a light had shown on life and shown it up in new colours. "We live," wrote Saint-Exupéry, "not on things, but on the meaning of things." The meaning of things is of the order of the person. When our eyes are open to the world of persons, things themselves become personal. It is just the reverse of the transformation of men into things of which we were speaking just now. Beasts, plants, and inanimate things take on the quality of persons. . . .

To become a person, to discover the world of persons, to acquire the sense of the person, to be more interested in people as persons than in their ideas, their party labels, their personage, means a complete revolution, changing the climate of our lives. Once adopted, it is an attitude which rapidly impregnates the whole of our lives. While at the Weissenstein conference I had occasion to congratulate one of my colleagues who had made an extremely good job of interpreting a talk I had given earlier in the day. "And do you know why?" he asked me. "It had been mentioned to me that one of our Scandinavian friends was finding it very troublesome following the speeches in foreign languages. So I interpreted for *him*; I never took my eyes off him, watching his face all the time to see if he had understood. And I found that through giving more attention to his person than to the ideas I was translating, I actually found it easier to express the ideas."

He had become an interpreter of the person, just as one can be a doctor of the person, or a teacher of the person, when one does not teach that impersonal thing, the class, but the persons of the pupils. In the same way, at a conference, one speaks quite differently if the audience is no longer an anonymous mass, if one seeks in it a few faces and exchanges glances with individuals, so that one's speech takes on the quality of a dialogue.

In the world of persons all one's professional relationships take on a new character. They become shot through with a joy that was absent when they were merely the fulfilling of a function. Everything becomes an occasion for personal contact, a chance to understand others and the personal factors which underlie their behavior, their reactions and opinions. It is much more interesting, as well as important, to understand why someone has a certain failing, than to be irritated by it; to understand why he maintains a certain point of view than to combat it; to listen to confidences than to judge by appearances.

The atmosphere of office, workshop, or laboratory is rapidly transformed when personal fellowship is established between those who previously criticized or ignored each other. In a recent lecture Professor F. Gonseth, professor of philosophy at the Zürich Polytechnic, the pioneer of the review *Dialectia*, spoke of the "law of dialogue" which he believes must govern the university of the future. By this phrase he means personal contact between teacher and student, so that the person is committed in the intellectual dialectic. The condition of this contact and commitment is that the teacher should not be so absorbed in his subject that he forgets all about the persons to whom he wishes to transmit it.

I was with some friends one day, and they were advising me to give more lectures and write less books, for, they said, in my writing they missed the personal accent of the spoken word. As you see, I am not following their advice. However precious one's friends are, one must not become their slave. Being a person means acting according to one's personal convictions, due regard of course being given to those of others. And my friends' observation is true. The living word remains the chief instrument of personal dialogue.

This is clearly seen in the case of those patients who send me beforehand—in writing—a long account of their lives. This is useful as information. But the point is that the purpose of a life-history is not so much to furnish information as to lead toward personal contact. Given by word of mouth it may be less intelligible, less systematic, but it is a method which calls for a much deeper commitment of the person.

I have my patients who write me letters after each consultation. They put in them the things they have not dared to say to my face. This has its value; it is for them a commitment, a way of forcing themselves to become more personal at the next consultation. But it is also a means of sparing themselves the intense emotion of a verbal explanation. It attenuates the dialogue, making it less direct because it uses a thing—paper—as an intermediary.

But even the spoken word itself can become a thing if it adopts the neutral and objective tone of information or discussion. Paradoxical though it may seem, the true dialogue is by no means a discussion. This is my answer to those of my colleagues who are perhaps afraid of not knowing what to reply to a patient who puts to them some moral problem that is on his conscience. It is important here to make a distinction between intellectual argument and personal encounter. Answer ideas with ideas, but answer the person with the person. Then often the heart's true response is silence.

Engaging in the dialogue, in the sense in which we understand it here, does not mean plunging into religious or philosophical theories about life, man, or God. The people who have helped me most are not those who have answered my confessions with advice, exhortation, or doctrine, but rather those who have listened to me in silence, and then told me of their own personal life, their own difficulties and experiences. It is this give and take that makes the dialogue.

If we answer with advice, exhortation, or theories, we are putting ourselves in a position of superiority, not equality. We are concerning ourselves with ideas, and not with the person, confining ourselves to the objective world of things, instead of entering the subjective world of persons. When someone lays bare to me the burning reality of his life, I am well aware that most of my replies could easily be only those of my personage....

The moment the personage reappears, with its system of thought and its claim to possess and express truth, our sincerest efforts to help others will finish by crushing and repressing them instead of liberating them. The dialogue between persons is replaced by a moralizing or proselytizing discussion. "Those who impose upon us their ready-made solutions," writes one of my patients, "those who impose upon us their science or their theology, are incapable of healing us."

You will see now how wide of the mark are those who describe the medicine of the person as "religious psychotherapy," in the belief that it consists in the indoctrination of the patient, denunciation of his failings, in moral uplift, or in exhorting him to accept his lot, and forcing him into confession and prayer. That indeed would be acting as a personage and not as a person. Then we should really be in danger of usurping the place of the minister of religion, and attempting to perform a function which is not proper to us.

The medicine of the person demands unconditional respect for the person of others. That does not mean putting one's own flag in one's pocket, but rather that we must state our convictions in a way that is truly personal, not theoretical, having at the same time a sincere regard for the convictions of others. In this way dialogue becomes possible where previously it has been shipwrecked on the rocks of religious, philosophical, political, or social prejudice. . . .

Review Questions

1. According to Tournier, what specifically is it about persons that forces us, if we want to perceive them accurately, not to treat them as things?
2. What does it mean to say that "We live not on things, but on the meaning of things"?
3. How broadly does Tournier say these ideas can be applied? Are they restricted to religious and other spiritual contexts?
4. Paraphrase this statement by Tournier: "But even the spoken word itself can become a thing if it adopts the neutral and objective tone of information or discussion."
5. What relationship does Tournier suggest between imposing and healing?

Probes

1. Do you think that Tournier's view is "anti-intellectual"? Is he saying, in effect, that we should feel our way into a relationship rather than think our way into it?
2. Would it be a revolutionary change for you to begin to look at the world as a world of persons rather than of things? How would your communication change?

I don't want to argue any more about how he "is." You see him one way, I see him another way, he sees himself a third way. Now if you want to talk about what how we see him indicates about us . . .

HUGH PRATHER

Chapter 7

Listening

I am afraid of your silence because of what it could mean. I suspect your silence of meaning you are getting bored or losing interest or making up your own mind about me without my guidance. I believe that as long as I keep you talking I can know what you are thinking. But silence can also mean confidence. And mutual respect. Silence can mean live and let live: the appreciation that I am I and you are you. The silence is an affirmation that we are already together—as two people. Words can mean that I want to make you into a friend and silence can mean that I accept your already being one.

HUGH PRATHER

A s the authors of this reading point out, most treatments of listening begin by arguing for the importance of good listening and then try to convince you that you're probably not an effective listener. But if you're studying listening, chances are you already know it's important and believe you could do it better. So rather than telling you what you already know, these authors begin their book on listening by discussing three misconceptions people commonly have about the listening process. Their idea is that it will be easier to improve your listening if you begin with an accurate rather than a distorted understanding of what's involved.

The first misconception is that listening is natural. The authors explain that hearing is the natural process, and that listening takes some thought, training, and effort. I've always believed that one of the most ironic things about listening is that, according to several surveys, we spend much more time listening than we spend reading, writing, or speaking, but we get almost no organized training in listening. So we are taught the least about the communication activity we engage in the most! Roach and Wyatt discuss this phenomenon.

The second misconception they discuss is the belief that listening is a passive act, a process of simply being open to what's available. This misconception exists primarily because we associate "work" with *visible* effort, and the effort you invest in listening is sometimes not very visible. But *every* person who listens for a living—therapist, lawyer, doctor, accountant, business consultant—has personally experienced the crushing fatigue that can come from working hard at listening.

The third misconception is that "I'm a good listener when I try." Some early listening research indicated that the average white-collar worker remembers about 25 percent of what he or she hears. So most of us start with a pretty low efficiency rate. Raw effort can improve that number, but not very permanently. It's most effective to get some listening training aimed at both attitudes and skills and then to practice what you learn long enough to make it habitual.

My primary purpose for including this brief reading is to set up the more developed articles that follow. If you're well informed about misconceptions, you'll be prepared to take on some new understandings and skills.

Listening and the Rhetorical Process

Carol A. Roach and Nancy J. Wyatt

Most texts on listening begin by establishing that listening skills are important to you in school, on the job, and in your personal relationships. Then they go on to convince you that you're not a very good listener. While these two observations may be true, we believe that you already know you could benefit by improving your listening skills or you wouldn't be taking this course. We will not, therefore, bore you by telling you what you already know. Instead, we will introduce you to some common misconceptions about listening and refute those misconceptions. . . .

Misconception Number One: Listening Is Natural

The misconception that listening is natural arises partly because we confuse the process of listening with the process of hearing. Hearing is certainly a natural process. Unless you have organic damage to some part of your ear, you will have been hearing since before you were born. Hearing is a matter of perception of small changes in atmospheric pressure, which goes on continuously, even when you are sleeping. How else would the alarm wake you in the morning? . . .

Humans can "hear" changes in air pressure in an effective range of frequencies from 20 to 20,000 cycles per second. Changes in air pressure impact the eardrum and are transmitted through the middle ear to the inner ear, where they are transformed into electrochemical messages and sent to the hearing center in the brain. That process is natural and automatic and outside conscious control. Problems start when we confuse this purely automatic physical process with the consciously purposeful psychological process of listening.

Listening is largely a process of discriminating and identifying which sounds are meaningful or important to us and which aren't. We actually focus our hearing in the same way we focus our sight. You can probably remember a time when you didn't "see" something that was in plain sight. Maybe you even fell over it. You have probably also had the experience of talking to someone—a parent, a teacher, a colleague, even a friend—who was thinking about something else and didn't "hear" what you said. In fact, they did hear in the sense that the sounds reached their ears, but they didn't hear what you said because they were paying attention to something else at the time. If you're sufficiently candid, you may also remember some times when you didn't hear something that was said to you because you weren't paying attention. We are all guilty of thinking about other things sometimes. The point is, you did hear, but you weren't listening.

> "Excuse me, Dr. Simpson, I'm having trouble thinking of a good attention getter for my speech."
> "What's your topic?"
> "I'm talking about Cambodia and the Khmer Rouge, all that killing."
> "In that case why don't you use the technique I just illustrated in class, the one from the acid rain speech?"
> "I didn't hear that one. I guess I wasn't listening."

The importance of distinguishing between hearing and listening is that we don't need training to hear well, but we do need training to listen well. In fact, if the hearing mechanism is damaged, no amount of training will improve its function. Real deafness can't be cured by trying harder. Faulty listening, on the other hand, can't be cured by medical science or by magic. To learn to listen more effectively, you have to try harder. You have to learn how to listen.

The idea that we learn to listen as children is partially true. Before they start to school, children learn many things by listening. But they only learn as well as they were trained. Unfortunately most of the training children receive in listening skills comes largely in the form of injunctions. "Now, you listen to me!" they are told, or "Listen carefully!" The usefulness of such training can be illustrated by comparing it to a similar injunction to a child to "Catch the ball!" Not very useful advice. It's more useful to show children how to hold their hands and tell them to keep their eyes on the ball. Then give them plenty of supervised practice and explain to them what they are doing right and what they're doing wrong, so they can improve. Without supervised practice, children can pick up bad habits of listening which serve them indifferently as they grow up. Learning to listen is a matter of training; it doesn't come naturally any more than playing ball does.

In one very interesting study, Nichols and Stevens (1957) found evidence that younger children listen better than older children. When the researchers stopped teachers in the middle of lectures and asked the students what the teachers were talking about, they found that 90 percent of the first graders could answer correctly, 80 percent of the second graders could answer correctly, but only 28 percent of the senior high school students could answer correctly. These results might even lead us to believe that we become worse listeners as we grow up. Far from being a natural process, listening is clearly a consciously purposive activity for which we need systematic training and supervision to learn to do well.

Another way to look at listening is as one part of the communication process, like speaking. While we could agree that speaking is a natural human function, no one could deny that children have to be taught how to speak. Certainly no one was born speaking standard English. If you have forgotten the process of learning to speak, spend a couple of hours in a supermarket listening to mothers talk to toddlers as they shop. You will hear careful and constant instruction, reiteration, correction, and reinforcement of correct language patterns and usage. Or, if you have studied a second language, remember how much time you had to spend memorizing, listening, and practicing to become fluent.

Listening and speaking are both consciously purposive activities for which we need training to do well. The idea that some people are born listeners or born speakers is a fiction. It's a copout for people who don't want to try harder.

Misconception Number Two: Listening Is Passive

One of the most common misconceptions we have in our American way of life is the idea that work is always active. We seem to think that if we don't "see" something happening, work is not being done. So thinking is not often defined as work. Children are encouraged to "do something"—join the Little League, scouts, clubs. They are enrolled in camps, dancing lessons, junior business associations, and extracurricular activities. Students are encouraged to "get involved"—join the students' government, join a club or fraternity or association, contribute time to charities, and attend social events. Time spent "doing nothing" is assumed to be time wasted. In businesses and corporations people spend much of their working day going to meetings, having lunch, traveling, doing anything to look busy. Employees learn very quickly how to "look busy" when the boss comes around, even though no specific action is required at the moment. Also, scholars, whose business is thinking, have to list specific activities to their administrators to prove they really are working. In our culture, movement is equated with work.

This American orientation toward a definition of work with visible activity leads us to view listening as passive. After all, you can't see anyone listening, so they must not be "doing" anything. What we have done instead is to define the visible signs of listening as the activity itself. You will understand this statement if you think back to when you were in high school. Think about the most boring class you had in high school. You didn't want to be caught daydreaming, so what did you do? You perfected the "student's stare." You put your chin in your hand, opened your eyes real wide, and nodded periodically as though you were agreeing with what was being said. If you were clever, you remembered to throw in a frown once in a while to show you were trying to understand something particularly difficult. You smiled occasionally to show you were glad to have something so interesting to listen to in school. Meanwhile your mind went on vacation. It worked perfectly. You had learned that activity equates with work.

> When I began teaching I learned very quickly that I couldn't tell by looking who was listening and who wasn't. I had one student who always sat in the back, tilted his chair against the wall, and seemed to go to sleep. Finally one day I got fed up and challenged him. I told him that if he only meant to sleep, he could do it at home on his own time. He sat up, pushed his hat back, and recited to me the last ten minutes of my lecture. Boy, was I embarrassed.

One consequence of defining listening by its visible signs is to deny the active nature of real listening. When you are listening, your mind is extremely busy receiving and sorting out new ideas and relating them to what you already know and making new connections with old information. Real listening involves taking in new information and checking it against what you already know, selecting important ideas from unimportant ideas, searching for categories to store the information in (or creating new categories), and predicting what's coming next in order to be ready for it. The explanation of hearing and listening in the next chapter will help to make the active nature of listening clearer. When you're listening, your brain is busy actively reconstructing what the speaker is saying into meaningful units in terms of your own experience. But all this activity takes place in your brain; none of it necessarily shows itself outwardly. So it often looks like nothing is being done.

> One of the things I found most frustrating about working in a group was that no one ever seemed to be listening to me. It was like I was always talking to myself. But then when it came time to prepare the final report, I discovered that the other group members knew a lot of the things I had been talking about. I was surprised to find out they had been listening after all. Especially John. I had thought he was a total deadhead.

Misconception Number Three: I'm a Good Listener When I Try

Most people vastly overestimate their own listening skills. One clever educator illustrates this to people who take his workshop on listening skills by having each person introduce herself to the class. Then he asks each of them to name the person who is sitting to her left. Most people can't do it.

If you ask most people what their listening efficiency is, they will tell you that they remember about 75 to 80 percent of what they hear. Most people think they are good listeners. Research findings directly contradict this perception. The research finding most often cited to illustrate this poor listening efficiency comes from the work of Nichols (1957) who found that the average white-collar worker demonstrates only about 25 percent listening efficiency. This means that the average person only remembers about one-quarter of what he or she hears. Both these percentages are in comparison to the ideal of 100 percent recall, a feat only accomplished by fictional detectives and a few unusual persons who have perfect auditory recall (like some people have photographic memories).

The real test of listening skills is, of course, not what you can do on a listening test, but how well you understand and remember the things you have to understand and remember to get along in your daily life. When the television news broadcast is over, how much of what you heard do you remember? Can you pick out the main points when someone is giving a speech? Can you understand and remember oral instructions? How good are you at discovering people's feelings when they are talking to you? Can you distinguish between a genuinely good business deal and a scam? Can you pick out the arguments and evidence in a political speech? Can you pick out the different instruments in a band or identify the theme of a symphony? All these tasks are related to your ability to listen effectively, and skill at these tasks is important to your welfare. But most people are only partially successful at any of these tasks.

The fact is that most of us would like to think we are better listeners (more intelligent, more sensitive, more beautiful) than we really are. Listening is hard work, and we don't apply ourselves to the task unless there is a clear payoff. But unless we practice and sharpen our listening skills and develop good listening habits, it may be too late when opportunity knocks. When you're in the middle of a business deal or in the middle of a physics lecture is not the time to start practicing listening skills.

References and Recommended Reading

Barbara, Dominick A. *How to Make People Listen to You.* Springfield, Ill.: Charles C. Thomas, 1971.

Barker, Larry L. *Listening Behavior.* Englewood Cliffs, N.J.: Prentice-Hall, 1971.

Hirsh, Robert O. *Listening: A Way to Process Information Aurally.* Dubuque, Iowa: Corsuch Scarisbrich, 1979.

Nichols, Ralph G. "Factors in Listening Comprehension." *Speech Monographs* 15 (1948): 154–163.

Nichols, Ralph G., and Leonard A. Stevens. *Are You Listening?* New York: McGraw-Hill, 1957, pp. 12–13.

Phillips, Gerald M., and Julia T. Wood. *Communication and Human Relations.* New York: Macmillan, 1983.

Steil, Lyman, Larry L. Barker, and Kittie W. Watson. *Effective Listening.* Reading, Mass. Addison-Wesley, 1983.

Wolff, Florence I., Nadine C. Marsnik, William S. Tracy, and Ralph G. Nichols. *Perceptive Listening.* New York: Holt, Rinehart and Winston, 1983.

Review Questions

1. What are the primary differences between hearing and listening?
2. What kind of listening training do we typically get as young children?

3. How is our attitude about listening affected by the typically North American belief that "movement is equated with work"?
4. What do your lecture notes say about your listening efficiency? Do they indicate that you're retaining more or less than 25 percent of what you hear in class?

Probes

1. Assume for a minute that human activities can be divided into the *physiological* (nerve impulses, skin reactions to chemicals, bleeding, etc.), *psychological* (attitudes, beliefs, fears, etc.), and *communicative* (involving coordination with at least one other person). Which type or types of activity are involved in *hearing*? Which ones characterize *listening*?
2. How would you describe some of the "invisible" activities that are involved in effective listening? What specifically is going on that can't be seen?
3. Think about your own listening efficiency. Do you remember more than 25 percent of what you hear in class? At a party? Around the dinner table at home? When talking to your boss at work? In the past, what factors have increased or decreased your listening efficiency?

 ach time I've searched the books and magazines for materials for earlier editions of *Bridges Not Walls*, I've had trouble finding a clear, fairly brief discussion that covers a broad range of listening topics, approaches its subject from a relational and nontechnical point of view, and includes some specific suggestions about how to do it better. This reading by Robert Bolton covers all those bases quite well. Bolton is the president of a communication consulting firm, and this material comes from his book *People Skills*, where he discusses how to assert yourself, listen, and resolve conflicts.

In the first section of this chapter Bolton introduces his topic by pointing out that we listen more than we do *anything* else, yet (1) most of us listen very poorly, partly because (2) we're never taught otherwise. Instead of listening, schools teach reading, writing, and some speaking, and at home many of us learn directly or indirectly to "pretend you don't notice" and to tune out or interrupt rather than listening effectively.

Bolton's alternative to this approach begins by distinguishing the physiological process of *hearing*—receiving sound waves—from the complex psychological and communicative process of *listening*—hearing plus interpreting, understanding, and checking your perceptions. Then he breaks the process down into three clusters of listening skills: Attending, Following, and Reflecting. I've reprinted his discussions of the attending and following skill clusters and some of his important introductory ideas about the skills of Reflecting or perception checking. There's more about the third skill cluster in the "Dialogic Listening" discussion by Milt Thomas and me later in this chapter.

One of the strong points of Bolton's essay is his discussion of *attending*. When you think about it, it's kind of obvious that you can't listen without *focusing* on the other person, but we often take this important fact too much for granted. Bolton emphasizes the point that, "What a person wants most of all from a listener" is that "the listener really be there for him" or her, and that without this kind of presence "no attending technique will work." I count nine specific suggestions about how to translate your intent-to-be-present into action: lean toward the speaker, face her squarely, maintain an open posture, position yourself at an appropriate distance, let your body "be moved by

the talker," avoid distracting motions, have good eye contact, cut environmental distractions, and minimize physical barriers. Bolton also notes that although most people
already know how to attend, focusing on attending communication motivates us to do
more often what we "know" but often neglect. At the end of the section he has some
useful things to say about how we can work hard to improve and still "act naturally."

In his discussion of *following* skills, Bolton continues to make helpfully explicit
several communication behaviors that are usually left undiscussed. The first *following*
skill is called a "door opener," and Bolton notes how some of our most well-meaning
responses—reassuring and advice-giving—often function to *close* the conversation door
rather than to facilitate talk. He identifies the four elements of door openers and gives
several examples of how they can work. "Minimal encourages" is Bolton's term for
another skill you already have but may not always use. "Mm-hmm," "Then?" "Really,"
"Tell me more" are all simple but effective ways to follow effectively. Bolton's discussion of questions emphasizes the importance of open rather than closed questions and
the wisdom of asking fewer questions. As he notes in the final part of this section, the
silence that can come when you rely less on questions can actually improve the quality
of your listening. In his words, "Most listeners talk too much."

If you listen thoroughly to what Bolton says here, I think you'll have laid a good
foundation for the rest of the readings in this chapter.

Listening Is More Than Merely Hearing

Robert Bolton

The Importance of Listening

If you are at all typical, *listening takes up more of your waking hours than any
other activity.* A study of persons of varied occupational backgrounds showed that
70 percent of their waking moments were spent in communication. And of that
time, writing took 9 percent, reading absorbed 16 percent, talking accounted for
30 percent, and listening occupied 45 percent.[1] Other surveys underscore the large
amount of time that people in different walks of life spend in listening.[2] It is important to listen effectively because of the sheer amount of it that you do each day.

Furthermore, many of the most important facets of your life are greatly influenced by your skills (or lack of skill) in listening. The quality of your friendships,
the cohesiveness of your family relationships, your effectiveness at work—these
hinge, in large measure, on your ability to listen.

From *People Skills* by Robert Bolton, pp. 30–48. Copyright © 1979 by Simon & Schuster, Inc. Reprinted
by permission of Simon & Schuster, Inc.

Unfortunately, few people are good listeners. Even at the purely informational level, researchers claim that 75 percent of oral communication is ignored, misunderstood, or quickly forgotten. Rarer still is the ability to listen for the deepest meanings in what people say. How devastating, but how common, to talk with someone about subjects of intense interest to oneself only to experience the stifling realization that the other person was not really listening and that his responses were simply automatic and mechanical. Perhaps it was after an experience like this that Jesus was quoted as saying, "Thou hearest in thy one ear but the other Thou has closed."[3]

Dr. Ralph G. Nichols, who developed innovative classes on listening at the University of Minnesota, writes:

> It can be stated with practically no qualification that people in general do not know how to listen. They have ears that hear very well, but seldom have they acquired the necessary ... skills which would allow those ears to be used effectively for what is called *listening*.... For several years, we have been testing the ability of people to understand and remember what they hear.... These extensive tests led to this general conclusion: immediately after the average person has listened to someone talk, he remembers only about half of what he has heard—no matter how carefully he thought he was listening. What happens as time passes? Our own testing shows ... that ... we tend to forget from one-half to one-third {more} *within eight hours*....[4]

All too often the speaker's words go "in one ear and out the other."

A major reason for the poor listening in our society is that most of us receive a very rigorous early training in nonlistening. The therapist Franklin Ernst says that "from the earliest years of life, a person's listening activity is the most heavily trained of all activities.... The person's listening ... is more attended to than his bowel training, his bladder activity, or his genital activity."[5] Ernst points out that the typical child, in his most impressionable years, receives a steady diet of antilistening edicts. Parents say things like:

"We don't listen to those things in our family."
"Don't pay any attention to him."
"Pretend you don't notice."
"Don't take it so seriously."
"He didn't mean what he said."
"Don't give them the satisfaction of knowing that you heard them" (and that it bothers you).

The typical parent not only verbalizes these antilistening comments, he demonstrates them daily in his own life. He is inattentive to persons speaking to him, may interrupt frequently, and responds with numerous roadblocks. By word and deed we are taught to be nonlisteners in our childhood.

Our schooling also conspires against the development of effective listening skills. About six years of training is given to reading in most school systems; additional opportunities are often available for remedial reading and speed reading. In the vast majority of schools, however, there are no effective training programs for developing listening skills. This makes little sense in a society where the graduated student will have to spend at least three times as much time listening as he spends reading.

Rather than receiving training in effective listening, the student in a typical school receives further antilistening training. Like his parents, most of his teachers will not be good listeners. They, too, will demonstrate inattentiveness, interruptions, and the use of many roadblocks throughout the school day. Furthermore, the typical classroom is structured for a larger ratio of listening time to talking time than the human being is capable of achieving. Some experts say that we can only listen effectively from one-third to two-thirds of the time. Whatever the specific ratio, each of us can recognize that when we listen for a long time without doing any talking or responding, our listening efficiency begins to drop drastically and finally our minds drift off to considering other topics than those about which the speaker is talking. Because the student cannot possibly listen effectively to all the talking to which school subjects him, he learns to turn off his mind when other people are speaking. This problem is compounded by the repetitions and boring nature of much teacher talk.

Most of us have been trained to be poor listeners, yet ironically, we spend more time listening than doing anything else, and the quality of our listening greatly affects both the personal and the vocational dimensions of our lives. The remainder of this chapter is devoted to defining *listening*, outlining the major clusters of listening skills, and teaching the more elementary of the listening skills.

Listening Defined

It is helpful to note the distinction between *hearing* and *listening*. "Hearing," says Professor John Drakeford, "is a word used to describe the physiological sensory processes by which auditory sensations are received by the ears and transmitted to the brain. *Listening*, on the other hand, refers to a more complex psychological procedure involving interpreting and understanding the significance of the sensory experience."[6] In other words, I can hear what another person is saying without really listening to him. A teenager put it this way: "My friends listen to what I say, but my parents only hear me talk."

I recall a time when I was talking with someone who seemed to ignore everything I said. "You are not listening to me!" I accused. "Oh, yes I am!" he said. He then repeated word for word what I had told him. He *heard* exactly. But he wasn't *listening*. He didn't understand the meanings I was trying to convey. Perhaps you have had a similar experience and know how frustrating it can be to be heard accurately by someone who isn't listening with understanding.

The distinction between merely hearing and really listening is deeply embedded in our language. The word *listen* is derived from two Anglo-Saxon words. One word is *hlystan*, which means "hearing." The other is *hlosnian*, which means "to wait in suspense." Listening, then, is the *combination* of hearing what the other person says *and* a suspenseful waiting, an intense psychological involvement with the other.

Listening Skill Clusters

Learning to be an effective listener is a difficult task for many people. Our approach simplifies the learning process by focusing on single skills or small clusters of skills so people can concentrate on one skill or one cluster at a time.

Focusing on a single skill when necessary, and on small clusters of skills when possible, enables people to learn most efficiently. This approach helps the reader master one cluster of skills, see himself readily improve in that area, and then move to a more advanced set of skills. When each of the separate listening skill clusters has been learned, the reader can integrate the various skills into a sensitive and unified way of listening.

The clusters of listening skills ... include:

Skill Clusters	Specific Skills
Attending Skills	• A Posture of Involvement
	• Appropriate Body Motion
	• Eye Contact
	• Nondistracting Environment
Following Skills	• Door Openers
	• Minimal Encourages
	• Infrequent Questions
	• Attentive Silence
Reflecting Skills	• Paraphrasing
	• Reflecting Feelings
	• Reflecting Meanings (Tying Feelings to Content)
	• Summative Reflections

Attending Skills

Attending is giving your physical attention to another person. I sometimes refer to it as listening with the whole body. Attending is nonverbal communication that indicates that you are paying careful attention to the person who is talking. Attending skills include a posture of involvement, appropriate body motion, eye contact, and a nondistracting environment.

The Impact of Attending and Nonattending

Effective attending works wonders in human relations. It shows the other that you are interested in him and in what he has to say. It facilitates the expression of the most important matters on his mind and in his heart. Nonattending, on the other hand, tends to thwart the speaker's expression.

Allen Ivey and John Hinkle describe the results of attending in a college psychology course. They trained six students in attending behavior. Then a session, taught by a visiting professor, was videotaped. The students started out in typical student nonattending classroom behaviors. The professor lectured, unaware of the students' prearranged plan. His presentation was centered on his notes. He used no gestures, spoke in a monotone, and paid little attention to the students. At a prearranged signal, however, the students began deliberately to physically attend. Within a half a minute, the lecturer gestured for the first time, his verbal rate increased, and a lively classroom session was born. Simple attending had changed the whole picture. At another signal, the students stopped attending, and the speaker, after awkwardly seeking continued response, resumed the unengaging lecture with which he began the class.[7]

It is an impressive experience to talk to a person who is directly and totally there for you. Norman Rockwell, the artist famed for his *Saturday Evening Post* covers, recounted his experience while painting a portrait of President Eisenhower:

> The general and I didn't discuss politics or the campaign. Mostly we talked about painting and fishing. But what I remember most about the hour and a half I spent with him was the way he gave me all his attention. He was listening to me and talking to me, just as if he hadn't a care in the world, hadn't been through the trials of a political convention, wasn't on the brink of a presidential campaign.[8]

Attending is often one of the most effective behaviors we can offer when listening to someone.

A Posture of Involvement

Because body language often speaks louder than words, a "posture of involvement" is extremely important in listening. In their book *Human Territories: How We Behave in Space-Time,* Drs. Albert Scheflen and Norman Ashcroft note, "Each region of the body can be oriented in such a way that it invites, facilitates, or holds an interpersonal relation. Or it can be oriented in order to break off, discourage, or avoid involvement."[9] Communication tends to be fostered when the listener demonstrates a relaxed alertness with the body leaning slightly forward, facing the other squarely, maintaining an "open" position and situating himself at an appropriate distance from the speaker.

The good listener communicates attentiveness through the *relaxed alertness* of his body during the conversation. What is sought is a balance between the relaxedness that communicates "I feel at home with you and accept you" and the alertness or productive tension that demonstrates "I sense the importance of what you are telling me and am very intent on understanding you." The blending of both of these body messages creates an effective listening presence.

Inclining one's body toward the speaker communicates more energy and attention than does leaning back or sprawling in the chair. When a public speaker has his audience enthralled, we say, "He has them on the edge of their seats." The people are not only leaning forward, but are sitting forward in their chairs. By contrast, some listeners slouch back in their chairs looking like propped-up cadavers. How demotivating that posture is to the speaker!

Facing the other squarely, your right shoulder to the other's left shoulder, helps communicate your involvement. The common phrase "He gave me the cold shoulder" suggests the indifference or rejection that can be communicated by not positioning yourself to face the other person. Because homes and offices are seldom arranged for good attending, you may have to rearrange some furniture to be able to position yourself properly.

Another aspect of facing the other squarely is to be at eye level with the speaker. This is especially important if you are an authority figure—a parent, teacher, or boss—of the speaker. Sitting on the edge of a desk when the other is in a chair or standing when he is sitting can be a major barrier to interpersonal contact. Parents of young children often comment on how important this aspect of attending is in their homes.

Maintaining an open position with arms and legs uncrossed is another important part of the posture of involvement. Tightly crossed arms or legs often communicate closedness and defensiveness. Baseball fans know what to expect when an umpire makes a call that is disputed by a team manager. The manager runs toward the umpire shouting and waving his arms. The umpire typically crosses his arms in a gesture of defensiveness, communicating that he will not budge from his position and that any argument will be fruitless. The very young do this same thing: they commonly cross their arms when defying their parents, indicating a psychological closedness to their parents' comments.

Positioning yourself at an appropriate distance from the speaker is an important aspect of attending. Too much distance between persons impedes communication. C. L. Lassen studied the effect of physical proximity in initial psychiatric interviews. The psychiatrists sat either three, six, or nine feet away from their clients. The clients' anxiety levels were measured, both by observable behaviors and through the clients' self-reports. Lassen discovered that a client's anxiety increased as the distance between himself and the psychiatrist increased.[10]

On the other hand, when a listener gets too close to another person, anxiety also increases. Some psychologists have demonstrated that the typical American feels uneasy when someone with whom he is not intimate positions himself closer than three feet for an extended time. Long periods of close physical proximity during a conversation can cause discomfort even when the persons are spouses or close friends. Cultural differences affect the optimal distance for conversing, as do individual differences within a given culture. The distance between yourself and another person that most facilitates communication can be discovered by watching for signs of anxiety and discomfort in the speaker and positioning yourself accordingly. Normally, about three feet is a comfortable distance in our society.

Appropriate Body Motion

Appropriate body movement is essential to good listening. In his book *Who's Listening?*, psychiatrist Franklin Ernst, Jr., writes:

> To listen is to move. To listen is to be moved by the talker—physically and psychologically.... The non-moving, unblinking person can reliably be estimated to be a non-listener.... When other visible moving has ceased and the eyeblink rate has fallen to less than once in six seconds, listening for practical purposes, has stopped.[11]

One study of nonverbal listener behavior noted that the listener who remains still is seen as controlled, cold, aloof, and reserved. By contrast, the listener who is more active—but not in a fitful or nervous way—is experienced as friendly, warm, casual, and as not acting in a role. People prefer speaking to listeners whose bodies are not rigid and unmoving.[12] When watching videotapes of effective listeners, I discovered that they tend to have a rhythm of less activity when the speaker is talking and somewhat more activity when they are responding. Occasionally, the listener becomes so in tune with the speaker that his gestures synchronize with the speaker's.

The avoidance of distracting motions and gestures is also essential for effective attending. The good listener moves his body in *response* to the speaker. Ineffective listeners move their bodies in response to stimuli that are unrelated to the talker. Their distraction is demonstrated by their body language: fiddling with pencils or keys, jingling money, fidgeting nervously, drumming fingers, cracking knuckles, frequently shifting weight or crossing and uncrossing the legs, swinging a crossed leg up and down, and other nervous mannerisms. Watching a TV program, waving or nodding one's head to people passing by, continuing with one's activities, like preparing a meal, or reading the paper can be very distracting when someone is talking to you.

Eye Contact

Effective eye contact expresses interest and a desire to listen. It involves focusing one's eyes softly on the speaker and occasionally shifting the gaze from his face to other parts of the body, to a gesturing hand, for example, and then back to the face and then to eye contact once again. Poor eye contact occurs when a listener repeatedly looks away from the speaker, stares at him constantly or blankly, or looks away as soon as the speaker looks at the listener.

Eye contact enables the speaker to appraise your receptiveness to him and his message. It helps him figure out how safe he is with you. Equally important, you can "hear" the speaker's deeper meanings through eye contact. Indeed, if effective listening means getting inside the other's skin and understanding the person's experience from his perspective, one of the best ways to enter that inner world is through the "window" of the eyes. Ralph Waldo Emerson said, "The eyes of men converse as much as their tongues, but with the advantage that the ocular dialect needs no dictionary, but is understood the world over."[13]

Many people have a difficult time establishing eye contact. Just as some people have a hard time knowing what to do with their hands in social interactions, other people do not know what to do with their eyes. People sometimes look away from another's face at the moment they sense he will show emotion on his face. Part of the reason for that behavior may be a desire not to be intrusive or embarrass the other.[14] (As we will see later, however, the effective listener hears feelings as well as content and understands what the other says with his body language as well as through words.) Another reason for not looking into the speaker's eyes is that it is one of the most intimate ways of relating to a person, and the fear of escalation of affection has made it somewhat taboo in many societies.[15]

Despite the fact that some people find it difficult to look into another's eyes, few of us enjoy carrying on a conversation with a person whose glance continually darts about the room. When I am listened to by that kind of person, I am distracted from what I am saying. For example, when a person talking with me at a party keeps looking around the room at other people, I often interpret that to mean that he would rather be someplace else—and I personally wish he would find out where he would rather be and go there! Lack of eye contact may be a sign of indifference or hostility. It can be experienced as a put-down.

The ability to have good eye contact is essential for effective interpersonal communication in our society. Sometimes it cannot be used maximally because others are uncomfortable with it. Often, however, it is one of the most effective of the listening skills. People who are uncomfortable with eye contact can develop the ability to communicate through the eyes. Awareness of the importance of eye contact helps many people overcome the inhibition. Additionally, people with this problem may have to work at looking at a person's face more often until they become more comfortable with this way of relating.

Nondistracting Environment

Attending involves giving the other person one's undivided attention. This is virtually impossible in environments that have a high level of distraction. An undistracting environment, one without significant physical barriers between people and one that is inviting rather than ugly—these conditions facilitate conversation.

The attending listener attempts to *cut environmental distractions to the minimum.* At home, the TV or stereo may be turned off in the room to provide the interruption-free and distraction-free environment that is so important for human interaction. If need be, the telephone receiver can be taken off the hook or unplugged, and a "Do not Disturb" sign can even be placed on the door. In many offices, the door can be closed, the music or intercom turned off, and the secretary can hold telephone calls until the conversation is completed. In the factory, finding an undistracting setting is difficult but not impossible. Good attending in a manufacturing plant may involve using the feet before using the ears—to get to an office or some other place where you will not be disturbed and where the environment is not distracting.

Removing sizable physical barriers fosters better communication. In offices the desk typically intrudes between the speaker and the listener. A. G. White's study of medical case-history interviewing discovered that 55 percent of the patients initially sat at ease when no desk separated the patient and the doctor; only 10 percent were at ease when a desk separated the patient from the doctor.[16] For some people, a desk is associated with a position of authority and can trigger feelings of weakness or hostility. When a listener sits behind a desk, the interaction is more likely to be role-to-role rather than person-to-person. If an office is too small to place two chairs away from the desk for conversation, it is desirable to have the visitor's chair beside the desk rather than across the desk.

Good attending fosters improved observation of the other's body language, which is an important part of listening. When a desk or other large physical barrier stands between you and the speaker, it is extremely difficult to note what the other's body is communicating.

Psychological Attention

What a person wants most of all from a listener is a sense of psychological presence. He wants the listener to really be there for him. Physical attending fosters psychological presence. When I am in a good environmental setting, have comfortable eye contact, appropriate body motion, and maintain the posture of involvement, my psychological attending usually improves. My physical attending skill also helps the other feel my psychological presence.

However, if I try to fake attention when listening to another, I deceive only myself. The listener who is truly present to another displays a vitality that registers on the face and body his interest and concern for what the other is saying. The person who is not really "there," even though his body takes an attending position, is inevitably detected. The speaker notes the glazed eyes, and his "antenna" picks up other signals that reveal that the listener's heart and mind are not with him. Without psychological presence, no attending technique will work.

Consciously Working at Attending

Surprisingly, we find that most people have a fairly accurate informal knowledge of attending before we teach them any attending skills. In our seminars, the trainer often says, "Position yourselves to show me that you are really interested in what I am saying." Most people in the group assume a fairly good attending position. Then the leader says, "Show me by your body posture that you couldn't care less about me or about what I am telling you." Virtually everyone demonstrates a clear idea of what nonattending behavior is like. So why do we make such an effort to teach attending skills? There are basically two reasons.

First of all, because the teaching of these skills does sharpen understanding of attending. People raise to the level of their awareness some understandings that were previously vague and hazy. People invariably learn something new and/or develop a deepened insight into what they already know.

Secondly, and more important, we find that a focus on the methods and merits of attending motivates many people to do what they already know how to do but often neglect to do. A focus on attending serves as a consciousness-raising experience that often motivates people to utilize these skills. Once people start attending at appropriate times, they are rewarded by a new quality of interpersonal relationships. Allan Ivey puts it this way:

> Some may question the possible artificiality of attending behavior or other skills.... They validly object to seeing life as a series of exercises in which the individual constantly dredges into a "handbag of skills" so he can adapt to each life situation. Our experience has been that individuals may sometimes begin attending in an artificial, deliberate manner. However, once attending has been initiated, the person to whom one is listening tends to become more animated, and this in turn reinforces the attender who very quickly forgets about attending deliberately and soon attends naturally. A variety of our clients and trainees have engaged in conscious attending behavior only to find themselves so interested in the person with whom they are talking that they lose themselves in the other.[17]

People tend to think of communication as a verbal process. Students of communication are convinced that most communication is nonverbal. The most commonly quoted estimate, based on research, is that 85 percent of our communication is nonverbal! So attending, the nonverbal part of listening, is a basic building block of the listening process.

Following Skills

Beatrice Glass's car collided with another auto. As soon after the accident as possible she telephoned her husband, Charlie, and reported that she had been in an accident. "How much damage did it do to the car?" was his immediate response. When he had that information, Charlie asked, "Whose fault was it?" Then he said, "Don't admit a thing. You phone the insurance company and I'll call our lawyer. Just a minute and I'll give you the number."

"Any more questions?" she asked.

"No," he replied, "that just about covers it."

"Oh, it does, does it?" she screamed. "Well, just in case you are interested, I'm in the hospital with four broken ribs!"

Charlie's responses may have been more callous and blatant than those of the average husband, but what he did is typical for many people. Because Charlie's wife had a problem (an automobile accident that resulted in her hospitalization), Charlie's role in the conversation should have been primarily that of a listener. But he did most of the talking.

One of the primary tasks of a listener is to stay out of the other's way so the listener can discover how the speaker views his situation. Unfortunately, the average "listener" interrupts and diverts the speaker by asking many questions or making many statements. Researchers tell us that it is not at all uncommon for "listeners" to lead and direct a conversation through the frequent use of questions. It is also common for the "listener" to talk so much that he monopolizes the conversation!

Four following skills foster effective listening: door openers, minimal encourages, open questions, and attentive silence.

Door Openers

People often send *nonverbal clues* when they are burdened or excited about something. Their feelings are telegraphed in facial expressions, tone of voice, body posture, and energy level. For example, Jerry, who is normally exuberant, had not laughed or entered into the family repartee for four days. When they were alone, his wife, Darlene, said, "You don't seem yourself these past few days. You seem burdened by something. Care to talk about it?" That was Darlene's way of sending a door opener.

A door opener is a noncoercive invitation to talk. There are times when door openers are not necessary. The speaker plunges right into his theme. Sometimes, however, you will sense that the other person wants to talk but needs encouragement as Jerry did. At other times, the speaker will be in the midst of a conversation and will show signs that he is unsure about continuing. A door opener like this may help him proceed: "I'm interested in hearing more about it."

People often send door closers (roadblocks) when door openers are much more appropriate. When a child comes home from school with dragging steps and an unhappy expression on his face, parents often respond in ways that tend to make the child withdraw into himself. *Judgmental* statements are apt to pour forth.

> "What a sourpuss you have on today."
> "What did you do this time?"
> "Don't inflict your lousy mood on me."
> "What did you do, lose your best friend?"

Sometimes, they try to *reassure:*

> "Cheer up."
> "Things will get better. They always do."
> "Next week you won't even remember what happened."

At such times, *advice giving* is another favorite tactic:

> "Why don't you do something you like to do?"
> "Don't mope around all day. That won't help anything."
> "I'm sure that whatever happened wasn't worth ruining your day over."

Instead of yielding to the temptation to use roadblocks, parents could send a door opener:

> "Looks like things didn't go well for you today. I've got time if you'd like to talk."
> "Something unpleasant happen to you? Want to talk about it?"

Door openers typically have four elements.

1. *A description of the other person's body language.* "Your face is beaming today." "You look like you are not feeling up to par."
2. *An invitation to talk or to continue talking.* "Care to talk about it?" "Please go on." "I'm interested in what you are saying."
3. *Silence—giving the other person time to decide whether to talk and/or what he wants to say.*
4. *Attending—eye contact and a posture of involvement that demonstrates your interest in and concern for the other person.*

All four parts are not necessarily present in every door opener. One day, a friend with whom I had shared a great deal of my thoughts and feelings saw that I was troubled. He motioned to a chair and said quietly, "Let's hear about it." On another occasion, he simply said, "Shoot." These brief door openers worked well because of the trust and frequent self-disclosure in the relationship. If other people had said those things to me, I might have clammed up. The personality of the listener, the nature of the relationship, and other factors will determine the most effective door opener in a given situation.

Silence and attending alone often constitute a strong inducement to talk. A housewife who complained that her husband seldom talked with her decided to try attending to him when *he* wanted to talk. She discovered, to her dismay, that he seemed most ready to converse when he got home from work—and that's when she was in the midst of dinner preparations! For years she had continued attending to her cooking while calling questions over her shoulder about how his day had gone—but received virtually no response. Her new approach was to serve dinner forty-five minutes later, to take fifteen minutes to relax before her husband came home, and to spend a half-hour talking with him alone. For that half-hour, both the children and her cooking tasks were excluded. She says her husband now engages in significant conversations with her.

Another housewife who found it inconvenient to postpone the dinner hour planned to cook much of the meal earlier in the day on three days a week so she could attend to her husband's conversation when he arrived home. She says, "What a difference that has made! Some days we talk the whole time. On other occasions, our conversations are quite brief—but even these are not the forced exchanges we had when I used to grill him with questions while I prepared dinner. Some days, of course, we do no more than exchange greetings. But the whole interpersonal atmosphere of our house is changing because of my quiet, attentive availability during those three half-hour periods a week before dinner."

A person sending door openers needs an awareness of and a respect for the other person's probable feelings of ambivalence—he may want to self-disclose, yet be hesitant to do so.

One way to deal with ambivalence is to recognize and reflect back to the speaker how difficult it is to talk about painful experiences. When the speaker seems to find it difficult to speak about the things he is saying, a listener can reflect: "It's pretty hard to talk about."

Another way of dealing with a person who is feeling very ambivalent is to make sure your door opener is an invitation rather than a directive to talk. Door openers should always be noncoercive.

Unfortunately, some people not only open the door, they try to drag the other through:

SAM: You look sad, John. Feel like talking?
JOHN: Not really.
SAM: I can tell you are troubled. You know you can talk to me.
JOHN: I don't feel like it right now.
SAM: You really ought to get it off your chest, you know.
JOHN: Yeah, I know. Later maybe.
SAM: But the time to talk is when you are feeling things ...

The empathic person respects the privacy of other people and is careful not to be intrusive. He honors rather than violates the other individual's separateness. When appropriate, empathic listeners invite conversation. They do not try to compel it.

It is difficult to offer a door opener, not to be taken up on it, and still let it go. However, in relationships where there is little trust or where communication has not been flowing well for some time, door openers will probably find little response from the other person. It takes time, skill, and goodwill to rebuild trust. Use of listening skills can help nurture this trust once more. If and when the relationship is restored, the door openers will probably find a welcome response.

Minimal Encourages

We have already stated that one of the listener's responsibilities is to allow the speaker room to talk about a situation as he sees and feels it. Many people, in their effort to stay out of the speaker's way, lapse into nonparticipation. Simple responses that encourage the speaker to tell his story in his way yet keep the listener active in the process are called *minimal encourages*. Minimal encourages are brief indicators to other persons that you are with them. The word *minimal* refers to the amount the listener says, which is very little, and to the amount of direction given to the conversation, which is also very little. The word *encourages* is used because these words and phrases aid the speaker to continue speaking. Just a few words can let the other know you are listening without interrupting the flow of talk or breaking the mood. Minimal encourages will be sprinkled throughout a conversation. In the early stages of an interaction, they may be used more frequently to help the conversation gain momentum.

The simple "mm-hmm" is probably the most frequently used of the minimal encourages. That brief phrase can suggest, "Please continue. I'm listening and I understand." There are many brief responses that the listener can use:

Tell me more.	You betcha!
Oh?	Yes.
For instance ...	Really?
I see.	Gosh.
Right.	And?
Then?	Go on.
So?	Sure.
I hear you.	Darn!

You undoubtedly have your own favorites. Repeating one or two of the speaker's key words or the last word or two of the speaker's statement also constitutes minimal encourages. When the speaker says, "I can't figure out what to do. I guess I'm just confused," the listener may respond "Confused?"

A skilled listener can communicate much empathy through voice and facial expressions even when only one or two words are said. I watched a film of one of America's leading therapists listening to a woman tell how furious she was at things her mother had done to her. His empathic "You betcha" seemed to give her the feeling, "He understands how angry I am and he still accepts me." When one of our children told my wife of a big disappointment at school, Dot simply said, "Darn!" but her tone of voice, facial expression, and other nonverbals made it a very feel-ing-ful response.

Minimal encourages do not imply either agreement or disagreement with what the speaker said. Rather, they let the other know he has been heard and that the listener will try to follow his meaning if the speaker chooses to continue. Thus, when I respond to a speaker with "Right," it does not mean that I agree with the speaker. Rather, it means, "Yes, I hear what you are saying—go on."

This kind of response has often been parodied. We hear tales of the psychi-atrist who says nothing but "mm-hmm" for fifty minutes and at the end of the session says, "That will be fifty dollars, please." Obviously, these expressions can be overdone or used mechanically. However, when sensitively orchestrated with a variety of other responses, they assist the speaker's self-exploration.

Infrequent Questions

Questions are an integral part of verbal interaction in our society. As with many other kinds of responses, questions have their strengths and their limitations. Comparatively few people in our culture know how to question effectively. We often rely on questions excessively and use them poorly. Questions usually focus on the intent, perspective, and concerns of the listener rather than on the speaker's orientation. When that happens, questions are a barrier to communication.

We distinguish between "closed" questions and "open" questions. *Closed questions* direct the speaker to give a specific, short response. They are often answered with one word like "yes" or "no." *Open questions,* on the other hand, provide *space* for the speaker to explore his thoughts without being hemmed in too much by the listener's categories. Closed questions are like true/false or multiple-choice test questions, while open questions are like essay questions. When an employee walks into her boss's office, the latter could ask either a closed or an open question:

Closed question: "Do you want to see me about the Rumsford job?"
Open Question: "What's on your mind, Ann?"

The open question is usually preferable because it does not suggest the agenda to the person who initiated the interaction.

When used skillfully and infrequently, open questions may help the listener better understand the speaker without directing the conversation. In the report on their study of open and closed questions, Moreland, Phillips, and Lockhart write:

Crucial to the giving of open-ended questions is the concept of who is to lead the interview. While the interviewer does ask questions while using this skill, his ques-tions are centered around concerns of the client rather than around concerns of the interviewer for the client. Questions should be designed to help the client clarify his own problems, rather than provide information for the interviewer.... If the interviewer relies on closed questions to structure his interview, he usually is forced to concentrate so hard on thinking up the next question that he fails to listen to and attend to the client.[18]

In addition to asking open rather than closed questions, it is important to *ask only one question at a time.* When two or more questions are asked in quick succession, the latter questions are usually closed questions. The tendency to ask more than one question seems related to the questioner's inner uncertainty. It rarely facilitates the conversation.

My experience in teaching communication skills leads me to conclude that *most people ask far too many questions.* Putting several questions in a conversation is risky to the interaction; it tends to put the listener opposite rather than beside the speaker, dictating the direction the conversation takes rather than giving the speaker an opportunity to explore his situation in his own way. Almost everyone I have taught would have been a better listener if he asked fewer questions. Furthermore, I believe that most questions can be expressed as statements and that doing so generally is far more productive in a conversation than repeated questioning.

When people try to give up their overreliance on questions, they usually feel very uncomfortable. They may feel the conversation is floundering because of more periods of silence. Skills taught in this [essay] will help you refrain from asking too many questions and at the same time not feel too much of a void in the conversation.

Attentive Silence

The beginning listener needs to learn the value of silence in freeing the speaker to think, feel, and express himself. "The beginning of wisdom is silence," said a Hebrew sage. "The second stage is listening."

Most listeners talk too much. They may speak as much or even more than the person trying to talk. Learning the art of silent responsiveness is essential to good listening. After all, another person cannot describe a problem if you are doing all the talking.

Silence on the part of the listener gives the speaker time to think about what he is going to say and thus enables him to go deeper into himself. It gives a person space to experience the feelings churning within. Silence also allows the speaker to proceed at his own pace. It provides time to deal with his ambivalence about sharing. In the frequent silences, he can choose whether or not to continue talking and at what depth. Silence often serves as a gentle nudge to go further into a conversation. When an interaction is studded with significant silences and backed by good attending, the results can be very impressive.

Through the years, I have returned again and again to these words of Eugene Herrigel that describe why silence can be such a powerful force for a person whose emotions are intense:

> The real meaning of suffering discloses itself only to him who has learned the art of compassion.... Gradually, he will fall silent, and in the end will sit there wordless, for a long time sunk deep in himself. And the strange thing is that this silence is not felt by the other person as indifference, as a desolate emptiness which disturbs rather than calms. It is as if this silence had more meaning than countless words could ever have. It is as if he were being drawn into a field of force from which fresh strength flows

into him. He feels suffused with a strange confidence.... And it may be that in these hours, the resolve will be born to set out on the path that turns a wretched existence into a life of happiness.[19]

Silence can be a balm for sufferers; it is also important in moments of great joy. How beautiful are the silences of intimacy. Thomas Carlyle and Ralph Waldo Emerson sat together for hours one night in utter silence until one rose to go and said, "We've had a grand evening!" I've had many experiences like that with my wife, Dot, when we sat quietly before a fire or gazed silently into each other's eyes, basking in each other's affection. As Halford Luccock says:

> This silence of love is not indifference; it is not merely poverty of something to say. It is a positive form of self-communication. Just as silence is needed to hear a watch ticking, so silence is the medium through which heartbeats are heard.[20]

More than half the people who take communication skills training with us are initially uncomfortable with silence. Even a few seconds' pause in a conversation causes many of them to squirm. These people feel so ill at ease with silences that they have a strong inner compulsion to shatter the quiet with questions, advice, or any other sound that will end their discomfort by ending the silence. For these people, the focus of attention is not on the speaker but rather on their own inner disquiet. They are like the character in Samuel Beckett's *Waiting for Godot* who said, "Let us try to converse calmly since we are incapable of keeping silent."[21]

Fortunately, most people can increase their comfort with silence in a relatively short period of time. When people find out what to do in silence, they become far less uptight in the verbal lulls that are so important to vital communication. During the pauses in an interaction, a good listener does the following:

> *Attends to the other.* His body posture demonstrates that he is really there for the other person.
> *Observes the other.* He sees that the speaker's eyes, facial expressions, posture, and gestures are all communicating. When you are not distracted by the other's words, you may "hear" his body language more clearly.
> *Thinks about what the other is communicating.* He ponders what the other has said. He wonders what the speaker is feeling. He considers the variety of responses he might make. Then he selects the one that he thinks will be most facilitative.

When he is busy doing these things, the listener does not have time to become anxious about the silence.

Some people are helped in their quest for comfort with silences by realizing that when the other person is conversing about a pressing need, the focus of attention is on him—not on the listener. If he does not want to talk further, that's his prerogative. Why should it bother a listener if the speaker doesn't want to continue the conversation? Many people believe that once a problem has been stated, it should be solved—in one sitting. Human behavior simply isn't that neat and efficient.

Before the birth of Jesus, the author of the book Ecclesiastes said there is a "time to keep silent and a time to speak."[22] The effective listener can do both. Some people sit quietly during a whole conversation, pushing the other into a monologue. Excessive silence can be as undesirable as no silence. To sit mute like a "bump on a log" does not constitute effective listening. It is rarely possible to listen effectively for a long time without making some kind of verbal response. Soon the mind of such an unresponsive "listener" dulls, his eyes become glazed, and it becomes obvious to the speaker that the "listener" is not with him. Silence, when overdone, is not golden—it is then merely a lack of response to the person with needs.

The effective listener learns to speak when that is appropriate, can be silent when that is a fitting response, and feels comfortable with either activity. The good listener becomes adept at verbal responses while at the same time recognizing the immense importance of silence in creative conversation. He frequently emulates Robert Benchley, who once said, "Drawing on my fine command of language, I said nothing."

Summary

Listening is a combination of hearing what another person says and involvement with the person who is talking. Its importance can be gauged by the fact that we spend more time listening than anything else we do in our waking hours and because our ability to listen directly influences our friendships, our family relationships, and our effectiveness at work. For ease of learning, this book treats listening in three skill clusters: attending skills, following skills, and reflecting skills. Attending is demonstrating by a posture of involvement, eye contact, appropriate body movement, and assurance of a nondistracting environment that the listener is psychologically present to the speaker. The skills of using door openers, minimal encourages, open questions, and attentive silence enable the listener to keep the focus on the speaker's communication....

Notes

1. Ralph G. Nichols and Leonard A. Stevens, *Are You Listening?* (New York: McGraw-Hill, 1957), pp. 6–7.
2. Ibid., pp. 6–10.
3. Quoted in B. Harvey Branscomb, *The Teachings of Jesus: A Textbook for College and Individual Use* (New York: Abingdon, 1931), p. 23. This saying comes from an apocryphal "New Testament" book.
4. Ralph G. Nichols and Leonard A. Stevens, "Listening to People," *Harvard Business Review* (September–October 1957).
5. Franklin Ernst, Jr., *Who's Listening? A Handbook of the Transactional Analysis of the Listening Function* (Vallejo, Calif.: Addresso 'set, 1973).
6. John Drakeford, *The Awesome Power of the Listening Ear* (Waco, Tex.: Word, 1967), p. 17.
7. Allen Ivey and John Hinkle, "The Transactional Classroom," unpublished manuscript, University of Massachusetts, 1970.
8. Norman Rockwell, "My Adventures as an Illustrator," ed. T. Rockwell, *Saturday Evening Post* (April 2, 1960), p. 67. President John Kennedy had this ability, too. See Drakeford, *The Awesome Power of the Listening Ear*, p. 65.
9. Albert Scheflen with Norman Ashcraft, *Human Territories: How We Behave in Space-Time* (Englewood Cliffs, N.J.: Prentice-Hall, 1976), pp. 6, 42.
10. C. L. Lassen, "Effect of Proximity on Anxiety and Communication in the Initial Psychiatric Interview," *Journal of Abnormal Psychology* 18 (1973): 220–232.

11. Ernst, *Who's Listening?* p. 113.
12. Charles Truax and Robert Carkhuff, *Toward Effective Counseling and Psychotherapy: Training and Practice* (New York: Aldine/Atherton, 1967), pp. 361–362.
13. Quoted in Gerald Nierenberg and Henry Calero, *How to Read a Person Like a Book* (New York: Pocket Books, 1975), p. 28.
14. Paul Ekman and Wallace Friesen, *Unmasking the Face: A Guide to Recognizing Emotions from Facial Expressions* (Englewood Cliffs, N.J.:Prentice-Hall, 1975), pp. 14–16.
15. Silvan Tomkins, in *Challenges of Humanistic Psychology*, ed. James Bugental (New York: McGraw-Hill, 1967), p. 57.
16. Anthony G. White, *Reforming Metropolitan Governments: A Bibliography* (New York: Garland, 1975).
17. Allen Ivey, *Microcounseling: Innovations in Interviewing Training* (Springfield, Ill.: Thomas, 1975).
18. John Moreland, Jeanne Phillips, and Jeff Lockhart, "Open Invitation to Talk," manuscript, University of Massachusetts, 1969, p. 1.
19. Eugene Herrigel, *The Method of Zen*, ed. Herman Tausend and R. F. C. Hull (New York: Pantheon, 1976), pp. 124–125.
20. Halford Luccock, *Halford Luccock Treasury*, ed. Robert Luccock, Jr. (New York: Abingdon, 1963), p. 242.
21. Quoted in Nathan Scott, *Man in the Modern Theater* (Richmond, Va.: John Knox, 1965), p. 86.
22. Ecclesiastes 3:7.

Review Questions

1. What percent of oral communication does Bolton say is "ignored" or not listened to?
2. Bolton claims that schooling sometimes teaches us bad listening habits. What aspects of your past school experience have had that effect?
3. What is the distinction Bolton makes between hearing and listening? Compare his approach to this issue with the view expressed by Carl Rogers in Chapter 15.
4. What's the difference between "focusing" and "attending"?
5. Some persons nod consistently while they're listening to you. Are they following Bolton's advice about "appropriate body motion"? Why or why not?
6. What does Bolton say is the relationship between physical and psychological attending?
7. In the section headed "Following Skills," Bolton suggests that sometimes questioning can actually decrease listening effectiveness. How so?
8. What is the greatest risk of using a "door opener"?
9. What is a "minimal encourage"?

Probes

1. Several research studies have concluded that most people listen effectively to only 25 to 33 percent of what they hear. Do those figures fit your experience? Is your listening efficiency about the same as that or different? How about those who listen to you?
2. What rules, norms, or habits did you learn as you were growing up that increased your listening effectiveness? What rules, norms, or habits decreased it?
3. In school, class periods typically run longer than the average person's attention span. Describe three additional features of your school experience that work against good listening. Do the same for your work situation. What characteristics of that environment make it harder to listen well?
4. In your experience, what is the difference between a posture of involvement that looks genuine and one that looks faked or phony?
5. What does Bolton mean when he says, in the words of Franklin Ernst, Jr., that the body of a person listening effectively is "moved by the talker"?

6. Give an example from your own experience of the importance of eye contact for good listening.

7. In the section "Consciously Working at Attending," Bolton addresses the question, "How can I work this hard and still be natural?" How do you respond to what he says there? Does it ring true for you?

8. After you read the essay entitled "Dialogic Listening" in this chapter, it might be useful for you to refer back to Bolton's discussion of following skills.

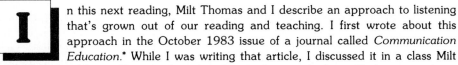 n this next reading, Milt Thomas and I describe an approach to listening that's grown out of our reading and teaching. I first wrote about this approach in the October 1983 issue of a journal called *Communication Education.** While I was writing that article, I discussed it in a class Milt was taking, and he really picked up the ideas and ran with them. He began applying them in his own teaching and encouraging me to do the same. So when I decided to include a discussion on this approach in *Bridges Not Walls*, I knew that Milt could contribute a great deal to the effort.

The most exciting thing about our collaboration on this piece—and we are both still smiling about it—is that our work together was an example of what we were writing about. Each time we talked, we seemed to get more evidence of the value of this approach to listening. In fact, after we were finished, when I discovered that I needed to cut thirty-five pages from this book before sending it to the publisher, I asked Milt to discuss the issue with me, because I knew that the ways we had learned to listen to each other would make that conversation very productive. I wasn't disappointed; the difficult decisions that emerged from that discussion still strike me as right.

So we encourage you to give dialogic listening a try. It's different from the kind of listening that Robert Bolton discusses, but only in the sense that it broadens and goes beyond his advice. We feel confident about it because we know it's solidly grounded in some well-developed philosophy of communication. But more important, we also know it can *work*.

Dialogic Listening: Sculpting Mutual Meanings

John Stewart and Milt Thomas

The two of us have recently had a number of communication experiences that have led us to substantially rethink our attitudes toward listening. In conversations with each other and in many of our contacts with students, family, friends,

*John Stewart, "Interpretive Listening: An Alternative to Empathy," *Communication Education*, 32 (October 1983): 379–391.

and co-workers, we have rediscovered in a concrete and exciting way the *productive* quality of interpersonal communication. In other words, we've experienced how in the most fruitful and satisfying conversations, our listening is focused less on repro-ducing what's "inside" the other person and more on co-producing, with the other person, mutual meanings *between* us. As a result, we've rediscovered how a good conversation can create insights, ideas, and solutions to problems that none of the conversation partners could have generated alone. It seems to us that a certain kind of listening has helped that happen.

For example, Milt was recently involved with two other people in an effort to design and conduct a training program for beginning university teachers. Jack, one of Milt's partners, came to the planning sessions with very definite ideas about the design and operation of the program. He assumed that Milt and Susan would also have their definite ideas and that their meeting times would be spent with each trainer bargaining for his or her own plan. You could say that Jack was mainly content-focused. Susan's primary concern was the quality of learning experienced by the beginning university teachers; she focused more on outcome or goals. She was willing to bargain with Jack, to advocate her own ideas, or to engage in what-ever process seemed to lead to the outcomes she valued.

Although Milt wasn't fully aware of the contrast at the time, his main con-cern was neither the content of the program nor outcomes for the participants, but the quality of the contact among the three planners. He was *not* just functioning as a "pure process" person; he brought his own ideas—for example, about how the new teachers could learn to handle the grading and the cross-cultural communi-cation problems they might encounter in their classrooms. But Milt found his ideas about content and outcomes entering the conversation somewhat like "counter-punches" in the sense that they were responses to Jack's or Susan's contributions. He seemed to use the momentum of the ongoing talk to create "holes" that his contributions helped fill.

Milt's efforts were not always greeted cheerfully. He often slowed down the planning process as he made sure that he understood the others, that they under-stood him, and that they comprehended one another. When Susan and Jack pre-sented their ideas, he would often raise questions or offer countersuggestions in order to build more talk about the ideas. Milt wasn't merely playing "devil's advo-cate" to stir things up; he was trying to help engage all three persons in a mutual building process. They were building conversation-texts, "chunks" of talk that developed ideas and suggestions, teased out nuances, and helped mold incomplete suggestions into refined ones.

While Jack's strength was content and Susan's strength was her outcome-focus, Milt's contribution to this effort came primarily from the way he *listened*. His attitudes and expectations, the questions he asked, the way he paraphrased others' comments, and even his nonverbal behavior—posture, tone of voice, rate of speak-ing, and so on—were all aimed not just toward *reproducing* what Jack or Susan said but toward *producing* with them a full response to the issues they faced.

We've come to call the kind of listening Milt engaged in *dialogic listening*. We use that term to label listening that values and builds mutuality, requires active involvement, is genuine, and grows out of a belief in and commitment to synergy— the idea that the whole actually can be greater than the sum of its parts. There are some important differences between dialogic listening and what's usually called "active listening" or "empathic listening." Let's start by briefly reviewing them.

"Active" or "Empathic" Listening

Recall for a minute some of what you've read or heard about listening, perhaps from Robert Bolton's excellent essay reprinted earlier in this chapter, from a listening text,[1] from your teacher, or in a listening seminar or workshop. For one thing, you may well have read or discussed some of the ironies of listening. For example, we spend much more time listening than we spend speaking, reading, or writing, but we're taught the most about writing and reading, a little about speaking, and almost nothing about listening.[2] Another irony is that we are worst at the activity we engage in the most. As Bolton notes, researchers claim that we usually remember only about one quarter of what we hear, and many people miss almost 100% of the feeling content of spoken communication.

To help remedy this situation, most books and articles emphasize that listening differs from hearing. Hearing is the physiological part of the process—the reception of sound waves. Good listening is traditionally defined as effective sensing, interpreting, and evaluating the other person's meanings. That definition is reflected in the anonymous maxim, "I know you believe you understand what you think I said, but I'm not sure you realize that what you heard is not what I meant." The idea behind this maxim is that listening involves *one* person grasping the *other* person's meanings, and since we can't get inside the other person's experience, the listening process is inherently flawed.

When people discuss empathic listening, they generally begin from this same basic understanding. Empathy is the process of "putting yourself in the other's place," or as Carl Rogers puts it,

> It means entering the private perceptual world of the other and becoming thoroughly at home in it. It involves being sensitive, moment by moment, to the changing felt meanings which flow in this other person.... To be with another in this way means that for the time being, you lay aside your own views and values in order to enter another's world without prejudice. In some sense it means that you lay aside yourself....[3]

One of the most important skills for achieving empathic understanding is paraphrasing. As Bolton puts it, "a *paraphrase* is a *concise response* to the speaker which states the *essence* of the other's *content* in the *listener's own words*."[4] Most traditional treatments of active or empathic listening also discuss several other parts of the process, including attending skills, clarifying skills, and perception checking.[5]

These traditional accounts are useful in several ways. For one thing, they call our attention to the fact that most of us don't listen as well as we could. We think of listening as a passive process, like "soaking up sense data," and as a result we often don't work at it. Good listening takes real effort and traditional listening texts and workshops almost always include helpful suggestions about how to do it better. There's also something intuitively appealing about discussions of empathic listening. Each of us knows what it's like to "walk a mile in the other person's moccasins," and we've also had the opposite experience where someone is so self-centered that he or she never really connects with any *else's* thoughts or feelings. Empathizing with someone's fear or pain—or having someone empathize with yours—can be very confirming and reassuring, and when it doesn't happen, it can hurt.

But there are also some problems with this view of listening. For one thing, it's based on a kind of fiction. As we mentioned, you cannot actually "get inside" the other person's awareness, and it can be confusing to try to think, feel, and act as if you could. It's also impossible to, as Rogers puts it, "lay aside your own views and values" or to "lay aside yourself." Any decision or effort to make that kind of move would be the decision or effort of a "self" and it would be rooted in that self's views and values. In other words, you cannot put yourself on the shelf because that move is an active choice that keeps yourself involved. "Laying aside yourself" is as literally impossible as lifting yourself by your ears—or your own bootstraps. So you may well decide to focus on the other person and to do your best to sense her meanings or feel his happiness, but these efforts will always be grounded in your own attitudes, expectations, past experiences, and world view. You *can't* "lay aside yourself." Neither can we.

A second problem is that empathic listening can get distorted into a frustrating or even manipulative process of parroting. The generally recognized "father" of empathic listening, Carl Rogers, often commented on how vulnerable to distortion the process can be. Consider, for example, how you'd feel if you were the client in this counselor–client conversation:

CLIENT: I really think he's a very nice guy; he's so thoughtful, sensitive, and kind. He calls me a lot. He's fun to go out with.
COUNSELOR: You like him very much, then.
CLIENT: Yeah, and I think my friends like him too. Two of them have asked me to double-date.
COUNSELOR: You are pleased that your friends accept him.
CLIENT: Yeah, but I don't want to get too involved right now. I've got a lot of commitments at school and to my family.
COUNSELOR: You want to limit your involvement with him.
CLIENT: Yeah.... Is there an echo in here?

When your conversation partner—whether counselor, lover, parent, or friend—is focusing only on sensing your meanings or feeling your feelings, it can begin to seem like you are talking to yourself. The contact between you is sacrificed to serve the other person's desire to "understand fully."

That brings us to a third shortcoming of many of the traditional approaches to active or empathic listening: They emphasize the "psychology" of the situation rather than the *communication*. By that we mean that these approaches make each person's "psyche" or internal state the focus of attention rather than the verbal and nonverbal transaction that's going on *between* them. As we've already said, it can be very helpful to try to sense another's feelings, and it is confirming and reassuring when someone does that for you. But we think there's more to effective listening than that. You definitely do not need to stop trying to listen actively or empathically, but we do think it can be helpful to broaden your repertoire by also learning to listen dialogically.

Dialogic Listening

In our thinking and talking we've identified four distinctive features of dialogic listening. In this section we want to outline them and to offer five suggestions for practicing this approach. We'll conclude with a brief discussion of some problems you might encounter as you try to apply what we suggest here.

Focus on "Ours"

The first distinctive feature of dialogic listening is that it focuses on "ours" rather than "mine" or "yours." Without listening training of any kind—and sometimes even with it—many of us fall into a pattern of communicating as if we were talking to ourselves—we focus on "mine." Sometimes this monologic communication "just happens"; we're not aware of the fact that we are only discussing our topic from our point of view, or we're not conscious of how long we've been talking or how few real questions we've asked. At other times we get caught up in our own agendas; we get so involved in and enthusiastic about our project or opportunity that we lose track of—and hence contact with—the other person. That happens often to one of John's friends. The friend's wife urges him to "be more sensitive," but he often can't seem to help himself. He gets going on his most recent idea or project and fifteen minutes pass before he takes a breath. Then he'll abruptly notice what he's done and apologize for "monopolizing the conversation—again."

Other persons concentrate on "mine" simply because they believe that their agenda is more significant than anyone else's. They fall into a "me focused" pattern when their excitement or worry about their own concerns overshadows everything else. And in still other cases a person sticks with his or her agenda because of the belief that "I can say it my way better than you can say it your way," and the possibility that *we* could say it even more effectively never occurs to them. In short, unconsciousness, honest enthusiasm, and a sense of superiority can all help us keep our communication focused on "mine."

The preceding quotations from Rogers and Bolton illustrate how treatments of empathic listening concentrate on "yours." A paraphrase states the essence of the *other's* content in the listener's own words, and empathizing means "entering the private conceptual world of the *other*." As we have already said, this can be a useful move for the very self-centered person, but it can also lead to the kind of communication illustrated in our counselor–client example.

The third alternative is to focus on *ours*. This is what we had in mind when we subtitled this discussion "Sculpting Mutual Meanings." The metaphor is Milt's and he uses it to suggest a concrete, graphic image of what it means to listen dialogically. Picture yourself sitting on one side of a potter's wheel with your conversation partner across from you. As you work (talk) together, each of you adds clay to the form on the wheel, and each uses wet fingers, thumbs, and palms to shape the finished product. Like clay, talk is tangible and malleable; it's out there to hear, to record, and to shape. If I am unclear or uncertain about what I am thinking or about what I want to say, I can put something out there and you can modify its shape, ask me to add more clay, or add some of your own. Your specific shaping, which you could only have done in response to the shape I formed, may move in a direction I would never have envisioned. The clay you add may be an idea I've thought about before—though not here or in this form—or it may be completely new to me. Sometimes these "co-sculpting" sessions will be mostly playful, with general notions tossed on the wheel and the result looking like a vaguely shaped mass. At other times, the basic shape is well defined and we spend our time on detail and refinement. Our efforts, though, are almost always productive and frequently very gratifying. Sometimes I feel that our talk helps me understand myself better than I could have alone. At other times we produce something that transcends anything either of us could have conceived separately. That's because the figure we sculpt is not mine or yours, but *ours,* the outcome of both of our active shapings.

Open-ended and "Playful"

The second distinctive feature of dialogic listening is its open-ended, tentative, playful quality. We notice that when we are listening dialogically, we actually do not know what the outcome of the conversation will be. For example, John initiated the collaboration on this chapter because he knew that Milt had done a lot of thinking about this approach to listening and had worked with these ideas in the interpersonal communication courses he teaches. Our first conversation about this essay occurred in the hallway outside the Speech Communication Department office, where we set a time to meet and talk about the project. At that point neither of us knew what the outcome of our longer conversation would be. One option was for John to write the essay and for Milt to read it and suggest changes and additions. Another possibility was that Milt would write it, based on his recent classroom experience, and then John would edit and polish it. A third was that each of us would draft different sections and then comment on what the other person wrote. In our meeting, we didn't discuss any of those options until after an hour and a half or so, when our tentative strategy emerged from our talk. We agreed that we would start by having John take the ideas that developed in our conversation—most of which Milt had initiated and given examples of—and would begin organizing the whole, and Milt would draft certain sections that he knew best. As the process has developed, Milt has written several sections, John has integrated Milt's contributions into the text, and Milt has critiqued, raised questions, and made additions to each draft. Our point is that this kind of open-endedness is one of the primary prerequisites for—and one of the greatest challenges of—dialogic listening.

It's a challenge especially because a great deal of what we learn in twentieth-century Western culture pushes us in the opposite direction, toward closure and certainty. For example, if you read John's "Interpersonal Communication—Contact Between Persons" essay in Chapter 2 of this book, you probably recall his discussion of the "Spiritual Child." Some people dislike that discussion because they think it is too "abstract" and "ambiguous"; they are impatient with it and want more "hard content." In his book on creativity, Roger von Oech addresses those concerns when he discusses "soft and hard thinking."[6] "Hard" thinking is logical, analytical, critical, propositional, digital, focused, concrete, and "left-brain." "Soft" thinking is speculative, divergent, symbolic, elliptical, analogical, ambiguous, metaphoric, and "right-brain." Both are vital to effective problem-solving. Yet von Oech describes how, especially in the twentieth-century Western world, we are taught that there is only one kind of *real* thinking that leads to *real* knowledge, and that's the "hard" kind. This same bias makes it difficult to practice the kind of openness and tentativeness that dialogic listening requires.

What von Oech calls "hard" thinking is thinking that values the three c's: certainty, closure, and control. Much of the "hard" sciences, like physics and chemistry, concentrate on the development of lawlike generalizations that apply with certainty in all situations.[7] Whether it's morning or evening, winter or summer, at

General Motors or General Mills, H_2O is always water and, given one atmosphere of pressure, H_2O will always boil at 100°C and freeze at 0°C. If you know these laws you can confidently *control* the "behavior" of water, and you can be sure that on these matters inquiry is *closed;* we know what we need to know.

Obviously, the hard sciences and the hard thinking that develops them are enormously powerful and effective. Holography and the space shuttle, to say nothing of diet soft drinks and word processing, would be impossible without them. But certainty, closure, and control are not always possible, and especially where persons are involved, they're often not even desirable.

In order to listen dialogically you need, in place of the three c's, a combination of some modesty or humility and some trust. The modesty comes from remembering that persons are choosers, choice-makers. That means that you cannot predict with certainty what they will think, feel, or do in any situation. We just don't have that power over people, although habits and patterns sometimes make it seem as if we do. John's grandmother "always" cries at weddings, and politicians "always" like publicity. So it seems that we could predict what they'll do in these situations "every time." But all you have to do is pay attention to the people around you, and you will discover how those "always" predictions turn into "usually" or "sometimes." So there's an inverse relationship between this kind of humility and your desire for conversational certainty and control. When you can acknowledge and affirm your partner's power, as a person, to choose, you can relax your grip on two of the three c's.

There's also an inverse relationship between conversational trust and the two c's of closure and control. By trust we don't mean a naive belief that the world is a completely friendly place and that nobody in it means you any harm. That's obviously foolish. What we do mean is that you trust the potential of the conversation to produce more than you could on your own, and that, at least until you're proven wrong, you trust the other person's presence to you. For us, the cognitive part of this trust seems to be a decision to let the talk work, a choice in favor of what William S. Howell calls the "joint venture" quality of the conversation.[8] The feeling part seems to be a combination of a relaxing-letting-go and a deep-breath-leap-of-faith. That may overstate things a bit; the point is that you relax whatever white-knuckled grip you might have on the conversation's direction or outcome—"How can I be sure she doesn't think I am being silly?" "What if he won't give me the time off?"—and trust it to work.

Playfulness is the icing on the cake. If you and your conversation partner can manage to be tentative and experimental and can manifest a sense of open-endedness, you'll frequently find yourself literally playing with the ideas. In the past couple of decades scholars from several disciplines have emphasized the "seriousness" of play, the many senses in which play isn't just for fun. Psychotherapists discuss "games people play," defense analysts engage in war games, and play therapy is one way to help both troubled and normal children. Even a couple of philosophers have discussed the "playful" nature of conversation.[9] They emphasize that the "to-and-fro" is the basic form of everything we call "play," including sporting events, board games, and even the play of light on the water. Another characteristic is indeterminacy, that is, that play constantly renews itself. No Super Bowl or World Series game is ever the definitive or final instance of the play of football or baseball; these activities are constantly renewed in each playing. In addition, we don't completely control our playing; in an important sense we are played by the game as much as we play it. This quality becomes clear if you think of the way the rules, the tempo, the setting, and the spectators all affect your playing of racquet-ball, chess, baseball, or poker.

The point is, when we are engaged in spontaneous conversation, the form of the to-and-fro itself can generate insight and surprise—if we are listening dialogically. No un-self-conscious conversation is ever simply outward *replay* of your inner intentions and meanings. Instead, you and your partner actually play together; the two of you enter a dynamic over which you do not have complete control, and the outcome of your talk can be a surprise to you both, a creation of your play. It's difficult to write down an example of open-ended playfulness, but we think the following conversation at least points in the directions we mean:

KIM: Can I talk to you, Professor Carbaugh?

DON: Sure, "Student Wells," what's up? Oh, yes, you missed the exam on Friday, didn't you.

KIM: Yeah. That's why I came by. And since you said at the beginning of the term that you didn't have a set policy on makeups, I don't know what to do about it.

DON: Well, you're doing it exactly right! There's no set policy, because the situation is a little different in each case. So we definitely *do* have to do something about it, or you will end up with a zero. But I don't know yet what that should be. Sit down and let's talk about it.

KIM: Can I take the exam now?

DON: Right now? I don't know.... let's back off a little and talk about what happened when the rest of the class was writing the exam.

KIM: I was sick. Well, not exactly *sick,* sick, but I couldn't do it. I was really not physically or mentally able to do it.

DON: Keep talking....

KIM: Well, I don't want to give you a pile of excuses.

DON: I don't want you to give me a pile either—*(smiling)* of anything. But I do want to hear what was happening with you.

KIM: We had a big party on Thursday at the house I'm in, and I was in charge of all the arrangements, and I stayed up most of Wednesday night getting ready for it, and then in the middle of the party my boyfriend and I had a big fight, and he left, and I fell apart that night and couldn't even get out of bed Friday until after noon. Actually, I knew the fight was coming; I wouldn't have gotten so upset except I was so tired. Anyway, I just blew it.

DON: Okay. I appreciate your honesty. Hmmm ... so you didn't have a certified, diagnosed disease, but it sounds like you *were* fairly well incapacitated—and probably a little hung over too.

KIM: I don't drink.

DON: I apologize. A dumb assumption on my part. I'm sorry.

KIM: It's okay. So what are we going to do?

DON: Well, what do you suggest? Sounds like you ought to be able to take a makeup, but that you aren't exactly in the same position as somebody who had the flu or who had to attend a funeral.

KIM: I don't know; I think it's the same. I don't know why I should be penalized at all. But you're the teacher.

DON: Yeah, and *both* of us are involved in this—as is the rest of the class, indirectly. I'm concerned that the exam was Friday and now it's Monday.

KIM: And I could have talked about it with other people in the class.

DON: Yeah, that's possible; and that would be less fair to the others. I don't care to put you "on the stand" to testify about that; I don't like playing judge and jury. So what if I modify the exam, you take it this afternoon, and we knock fifteen points off the top because, as you put it, you did kind of "blow" it.

KIM: All of that's fine but the fifteen-point penalty. I think I was as sick as anyone who has the twenty-four-hour flu.

DON: Okay, let's run that part of it briefly by the class. I'll keep you anonymous and see how they feel about makeups under these general circumstances—whether they feel any unfairness.

KIM: Well, if you feel you have to do that.

DON: Sounds like you don't. What are you thinking?

Don's open-endedness is evident here in his unwillingness to set a rigid policy in advance, his concern that the two of them discuss the situation before arriving at a conclusion, and his willingness to admit his own errors and to acknowledge the validity of Kim's viewpoint. Obviously, he does have principles here, and the fact that he is open to play does not mean he's wishy-washy. In this case, his position is clear: "We definitely *do* have to do something about it, or you will end up with a zero," but he is willing to let the conversation guide the two of them toward their specific solution. There's also a little play here around titles—"professor" and "student"—and the "pile of excuses" metaphor. In addition, once Don enters into a discussion that is this open, he cannot not take Kim's arguments seriously. He has to at least listen to her; in that sense Don is "being played by the game." The same is obviously true for Kim. We end the example before a final resolution is reached to emphasize that even after this much talk it may still be important to stay open.

In Front Of

The third distinctive feature of dialogic listening is that it emphasizes what's in front of or between the conversation partners rather than what's "behind" them. One influential definition of empathy includes this sentence: "It is an experiencing of the consciousness 'behind' another's outward communication, but with continuous awareness that this consciousness is originating and proceeding in the other."[10] That's the opposite of dialogic listening. Instead of trying to infer internal "psychic" states from the talk, when you are listening dialogically you join with the other person in the process of co-creating meaning *between* you.

Again, we don't mean to be making an artificial dichotomy. "Internal states" cannot be separated from external ones, and thoughts and feelings are obviously a part of all communication. But it makes a big difference whether you are *focusing* on those internal states, trying to make an educated guess about where the other person is coming from, or focusing on building talk between the two of you. In other words, it can make a big difference whether your metaphor is "figuring out where she's coming from" or "sculpting mutual meanings." When your focus is "behind" you spend your time and mental energy searching for possible fits between what you're seeing and hearing and what the other person "must be" meaning and feeling. In other words, you're engaging in a form of psychologizing, treating the talk as an indicator of something else that's more reliable, more important, more interesting.

On the other hand, when you're listening dialogically, your focus, as we said before, is on the communication not the psychology. We don't mean that you are insensitive to the other person's feelings. In fact, your sensitivity may well be heightened, but it is focused *between* rather than behind. You concentrate on the verbal and nonverbal text that the two of you are building together. In one sense you take the talk at face value; you attend to it and not to something you infer to be behind it. But this doesn't mean you uncritically accept everything that's said as the "whole truth and nothing but the truth." You respond and inquire in ways that make the mutual text as full and reliable as possible. You work to co-build it into a text you *can* trust. That leads us to the final distinctive feature we want to mention.

Presentness

When you're listening dialogically, you focus more on the present than on the past or future. Once again, please don't hear an absolute; the future is not irrelevant and neither is the past. When we met to discuss our collaboration on this essay, we felt the pressure of a future deadline, and we were encouraged by the success of past interactions. But as we talked, our attention was on the present; we were open to what *could* be co-built, we focused on the "ours" *between* us, and all that helped keep us in the here-and-now.

The philosopher of communication, Martin Buber, was once described by his friend and biographer Maurice Friedman as a person with a unique ability to be "present to the presentness of the other and able to call the other into presence with him." Friedman speaks of how, when he met Buber, he first noticed his eyes. Others mentioned too how Buber's look was penetrating but gentle. His gaze and his look seemed both to demand presentness and to reassure. One person said that the message from Buber's eyes was always, "Do not be afraid." And it was difficult not to respond in kind, with as much presentness as one could muster. This quality of Buber's communication is what we mean by this characteristic of dialogic listening.

Buber also had another way of making the point we are making here: he talked of the desirability of working toward a unity of one's saying, being, and doing. In one of his books, Buber wrote that human life can be thought of as consisting of three realms: thought, speech, and action. "Whoever straightens himself out in regard to all three will find that everything prospers at his hand."[11] Later in the same book he added, "The root of all conflict between me and my fellow man is that I do not say what I mean and I do not mean what I say."[12]

It seems to us that if you are going to work toward unifying your saying, being, and doing, you are going to have to focus on the present. You can't connect and coordinate your actions, speech, and be-ing in any other way. It also seems that when we focus on the present as a way toward unifying these three realms, our efforts tend to make it easier for the other person to do the same thing. So the whole process can spiral in a very positive way.

"But," you may be asking, "what if the other person is lying? What if the 'present talk' *cannot* be trusted? Isn't your advice a little naive?" Our response, as we mentioned earlier, is that we are not suggesting blind naiveté. If you allow us one other personal example, trust was an issue for us as we collaborated on this essay. John is clearly "one up" on the power scale in this partnership, because he's an associate professor and Milt is a teaching assistant. In order for us to be able to practice what we are preaching about dialogic listening, John has to be willing and able to participate in genuine power *sharing,* and Milt has to *trust* him to do that. It isn't enough for John just to "give Milt power" by letting him have his say while reserving the right to make the final decision. He has to actually share responsibility, to leave the outcomes genuinely open. Both of us also need to trust each other to work constructively with incomplete, fuzzy, and sometimes off-the-point ideas. Especially because he's power-down, Milt needs to trust John, first to criticize rather than just to superficially agree with everything, and second, to criticize in constructive ways and not to ridicule unfinished ideas. We've been excited by the power sharing and trust that's been generated. We think it's materially improved the finished product.

If you aren't that fortunate and find that you mistrust the other's presence or his truthfulness, you can make that fact part of your conversation. There are ways to raise that issue without ridiculing or rejecting the other person. You can describe your reservations or ask your questions in ways that keep the conversation going, and that brings us to our "how to do it" section.

Applications

When we first began to think seriously about dialogic listening, we both moved almost immediately to this point. "What behavioral differences," we asked ourselves and each other, "are there between active or empathic listening and dialogic listening? What do you *do* differently?" For a while we felt like we'd run up against a brick wall. We could identify two or three important behaviors, "moves" or "techniques," but (1) there seemed to be much more to the process than just those behaviors and (2) strictly speaking, there was at least a mention in a "traditional" treatment of listening of each behavior on our list. After about two years of periodic thinking, discussing, and classroom experimenting, we began to understand our struggle. There are at least five ways of applying this approach to listening, but the most important element is the listener's *attitude, intent, awareness,* or *perspective.*

The first and most important application advice is that you define your specific listening situation as "ours," "open-ended," "between," and "present." Try not to focus your attention on "mine" or "his/hers," "control," "what's behind," or the past or future. When you're able to do that you will notice how "attitudes" and "behaviors" are not really separate. What you do—the behaviors—will *feel* different as your attitude or perspective shifts. At least that is our experience. For example, the ways we paraphrase (we'll discuss that skill in a minute) actually change as we shift from empathic to dialogic listening. We believe you may well discover the same. The point is, if you can genuinely achieve the mind-set we've discussed here, you'll have gone a long way toward listening dialogically.

"Say More"

One communication behavior that seems to be an application of that mind-set is the response, "Say more." As we explained when we discussed the sculpting metaphor, talk is tangible and malleable, and one of the primary goals of dialogic listening is to build more "chunks" of talk that develop ideas and suggestions, tease out nuances, and help define incomplete ideas. As a listener, you can most directly contribute to that process by simply encouraging your conversation partner to keep talking.

One common situation where "say more" can help is when someone makes a comment that sounds fuzzy or incomplete. Frequently, our inclination is to try to paraphrase what's been said or to act on that information even though we don't feel like we have the materials to do so. When Milt is in this situation, he finds himself feeling frustrated because he seems to have a disproportionate share of the burden to "make things clear." When he feels that frustration, he uses it as a signal to ask the person to "say more." The indirect message is that Milt wants the other person's help; he's saying, in effect, "I can't continue our sculpture until you add some definition to the form you began."

In this situation and in others, you might expect that your "say more" will just promote repetition and redundancy, but that's not been our experience. We find that if our encouragement is genuine, we frequently get talk that clarifies ideas, gets more specific, and substantially reduces misunderstanding. Like each of our suggestions, this one has to be used appropriately. It'd be pretty ridiculous to respond to "Could you tell me what time it is?" with "Say more about that." But each time you hear a new idea, a new topic, or an important point being made, we suggest you begin your listening effort at that moment not by guessing what the other person means but by asking them to tell you. "Say more," "Keep talking," or some similar encouragement can help.[13]

Run with the Metaphor

Our second suggestion is that you build more conversation-text, in part by extending whatever metaphors the other person has used to express his or her ideas, developing your own metaphors, or encouraging the other person to extend yours. As you know, a metaphor is a figure of speech that links two dissimilar objects or ideas in order to make a point. "My love is a red, red rose," "He's built like King Kong," and "The table wiggles because one leg is shorter than the other" all include metaphors. The first links my love and a rose in order to make a point. The second links his build and King Kong's, and the third links a table support with the appendage an animal uses to walk. As the third example suggests, metaphors are more common than we sometimes think. In fact, some people argue that virtually *all* language is metaphoric.[14]

We use the example, though, to encourage you to listen for both subtle and obvious metaphors and to weave them into your responses. We've found that when the other person hears his metaphor coming back at him, he can get a very quick and clear sense of how he's being heard. For example, notice how the process works in this conversation:

VICE PRESIDENT: This is an important project we're going after. Water reclamation is the wave of the future, if you'll pardon the pun, and we want to do as much of it as we can.

PROJECT MANAGER: I agree completely. But I am not sure the people from the other firms on our team are as enthusiastic as you and I are.

VICE PRESIDENT: Well, if they aren't, part of your job as quarterback is to get them charged up and committed. We can't go into this with a half-hearted attitude and expect to do well.

PROJECT MANAGER: Okay, I realize I am quarterbacking the effort, but it seems to me that the coach can also help "fire up the troops," and I haven't heard you doing much of that yet. Are you willing to help me increase their enthusiasm?

VICE PRESIDENT: Sure. What do you want me to do?

PROJECT MANAGER: I think part of the problem is they already think they've won the game. I don't. We haven't got this contract yet, and we won't get it unless we convince the city we *want* it. You could help by giving sort of half-time talk before the kickoff.

VICE PRESIDENT: Sure, no problem. I'll talk to everybody at the start of tomorrow's meeting.

In this situation the project manager develops his boss's "team" and "quarterback" metaphors by talking about what a "coach" can do with a "half-time talk." On the other hand, sometimes the process is more subtle.

CHIP: You look a lot less happy than when I saw you this morning. What's happening?

THERESE: I just got out of my second two-hour class today, and I can't believe how much I have to do. I'm really feeling squashed.

CHIP: "Squashed" like you can't come up for air, or "squashed" as in you have to do what everybody else wants and you can't pursue your own ideas?

THERESE: More like I can't come up for air. Every professor seems to think this is the only class I'm taking.

Again, the purpose of running with each other's metaphors (notice that "running with" is a metaphor too) is to co-build talk between you in order to produce as full as possible a response to the issues you face together. In addition, the metaphors themselves reframe or give you a new perspective on the topic of your conversation. A project manager who sees himself as a "quarterback" is going to think and behave differently from one who sees himself as a "general," a "guide," or a "senior-level bureaucrat." And the work stress that "squashes" you is different from the pressure that "keeps you jumping like a flea on a griddle." Listen for metaphors and take advantage of their power to shape and extend your ideas.

Paraphrase Plus

Our third suggestion is that you apply that most useful of all communication techniques, paraphrasing, but that you do it in a couple of new ways: Paraphrase not to *re*produce the other's meaning but to *pro*duce a fuller conversation-text between you, and ask the other person to paraphrase you. As we've noted, paraphrasing is usually defined as restating the other person's meaning in your own words. It's an enormously useful thing to do in *many* communication situations, including conflict, parent–child contacts, classroom, and on the job.

In a way, though, if you only spend your conversational time checking to see if you are following the same path as the other person, you aren't fully carrying your share of the conversational load. To do more of that, you can add to your paraphrase your own response to the question, "Now what?" In other words, you start by remembering that the meanings you are developing are created between the two of you, and individual perspectives are only a part of that. So you follow your perception-checking with whatever your good judgment tells you is your response to what the person said. The spirit of a paraphrase plus is that each individual perspective is a building block for the team effort.

When we suggest that paraphrasing can include new information—your contribution—we are not implying that the person listening dialogically has license to poke fun at or to parody the other person. Notice the difference among these three responses:

RITA: I like being in a "exclusive" relationship, and your commitment to me is important. But I still sometimes want to go out with other people.

MIKE'S RESPONSE: So even though there are some things you value about our decision not to date others, you're still a little uncertain about it.

TIM'S RESPONSE: Oh, so you want me to hang around like a fool while you go out and play social butterfly! Talk about a double standard!

SCOTT'S RESPONSE: It sounds like you think there are some advantages and disadvantages to the kind of relationship we have now. I like it the way it is now, but I don't like knowing that you aren't sure. Can you talk some more about your uncertainty?

Mike responded to Rita's comment with a paraphrase. That tells us that Mike listened to Rita, but not much more. Tim made a caricature of Rita's comment, masking an editorial in the guise of a paraphrase. Scott offered a paraphrase plus. He made explicit his interpretation of what Rita was saying, then he moved the focus of the conversation back to "the between," back to "the middle" where both persons could work on the problem together. Because of what Rita said, Scott may have felt hurt or mad or both, and maybe he wouldn't have been so constructive as we've made him sound, but the point is that he not only paraphrased but also interpreted and responded to her comments. When this happens both the paraphrase and the interpretation keep understanding growing between the individuals, instead of within them.

Another way to think about the paraphrase plus is that you're broadening your goal beyond "fidelity" or "correspondence." If you're paraphrasing for fidelity or correspondence, you're satisfied and "finished" with the task as soon as you've successfully reproduced "what she means." Your paraphrase is a success if it corresponds accurately to the other person's intent. We're suggesting that you go beyond correspondence to creativity, beyond reproducing to co-producing. It's the same point we've made before.

It's easy to see that this kind of listening takes energy, even more so if only one person in a conversation is committed to dialogue. One way to elicit help from the other participants in a conversation is to *ask for paraphrasing* from them. Whenever you're uncertain about whether the other person is listening fully, you can check their perceptions by asking them for talk. This works best if you don't demand a paraphrase, and if you don't say, "Ha! Gotcha!" if the other person cannot respond well. The other person's paraphrase can, however, let both of you check for mutual understanding, and it can also keep the other's interpretations and responses in the talk between you where they can be managed productively.

Context-Building

We've mentioned that your conversation partner(s) may sometimes not be as eager or as willing as you are to work toward shared understanding. Their indifference sometimes surfaces in semi-messages, such as a blank stare or a dirty look, an indistinct blob of words, or silence. Paraphrasing and asking for a paraphrase can help produce more talk to build on between you, but what else can you do? We've found that what we call context-building can help.

By "context" we mean the circumstances that surround or relate to a topic, idea, opinion, or statement. When someone says something, it is spoken in a particular context or situation, which is made up of at least the physical location, feelings and thoughts, and the comment it is a response to. When you are listening dialogically, you can thematize and help develop or flesh out this contextual information so it can become part of the material you are co-sculpting.

For example, often ideas come out initially as vague judgments such as, "That's stupid!" or, "What a jerk!" That's like slamming some clay down hard onto the potter's wheel. But there is potential value in a move like that, if you are willing to initiate talk that helps turn the clay from a blob into a more distinct shape. As difficult as it sounds, one of the best ways to respond to comments like these is to say, "What do you mean by 'stupid'?" or "Tell me more," or, "Where did that come from?" These contributions all help elicit additional talk.

Although many discussions of communication suggest that skillful communicators need to learn to describe their feelings, there is nothing particularly enlightening about, "I feel like hell!" thrown into the middle of a conversation. Feelings are accompanied by circumstances and desires—their context—and you can help sculpt mutual meanings by trying to find out what preceded the feelings, what they are a response to, and what desires accompany them. Try, "Are you disappointed by what she did to you or are you angry?" "I notice that whenever I offer a suggestion, you dismiss it. Do you see that happening too?" or, "What do you want to have happen?"

Of course, it's not always just the other person who offers de-contextualized comments. You too will catch yourself throwing out cryptic judgments and incomplete exclamations that contribute little to shared understanding. In fact, sometimes all of us do that on purpose. But when you are not trying to be vague, you can follow an "I'm bored," with talk about the parts of the context that you feel bored about and what you would like to have happen. These individual contributions can be part of a text of conversation that can help all the participants create shared meanings.

Potential Problems

We don't want to stop without at least mentioning some of the negative responses we've gotten to our efforts to listen dialogically. We assume that if you are actually going to try what we've outlined here, you may appreciate being forewarned about some potential difficulties.

Time   The first is most obvious: It takes *time*. Dialogic listening is not efficient. Open-endedness and play, a commitment to developing full conversation-texts and even presentness all extend and prolong talk-time. When you ask someone to "Say more," they usually do. Running with metaphors can fill up the better part of an afternoon. Be ready for that increased time commitment, and realize that when there just *isn't* time, most of your efforts to listen dialogically will be frustrated.

On the other hand, we've also found that the time issue becomes less important when we recognize (1) that the gain in quality of contact can more than balance the "loss" of time, (2) that dialogic listening generates "economies of clarity" that can increase subsequent communication efficiency, and (3) that it often doesn't take all *that* much time. By (1) we mean that yours and your conversation partner's feelings of confirmation, comfort, and even intimacy can be enhanced enough by dialogic listening that the time investment is more than worth it.

This kind of listening can also help a group handle misunderstanding before it gets serious and can help a couple build a firm foundation of mutual agreement under their relationship. Both those outcomes are examples of "economies of clarity." Our parallel here is the "economies of scale" that manufacturers get. As they get into larger-scale production—they build more widgets—their cost per widget goes down, and that's an example of "economy of scale." Similarly, as your listening builds clearer and clearer foundations, you can move through more fuzzy or problematic issues faster. That's what we mean by an "economy of clarity."

We've also found that though dialogic listening definitely takes time, it doesn't need to go on forever. A ten-minute conversation may be extended to fifteen minutes, and a one-hour meeting to an hour and twenty minutes. And usually that's not too much to pay for what you can get.

What Are You Up To?　After experiencing some openness, some presentness, a few "Keep talking'" and "Paraphrase what I just said" responses, some people want to stop the conversation to find what's going on. They perceive those communication behaviors as a little unusual, and they jump to the conclusion that we must be up to something. "Is this a study of some kind?" "Are you just answering every question with a question, or what?" Some people may perceive your efforts to co-build more talk as disruption just for the sake of disruption. Others may even hear this kind of listening as manipulative.

We believe there are two ways to respond to this challenge. The first is to examine your own motives. *Are* you "listening for effect"? *Are* you obstructing or manipulating? In order for this kind of listening to work, your attitude needs to be one of genuine open-endedness focusing on ours, and so on.

The second way is to give a brief account of what you're doing, to *meta*communicate. Metacommunication simply means communication about your communication, talk about your talk, (see Chapter 3 above) and it can help facilitate your dialogic listening, especially where someone's feeling manipulated. Try, "I want us to talk about this more before we decide," or, "I'd really like to hear more talk; I don't think we've gotten everything out on the table yet and I'd like us to play with as full a deck as we can." You may even want to go into more detail about the value of focusing on the between and staying present—expressed in your own words, of course. Or in other situations you may want to begin a discussion with something like, "Let's just play with this question for a while. We don't have to come up out of this discussion with a solid decision or conclusion." The point is, if your motives are genuine and you can metacommunicate or give an account of your motives, you should be able to diminish much of the other person's defensiveness and sense of being manipulated.

"Give Me a Break!"   Sometimes when one of us asks another person to paraphrase what he just said or when we slow down a group discussion with meta-communication or a request for someone to "Say more," others respond with exasperation. "Ease up," they might say, "Give me a break," or "Get off my back." Dialogic listening both takes and demands effort, and sometimes people don't feel like they have the energy to invest in it. During the group experience Milt described at the beginning of this essay, his dialogic listening efforts were sometimes met with responses that indicated that Susan and Jack were just "tolerating Milt's little digressions." And that can be frustrating; it can even hurt. At other times people can simply refuse to engage with you—they ignore your request to "Say more" or they simply stop talking.

There is no easy solution to this set of problems. Another dose of self-examination can help: *Are* you coming across like a pushy true-believer? Have you let your efforts to listen dialogically become a new task that you're trying to force on the group? Sometimes "give-me-a-break" responses really mean, "Let me be lazy," and you need to gently persevere. But at other times you need to remember that all you can do is all you can do, and it's time to back off a bit.

Conclusion

We believe that dialogic listening is little different from some other approaches to listening. We experience the focus on "ours" as an actual shift of awareness, the open-ended playfulness as a real challenge, and the concentration on the between and on presentness as ways to highlight the productive, co-creating that we are engaging in with our conversation partners. We also notice some different communication behaviors, although they feel different mainly because of our shift from an empathic to a dialogic perspective, attitude, or point of view. Of the five we've discussed here, the commonest and most useful behaviors for us are "Say more," running with the other's metaphor, and the paraphrase plus.

But we don't want to overemphasize the differences. The communication attitudes and behaviors that are discussed under the headings of active and empathic listening can also promote genuine understanding. Even more important, though we've discussed these ideas and skills as an approach to dialogic *listening,* they can also serve as the guidelines for a complete approach to interpersonal communicating. That's because they are based on the works of two philosophers of dialogue, Martin Buber and Hans-Georg Gadamer. Buber's and Gadamer's writing and teaching offer an approach to all your communicating that is only partly developed and applied in what we say here about listening. It's the approach that's behind this entire book, and we hope that by the time you've read through all these materials, you'll see how these fit together. (We especially recommend that you compare this essay with the final one in the book, Buber's "Elements of the Interhuman.")

Listening is only part of the entire communication process. But if it's dialogic listening, it can promote the richest kind of interpersonal-quality contact. Listening dialogically involves focusing on what you share with the persons you are talking with, playing with the conversation in an open-ended way, concentrating mostly on the ideas talked about together, and maintaining an emphasis on "Here and now." Some ways to instill in your communication these aspects of a dialogic approach to listening are to encourage others to "Say more," to run with metaphors, to include new information in paraphrasing (and request paraphrasing from others), and to build in as much contextual information as you can to facilitate clarity. We encourage you to develop the attitudes and skills associated with a dialogic perspective in listening and see if you find them helpful.

References

1. See, for example, Lyman K. Steil, Larry L. Barker, and Kittie W. Watson, *Effective Listening: Key to Your Success* (Reading, Mass.: Addison-Wesley, 1983); Madelyn Burley-Allen, *Listening: The Forgotten Skill* (New York: Wiley, 1982); and Florence I. Wolff, Nadine C. Marsnik, William S. Tracey, and Ralph G. Nichols, *Perceptive Listening* (New York: Holt, Rinehart & Winston, 1983).
2. Steil, Barker, and Watson, p. 5.
3. Carl R. Rogers, *A Way of Being* (Boston: Houghton Mifflin, 1980), pp. 142–143.
4. Robert Bolton, "Listening Is More than Merely Hearing," in *People Skills: How to Assert Yourself, Listen to Others, and Resolve Conflicts* (Englewood Cliffs, N.J.: Prentice-Hall, 1979), p. 51.
5. See, e.g., Lawrence M. Brammer, *The Helping Relationship: Process and Skills,* 2nd ed. (Englewood Cliffs, N.J.: Prentice-Hall, 1979), Chapter 4.
6. Roger von Oech, *A Whack on the Side of the Head: How to Unlock Your Mind for Innovation* (Menlo Park, Calif.: Creative Think, 1982), pp. 29–39.
7. There is, however, a large and important "metaphoric" or "soft" side of physics, especially theoretical and nuclear physics, and of mathematics.
8. William S. Howell, *The Empathic Communicator* (Belmont, Calif.: Wadsworth, 1982), pp. 9–10.
9. We're thinking of Hans-Georg Gadamer and Paul Ricoeur. See, e.g., Gadamer's *Truth and Method* (New York: Seabury Press, 1975), pp. 91ff. and Ricoeur, "Appropriation," in *Hermeneutics and the Human Sciences,* ed. and trans. by John B. Thompson (Cambridge: Cambridge University Press, 1981), pp. 182–186.
10. G. T. Barrett-Lennard, "Dimensions of Therapist Response as Casual Factors in Therapeutic Change," *Psychological Monographs,* 76 (1962), cited in Rogers, *A Way of Being,* p. 144.
11. Martin Buber, "The Way of Man," in *Hasidism and Modern Man,* ed. and trans. Maurice Friedman (New York: Harper & Row, 1958), p. 155.
12. Ibid., p. 158.
13. Our suggestion here is similar to Step 2 of Robert Bolton's discussion of "door openers."
14. Paul Ricoeur, *The Rule of Metaphor: Multi-Disciplinary Studies of the Creation of Meaning in Language,* trans. Robert Czerny with Kathleen Mclaughlin and John Costello, SJ (London: Routledge and Kegan Paul, 1978).

Review Questions

1. In your own words, describe the essential features of what has been called "empathy."
2. What shortcomings of the concept of "empathy" do Milt and I discuss?
3. Paraphrase the difference we discuss between *reproductive* listening and *productive* listening.
4. Develop an example of the potter's wheel image we describe. Choose a person who's "seated at the wheel" with you (i.e., a person you're having a conversation with). Describe what the "clay" is (the conversation topic; what each of you says). Continue in this way until you've described a hypothetical conversation about this topic between the two of you using our "sculpting" metaphor.
5. What are the "three c's" we discuss? How do the three c's relate to dialogic listening?
6. Describe the distinction we make between psychology and communication.

7. What does it mean to "unify your saying, being, and doing"?
8. Describe the basic difference between a "paraphrase" and a "paraphrase plus."
9. What's "context-building"?

Probes

1. "I know you believe you understand what you think I said, but I'm not sure you realize that what you heard is not what I meant." It strikes us that dialogic listening is a good *solution* to the *problem* that this quotation describes. Do you agree? Discuss.
2. Paraphrase our point that it's impossible to "lay aside yourself." Give an example from your own experience of this impossibility.
3. How well does the "sculpting" metaphor work for you? In what ways is it especially illuminating? In what ways does it seem inappropriate? What alternatives or additional metaphors would you suggest for the process we discuss here?
4. The idea that you can work with talk itself, that it is tangible and malleable and can be productively shaped, is a little unusual for some people. How is that idea different from some of what you've been taught in the past about human communication?
5. Do you agree that there are many pressures on us today pushing us toward the three c's—certainty, closure, and control? How do they affect your communicating?
6. Give an example from your own experience of conversational *play*. Discuss it with others. Which of the characteristics of play that we discuss do you notice in your own communicating?
7. Assume you are talking with a group of friends and one of them makes a racist or sexist remark that you don't like. In this situation how might you "unify your saying, being, and doing"?
8. What happens when you try the "Say more" response we suggest?
9. Identify two metaphors in this essay that we did not discuss as examples of metaphorizing. Notice how many there are to choose from.
10. Explain what it means to shift your paraphrasing-goal from fidelity or correspondence to creativity. (And, if you want to, pinpoint which previous Probe in this set asks essentially this same question.)
11. Which of the three potential problems that we discuss seems to you to be the most difficult?

Part 3

Openness as "Exhaling"

Chapter 8

Self-Disclosure

In order to see I have to be willing to be seen. If a man takes off his sunglasses I can hear him better.

HUGH PRATHER

I think/feel that it's important, before you read about how self-disclosure works, to be sure that you and I agree on what we're talking about. Self-disclosure is *not* interpersonal exhibitionism; it's *not* the communication equivalent of jumping onto the nearest desk or table and ripping your clothes off. People who fear the process or who want to attack the whole idea of communicating interpersonally often treat disclosure as if it *were*.

Self-disclosure is the act of verbally and nonverbally sharing with another some aspects of what makes you a person, aspects the other individual wouldn't be likely to recognize or understand without your help. In other words, self-disclosure is verbally and nonverbally making available information about your uniqueness, your choice-making, your addressability, and the unmeasurable or reflective parts of you—for example, your feelings.

It's very important, I think, to remember that self-disclosure is a process that can improve a *transaction,* that can positively affect what's happening *between* persons. Disclosure is not meant to meet just one person's needs, but rather to enhance the *relationship.* Consequently, effective self-disclosure is disclosure that's *appropriate,* appropriate to the situation and appropriate to the relationship between the persons communicating. A crowded theater or a football game is not the place to discuss a profound religious experience even with your closest friend. Intimate sexual fantasies are usually not appropriate topics for a teacher to discuss with a student or for an employer to discuss with an employee. In short, you don't disclose just to make *you* feel better, but to facilitate the relationship. So, some disclosures are appropriate and some are not.

Self-disclosure is also not necessarily negative and not necessarily profound. You can help another know you as a person by sharing your joy, your excitement, your anticipation, or enthusiasm, and it doesn't have to be about the most weighty topic in your life. Small joys, small compliments, small successes, or even small disappointments can help others know who you are.

You might look at my comments in the introduction to this book as an example of what I'm talking about. I do want you to know more about me than just that I'm "author" or "teacher." I do want you to see some of my personness. But I'm convinced that you would probably be bored, offended, or both by a detailed account of every heavy happening I've experienced in the past several years. So I want to tell you something, but not everything, of what distinguishes me from other persons, something of the choices I've made and the changes I've experienced recently, something of my feelings about what I'm doing. Since you're not here to respond in person, I'm not sure that what I've said is appropriate to the relationship between you and me, but I am working to make it that. I chose to disclose some of my self to you because I want our relationship to be more than just "writer–reader," but I also chose *what* to disclose because I know that our relationship cannot be intimate or long-term. I would encourage you to treat self-disclosure in the same way: choose to do it because it will help others know you as a person, but base your choices on a clear understanding of what's desirable and what's possible for the *relationship.*

One more thing. Sometimes people fear self-disclosure because they feel that their self is their most precious possession and that if they give much of it to others, they are liable to run out, to end up without any self left. This fear is based on the assumption that selves are like money or the hours in a day—there is only so much and when it's gone, it's gone. But the assumption simply isn't accurate. Selves are not governed by the economic law of scarcity. Since each of us is continually growing and changing— becoming—the more we share, the more there is to share. To put it another way, when I give you something of myself, I don't give it "up"; I still "have" it, but as a result of my disclosure, now you "have" it too. As many couples who have enjoyed a long-term intimate relationship have learned, you can never succeed in disclosing everything about yourself. Similarly, the more you know about the other, the more clearly you realize how much more there is to know. Self-disclosure doesn't eliminate what Jourard calls the "mystery" of the other person; it can enhance it. In short, the fear that if you disclose you risk giving up all of your self is groundless.

It *is* true, though, that disclosure is risky. When I share something of my personness with you, I take the risk that you might reject it. That kind of rejection could hurt. But I take the risk because I know that if I don't, we cannot meet as persons. Although disclosing is risky, the relationship that can come with appropriate disclosure makes the risk, for me, worth it.

Elaine Hatfield's discussion of disclosure comes from a book called *Communication, Intimacy, and Close Relationships.* As a result, her article treats self-disclosure not as an end in itself but as a prerequisite for the achievement of intimacy. Intimacy, of course, happens most often between spouses, lovers, and friends. And we often assume that intimacy involves some kind of sexual contact. But I think it's useful when reading this essay to think of intimacy as a more general phenomenon. Professionals often develop intimate—although completely nonsexual—relationships with their clients. My wife Kris, for example, is an attorney, and she's found that you cannot go through a lengthy trial or negotiation process without developing attorney-client relationships that are intimate in some ways. Other long-term business relationships with accountants, stockbrokers, doctors, therapists, consultants, or even clothing or shoe salespersons sometimes also develop toward intimacy. In addition, long-term work relationships can take on some similar features. After several years in the same office, store, or factory, people commonly develop relationships close enough to be called "intimate." Hatfield implies this when she defines intimacy as a process in which "we attempt to get close to another; to explore similarities (and differences) in the ways we both think, feel, and behave." That happens in more than just dating and sexual relationships.

After sketching the cognitive, emotional, and behavioral aspects of intimacy, Hatfield talks about six common fears that make us reluctant to become intimate with others. I won't repeat what she says here, but I do think she makes some especially important points about abandonment, control, and being engulfed. As she explains, one reason we sometimes avoid intimacy is the fear that, if we get close, it will hurt more when the person leaves. Another fear regards the loss of control over our lives that genuine intimacy can often bring. Intimacy develops a kind of interdependent or even dependent relationship, and that means I alone am no longer 100 percent responsible for my happiness. Some people fear that loss of control. The fear of being engulfed is similar. Some are worried that they will get lost in the other person. Hatfield discusses a family that was plagued by that fear.

In the second half of her article, Hatfield offers a "prescription for intimacy." She begins by emphasizing the complementary relationship between independence and intimacy. You literally cannot have one without the other. Then she outlines four skills for developing intimacy. Her approach here is consistent with much of what you've already read in *Bridges Not Walls,* and a great deal of what appears in Part 5 of this book.

The Dangers of Intimacy

Elaine Hatfield

I have two careers—I am chair of the psychology department at the University of Hawaii and a family therapist at the King Kalakaua Center in Honolulu, Hawaii. In both roles, I'm bombarded with questions about love, sex, and intimacy. One of the most common dilemmas people face is "How intimate dare I be with friends and lovers?"

Theorists and therapists take it for granted that people need intimacy.... In intimate encounters we discover our own and other people's innermost natures. Close family relationships spark the deepest of feelings. It is in our early intimate encounters that we learn our basic strategies for dealing with the world.

Yet most people are wary of intimate encounters. My cotherapist Dr. Richard Rapson and I spend most of our time dealing with people's fears of intimacy. Why? Their caution is not without reason....

Intimacy: What Is It?

The word intimacy is derived from the Latin *intimus*, meaning "inner" or "inmost." In a wide variety of languages, the word intimate refers to a person's innermost qualities. For example, the French *intime* signifies "secret, deep, fervent, ardent." The Italian *intimo* conveys "internal, close in friendship." In Spanish, *intimo* means "private, close, innermost." To be intimate means to be close to another.

..., we will define *intimacy* as: A *process* in which we attempt to get close to another; to explore similarities (and differences) in the ways we both think, feel, and behave.

Intimate relationships have a number of characteristics.

Cognitive   Intimates are willing to reveal themselves to one another. They disclose information about themselves and listen to their partners' confidences.

Research supports the contention that men and women are willing to disclose far more about themselves in intimate relationships than in casual ones. In casual encounters, most people reveal only the sketchiest, most stereotyped information about themselves. Yet, as the French essayist Montaigne (1948) observed, everyone is complex, multifaceted:

> All contradictions may be found in me ... bashful, insolent; chaste, lascivious; talkative, taciturn; tough, delicate; clever, stupid; surly, affable; lying, truthful; learned, ignorant; liberal, miserly and prodigal: all this I see in myself to some extent according to how I turn ... I have nothing to say about myself absolutely, simply and solidly, without confusion and without mixture, or in one word. (p. 242)

In deeply intimate relationships, friends and lovers feel free to reveal far more facets of themselves. They reveal more of their complexities and contradictions. As a result, intimates share profound information about one another's histories, values, strengths and weaknesses, idiosyncracies, hopes, and fears (Altman & Taylor, 1973; Huesmann & Levinger, 1976; Jourard, 1964; Worthy, Gary, & Kahn, 1969)....

Emotional   Intimates care deeply about one another. When discussing intimate encounters, most theorists seem to assume that the more intimate a relationship, the more friends and lovers like and love one another. In fact, most scales of liking and loving assume love and intimacy are unidimensional concepts—that human feelings range from love (the high point), through liking, through neutrality, through dislike to hatred (the low point) (Berscheid and Walster {Hatfield}, 1968).

Yet folk wisdom and our own experiences tell us that there is something wrong with such a unidimensional view of love—often love and hate go hand in hand. The opposite of love is not hate, but indifference. It is in intimate relationships that we feel most *intensely*. True, we generally feel more intense love for intimates than for anyone else. Yet, because intimates care so much about one another, they have the power to elicit intense pain as well; the dark side of love is jealousy, loneliness, depression, and anger. It is this powerful interplay of conflicting emotions that gives vibrancy to the most intimate of relationships. (See Berscheid, 1979, 1983; Hatfield and Walster, 1981).

Basic to all intimate relationships, of course, is trust.

Behavioral   Intimates are comfortable in close physical proximity. They gaze at one another (Argyle, 1967; Exline, 1972; Rubin, 1970), lean on one another (Galton, 1884; Hatfield, Roberts, & Schmidt, 1980; Mehrabian, 1968), stand close to one another (Allgeier & Byrne, 1973; Byrne, Ervin, & Lambreth, 1970; Goldberg, Kiesler, & Collins, 1969; Sheflen, 1965), and perhaps touch.

For most people, their intimate relationships are the most important thing in their lives. (See Berscheid & Peplau, 1983; Cook & Wilson, 1979; Duck & Gilmour, 1980, 1981a, 1981b, 1982; Fisher & Stricker, 1982; Pope, 1980.) Clients who come to see us at King Kalakaua clinic are usually seeking intimacy—they are eager to find someone to love, to maintain a faltering love affair, or are adjusting to separation or divorce. Everyone needs intimacy. Why then is it so hard to find? Why are people reluctant to risk it? To understand this, theorists must focus not just on the advantages of intimacy, but on its *risks*. In the following section, we focus on the dangers of intimacy. In the section called "Prescription for Intimacy" we review what theorists and scientist-practitioners know about securing the benefits of intimacy while minimizing its risks.

Intimacy: Why Not?

Why are people reluctant to become intimate with others? There are many reasons:

Fear of Exposure

In deeply intimate relationships we disclose far more about ourselves than in casual encounters. As a consequence, intimates share profound information about one another's histories, values, strengths and weaknesses, idiosyncracies, hopes, and fears. (See Altman & Taylor, 1973; Huesmann & Levinger, 1976; Jourard, 1964; Perlmutter & Hatfield, 1980; Worthy *et al.*, 1969.)

One reason, then, that all of us are afraid of intimacy, is that those we care most about are bound to discover all that is wrong with us—to discover that we possess taboo feelings ... have done things of which we are deeply ashamed.

Such fears are *not* neurotic. The data make it clear that people who reveal too much to others, too soon, *are* judged to be a little peculiar. (See Derlega & Chaikin, 1975, for a review of this literature.)

Fear of Abandonment

A second reason people fear exposure is because they are concerned that if others get to know them too well, they will abandon them. Such concerns, too, are sometimes realistic.

We can think of examples:

One of my favorite graduate students was a beautiful Swedish woman. At one time, three sociologists at the University of Wisconsin were in love with her. Her problem? She pretended to be totally self-confident, bright, charming. In intimate affairs, each time she tried to admit how uncertain she was, to be herself, the men lost interest. They wanted to be in love with a *Star*, not a mere mortal like themselves.

A second reason, then, that people are reluctant to risk intimacy, to admit how needy they are, is that they are terrified that their friends and lovers will abandon them.

Fear of Angry Attacks

Another reason people are reluctant to reveal themselves to others is the fear that "anything they say will be used against them." Most of us worry that if we reveal confidences to our friends, they will reveal the confidences to their friends, who will reveal them to their friends, etc.

One of my clients was Sara, a Mexican-American army wife. Her parents had divorced when she was three. Her father was granted custody, thereafter she was abused both sexually and physically. Sara was justifiably proud of the fact that she learned to be "a perfect lady" in even the most impossible of circumstances. Her voice was always calm, her emotions in control. She took pride in not ever needing anyone for anything. Her only problem was that she didn't have a single friend in whom to confide. At long last, she decided to trust one of her sisters. She painfully revealed that her marrige was falling apart and that she was thinking of leaving. Her sister became enraged and denounced her. What kind of a Catholic was she!

Similarly, a powerful businessman I interviewed observed that if he were to reveal that he was worried about getting old, worried that he was not as smart as his computer-age competition, he could expect his competitors to seize on his revelations with glee.

Sometimes it *is* dangerous to trust.

Fear of Loss of Control

Men and women are sometimes afraid to risk becoming intimate for yet another reason—they fear losing control. Some theorists have speculated that *men* may be particularly afraid of intimacy and the loss of control it brings. (See Hatfield, 1982.) Traditionally, men are supposed to be in control—of themselves, of other people, and of the situation. The ideal man carefully controls his *thoughts;* is logical, objective, and unemotional. He hides his *feelings,* or if he does express any feelings, he carefully telescopes the complex array of human emotions into a single powerful emotion: anger. A "real man" is even supposed to dominate nature.

In contrast, the ideal woman is supposed to be expressive and warm. She is comfortable expressing a rainbow of "feminine" feelings—love, anxiety, joy, and depression. (She may be less in touch with anger.) She is responsive to other people and the environment.

Broverman and her colleagues (1972) asked people what men and women *should* be like and what they really *are* like. Their answer was clear: men should be/ are in control and instrumental. Women should be/are expressive and nurturant.

According to theorists, there are marked gender differences in three areas: (1) desire to be "in control"; (2) desire to dominate their partners versus submit to them, and (3) desire to "achieve" in their love and sexual relations. If such gender differences exist, it is not surprising that women feel more comfortable with intimacy than do men. Unfortunately, although a great deal has been written about these topics, there is almost no research documenting that such gender differences exist. (See Hatfield, 1982.)

Fear of One's Own Destructive Impulses

Men and women sometimes fear intimacy for yet another reason.

Many of my clients keep a tight lid on their emotions. They fear that if they ever got in touch with what they are feeling, they would begin to cry ... or kill.

One of my Korean clients was a traditional macho man. As he sat in my office he often explained that men *had* to be cool. He refused to even allude to the things that were bothering him. As a therapist, it was obvious to me that he was anything but cool. He looked like a seething volcano. He was an enormous, powerful man— a Tai Chi expert. As he explained "analytically" how he felt about things, his eyes blazed, his jaw clenched, he smashed his fist into the palm of his other hand. People were terrified of him. He had to stay cool at all times, he insisted ... otherwise he would kill.

He was undoubtedly wrong. In therapy, I have found that as people learn to be ever more aware of what they're feeling, they find that their emotions are not as powerful, not nearly so overpowering as they had assumed, that somehow they can learn to express their feelings in a controlled way. Yet the fear is real.

Fear of Losing One's Individuality or of Being Engulfed

When I first began reading the intimacy literature, I discovered that theorists believed that one of the most primitive fears of intimacy was the feeling that one would be engulfed by another, the fear that one would literally disappear as he or she lost himself in another. (See Diamond and Shapiro, 1981, for a discussion of this point.) To me, such a concern was inconceivable.

Then I met the Watsons in therapy, and for the first time got some sense of what it meant to fear engulfment. The Watsons were a bright, delightful, and thoroughly crazy family. The father and the mother insisted that they wanted their girls to become independent, to leave home and build families of their own. However, every time the "girls" (who were 50) showed the least independence, their parents got angry. They complained that the girls weren't doing "it" right. They should be more relaxed about their endeavors. They should be breezy ... while succeeding spectacularly. The daughters were the first people I ever heard say they were afraid to get close to anyone for fear that they would be "swallowed up." Basically, Patti and Mary were confused about what they wanted versus what everyone else in the family wanted. Each time they were tempted to express themselves, they would be overtaken by guilt. They began a tortured internal dialogue. Why were they so ungrateful? Demanding? Their parents would be hurt terribly. Was it fair to do that to them? "No." They inevitably decided to remain mute.

Nor were Patti and Mary capable of really listening. If they listened, if they permitted themselves to see what their parents needed, they would be responsible for sacrificing themselves completely to provide it. They would lose their freedom. Even then what could they do? They were too weak.

So everyone stayed in their own shell. No one could ever be really independent: no one could ever be really intimate with others for fear that they would be engulfed.

A Prescription for Intimacy

Everyone needs a warm intimate relationship. At the same time, one must recognize that in every social encounter there are some risks. What, then, is the solution? Social psychological research and clinical experience gives us some hints (See Sprecher & Hatfield, 1986).

A basic theoretical assumption provides the framework we use in teaching people how to be intimate with others. People must be capable of independence in order to be intimate with others; capable of intimacy, if they are to be independent. Independence and intimacy are not *opposite* personality traits, but *interlocking* skills. People who lack the ability to be independent *and* intimate can never really be either. They are never really with one another, never really without them.

What we set out to do, then, is to make people comfortable with the notion that they and the intimate are separate people, with separate ideas and feelings, who can sometimes come profoundly close to others.

According to theorists, one of the most primitive tasks people face is to learn how to maintain their own identity and integrity while yet engaging in deeply intimate relationships with others. (For a fuller discussion of this point, see Erikson, 1968; Fisher & Stricker, 1982; Freud, 1922; Hatfield and Walster, 1981; Kantor & Lehr, 1975; Kaplan, 1978; Maslow, 1954; Pope, 1979.)

Once individuals have the skills to be independent/intimate, they must find an appropriate lover or chum on which to practice their art.

In a few situations, the only thing one can do is to play out a stereotyped role. In most situations, one has to be at least tactful; in a few, downright manipulative, in order to survive. But on those occasions when real intimacy is possible, men and women can recognize its promise, seize their opportunities, and take a chance. . . .

People need intimacy; yet they have every reason to fear it. What advice can social psychologists give men and women as to how to secure the benefits of deep encounters while not being engulfed by their dangers?

The advice we would give follows directly from the theoretical paradigm we offered earlier—one must be independent before one can be intimate; intimate before one can be independent. How do we teach the impossible? It's easy.

Developing Intimacy Skills

Encouraging People to Accept Themselves as They Are   It is a great temp-tation to dwell in the realm of absolutes. One is either a saint or a sinner. Many people are determined to be perfect (at least); they can't settle for less.

Yet Saintliness/Evil are the least interesting of human conditions. Real life is lived in the middle zone. Real people inevitably have some real strengths; yet every-body possesses small quirks that makes them what they are. The real trick to enjoy-ing life is not just to accept diversity, but to learn to take pleasure in it.

The first step in learning to be independent/intimate, then, is to come to accept the fact that you are entitled to be what you are—to have the ideas you have, the feelings you feel, to do the best that you can do. And that is good enough.

In therapy, we try to move people from the notion that one should come into the world perfect and continue that way to a realization that one can only gain wisdom in small steps. People must pick one small goal and work to accom-plish that. When that's accomplished, they can move on to another. That way change is manageable, possible (Watson & Tharp, 1981). You can never attain per-fection, only work toward it.

Encouraging People to Recognize Their Intimates for What They Are   People may be hard on themselves, but they are generally even harder on their partners. Most people have the idea that everyone is entitled to a perfect partner, or at least one a little bit better than the one available. (See Hatfield, Traup-mann, Sprecher, Utne, & Hay, 1986.) If people are going to have an intimate rela-tionship, they have to learn to enjoy others as they are, without hoping to fix them up.

It is extraordinarily difficult for people to accept that their friends are entitled to be the people they are. From our own point of view, it seems so clear that things would be far better if our mates were only the people we wanted them to be. It would take so little for them to change their whole character structure. Why are they so stubborn?

If we can come to the realization that our lover or friend is the person who exists right now—not the person we wish he was, not the person he could be, but what he is—once that realization occurs, intimacy becomes possible.

Encouraging People to Express Themselves   Next, intimates have to learn to be more comfortable about expressing their ideas and feelings. This is harder than one might think.

People's intimate relations are usually their most important relationships. When passions are so intense, consequences so momentous, people are often hes-itant to speak the truth. From moment to moment, they are tempted to present a consistent picture. If they're in love, they are hesitant to admit to their niggling doubts. (What if the person they love is hurt? What if their revelations destroy the relationship?) When they are angry, they don't want to speak about their love or their self doubts, they want to lash out.

To be intimate, people have to push toward a more honest, graceful complete, and patient communication; to understand that a person's ideas and feelings are necessarily complex, with many nuances, shadings, and inconsistencies. In love, there is time to clear things up.

One interesting thing that people often discover is that their affection increases when they begin to admit their irritations. People are often surprised to discover that sometimes, when they think that they have fallen out of love—they are "bored" with their affair—that as they begin to express their anger and ambivalence, they feel their love come back in a rush.

In *The Family Crucible* Napier and Whitaker (1978) describe just such a confrontation.

> 1) What followed was a classic confrontation. If John's affair was a kind of reawakening, so now was this marital encounter, though of a very different sort. Eleanor was enraged, hurt, confused, and racked with a sense of failure. John was guilty, also confused, but not apologetic. The two partners fought and cried, talked and searched for an entire night. The next evening, more exhausting encounters. Feelings that had been hidden for years emerged; doubts and accusations that they had never expected to admit articulated.
>
> Eleanor had to find out everything, and the more she discovered, the more insatiable her curiosity became. The more she heard, the guiltier her husband became and the angrier she grew, until he finally cried for a halt. It was his cry for mercy that finally led to a temporary reconciliation of the couple. They cried together for the first time either of them could remember.
>
> For a while they were elated; they had achieved a breakthrough in their silent and dreary marriage. They felt alive together for the first time in years. Somewhat mysteriously, they found themselves going to bed together in the midst of a great tangle of emotions—continuing anger, and hurt, and guilt, and this new quality: abandon. The lovemaking was, they were to admit to each other, "the best it had ever been." How could they have moved through hatred into caring so quickly? (p. 153)

Love and hate tend to flow together (Hatfield & Walster, 1981; Kaplan, 1979).

Teaching People to Deal with Their Intimate's Reactions   To say that you *should* communicate your ideas and feelings, *must* communicate if you are to have an intimate affair, does not mean your partner is going to like it. You can expect that when you try to express your deepest feeling, it will hurt. Your lovers and friends may tell you frankly how deeply you have hurt them and that will make you feel extremely guilty. Or they may react with intense anger.

Intimates have to learn to stop responding in automatic fashion to such emotional outbursts—to quit backing up, apologizing for what they have said, measuring their words. They have to learn to stay calm, remind themselves that they are entitled to say what they think, feel what they feel, listen to what their partners think and feel and keep on trying.

Only then is there a chance of an intimate encounter.

References

Allgeier, A. R., & Byrne, D. (1973). Attraction toward the opposite sex as a determinant of physical proximity. *Journal of Social Psychology, 90,* 213–219.

Altman, I. (1973). Reciprocity of interpersonal exchange. *Journal for the Theory of Social Behavior, 3,* 249–261.

Altman, I., & Taylor, D. A. (1973). *Social penetration: The development of interpersonal relationships.* New York: Holt.

Argyle, M. (1967). *The psychology of interpersonal behavior.* Baltimore, MD: Penguin Books.

Berscheid, E. (1979). *Affect in close relationships.* Unpublished manuscript.

Berscheid, E. (1983). Emotion. In H. H. Kelley *et al.* (Eds.), *Close relationships* (pp. 110–168). NY: Freeman.

Berscheid, E., & Peplau, L. A. (1983). The emerging science of relationships. In Harold H. Kelley *et al.* (Eds.), *Close relationships* (pp. 1–19). NY: Freeman.

Berscheid, E., & Walster (Hatfield), E. (1968). *Interpersonal attraction.* Reading, MA: Addison Wesley.

Broverman, I., Vogel, S., Broverman, D., Clarkson, F., & Rosenkrantz, P. (1972). Sex role stereotypes: A current appraisal. *Journal of Social Issues, 28*(2), 59–78.

Byrne, D., Ervin, C. R., & Lamberth, J. (1970). Continuity between the experimental study of attraction and "real life" computer dating. *Journal of Personality and Social Psychology, 16,* 157–165.

Cook, M., & Wilson, G. (Eds.) (1979). *Love and attraction.* NY: Pergamon.

Cozby, P. C. (1973). Self-disclosure: A literature review. *Psychological Bulletin, 79,* 73–91.

Davis, J. B., & Skinner, A. E. (1978). Reciprocity of self-disclosure in interviews: Modeling of social exchange. *Journal of Personality and Social Psychology, 29,* 779–784.

Derlega, V. J., & Chaikin, A. L. (1975). *Sharing intimacy: What we reveal to others and why.* Englewood Cliffs, NJ: Prentice-Hall.

Diamond, M. J., & Shapiro, J. L. (1981). *The paradoxes of intimate relating.* (Available from Dr. J. L. Shapiro, King Kalakaua Center for Humanistic Psychology, Honolulu, HI 96821.)

Duck, S., & Gilmour, R. (Eds.) (1980). *Personal relationships.* Vol. 1. *Studying personal relationships.* London: Academic Press.

Duck, S., & Gilmour, R. (Eds.) (1981a). *Personal relationships.* Vol. 2. *Developing personal relationships.* London: Academic Press.

Duck, S., & Gilmour, R. (Eds.) (1981b). *Personal relationships.* Vol. 3. *Personal relationships in disorder.* London: Academic Press.

Duck, S., & Gilmour, R. (1982) *Personal relationships.* Vol. 4. New York: Academic Press.

Erikson, E. H. (1968). *Childhood and society* (rev. ed.). New York: Norton.

Exline, R. (1972). Visual interaction: The glances of power and preference. In J. Cole (Ed.), *Nebraska Symposium on Motivation 1971.* Lincoln: University of Nebraska Press.

Fisher, M., & Stricker, G. (Eds.) (1982). *Intimacy.* NY: Plenum.

Freud, S. (1922). *Group psychology and the analysis of the ego.* London: Hogarth.

Galton, F. (1884). Measurement of character. *Fortnightly Review, 36,* 179–185.

Goldberg, G. N., Kiesler, C. A., & Collins, B. E. (1969). Visual behavior and face-to-face distance during interaction. *Sociometry, 32,* 43–53.

Hatfield, E. (1982). What do women and men want from love and sex? In E. R. Allgeier & N. B. McCormick (Eds.), *Gender roles and sexual behavior: The changing boundaries.* Palo Alto, CA: Mayfield.

Hatfield, E., Roberts, D., & Schmidt, L. (1980). The impact of sex and physical attractiveness on an initial social encounter. *Recherches de psychologie sociale, 2,* 27–40.

Hatfield, E., Traupmann, J., Sprecher, S., Utne, M., & Hay, J. (1986). Equity and intimate relations: Recent research. In W. Ickes (Ed.), *Compatible and incompatible relationships.* NY: Springer-Verlag.

Hatfield, E., & Walster, G. W. (1981). *A new look at love.* Reading, MA: Addison-Wesley.

Huesmann, L. R., & Levinger, G. (1976). Incremental exchange theory: A formal model for progression in dyadic social interaction. In L. Berkowitz and E. Hatfield-Walster (Eds.), *Equity theory: Toward a general theory of social interaction.* New York: Academic Press, 9, 192–230.

Jourard, S. M. (1964). *The transparent self.* Princeton, NJ: Van Nostrand.

Jourard, S. (1971). *Self-disclosure: An experimental analysis of the transparent self.* New York: Wiley.

Jourard, S., & Friedman, R. (1970). Experimenter–subject distance in self-disclosure. *Journal of Personality and Social Psychology, 15,* 278–282.

Kantor, D., & Lehr, W. (1975). *Inside the family.* San Francisco: Jossey-Bass.

Kaplan, H. S. (1979). *Disorders of sexual desire.* New York: Simon & Schuster.

Kaplan, L. J. (1978). *Oneness and separateness: From infant to individual.* NY: Simon & Schuster.

Marlatt, G. A. (1971). Exposure to a model and task ambiguity as determinants of verbal behavior in an interview. *Journal of Consulting and Clinical Psychology, 36,* 268–276.

Maslow, A. H. (1954). *Motivation and personality.* NY: Harper.

Mehrabian, A. (1968). Relationship of attitude to seated posture, orientation, and distance. *Journal of Personality and Social Psychology, 10,* 26–30.

Montaigne, M. de. (1948). Of the inconsistency of our actions. In D. M. Frame (Trans.), *Complete essays of Montaigne* (p. 242). Stanford, CA: Stanford University Press.

Napier, A. Y. (1977). *The rejection–intrusion pattern: A central family dynamic.* Unpublished manuscript, School of Family Resources, University of Wisconsin–Madison.

Napier, A. Y., & Whitaker, C. (1978). *The family crucible.* New York: Harper & Row.

Perlmutter, M., & Hatfield, E. (1980). Intimacy, intentional metacommunication and second-order change. *American Journal of Family Therapy, 8,* 17–23.

Pleck, J. H., & Sawyer, J. (Eds.) (1974). *Men and masculinity.* Englewood Cliffs, NJ: Prentice-Hall.

Pope, K. S. (1980). Defining and studying romantic love. In K. S. Pope and Associates (Eds.), *On love and loving.* San Francisco, CA: Jossey-Bass.

Rubin, A. (1970). Measurement of romantic love. *Journal of Personality and Social Psychology, 16,* 265–273.

Rubin, A., Hill, C. T., Peplau, L. A., & Dunke-Schetter, C. (1980). Self-disclosure in dating couples: Sex roles and the ethic of openness. *Journal of Marriage and the Family, 42,* 305–317.

Scheflen, A. E. (1965). Quasi-courtship behavior in psychotherapy. *Psychiatry, 28,* 245–257.

Sprecher, S., & Hatfield, E. (1986). Interpersonal attraction. In G. Stricker & R. Keisner (Eds.), *The implications of non-clinical research for clinical practice.* New York: Plenum.

Watson, D. L., & Tharp, R. G. (1981). *Self-directed behavior* (3rd ed.). Monterey, CA: Brooks-Cole.

Worthy, M. A., Gary, L., & Kahn, G. M. (1969). Self-disclosure as an exchange process. *Journal of Personality and Social Psychology, 13,* 63–69.

Review Questions

1. What distinction does Hatfield make between the cognitive, emotional, and behavioral aspects of intimacy? Give an example of each.
2. How is fear of abandonment similar to fear of loss of control?
3. How is fear of being engulfed similar to fear of loss of control?
4. What does Hatfield mean when she says that independence and intimacy are "not *opposite* personality traits, but *interlocking* skills"?
5. What does Hatfield say about the relationship between self awareness and self-disclosure?
6. Hatfield says that our disclosive communication ought to be "honest, graceful, complete, and patient." Explain what she means by each of these adjectives.

Probes

1. Which of the six fears of intimacy are most commonly experienced by young people, and which are experienced most as we get older? Are you aware of any developmental patterns in these fears?
2. Which one of the six fears of intimacy do you experience most? In what ways is your fear legitimate? In what ways is it exaggerated? What steps might you take to lessen the fear?
3. Can you think of a time when your fear of exposure was legitimate—when someone discovered something "wrong" with you and rejected you for it? Can you think of a time when that fear was unfounded? What were the differences between the two situations?

4. Logically it would appear that independence is the opposite of togetherness or intimacy. So how can Hatfield support her claim that the two are "interlocking" or complementary? Can you give an example from your own experience or the experience of someone you know that demonstrates the complementarity of independence and intimacy?
5. How does Hatfield deal with the point that you cannot force intimacy on another person?

John and Kris Amodeo are family counselors who've written a book called *Being Intimate*. This chapter of their book focuses on what they call self-revealing communication. The Amodeos first repeat a very useful distinction others have made between "I-statements" and "You-statements." They point out that, while the difference might be obvious, the effect of using one versus the other can be profound. You-statements are almost always heard as blaming, fault-finding, or self-centered acting-out. None of that contributes much to interpersonal communication. I-statements, on the other hand, can be heard as clean, self-revealing comments that promote interpersonal contact.

It's important to note that they aren't always heard that way. One person's I-statements can be heard by another person as thinly-disguised criticisms. When this happens, the conversation partners need to work harder to develop mutual understanding. The point is, your word choice is important, but it won't guarantee success.

The second section of this article discusses several benefits of self-revealing communication. The Amodeos describe how it can, among other things, deescalate interpersonal tension, heal the wounds between oneself and a friend or partner, and invite others to change their behavior while respecting their autonomy.

The final section focuses on an important paradox of self-disclosure that these authors call "the power of vulnerability." Many people—for example, macho males—believe that aggressive, loud posturing will always be interpreted as a sign of confidence and strength. But just a little reflection will remind you that the reverse is often true. When we see someone acting aggressive, we often understand that he or she is actually trying to mask insecurity. Belligerence is often a cover-up for fear. Vulnerability, on the other hand, can be an extremely strong posture. As the Amodeos point out, "a special kind of inner strength is required to 'hold our own' as we experience and assert our genuine feelings, as opposed to aggressively reacting with blame, attacks, moralizing, or other forms of manipulation. . . ." They make some very useful points about this paradox in this article.

The essay concludes by encouraging you to consider how you might take the risk of revealing more about yourself in order to build some relationships that move toward genuine intimacy.

Self-Revealing Communication: A Vital Bridge Between Two Worlds

John and Kris Amodeo

Structuring Our Language to Invite Contact

The complex art of verbal communication is a learned skill that can enhance intimacy and mutual understanding when the structure of our language conveys the trust-promoting attitudes of honesty, acceptance, caring, and respect. The ability to state our experience in a simple, direct, noncoercive manner can serve the dual purpose of communicating what is happening in our inner world while honoring other people's right to respond to us in a manner that preserves the integrity of their own felt experience. Integrating this respectful attitude into the very structure of our language can do much to promote trust and create genuine contact between two autonomous individuals.

Thomas Gordon, in a landmark book entitled *Parent Effectiveness Training,* describes how communication is more effective when we express ourselves using "I statements" as opposed to "you statements." "I statements," or what we will call "self-revealing communications," are those that disclose our experience without attacking others, invalidating their feelings, or criticizing them for not meeting our needs or conforming to our point of view. Self-revealing communications invite others into our tender world of feelings and meanings. They reflect a willingness to risk being vulnerable, rather than resort to strategies of control or manipulation in order to get what we want.

For example, we might say, "I'm feeling frustrated about our conversation because I imagine that I'm not being understood." This way of expression effectively says how we feel ("frustrated") and gives the additional input of sharing what this feeling means to us ("being misunderstood").

Instead of this self-disclosing communication, we could resort to a variety of what Gordon calls "you statements," or what we prefer to call "intrusive communications." For example, instead of cleanly communicating that we feel frustrated or sad, we could blame the other person for not understanding us by saying something such as, "We're not resolving our conflict because you don't listen to my side of the story!" We could also criticize the other by a hostile statement such as, "You never want to listen to me!" Or, we may wage a personal attack by responding, "You're really selfish, childish, and stupid!"

The above reactions are impulsive ways of acting out our feelings, as opposed to simply sharing them. This can quickly lead to a downward spiral in the communication process. Mistrust grows and communication falters (if it ever existed in the first place), because people then feel judged rather than respected, criticized instead of accepted, intruded upon rather than invited to openly explore disagreements. Feeling less safe to be open and vulnerable, individuals will tend to react by either increasing their verbal attacks, which can further escalate a counter-productive power struggle, or withdrawing entirely in order to protect themselves from further hurt.

Self-revealing communications reflect a wise willingness to take responsibility for how we feel, rather than transfer blame or make judgmental decrees that infringe upon people's basic humanness. For instance, we may say, "I feel hurt when you joke about my weight. That's a sensitive area because people have kidded me about it all of my life." This statement is a simple, open description of how we feel. It also offers information to the other person that may assist him or her in understanding how past experiences have contributed to our present feeling. It does not counter-attack by saying, "Well, you're pretty flabby, too!" It does not criticize by exclaiming, "You're always nagging me about my weight." It does not place demands or pose threats as by stating, "If you don't stop, you'll be sorry!" All of these intrusive statements are manipulations in that they are intended to coerce the other to change his or her behavior, rather than to simply express our feelings. Such assertions represent a lack of trust in the other person's propensity to respond favorably to us if we reveal our more tender, vulnerable feelings. And, practically speaking, these intrusive statements rarely, if ever, produce lasting changes. Although one or the other may temporarily give in, resentments will continue to mount. As the basic humanness of the organism is wounded by this judgmental, coercive process, a cycle of damaging communications is generated. Allowing this to continue, a relationship can degenerate to the point where all openness and warmth are crushed. The two vulnerable and hurting human beings then take care of themselves the best way they know how—by retreating behind walls of self-protection and defense. However, the periodic eruption of vindictive, embittered fights will reveal the layer upon layer of unresolved resentment, hurt, and mistrust. . . .

Learning to communicate in a more reflective, self-revealing manner can halt a painful escalation of interpersonal tension by removing the fuel that has been intensifying the conflict. Hostilities may then cease long enough for us to explore what is really going on—that is, the unacknowledged feelings, meanings, and unmet needs that are at the source of the difficulties. As these are openly shared, some trust may re-emerge.

Whether we long to heal the wounds with a friend or partner, improve a satisfying relationship, or initiate a new one, self-revealing communications can be instrumental in eliciting responses from others that lead to greater love and intimacy in our lives. Such expressions shine a gentle light on our inner world, offering a glimpse of what we really feel and how we see things. This more self-searching and self-disclosing approach to interpersonal relating holds the prospect that another will treat us with loving care and human sensitivity as we become willing to be transparent. Lowering our defensive shield, we open ourselves to the possibility of being seen and warmly embraced, which is our quiet hope, although we risk being hurt, which is an ever-present possibility.

Focusing attention on the dimension of disclosing our feelings, instead of on the nearly impossible task of trying to change others' behavior, can drastically shift the typical interactional scenario. By simply sharing how we feel in response to people's words or actions, we reveal our hurt, fear, anger, or other vulnerable feelings that are evoked by their words or deeds. Communicating in this way becomes an invitation for others to sensitively respond to our feelings and concerns, and, perhaps, to voluntarily modify their behavior.

A basic assumption behind self-revealing expressiveness is that if people see who we really are, how we really feel, and what we really need, they will tend to respond to us in an accommodating manner; at ground level, people do care about one another, and wish to be helpful if they can.…

In order for others to care about us they need to know what we are feeling. And, rather than assume that they already understand or "should" know how we feel, it is our responsibility to tell them. Self-revealing statements can be an empowering, effective way to communicate feelings and needs. An honest self-disclosing expression of our real feelings can make the crucial difference that leads to greater trust. Being non-manipulative, such expressions encourage others to concretely express their caring for us by allowing themselves to be touched by our feelings, and, as a result, respond to us in a more loving, cooperative way.

By communicating in a more vulnerable, self-revealing manner, we give people a chance to change while respecting their autonomous right to choose whether or not they want to change or give us what we are asking for. If they minimize our concerns, resist communicating about them, or refuse to be touched by our experience, then, of course, we may not feel very safe to continue exposing our vulnerable feelings. Our sense of trust will most likely diminish because we are not receiving caring in the way we need it. A vital, growing relationship requires two individuals who are willing and able to be touched by one another's feelings and be responsive to each other's felt concerns.

The communication of feelings is best done when others have the time and interest to hear what we have to say, rather than trying to make contact during a football game or after a tiring day at work. Eliminating or minimizing the distracting influences of the television, telephone, children, or pets enables us to attend more carefully to our subtle feelings and understand each other's concerns. It is often helpful to set aside time on a regular basis, such as one evening each week, in order to discuss ongoing issues or share recent upsets so that they may be resolved before they grow into more serious conflicts.

Creating undistracted time to open to each other's feelings, can create a refreshingly safe environment in which to become better acquainted with one another, and, as trust builds, to enjoy the flourishing of love and intimacy.

The Power of Vulnerability

Although using self-revealing statements to sensitively share our feelings and needs may appear to reduce us to a weaker position in terms of getting what we want from a relationship, in reality, the opposite is true. On the surface, it may seem that we rise to a stronger position by fighting for the changes we would like to see in the other person. We often fool ourselves by thinking that if only we could assert ourselves a little more convincingly or forcefully, then the other person would finally change.

Those who have discovered the hidden power of vulnerability realize that being vulnerable does not mean being weak. In fact, a special kind of inner strength is required to "hold our own" as we experience and assert our genuine feelings, as opposed to aggressively reacting with blame, attacks, moralizing, or other forms of manipulation that create an adversarial position. Even the intense emotion of anger can be expressed "cleanly" without being contaminated by blame, criticism, or self-righteousness.

As we learn to caringly accommodate our softer feelings, we can breathe more deeply and take greater risks in relation to others. Feeling strong and confident within ourselves, our communications can embody an integrity that respects another's freedom of response while affirming our right to our feelings and to make crucial life decisions based upon our growth needs.

Responding from a confident center within our vulnerable inner world reflects a special kind of inner strength. Reacting in a demanding or hostile way usually masks a personal sore spot or long-term unexpressed and unsatisfied need. What is sometimes considered to be a "strong" or courageous position often camouflages a host of unacknowledged fears or unexplored areas within ourselves that we have yet to understand, accept, or befriend.

For example, Rose, who wanted the best for her son, Ira, pressured him to enter medical school, which he reluctantly agreed to do. Finding the stresses of school overwhelming, he wanted to drop out, a decision his mother found difficult to accept. Needing her love and respect (and having an undeveloped inner caretaker), he agreed to push ahead in school. Shortly thereafter, Ira died of cancer. Only then was Rose able to acknowledge her fear of being embarrassed or ashamed if her son did not enter a prestigious profession.

What seemed a strong position by Rose was actually a reaction to her unexplored fears of being an inadequate parent. Unskilled at contacting and communicating her more vulnerable feelings, and unwilling to trust Ira to make decisions consistent with his own best interests, she remained invested in her own decision regarding what he should do. This led to pressuring him in ways that she later regretted.

Trying to achieve resolution on the dimension of feelings, rather than being preoccupied with what we think is the "right" thing for someone to do (the dimension of behavior), is more likely to produce the changes we want. For example, Lynn became very upset when Gary became attracted to another woman and was considering becoming more deeply involved with her. Lynn was aware of her hurt while maintaining respect for his choices. She expressed her hurt and allowed herself to cry without being accusatory or demanding, although she reserved the option to move out in case she needed to take care of herself in this way.

Gary was touched by her vulnerable sharing and appreciated not being criticized or told that he was acting immaturely or insensitively—invalidating accusations that had hurt him in previous relationships. Allowing himself to be affected by her hurt, he experienced a shift from being confused about what to do to feeling a deeper sense of intimacy with her. Lynn also discovered that expressing her real feelings produced an outcome in which she felt closer to Gary. Interestingly, it is this feeling of closeness that each of them had really been wanting, and which never would have resulted had she tried to make him feel guilty or change his behavior in some coercive way. It is likely that he would have then simply rebelled against the threat to his autonomy. In other words, her willingness to be vulnerable (and not controlling) had a surprisingly powerful effect that, indirectly, led to the deeper commitment she had been wanting.

Self-revealing statements create a climate in which it is vastly easier for another to remain attentive and interested in what we are saying. Reflecting an open-handed approach, they act as a gesture of goodwill and trust. Rather than condemn, insult, or defy, they open a door through which our real selves can be seen and empathetically understood. Consequently, conflicts or differences can be more easily resolved because the other is invited to visit and participate in our inner world of feelings and meanings....

As human beings we possess the unique capacity to discover a serene territory that exists somewhere beneath the biologically programmed "fight or flight" response. The key to that territory lies in our capacity to simply experience the threatening feelings that exist immediately prior to our impulse to attack or flee. The major ones, as we have been mentioning throughout, are fear (or terror), sadness (or grief), hurt (or woundedness), anger (or rage), embarrassment (or shame), loneliness (or isolation), and longing (or intense desire). Personal growth is largely a function of our capacity to be with these feelings in an accepting, sensitive manner. The goal is to befriend them, not transcend them.

The ability to be caretakers for ourselves in regard to these feelings—that is, to simply be with them in an allowing way—can have a surprisingly transformative effect upon our lives and relationships. When we become capable of welcoming and being with these feelings as they arise within ourselves, our hearts and minds can remain open as we experience difficulties in relation to another person. As we face the "demons" (scary unwanted feelings) within ourselves and communicate these feelings to another, an interesting thing tends to happen. Being with and sharing intense feelings with another person are two essential ways of moving toward a deep place of restful contact within ourselves and in relation to another being. As we learn to stabilize in our capacity to identify and be present to a full range of human feelings, we become more and more at home with ourselves. From this base we can then openly communicate our experience to another person. Doing so, we come to know and understand one another more deeply. Communication becomes the bridge between our two separate worlds.

Those moments during which basic emotions, insistent needs, and personal concerns and dissatisfactions are no longer coursing through us are rare ones. However, these quiet moments are often the most rich and meaningful ones of our lives. We sometimes experience this after a poignant sharing of threatening or tender feelings. Engaging one another in a real, honest manner, we may find that communication at times, progresses into a non-verbal sense of contact or intimacy that can be referred to as a state of union or an experience of love. Free of unsettling feelings or undercurrents of dissatisfaction, we simply become present with one another—two beings free of struggle and pretensions, simply breathing and being together....

Review Questions

1. When the Amodeos discuss how to structure our language to invite contact, which linguistic element do they focus on?
2. According to the authors, how can you-messages lead to "a downward spiral in the communication process"?
3. List the benefits of self-revealing communication that the Amodeos discuss.
4. What is the paradox of power and vulnerability?
5. What do the authors mean when they say that self-revealing communication can help us respond in ways that involve neither "fight nor flight"?

Probes

1. Some people argue that you cannot actually change other people; the only person you can change is yourself. Do John and Kris Amodeo appear to agree or disagree with this generalization? How does their position on this issue affect what they say about self-revealing communication?

2. Recount an example that you either experienced or observed where vulnerability was powerful. What features of the communication situation helped it be interpreted that way?

3. How realistic do you think John and Kris Amodeo are about self-revealing communication? Is the position they take a naive one? Or do you think you can apply their advice in communication situations you experience?

I n this reading Neil Postman presents the viewpoint of "the opposition." Postman offers a sensible and compelling argument *against* the notion that all we have to do to solve our problems is to communicate more effectively. Better communication, he says, is *not* a panacea, especially if by better communication we mean self-disclosing, that is, "saying what's on your mind," and "expressing your feelings honestly."

Postman reminds us, as do some communication researchers, that one of the important functions of speech communication is concealment.[1] Civility is a necessary part of society, he argues, and civility sometimes requires that we keep our feelings to ourselves. It's pretty hard to ignore the way he makes his point; as he puts it in one place, "There is no dishonesty in a baboon cage, and yet, for all that, it holds only baboons."

Postman maintains that when people disagree fundamentally—for example, about racial issues—"honest openness may not help at all." He writes, "There is no good reason . . . for parents always to be honest with their children."

You may find it tempting to dismiss Postman as some kind of fascist and to reject his remarks as inflammatory hate-mongering. Try not to take that easy way out. His main point is, as he puts it, "that 'authentic communication' is a two-edged sword," and I think that's an idea that's well worth thinking about and discussing.

I feel frustrated and disappointed when my students—or readers of this book—conclude that the main message in all of this is just that we need to "be open and honest." That's a vast oversimplification, and it's also a dangerous one. One of Postman's most important points is that in any given situation we do not have *an* "honest feeling" but a complex of often conflicting "authentic" feelings. So the expression of one may be no more or less "honest" or "dishonest" than the expression of another.

I hope this essay will prompt the kind of reflection and discussion that can move well beyond a simplistic belief in the universal value of "being open and honest."

Reference

1. Malcolm Parks, "Ideology in Interpersonal Communication: Off the Couch and into the World," *Communication Yearbook 5,* ed. Michael Burgoon (New Brunswick, N.J.: Transaction Books, 1982), pp. 79–107.

The Communication Panacea

Neil Postman

In the search for the Holy Grail of complete harmony, liberation, and integrity, which it is the duty of all true Americans to conduct, adventurers have stumbled upon a road sign which appears promising. It says in bold letters, **"All problems arise through lack of communication."** Under it, in smaller print, it says: "Say what is on your mind. Express your feelings honestly. This way lies the answer." A dangerous road, it seems to me. It is just as true to say, This way lies disaster.

I would not go so far as Oliver Goldsmith, who observed that the principal function of language is to *conceal* our thoughts. But I do think that concealment is one of the important functions of language, and on no account should it be dismissed categorically. As I have tried to make clear earlier, semantic environments have legitimate and necessary purposes of their own which do not always coincide with the particular and pressing needs of every individual within them. One of the main purposes of many of our semantic environments, for example, is to help us maintain a minimum level of civility in conducting our affairs. Civility requires not that we deny our feelings, only that we keep them to ourselves when they are not relevant to the situation at hand. Contrary to what many people believe, Freud does not teach us that we are "better off" when we express our deepest feelings. He teaches exactly the opposite: that civilization is impossible without inhibition. Silence, reticence, restraint, and, yes, even dishonesty can be great virtues, in certain circumstances. They are, for example, frequently necessary in order for people to work together harmoniously. To learn how to say no is important in achieving personal goals, but to learn how to say yes when you want to say no is at the core of civilized behavior. There is no dishonesty in a baboon cage, and yet, for all that, it holds only baboons.

Now there are, to be sure, many situations in which trouble develops because some people are unaware of what other people are thinking and feeling. "If I'd only *known* that!" the refrain goes, when it is too late. But there are just as many situations which would get worse, not better, if everyone knew exactly what everyone else was thinking. I have in mind, for example, a conflict over school busing that occurred some time ago in New York City but has been replicated many times in different places. Whites against blacks. The whites maintained that they did not want their children to go to other neighborhoods. They wanted them close at hand, so that the children could walk home for lunch and enjoy all the benefits of a "neighborhood school." The blacks maintained that the schools their children attended were run-down and had inadequate facilities. They wanted their children to have the benefits of a good educational plant. It was most fortunate, I think, that these two groups were not reduced to "sharing with each other" their real feelings about the matter. For the whites' part, much of it amounted to, "I don't want to live, eat, or do anything else with niggers. Period." For the blacks' part, some of it, at least, included, "You honky bastards have had your own way at my expense for so long that I couldn't care less what happens to you or your children." Had these people communicated such feelings to each other, it is more than likely that there could have been no resolution to this problem. (This seems to have been the case in Boston.) As it was, the issue could be dealt with *as if* such hatred did not exist, and therefore, a reasonable political compromise was reached.

It is true enough, incidentally, that in this dispute and others like it, the charge of racism was made. But the word *racism,* for all its ominous overtones, is a euphemism. It conceals more than it reveals. What Americans call a *racist* public remark is something like "The Jews own the banks" or "The blacks are lazy." Such remarks are bad enough. But they are honorifics when compared to the "true" feelings that underlie them.

I must stress that the "school problem" did not arise in the first place through lack of communication. It arose because of certain historical, sociological, economic, and political facts which could not be made to disappear through the "miracle of communication." Sometimes, the less people know about other people, the better off everyone is. In fact, political language at its best can be viewed as an attempt to find solutions to problems by circumventing the authentic hostile feelings of concerned parties.

In our personal lives, surely each of us must have ample evidence by now that the capacity of words to exacerbate, wound, and destroy is at least as great as their capacity to clarify, heal, and organize. There is no good reason, for example, for parents always to be honest with their children (or their children always to be honest with them). The goal of parenthood is not to be honest, but to raise children to be loving, generous, confident, and competent human beings. Where full and open revelation helps to further that end, it is "good." Where it would defeat it, it is stupid talk. Similarly, there is no good reason why your boss always needs to know what you are thinking. It might, in the first place, scare him out of his wits and you out of a job. Then, too, many of the problems you and he have do not arise from lack of communication, but from the nature of the employer-employee relationship, which sometimes means that the less money you make, the more he does. This is a "problem" for a labor organizer, not a communication specialist.

Some large American corporations have, of late, taken the line that "improved communication" between employees and management will solve important problems. But very often this amounts to a kind of pacification program, designed to direct attention away from fundamental economic relationships. It is also worth noting that a number of such corporations have ceased to hold "communication seminars" in which executives were encouraged to express their "true" feelings. What happened, apparently, is that some of them decided they hated their jobs (or each other) and quit. Whether this is "good" or not depends on your point of view. The corporations don't think it's so good, and probably the families of the men don't either.

The main point I want to make is that "authentic communication" is a two-edged sword. In some circumstances, it helps. In others, it defeats. This is a simple enough idea, and sensible people have always understood it. I am stressing it here only because there has grown up in America something amounting to a holy crusade in the cause of Communication. One of the terms blazoned on its banners is the phrase *real* (or *authentic*) feelings. Another is the motto "Get in touch with your feelings!" From what I have been able to observe, this mostly means expressing anger and hostility. When is the last time someone said to you, "Let me be *lovingly* frank"? The expression of warmth and gentleness is usually considered to be a façade, masking what you are really thinking. To be certified as authentically in touch with your feelings, you more or less have to be nasty. Like all crusades, the Communication Crusade has the magical power to endow the most barbarous behavior with a purity of motive that excuses and obscures just about all its consequences. No human relationship is so tender, apparently, that it cannot be "purified" by sacrificing one or another of its participants on the altar of "Truth." Or, to paraphrase a widely known remark on another subject, "Brutality in the cause of honesty needs no defense." The point is that getting in touch with your feelings often amounts to losing touch with the feelings of others. Or at least losing touch with the purposes for which people have come together.

A final word on the matter of "honesty." As I have said before, human purposes are exceedingly complex—multileveled and multilayered. This means that, in any given situation, one does not have *an* "honest feeling," but a whole complex of different feelings. And, more often than not, some of these feelings are in conflict. If anger predominates at one instant, this does not mean it is more "authentic" than the love or sorrow or concern with which it is mingled. And the expression of the anger, alone, is no less "dishonest" than any other partial representation of what one is feeling. By *dishonesty*, then, I do not merely mean saying the opposite of what you believe to be true. Sometimes it is necessary to do even this in the interests of what you construe to be a worthwhile purpose. But more often, dishonesty takes the form of your simply not saying *all* that you are thinking about or feeling in a given situation. And, since our motives and feelings are never all that clear, to our own eyes in any case, most of us are "dishonest" in this sense most of the time. To be aware of this fact and to temper one's talk in the light of it is a sign of what we might call "intelligence." Other words for it are discretion and tact.

The relevant point is that communication is most sensibly viewed as a means through which desirable ends may be achieved. As an end in itself, it is disappointing, even meaningless. And it certainly does not make a very good deity.

Review Questions

1. What does Postman mean by "civility"?
2. Some persons insist that *whenever* humans disagree, to *some* extent there's a communication problem. Postman clearly doesn't agree. What is his position on this issue?
3. True or false: Postman urges the reader *not* always to "be honest." Explain.
4. What does Postman mean by "the Communication Crusade"? Where have you experienced this "crusade"?

Probes

1. Postman may sound like he is disagreeing with everything written by the other authors in this chapter. But I'm not so sure. What specific comments and suggestions by John and Kris Amodeo and Elaine Hatfield is Postman emphasizing and developing? Where is he agreeing with points that they make?
2. In your experience is what Postman calls "civility" more a function of keeping feelings to one's self or expressing them in "constructive" ways? How so?
3. Do you agree or disagree with Postman's characterization of the perceptions and feelings that are "really" behind racist remarks? Discuss.

4. What's an example from your own experience of the accuracy of Postman's claim that "sometimes, the less people know about other people, the better off everyone is"?
5. In what specific ways do you agree or disagree with what Postman says about parenting?
6. What does Postman mean when he says that authentic communication is a two-edged sword? What are the two "edges"? How can the sword "cut" two ways?
7. Discuss an example from your own experience where you felt a complex of inconsistent or perhaps contradictory "honest feelings." How did you handle them in that situation?

Chapter 9

Confirmation

The human person needs confirmation. . . . An animal does not need to be confirmed, for it is what it is unquestionably. It is different with {the person}. Sent forth from the natural domain of species into the hazard of the solitary category, surrounded by the air of a chaos which came into being with him, secretly and bashfully he watches for a Yes which allows him to be and which can come to him only from one human person to another. It is from one {person} to another that the heavenly bread of self-being is passed.

MARTIN BUBER

onfirmation means actively acknowledging a person as a person, recognizing him or her as a subject, a unique, unmeasurable, choosing, addressable human. As Cissna and Sieburg point out, Martin Buber was the first to use the term in this interpersonal sense.* As the quotation that begins this paragraph shows, Buber identifies confirmation as a phenomenon that distinguishes the human world from the nonhuman. His point is that we discover our personhood or humanness as we make contact with others. I learn that I am a person when I experience confirmation from another person. That's one of the crucial functions of communication; to confirm others and experience confirmation myself.

Ken Cissna and Evelyn Sieburg are two speech communication teachers who've been studying confirmation for several years. This essay is nicely organized into a section that defines and describes confirmation, a section that identifies its four main dimensions, and then a longer section that talks systematically about confirming and disconfirming behaviors.

The authors describe and illustrate how what they call indifferent responses, impervious responses, and disqualifying responses are all disconfirming. Indifference denies the other's existence, while imperviousness means responding only to my image of you, even if it contradicts your perception of yourself. We communicate indifference, for example, by avoiding eye contact or physical contact or by ignoring topics the other person brings up. Imperviousness can be communicated, for example, with "Don't be silly—of course you're not afraid," or, "Stop crying, there's nothing the matter with you!" Disqualification is the technique of denying without really saying "no," as we do when, for example, we utter the "sigh of martyrdom," respond tangentially to the other person, or say something like, "If I were going to criticize, I'd say your haircut looks awful, but I wouldn't say that."

Responses that confirm, the authors point out, are less clearly defined than disconfirming ones. However, they identify three clusters of communication, recognition, acknowledgment, and endorsement. They also emphasize that "confirming response is dialogic in structure; it is a reciprocal activity involving shared talk and sometimes shared silence." That echoes the points about contact and the between that I've made and that have been made by several other contributors to this book.

---

*Martin Buber, "Distance and Relation," in *The Knowledge of Man,* ed. Maurice Friedman, trans. Maurice Friedman and R. G. Smith (New York: Harper & Row, 1965), p. 71.

Patterns of Interactional Confirmation and Disconfirmation

Kenneth N. Leone Cissna and Evelyn Sieburg

The term "confirmation" was first used in an interpersonal sense by Martin Buber (1957), who attributed broad existential significance to confirmation, describing it as basic to humanness and as providing the test of the degree of humanity present in any society. Although Buber did not explicitly define confirmation, he consistently stressed its importance to human intercourse:

> The basis of man's life with man is twofold, and it is one—the wish of every man to be *confirmed* as what he is, even as what he can become, by men; and the innate capacity in man to confirm his fellow men in this way.... Actual humanity exists only where this capacity unfolds. {p. 102}

R. D. Laing (1961) quoted extensively from Buber in his description of confirmation and disconfirmation as communicated qualities which exist in the relationship between two or more persons. Confirmation is the process through which individuals are "endorsed" by others, which, as Laing described it, implies recognition and acknowledgment of them. Though Laing developed confirmation at a conceptual level more thoroughly than anyone prior to him, his focus remained psychiatric: he was concerned with the effects of pervasive disconfirmation within the families of patients who had come to be diagnosed as schizophrenic. In such families, Laing noted, one child is frequently singled out as the recipient of especially destructive communicative acts by the other members. As Laing explained it, the behavior of the family "does not so much involve a child who has been subjected to outright neglect or even to obvious trauma, but a child who has been subjected to subtle but persistent *disconfirmation*, usually unwittingly" (1961:83). Laing further equated confirmation with a special kind of love, which "lets the other be, but with affection and concern," as contrasted with disconfirmation (or violence), which "attempts to constrain the other's freedom, to force him to act in the way we desire, but with ultimate lack of concern, with indifference to the other's own existence or destiny" (1967:58). This theme of showing concern while relinquishing control is common in psychiatric writing and is an important element in confirmation as we understand it. Although Laing stressed the significance of confirmation, he made no attempt to define it in terms of specific behaviors, noting only its variety of modes:

> Modes of confirmation or disconfirmation vary. Confirmation could be through a responsive smile (visual), a handshake (tactile), an expression of sympathy (auditory).

From Kenneth N. Leone Cissna and Evelyn Sieburg, "Patterns of International Confirmation and Disconfirmation," in *Rigor and Imagination*, Carol Wilder-Mott and John Weakland, eds. (Praeger Publishers, New York, 1981), pp. 230–239. Copyright © 1981 by Praeger Publishers. Abridged and reprinted with permission.

> A confirmatory response is *relevant* to the evocative action, it accords recognition to the evocatory act, and accepts its significance for the other, if not for the respondent. A confirmatory reaction is a direct response, it is "to the point," "on the same wavelength," as the initiatory or evocatory action. [1961:82]

In 1967, Watzlawick, Beavin, and Jackson located confirmation within a more general framework of human communication and developed it as a necessary element of all human interaction, involving a subtle but powerful validation of the other's self-image. In addition to its content, they said each unit of interaction also contains relational information, offering first, a self-definition by a person (P) and then a response from the other (O) to that self-definition. According to Watzlawick *et al.*, this response may take any of three possible forms: it may confirm, it may reject, or it may disconfirm. The last, disconfirmation, implies the relational message, "You do not exist," and negates the other as a valid message source. Confirmation implies acceptance of the speaker's self-definition. "As far as we can see, this confirmation of P's view of himself by O is probably the greatest single factor ensuring mental development and stability that has so far emerged from our study of communication" (p. 84). The descriptive material provided by Watzlawick *et al.* to illustrate disconfirmation includes instances of total unawareness of the person, lack of accurate perception of the other's point of view, and deliberate distortion or denial of the other's self-attributes.

Sieburg (1969) used the structure provided by Watzlawick as well as the concept of confirmation/disconfirmation to begin distinguishing between human communication which is growthful, productive, effective, functional, or "therapeutic," and communication which is not. She developed measurement systems for systematically observing confirming and disconfirming communication (1969, 1972); she devised the first scale which allowed for measurement of an individual's feeling of being confirmed by another person (1973). She has continued to refine the basic theory of confirmation (1975), and has recently used the concepts to describe both organizational (1976) and family (in preparation) communication systems. During this time, a growing body of theoretical development and empirical research has attempted to explore these important concerns (cf. Cissna, 1976a, 1976b)....

Dimensions of Confirmation

In the few direct allusions in the literature to confirmation and disconfirmation, several different elements are suggested. Confirmation is, of course, tied by definition to self-experience; our first problem, therefore, was to identify the specific aspects of self-experience that could be influenced positively or negatively in interaction with others. Four such elements seemed significant for our purpose:

1. The element of existence (the individual sees self as existing)
2. The element of relating (the individual sees self as a being-in-relation with others)
3. The element of significance, or worth
4. The element of validity of experience

Thus, it was assumed that the behavior of one person toward another is confirming to the extent that it performs the following functions in regard to the other's self-experience:

1. It expresses recognition of the other's existence
2. It acknowledges a relationship of affiliation with the other
3. It expresses awareness of the significance or worth of the other
4. It accepts or "endorses" the other's self-experience (particularly emotional experience)

Each unit of response is assumed to evoke relational metamessages with regard to each of the above functions, which can identify it as either confirming or disconfirming:

Confirming	Disconfirming
"To me, you exist."	"To me, you do not exist."
"We are relating."	"We are not relating."
"To me, you are significant."	"To me, you are not significant."
"Your way of experiencing your world is valid."	"Your way of experiencing your world is invalid."

In attempting to find behavioral correlates of these functions, we acknowledge that it is not possible to point with certainty to particular behaviors that universally perform these confirming functions for all persons, since individuals differ in the way they interpret the same acts; that is, they interpret the stimuli and assign their own meaning to them. Despite this reservation about making firm causal connections between the behavior of one person and the internal experience of another, we have followed the symbolic interactionist view that certain symbolic cues *do* acquire consensual validation and therefore are consistently interpreted by most persons as reflecting certain attitudes toward them on the part of others. Such cues thus have message value and are capable of arousing in the receiver feelings of being recognized or ignored, accepted or rejected, understood or misunderstood, humanized or "thingified," valued or devalued. This assumption was borne out in a very general way by our research to date (Sieburg & Larson, 1971)....

Systematizing Disconfirming Behavior

A variety of specific acts and omissions have been noted by clinicians and theoreticians as being damaging to some aspect of the receiver's self-view. We have arranged these behaviors into three general groupings, or clusters, each representing a somewhat different style of response:

1. Indifferent response (denying existence or relation)
2. Impervious response (denying self-experience of the other)
3. Disqualifying response (denying the other's significance)

These clusters include verbal/nonverbal and vocal/nonvocal behaviors. Since they encompass both content and process features of interaction, it meant that scorers must be trained to evaluate each scoring unit in terms of its manifest content, its transactional features, and its underlying structure. In either case, no single utterance stands alone since it is always in response to some behavior or another, and is so experienced by the other as having implications about his or her self.

Disconfirmation by Indifference

To deny another's existence is to deny the most fundamental aspect of self-experience. Indifference may be total, as when presence is denied; it may imply rejection of relatedness with the other; or it may only deny the other's attempt to communicate.

Denial of Presence   The absence of even a minimal show of recognition has been associated with alienation, self-destructiveness, violence against others, and with psychosis. Laing used the case of "Peter," a psychotic patient of 25 to illustrate the possible long-term effects of chronic indifference toward a child who may, as a consequence, come to believe that he has no presence at all—or to feel guilty that he *does,* feeling that he has no right even to occupy space.

> Peter ... was a young man who was preoccupied with guilt *because* he occupied a place in the world, even in a physical sense. He could not realize ... that he had a right to have any presence for others ... A peculiar aspect of his childhood was that his presence in the world was largely ignored. No weight was given to the fact that he was in the same room while his parents had intercourse. He had been physically cared for in that he had been well fed and kept warm, and underwent no physical separation from his parents during his earlier years. Yet he had been consistently treated as though he did not "really" exist. Perhaps worse than the experience of physical separation was to be in the same room as his parents and ignored, not malevolently, but through sheer indifference. {Laing, 1961:119}

That such extreme indifference is also devastating to an adult is evident in the following excerpt from a marriage counseling session (Sieburg, personal audiotape). It is perhaps significant that throughout his wife's outburst, the husband sat silent and remote:

THERAPIST: ... and is it okay to express emotion?

WIFE: Not in my house.

THERAPIST: Has he {the husband} ever *said* it's not okay to talk about feelings?

WIFE: But he never *says* anything!

THERAPIST: But he has ways of sending you messages?

WIFE: {loudly} Yes! And the message is *shut out*—no matter what I say, no matter what I do, I get no response—zero—shut out!

THERAPIST: And does that somehow make you feel you are wrong?

WIFE: Oh, of course not wrong—just *nothing!*

THERAPIST: Then what is it that makes you feel he disapproves of you?

WIFE: Because I get nothing! {tears} If I feel discouraged—like looking for a job all day and being turned down—and I cry—zero! No touching, no patting, no "Maybe tomorrow"—just *shut out*. And if I get angry at him, instead of getting angry back, he just walks away—just nothing! All the time I'm feeling shut out and shut off!

THERAPIST: And what is it you want from him?

WIFE: {quietly} Maybe sometimes just a pat on the back would be enough. But, no!—he just shrugs me off. Where am I supposed to go to feel real? {tears}

Avoiding Involvement   Extreme instances of indifference like those above are presumed to be rare because even the slightest attention at least confirms one's presence. Lesser shows of indifference, however, still create feelings of alienation, frustration, and lowered self-worth. Although recognition is a necessary first step in confirming another, it is not in itself sufficient unless accompanied by some further indication of a willingness to be involved.

The precise ways in which one person indicates to another that he or she is interested in relating (intimacy) are not fully known, but several clear indications of *unwillingness* to relate or to become more than minimally involved have emerged from research and have been included in our systemization of disconfirming behaviors. Of particular significance are the use of:

- Impersonal language—the avoidance of first person references (I, me, my, mine) in favor of a collective "we" or "one," or the tendency to begin sentences with "there" when making what amounts to a personal statement (as, "there seems to be ... ")
- Avoidance of eye contact
- Avoidance of physical contact except in ritualized situations such as hand-shaking
- Other nonverbal "distancing" cues

Rejecting Communication   A third way of suggesting indifference to another is to respond in a way that is unrelated, or only minimally related, to what he or she has just said, thus creating a break or disjunction in the flow of interaction.

Totally irrelevant response is, of course, much like denial of presence in that the person whose topic is repeatedly ignored may soon come to doubt his or her very existence, and at best will feel that he or she is not heard, attended to, or regarded as significant. Perhaps for this reason Laing called relevance the "crux of confirmation," noting that only by responding relevantly can one lend significance to another's communication and accord recognition (Laing, 1961:87).

The most extreme form of communication rejection is monologue, in which one speaker continues on and on, neither hearing nor acknowledging anything the other says. It reflects unawareness and lack of concern about the other person except as a socially acceptable audience for the speaker's own self-listening. A less severe communication rejection occurs when the responder makes a connection, however slight, with what the other has said, but immediately shifts into something quite different of his or her own choosing.

Disconfirming by Imperviousness

The term "imperviousness" as used here follows Laing's usage and refers to a lack of accurate awareness of another's perceptions (Watzlawick *et al.*, 1967:91). Imperviousness is disconfirming because it denies or distorts another's self-expression and fosters dehumanized relationships in which one person perceives another as a pseudo-image rather than as what that person really is. Behaviorally, the impervious responder engages in various tactics that tend to negate or discredit the other's feeling expression. These may take the form of a flat denial that the other *has* such a feeling ("You don't really mean that"), or it may be handled more indirectly by reinterpreting the feeling in a more acceptable way, ("You're only saying that because ... "), substituting some experience or feeling of the *listener* ("What you're trying to say is ... "), challenging the speaker's right to have such a feeling ("How can you *possibly* feel that way after all that's been done for you?"), or some similar device intended to alter the feeling expressed....

A slightly different form of imperviousness occurs when a responder creates and bestows on another an inaccurate identity, and then confirms the false identity, although it is not a part of the other's self-experience at all. Laing calls this pseudo-confirmation (1961:83). Thus a mother who insists that her daughter is always obedient and "never any trouble at all" may be able to interpret her daughter's most rebellious aggression in a way that fits the placid image she holds of her daughter, and the parents of even a murderous psychopath may be able to describe their son as a "good boy." Such a false confirmation frequently endorses the fiction of what the other is *wished* to be, without any real recognition of what the other is or how he/she feels. As noted earlier, this form of disconfirmation also appears as simply a well-meaning attempt to reassure another who is distressed, which too is usually motivated by the speaker's need to reduce his or her own discomfort.

> "Don't be silly—of course you're not afraid!"
> "You may think you feel that way now, but I know better."
> "Stop crying—there's nothing the matter with you!"
> "How can you possibly worry about a little thing like that?"
> "No matter what you say, I know you still love me."

Such responses constitute a rejection of the other person's expression and often identity, raising doubts about the validity of his/her way of experiencing by suggesting, "You don't really feel as you say you do; you are only imagining that you do."

A subtle variation of the same tactic occurs when the speaker responds in a selective way, rewarding the other with attention and relevant response *only* when he or she communicates in an approved fashion, and becoming silent or indifferent if the other's speech or behavior does not meet with the responder's approval. This may mean that the speaker limits response to those topics initiated by self, ignoring any topic initiated by the other person.

Imperviousness is considered disconfirming because it contributes to a feeling of uncertainty about self or uncertainty about the validity of personal experiencing. Imperviousness occurs when a person is told how he or she feels, regardless of how he or she experiences self, when a person's talents and abilities are described without any data to support such a description, when motives are ascribed to another without any reference to the other's own experience, or when one's own efforts at self-expression are ignored or discounted unless they match the false image held by some other person....

Disconfirmation by Disqualification

According to Watzlawick (1964) disqualification is a technique which enables one to say something without really saying it, to deny without really saying "no," and to disagree without really disagreeing. Certain messages, verbal and nonverbal, are included in this group because they (a) disqualify the other speaker, (b) disqualify another message, or (c) disqualify themselves.

Speaker Disqualification   This may include such direct disparagement of the other as name-calling, criticism, blame, and hostile attack, but may also take the indirect form of the sigh of martyrdom, the muttered expletive, addressing an adult in a tone of voice usually reserved for a backward child, joking "on the square," sarcasm, or any of the other numerous tactics to make the other appear and feel too incompetent or unreliable for his message to have validity. This creates a particularly unanswerable put-down by evoking strong metamessages of insignficance or worthlessness. The following examples are spouses' responses from conjoint counseling sessions:

- "Can't you ever do anything right?"
- "Here we go again!" {sigh}
- "We heard you the first time—why do you always keep repeating yourself?"
- "It's no wonder the rear axle broke, with you in the back seat!" {laughter}
- "Why do you always have to get your mouth open when you don't know what you're talking about?"

Message Disqualification   Without regard to their content, some messages tend to discredit the other person because of their irrelevance—that is, they do not "follow" the other's prior utterance in a transactional sense. (This is also a tactic of indifference and may serve a dual disconfirming purpose.) Such disjunctive responses were studied by Sluzki, Beavin, Tarnopolski, and Veron (1967) who used the term "transactional disqualification" to mean any incongruity in the response of the speaker in relation to the context of the previous message of the other. A relationship between two successive messages exists, they noted, on two possible levels: (a) continuity between the content of the two messages (are both persons talking about the same subject?), and (b) indication of reception of the prior message (what cues does the speaker give of receiving and understanding the previous message?). If a message is disjunctive at either of these levels, transactional disqualification of the prior message is said to have occurred.

A similar form of message disqualification occurs when a speaker reacts selectively to some incidental clue in another's speech, but ignores the primary theme. Thus the responder may acknowledge the other's attempt to communicate, but still appears to miss the point. This "tangential response" was identified and studied by Jurgen Ruesch (1958), who noted that a speaker often picks up on a topic presented, but then continues to spin a yarn in a different direction. The response is not totally irrelevant because it has made some connection, although perhaps slight, with the prior utterance. Because it causes the first speaker to question the value or importance of what he or she was trying to say, the tangential response is reported to affect adversely a speaker's feeling of self-significance, and is therefore included as a form of disconfirmation.

Message Disqualifying Itself

A third way in which a speaker can use disqualification to "say something without really saying it," is by sending messages that disqualify themselves. There are many ways in which this may be done, the commonest devices being lack of clarity, ambiguity, and incongruity of mode. These forms of response are grouped together here because they have all been interpreted as devices for avoiding involvement with another by generating the metamessage "I am not communicating," hence "We are not relating."

Systematizing Confirming Behaviors

Responses that confirm are less clearly defined than disconfirming behaviors because there has been less motivation to study them. In fact, identification of specific acts that are generally confirming is difficult unless we simply identify confirmation as the absence of disconfirming behaviors. More research in this area is clearly needed, but, in general, confirming behaviors are those which permit people to experience their own being and significance as well as their interconnectedness with others. Following Laing (1961), these have been arranged into three clusters: recognition, acknowledgment, and endorsement.

The Recognition Cluster   Recognition is expressed by looking at the other, making frequent eye contact, touching, speaking directly to the person, and allowing the other the opportunity to respond without being interrupted or having to force his or her way into an ongoing monologue. In the case of an infant, recognition means holding and cuddling beyond basic survival functions; in the case of an adult, it may still mean physical contact (touching), but it also means psychological contact in the form of personal language, clarity, congruence of mode, and authentic self-expression. In other words, confirmation requires that a person treat the other with respect, acknowledging his or her attempt to relate, and need to have a presence in the world.

The Acknowledgment Cluster   Acknowledgment of another is demonstrated by a relevant and direct response to his or her communication. This does not require praise or even agreement, but simple conjunction. Buber (Friedman, 1960) recognized this aspect when he wrote that mutually confirming partners can still "struggle together in direct opposition," and Laing (1961) made a similar point when he said that even rejection can be confirming if it is direct, not tangential, and if it grants significance and validity to what the other says. To hear, attend, and take note of the other and to acknowledge the other by responding directly is probably the most valued form of confirmation—and possibly the most rare. It means that the other's expression is furthered, facilitated, and encouraged.

The Endorsement Cluster   This cluster includes any responses that express acceptance of the other's feelings as being true, accurate, and "okay." In general, it means simply letting the other *be*, without blame, praise, analysis, justification, modification, or denial.

Confirming response is dialogic in structure; it is a reciprocal activity involving shared talk and sometimes shared silence. It is interactional in the broadest sense of the word. It is not a one-way flow of talk; it is not a trade-off in which each speaker pauses and appears to listen only in order to get a chance to speak again. It is a complex affair in which each participates as both subject and object, cause and effect, of the other's talk. In short, confirming response, like all communication, is not something one does, it is a process in which one shares.

References

Buber, M. "Distance and Relation," *Psychiatry* 20 (1957): 97–104.

Cissna, K. N. L. "Facilitative Communication and Interpersonal Relationships: An Empirical Test of a Theory of Interpersonal Communication." Doctoral dissertation, University of Denver, 1975.

Cissna, K. N. L. "Interpersonal Confirmation: A Review of Current/Recent Theory and Research." Paper presented at the Central States Speech Association Convention, Chicago, 1976, and the International Communication Association Convention, Portland, Oregon, 1976.

Cissna, K. N. L. *Interpersonal Confirmation: A Review of Current Theory, Measurement, and Research*. Saint Louis: Saint Louis University, 1976.

Cissna, K. N. L. "Gender, Sex Type, and Perceived Confirmation: A Response from the Perspective of Interpersonal Confirmation." Presented at the International Communication Association Convention, Philadelphia, 1979.

Cissna, K. N. L., and S. Keating. "Speech Communication Antecedents of Perceived Confirmation," *Western Journal of Speech Communication* 43 (1979): 48–60.

Friedman, M. S. "Dialogue and the 'Essential We': The Bases of Values in the Philosophy of Martin Buber," *American Journal of Psychoanalysis* 20 (1960): 26–34.

Laing, R. D. *The Self and Others*. New York: Pantheon, 1961.

Laing, R. D. "Mystification, Confusion and Conflict," in *Intensive Family Therapy*, ed. I. Boszormenyi-Nagy and J. L. Framo. New York: Harper & Row, 1965.

Laing, R. D. *The Politics of Experience*. New York: Ballantine, 1967.

Laing, R. D. *The Self and Others*. 2nd ed. Baltimore: Penguin, 1969.

Laing, R. D. *Knots*. New York: Vintage, 1970.

Laing, R. D., and A. Esterson. *Sanity, Madness, and the Family*. Baltimore: Penguin, 1964.

Ruesch, J. "The Tangential Response," in *Psychopathology of Communication*, ed. P. H. Toch and J. Zuben. New York: Grune & Stratton, 1958.

Ruesch, J. and G. Bateson. *Communication: The Social Matrix of Psychiatry*. New York: Norton, 1951.

Sieburg, E. "Dysfunctional Communication and Interpersonal Responsiveness in Small Groups." Doctoral dissertation, University of Denver, 1969.

Sieburg, E. "Toward a Theory of Interpersonal Confirmation." Unpublished manuscript, University of Denver, 1972.

Sieburg, E. *Interpersonal Confirmation: A Paradigm for Conceptualization and Measurement*. San Diego: United States International University, 1975.

Sieburg, E. "Confirming and Disconfirming Organizational Communication," in *Communication in Organizations*. eds. J. L. Owen, P. A. Page, and G. I. Zimmerman. St. Paul: West Publishing, 1976.

Sieburg, E. *Family Communication Systems* (in preparation).

Sieburg, E. and C. E. Larson. "Dimensions of Interpersonal Response." Paper presented at the annual convention of the International Communication Association, Phoenix, 1971.

Watzlawick, P. *An Anthology of Human Communication*. Palo Alto: Science and Behavior Books, 1964.

Watzlawick, P., J. Beavin, and D. D. Jackson. *Pragmatics of Human Communication: A Study of Interactional Patterns, Pathologies, and Paradoxes*. New York: Norton, 1967.

Review Questions

1. Give a one-sentence definition of the term "confirmation."
2. Discuss the distinctions between the four elements of confirmation that Cissna and Sieburg outline—existence, relating, significance, and validity of experience.
3. According to these authors, which are more important in the confirmation/disconfirmation process, verbal cues or nonverbal cues?

4. "The most extreme form of communication rejection is _____."
5. Which kind of disconfirmation is happening in the following example:
   Rae: "Damn! I wish that test wasn't tomorrow! That really ticks me off!"
   Kris: "You aren't mad, you're just scared because you haven't studied enough."
6. Give an example of a person "saying something without really saying it."
7. Explain the authors' distinction between recognition and acknowledgement.

Probes

1. What makes the term "confirmation" appropriate for what's being discussed here? You can confirm an airplane reservation and in some churches young people are confirmed. How do those meanings echo the meaning of confirmation that's developed here?
2. Notice how, in the first paragraph under the heading "Dimensions of Confirmation," the authors emphasize the transactional or relational quality of the phenomenon. Paraphrase what you hear them saying there.
3. All of us experience disconfirmation, sometimes with destructive regularity. Give an example where you have given an *indifferent* response. Give an example of where you've received one. Do the same for *imperviousness* and *disqualification*.
4. When a person is "impervious," what is he or she impervious *to?* Discuss.
5. Create an example of well-meant imperviousness, that is, imperviousness motivated by a genuine desire to comfort or to protect the other person. Do the same with a disqualifying response.
6. Identify five specific confirming communication events that you experienced in the last four hours.

aurice Friedman's comments about confirmation grow out of his lifelong study and application of Martin Buber's ideas. In fact, Friedman's recent book, which includes this excerpt, is called *The Confirmation of Otherness in Family, Community, and Society.* I especially like the way Friedman emphasizes that confirmation happens *between* persons. As he notes, one implication of that fact is that we cannot *make* confirmation happen; we cannot *will* it. We can, however, choose to be closed to it; we can shut out even the others who are genuinely trying to contact us. That's the point of Friedman's brief discussion of St. Francis of Assisi.

Another implication of the "between" quality of confirmation is that no one can offer or give a blanket of unconditional confirmation. We can only give as much of our personal selves as we can bring to the concrete situation, and we can only confirm the other in his or her uniqueness, as a person also conditioned by this concrete situation. Confirmation also differs from acceptance in that it can include a commitment to growth and change. At the end of this selection, Friedman discusses the dangers of the confirmation-with-strings-attached and the confirmation that smothers.

I hope that the combination of Cissna and Sieburg's quasi-social scientific treatment and Friedman's more philosophical discussion will give you a reasonably firm grasp of this crucial interpersonal phenomenon. Then Paul Rabinow's example in the final reading of this chapter should round out your understanding.

Confirmation and the Emergence of the Self

Maurice Friedman

Confirmation, as we have seen, is an integral part of the life of dialogue. Dialogue may be silent and monologue spoken. What really matters in genuine dialogue is my acceptance of the "otherness" of the other person, my willingness to listen to her and respond to her address. In monologue, in contrast, I only allow the other to exist as a content of my experience. Not only do I see her primarily in terms of her social class, her color, her religion, her IQ, or character neurosis; I do not leave myself open to her as a person at all. The life of dialogue is not one in which we have much to do with others, but one in which we really have to do with those with whom we have to do....

Confirmation is central to human existence, but human existence is itself problematic, and the heart of its problematic is that of confirmation. This problematic can be grasped most clearly if we look at what we ordinarily take as a self-evident reality and as the foundation of our personal existence—our "I." The "I" is not an object or a thing. Indeed, it escapes all attempts to objectify it. But even as a subjective reality, it is not something continuous, secure, or easily discernible. It is elusive and insubstantial, paradoxical and perplexing to the point of illusion or even downright delusion. It cannot be understood as something taken by itself, outside of all relationship, but neither is it a part of a whole. It rests on the reality of the "between," the interhuman. I cannot regard my "I" as merely a product of social forces and influences, for then it is no longer an "I." There has to be that in me which can respond if I am going to talk about any true personal uniqueness. Therefore, I cannot say with George Herbert Mead, "The self is an eddy in the social current." I cannot turn the self into a mere confluence of social and psychological streams.

On the other hand, if I speak of the "I" as an "essence," that is misleading because it suggests something substantive that is within us as a vein of gold within a mountain waiting to be mined. Our uniqueness is our personal vocation, our life's calling that is discovered when we are called out by life and become "ourselves" in responding. We must respond to this call from where we are, and where we are is never merely social nor merely individual but uniquely personal. We need to be confirmed by others. Our very sense of ourselves only comes in our meeting with others. Yet through this confirmation we can grow to the strength of Socrates, who said, "I respect you, Athenians. But I will obey the god and not you." Socrates made his contribution to the common order of speech-with-meaning—he expressed his responsibility to his fellow Athenians precisely in opposing them. But if Socrates had not had seventy years in Athens in which he was part, first of his family of origin and then of his own family of wife and children, and if he had not been confirmed by the Athenian youth with whom he met in daily discussion, confirmed even when they opposed him, he would not have been able to stand alone.

The religious person sometimes imagines that one can be confirmed by God without any confirmation from one's fellow human beings. This is possible for a Jesus or a Buddha when they are adults. We are really set in existence, and existence is social existence. Once you have had real dialogue with human beings, you may then leave them for a desert island where you relate only to the chameleon, the Gila monster, or the waves lapping on the shore. But if you had no such relationship to begin with, you would not become a self. Or if you had such relations but were not confirmed or were even disconfirmed as an infant and young child, then your self will exist only in that impairment with which we are familiar in the schizophrenic, the paranoid, or the severe neurotic.

One of the paradoxes of confirmation is that, essential as it is to our and to all human existence, we cannot *will* to be confirmed. We cannot even *will* to confirm. When we do so we fall into what Leslie Farber has called willfulness, that sickness of the disordered will that seeks an illusory wholeness through trying to handle both sides of the dialogue.... Hence the futility and frustration of the lovelorn and the jealous who try to give up the beloved in order to receive her back and only make things worse in doing so. A large part of the pain of unrequited love as of jealousy comes from just this fact—that we cannot control others, that we must leave them really free to handle their side of the dialogue, to respond freely to our address rather than react as the effect of which *we* are the cause.

If we cannot *will* what the other side will give us, we *can* will not to receive. This is the other side of the coin. In a saying that Martin Buber has entitled "Give and Take," one Hasidic master says: "Everyone must be both a giver and a receiver. He who is not both is like a barren tree." There are people who so habitually see themselves and are seen by others in the role of helper, responsible person, or giver, that they have never learned how to accept and still less how to ask for what they need. Once Rabbi Mendel sat motionless at his plate when everyone else at the Sabbath dinner was eating soup. "Mendel, why do you not eat?" asked Rabbi Elimelekh. "Because I do not have a spoon," Mendel replied. "Look," said Rabbi Elimelekh, "you must learn to ask for a spoon and if need be for a plate too." Rabbi Mendel took the words of his teacher to heart, and from that time on his fortunes mended.

I have always been deeply moved by St. Francis' prayer, which for many years I said every night before going to sleep:

> O Lord,
> Make me an instrument of Thy peace.
> Where there is hatred, let me sow love;
> Where there is despair, hope;
> Where there is darkness, light;
> Where there is sadness, joy.
>
> O Divine Master
> Grant that I may not so much seek
> To be understood as to understand,
> To be consoled as to console,
> To be loved as to love.

For it is in giving that we receive,
It is in pardoning that we are pardoned,
And it is in dying that we are born into eternal life.

However, I have come increasingly to recognize that this prayer presents only one aspect of reality. A person has also to allow himself to be understood, to be consoled, to be loved. Toward the end of his life, St. Francis said, "I was too hard on Brother Ass," by which he meant his own body. Even by medieval standards, his asceticism was unbelievably harsh. St. Francis loved every person and every thing, but he did not love himself quite enough. There is a compassion for oneself which is the opposite of self-pity and self-indulgence because it arises from a distancing from oneself rather than from a wallowing in subjective emotions. Such compassion is a form of humility whereas being too hard on oneself is a form of pride. "Everyone must have two pockets to use as the occasion demands," said Rabbi Bunam. "In one pocket should be the words: 'For my sake the world was created,' and in the other, 'I am dust and ashes.'"

To exist as human beings we must, as long as we live, enter ever anew into the flowing interchange of confirming and being confirmed, of addressing and responding. This means that we must have that courage to address and that courage to respond which rests on, embodies, and makes manifest existential trust. It also means a new and deeper understanding of responsibility and of its relation to confirmation. Responsibility means to respond, and genuine response is response of the whole person. In every situation we are asked to respond in a unique way. Therefore, our wholeness in that situation is unique too, even though we become more and more ourselves through such response—hence, more and more recognizable by others in a personal uniqueness that extends beyond the moment.

Because confirmation is a reality of the between, no one can offer another a blanket of unconditional confirmation, regardless of what that other says, does, or is. We can only give what we have, and what we have, first of all, is not a technique of confirmation but our personal selves—selves which can make another present and "imagine the real" but selves which also respond from where we are. Further, because confirmation means a confirmation of our uniqueness, a blanket confirmation would be valueless. We need to be confirmed in our uniqueness as what we are, what we *can* become, and what we are called to become, and this can only be known in the give and take of living dialogue. Therefore, as Martin Buber stressed in his 1957 dialogue with Carl Rogers, that affirmation which says "I accept you as you are" is only the beginning of dialogue and must be distinguished from that confirmation which has to do with the development of the person over time. Rogers emphasized an unqualified acceptance of the person being helped, whereas Buber emphasized a confirmation which, while it accepts the other as a person, may also wrestle *with* him against himself. Rogers spoke of acceptance as a warm regard for the other and a respect for him as a person of unconditional worth, and that means "an acceptance of and regard for his attitudes of the moment, no matter how much they may contradict other attitudes he has held in the past." Buber, in response, said:

> I not only accept the other as he is, but I confirm him, in myself, and then in him, in relation to this potentiality that is meant by him and it can now be developed, it can evolve, it can answer the reality of life.... Let's take, for example, man and wife. He

says, not expressly, but just by his whole relation to her, "I accept you as you are." But this does not mean, "I don't want you to change." But it says, "I discover in you just by my accepting love, I discover in you what you are meant to become."[1]

To Rogers' statement that complete acceptance of the person as he is is the strongest factor making for change, Buber countered with the problematic type of person with which he necessarily had to do. By this Buber meant the person whose very existence had run aground on the problematic of confirmation, a person whom simple acceptance could not help:

> There are cases when I must help him against himself. He wants my help against himself.... The first thing of all is that he trusts me.... What he wants is a being not only whom he can trust as a man trusts another, but a being that gives him now the certitude that "there *is* a soil, there *is* an existence." And if this is reached, now I can help this man even in his struggle against himself. And this I can only do if I distinguish between accepting and confirming.[2]

As babies we are really at the mercy of "significant others." Some people in their early years do not receive enough confirmation to enable them to be human. It is even possible that a nursery-school teacher could make all the difference for a deprived child's capacity to grow up human. Although once we are grown we imagine ourselves as independent "I"'s, as babies and little children we are totally dependent upon being called into existence as persons. Our notion of ourselves as separate consciousnesses that then enter into relation is an error produced by the individuation that we experience later. When we grow up, we think of ourselves as first and foremost "I" and imagine that we enter into relationship with others as one nation might send out ambassadors to foreign countries. Actually, as John Donne said, "No man is an island, entire of itself; every man is a piece of the continent," a continent that is based on the distancing and relating of our person-to-person relationships and of the "essential We" of family, group, community, and society.

To say that all men are created equal means, if anything, that each person may be and deserves to be related to as Thou. It does not mean, however, that this actually happens. There is a fundamental *inequality* insofar as the actual confirmation that each person receives is concerned. No one can ever change the fact of being an older brother or sister or a younger one or, for that matter, of being born with a gold, silver, lead, or copper spoon in his mouth. In every social group there is a sense of status, and in every social group there are those who have come out on the short end of the stick as far as confirmation is concerned.

What makes the emergence of the self still more problematic is that even where confirmation is given and given lavishly, it is usually with strings attached. It takes the form of an unspoken, invisible contract which reads: "If you are a good boy or girl, student, churchgoer, citizen, or soldier, we shall confirm you as lovable. If you are not, not only will you not be confirmed but you will have to live with the {introjected} knowledge that you are fundamentally unlovable." This is a contract that most of us buy, more or less, and there is no human way to be wholly free of it. This means that most confirmation is *not* unconditional, however much it may be "positive." As we grow older, this problematic is complicated still further by the need people have to fix each other in social roles. This is, if you like, a tragedy, but it is a well-nigh universal one. There are people who are made so anxious by not being able to put you in a given cubbyhole that they will never accept you. How many parents love their child but love him or her only as "my child" and will never allow that child to grow up—to become a person with a ground of his or her own....

There is a distinction that must be made between a basic confirmation that gives us our ticket to exist and the confirmation along the road which has to do with the way in which we exist. If we are so fortunate as to have been confirmed in our right to exist, that does not mean that the confirmation then extends to everything we do. If, on the other hand, we have not been confirmed in our existence itself, then all the later confirmation we receive is not likely to fill the vacuum within.

Other people fix us in their images of us, and we in turn internalize those images and fix ourselves in them. Why is it so important to a child who goes to college not to be called by the nickname which his or her family and friends used when s/he was at home? It is because the young person wants to feel "I am growing up now." When such a young person goes home for vacation and the family calls him or her by the nickname he or she feels s/he has outgrown, they are imprisoning that young person in an image of him- or herself which has power over his or her self. It leads one to limit one's sense of what one can do. It gets in the way. Eventually, of course, one reaches the strength to say, "I am not this," and the still greater strength of standing one's own ground without being made anxious, defensive, or upset. If it remains a conflict situation, one can accept the tragedy for what it is. Unfortunately, some people never attain this courage and strength and, even if they succeed in getting their families to call them by different names, they remain bound to the roles in which their family has cast them.

References

1. Martin Buber, *The Knowledge of Man,* ed. Maurice Friedman, trans. Maurice Friedman and Ronald Gregor Smith (New York: Harper & Row, 1965), p. 182.
2. Ibid., p. 183.

Review Questions

1. What does Friedman mean when he says, "The life of dialogue is not one in which we have much to do with others, but one in which we really have to do with those with whom we have to do"?
2. What does it mean to say that "human existence is itself problematic"?
3. When Friedman talks about the "misleading" idea that there is an "I" as an "essence," he is making a point Bill Wilmot makes in Chapter 5. What is this point?
4. What is Friedman's main point about the relationship between confirming and being confirmed?
5. What does it mean to say that confirmation is "a reality of the between"? How is this point related to what I write in Chapter 1?
6. What is the "fundamental *inequality*" of actual confirmation that Friedman discusses?

Probes

1. Friedman says that you need others in order to be an I, a self. How do you respond to this point?

2. What are some practical implications of Friedman's point that we cannot *will* to be confirmed or to confirm?

3. If Friedman is right that we cannot will to be confirmed or to confirm, why study the process? If we can't control it, why learn about it?

4. What difference do you hear Friedman making between confirmation and acceptance? Is that consistent with Cissna and Sieburg's uses of these terms?

5. What's the relationship between what Friedman calls the "basic confirmation that gives us our ticket to exist" and the confirmation "which has to do with the way in which we exist"?

The next selection comes from a small book that describes the experiences of a young, Jewish-American anthropologist who went to Morocco to live and study the culture there. I discovered this excerpt in a conversation with Tamar Katriel, an Israeli who was studying interpersonal communication in our department. Tamar noticed how the event Rabinow describes here is an excellent example of confirmation, which we were discussing in class.

One question we had discussed was whether confirmation is important in all cultures or just in Western ones. We know, for example, that the direct eye contact that can be so confirming to whites can often be inappropriate and uncomfortable for persons from Japanese or other nonwhite cultures. And there are many other differences.

Tamar noticed that Rabinow's description of his confrontation with Ali suggested that confirmation is also vital in nonwhite cultures but that it is communicated in radically different ways. Rabinow thought he could affirm Ali as a person by being passive, accepting, and deferent. When he blew up at Ali he thought he'd ruined their relationship. But he discovered that in Ali's culture it was more confirming to be confronted than to be treated gently and with total acceptance. It impressed me to read that only *after* their argument and the strong mutual confirmation it established were Rabinow and Ali able to talk about Ali's involvement in a radical religious group and prostitution, two very private topics. This article also introduces one of the main points of Chapter 13, "Communicating Across Cultures." As the readings there demonstrate, the basic elements of effective interpersonal communication—contact, confirmation, understanding, clarity, responsiveness—are important in all cultures, but the way you communicate each of these differs significantly from culture to culture. In other words, the mode of communicating described in this book is not restricted just to Western white majority cultures; it applies to all human contacts, so long as it is adapted to the cultural setting.

Confrontation with Ali

Paul Rabinow

Ali promised to take me to a wedding in the village of Sidi Lahcen Lyussi. I had already been to several urban weddings. The best Moroccan food, music, and ceremonial were displayed on these occasions. It was a nice change of pace, a break in the routine. The wedding would be an excellent opportunity for me to see the village, and for the villagers to see me.

That afternoon, Ali came by. I told him I wasn't sure I would be able to go with him because I was suffering from a stomach virus. The prospect of being in a strange and demanding situation where I wanted to please, for such a long period, seemed overwhelming, especially in my present condition. Ali expressed keen disappointment at this. He had clearly counted on transportation in my car and the mixed prestige of arriving with the most auspicious guest (if not the guest of honor).

When he returned the next day I was feeling a bit better. He assured me that we would stay only for a short time. He stressed all the preliminary politicking and arranging he had done; if I didn't show up it would not be good for either of us. So I agreed, but made him promise me that we would stay only an hour or so because I was still weak. He repeated his promise several times saying we would leave whenever I felt like it.

Ali and Soussi came to my house around nine that evening and we were off. I was already somewhat tired and repeated clearly to Soussi, a renowned partygoer in his own right, that we would stay only for a short time and then return to Sefrou. *Waxxa*, O.K.?

It was already growing dark as we left Sefrou. By the time we turned off the highway onto the unpaved road which leads to the village, it was nearly pitch black, depriving me of a sense of the countryside, while adding to my feelings of uncertainty about the whole affair. Nonetheless, on arriving in the village I was exhilarated.

The wedding itself was held in a set of connected houses which formed a compound. A group of sons had built simple mud and mortar houses next to each other as they married, and by now these formed an enclosed compound. Each part of the enclosure was made up of a two-story building. The facilities for the animals and cooking areas were downstairs, the sleeping quarters were on the top level, connected by a rickety staircase. That night the center of the compound area had been covered with straw for the dancing. We were welcomed and ushered up the stairs into a long narrow room furnished with thin cushions along the perimeters. Perhaps five tables were arranged parallel to each other, running the length of the room. I told myself it was a good thing we had come, a wise decision. Everyone was friendly and seemed to know who I was. We had tea, then after perhaps an hour of chatting and banter, dinner was served on battered but polished metal trays. The hour of talk had passed amicably enough, even though my minimal Arabic

From *Reflections on Fieldwork in Morocco* by Paul Rabinow, pp. 40–49, published by the University of California Press. © 1977 The Regents of the University of California.

did not permit much expansive conversation. I still had a beard at this point, and there was much friendly but insistent joking that this was improper for such a young man. The dinner was simple but nicely prepared, consisting of goat meat in a sort of olive oil stew with freshly baked bread, still warm from the oven.

After we ate and drank more tea, we went down to the courtyard, where the dancing began. I watched from a corner, leaning against a pillar. The dancers were all men, of course, and they formed two lines facing each other, their arms draped over one another's shoulders. Between the two lines was a singer with a crude tambourine. He sang and swayed back and forth. The lines of men responded in turn to his direct, insistent beat, answering his verses with verses of their own. The women were peeping out from another part of the compound where they had eaten their dinner. They were all dressed in their best clothes, brightly colored kaftans. They answered the various verses with calls of their own, enthusiastically urging the men on. Since I did not understand the songs and was not dancing, my excitement wore off rapidly. Ali was one of the most dedicated of the dancers, and it was difficult to catch his attention. During a break when the central singer was warming his tambourine over the fire to restretch the skin, I finally got Ali's ear and told him politely but insistently that I was not feeling well, that we had been here three hours already. It was midnight, could we leave soon after the next round of dances maybe? Of course, he said, just a few more minutes, no problem, don't worry, I understand.

An hour later I tried again and received the same answer. This time, however, I was getting angrier and more frustrated; I was feeling truly ill. The mountain air was quite cold by now, and I had not dressed warmly enough. I felt entirely at Ali's mercy. I didn't want to antagonize him, but neither did I want to stay. I continued to grumble to myself but managed to smile at whoever was smiling at me.

Finally, at three in the morning, I could stand it no longer. I was feeling terrible. I was furious at Ali but loath to express it. I was going to leave, regardless of the consequences. I told Soussi, let's go; if you want a ride, get Ali and that's it. Ali at this point was nowhere in sight. Soussi went off and returned to the car with a smiling and contented Ali. I was warming the engine up, publicly announcing my readiness to leave. They climbed in, Soussi in the front and Ali in the back, and we were off. The road for the first five miles is little more than a path—untarred, pitted, and winding and steep in places. I was a novice driver and unsure of myself, so I said nothing, concentrating all my energy on staying on the road and keeping the car going. I managed to negotiate this stretch of road successfully and heaved a sigh of relief when we reached the highway.

Soussi had been keeping up a steady flow of chatter as we bumped over the country road. I had kept my silence, ignoring Ali in the back, who said little himself. When we reached the highway and began rolling smoothly toward Sefrou, he asked in a nonchalant manner, *wash ferhan?*, are you happy? I snickered and said no. He pursued this. Why not? In simple terms I told him that I was sick, that it was three-thirty in the morning, and all I wanted to do was go home to bed—adding that I sincerely hoped he had enjoyed himself. Yes, he said, he had enjoyed himself, but if I was unhappy then the whole evening was spoiled, he was getting out of the car. Please, Ali, I said, let's just get back to Sefrou in peace. But why are you unhappy? I reminded him of his promise. If you are unhappy, he said, then I will walk back. This exchange was repeated several times, Soussi's vain attempts at mediation being ignored by both sides. Finally I told Ali he was acting like a baby, and yes, I was unhappy. He never offered any specific excuses but only insisted that if I was unhappy he would walk. He started to lean over and open the door on Soussi's side, scaring Soussi witless. We were traveling at forty miles an hour, and it scared me too, and I slowed down to ten. He challenged me again asking me if I was happy. I just could not bring myself to answer yes. My superego told me I should. But the events of the evening combined with the frustration of not being able to express myself fully to him in Arabic got the better of me. After another exchange and bluff on his part, I stopped the car to let him get out, which he now had to do. He did, promptly, and began striding down the dark highway in the direction of Sefrou. I let him get about one hundred yards ahead and then drove up alongside and told him to get in the car. He looked the other way. Soussi tried his luck with the same results. We repeated this melodrama two more times. I was confused, nauseous, and totally frustrated. I stepped on the gas and off we went to Sefrou, leaving Ali to walk the remaining five miles.

I went to sleep immediately, but woke from a fitful night saying to myself that I had probably made a grave professional mistake, because the informant is always right. Otherwise I was unrepentant. It was quite possible that I had ruined my relationship with Ali and that I had done irreparable damage to my chances of working my way into the village. But there were other things worth studying in Morocco, and it was something I would just have to make the best of. I took a walk through the tree-lined streets of the Ville Nouvelle and remembered a story a friend had told me before we took our doctoral exams; he had had nightmares for a week before the exams in which he saw himself as a shoe salesman. I mentally tried several occupations on for size as I drifted aimlessly among the villas. I felt calm; if this was anthropology and if I had ruined it for myself, then it simply wasn't for me.

The parameters seemed clear enough. I had to clarify for myself where I stood. If the informant was always right, then by implication the anthropologist had to become a sort of non-person, or more accurately a total persona. He had to be willing to enter into any situation as a smiling observer and carefully note down the specifics of the event under consideration. If one was interested in symbolic analysis or expressive culture, then the more elusive dimensions of feeling tone, gesture, and the like would be no exception. This was the position my professors had advocated: one simply endured whatever inconveniences and annoyances came along. One had to completely subordinate one's own code of ethics, conduct, and world view, to "suspend disbelief," as another colleague was proud of putting it, and sympathetically and accurately record events.

All of this had seemed simple enough back in Chicago (where, more accurately, no one paid more than lip service to these problems), but it was far from simple at the wedding. Ali had been a steady companion during the previous month and I had established a real rapport with him, more as a friend than as an informant; I was getting acclimated to Sefrou, and my Arabic was still too limited for us to do any sustained and systematic work together. I found the demands of greater self-control and abnegation hard to accept. I was used to engaging people energetically and found the idea of a year constantly on my guard, with very little to fall back on except the joys of asceticism, productive sublimation, and the pleasures of self-control, a grim prospect....

At the wedding Ali was beginning to test me, much in the way that Moroccans test each other to ascertain strengths and weaknesses. He was pushing and probing. I tried to avoid responding in the counter-assertive style of another Moroccan, vainly offering instead the persona of anthropologist, all-accepting. He continued to interpret my behavior in his own terms; he saw me as weak, giving in to each of his testing thrusts. So the cycle continued: he would probe more deeply, show his dominance, and exhibit my submission and lack of character. Even on the way back to Sefrou he was testing me, and in what was a backhanded compliment, trying to humiliate me. But Ali was uneasy with his victories, and shifted to defining the situation in terms of a guest-host relationship. My silence in the car clearly signaled the limits of my submission. His response was a strong one: Was I happy? Was he a good host?

The role of the host combines two of the most important of Moroccan values. As throughout the Arabic world, the host is judged by his generosity. The truly good host is one whose bounty, the largesse he shows his guests, is truly never-ending. One of the highest compliments one can pay to a man is to say that he is *karim*, generous. The epitome of the host is the man who can entertain many people and distribute his bounty graciously. This links him ultimately to Allah, who is the source of bounty.

If the generosity is accepted by the guest, then a very clear relationship of domination is established. The guest, while being fed and taken care of, is by that very token acknowledging the power of the host. Merely entering into such a position represents an acceptance of submission. In this fiercely egalitarian society, the necessity of exchange or reciprocity so as to restore the balance is keenly felt. Moroccans will go to great lengths, and endure rather severe personal privation, to reciprocate hospitality. By so doing, they reestablish their claim to independence.

Later in the day, I went down to Soussi's store in search of Ali to try and make amends. At first he refused even to shake hands, and was suitably haughty. But with the aid of Soussi's mediation and innumerable and profuse apologies on my part, he began to come round. By the time I left them later that afternoon it was clear that we had reestablished our relationship. Actually, it had been broadened by the confrontation. I had in fact acknowledged him. I had, in his own terms, pulled the rug out from under him—first by cutting off communication and then by challenging his gambit in the car. There was a fortuitous congruence between my breaking point and Moroccan cultural style. Perhaps in another situation my behavior might have proved irreparable. Brinkmanship, however, is a fact of everyday life in Morocco, and finesse in its use is a necessity. By finally standing up to Ali I had communicated to him.

Indeed, from that point on, we got along famously. It was only after this incident that he began to reveal to me two aspects of his life which he had previously concealed: his involvement in an ecstatic brotherhood, and his involvement in prostitution.

Review Questions

1. What professional mistake did Rabinow think he had made with Ali? What "rule all good anthropologists should follow" did he think he had violated?
2. Why does Rabinow talk about enduring annoyances and inconveniences as "suspending disbelief"?
3. What does it mean in the Moroccan culture to be *karim*? What is the significance of this characteristic?

Probes

1. Notice how space is organized and used in the Moroccan village Rabinow describes. For example, how are the houses arranged and built? Where are the men and the women during the dancing? What messages about culture do you get from these uses of space?
2. How do you account for the radical response Rabinow first had to the argument with Ali—he actually considered having to become a shoe salesperson or something other than an anthropologist. Why do you suppose he responded so strongly?
3. What does Rabinow's experience say about the relationship between theory and practice?
4. Paraphrase Rabinow's explanation of the guest–host, dominant–submissive dynamic he found in Moroccan culture.
5. Notice that, for Rabinow, the key outcome of the confrontation with Ali was that "I had in fact acknowledged him." What does he mean by that?

Part
4

Bridging
Differences

Chapter 10

Relationships

I n 1981, Roger Fisher and William Ury published a book called *Getting to Yes: Negotiating Agreement Without Giving In* (Boston: Houghton Mifflin). The book was based on the Harvard Negotiation Project, a program jointly created and executed by the law and business schools at Harvard University. The book became a best-seller, primarily because of Fisher and Ury's ability to translate the findings from extensive and rigorous research into practical suggestions for people involved in negotiation. In 1988, Roger Fisher and Scott Browning published a book called *Getting Together: Building a Relationship That Gets to Yes*. Their second book is undoubtedly designed to exploit the popularity and financial success of their first one. But it also includes some excellently clear discussions of some well-researched and well-tested ideas.

This next reading consists of most of Chapter 6 of Fisher and Browning's 1988 book. I've included it here because it provides an excellent introduction to the topic of relationships. Fisher and Browning begin by recognizing that "To have a working relationship, we have to communicate," and that "Many people measure the quality of a relationship by the quality of communication." These generalizations apply to all kinds of relationships — superior-subordinate and other business relationships, political affiliations, friendships, and the relationships among family members, dating partners, and spouses.

In the spirit of many books addressed to general nonacademic readers, Fisher and Browning develop their ideas about relationships by describing "three barriers to effective communication" and "three ways to strengthen the relationship." There's nothing magic in their six ideas, but most of them are insightful, and they do outline a basic approach to the development and management of relationships that can, I believe, serve you well.

All three of their barriers to effective communication will be familiar to you, either from your earlier reading in this book or from your own experience. Fisher and Browning are right when they say that (1) we assume there is no need to talk, (2) we communicate only in one direction, and (3) we send mixed messages. They also have some helpful things to say about the various reasons why our messages are often "mixed" — because of mixed purposes, multiple audiences, and mixed emotions.

Their first prescription for improvement is the "ACBD" rule: Always Consult Before Deciding. This is the kind of advice that it's almost impossible to argue with. And the way Fisher and Browning present and discuss it helps make it clear and effective. They also explain six goals that your consultation can help to achieve.

Since I've already expressed my opinion about the importance of listening in Chapter 7, you can understand why I agree with Fisher and Browning's second piece of advice: "Listen actively." The four suggestions they make about listening are incomplete, but they do characterize the general form of this part of your communication. I especially like what they say about their fourth suggestion, "Speak clearly in ways that promote listening."

The authors' advice about how to avoid mixed messages follows the same organization as their discussion of the problem. They offer suggestions about how to clarify purposes, use privacy to minimize the problem of multiple audiences, and minimize emotional interference.

The summary chart on the final page of the essay applies to Fisher and Browning's ideas to a superior-subordinate relationship. But the primary purpose of the essay is to overview some essential communication features of *all* relationships. The rest of Chapter 10 offers individual discussions of (1) superior-subordinate, (2) friend, (3) family, and (4) couple relationships.

Communication: Always Consult Before Deciding—and Listen

Roger Fisher and Scott Browning

To have a working relationship, we have to communicate. What we communicate and how we do it—whether with a friend, a spouse, an employer, or a government—affect our ability to deal with differences. Poor communication can lead to misunderstanding, unhelpful emotions, distrust, sloppy thinking, and poor outcomes.

Communication is a broad field. It has many aspects beyond those involved in developing a working relationship. This chapter focuses on three barriers to good communication and some unconditionally constructive strategies that anyone in a relationship can use to improve communication in ways that help solve problems.

Many people measure the quality of a relationship by the quality of the communication. "We don't talk" means that the relationship has broken down, while "we talk about everything" means the relationship is healthy. The way we communicate reveals the nature of a relationship. Just the tone of voice used by a parent to a child, one spouse to another, or a superior to a subordinate tells us much about how they deal with each other. A hostile tone, interruptions, and shouting indicate a relationship that is likely to foster more problems than it can solve. A short telegram, an aide-mémoire, or an impersonal business letter may convey more by its form than its content.

Good communication need not indicate friendship. Communicating effectively with those with whom we have fundamental disagreements is more difficult but often more important than communicating with those we like. The United States and Soviet governments recognize their interest in maintaining communication *especially* when disagreements are most serious. In 1987, the two governments agreed to upgrade the "hot line" between their capitals and establish crisis communication centers so that their communication will be most direct when it's most needed.

Communication is complex. We communicate with every movement and action, often without conscious intent. Silence itself can send a powerful signal. It may mean, "I am upset, don't bother me," or "I am thinking hard about what you just said." Body position and movement may convey warm openness or cold rejection.

The emotional impact of my communication may determine whether someone will *want* to work with me. All of us have had the experience of meeting someone for the first time and feeling an instant rapport. After a few brief words, I understand what you are trying to say and you seem to understand me precisely. I am comfortable with you and enjoy your company. There is a mutual rhythm in the conversation and both of us are fully engaged.

If we are communicating poorly, on the other hand, the symptoms may be equally clear. I am uncomfortable and ill at ease. When I am talking, you look away. You appear to assume that you know all you need to know about me and do not care to learn more. There are uncomfortable pauses in the conversation, forced laughs at jokes that are not funny. Neither of us learns anything from the conversation; neither listens. Unless I can do something to change the way we are communicating, I am likely to leave such a conversation feeling frustrated and unproductive. I will want to avoid you in the future. The feeling will be mutual.

Each communication helps establish a pattern of interaction that plays a crucial role in the ability to deal with future problems. A mother who yells at her daughter may see an immediate response, but may find that she has created a barrier between herself and her child as that daughter grows older. Any message that cuts off future communication handicaps both sides.

Poor communication can hurt every element of a good working relationship. What prevents our communicating in ways that help us deal with differences?

Three Barriers to Effective Communication

Communications go awry in many ways and for many reasons. Some are beyond our control. But there are others each of us can affect with modest effort and no risk:

- We assume there is no need to talk.
- We communicate in one direction: we "tell" people.
- We send mixed messages.

1. We Assume There Is No Need to Talk

Perhaps the most important explanation for failed communication in a relationship is the common assumption that there is no reason to discuss a particular matter. A husband, for example, without consulting his wife, may have made a decision that affects her. He may have done so because:

- it didn't occur to him to talk with her about it;
- his mind was focused on the substance of the matter;
- he thought he knew what the right decision was;
- he thought he knew what she would say; or
- in the last analysis, the decision was one he himself would have to make.

His wife may have had an interest in the decision, known things that would have led him to decide otherwise, or had views quite different from those he imagined. His decision may have been a mistake. But even if he made the right decision and correctly guessed what she would say, the process was unwise. The husband may have surprised his wife, thereby appearing a little less reliable in her eyes. He confronted her with a fait accompli, tending to make her feel coerced, not persuaded. And by unilaterally deciding something that affects her, he sent the implicit message that she, her interests, and her views were not worthy of consideration— a view exactly contrary to the kind of acceptance that helps build a working relationship....

2. We Communicate in One Direction: We "Tell" People

Even when we do see the need to communicate, we often assume that it simply means telling something to somebody else. For communication to be effective, it needs to be two-way: there must be not only transmission, but reception. Listening is essential.

We may talk so much that we discourage the other side from listening. Consider the case of a couple in which the husband is talkative and the wife quiet. If an observer were to interrupt the husband's flow of words at some point and ask the wife what he had been saying, the answer might be, "I have no idea." One way to adapt to an extremely talkative person is to stop listening. Why listen? There is no interchange. Building a relationship with such a person is as difficult as building one with a loudspeaker....

The consequences of one-way communication can be as bad as those of none at all. Like the husband who failed to consult his wife, if we communicate solely by transmitting our opinions, we cut off the chance to learn things we don't know and discourage the other side from contributing to a solution. Further, we reduce their commitment to any solution.

3. We Send Mixed Messages

To be effective, communication should be consistent: what I say today should agree with what I said yesterday and what I will say tomorrow. What you heard me telling someone else should fit with what I told you. My words should be consistent with each other and with my actions. Mixed messages undermine each other and prevent effective communication.

Inconsistency is particularly damaging to our ability to build a working relationship. On a personal level, we feel uneasy with someone who gives lip service to one way of living and acts differently. We get mixed messages from the fundamentalist evangelist who has an affair with a secretary and defrauds the church. Some people may succeed in ignoring one message or the other, but most will find the conflict disturbing: something does not ring true.... When we hear such conflicting messages, we become skeptical and confused, not only about the speaker's interest, but also about his or her reliability; we do not know which message, if either, to believe. As a result, future joint problem-solving will be more difficult.

Mixed messages are common in our communication for three reasons: we communicate about mixed interests; we address ourselves to multiple audiences; and our mixed emotions may send out confusing signals.

Mixed Purposes   One of my goals may be to improve a working relationship, but I always have a number of other goals as well. Because my short- and long-term interests often conflict, an explicit message I transmit to further one set of interests may contain implicit messages that conflict with the other set. Long-term concerns are drowned out by short-term goals that seem—at the moment—more urgent. If I tell my young daughter, "I'm busy; please don't bother me," hoping to finish an urgent piece of work, she may hear a far more general message that I am not interested in her. That second, implicit message might have been avoided if, aware of the problem, I had added, "Could you come back in twenty minutes with a book you'd like me to read to you?"

A message we send one day in pursuit of one goal may be inconsistent with one we send the next day, when we have a different interest in mind. If I angrily rebuke a supplier for missing a deadline, hoping that he won't miss another, he may hear that I want to change suppliers. And he may pay no attention to my later comment about wanting an ongoing business relationship.

Multiple Audiences   We often want to say different things to different audiences, for reasons that are perfectly legitimate. The CEO of a publicly held corporation faces this situation when writing an annual report, which must satisfy several constituencies; shareholders, employees, and investment analysts. To each, the CEO may wish to emphasize different points. If the report says the company expects to reduce labor costs in the coming year, the shareholders may be pleased, but the employees upset. To improve the company's ability to work with each, the CEO will have to choose his words carefully.

Mixed Emotions   Suppose I tell my staff that they can interrupt me at any time to voice strong concerns about the office. The week after I announce this policy, however, I have a run-in with my boss that upsets and angers me. If my assistants come in that morning to tell me they are unhappy with the vacation schedule, I may show irritation and anger even as I try to listen to them. I may still say, "Thank you for bringing this to my attention. You can do so anytime," but they will get a quite different message, one that says, "Don't bother me when I have something else on my mind...."

Emotions play a large role in determining not only what we say and how we say it but what we hear. If I am upset, angry, or frightened, I will interpret what you say in the light of my emotional state. An innocuous statement of fact—such as "I'll be talking with your boss tomorrow"—may be interpreted as a threat. A silence may appear highly suspicious. A failure to return a phone call may seem proof of personal rejection.

Three Ways to Strengthen the Relationship

To overcome these barriers to an effective problem-solving relationship, we need both a general strategy and some specific techniques to deal with particular communications problems. The suggested general strategy has three components:

1. Always consult before deciding.
2. Listen actively.
3. Plan the process.

1. ACBD: Always Consult Before Deciding

As a general rule, if you and I have an ongoing relationship and I would like to improve our ability to deal with differences, then I should consult you before making a decision that would significantly affect you. To consult means to ask your advice. It is not enough to tell you a decision after it has been made. Consultation does not require that we agree or that I give up such authority as I may have to make a decision. But it does require that I inform you of a matter on which I may decide, that I request your advice and views and listen to them, and that I take them into account in making a decision.

For instance, the president of a company is facing her third straight quarter of losses. She believes she must reduce the payroll, but she has to worry about a union. She might invite the union leaders to her office, explain the reasons for the cutback, and say something along the following lines:

> Ultimately, it is my responsibility to the company and its shareholders to decide how best to reduce our payroll. But before I make any decision, I'd like to learn your views of the employees' interests and how you think they might be affected by various options. I would also like to hear any ideas you may have on how our production could be restructured to make it more competitive. We want to be expanding, not contracting. I can't promise to implement your suggestions, but I'll certainly consider them and use them if I think they'll help.

Consultation of this kind should be the norm of every working relationship. It should take place whether I am making plans for next weekend (I should consult my spouse) or the U.S. government is makings plans to send a fleet to the Persian Gulf (it should consult allies and friendly governments in the area).

We cannot adopt a rigid rule to consult relationship partners before making any decision that may affect them. Some circumstances will require quick decisions. In other cases, a decision may affect so many people (perhaps every employee in a factory of every citizen in a city) that advance consultation with each one is out of the question. Perhaps the impact of our decision on someone will be slight. Or perhaps there is a risk that disclosure of a proposed decision will generate opposition that will cause serious problems for both of us. This consultation guideline, like others, is subject to reasonable explanations.

Nonetheless, the practice of consulting relationship partners before making decisions that significantly affect them—whether they are family members or foreign governments—is unconditionally constructive. It will be good for the working relationship and good for me whether or not you follow the same practice. We can see this by examining how a practice of consulting before deciding improves each of the elements of a good working relationship.

Consult to Help Balance Emotion with Reason   We cannot avoid our emotions and those of others—nor should we try to. But we can often avoid the damaging impact that emotions can have on communication and that emotional communications, in turn, can have on a working relationship. A policy of consulting a relationship partner gives us time to think and reduces the risk of a hasty decision.

Consult to Promote Better Understanding If I routinely consult you before making any significant decision that will affect you, I will promote mutual understanding. I let you know what I am thinking of doing and why, and I ask for your concerns, ideas, and suggestions. I listen and take them into account. The process improves our understanding of each other's thinking.

Consult to promote two-way communication The general guideline of consulting before deciding engages both parties in talking and listening. Consultation *is* two-way communication: I tell you of a situation, I ask your advice, and (if you are willing to give it) I receive it. One person can stimulate two-way communication. The best advice is to ask advice.

Consult to Be More Reliable If, without advance notice, I make decisions that affect you, you will often be caught by surprise. The more often this happens, the less able you will be to predict my behavior and the less reliable I will appear in your eyes. You are likely to trust me less, not knowing what I am going to do next. If I ask your views before making a decision, you are less likely to be surprised and my behavior will tend to be more predictable. By simply giving advance notice—and doing what I tell you I am going to do—I can become more trustworthy.

Consult to Avoid a Coercive Fait Accompli A unilateral decision by one that confronts the other with no chance to affect it will often feel coercive. Simply *informing* you before I take action may be enough to avoid damage to my reliability in your eyes. But to avoid your feeling coerced, I will need to *consult* you before making a decision and give you an opportunity to persuade me.

Consult to Establish Acceptance The final element of a good working relationship is acceptance. If, without giving you an opportunity to help shape a decision, I decide the matter by myself, I am to that extent treating you as someone I will not deal with, whose interests and views deserve little consideration. Such behavior will prevent our having a good working relationship. If, on the other hand, I do consult you, I demonstrate that I am willing to deal with you and willing to consider your interests and views.

2. Listen Actively

Sometimes in a relationship one of us is talking too much and listening too little. Perhaps, more commonly, neither of us—however much we are talking—is listening effectively to the other.

Find the Listening Needs and Match Them The first step in active listening is to become aware of any listening problem. If you think you tend to dominate conversation, check yourself. Ask friends or colleagues to tell you if they observe you talking too much or not listening enough. Try recording the length of time you spend talking versus the length of time you spend listening.

Next, design an opportunity and setting that will be conducive to listening. Some marriage counselors, for example, advise their clients to make a "listening contract." The couple agrees to allow each spouse to talk without interruption for a period of time. Even without such ground rules, self-restraint will help. We some-times talk every time we can think of something to say. If we are talking too much, a better rule is to talk only for a purpose, and to keep that purpose in mind.

Engage the Other Person My active listening means more than sitting silently, although that is sometimes needed. It also means establishing conditions and asking questions that will draw you out and engage you. As we begin a con-versation, I can use several techniques to establish personal rapport. I can adopt a manner that is harmonious with yours in terms of pace, volume and tone of voice, formality or informality, degree of relaxation, and so forth. We can sit more or less side by side with a pad of paper, chart, or other symbolic representation of "the problem" in front of us on which we can work jointly. And I can learn as much as possible about you in advance, so that my questions will reflect a genuine curiosity.

A variety of techniques can help me understand the specific content of what you wish to communicate. These include making short interjections that acknowl-edge points made, paraphrasing in my own language what I have heard to make sure that I have it right, taking short notes, maintaining intermittent eye contact, and asking follow-up questions. It can be particularly useful to repeat points that surprised me so that I will remember them instead of slipping back to a prior assumption. With careful listening, I will learn things that will help us improve our relationship in the future.

Inquire No matter how sensitive I am when I listen, I will not be able to grasp fully what you are saying unless I understand something about you. Each of us may be transmitting ideas in our own jargon or conveying highlights that pre-sume a common base of information that the other does not have. Just as under-standing another person requires some communication, so communication requires some understanding of the other person's frame of reference and culture....

We can measure our listening skills by asking ourselves how much we know about our relationship partners. Do we know how our friends feel about current political or social issues? about art? Do we know what is important in their lives? Do we know how our employees feel about their schedules or benefits? how the Mexican government feels about the new U.S. immigration law? If we draw blanks on questions like these, especially about matters on which we differ, we should probably be listening more carefully.

Speak Clearly in Ways That Promote Listening If our communication is to be truly two-way, you will need to understand what I am trying to say. While I cannot force understanding on you, I can communicate in ways that make it more likely that you will understand me.

Speak for ourselves, not them. In general, we can speak in the first person, talking about what we have observed, what we think, and what we fear. And we can avoid putting words in their mouth, attributing motives to them, or telling them what they really think. "I'm feeling ignored" is likely to be more effective and construc-tive than "you're ignoring me."

Use short clear statements—and pause. With every statement I make, there is some risk, however small, that you will misinterpret what I mean. I may misspeak, use ambiguous words, forget critical points, use unfamiliar terms, and so on. The longer my statement, the greater the chance that one misinterpretation will confuse other points that I have tried to make. I can reduce that risk by avoiding long lectures, breaking complex messages into small parts, encouraging interchange, and allowing pauses so that each of us can digest what we have heard. If I have several important points, I can make them one at a time and give you an opportunity to confirm your understanding as we talk.

Help them be active listeners. We can ask others to confirm in their own words what they've heard us say. If they have not understood, we should try a fuller explanation that may help them understand both our words and our context.

3. Plan the Communication Process to Minimize Mixed Messages

If we want to improve our communication process in ways that enhance our ability to solve problems, we will need to think about why we want to communicate in the first place, what we need to learn or transmit, which channels or forums to use, and how we will communicate. We will need to implement our plans and monitor the results.

Clarify Our Purposes We frequently convey messages that work at cross purposes when we have interests that genuinely conflict with each other. A professional woman would like to be successful at the office. She might also like to see herself as a full-time nurturing mother, an author, a loving wife, and an outstanding civic leader. As she communicates her honest interests to her family and colleagues, one message may undermine another so that she appears insincere....

Use Privacy to Minimize the Problem of Multiple Audiences When we try to talk to many people at the same time, our messages are bound to be confused. When the president of the United States, for example, is making a public statement nominally directed to the Soviet Union, he is aware that his statement will also be heard and noted by, among others:

- the secretaries of state and defense;
- senators and members of Congress;
- those who select stories for the evening television news;
- a large number of American voters; and
- our European allies.

At any one time, the purpose of a given communication may be primarily to have an impact on one or another of those audiences. But when a presidential message to the Soviet Union has been edited and revised in an attempt to satisfy all of them, the final text may end up murky to all. Worse, that text is likely to be accompanied by background statements and television interviews of various other officials, each of whom has a different audience in mind. The resulting "message" is unlikely to improve the president's ability to work with the Soviet Union....

At every level, the confusion that comes from dealing with multiple audiences can be reduced by avoiding the multiple audience and by increasing the amount of one-on-one private discussion. In a family situation, the same principle applies. If you have difficulty working through an issue with your mother-in-law when your spouse is present, consider having a one-on-one lunch. The difference between a talk among three people and a talk between two is enormous. Among three people, every comment is directed to two listeners. There is no chance, for example, to say something to your mother-in-law without the risk that your spouse will react, respond, or change the subject.

Plan Encounters to Minimize Emotional Interference   Planning can build confidence and reduce anxiety about communication in general.

Plan an approach to troublesome questions. We can reduce fears of revealing too much of our own uncertainty by thinking things through in advance. For example, suppose I am negotiating to buy a house that I want so desperately that I am willing to pay much more than the market value. I fear that the seller will ask me to name the highest price I would be willing to pay. I may plan an approach to any such question along the following lines:

> I don't want to close my mind on that subject. You may be able to persuade me that your house is worth more than I think it is. And if you were to pay any attention to some figure I named as the highest I would pay, you would be encouraging me to name a very low figure and try to deceive you. Let me tell you this: I like the house. If I can afford to do so, I will pay what it's worth. Let's discuss what it's worth.

These are not lines I memorize, but having thought through this approach, I no longer fear questions about the most I would pay (or, if I am a seller, the least I would take). Similarly, if I am afraid of divulging sensitive information, I can prepare a safe way to deal with that subject.

Think ahead about candor. If I want to understand you, I will want you to talk about yourself. If I have thought ahead of time about what might be troubling you or why you might be reluctant to talk, I can prepare what I might say to make you more comfortable talking with me. I may want to reveal a bit of personal information about myself and then be open to listening should you want to talk; such as:

> My husband and I went through some tough times two years ago, and it affected me so much that I couldn't get myself out of bed in the morning. I stopped exercising, eating well, and visiting friends. But after several months, therapy began to help.

In many situations, such as in dealing with a friend who has just been divorced, I can predict that a large emotional element is likely to affect our communications. The more I think in advance about those emotions, and about what I want to learn and what I want to convey, the better our communication is likely to be and the better able we will be to deal with substantive problems.

Plan where and how to communicate. If we are part of a relationship that is not working well, we may have a pattern of communication that is both ineffective and difficult to break. One way to avoid verbal logjams is to create in advance a forum that will facilitate clear communication.

Such a forum might be on neutral ground to promote a sense of security, equality, and mutual respect, and thus reduce anxiety. A known place and context, which can help people treat otherwise emotional issues in a familiar and business-like manner, can improve the clarity and quality of communication. It helps to have a regular place, time, and process. Unions and management frequently create committees to deal with workers' grievances. Two companies that work together sometimes designate one person from each to handle jointly any problem that may come up between them. Married couples may designate a particular time of the week to discuss their individual calendars and any issues that may have accumulated. One couple agreed to discuss all divisive issues in the meat department of a nearby supermarket where they had once resolved a major argument. For them, the place had a "spirit of agreement" about it, and each was confident that tempers would stay under control. Anticipating and preparing for divisive issues in some way can alleviate negative patterns that prevent effective communication.

Even if we don't prepare a particular place for sensitive conversations, we may want to set forth some ground rules that will make each of us feel more secure. During a dispute, one person may not want to advance a suggestion for fear that it will be taken as a commitment. In these circumstances, it may help to designate a time and place for brainstorming only—a session in which either person can suggest any solution or wild idea without commitment or attribution.

Implementation: Monitor Communications with the Relationship in Mind   As carefully as we might design the communications process to improve the relationship, we may still fall shy of our goal. But we can do better over time if we monitor our communications and take steps to correct problems. ....

Institutions such as businesses and trade unions could benefit from organized thinking about a communication program intended to improve their working relationships. Even in the case of two individuals at the office, it may be useful to do some planning about communication. Such a plan might be a simple checklist along the following lines:

Notes for Improving My Relationship with the New Account Manager

Communication

1. **Acceptance.** Make sure she knows that she's a member of the team and that I am interested in her point of view.
2. **Frequency.** Speak with her every day.
3. **Audience.** Talk *with* her, not about her. If there is anything I might say to others about her, arrange a time to talk about it with her. Identify goals for the future. Give her constructive feedback about her performance.
4. **Listen.** What's on her mind? Share my perceptions with her and ask how she sees the same things. Does she understand my concerns? Ask her to try to spell them out.
5. **Quality time.** Every now and then, set aside a fair amount of time—perhaps a lunch—for an unhurried discussion of what's on her mind.
6. **Consult.** Before making any decision that might have a significant impact on her, ask for her advice. Repeat it back in my words to make sure she knows I am listening and interested.

Communication is the lifeblood of a working relationship. No matter how good our communication is now, we can undoubtedly find ways to improve it. Common barriers to effective communication—such as assuming there is no need to talk, communicating one-way, and sending mixed messages—can be worn away by planning and active listening. But the simplest and most powerful rule of thumb is to consult the relationship partner. Really consult. Ask advice before making a decision—and listen carefully.

Review Questions

1. What do the authors of this essay mean by "relationship"? Are they talking primarily about spouses? Dating partners? Lovers?
2. According to the authors, what role does communication play in relationships?
3. Which of the three barriers to effective communication affects you the most?
4. What is a "mixed message"?
5. What do the authors mean when they say that "consultation should be the norm of every working relationship"?
6. How can consultation enable one person to be perceived as "more reliable"?
7. What are the three ways Fisher and Browning suggest that you plan your communication to minimize emotional interference?
8. Consider using the checklist on the last page of the essay to guide your communication in relationships that are important to you.

Probes

1. Fisher and Browning give an example of a wife and husband operating on the assumption that there is no need to talk. Give an example of this same phenomenon affecting organizational communication.
2. What similarity do you notice between the first two barriers the authors discuss? How is the assumption that there's no need to talk similar to the act of communicating by "telling"?
3. Fisher and Browning identify three kinds of "mixed messages." Can you think of a fourth and fifth kind?
4. Sometimes one person's effort to "consult before deciding" is misinterpreted by the person being consulted. What kinds of misinterpretations can especially be promoted by efforts to consult?
5. What are the specific similarities between what Fisher and Browning say about listening and what Milt Thomas and I say about it in Chapter 7?
6. Does the problem of privacy and multiple audiences affect only CEOs and people speaking in public? Explain.
7. Fisher and Browning suggest that you use "planning" to "minimize emotional interference." Do you believe that emotions can be managed by planning? Why or why not?

The next essay discusses the first of four kinds of relationships that this chapter focuses on, the one between a superior and a subordinate. Many writers are interested in superior-subordinate relationships, including specialists in organizational communication, business school professors, consultants, and sociologists. But this is the only treatment I know of written from the perspective of a person interested in androgyny. I include it because I think it highlights an increasingly important dimension of the superior-subordinate relationship, and it suggests some very useful ways to improve communication in the workplace.

Andro is the Greek root for male and *gyne* is the Greek root for female, so the term "androgyny" suggests a blend between male and female characteristics. As Alice Sargent points out early in this reading, her thesis is that "an adrogynous mix of behaviors is the most effective management style" in the workplace of the 1980s and beyond. In the past, certain superior-subordinate behaviors have been considered to be typically "male" and others to be typically "female." Sargent argues that enlightened managers need to learn to blend these two kinds of behaviors.

Sargent's work draws heavily on the extensive research of psychologist Sandra Bem, who developed the widely used Androgyny Scale. In a portion of this reading that I omitted, Sargent notes that "An increasing body of literature and experience suggests that androgyny in management makes not only for happier people but also for better managers."

Sargent begins her discussion of effective interpersonal relationships in organizations by describing how the best-planned and most carefully designed management systems, like those for performance appraisal, management by objectives, and zero-based budgeting, are often sabotaged by poor interpersonal relationships. I have experienced what she's talking about. Over the past ten years I've worked as a communication consultant for a management consulting firm that provides services to engineers and architects all over the United States. I have witnessed how defensiveness, petty jealousy, stereotyping, unrealistic expectations, poor listening, and other interpersonal problems have undermined the effectiveness of some very well conceived and thoroughly implemented management systems. I have also noticed how stereotypically male and stereotypically female attitudes and behaviors have contributed significantly to these problems.

When Sargent talks specifically about manager-subordinate communication, she emphasizes the importance of both instrumental and expressive behaviors. She notes, in other words, that both task-related and relationship-focused communication are necessary if a pair of people are going to work well together. Moreover, since the success of the relationship is the responsibility of both parties, "Boss and subordinate need to challenge each other, inform each other, ask each other for feedback, give feedback, share needs, build trust, acquire self-awareness, confront each other, and back off from each other." The Interpersonal Relationships at Work Inventory, which she reprints here, operationalizes the attitudes and skills that Sargent believes are vital to a good superior-subordinate relationship.

These attitudes and skills also figure prominently in a manager's work with a group, Sargent's next topic. One set of important group leadership skills has typically been associated with females—the ability to establish supportive relationships in which people share their thoughts and feelings, the ability to respond to self-expression with genuine interest and concern, and the ability to confirm others as significant and worthwhile. Other important skills have typically been considered "male," for example the ability to focus on the task, to be objective, to confront others, and to establish control. Sargent argues that "Effective group work, like so much of management, places a premium on an androgynous mix of skills."

By the time you reach the conclusion of Sargent's essay, I hope you will be convinced that the concept of androgyny can be useful to the person interested in thinking about and improving the superior-subordinate relationship.

The Androgynous Manager

Alice G. Sargent

As women, Blacks, Hispanics, Asians, and American Indians began to move into the world of management, the emphasis was not on learning from them. Efforts focused, instead, on fitting minorities and women into what once was the domain of white men. These efforts almost totally missed the point by failing to take advantage of the new resources being brought to the management world. Interestingly, though, as affirmative action has gained ground, management theory and practice are expanding the concept of what makes a good manager. The new members of the workforce exhibit many of the behaviors that are being discussed and very tentatively tried out by managers.

As concern for people inches toward parity with concern for getting the job done, managers will have to exercise greater skills in dealing with people. They will need to express and accept emotions, nurture and support colleagues and subordinates, and promote interactions between bosses and subordinates and between leaders and members of work teams. These behaviors are desirable not only for their own sake, but because they can increase organizational effectiveness and efficiency. Since many of these behaviors traditionally have been regarded as "feminine," and therefore not acceptable in the marketplace, both male and female managers have avoided them. Instead managers have been expected to be aggressive, rational, autonomous, task-oriented, and tough-minded.

The new management style does not call for abandoning traditional "masculine" behaviors but for blending them with "feminine" behaviors. As we shall see, the demands of the workplace increasingly require this balance. In addition, the greater number of options promise a richer, fuller life at work and at home for both men and women. In order to be effective and healthy, all of us need a mix of both masculinity and feminity.

The word *androgyny* describes this new management mode. As a psychological term, androgyny suggests that it is possible for people to exhibit both masculine and feminine qualities and that such values, attitudes, and behaviors reside in varying degrees in each of us. My thesis is that an androgynous mix of behaviors is the most effective management style in the workplace in the 1980s—a style that blends behaviors previously deemed to belong exclusively to men or women.

What is equally significant, if not more so, is that androgyny is also the best route to fulfillment in our personal lives. It holds out the possibility that we might feel human and whole in both the workplace and the home—that we might express autonomy and interdependence in all our relationships and feel like balanced emotional and rational people wherever we go. Certain aspects of intimate relationships are becoming relevant to organizational life. Both at home and at work we need a supportive culture that includes the opportunity to have intellectual and emotional rapport with those around us; the chance to be vulnerable and to take risks in order to learn; and the chance to utilize a problem-solving approach rather than a blaming one....

Masculinity and femininity may become negative and even destructive when they are represented in extreme and unadulterated form. This point is made clear by psychologist Sandra Bem, who developed the Androgyny Scale and has been instrumental in fostering the concept of psychological androgyny: "Extreme femininity, untempered by sufficient concern for one's own needs as an individual, may produce dependency and self-denial, just as extreme masculinity, untempered by a sufficient concern for the needs of others, may produce arrogance and exploitation.[1] What I am suggesting is an integration rather than a polarization of the characteristics of toughness and tenderness, of connectedness and autonomy. Then a manager may combine being a tough battler, friendly helper, and logical thinker....

You may be saying, "We want to live in a sex-role-free society. Doesn't androgyny encourage sex-role stereotyping? We want behavior to have no gender." There is an irony there. As Sandra Bem says:

> The concept of androgyny contains an inner contradiction and, hence, the seeds of its own destruction.... Androgyny necessarily presupposes that the concepts of masculinity and femininity themselves have distinct and substantive content. But to the extent that the androgynous message is absorbed by the culture, the concepts of masculinity and femininity will cease to have such content and the distinctions to which they refer will blur into invisibility. Thus, when androgyny becomes a reality, the concept of androgyny will have been transcended.[2]

We are not at that point in our culture in the 1980s. We may not reach that point in our lifetimes. As sociologist Philip Slater said in a recent speech, "The women's movement is the most important liberation movement in history. All other social upheavals in history usually have ended, even after considerable progress, with a patriarchal hierarchy; but this one gradually is forcing both sexes into a more holistic perspective on the world."

.... A move toward androgynous behaviors may, in the short run, increase the inner turmoil for a boss or subordinate, a wife or husband. But in the long run such behaviors are critical to being effective in organizations, content in family life, and successful in achieving self-expression and meaningful contact with others.

An androgynous organization is one that strives to develop its people at the same time that it increases its productivity, and not to do either activity to the exclusion of the other. An androgynous person is one who strives to attain a balance in all relationships—at work, at home, and in the community; while playing racquetball, loving other people, starting a new project, having fun with kids, or taking long walks on the beach. Achieving this balance is a significant next step in moving us beyond our sex roles. It seems quite a lot to aspire to in one lifetime.

Effective Interpersonal Relationships in Organizations

Traditionally, it has been the manager's job to ensure that a work group functioned well. But in the past this has largely meant a focus on task-oriented activity.

It is only recently, as we recognize the diversity of the needs of the new workforce and the importance of responding effectively to these needs, that bosses are being encouraged to show greater concern for human factors. People skills—traditionally regarded as feminine (and therefore given second-class status in many organizations)—are coming to the fore as a crucial part of managerial effectiveness.

The benefits of the most refined management systems become lost if the manager-subordinate relationship or the work team is not effective. Systems presumably employing performance appraisal, management by objectives, and zero-base budgeting have been sabotaged time and again because people in the organization do not really talk to one another about what is on their minds. In one large organization, over half of a group of senior managers indicated they spent less than half an hour a year on performance appraisal, even though the results were a central factor in promotion decisions.

To be effective as bosses or subordinates, team leaders or team members, employees need to increase their interpersonal skills. They need greater self-awareness (particularly a sense of their own power needs) as well as skill in providing open communication and candid performance feedback. They need to know how to work in groups or teams, how to encourage development among their subordinates, and how to deal effectively with authority.

The work relationship can be an intense one, particularly when issues of attraction and power are at stake. Among men, the issue may be framed as loyalty. Among men and women, it may take the form of sexual attraction. As one woman manager told me:

> I asked my boss if he felt comfortable giving me constructive criticism. He said, "I'm afraid of your anger." It attacks his sexuality. It's very important for my boss to feel that he's central to my development. He experiences my anger as a form of sexual rejection. He uses me for personal and interpersonal discussions, still not for technical discussions as much. I am afraid of the attraction. He needs me to be attracted to him—demands it, like the way he wants loyalty from the guys.

Some major corporations as well as such government organizations as the General Accounting Office and NASA are beginning to require human resources management functions from their line managers. The U.S. General Accounting Office holds managers responsible for the following four functions: (1) coaching and counseling employees to increase their effectiveness; (2) developing subordinates' careers; (3) managing subordinates' performance; and (4) dealing with problem employees. (NASA adds dealing with high-potential employees.)

Manager-Subordinate Communication

Communication is undoubtedly one of the most important management functions. It helps advance relationships as well as ideas. Henry Mintzberg says managers spend between 50 percent and 90 percent of their time in interpersonal communications.[3] They are likely to spend about 10 percent of this time communicating with their bosses, 40 percent with subordinates, and 50 percent with people outside the chain of command. To do this effectively requires a great deal of interpersonal skill and concern for relationships.

Full communication requires both instrumental and expressive behaviors, especially between boss-subordinate pairs and in group settings. Instrumental acts

3. The planning for our team is done by_____

4. Taking stock of our relationship is done by_____

5. Decisions about how much time we spend working together are made by_____

IV. *Expressing Feelings*

1. I feel *most* free with you to express ( ) frustration, ( ) anger, ( ) disagreement, ( ) feelings of failure, ( ) fear, ( ) sadness, ( ) feelings of success. (Rank in order.)
2. I feel *least* free with you to express ( ) frustration, ( ) anger, ( ) disagreement, ( ) feelings of failure, ( ) fear, ( ) sadness, ( ) feelings of success. (Rank in order.)

V. *Communiction*

1. I feel free to talk openly to you because_____

2. You encourage me to bring good news and bad news to your attention by_____

VI. *Roles*

1. I have difficulty being assertive when you_____

2. You have difficulty being assertive when I_____

3. If I were you, I would do the following differently at work:_____

4. Since I am not you, I cannot object to your_____

5. The strengths of our relationship are_____

6. The weaknesses of our relationship are_____

7. Our relationship would be more effective if you_____

8. Significant people in my life would characterize our work relationship as_____

VII. *Description*

1. A metaphor that describes our relationship is_____

   A descriptive song title is_____

A descriptive book title is_____

A hero or heroine from literature who describes me is_____

_____

A hero or heroine from literature who describes you is_____

_____

VIII. *Action Plan*

1. If I could change one thing about our relationship, it would be_____

   _____

2. If I could change one thing about you it would be_____

   _____

3. If I could change one thing about myself it would be_____

   _____

Effective Managers as Group Leaders and Group Members

Today's managers must increasingly rely on groups and work teams to get the job done. Much of the work of organizations takes place in groups—task forces, study groups, work groups, management teams, committees, and so on. And much frustration accompanies work in groups. The concept of androgyny helps to shed light on the issues. Working with groups may be difficult for male managers, who have traditionally been rewarded for rationality, independence, competitiveness, a win-lose style, living by rules and procedures, and entrepreneurial skills. Working with groups may also be difficult for women managers, who have been socialized to be more reactive than proactive, to moderate or sidestep conflict rather than confront it head on, and to refrain from expressing their boundaries by saying yes when they should say no. Given these norms, it is frequently difficult to achieve collaboration and teamwork in organizations.

In addition, few managers receive training in group effectiveness skills, in sharp contrast to the numerous sessions of technical training they undergo. Thus engineers who become project managers quickly realize how unprepared they are to build a work group when all they can rely on is their technical background. Working with groups means dealing with all kinds of needs. Clayton Aldefer, a professor of organizational behavior at Yale University,[5] refers to these group effectiveness skills as relatedness needs:

- The need to establish supportive relationships in which people share their thoughts and feelings.
- The need to be heard and understood on significant matters and to find others who will respond to self-expression with genuine interest and concern.
- The need to be liked, to be accepted, and to belong to the group.
- The need to be confirmed by others as significant and worthwhile.
- The need to maintain some degree of influence or power when trying to exert leadership.

An effective group needs to concern itself both with task accomplishment (getting on with the job) and with social, emotional, and maintenance needs. Task accomplishment includes identifying mutual concerns, analyzing the problem, evaluating proposed solutions, and making and implementing decisions. Social, emotional, and maintenance needs involve dealing with the feelings and interactions of group members—factors that affect the intensity of member participation and the level of conformity and manipulation in the group.

High-pressure organizational life makes it too easy to focus exclusively on the task at hand and to ignore the fact that the interaction of group members substantially affects the functioning of the team. For example, a group may let one or two highly verbal or dominant people determine the course of action and ignore the involvement and collaboration of all group members. Yet we know from research and experience that if people begin to feel disenfranchised, they may remain silent for a time but later sabotage group decisions through lack of commitment. Typically, groups stifle spontaneity and creativity through overly rigid procedures and rules or through too little structure, which leads people to feel that nothing has been accomplished.

If groups are to function well, managers need to remember that collaboration takes longer than unilateral decision making, requires compromise, and hampers feelings of autonomy, but it may also produce better decisions, over which group members feel greater ownership. A manager accustomed to fast-paced, high-energy situations will have to exercise patience and compassion in order to nurture the collaborative process. In addition, the manager and group members need to play participant-observer roles with respect to the process so that they can make midcourse corrections if necessary....

Effective group work, like so much of management, places a premium on an androgynous mix of skills. As Professor William Eddy notes:

> Traditional male traits of task focus, objectivity, confrontation, and control are clearly important in many situations. Without them, as some free-floating counterculture groups found out in the 1960s, you have disorganization, wasted motion, and anarchy. But to build and lead groups that attain effectiveness and viability by fully utilizing their human resources, you also need some of the traits traditionally thought of as female. Sensitivity to feelings, development of support and trust, and collaboration rather than competition are important aspects of long-term group effectiveness.
>
> It is not surprising, when you think about it, why an androgynous combination of skills is best. Much of our work with groups of male managers involves helping them get in touch with important aspects of the group which are normally lost from their view—the expression of their own and others' feelings, the need for positive and supportive interaction, and the hazards of overuse of logical-rational modes. With women, in contrast, our work involves encouraging directness, dealing openly with power issues, and being clear about their boundaries. The basic point is, of course, that the full range of human characteristics is present in groups at all times. It's just a question of whether we decide to understand and deal with them.[6]

As the interpersonal side of management continues to gain in importance, androgynous behavior will become all the more valuable. Today, more and more of the manager's time is spent working collaboratively. The manager needs to conduct career development sessions and performance appraisals, run productive meetings, develop short-range and long-range plans in groups, lead task forces and study groups, and build open communications to improve the quality of work. Thus an androgynous blend of skills—of task-focused and people-focused behavior—is no longer a luxury but a crucial part of managerial effectiveness.

Notes

1. Sandra Bem, "Androgyny and Mental Health." Paper presented at The American Psychological Association meeting, Chicago, 1975.
2. *Ibid.*
3. Henry Mintzberg, *The Nature of Managerial Work* (New York: Harper & Row, 1973).
4. Leslie This, *Guide to Effective Management* (Reading, Mass.: Addision-Wesley, 1974).
5. Clayton Aldefer, *Existence, Relatedness, and Growth: Human Needs in Organizational Settings* (New York: Free Press, 1972).
6. William B. Eddy, "The Manager and the Working Group." Unpublished manuscript, 1980, School of Public Administration, University of Missouri, Kansas City (copyright by the author).

Review Questions

1. Define the word "androgyny." Use it in a sentence.
2. True or false: Androgynous managers need to abandon a number of traditional "masculine" behaviors. Explain your response.
3. According to Sandra Bem, what change in our culture may do away with the need for the concept of androgyny?
4. According to Sargent, what is the connection in the work relationship between power and sexual attraction?
5. Give an example of each of the barriers to effective downward and upward communication that Sargent lists.
6. In your opinion, what are the most important questions in the Interpersonal Relationships at Work Inventory?
7. What are "instrumental" behaviors? What are "expressive" behaviors? How are they relevant to this reading?

Probes

1. How do you respond to Sandra Bem's argument that the concept of androgyny will become obsolete when our culture has grown beyond its current tendency to stereotype sex roles?
2. Sargent argues—and I concur in the introduction—that the best management systems are virtually worthless unless the people applying them have good interpersonal skills. *Why* do you think this is the case?
3. Sargent presents her Interpersonal Relationships at Work Inventory as an operationalization of her approach to superior-subordinate communication. How does it function that way? What specific all do you learn about her approach by reading the Inventory?
4. Assume you are the leader of a work group that has to produce a lengthy report for a customer or client in a very short time. What are some examples of "male" leader behaviors that would probably be important in this situation? What are some examples of necessary "female" behaviors?

riendship is a relationship that we all experience. At the same time, as these authors point out, it is not a well-defined phenomenon. In order to enrich the friendships we have, it can help to understand the nature of this type of relationship and to know how friendships develop over time. These are the two topics of this essay.

Mara Adelman, Mac Parks, and Teri Albrecht are friends and colleagues of mine.

This is a recent piece of their work, and it is based on a great deal of research and reflection. Mac, especially, has thought, studied, and written about close relationships for a number of years. So you can trust the generalizations that they make here.

After acknowledging the difficulty of defining something as pervasive and amorphous as friendship, the authors focus on five distinctive features of this kind of relationship: (1) voluntariness, (2) status equality, (3) assistance, (4) activity sharing, and (5) confidentiality and emotional support. Then they briefly discuss how each functions and, by the end of this discussion, we have a rather clear picture of the nature of friendship.

Their treatment of the development of friendship relations is equally thorough and helpful. They talk about the development toward increasing intimacy and attachment, toward increasing breadth or variety of interaction (friends can talk about almost anything almost anywhere), toward increasing interdependence, toward increasing communication code specialization (friends "speak the same language"), toward decreasing cognitive uncertainty (I can usually predict what my friend's going to do), and toward increasing network contact and overlap (My friends are your friends, your friends are my friends, and our friends are often friends). They also note that changes in each of these dimensions affect all the other factors. As with the first section of this essay, each dimension of relationship development the authors discuss is important and, when taken together, they cover just about all the crucial aspects of this topic.

Mara, Mac, and Teri don't try to tell you how to make friends or even specifically how to communicate with them. But they do provide a wealth of useful insights into this most common and often most important of all our relationships.

The Nature of Friendship and Its Development

Mara B. Adelman, Malcolm R. Parks, and Terrance L. Albrecht

The Nature of Friendship

Friendship is a slippery concept. Even if we limit the problem of defining friendship to North American and Western European models, consensus regarding the nature of friendship exists only at the most general level. Reisman (1979, p.

108), for example, defines a friend as "someone who likes and wishes to do well by someone else and who believes those feelings and good intentions are reciprocated." Argyle and Henderson (1985, p. 64) can be no more specific than to define friendship in this way:

> Friends are people who are liked, whose company is enjoyed, who share interests and activities, who are helpful and understanding, who can be trusted, with whom one feels comfortable, and who will be emotionally supportive.

The difficulty with such definitions, of course, is that they do not neatly differentiate friendship from other close relationships. In fact, most of the characteristics of friendship can, to one degree or another, be found in other close relationships (see Argyle & Henderson, 1985). Given this ambiguity, we believe that concepts like "friend" and "close friend" are best treated as social and cognitive lables. Their meaning is derived from the individual's act of labeling a relationship as a friendship rather than from some unique and theoretically specified conceptual domain.

Friendship is also a slippery concept because it is both a type of relationship and a quality that people attribute to other types of relationships. For example, people often view other types of close relationships as if they were friendships (e.g., "She's my cousin, but mostly she's my friend" or "My wife is my best friend"). People frequently count kin among their close friends. Conversely, people often treat close friends as if they were members of the family (e.g., "You're like a brother to me").

None of these observations should suggest that the vessel of friendship is an empty one, only that many other relationships also carry its cargo. Perhaps friendship can be distinguished from other relationships by negation. Marriage, for example, carries all of the expectations of friendship, but friendship does not carry all of the expectations of marriage. This naturally begs the question of what the expectations and characteristics of friendship are. Our admittedly nonexclusive manifest of characteristics includes the following factors: (1) voluntariness, (2) status equality, (3) assistance, (4) activity sharing, and (5) confidentiality and emotional support.

Voluntariness   We are born into a family, but we choose our friends. The perception of choice distinguishes friendship from most family, kin, and work relationships. No other close relationship except marriage contains such a strong aura of voluntariness. The perception of voluntariness may give the support received from friends enhanced value just because the recipient knows that it was given more as a matter of choice than of obligation. However, even this perception is subject to restrictions. The amount of contact one has with kin becomes increasingly a matter of choice in adulthood (Arglye & Henderson, 1985). Moreover, because friendships are often developed within a network of other friendships, one's actual freedom of choice may be bounded by definite social pressures to either develop or to maintain a given friendship within the network.

Equality   Close friendships are usually based on the shared perception that the participants are social equals (Reisman, 1979, 1981). In her study of adult friendship choices in the United States and Germany, for instance, Verbrugge (1977) found that equality in social status was a major factor in close friendship choices. Less developed friendships, on the other hand, need not always be among equals. Many relationships growing out of work settings are "mixed friendships" in that they contain both elements of equality and inequality. Superiors and their favored subordinates, for example, often mix both a work relationship and a friendship. Elaborate rule systems are often needed to signal shifts from one relational domain to another. In general, however, the closer the friendship is perceived to be, the more equality the participants will perceive.

Assistance   Most studies of friendship emphasize that friends are people who help each other (e.g., Argyle & Henderson, 1985; Crawford, 1977; Parlee, 1979; Reisman, 1981; Reisman & Shorr, 1978). In contemporary U.S. and Western European cultures, however, there are definite limits to the amount of tangible and task assistance expected from friends. As Allan (1983) notes, friends typically "care about" rather than "care for" each other. While short-term and minor assistance can be expected, long-term and significant assistance must usually come from kin or public agencies. In a study of men who had suffered from myocardial infarctions, for example, Croog, Lipson, and Levine (1972) found that support from friends was more of a supplement to support from family rather than a primary or compensatory form of support.

Activity Sharing   Argyle and Henderson (1985, p. 84) observe that "above all we need friends to do things with, especially leisure activities, going out, and having fun." Obviously marital and family relationships also engage in activity sharing, but many of these shared activities are experienced with a sense of obligation rather than sharing for the joy of the activity alone. Shared leisure activities among friends can be more easily enjoyed purely for their intrinsic value. Friends also provide opportunities to share activities that are less enjoyable to the spouse or to other family members. Thus friends support us by giving us an outlet for activities not shared with family members and by giving us opportunities for enjoying activities without the larger relational implications so frequently a part of family life.

Confidentiality and Emotional Support   A major theme in the social support literature on friendship is the provision of emotional support, intimate confiding, and felt attachment (e.g., Allan, 1983; Argyle & Henderson, 1985; Bankoff, 1981; O'Conner & Brown, 1984; Quam, 1983). Friendships may serve as the primary sources of emotional support for unmarried persons, for adolescents experiencing the stresses of developing an independent identity, for men and women whose spouses are unsupportive, and for the elderly who have no kin living nearby (Argyle & Henderson, 1985). Friends may therefore at least partially compensate for inadequacies in other types of relationships. Even for those with many close family relationships, however, friends may serve as important sources of emotional support for at least two reasons. Because friendship networks tend to be less densely connected than family networks, individuals have a generally easier time keeping information confidential. Concerns for confidentiality and privacy figure prominently in people's subjective definitions of friendship (Argyle & Henderson, 1985; Crawford, 1977; Reisman & Shorr, 1978). In addition, friendships are sometimes more easily terminated than family and kin relationships. This fact provides individuals with a kind of "emergency exit" when the issues raised by the pursuit of emotional support become too disruptive to the relationship.

Dimensions of Relationship Development

... What does it mean to say that a relationship has "developed"? Relationships "develop" in several directions at the same time and so there is no one answer to such a question. However, we believe that the following six dimensions provide a relatively comprehensive view of relationship development. Personal relationships can be said to develop as (1) intimacy and emotional attachment increase, (2) the breadth or variety of interaction increases, (3) the degree of interdependence or contingency increases, (4) communication codes become specialized, (5) cognitive uncertainty about the self and other decreases, and (6) the participants' social networks become intertwined. Changes in each of these factors are presumed to affect the others. Moreover, while our primary concern is with the development of friendships, these dimensions of development are general ones that can be applied to the development of virtually any close relationship.

Increasing Intimacy and Attachment   The most obvious and researched aspect of relationship development is self-disclosure and intimacy. This is the "depth" dimension of relationship development (Altman & Taylor, 1973; Levinger & Snoek, 1972). As a relationship develops, the participants typically disclose more personal information, express more positive and negative feelings, and express praise and criticism more openly (Altman & Taylor, 1973; Huston & Burgess, 1979). At a general level, this implies that the value or magnitude of rewards and punishments exchanged tends to increase as a relationship develops (e.g., Altman & Taylor, 1973; Aronson, 1970; Hatfield, Utne, & Traupmann, 1979; Huesmann & Levinger, 1976). In a longitudinal study of friendship development, Hays (1984), for example, found that development was associated with increases in the intimacy of behaviors exchanged. At a more specific level, the depth dimension implies that the intimacy of participants' conversations increases as their friendship develops (e.g., Altman & Taylor, 1973; Naegele, 1958; Parks, 1976). Interaction becomes more oriented around the distinctive characteristics of the individual than around the more generalized characteristics they may stereotypically share with others (Miller & Steinberg, 1975).

Along with increases in the intimacy of interaction come increases in a series of affective variables such as liking and loving (e.g., Huston & Burgess, 1979) and a number of cognitive variables associated with them. In one recent study of friendship development, for instance, Eggert and Parks (1987) found strong positive correlations among measures of liking, love, intimacy, perceived similarity, satisfaction with communication, and the expectation that the friendship would continue into the future.

These findings suggest that the depth dimension of friendship development is reciprocally related to social support. As a relationship develops, the opportunities to provide the more intimate forms of social support such as emotional support increase and the participants place greater value on the support they receive.

And as the opportunity for and value of support increases, the development of the relationship is spurred onward.

Increasing Breadth or Variety of Interaction　As a friendship develops, the participants come to interact not only about increasingly intimate concerns, but also about an increasing variety of concerns. This is the "breadth" dimension of relationship development (Altman & Taylor, 1973). Disclosure and conversation occur along a greater variety of topics (e.g., Altman & Taylor, 1973; Naegele, 1958; Parks, 1976). In the parlance of exchange theory the variety of resources exchanged increases as a relationship develops (e.g., Hatfield et al., 1979). This point is nicely illustrated by Hays's (1984) longitudinal study of same-sex friendship development. Hays found that pairs whose friendship developed tended to engage in more behaviors in more categories of interaction (i.e., activity sharing, task assistance, mutual disclosure, expressing emotion) than did pairs that terminated or failed to become closer over the three month period of the study. These findings suggest that closer friendships provide more different types of social support for the individual and that the ability to provide such variety contributes to the overall development of the relationship.

As a relationship develops, the participants also tend to interact in an increasing variety of settings and contexts (e.g., Huston & Burgess, 1979). Closer relationships are more portable, less dependent upon the particular situational context. This implies that close relationships can serve as sources of social support in a greater range of settings than can "weaker," less developed relationships.

Increasing Interdependence and Contingency　Relationships develop to the degree that the participants become increasingly interdependent (see Kelley, 1979; Kelley & Thibaut, 1978). What each receives becomes more contingent upon the actions of the other. Their individual goals and actions become more synchronized and intermeshed (e.g., Altman & Taylor, 1973; Huston & Burgess, 1979). Indeed, if the participants believe that the benefits of the relationship can also be obtained from a variety of other sources, the relationship is less likely to develop (Huston & Burgess, 1979).

Interdependence and contingency have several implications for the social support process. First, increasing interdependence creates increasing substitutability in the resources or types of social support. The individual who gives support in one area may be repaid by support in another area. Less developed or "weaker" social ties, on the other hand, tend to operate more often on a give and take of like resources (Hatfield et al., 1979). While this characteristic makes the coordination of a close relationship a more difficult task, it also increases the range of behaviors that can be used to reciprocate support and thereby decreases the probability that an inability to reciprocate with like resources will disrupt the overall relationship. In addition, increasing interdependence is usually associated with a lessening concern for immediate repayment of favors and assistance received. Close friends tend to be more tolerant of inequities in the support taken and given because, unlike those in less developed relationships, they can believe that they have a good deal of time and many ways to restore equity (Hatfield et al., 1979). Finally, these characteristics of interdependence imply that methodologies that examine only those support requests that are immediately reciprocated with similar resources will miss much of the richness of the support process in close relationships.

Increasing Communication Code Specialization   Relationship development is not only characterized by an increasing depth and breadth of communication, but also by changes in the structure of communication. Waller and Hill's
(1951, p. 189) comments about the communication of courtship pairs apply equally
well to the communication of close friends:

> As a result of conversations and experience, there emerges a common universe of
> discourse characterized by the feeling of something very special between two per-
> sons.... They soon develop a special language, their own idioms, pet names, and jokes;
> as a pair, they have a history and a separate culture.

Code specialization occurs at several levels (Bernstein, 1964; Hopper, Knapp,
& Scott, 1981; Knapp, 1984). Private slang or jargon may be developed. Conventional language forms may be given new meanings that are fully understood only
by the participants themselves. Verbal statements may become abbreviated, incomplete. Or that which used to be verbally communicated may become communicated
nonverbally.

Code specialization has both methodological and substantive implications for
the study of social support. Observers given the task of coding interaction for its
support value may simply miss much of what is happening in a close relationship
unless directly aided by the participants. Moreover, the presence of a specialized or
"restricted" code implies that the conversation of close friends subtly reinforces and
supports their relationship in an ongoing way that is independent of its overt content (see Bernstein, 1964). However, because so much is implicit in these codes, their
presence can also be a barrier to renegotiation and change when partners have
difficulty talking about their relationship (metacommunicating) at a more explicit
level (see Adelman & Siemon, 1986).

Decreasing Cognitive Uncertainty   Humans have a deeply set need to
"make sense" of their social interactions (Heider, 1958). Much of what happens as
a personal relationship develops is therefore contingent upon the participants'
abilities to predict and explain each other's behavior; that is, to reduce uncertainty
(Berger & Calabrese, 1975). Most theories of relationship development recognize
the centrality of uncertainty reduction processes either explicitly or implicitly. As
Parks and Adelman (1983, p. 56) point out, "No theory presumes that interpersonal relationships can develop when participants are unable to predict and
explain each other's behavior." And, as we have emphasized elsewhere (see
Albrecht & Adelman, 1984), uncertainty reduction processes are also at the heart
of the process of social support.

Uncertainty reduction involves creating the sense that one knows how to act
toward the other, knows how the other is likely to act toward the self, and understands why the other acts the way he or she does (Berger & Calabrese, 1975; Berger,
Gardner, Parks, Schulman, & Miller, 1976; Parks, 1976). As uncertainty is reduced,
predictive and attributional confidence grow. So, too, do most other dimensions of
the relationship between the participants. Measures of uncertainty reduction have
been empirically linked to increases in the breadth and depth of communication,
the frequency of communication in general and metacommunication in particular,
measures of emotional attachment and attraction, contact with and support from
the partner's network, perceived similarity, relationship satisfaction, commitment

to the future of the relationship, and even with the overall stability of personal relationships over time (e.g., Berger & Calabrese, 1975; Berger et al., 1976; Eggert & Parks, 1987; Parks, 1976; Parks & Adelman, 1983).

Increasing Network Contact and Overlap　Whatever our inner experience of them may be, our personal relationships are also social objects existing within the broader context created by our surrounding social networks. How the participants in a developing relationship relate to those networks is therefore a vital dimension of the relationship itself.

The developmental course of a personal relationship is deeply influenced by network factors such as the extent to which the partners create an overlapping network of friends, perceive that each other's friends and family support their relationship, communicate with each other's networks, and are attracted to each other's friends and family. Research on friendship and romantic relationship development has shown that these factors are positively linked with the partners' emotional attachment for each other, their intimacy, commitment, perceived similarity, satisfaction, the frequency of their communication, and the stability of their relationship over time (e.g., Eggert & Parks, 1987; Lewis, 1973; Milardo, 1982; Parks & Adelman, 1983; Parks, Stan, & Eggert, 1983). . . .

Summary

Friendship is among the most malleable of human relationships. It is best understood as a social and cognitive label given to relationships that are characterized by relative voluntariness, perceived equality, the give and take of assistance, sharing activities, confidentiality, and emotional support.

References

Adelman, M. B., & Siemon, M. (1986). Communicating the relational shift: Separation among adult twins. *American Journal of Psychotherapy, 60,* 96–109.

Albrecht, T. L., & Adelman, M. B. (1984). Social support and life stress: New directions for communication research. *Human Communication Research, 11,* 3–32.

Allan, G. (1983). Informal networks of care: Issues raised by Barclay. *British Journal of Social Work, 13,* 417–433.

Altman, I., & Taylor, D. A. (1973). *Social penetration: The development of interpersonal relationships.* New York: Holt, Rinehart, & Winston.

Argyle, M., & Henderson, M. (1985). *The anatomy of relationships.* London: Heinemann.

Aronson, E. (1970). Some antecedents of interpersonal attraction. In W. J. Arnold & D. Levine (Eds.), *Nebraska Symposium on Motivation* (pp. 143–173). Lincoln: University of Nebraska Press.

Bankoff, E. A. (1981). Effects of friendship support on the psychological well-being of widows. In H. Z. Lapota & D. Maines (Eds.), *Research in the interweave of social roles: Friendship* (pp. 109–139), Greenwich, CT: JAI.

Berger, C. R., & Calabrese, R. J. (1975). Some explorations in initial interaction and beyond: Toward a developmental theory of interpersonal communication. *Human Communication Research, 1,* 99–112.

Berger, C. R., Gardner, R. R., Parks, M. R., Schulman, L., & Miller, G. R. (1976). Interpersonal epistemology and interpersonal communication. In G. R. Miller (Ed.), *Explorations in interpersonal communication* (pp. 149–171). Newbury Park, CA: Sage.

Bernstein, B. (1964). Elaborated and restricted codes: Their social origins and some consequences. *American Anthropologist, 66*(2), 55–69.

Crawford, M. (1977). What is a friend? *New Society, 42* (116–177).

Croog, S. H., Lipson, A., & Levine, S. (1972). Help patterns in severe illness: The roles of kin network, non-family resources, and institutions. *Journal of Marriage and the Family, 32,* 32–41.

Eggert, L. L., & Parks, M. R. (1987). Communication network involvement in adolescents' friendships and romantic relationships. In M. L. McLaughlin (Ed.), *Communication Yearbook 10.* Newbury Park, CA: Sage.

Hatfield, E., Utne, M. K., & Traupmann, J. (1979). Equity theory and intimate relationships. In R. L. Burgess & T. L. Huston (Eds.), *Social exchange in developing relationships* (pp. 99–133). New York: Academic Press.

Hays, R. B. (1984). The development and maintenance of friendship. *Journal of Social and Personal Relationships, 1,* 75–98.

Heider, F. (1958). *The psychology of interpersonal relations.* New York: John Wiley.

Hopper, R., Knapp, M. L., & Scott, L. (1981). Couples' personal idioms: Exploring intimate talk. *Journal of Communication, 32,* 23–33.

Huesmann, L. R., & Levinger, G. (1976). Incremental exchange theory: A formal model for progression in dyadic social interaction. In L. Berkowitz & E. Walster (Eds.), *Advances in experimental social psychology* (Vol. 9, pp. 191–229). New York: Academic Press.

Huston, T. L. & Burgess, R. L. (1979). Social exchange in developing relationships: An overview. In R. L. Burgess & T. L. Huston (Eds.), *Social exchange in developing relationships* (pp. 3–28). New York: Academic Press.

Kelley, H. H. (1979). *Personal relationships: Their structures and processes.* Hillsdale, NJ: Lawrence Erlbaum.

Kelley, H. H., & Thibaut, J. W. (1978). *Interpersonal relations: A theory of interdependence.* New York: John Wiley.

Knapp, M. L. (1984). *Interpersonal communication and human relationships.* Boston: Allyn & Bacon.

Levinger, G. & Snoek, J. D. (1972). *Attraction in relationship: A new look at interpersonal attraction.* Morristown, NJ: General Learning Press.

Lewis, R. (1973). Social reaction and the formation of dyads: An interactionist approach to mate selection. *Sociometry, 36,* 409–418.

Milardo, R. M. (1982). Friendship networks in developing relationships: Converging and diverging social environments. *Social Psychology Quarterly, 45,* 162–172.

Miller, G. R., & Steinberg, M. (1975). *Between people: A new analysis of interpersonal communication.* Chicago: Science Research Associates.

Naegele, K. D. (1958). An exploration of some social distinction. *Harvard Educational Review, 28,* 232–252.

O'Connor, P., & Brown, G. W. (1984). Supportive relationships: Fact or fancy? *Journal of Social and Personal Relationships, 1,* 159–175.

Parks, M. R. (1976). Communication and relational change processes: Conceptualization and findings. Unpublished Ph.D. dissertation, Department of Communication, Michigan State University.

Parks, M. R., & Adelman, M. B. (1983). Communication networks and the development of romantic relationships: An expansion of uncertainty reduction theory. *Human Communication Research, 10,* 55–79.

Parks, M. R., Stan, C. M., & Eggert, L. L. (1983). Romantic involvement and social network involvement. *Social Psychology Quarterly, 46,* 116–131.

Parlee, M. B. (1979). The friendship bond. *Psychology Today, 13,* 43–54.

Quam, J. K. (1983). Older women and informal supports; Impact of prevention. *Prevention in Human Services, 3,* 119–133.

Reisman, J. M. (1979). *Anatomy of friendship.* New York: Irvington.

Reisman, J. M. (1981). Adult friendships. In S. W. Duck & R. Gilmour (Eds.), *Personal relationships 2: Developing personal relationships* (pp. 205–230). London: Academic Press.

Reisman, J. M., & Shorr, S. E. (1978). Friendship claims and expectations among children and adults. *Child Development, 49*, 913–916.

Verbrugge, L. M. (1977). The structure of adult friendship choices. *Social Forces, 56*, 576–597.

Waller, W., & Hill, R. (1951). *The family: A dynamic interpretation.* New York: Holt, Rinehart & Winston.

Review Questions

1. According to the authors, what makes friendship a "slippery concept"?
2. What's the relationship between the features of friendship called "assistance" and "activity sharing"? How do they overlap?
3. How is "contingency" the same as "interdependence"?
4. Give an example from your own experience of increasing communication code specialization between you and a friend.
5. What do the authors mean by "increasing network contact and overlap"?

Probes

1. The authors claim that "status equality" is one defining characteristic of friendship. But they also note that some friendships negotiate elements of equality and inequality. It strikes me that inequality may be more of the norm than equality. What do you think? Is social equality a defining characteristic of your friendships?
2. The authors note that changes in one dimension of development affect the other dimensions. Give an example of this phenomenon. For example, how is increasing the variety of interactions likely to affect a friendship's intimacy and attachment? How might increasing code specialization affect network contact and overlap?
3. Sometimes communication seems to increase rather than decrease cognitive uncertainty. The more we get to know a friend, for example, the less we take him or her for granted. Does that phenomenon or your own experience challenge what the authors say here about uncertainty reduction?
4. One implication of the network research is that, if my family and friends don't like a friend I have, the probability that we'll stay friends is significantly reduced. Does that tendency match your experience? Discuss.
5. Do you agree with the authors that friendship is "the most malleable of human relationships"? Why is this important?

few years ago, newspaper columnist and speaker Dolores Curran was asked by her church to write a paper on the topic "Family—A Church Challenge for the Eighties." As she did her research, she noticed how many family experts were calling for someone to study healthy families in order to learn what similarities they had. Curran began paying attention to the traits the experts believed characterized healthy families, and a talk she developed about this topic became very popular. She then decided to study healthy families in depth and designed a survey that she sent to 500 family professionals. The professionals—affiliated with educational institutions, churches, health facilities, voluntary organizations, and family counseling centers—were apparently intrigued by her survey, because some passed the questionnaires on to others and Curran ended up with 551 completed surveys for the 500 she sent out. This nonscientific but informative study enabled Curran to generate a list of fifteen Traits of a Healthy Family. Curran discusses these traits in a book of that name, and the next reading is an excerpt from that book.

The experts who identified these traits work with a range of lower-middle-, middle-, and upper-middle-income families who live in urban, suburban, and rural areas. As Curran notes, "Most work with Anglo-American families, although I had significant response from those working with Hispanics in the Southwest and those working with the interesting racial mix that makes up Hawaii." She allowed each professional respondent to decide what the term "healthy" meant. Here are the fifteen traits these experts identified, listed in the order in which they were most often mentioned:

1. Communicates and listens.
2. Affirms and supports one another.
3. Teaches respect for others.
4. Develops a sense of trust.
5. Has a sense of play and humor.
6. Exhibits a sense of shared responsibility.
7. Teaches a sense of right and wrong.
8. Has a strong sense of family in which rituals and traditions abound.
9. Has a balance of interaction among members.
10. Has a shared religious core.
11. Respects the privacy of one another.
12. Values service to others.
13. Fosters family table time and conversation.
14. Shares leisure time.
15. Admits to and seeks help with problems. (pp. 26–27)

The reading consists of excerpts from the chapter in Curran's book that discusses traits 1 and 13. She begins by noting that a generation ago communication wasn't considered to be nearly as important as it is now. But today, as she puts it, "the major function of family is relational. Our needs are emotional, not physical." Family members are valued not just because of their ability to bring home a paycheck or clean the house but because of our relationships with them.

Curran develops what is meant by trait 1 in a discussion of eight specific characteristics of the communication in healthy families. The first is that the family exhibits an unusual relationship between the parents. The parents complement rather than dominate each other, and they feel and express love for one another. The second is that the family has control over television. TV can be beneficial, but in many families it detracts from quality interpersonal contact.

The third specific feature is that the family listens and responds rather than just reacting to what other members say. Curran is another observer of communication who recognizes how crucial listening is to the process. The fourth feature is that the family recognizes nonverbal messages. Members of healthy families are sensitive not just to what is said but to tone of voice, posture, facial expression, timing, and the other nonverbal cues discussed above in Chapter 4.

Healthy families also encourage individual feelings and independent thinking.

They accept differing opinions and engage in discussions with a good deal of give and take. These families also recognize what Curran calls "turn-off words and put-down phrases." Family members don't typically use words and phrases to "zap" each other. The next specific feature—the seventh—is related. In healthy families members do tend to interrupt one another, but equally. It's impossible to have a genuine give-and-take conversation without interruptions, but the key is that no one person gets interrupted much more than anyone else. And finally, healthy families are able to develop a pattern of reconciliation, a way to put arguments behind them, to pick up and go on after a fight has occurred.

This list may make the "healthy" family sound like a convention of angels. But as Curran's discussion clarifies, no family is perfect; none communicates flawlessly all the time. The key, though, is that the patterns that characterize communication in healthy families tend to resemble these eight specific features.

In the final part of this reading, Curran briefly discusses trait 13, "The healthy family values table time and conversation." She argues for the cultural importance of sharing food—a theme echoed by many anthropologists—and describes differences in the eating patterns of healthy and less healthy families.

As I mentioned, Curran's research would not meet the standards of a careful social scientist. But many of her findings are consistent with other studies of family relationships, and she presents them in a very accessible format. I've included this reading because I believe it can help you understand some important features of what are, for most of us, our most formative relationships. Curran's findings can also help direct your thinking about how you'd like communication to develop between you and your own spouse and children.

Traits of a Healthy Family

Dolores Curran

TRAIT 1: The Healthy Family Communicates and Listens.
TRAIT 13: The Healthy Family Values Table Time and Conversation.

Communicating and listening was chosen as the number one trait found in healthy families by my 551 survey respondents. This is consistent with the findings of the National Study of Family Strengths and in the work done on the healthy family by Dr. Jerry M. Lewis of the Timberlawn Foundation in Dallas.

Excerpts from "Communicating," from *Traits of a Healthy Family* by Dolores Curran, Harper & Row Publishers, San Francisco, 1983.

It's intriguing to ponder the fact that this trait wasn't even considered an important marital trait a generation ago. Why? Why was communication and listening perceived by today's family professionals to be the single most important characteristic of health in the family today? One family counselor I surveyed answered the question for me when he said, "Because without communication you don't know one another. If you don't know one another, you don't care about one another, and that's what the family ballgame is all about." . . .

Today the major function of family is relational. Our needs are emotional, not physical. We want to be valued for more than our ability to bring home a paycheck or to cook and clean. It isn't enough. Our affluence as a people has freed most of us from haunting hunger and the fear of physical survival. We aren't loved today for what we can do, but we still need to be loved and to love. We need to know we're needed and appreciated. We want to share our intimacies, not just physical intimacies but all the intimacies in our lives.

The kind of man our earlier family called for was the masculine one who never feared, doubted, flinched, or—heaven forbid—cried. The kind of woman our earlier family called for was the soft, dependent women who was ever patient and satisfied with her womanly skills, and who—heaven doubly forbid—never yearned for those things that belonged to the world of men. If either the man or woman experienced feelings traditionally assigned to the other gender, it was best to hide those feelings.

Those traditional sex roles linger on. At a workshop designed for mothers of young children, one young mother disclosed an archetypal problem: the insensitivity of a husband toward his wife and the children when they get sick or are hurting in some way. "My husband gets angry when I get sick," she reported. "And when the kids hurt themselves, he tells them to be tough, not to be pansies and give in to every little hurt. It worries me that when they get older they won't come to him when they're hurting."

They won't, and neither does she now. We probed a little and discovered what I had suspected, that her husband couldn't handle any sign of weakness because it scared him. He was supposed to be in charge at all times. So when his wife got sick, he got angry. He couldn't control her illness. When the kids got hurt, he wouldn't allow himself to be sensitive and caring. He had to become gruff and strong and in charge. Incidentally, guess what kind of father he had? Right—a strong, silent, insensitive man who felt ashamed when he had a stroke and had to be hospitalized because, to him, it was a sign of weakness in a world where men aren't supposed to be weak. . . .

Such men are rapidly becoming anachronisms in today's families. They exist, but they aren't good providers in that they don't provide what is needed. . . . Honest communication calls for courage of a kind different from machismo, and patience of a kind different from motherliness. It means risking ourselves to let another know who we really are underneath all these layers of societal musts, shoulds, oughts, and tsk-tsks. . . .

Communication is at the top of the family specialists' list because it is basic to loving relationships. It's the energy that fuels the caring, giving, sharing, and affirming. Without genuine listening and sharing of ourselves, we can't know one another. We become a household of roommates who react rather than respond to one another's needs. Let's look carefully at this all-important trait.

TRAIT 1: The Healthy Family Communicates and Listens.

Families ask, "How do we know if we are communicating? What are the signs of good and poor communication in the family?" I perceive these hallmarks in the communicating family.

1. The Family Exhibits an Unusual Relationship Between the Parents.

According to Dr. Jerry M. Lewis ... research data strongly suggest that intimacy, or the capacity of two people to share deep feelings, is strongly correlated with shared power. Rather than dominating one another, healthy spouses complement one another. In an exciting study of families undertaken by his center, he found that in the healthy families, husbands and wives were of equal power. Either could be leader, depending on the circumstances. In the unhealthy families he studied, the dominant spouse had to hide feelings of weakness while the submissive spouse feared being put down if he or she exposed a weakness or fear.

Acknowledging that this finding might be unpopular—touching as it does upon some people's moral conviction that spousal roles must remain in their traditional mold—Dr. Lewis nevertheless insists that equality exists in the healthy marriage. He stresses that children in the healthy family have no question about which parent is boss. Both parents are. If children are asked who is boss, they're likely to respond, "Sometimes, Mom, sometimes Dad." And, in a wonderful statement, Dr. Lewis adds, "If you ask if they're comfortable with this, they look at you as if you're crazy—like there's no other way it ought to be."[1]

My survey respondents echo Dr. Lewis's finding. An administrator in a degreed family program wrote on her survey, "The healthiest families I know are ones in which the mother and father have a strong, loving relationship between themselves. This seems to flow over to the children and even beyond the home. This strong primary relationship seems to breed security in the children, and, in turn, fosters the ability to take risks, to reach out to others, to search for their own answers, become independent, and develop a good self-image."

2. The Family Has Control over Television.

Television in the family has been maligned, praised, damned, cherished, and thrown out. It has changed family weekend-living patterns, it has been called the new hearth, and it has more influence on children's values than anything else except their parents. A friend of mine who is a marriage therapist lists football as one of the top five causes of marital discord, competing with money, in-laws, children, and jobs. Television's impact on the family is a book in itself, and a number of books on the subject are on the market for families who feel controlled by the media, who worry about values, consumerism, and passivity brought about by television. . . .

Here, I want specifically to discuss the effect of TV on family communication. Over and over when I'm invited to help families mend their communication ruptures or learn to celebrate together, I hear "But when can we do this?" Probing, I find that these families have literally turned their family-together time over to television. Even those who control the quality of programs watched and set home-workfirst regulations feel reluctant to intrude upon the individual's right to spend all spare time in front of the set. Or sets. Many families, in the ultimate attempt to offer freedom of choice, avoid clashes over program selection by furnishing a set for each family member. Indeed, one of the women who was most desperate to establish a better sense of communication in her family confided to me that they owned nine sets. Nine sets for seven people.

Whether the breakdown in family communication leads people to excessive viewing or whether excessive television breaks into family lives so pervasively as to literally steal it from them, we don't know. It's the chicken and egg dilemma. But we do know that we can become out of reach to one another when we're in front of a TV set. The term *television widow* is not humorous to thousands whose spouses are absent though present. . . .

When someone in the family does want some uninterrupted time to share some problems or feelings, he or she often hears "Shhh, I'm watching TV." That phrase is a strong clue that in that family television is the basic presence, with all other presences considered interruptive. It tells us a lot about the value of persons in that home. . . .

We shouldn't get the impression that television always plays the role of villain in family communication patterns. Although a 1980 Gallup Poll undertaken for the White House Conference on Families cited the negative effect of television on families, it also found that the public sees great potential for television as a help in families. It can be a tremendous device for initiating discussion between generations on subjects that aren't likely to come up elsewhere, subjects such as sexuality, sexual mores, corporate ethics, sportsmanship, marital fidelity, and consumerism.

Even very bad programs can by their badness offer material for value clarification in the family if members view them together. I recently observed my sixteen-year-old son and his father viewing a program in which hazardous driving was part of the hero's characterization. At one point, my son turned to his dad and asked, "Is that possible to do with that kind of truck?"

"I don't know," replied my husband, "but it sure is dumb. If that load shifted. . . ." With that they launched into a discussion on the responsibility of drivers that didn't have to originate from a parental lecture base. I also noted with interest that as the discussion became more engrossing to them, the TV program became less so, and they eventually turned the sound down in order to continue their conversation.

Parents frequently report this kind of use of television, which, incidentally, is the method that the widely publicized 1972 Surgeon General's report suggested as the most effective television gate-keeping by parents. The report suggested that instead of turning off the set, parents should view programs with their children and make moral judgments and initiate discussion. . . .

In 1981, the A.C. Nielsen Company announced that the average American television set is on for forty-three hours and fifty-two minutes a week. That's more than six hours a day. Whether the family uses television to replace or enhance communication depends on the family. Unfortunately, the level of family communication tends to go down as the level of television goes up, according to the opinion of professionals who work with families.

3. The Family Listens and Responds.

"My parents say they want me to come to them with problems, but when I do they're either busy or they only half listen and keep on doing what they were doing—like shaving or making a grocery list. If a friend of theirs came over to talk, they'd stop, be polite and listen," said one of the children quoted in a *Christian Science Monitor* interview by Ann McCarroll.[2] This child put his finger on the most difficult problem of communicating in families: the inability to listen and respond.

Most of us react rather than respond. When we react, we reflect our own experiences and feelings onto what we've just heard; when we respond, we get into the other person's feelings and are empathetic. Here are a couple of examples to show the difference.

TOM, AGE 17: "I don't know if I want to go to college. I don't think I'd do very well there."
FATHER: "Nonsense. Of course you'll do well."

That's reacting. Although this father may think he's fostering confidence, he's actually cutting off communications. He's labeling his son's fear as baseless and telling him he'll do well. He's refusing either to hear his son's fears or to consider his son's feelings, possibly because he can't accept the idea of his son's not attending college. Paradoxically, if the father cared less about college, he probably would be more open and responding, as in this father's handling of the same situation.

TOM: "I don't know if I want to go to college. I don't think I'd do very well there."
FATHER: "Why not?"
TOM: "Because I'm not that smart."
FATHER: "Yeah, that's scary. I worried about that, too."
TOM: "Did you ever come close to flunking out?"
FATHER: "No, but I worried a lot about it before I went because I thought college would be full of brains. Once I got there, I found out that most of the kids were just like me."

This father has responded rather than reacted to his son's fears. Notice what the father did: First, he searched for the reason for Tom's lack of confidence and found it was academic fear (it could have been fear of leaving home, of a new environment, of peer pressure, of any of a number of things); second, he accepted the fear as legitimate; third, he empathized by admitting to having the same fear when he was Tom's age; and finally, he explained why his, not Tom's, fears turned out to be groundless. He did all of this without denigrating or lecturing Tom.

And that's tough for parents to do. Often we don't want to hear our children's fears because they frighten us or their dreams because they aren't what we have in mind for them. Parents who deny such feelings will allow only surface kinds of conversation. It's fine as long as a child says "School was okay today," but when she says, "I'm scared of boys," the parents are uncomfortable, and they react instead of responding. They don't want her to be scared of boys, but since they're afraid they won't handle it well, they react with a pleasant "Oh, you'll outgrow it." She probably will, but what she needs at the moment is someone to hear and understand her pain.

Listening is crucial to communication.... A careful empirical study (S. Min-uchin and others, *Families of the Slums,* 1967) has documented that multiproblem families are groups of people who do not listen to one another.... It has been discovered that in such families no one expects to be heard. They are noisy families where people are used to tuning each other out. Or if on occasion people are heard, they do not expect a response. There is no experience of making contact, of count-ing as a person, or of making a significant impression. If there is some response, it is not usually relevant. Rather than connect with the other person's message, the response indicates disregard for it and changes the subject...."[3]

Often children need no more than to know that their parents are listening. They don't really need any active response. They simply want an opportunity to vent some feelings, to expose some opinions, to share some experiences. Pastoral counselor Norman Calloway suggests a counseling procedure for parents: When they listen to a spouse or child, they should ask themselves before responding, "Do I need to do any more than know this?" Often just attentively listening to another's words is all that's required in order to be empathetic. The speaker may not want a solution, just an ear. A five-year plan doesn't have to be designed to meet every problem that's expressed.

In Ann McCarroll's interviews, she ran into fifteen-year-old Bob, who said he had "some mother." And he described what he meant by that. "Each morning she sits with me while I eat breakfast. We talk about anything and everything. She isn't refined or elegant or educated. She's a terrible housekeeper. She uses double negatives. But she's interested in everything I do and she always listens to me— even if she's busy or tired."[4]

That's the kind of listening behavior found in families who experience real communication. Answers to the routine question "How was your day?" are really heard, with the eyes and heart as well as the ears. Nuances are picked up and ques-tions are asked. Every statement isn't met with "That's nice, dear." Members of a family that really listens to one antoher instinctively know that if people listen to you, they are interested in you. And that's enough for most people....

4. The Family Recognizes Nonverbal Messages.

Once one of my sons came home from school and I knew instantly that some-thing was wrong. I ventured a question, "What's wrong, Mike?" and his quick answer, "Nothing," told me that indeed something was amiss. If it wasn't, I knew him well enough to know that he would have looked up questioningly and asked, "Nothing. Why?" His abrupt "Nothing" also told me not to meddle, so I didn't.

But a while later, when he was ready to talk about it, he came and told me he had been the last one chosen that day for football. Remember how painful that was? You stood there praying silently to be chosen and as the list got lower and lower, your stomach cramps got stronger and stronger. And there was an ultimate indignity. If you were really bad, as I was in baseball, even when you were the last one chosen, once in a while the team would ask, "Do we have to take her?"

So when Mike told me he had been the last one chosen, primarily because he was short then and the game was football, I knew how he felt. "That's a terrible feeling," I said, "standing there and watching everyone else get picked."

His head snapped up. It never occurred to him that a parent could have been the last one chosen. He asked a lot of questions, shifting the attention from his pain to my experiences as a child. After a while, he ate a couple of bananas and went out to play.

So often we parents neglect to share with our children our past—and present—feelings of being inadequate, awkward, ugly, not loved, or not treated fairly. Unless we share ourselves with them, they think we've come full-blown to adulthood, never once doubting ourselves. They're much more likely to communicate their feelings to us if they know we experienced such feelings, too.

The healthy family responds to feelings as well as to words. "I know how you feel" can be as effective as a dozen admonishments. Dr. Jerry M. Lewis defines empathy as that characteristic in which someone responds to your feelings in such a way that you feel deeply understood. He says, "There is probably no more important dimension in all of human relationship than the capacity for empathy. And healthy families teach empathy."[5]

In the healthy family, members are allowed to be mad, glad, and sad; however, other members aren't always condemned to be around them. There's no crime in being in a bad mood—nor is there betrayal in being happy while someone else is feeling moody. The family recognizes that bad days and good days attack everyone at different times. . . .

Nonverbal expressions of love are the best way to show children that parents love each other. Verbalizing love to children isn't enough. Or even necessary if the nonverbal messages come through clearly. A spouse reaching for the other's hand, a wink, a squeeze on the shoulder, a "How's-your-back-this-morning?", a meaningful glance across the room, a peaceful silence together—all of these tell children that their parents love one another. . . .

On the reverse side, the most destructive kind of nonverbal communication in marriage is silence. Silence on the part of a spouse can mean disinterest, hostility, denigration, boredom, or outright war. On the part of a teen or preteen, silence usually indicates pain, sometimes very deep pain. I recall a mother who testified on family needs at a national church hearing. She listened to other parents complain about the quality of religious education offered their teens. Then she said, "I can't get overly worried about what my thirteen-year-old son is or isn't learning in religion class when he hasn't spoken to anyone in the family for three weeks."

This mother recognized prior needs. She knew that simply furnishing a better religion teacher or a more appealing youth group wasn't going to touch the pain that was keeping her son from being a part of their family.

The most common reaction techniques of youths in conflict with their families is silence. Often silence is the only reaction acceptable in the family. If youths can't expose what's bothering them for fear of ridicule or censure, or if they aren't allowed to argue, then they will revert to silence. The sad irony discovered by so many family therapists is that parents who seek professional help when their teenager becomes silent have often denied him or her any other route but silence in communicating. And although they won't permit their children to become angry or to reveal doubts or to share depression, they do worry about the silence that results. Rarely do they see any relationships between the two.

Many adolescents feel ugly and unlovable most of the time. They need constant reassurance that they are attractive and loved. I remember particularly the great number of teenage girls I taught in high school who were never made aware of their unique and appealing traits, such as an engaging smile, a special zest, or a keen wit. But they knew about their acne or their extra five pounds, and that was all that counted. . . .

The healthy families I know recognize positive nonverbal communication as crucial to family life. They use signs, symbols, body language, smiles, and other physical gestures to express their feelings of caring and love. They deal with silence and withdrawal in a positive, open way. Communication to them doesn't mean talking or listening alone. It includes all the clues to a person's feelings—his bearing, her expression, their resignation. Such families have a highly developed form of communication. Members don't have to say "I'm hurting" or "I'm in need." A quick glance tells other members that. And they have developed ways of responding without words—ways that indicate empathy and love, whether or not there's an immediate solution to the pain. And that's what counts in the healthy family.

5. *The Family Encourages Individual Feelings and Independent Thinking.*

It is a paradox that healthy families tend to be alike in their differences, that is, their similarity lies in their ability to encourage and accept the emergence of individual personalities via open sharing of thoughts and feelings. Unhealthy families tend to be less open, less accepting of differences of opinion among members, more interested in thought control. The family must be Republican, or Bronco supporters, or gun-control advocates, and woe to the individual who says "Yes, but. . . ."

In discussing his study on the healthy family, Dr. Jerry M. Lewis called communicating patterns in his healthy families "a joy to witness." He saw very little group-think. He explained that the healthy family encouraged "I" statements, such as "I think . . ." and "I feel. . . ." According to Dr. Lewis, one way a human being identifies himself or herself as a separate being is by making such individual statements. . . .[6]

The healthier the family, the better able it is to accept differing opinions in its midst. Instead of finding these opinions threatening, this family finds them exhilarating. And what Dr. Lewis found is true. It is exciting to witness such a family discussing politics, sports, or the world. Members freely say "I don't agree with you" without risking ridicule or rebuke. They say "I think it's wrong . . ." immediately after Dad says "I think it's right . . ." and Dad listens and responds.

Teachers often are able to identify students who come from such families. These students seem confident that their opinions are respected, even if they aren't shared. Students from families that don't encourage individuality in thought often seem afraid to venture their own thoughts on a subject. Instead, they wait until they discover the tenor of the class's thinking, and then they feel safe to go along. It takes a strong identity to express a belief or a feeling in a group before the group's opinion is known, but people in healthy families establish strong identities early in life.

The give-and-take of good family discussion is valuable for another reason: It gives children practice in articulating their thoughts at home so that eventually they'll feel confident outside the home. What seems to be chaotic, and even contradictory, verbal rambling on the part of preteens during a family conversation is an important prelude to their sorting out their thinking and putting words to their thoughts. Later, they'll be able to do this without verbalizing first, but speaking is the earliest way of discovering one's thoughts on a subject, the "how do I know what I think until I say it" level of articulation.

Rigid families don't understand the dynamics of this give-and-take. Some label it disrespectful and argumentative, others confusing. I like the words of Dr. John Meeks, medical director of the Psychiatric Institute of Montgomery County, Maryland, who claims that argument is a way of life with normally-developing adolescents. "In early adolescence they'll argue with parents loud and long about anything at all; as they grow older the quantity of argument decreases but the quality increases." According to Meeks, arguing is something adolescents need to do. If the argument doesn't become too bitter, they have a good chance to test their own beliefs and feelings. "Incidentally," says Meeks, "parents can expect to 'lose' most of these arguments, because adolescents are not fettered by logic or even reality."[7] ...

Cutting off discussion of behaviors unacceptable to us, making our young feel guilty for even thinking about values contrary to ours, and insisting upon group-think only makes contrary values more attractive to them. The healthy family risks openness in discussion rather than later regrets in experimental behaviors.

6. The Family Recognizes Turn-Off Words and Put-Down Phrases.

Some families deliberately use hurtful language in their daily communication. "What did you do all day around here?" can be a red flag to a woman who has spent all day on household tasks that don't show unless they're not done. "If only we had enough money" can be a rebuke to a husband who is working as hard as he can to provide for the family. "Got a new zit, David?" "Flunk any tests today, John?" "Don't pass her the bread. She sure doesn't need it."

Healthy families seem to develop a sensitivity to turn-off words and put-down phrases. They recognize that a comment made in jest to one person may be insulting to another. All of us are sensitive, only on different subjects. A father in one of my parenting groups confided that he could tease his wife about everything but her skiing. "I don't know why she's so sensitive about that, but I back off on it. I can say anything I want to about her cooking, her appearance, her mothering—whatever. But not her skiing." He shook his head, mystified.

Sometimes we try too hard to discover why a certain sensitivity exists when all we need to know is that it does exist and then respect it. One of my favorite exercises with families is to ask them to reflect upon phrases they most like to hear and those they least like to hear. It's an interesting challenge because we rarely give thought to it. ...

Another good exercise to clue a family in on the level of its sensitivity is that of keeping a record for a couple of weeks of the comments heard most often in daily family life. At the end of each day, parents can think of what phrases they've heard more than once that day and tally an approximate number of times they were used. If a family finds that its most-used phrases are of a helpful and caring nature—words such as "How was your day?" and "Can I help?"—then its level of sensitivity is high. If the words most commonly heard are negative—for example, "Shut up" and "Stop it"—then that family needs to pay more attention to its inter-relationships, especially the role that communication plays in them.

7. The Family Interrupts, but Equally.

When Dr. Jerry M. Lewis began to study the healthy family, he and his staff videotaped families in the process of problem-solving. The total family was given a question such as "What's the main thing wrong with your family?" Answers would vary from favoritism to lack of money to too much noise, but the answers themselves weren't important to the researchers. What was of significant interest was how the family dealt with problem-solving—who took control, how individuals responded or reacted, what were the putdowns, and whether some members were more entitled to speak than others. Among other results, the researchers found that healthy families were very clear in their communication. These families expected everyone to articulate clearly their words and feelings. Nobody was encouraged to hold back.

But in addition a most interesting discovery emerged. *Members of healthy families interrupted one another more than did members of less healthy families, but no one person got interrupted more than anyone else.* This should make many parents feel better about their family's dinner conversation. One dad reported to me that at their table, they had to take a number to finish a sentence. However, finishing sentences doesn't seem all that important in the communicating family.

So manners, particulary polite conversation techniques, are not high hallmarks of the communicating family. Spontaneity is. The family that communicates well doesn't need to finish its statements—others know what they're going to say. Members aren't sensitive to being interrupted, either. The intensity and spontaneity of the exchange are more important than propriety in conversation.[8]

8. The Family Develops a Pattern of Reconciliation.

"We know how to break up, but who the hell ever teaches us to make up?" These words, written in a letter to me from a reader in his thirties, sum up the situation in many families....

Following up on that reader response, I studied the healthy families pinpointed by professionals and also interviewed several professionals who counsel families. Both groups indicated that there is, indeed, a pattern of reconciliation developed in healthy families that is missing in others. "It usually isn't a kiss-and-make-up situation," explained a family therapist, "but there are certain rituals developed over a long period of time that indicate it's time to get well again. Between husband and wife, it might be a concessionary phrase to which the other is expected to respond in kind. Within a family, it might be that the person who stomps off to his or her room voluntarily reenters the family circle, where something is said to make him or her welcome. The most revealing characteristic lies in how the spouse or the family responds to the first gesture of reconciliation."

When I asked some families how they knew a fight had ended, I got remarkably similar responses from individuals questioned separately. "Everyone comes out of their room," responded every single member of one family. Three members of another family said, "Mom says, 'Anybody want a Pepsi?'" My favorite, though, was the little five-year-old who scratched his head and furrowed his forehead in deep thought after I asked him how he knew the family fight was over. Finally, he said, "Well ... Daddy gives a great big yawn and says, 'Well....'" This scene is easy to visualize and even somewhat stereotypic of the healthy family in which one parent decides that the unpleasantness needs to end and makes a gesture that comes to be known as the beginning of peace. The great big yawn and the "Well" say a lot more than a stretch to this family. They say it's time to end the fighting and to pull together again as family.

Why have we neglected to teach families the important art of reconciling? I asked the family therapist mentioned earlier. "Because we have pretended that good families don't fight, They do. Everybody does. It's essential to fight for good health in the family. It gets things out into the open. But we need to learn to put ourselves back together—and many families never learn this." ...

I also found that healthy families know how to time divisive and emotional issues that may cause friction. They don't bring up potentially explosive subjects right before they go out or before bedtime, for instance. Over and over I heard the phrase "the right time." The right time seemed to be one in which there was enough time to discuss the issue heatedly, rationally, and completely—*and* enough time to reconcile. "You got to solve it right there," said the dad in one of the healthiest families I studied. "Don't let it go on and on. It just causes more problems. Then when it's solved, let it be. No nagging, no remembering." ...

Reconciliation is a basic part of communication. It allows the surfacing of occasional discord, unhappy feelings, anger, sadness, disappointment, and frustration. The healthier the family, the more refined its pattern of reconciliation.

These, then, are eight hallmarks of the family that is able to communicate and listen—the trait most often selected by professionals as evident in the healthy families they observe....

TRAIT 13: The Healthy Family Values Table Time and Conversation.

My survey respondents valued family table time and conversation so highly that they placed it thirteenth in a list of fifty-six possible traits. Because this trait is so obviously a part of the family communication process, I am discussing it here.

Traditionally, the family table has been a symbol of socialization. It's the gathering place for the clan, the one time each day that parents and children are assured of uninterrupted time with one another.... Cartoonists use drawings of a family at table in order to quickly characterize that family. Breakfast scenes with people hidden behind newspapers show us a certain family style. A round dinner table with lots of people conversing is often used to suggest family closeness. The classic long, narrow table with the matriarch at one end and the patriarch at the other, with perhaps a child or two equidistant, easily indicates distance among family members.

In discussing the problem of family listening and sharing, Dr. Lee Salk, Cornell's popular child psychologist, writes, "Meal time is incredibly important in this regard. People used to talk and listen at meal time, but now they sit in front of their television sets with their dinner. I don't care how busy you are—you can take that time with your children. You can talk about your dreams; you can talk about your day; you can talk about your frustrations. The busier you are, the more valuable meal time is for your child. If we don't spend this time with our youngsters, they are not going to develop healthy attitudes toward family life...."[9]

Although my respondents placed family table time high in the traits of the healthy family, the trend is away from families having table time together. Yankelovich, Skelly and White, a research firm specializing in attitudes and life-styles, have found that fast-food dining is becoming a way of life for Americans. According to Florence Skelly, we are eating an average of five times per day and we are eating light and fast. Ironically, while there is a trend toward eating more meals at home, the variety of working patterns in our culture *has led to more unplanned meals that families no longer eat together.*[10] This finding is seconded by George Armelagos, coauthor of *Continuing Passions: The Anthropology of Eating,* who says that fast food is a reflection of a society in which social encounters are short and intense. When asked if the tradition of families eating together is dying, he replied, "Yes. There are so many things we have to do, often with work schedules that don't coincide. Women are working outside the home, and, in general, men and women are becoming more independent."[11]

Independent of what, we might ask? Of our children and spouses? Of our need to share while breaking bread together in the age-old ritual of family life? Or of our need for the closeness and communication that the family table presumes? ...

Families who do a good job of communicating make the dinner meal an important part of their day. They don't allow personal grudges and unpleasantness to be expressed, even though they do encourage differences of opinion. These families are very protective of the time allotted to the family dinner hour and often become angry if they're asked to infringe upon it for work or pleasure. A good number of respondents indicated that adults in the healthiest families they know refuse dinner business meetings as a matter of principle. They discourage their children from sports activities that presume upon the dinner hour as a condition for team participation. ("We know which of our swimmers will or won't practice at dinner time," said a coach, with mixed admiration. "Some parents never allow their children to miss dinners. Others don't care at all.") These families pay close attention to the number of times they'll be able to be together in an upcoming week, and they rearrange schedules to be assured of spending this time together. And they never allow television to become part of the menu.

A family counselor commented, "The best way to discover the health of a family is to eat a few meals with them. They can't fake it. Too many ingrained eating patterns. Some are miserable, but others are beautiful to behold."

According to professionals, the family that wants to improve its level of communication should look closely at its attitudes toward the family table. Is family table time and conversation important? Is it optional? Is it open and friendly or warlike and sullen? Is it conducive to sharing more than food—does it encourage the sharing of ideas, feelings, and family intimacies? Is it a battleground between cook and eaters? Does it exist at all? ...

Dinner can still be the daily gathering point for the family, the time when many kinds of sustenance are offered. Although the national trend seems to be away from the family table, the healthy families we studied are making a determined effort to offset that trend.

Notes

1. Jerry M. Lewis, address delivered at The Ecumenical Center for Religion and Health, San Antonio, Texas, 1979.
2. Ann McCarroll, "Getting to Know Children Requires Lots of Good Talk," Christian Science Monitor News Service. Reprinted in *The Denver Post,* June 19, 1980.
3. Paul F. Wilczak, "Listening as Ministry," *Marriage and Family Living,* March 1980.

4. McCarroll, op. cit.
5. Jerry M. Lewis, address in San Antonio, Texas.
6. Jerry M. Lewis, address in San Antonio, Texas.
7. Jayne L. Greene, "Adolescence: The Time of Life You Love to Hate," *The Sentinel*, Montgomery County, Md., March 11, 1981.
8. Jerry M. Lewis, address in San Antonio, Texas.
9. "The Traditional Family Will Make a Comeback," interview with Dr. Lee Salk, *U.S. News and World Report*, June 16, 1980.
10. Kim Upton, "Food Goals Include Cheap, Fast and Good." *The Denver Post*, December 3, 1980.
11. "Culturally Speaking: A Tasty Tale," *Weight Watchers Magazine*, February 1981.

Review Questions

1. What's the primary difference Curran notices between families a generation ago and families today?
2. Paraphrase Curran's account of the way changed sex roles have changed communication patterns in healthy families.
3. According to Curran, how can television *help* family communication?
4. According to Curran, what's the difference between reacting and responding?
5. What does Curran say about silence as a form of nonverbal communication?
6. Explain the paradox Curran discusses regarding the ability of healthy families to tolerate and encourage individual differences.
7. What does Curran mean by "a pattern of reconciliation"? What does she say about the importance of having such a pattern in a family?
8. Curran argues that table time and conversation are valuable. What makes them valuable? Why are they important?

Probes

1. What sex-role definitions have to exist in order for there to be the kind of parental power sharing that Curran discusses?
2. What are the links between Curran's discussion of the function of listening in family communication and the concept of confirmation discussed in Chapter 9?
3. Translate Curran's advice and your own experience into three or four principles of dealing positively with silence and withdrawal in a family.
4. If it's "good" to express individuality and independent feelings and to interrupt, why is it so "bad" to use "turn-off words and put-down phrases"?
5. Describe what you believe are the two or three general attitudes that characterize all eight of the specific features of communication that Curran discusses.

s you can tell from earlier chapters, my inclination is to vary the authors whose works I reprint here. But when I was looking for a brief but useful discussion of the couple relationship, I found the next reading in another book by Dolores Curran. The book is called *Stress and the Healthy Family*, and it's a follow-up to her *Traits of a Healthy Family*.

Curran's approach to the couple relationship is similar to her approach to the family relationship. But this time, rather than contacting professionals who worked with couples, she interviewed thirty-two sets of spouses and eight single parents. She focused on how the couples handled stress, and my assumption is that the ability to handle stress is one feature of a healthy, strong relationship.

Curran identifies five characteristics of couples who handle stress in a healthy way: (1) they view stress as a normal part of family life, (2) they share feelings as well as words, (3) they develop conflict-resolution skills and creative coping skills, (4) they make use of support people and systems, and (5) they are adaptable. As Curran discusses each of these characteristics, you will probably notice similarities between what she found and what Adelman, Parks, and Albrecht found in their research on friendship.

Curran makes two key points about the first characteristic. One is that healthy couples expect stress; they don't have an unrealistically romantic view of "the perfect relationship." A related point is that stress is usually generated by expectations. When you can manage your expectations, you can often manage your stress.

Her discussion of the second trait emphasizes the importance of what other authors discuss in Chapter 8, self-disclosure. Healthy couples were willing to take the risk of openness, and they developed nonthreatening ways to communicate feelings. Curran also notes that these couples' relationships typically developed into intimate *friendships*.

I omitted some parts of Curran's discussion of characteristic 3 because it overlaps material in this book's chapter on conflict. But Curran's treatment is useful because it reminds us of the central importance of conflict in all long-term, healthy relationships. Curran notes the importance of both conflict-resolution and coping skills.

Characteristic 4 echoes a point Adelman, Parks, and Albrecht made earlier: healthy couples pay attention to and use their networks to help them cope with stress. Frequently couples with short histories and newlyweds overlook the importance of strong support systems. They believe that their love can "conquer all" and that the two of them should be able to survive just fine on a desert island. The first really difficult problem or conflict reminds them of the truth of what Curran discusses here.

The final characteristic is adaptability. Given the pervasiveness of change in couple relationships—job change, geographic change, economic change, the changes caused by children, etc.—couples have to relax whatever white-knuckled grip they have on future plans so they can adapt to the circumstances that confront them.

Once again, the goal is not to lay out a prescription for the "perfect" couple relationship. But the guidelines suggested here can help you work toward a relationship that deals creatively rather than destructively with the problems you encounter.

The Couple Relationship

Dolores Curran

"I notice that when things are going well between us, other pressures disappear. But if we're not clicking, even the cat becomes a stress."

— FORTY-ONE-YEAR-OLD HUSBAND

"Clicking" is an apt word to use in looking at the basic factor in controlling everyday stress in the family. What makes couples click? What goes on inside the healthy spousal relationship that enables some couples to deal more effectively with time, money, work, and children than others? In an attempt to isolate commonalities among stress-effective couples, I interviewed and studied thirty-two couples and eight single parents identified as healthy by professionals who responded to my earlier research for *Traits of a Healthy Family*. Certain attitudes and characteristics surfaced among these families that give a clue to the dynamic which enables them to control normal stress well in their families.

Because the word *couple* in this book is necessary in discussing the two-parent family structure, I have used it frequently. However, the discussion applies to single-parent families as well. I suggest single parents substitute the word *family* where couple is used because in the single-parent family, the couple interaction usually transfers into a parent/children interaction, a parent/grandparent interaction, or a parent/friend interaction. I leave it to the single-parent reader to substitute whichever grouping is most appropriate. At times, of course, the use of couple is fitting for the single parent if the former spouse is involved in the issue under discussion.

The following are five characteristics of couples who handle stress in a healthy way:

- They view stress as a normal part of family life.
- They share feelings as well as words.
- They develop conflict-resolution skills and creative coping skills.
- They make use of support people and systems.
- They are adaptable.

I. The Healthy Couple Views Stress as a Normal Part of Family Life.

Healthy couples do not equate family life with perfection. Their expectations and goals are frequently lower than those of other couples. These couples don't link problems with self-failure, but rather anticipate stresses like children's behavior and occasional disagreements over money as a normal part of married life, and they develop ways of coping that are both traditional and unique.

Expectations in marriage play a foundational role in a couple's satisfaction with marriage. For example, if he expects her to be satisfied with his role as a good provider while finding his primary need for intimacy satisfied in his work, and she expects him to find his primary intimacy needs satisfied within the family, stress is predictable. Family scholars are bending their attention to this expectation factor in marriage to predict marital satisfaction. A recent paper delivered before the National Council on Family Relations provides an instrument to measure the degree of contrast between couple expectations in their relationship and complaints about the relationship.[1] If such an instrument becomes commonplace, couples may eventually be able to name their expectations before marriage rather than presume they share the same ones.

Couples often have very different expectations of what marriage and marriage roles mean. [One] woman said, "When we got married I was expected to stay home and be ready to be 'together' with my husband at a moment's notice. We had many arguments when I wanted to go back to school for a degree in social work; he deeply believed it was an insult to his masculinity and pride to have a wife who worked. Then it was OK with him if I worked—in fact, he was secretly very proud of me—as long as I didn't make much money or question the priority of his career." This couple had to renegotiate their expectations in order to deal with the normal stresses change brought. Later on, she ruefully reported, "Now I think he'd be happy to let me support him!"[2]

Couples with a strong spousal relationship expect change as part of growth and expect stress to result as part of this change. The first skill, then, in dealing with family stress springs from the couple's expectations and their ability to express them to one another.

2. The Healthy Couple Shares Feelings as Well as Words.

"In a survey, 5,000 German husbands and wives were asked how often they talked to each other. After two years of marriage, most managed two or three minutes of conversation at breakfast, more than 20 minutes over dinner, and a few minutes in bed. By the sixth year, the total was down to 10 minutes a day. A state of 'almost total speechlessness' was reached by the eighth year of marriage."[3]

Lack of communication is not an exclusively German phenomenon. "Whenever my husband is in a deep gloom, I have to play search and destroy," said an American wife. "Why won't he share his feelings? The more I search, the gloomier he gets." . . .

When I interviewed the couples who communicated effectively, I was struck by the many nonthreatening techniques they developed to get in touch with their own and their partners' feelings. "I learned early in our marriage not to say, 'What's bothering you?'" one women said. "His answer was always, 'Nothing.' And if I pushed he became angry or silent. One day I told him, 'I feel so lonely when something's bothering you and you won't tell me . . . like I've failed.' And I meant it.

"He was astonished at my reaction. He said, 'I don't want you to feel like that. The reason I don't tell you my worries is because I don't want to worry you.'

"Here we were, both concerned about the other's feelings but I was accusing him of being unfeeling and he was accusing me of intruding. I convinced him that hiding his feelings was more painful to me than any worry he could share. We agreed that when I felt he was shutting me out, I would say to him, 'I'm feeling lonely,' and he'd try to be more open. It's taken a long time for us but it works. Sometimes it's a risk, though."

Risk is a word we hear often from couples when they talk about feelings. "He won't risk confrontation." "I can't risk telling her." Yet, intimacy is built upon risk. It implies being able to risk one's vulnerability by sharing feelings that might not be acceptable to the other. When partners risk and there's belittlement or no response at all, another layer of protection is built around feelings. Some couples have such thick walls that the only time feelings emerge is in explosive anger.

In an article, "The Stresses of Intimacy," Michael Griffin writes, "If there is going to be deep intimacy, there will be stress. There can be no deep intimacy between a couple unless there is a great deal of fighting about what is important. Two people who care deeply about what is important to them are bound to come into conflict. If intimacy is the most important thing in life then the price must be paid to achieve this in conflict and struggle. But the rewards can be enormous."[4]

Love and intimacy don't come easily, however. We know how to work and how to cook because these skills were prized in an earlier economic model of family. We accepted honorable labels like the "hardworking man" and the "good little mother" as applied to husbands and wives. As a consequence, persons who fit such labels became enshrined as the underpinning of successful marriages.

Today we find ourselves seeking intimacy at its deepest level in a highly technological society, but we (particularly men) don't know how to be intimate. Intimacy is a skill to be learned and to share, and yet we're novices as far as understanding it. How often I hear a wife say, "He's a wonderful provider, a good father, and never unfaithful *but* ... ," and then she indicates that they can't talk or share feelings.

Psychiatrist Harold Lief, director of the Institute for Marital and Sexual Health in Philadelphia, believes that many people never learn to recognize and express feelings. "Fearful of sounding foolish or of bruising another's feelings, they're also tongue-tied by the risks of exposing themselves, of being vulnerable, of getting hurt. It *is* scary," Dr. Lief concedes, "but, if you play it too safe, your relationship will suffer. In effect, every couple truly committed to staying together have to create a language, a special code of words, gestures and actions that only they fully understand."[5]

I found that many healthy couples create their own code. Certain words give permission to open up while others warn, "Stay away." A letter from a reader of an article I wrote on family communication caused me to reflect on fear and lack of adequate language. She wrote, "I just finished reading your article and just have to tell you how much I enjoyed it. I only wish my husband would read it. *I intend to cut it out and mail it to his office* and hope he will take the time to read it as we could benefit from it." What an obvious communication problem right there. She has to mail the article to his office to get his attention. Their level of communication has become so impersonalized that it takes place through the U.S. mail, even though they live together....

When couples begin to share feelings, they begin to become friends, not just spouses or lovers. This element of friendship is mentioned frequently by couples in good relationships. "We're good friends. We can talk about anything." Because most marriages begin with a sexual attraction rather than friendship, some couples never become good friends....

I see a reluctance on the part of many young people today to cross the line from a friendship to a dating relationship. They realize that the nature of the relationship will change, and they don't want to jeopardize the friendship. It's a sad commentary on our cultural attitudes toward marriage—that spouses can't be friends....

Thousands of "unmarried" marrieds in the world are lonely in their couple lives. For reasons of their own, they choose to remain in a relationship that began with love but deteriorated through the years. Carin Rubinstein and Phillip Shaver, authors of *In Search of Intimacy*, found that one out of every four Americans suffers from loneliness and that 13 percent of married people say they are lonely and not in love. Their research also showed that men need women more than women need men because women are intimacy-givers while men tend to be intimacy-takers.[6]

Even within couples who develop friendship, life is not always smooth because one may not enjoy what the other enjoys. I worked with a couple who had very different social preferences. He hated parties and socializing, and she loved them. "At first I tried to change him," she admitted. "I'd drag him to a cocktail party where he'd head for a corner and stand there while I flitted around having a wonderful time. Then I'd be angry with him on the way home for being antisocial."

He nodded and said, "It was a no-win situation. I didn't want to go in the first place because I knew I would fail her and get scolded for it. We had an argument after every party. What she didn't know was how I envied her ability to talk with strangers and have a good time. I'm not good at that but I wish I was."

How did they deal with the stress affecting their relationship? He gathered the courage to tell her his real feelings—not that he disliked parties but that he was intimidated by them. A basic shyness, which she perceived as antisocial behavior, underlay his reluctance to attend that particular kind of social function. Once he risked his vulnerability to tell her he felt insecure in chatting with strangers, she reacted differently to his social needs.

"I felt awful," she said. "I didn't know he was shy and intimidated because he isn't that way with me or with our close friends."

Here is a common attitudinal change that takes place in healthy couples once they dare to risk sharing feelings. He risked, and she followed through with an important response to that risk: She accepted his feelings rather than discounting them by reacting with, "Nonsense. What's there to be shy about? Nobody's going to hurt you. Just get out there and start talking." ...

We behave similarly with teenagers, and it drives *them* crazy, too. When they share with us that they're fat or ugly, we tell them they're not. Then we wonder why they become angry with such a loving response. If they feel fat and ugly, our words inflame them because we're actually telling them their feelings are worthless. (Besides, they expect parents to say such things. Didn't we tell them their kindergarten artwork was beautiful?)

A more effective response would be, "I know how you feel ... I feel that way at times, too," or, "I'm sorry you feel ugly because I see such a lovely person in front of me." This doesn't discount their feelings but lets us share ours in a reassuring and supportive way....

How did the couple with the party stress respond ultimately to their diverse social needs? Once the wife realized the basis for her husband's dislike of cocktail parties, she didn't insist they attend as many, and she no longer left him alone in a corner but led him into conversations. She also no longer criticized him for his antisocial behavior. They gravitated toward smaller functions, inviting close friends with whom he was comfortable.

In talking about it, they indicated they both tried harder to collaborate, he attempting to join in more and she expecting less. They dealt with the actual stress—his shyness—to change the perceived stress—parties. In order to do this, they had to risk sharing some deep feelings of insecurity and compassion....

3. The Healthy Couple Develops Conflict-Resolution Skills and Creative Coping Skills.

Quite simply, the couples best able to deal with everyday stresses are those who develop workable ways of solving their disagreements and a fat supply of coping skills. Resolving conflict and coping are related, but not identical, skills.

Conflict-resolution skills depend largely on communication, while *coping skills* depend upon creativity, ingenuity, and perseverance. Some couples can have one set of skills and not the other. I met a couple who had excellent conflict-resolution skills. They could talk anything to death, share feelings, and emerge feeling good about themselves, but their family life was chaotic because they never *did* anything about the stresses attacking them. They just talked about them. The stresses went on and multiplied, and the couple finally sought help.

On the other hand, there are families in which stresses are addressed but not the conflict their resolution engenders. Maybe insufficient money stress is resolved by a husband's taking a second job, but the resentment this instills in him can be explosive. Such couples are constantly putting out brush fires as a response to stress rather than dealing with the dry prairie.

Let's look at *conflict resolution* first. Philip Blumstein and Pepper Schwartz, authors of *American Couples: Money, Work, Sex*, an exhaustive study on how couples interact, explained their purpose in studying how American couples deal with stresses: "Today's marriages require a new level of awareness and more commitment to problem solving. When marriage was forever, issues could be left alone because there was the understanding that the couple had a lifetime together to work them out. Because this is no longer the case, we hope that a little information can help people to spot vulnerabilities and give their marriage the best chance it has to be a satisfying lifetime experience."[7]

All stressors do not lead to conflict, but many do, particularly those that have to do with money, sex, children, and shared responsibility in the family. When these reach a high stress level, they can damage the spousal relationship if the couple lacks the skills needed to resolve conflict....

And single parents, too, suffer increased stress if they are in continual conflict with former spouses. Robert E. Emery reviewed research findings that suggest that children's behavior may be affected more by the level of "family turmoil" surrounding the divorce than the separation itself; that many of the problems evident in the children of divorced parents were present long before the divorce occurred; and most significant, *that children of divorced parents whose family members are not in conflict exhibit fewer problems than those from two-parent families in which discord does exist.* From his evidence, the author suggests that parents try to keep children out of their conflicts and do everything they can to keep their individual relationships with their children supportive ones.[8]

Osolina Ricci, family therapist and author, says that divorced parents should get away from the idea that only mothers are important. "The parent who ends up with the least amount of time with the child is just as important to the child as the parent with the most amount of time," she says. "The good divorce is not a mystery, even though there are a lot of hard feelings ... It's hard work to have a good divorce, but the amount of time the parents spend to make it a good divorce the first couple years will come back to reward them one hundred-fold three and four years down the line."[9] ...

Coping skills are discussed throughout this book so I will not develop them in depth here other than to say that the effective parents tend to collect, devise, and use a variety of coping skills rather than to depend upon the one or two most commonly used in our culture. For example, they don't automatically turn to grounding for every adolescent infraction but work out other consequences. When money gets tight, they don't automatically send a wife to work but try other methods of simplifying their life-style or share goods and services with others. Instead of automatically saying no to a child, they develop other responses. I loved the reaction of the mother whose eleven-year-old daughter wanted to use eye makeup. "You can use it as long as I can't see it," she said. It was a creative solution to a common family stressor.

Families who deal most effectively with stresses have hundreds of little solutions to share on allowances, television, sibling fighting, time pressures, and shared responsibility, and I will pass them on to you in the chapters ahead.

4. The Healthy Couple Makes Use of Support People and Systems.

"We couldn't have survived without our friends ..."; "If I didn't have my family nearby ..."; "The neighbors were there when we needed them ..."; "I couldn't get over the support I got from our church ..."

Stress-effective families and stressed families view support systems quite differently from one another. Stress-effective families see relatives, friends, groups, and community as valuable supports in dealing with stresses, while highly stressed families view them as evidence of their own inability to deal with stresses. Culturally, we came to believe that a good family was one that could handle its own problems. If it had to call upon relatives or neighbors for help in other than an emergency, it was not quite as "good" as other families.

Whatever the origin of this myth, I am appalled to find it still operating within pockets of our culture. We find, for example, cases of child abuse in which parents refuse to ask for help because they see such a request as a sign of weakness. The supports are there for them—loving family, hot lines, church mother's-day-out programs, friendly neighbors, a good community social service system which offers preventive skills—but even so these parents will risk abusing their children when stresses get too high rather than admit they need support and help.

Clearly, the most stress-effective families make the most use of support systems. When they need sudden childcare or when there's an illness or a problem, they have people to call upon, people who will call upon them as freely in return. I know a single mother, never married, who has a ten-year-old daughter. When she decided to keep her baby, her disapproving parents told her not to come to them if she needed help.

"I tried to prove to them that I could do it alone," she told me, "and as a result I nearly collapsed in stress overload. My therapist suggested a support group of other single parents and it has been my salvation. We call each other when we need support. We sit each other's children, loan dishes, furniture, even money. But most of all, we're family to one another. They are far more family to me than my own family."

Her experience is echoed in many studies of family support systems, particularly one by Nancy Colletta (1981), who found that those parents with high levels of support were more affectionate toward, closer to, and more positive with their children, while those with low levels of support were more hostile to, indifferent toward, and rejecting of their chidlren.[10]

In today's highly mobile and technological society, we're not likely to find our relatives and old friends nearby. They may be a thousand miles away and available as support in an emergency but not in an everyday stress situation.

But we find the structured support group stepping in to meet the need for close family and friend networking. In the past few years, I have worked with support groups for families of Vietnam veterans, parents of unwed teenage mothers, bereaved parents, single-parent and stepparent families, pregnant women, parents of chronically ill family members, parents of adolescents, and others. I have great respect for these groups and often encourage stressed couples to consider becoming part of a support group to give them affirmation and confidence in their parenting....

5. The Healthy Couple Is Adaptable.

Although many of these couples speak of entering marriage with set ideas of marriage and family life, they then mention—often with humor—how quickly they came to recognize and negotiate individual differences. Some spouses marry intending to change their partner to their own way of thinking.

Healthy couples adapt and borrow each other's techniques in resolving conflict and dealing with stress. One couple I interviewed spoke laughingly of their attitude toward sleeping late on Saturday morning. "When we married I was up at 6:00 A.M. to get at the housework," admitted the wife. "My husband slept until noon and I thought that was immoral. Now we both sleep until nine. We never made a conscious agreement about it—we just sort of evolved into it."

Whether or not to sleep late on Saturday is hardly a major point of stress, but the example does show how couples gradually come to respect each other's habits and needs. Adaptability is a feature found in stress-effective families.

When faced with a stress, adaptable couples are able to modify attitudes and habits to best meet it. An example of this ability may occur when a couple's employment conditions change. "When Peter lost his job, I was concerned, of course. But I knew we could scale down and get through it," reported one wife. "Our biggest problem was relatives who thought the world was going to end. We ended up reassuring them rather than the reverse."

Recently there has been intensive study on the family life cycle, particularly as it relates to stress and change. Dr. Hamilton I. McCubbin and Dr. Charles R. Figley invited top family scholars to contribute their insights and research on families and the stresses families experience as they move along the life cycle from courtship to old age. These scholars came from many different perspectives. But, according to the authors, "In spite of these differences in perspective, it is remarkable how much similarity these scholars see in how families respond to different stressors. The methods of functional coping are very similar across the different transitions and demands. These coping strategies include seeking information and understanding of the stressor event; seeking social support from relatives, friends, neighbors, others in similar situations, and professionals; being flexible about family roles; taking an optimistic view of the situation; and improving family member communication."[11]

Notes

1. Ronald M. Sabatelli, "The Marital Comparison Level Index: A Social Exchange Measure of Marital Satisfaction," unpublished paper.
2. Carol Tavris, "The Myth of the 50/50 Marriage," *Woman's Day,* March 6, 1984.
3. "Around the Network," *Family Therapy NetWorker,* March–April 1984.
4. Michael Griffin, O.C.D., "The Stresses of Intimacy," *Spiritual Life,* 1979.
5. Diane Hales, "Marriages That Get Better and Better," *McCall's,* January 1983.
6. Carin Rubinstein and Phillip Shaver, *In Search of Intimacy* (New York: Delacorte Press, 1982).
7. Philip Blumstein and Pepper Schwartz, "What Makes Today's Marriages Last?" *Family Weekly,* November 13, 1983.
8. Robert E. Emery, "Interpersonal Conflict and the Children of Discord and Divorce," *Psychological Bulletin* (92) 2.
9. Mary Meitus, "Therapist Supports Shared Parenting," *Rocky Mountain News,* February 12, 1984.
10. Hamilton I. McCubbin and Charles R. Figley, eds., *Stress and the Family: Coping with Normative Transitions,* vol. I (New York: Brunner/Mazel, 1983).
11. Ibid.

Review Questions

1. According to Curran, what's the relationship between expectations and stress?
2. What's the relationship between intimacy and risk?
3. Give an example from your own experience of a time you and a close friend created your own code.
4. According to Curran, what's the relationship between stress and conflict in a couple relationship?
5. Which kind of support system does Curran believe is most helpful for a couple, an informal system of friends, or a more formal group?

Probes

1. What are some weaknesses in Curran's research methods? To what degree do those weaknesses undermine the validity of the points she makes? How does your own experience lead you to verify or to challenge what she says?
2. Ask a married person you know to keep track over a one-week period of the number of minutes per day that person spends communicating with his or her spouse. How do your results compare with the ones Curran cites?
3. How do you view the connection between a dating relationship and a friendship? Which has to come first? Do they both need to go together?
4. Recall when you were a teenager. How do you respond to what Curran says about how parents behave with teenagers?
5. In your opinion, what is the most important/useful kind of support system for a couple?

Chapter 11

Conflict

No one is wrong, At most someone is uninformed. If I think a man is wrong, either I am unaware of something, or he is. So unless I want to play a superiority game I had best find out what he is looking at. "You're wrong" means "I don't understand you"—I'm not seeing what you're seeing. But there is nothing wrong with you, you are simply not me and that's not wrong.

HUGH PRATHER

ll of us experience conflict. We argue with our parents, disagree with our spouses, dispute the merits of television shows and political candidates with friends, and sometimes even quarrel with strangers at the bus stop. At times we lose sight of the fact that all this conflict is "normal" and "natural." So long as persons are individuals, there will be the potential for conflict each time they meet. In other words, conflict in and of itself is not evidence of a communication "failure" or "breakdown." It just shows that two or more individuals happen to be in a contact on a topic that reflects part of their individuality.

That's the first thing to learn about conflict: It isn't "wrong" or "bad"; it's just part of being a person who's in contact with other persons. The only people who don't experience conflict are hermits.

Since you can't prevent conflict, the most important thing is to learn how to *handle* or *manage* it in productive rather than destructive ways. One key to effective conflict management is determining how it happens and what you can do to help your experience be productive rather than person-destroying.

The author of the next reading has dedicated a major part of his life to helping conflicts be productive. Sam Keltner is now retired from his duties as a speech communication professor in Oregon, but he is still active as a mediator in family and labor-management disputes and a teacher of mediation and conflict management. Sam's been working in this arena for over thirty years, and this summary of part of what he's learned was written especially for *Bridges Not Walls*.

In this essay he shows how each struggle that we experience fits somewhere on a sliding scale that runs from "Mild Difference" to "Fight or War." This sliding scale is the "Struggle Spectrum" referred to in the title. The kind of struggle we experience depends on nine different factors: the processes we're engaging in, our behaviors, our relationship, our goals, our orientation to each other, our communication choices, the decision-making structure, intervention possibilities, and possible outcomes of the struggle. Sam explains each of these and gives several examples of the different stages.

This reading is valuable partly because it enables you to understand how mild differences can escalate into intense disputes and then even into violent fights. The spectrum demystifies an escalation process that each of us sometimes gets caught up in. When you understand the struggle spectrum you have the ability to stand back from what's happening and recognize what will occur if you move from one kind of behavior, communication choice, or decision-making style to another. It can also help tell you exactly what to do to cool down a struggle. Finally, this reading gives an overview of all the different kinds of struggles humans experience, so you can see how your disagreement with your friend fits into the larger context of business negotiations, political campaigns, and legal disputes.

You'll notice that Sam labels things a little differently from the way I label them. I call this chapter, "Conflict," and he uses that term for a specific stage in the spectrum. Sam prefers "Struggle" as his general term. You'll also notice that Sam's extensive experience as a mediator influences what he writes about. At the end of the article you'll see that Sam's work with the "Struggle Spectrum" is part of his larger concern with peace issues. As he says, peace "is a concrete reality that can occur only through our ability to understand and track the internal and external pathways of struggle that lead us toward violence and distruction. . . . Understanding the struggle spectrum and using it to aid in plotting the resolution of disputes and conflicts is not an abstract exercise. It is a daily process that challenges each of us to confront our own struggles and their effect on all those around us."

From Mild Disagreement to War: The Struggle Spectrum

John (Sam) Keltner

Jack and Jane were just returning home from work and as they entered the kitchen of their apartment, Jane threw her jacket over the back of one of the chairs and with a big sigh said, "I don't feel like cooking tonight, Jack. Could we go out to dinner?" Jack went into the living room, plopped down with some exhaustion into an easy chair and said with approval, "That's a good idea. You deserve a break and I'm tired too. Where shall we go?"

"Hmmmm, ... I think I'd like some seafood tonight," replied Jane as she came into the living room and sat opposite Jack. "We haven't had good sea food for a long time."

Jack closed his eyes for a minute and scratched his head. "Well, the best place I know for sea food is only four blocks away ... Captain Kidd's ... you know."

Jane brightened and started to answer then sighed, "Darn, it's Monday and they're not open on Monday. Depend on me to want something I can't get. Let's see ... maybe some oriental type. I know," she said leaning forward in her chair, "Chinese! There's that wonderful little Chinese place down on Fourth Street. And some good Chinese food would go just right tonight. Don't you agree?"

"I don't think so, Jane," Jack said with a pat on his stomach. "The last time I ate there I was miserable for two days. I'm afraid of what they put into it. But how about that Thai place over on Fifth? I've always wanted to try that out, and people say its very good, and the food is carefully prepared. It's kinda Chinese, too, I guess. Whaddya say?"

"No way, Jose!" snapped Jane. "It looks dirty and smells worse." She leaned back in her chair and with a frown said slowly, "Besides, I guess I really don't want Chinese after all."

"But all reports are that it's very good food. And what's wrong with Chinese food? You've always liked it," answered Jack with some irritation.

Jane seemed confused, tired, and was beginning to get frustrated. "Maybe we could just go to Bennies Hamburger Haven," she said. "After all, it's cheaper and we can save our money for one of your more fancy dinners over the weekend or something like that."

"For God's sake, Jane," Jack blurted as his patience seemed to give way. "Make

This selection was specially written for this book. It is printed with the permission of the author.

up your mind. First you want fish, then you want Chinese, and now you want nobody knows what."

Jane looked at him with irritation. "Well, whatever I suggest you seem to veto." And she turned away from him and picked up a newspaper.

Jack sat upright in his chair, put his hand on his head and stared at Jane. "I veto! You just vetoed the Thai place and Chinese food and that was your suggestion! You can't make up your mind and you blame it on me. Just like your mother, always avoiding the...."

Jane slammed the paper down and leaned forward in her chair her face red and angry. "My mother!" she shouted. "What's my mother got to do with this? Here we were simply discussing where to go to dinner and you make nasty remarks about my mother!" She jumped up and took a step toward Jack. "You miss no opportunity to make snide references about my mother! Damn you!"

"I did not make a nasty remark about your mother," Jack shouted back. "Anyway, the fact is you do have a number of your mother's dumb habits and...."

"You keep my mother out of this, you bully," shouted Jane. "I'm really getting tired of your constant nasty remarks about my mother and my family...."

Jack jumped out of his chair and stood close to Jane facing her with an angry look.

"And I'm getting completely disgusted with your holding your mother and your family high on a pedestal that they could never reach no matter what. You are so unrealistic about them," he countered. "If you'll let go of your obscene preoccupation with your family, I'll quit reminding you of it."

"You never have liked my family, you bastard!" screeched Jane, almost to tears. "And you keep battering me with your shit about them! I'm getting real tired of this."

"You're getting tired, well so am I getting tired of your bitchiness and always carrying a chip around on your shoulder about your God-awful family!"

Jane stared at Jack in violent anger, rushed toward him and with a wide swinging right arm slapped him on the left side of his head so hard that it knocked his glasses off. He recoiled from the blow. With one hand he grabbed his glasses and with the other hand he speared her arm and held it in a tight grip as she started to swing the other fist.

"I've had it with you!" Jane snarled. "We'll never get this settled. I'm going to a lawyer. I want a divorce!"

"If that's what you want, that's what you'll get," snapped Jack as he pushed her violently so that she fell back on the sofa. "And when I get through with you everybody in town will know what a cheat and sleazy trick you really are."

Jane jumped up, screaming, "You lousy bastard! I always knew you were a bum. I've had enough!" And with that she rushed to the kitchen, grabbed her coat and charged out the back door slamming it after her. She got into her car and drove wildly to her parents' home, some five miles across town.

Within the next few days Jack moved out of the apartment, took most of his things with him and refused to pay the back rent. Jane spent much of her time with her parents, family, and her friends discussing the details of the struggle with Jack and painting him not only as an undesirable partner but also a criminal type and woman chaser. She seemed determined to destroy any reputation that he might have had. Jack, on the other hand, went to their mutual friends and told them the story, with the result that the friends became quite cold toward Jane.

Their struggle seemed to get worse. Jane gathered up all Jack's things that he left in the apartment, put them into a box and put it in the apartment trash dumpster. When Jack came back to get these things and found them gone he wrote a violent note and left it on the kitchen table. The note threatened legal action if she didn't return his belongings.

There was no effort to come back together. Jack and Jane went to separate lawyers, and shortly thereafter their divorce case was filed. When they eventually came to court, the dispute was bitter. Each was determined to make the other person lose and to smear the other's reputation. The court granted the divorce but refused Jane any alimony, support, or legal fees. Jack was ordered to pay the rent on the apartment up to the time he left.

Jane was violently angry with the decision as were her family who gathered in her defense. Following the court decision Jane made considerable effort to find occasions to make things uncomfortable for Jack. She wrote letters to his employer complaining of his behavior, called the police to accuse him of harassing her, called all his friends she knew and represented him as really not their friend.

Jack, on the other hand was busy trying to counter the negative gossip that she created, and at the same time he told many of her friends of her unfaithfulness in the past, of her "unhealthy" preoccupation with her family, and of their generally bad marriage.

Jane's family picked up her cry of woe and conducted its own campaign. Jack found his tires slit one morning. On another occasion, the windows on his car were broken. Two of his old friends refused to talk to him. His employer told him that if he couldn't keep his personal affairs away from the job he would be fired.

Finally, in desperation, Jack resigned from his job and prepared to move out of town and seek another job. On the night before he planned to leave he arrived at his apartment around midnight to find the lights on and as he walked into the living room there stood Jane with a gun in her hand aimed directly at him ...

The story of Jane and Jack is based on an actual situation. It represents the classic escalation of mild disagreements through various stages until they reach the level of violence. I have discovered, during thirty years of studying the nature of conflict and practicing methods of managing the process, that we can track this escalation as struggle becomes increasingly violent and uncontrolled. Almost every struggle between individuals, groups, and nations can be tracked as it follows a sequence of events that seem to lead toward violence. I call this sequence the "Struggle Spectrum."

This spectrum is based on a natural process that occurs between individuals, groups, social entities, or nations as they seek to resolve differences.

Violent conflict such as fighting and even war generally grow through a step-by-step process. Unless the steps are interrupted, unresolved intrapersonal and interpersonal tension leads inevitably into larger and larger contexts of struggle. Thus, when Jane and Jack did not resolve their differences over where they were to eat, the matter began to escalate and other differences that existed began to emerge. As these other differences were unresolved, the intensity of the struggle increased and precipitating acts of violence began to occur. The "snowball" was rolling and it seemed that it could not be stopped.

It is important to understand the nature of this struggle spectrum and the conditions under which we experience escalation of disagreement to destruction. One reason is that this understanding helps us see where various methods of dispute resolution may be appropriately and successfully applied. My experience in dispute resolution as a mediator, arbitrator, advocate, and student has taught me that there are many situations where certain dispute resolution tools are not effective. By using the struggle spectrum as a guide, I can see more clearly where and why various dispute resolution systems may have value and where they may be useless. The nonprofessional will also find a knowledge of the spectrum highly valuable. Understanding the stages of the spectrum allows us to recognize them when we encounter them and to adjust our style of communication to one that is more likely to lead to a settlement. It also enables us to recognize the styles used by our counterparts and to accommodate to them as we choose. Further, it is highly valuable in determining when to request neutral third party assistance. Since mediation and arbitration are voluntary methods, the knowledge of the spectrum is vital in making the decision to seek them.

Why the Term "Struggle"?

Struggle is an act of striving against some form of resistance or opposition. Struggle involves an effort to move from or sustain the immediate position. We struggle all the time in many ways. The origins of conflict are found in the struggle between people as they seek to cope with conditions that resist their direction, goals, or desires. Struggle is the basic experience that underlies all the forms of tension humans experience from mild disagreement to violence. I use the term "conflict" to designate an *advanced form of struggle* where the threads of the relationship between people, groups, or nations take on a more polarized state and where forms of violence become characteristic.

From Peace to War in Inevitable Stages

Jane and Jack went through a process that led from calm and peaceful efforts at joint decision making to fighting and violence. In their experience we can see clearly the flow of the struggle from mild difference to disagreement to dispute, to litigation, to campaign, and finally to armed violence. Each stage involved different processes, behaviors, and forms of communication between Jane, Jack, and others. Each stage also involved different orientations between parties and different decision making possibilities. All along the way there were times when some kind of intervention may have stopped or stalled the escalation to more violent alternatives. The Struggle Spectrum chart summarizes all these features.

Some Assumptions About Struggle and Conflict

The function of the struggle spectrum is to provide a framework we can use to study struggle and the ways of managing the processes involved. Several basic assumptions underlie it.

1. *Conflict does not emerge suddenly from a peaceful context.*

   It has antecedents in the relationships between the parties and the contexts of those relationships. Jane and Jack had a relationship history that included differences and painful experiences. When they finally came to a struggle crisis, these old issues emerged to aggravate the situation.

2. *It is important for us to understand these antecedents if we are to mount effective systems of managing the process of struggle, so that it does not escalate to the destructive stages.*

   If Jane and Jack had understood the nature of struggle better, they may have been able to modify the manner in which they dealt with their unresolved issues and to prevent the ultimate tragedy.

The Struggle Spectrum: From Differences to Disputes to Litigation to War

	Stage 1 Mild Difference	Stage 2 Disagreement	Stage 3 Dispute	Stage 4 Campaign	Stage 5 Litigation	Stage 6 Fight or War
Processes	Discussion	Discussion negotiation	Argument bargaining	Persuasion pressure	Advocacy debate	Violent conflict
Behavior	Joint problem solving	Contentions over choices	Rational proof & game playing by rules	Emotional and logical strategies	Selective proofs before judges or juries	Psychological or physical violence
Relationships	Partners, friends & acquaintances	Rivals	Opponents	Competitors	Antagonists	Enemies
Goals	Includes other	Includes other	Excludes other	Excludes other	Excludes other	Eliminates other
Orientation to each other	Cooperative & amicable	Disputative conciliatory	Win-lose (a) hostile	Win-lose (b) estranged	Win-lose (c) alienated	Irreconcilable
Communication	Open-friendly	Open but strained	Limited tense	Restricted & planned antagonistic	Blocked and controlled hostile	Closed except for violence
Decision making	Mutual decisions	Joint decisions and agreements	Joint decisions in mediation third-party decisions in arbitration	Vote by constituents or third-party decisions	Third-party courtroom decisions by judge or jury	Each side seeks control by forcing other
Intervention possibilities	None needed	Mediation by neutral party	Mediation or arbitration by neutral party	Arbitration by neutral party or election-vote	Arbitration or judge or jury	Force of police or other military intervention
Possible outcomes	Integrated agreement satisfaction	Accommodated agreement both pacified	Compromise agreement or one wins	A win or draw winner pleased loser accepting	One wins winner celebrates	One prevails other or both destroyed or harmed

A. Mediation is relatively useless in stages 1, 4, 5, and 6, but may be used in 4 under special arrangement.

B. Win-lose escalates from level (a) to level (c). The longer it exists, the more intense it becomes.

C. Neutral third parties have no stake in the outcome of the struggle and include mediators, arbitrators, judges, and juries.

D. Parties lose their joint decision-making power when mediation is no longer available.

E. When issues are not resolved at one stage, the tendency is to move to the right on the continuum.

Source: From John (Sam) Keltner, *Mediation: Toward a Civilized System of Dispute Resolution*, p. 4. Annandale, Va.: SCA, 1987. Copyright 1986 by John (Sam) Keltner.

3. *Struggle is a multiple condition that affects individuals, partners, groups, states, and nations.*

   The spectrum applies to all. It is just as descriptive of what happens between nations as it is of what happens between husband and wife, neighbors, or competing businesses.

4. *The structure of our present society is such that it almost forces us to the dispute level of struggle in many contexts.*

   The "win-lose" condition is rampant. If we expect to reduce the dangers of escalating to the violent end of the struggle spectrum, we must eventually work to change the personal, social, political, national, and international structures that make disputes "normal" and that leave no room for the management of mild differences and disagreements. (See Keltner, 1987, p. 4–5, and Kohn, 1986.)

5. *The management of struggle must begin with individual behaviors and perceptions before it can be expected to occur in groups and nations.*

   The Janes and Jacks of our society must learn how to deal with their own disputes before they can help to deal with the struggles of their neighbors, their city, their state, and their nation. Peace begins within each person.

6. *We need to develop and use neutral third parties as agents in the management of struggle.*

   It is clear from the nature of the spectrum that there are levels where a mediator or an arbitrator can play a vital role in struggle management. There are other stages where these agents are relatively helpless.

7. *The relation of "internal intentional competition" (the desire of a person to be "number 1") and the "external structural competition" (the "win-lose" condition) needs to be more thoroughly studied.*

   We have evidence that structural competition can induce internal competition. Are we likewise able to predict structural competition from the presence of internal intentional competition? I believe we can predict that people who are at war within themselves will be more likely to struggle with others than people who are at peace within themselves. (See Kohn, 1986.)

The Stages of the Struggle Spectrum

The story of Jane and Jack typifies the struggle spectrum. We saw the move from calm and peaceful joint decision making to fighting and the equivalent of war. Let's look at the stages in this spectrum.

Stage 1. Mild Difference

Struggle between people appears to begin with mild differences and a relatively limited collision of interests. These differences emerge from many types of conditions.

A *change in status quo* is involved when one partner, for instance, wants to move an office desk from where it had been for some time, and the other partner would rather it be left where it is.

A *collision of time commitments* is involved when wife wants husband to pick up the children from school today in order to allow her to visit a sick friend, and he expects not to be free at that time.

Varying goals are involved when an employer wants an employee to work extra hours, and the employee has already made plans for that time.

Changes in practice are involved when one group wants some minor changes in a contract for services between them and the other group would prefer to keep the contract as it is.

Different preferences are involved when a couple is trying to decide on where to go to dinner and one prefers Chinese food while the other prefers seafood. These are mild differences and do not represent, at this point, serious difficulties. I do not identify them as "conflicts" since the differences are not expressed in destructive interactions.

Usually the *behavior* exhibited at this level is a joint problem solving activity where the parties, in a friendly and collaborative manner, explore the problem and reach decisions together. Their *goals* are mutually inclusive, that is, they include each other. In general, their *orientation* to each other is cooperative and friendly. Their *communication* is open and reasonably clear and unobstructed. That is, there are no blocks or interferences that prevent them from saying what they think and feel to each other, and each respects the other's different point of view. The *decision making* is predominantly by mutual agreement and is consensus-based, that is, all parties agree.

At this stage there are no reasons for intervention by other parties. In fact, well-meaning meddling by others at this stage could create tension where tension did not exist before.

The *outcomes* of this stage can be integrated agreement and satisfaction by both parties. For example, Jack and Jane could have decided to go to another Chinese restaurant since they had fish the night before. Or, union representatives and management, after some discussion, could agree to change the shift schedules to improve efficiency and provide workers with better shift preferences.

At this mild difference level hidden motives are relatively insignificant in relation to the issue at hand, or are quite openly recognized but not considered relevant to the points of discussion. For example, Jane's and Jack's particular appetites were important to the selection of the place to eat, but they did not stand in the way of the decision. Some shift workers would be temporarily inconvenienced by the change in shift schedules, but the larger effect was perceived to benefit everyone. There are many examples of this kind of mild disagreement and resolution in our daily lives.

This stage is usually accompanied by good will and good faith between the parties. Neighbors deal with the problems by willingly joining together and discussing the matters openly and forthrightly. Friends and partners openly discuss problems that arise between them.

When satisfactory outcomes are not forthcoming and there is no resolution, the struggle may shift to the next level.

Stage 2. Disagreement

When mild differences are not resolved, they may be laid aside and forgotten, stored in "memory" for future reference, avoided, or they may escalate into disagreements. When they escalate, the usual development is toward a more apparent level of disagreement. Here people begin to show signs of being *polarized*. The mild differences become more explicit. The intensity of the interaction increases. The agreement level diminishes, and each party begins to search for ways to support, defend, and justify the positions taken and to gain concessions from the other. Notice how Jane and Jack began to find fault with each other's suggestions and to seek concessions from each other.

The initial processes at this stage are *joint deliberation* and *problem solving* between the parties, but as the stage progresses and resolution of the differences does not occur, the parties begin *negotiating* with each other. Negotiation is a complex process that involves several possible functions: the parties may present their positions in order to gain concessions, or suggest alternative ideas in order to accommodate to the other without losing their own goal, or attempt to find ways of cooperating or compromising in order to find some satisfactory settlement outcome. (See Rule 1962, pp. 5–6; Schatzki, 1981, p. 9; Nierenberg, 1968, p. 2; Pruit, 1981, p. 1; Rangarajan, 1985, pp. 4–7; and Lewicki and Litterer, 1985.)

If these efforts do not bring a resolution, both parties begin to *contend* over their choice of position and begin to formulate and present persuasive statements in support of their choices. The *polarization* between them becomes increasingly apparent to them and to outside observers. The contentions are usually stated to each other. Soon they begin to see themselves as *rivals* or opposing advocates.

When Jane and Jack could not agree on where to go to dinner, each began to support a favored position with some contentions and persuasive efforts. They each began to see that they must change the other's position in order to reach an agreement.

When management's proposal to change the shift hours runs counter to the personal schedules of a number of workers, each side will begin to bring forward their justifications for their position while at the same time the spokespersons may begin to realize that changes in both sides may have to occur.

The parties' *goals* at this stage are still mutually inclusive; that is, both parties seek a solution that provides satisfaction for themselves as well as their rivals. Their *orientation to each other* is ambivalent. On the one hand, the parties are still conciliatory. On the other hand, each side begins to dispute the other's position and to feel some frustration at the other side for not accepting their proposals.

Decision making at this stage can still be accomplished through joint decisions and agreements. By sharing their differences and making special efforts to accommodate each other's goals, the parties can reach decisions together and build on the possibility of consensus.

Communication at this stage is less open than it was in the preceding stage. There begin to appear guarded statements, and more conditional comments appear in the talk. Such statements as, "If you can't accept this then, . . ." begin to appear. The openness is modified by strains in the communication exhibited by fewer complimentary phrases to each other, occasional accusatory or derogative remarks, and sometimes outright expressions of anger or frustration.

The *outcome* of this stage may be an agreement that accommodates both parties. Here compromise plays an important role. Jane and Jack seemed unable to find a compromise.

Because of the increasing difficulty in communicating, this stage often results in a stalemate where the parties are unable to find a solution to their differences. At this point the situation may escalate to the dispute level or a neutral third party may be invited in to function as a *mediator*. (See Keltner, 1987.) The mediator can serve effectively at this stage, because the polarization has not become excessively intense and there is still a mutual desire to find a solution that can satisfy both parties. At the point where Jane and Jack were beginning to get angry and frustrated with each other, they could have used a neutral third person as a mediator to help them. The mediator could facilitate Jane and Jack's efforts to communicate with each other, to look at alternatives, to find accommodation for each other, and to reach a solution that is satisfactory to them.

Stage 3. Dispute

When we fail to resolve a disagreement, the matter tends to escalate to more intense interaction between the parties. Many disputes break open first at this stage, because the previous stages have been relatively hidden or the struggle has been avoided or ignored as the issues developed.

When we become involved in the dispute stage, arguments become more heated, and the polarization becomes quite powerful and controlling. Each person in the dispute views the one on the other side in an increasingly negative way. Each sees him or herself as more on the "right" side and the other as on the "wrong" side.

At this point the parties may move into two different kinds of interaction: formal rule-controlled, structured activities and/or intense attack and defense behaviors.

In the case of structured competitive situations, special activities begin at this stage. In the labor-management field when a grievance has remained unresolved after having been discussed at least on two levels of the organization, the dispute becomes more intense. The polarization of the parties around their point of view becomes firmer, the groups and the principals involved become more alienated, and the system seems increasingly unable to bring the matter to a resolution through joint deliberation.

Here is where Jane and Jack found themselves shouting at each other, accusing each other of spiteful intents and behaviors and of improper attempts to manipulate each other. Often at this stage other issues will be introduced into the dispute. Frequently these issues have nothing to do with the matter over which the disagreement began. Emotions become aroused and the atmosphere is charged with feelings. Old unresolved issues get dragged into the dispute and become points of contention. Thus, in the heat of the dispute when Jane accused Jack of maligning her mother, the direction suddenly changed and the intensity of the dispute escalated rapidly.

The characteristic processes at this stage of struggle are intense arguments and *bargaining*.[1] Bargaining involves argument, persuasion, threats, proposals, counter proposals, "horse trading," all in the context of mutually exclusive goals. The interplay of power and tactics is an essential characteristic of this bargaining (Bacharach and Lawler, 1981, p. 40). The attempts to reach resolution are usually suffused with a "quid pro quo" kind of interaction. Each party may be willing to give up or give

---

[1] I separate negotiation and bargaining in this spectrum for the purpose of showing degrees of intensity and also because there are some important differences between them. This is much like what Fisher and Ury have done when they separate "soft" and "hard" bargaining. What they would call "soft" bargaining I prefer to identify as negotiation and what they call "hard" bargaining I prefer to identiy as bargaining (Fisher and Ury, 1981, p. 9). Negotiation, as I perceive it in this spectrum, involves much more joint interest and mutual goal sharing than does bargaining.

in on a point, but only if the other party does too. What may have been more calm and thoughtful negotiations can also escalate into more acrid accusation and defense.

In many situations such as the labor-management context, the parties become involved in game-playing by a set of rules established by their prior agreement or contractual relationship. Each side takes its turn to present its arguments and rebuttals. There is an attempt to cloak the dispute in logical terms, to find evidence to support the arguments, to bring witnesses to testify in favor or against the participants. In less formal dispute situations there may be attempts to control the dispute by outsiders insisting that the parties follow some rules of behavior in their attacks on each other. Two neighbors involved in a heated dispute over where their mutual property line exists are restrained from certain types of behavior by civil and criminal law.

Many sporting events have the character of disputes in that they are run by a set of rules which have been agreed to by the parties to the game. These rules are administered by persons outside the dispute and there are penalties for violation of the rules. There are also clearly identified winners and losers in these events. These are cases of *structured competition* and dispute.

Perhaps the most significant difference between the dispute stage and those which precede it are the *goal and orientation* conditions. In the dispute stage the matter has now become a *win-lose* situation (Keltner, 1987, p. 4–5). Each party is convinced that it must overcome the other and gain its own point of view or objective. The goals are perceived to have become mutually exclusive and the result is a highly competitive situation (Kohn, 1986, pp. 3–9); that is, what one gets the other cannot have. While the goals may in fact still be mutually inclusive, the parties to the dispute have, in their intensity and polarization, come to *perceive* them as being exclusive, and that perception controls their behaviors toward each other. If Jane and Jack each believes that they must win and defeat the other, they will act on that perception and no agreement can be reached. The *orientation* to each other therefore becomes a hostile one. The friendliness of the prior stages seems to melt away and in its place appears an animosity and a fervent hostility that is highly emotional.

Communication between the parties becomes tense and limited. Each party restricts the information that it sends to the other. Each party is actually unable to perceive or hear what the other side may be saying. Emotional barriers to understanding are very strong. There is a high incidence of accusatory messages. The husband accuses the wife of destructive "hidden" motives and cheating; the union accuses the management of wrongful acts toward the workers; one neighbor accuses the other of being a "land hungry liar"; the developer accuses the county commissioners of petty politics and restraint of trade; one nation accuses the other of violating treaties or agreements.

The *outcomes* of this stage are, of course, related to the perception of "who wins?" Because of the win-lose orientation the common conception is that the winner takes the rewards and the game (dispute) is over. In many situations, however, the loser retreats for a while to plan future attacks in order to win back what was lost and the dispute is really not resolved. Japan was the military loser of World War II, but in recent years we have seen a resurgence of economic power in Japan that now makes it one of the most powerful economic forces in the world.

In this stage it is still possible for the parties to find ways to work toward joint decision making and compromise. The most significant and useful way is through the intervention of a neutral mediator who facilitates the parties in their attempts to find resolution. The mediator does not make decisions or direct the decision making toward one solution or another. The mediator's function is facilitative, and in the process the parties are often led to de-escalate the dispute to the prior stages, so that more open communication can take place and more open consideration of alternatives can occur. The mediator actually helps the parties to overcome the barriers to joint decision making and facilitates them in making their own decisions.[2]

Mediation is impossible, however, if the parties do not have a desire to work out a solution to the dispute. If the parties are simply frozen into a win-lose attitude it is very difficult for a mediator to "defuse" the situation so that other conditions can be considered. Once Jane and Jack are in a position where each feels that winning is the only acceptable alternative, there is not much place for mediation.

But when skilled intervention takes place, it may be possible to modify the win-lose condition so that compromises can be designed that will allow for resolution of the dispute. Compromises are important and valuable when they allow for settlements that extend the values of an agreement to both sides of a dispute. They do, however, require a modification of the win-lose orientation.

Stage 4. Campaign

When the parties fail to find resolution of their differences at Stage 3, the dispute escalates to campaign or litigation. While I have identified these stages in a continuum relationship to each other, they are, in reality, interchangeable and may often be taking place at the same time. Stage 4, Campaign, may not be encountered until after Litigation (Stage 5) has taken place, or it may not take place at all. Jane and Jack mounted campaigns against each other before, during, and after the litigation proceedings in the court.

When campaign and/or litigation are not perceived as having potential for resolution, failure to settle a dispute at Stage 3 may be followed by fight or war. Jane, for example, might have despaired of going through a divorce and the subsequent campaigns and just stabbed or shot Jack instead of going to a lawyer. That tragedy has occurred many times.

If no resolution appears in previous stages, the disputants may then begin to expand the struggle to involve more and more participants. Here the dispute "goes public." The goal is to get supporters, to gather power by increasing the number of people who will "join up" with the parties involved. The efforts often move toward the use of the media and group meetings or rallies where others can be drawn into the dispute. Thus the husband and wife in a family dispute will seek to gain the support of their neighbors, their relatives, and of others who might be able to bring some pressure to bear.

Political struggles move quickly to this stage as the competitors campaign for votes. The disputants in a land-use dispute will organize a public meeting where their point of view can be presented. The union and/or the employer will prepare

[2]Marriage counselors, friends, church pastors, and others with substantial training in mediation can often help people deal with their struggles. However, they must be specifically trained in mediation, for these processes are different from the traditional functions performed by these people. Warning! Be sure to check carefully the *mediation* credentials of anyone you seek to mediate a struggle in which you are involved (see Keltner, 1987).

press releases that support their positions. Nations will seek to build coalitions by involving other nations in the support of their goals. The thrust of the campaign stage is not directed specifically at the opponent or competitor but at people surrounding the situation who can ultimately influence the behavior of the opponent. The function is to mold constituencies that will provide power to the advocate.

Persuasion becomes the critical tool in the campaign stage. Although persuasion may also be used in the disagreement and dispute stage, the primary emphasis there is usually on forms of "logical" support. In this stage all of the persuasive tools are brought to bear to bring about changes in and to build constituencies. Emotional and logical strategies are employed by the parties in their process of "going public" with the dispute. The various media are drawn into the process with newspaper and radio-TV releases, pamphlets and books, mass meetings, small group sessions, brochures, signs, etc. Skilled speakers are enlisted in the campaign. House-to-house solicitation is often used. In some instances theater is even mobilized as plays are written and produced dramatizing the theme and presenting one side's case. "Uncle Tom's Cabin," for example, played a very important role in the American Civil War.

By this time the goals are highly exclusive. Signs of compromise or joint agreement are hardly admissable to the campaign positions. The "win-lose" context is paramount. Each side seeks to exclude the other and the other's position in any resolution.

Communication between the parties themselves becomes almost totally blocked. The walls separating the adversaries become so thick and so high that it is almost impossible for them to send or receive information directly. Jane and Jack refused to talk to each other and the only communication between them was the violent note that Jack wrote and the secondhand information that was transmitted through their lawyers. Roommates who have allowed a dispute to reach this stage will refuse to talk to each other, will try to avoid being together on any occasion, and will send what messages are necessary through others who are not directly involved in the struggle.

In other contexts adversaries and/or their representatives may appear together on a platform or in a meeting, but each speaks primarily to the audience rather than to the other. They listen to each other only to the degree that they can find errors in what their opponent may be saying. It is in this context that attempts to destroy the credibility of the opponent often occur. Notice the efforts during political campaigns to raise questions about the honesty and integrity of the candidate.

The *decision-making* processes at this stage reach beyond that of the parties themselves. In fact, the adversaries have functionally abandoned the responsibility for resolving the dispute themselves. Having "gone public" the decision may depend on the pressure of others who have been drawn into the campaign. Here the actions of constituents become the decision-making standard. The power of numbers becomes important.

There are several *outcomes* of the campaign stage. A winner can emerge. There can be an impasse from a tie vote. One side may so sway the audience that it will prevail. The audience can become involved in the struggle and many side-struggles can emerge with their roots in the initial one. Two fans at a football game, each supporting the other side, got into a fist fight over the outcome of the game even though they were not a part of the struggle on the field. Two neighbors, after being "campaigned" by a couple in dispute, found themselves struggling with each other. Two friends who supported different candidates for president of the fraternity found themselves in dispute over other fraternity matters.

There are situations in which, no matter what the outcome of the campaign, its results are not accepted by the parties to the dispute. At this point there may be a de-escalation of the struggle to the point where more negotiation and bargaining can take place. The parties may become so impassioned by their frustrations that they will engage in physical fighting or war. Or, the parties may go to litigation either by choice of one or the other, or by law.

Stage 5. Litigation

Taking legal action becomes an alternative stage in dispute resolution when other means fail. There are two levels of litigation: the formal judicial, as in the court, and the quasi judicial, as in the arbitration process. The principal process in litigation is the use of *advocacy, formal argument, debate, and persuasion.* In the court this means that legal rules of evidence must be followed, formal briefs filed, and a prescribed order of events takes place. Arbitration is somewhat less formal.

In court, the representatives of the parties present selected proofs before the judge, jury, or arbitrator. Witnesses are brought forth to testify in favor of or against each of the principals in the dispute. The *orientation* of the principals is antagonistic and each seeks to prevail over the other. The win-lose condition is probably at its next most intense level, and the parties are highly alienated toward each other.

Arbitration by a neutral third party may be an alternative to formal court litigation. Arbitration is a quasi-judicial process whereby the parties agree to abide by the decision of a third person whom they mutually choose. Sometimes even reaching that level of agreement is difficult when a situation has escalated to the campaign or litigation stage or beyond. There can be a decision by an arbitrator that allows neither side to actually prevail or "win," yet both parties have agreed to accept the decision. An arbitrator can also rule so as to provide a winner and loser.

Arbitration can be considered a milder form of litigation particularly when lawyers are brought into the dispute to represent the parties. One of the significant differences between court litigation and arbitration is that court litigation most typically involves alleged violations of the law or matters of equity whereas arbitration can involve almost any kind of dispute.

When the parties are unable to agree on arbitration or any other means of settling the dispute short of violence, either one can move the dispute to the court. At this point the parties give up any freedom they may have in working out the solution to the struggle themselves. By the act of referral to a court, Jane and Jack put in someone else's hands the resolution of their dispute.

Communication between the parties themselves is blocked and controlled by the conditions of the litigation. Usually any communication between the parties is conducted through the services of the "hired guns." The parties themselves, at this stage, rarely communicate with each other directly. If they do, it is usually hostile and highly inflammatory.

The *decision making* in the court litigation is done by the judge or jury, and the parties to the dispute have no function in the making of that decision. It is entirely out of their hands.

The *outcome* of the litigation stage comes when one of the parties wins and the other loses. Sometimes a wide jurisdiction is allowed by the court, permitting it to divide up the available resources, as in a divorce proceeding. In that case there could be a division of the resources that would not represent a clear win by one or the other of the disputants. This was not the result in the case of Jane and Jack.

When the court or arbitration decision does not satisfy the parties to the dispute, the alternatives become very limited. They must abide by the decision handed down to them or violate the law and abandon the effort, de-escalate, or become engaged in the ultimate and destructive level of struggle through fighting or war.

Stage 6. Fight and/or War

The critical characteristic of this stage is the presence of *violence* and destructive behavior. (It is this kind of behavior that I usually call conflict.) Fights involve forms of violence toward each other as when two neighbors try to "punch each other out," a union strikes a company, one country invokes sanctions against another, or when Jane slugs Jack, and certainly when she faces him with a pistol. War is a more extreme level of violent fighting where the parties to the struggle *take up weapons* to extend their power to hurt and destroy. Jane slugged Jack and that was fighting. But when she pulled the gun on him she was at war. War is a kind of fighting that aims to destroy people, resources, facilities, and relationships. War has always been the extreme effort to resolve disputes by eliminating a party to the dispute.

All the prior stages in the struggle spectrum have alternatives that do not involve violence and destruction. But when parties reach this level of a dispute the only alternative short of the outcomes of the battles is to de-escalate into other levels of the struggle spectrum. When we reach this level we have come to the point from which there is not much retreat. Rational processes no longer function in the relations between the parties except as tools of destruction. *Polarization* is so great that changes in position are extremely difficult.

It is important to recognize that all fighting and war need not be purely physical in nature. Psychological and economic violence can be equally destructive. Psychological warfare is very powerful whether between persons or nations. Economic violence is similar. High tariffs on manufactured products from another country can destroy the production enterprises of that country and can result in actual physical deprivation and death through the loss of jobs and economic means of survival.

In fighting and war the parties to the dispute view each other as enemies, and their *goal* is to eliminate each other or to reduce the other's capacities to respond. The goals of the parties are irreconcilable. This irreconcilability brings on the violent action. In spite of the often-cited instances of where a single mistake or error triggered a war, the essential context that makes that war possible is the existence of perceived mutually irreconcilable goals.

There is *communication* in warfare. The throwing of a punch, the firing of a shell, the dropping of a bomb, all are messages about a party's intent and desire. When an enraged wife slaps her husband or pulls a gun and shoots him, she has sent a clear message. In warfare there is a difference between dropping an atom bomb on a country and setting up a blockade of its commerce.

The only *interventions* that are available in fighting or war are those of physical, psychological, or economic force. When neighbors become embroiled in acts of physical destruction of each other or each other's property, the basic intervention is from the police or others who use physical force to subdue the combatants. Sometimes the others in the neighborhood will boycott the fighters or use psychological pressures to force them to abandon their destructive behavior. These interventions, however, rarely actually resolve the struggle between the parties and may initiate other struggles.

The *outcomes* of fights and war are destruction of one or both of the disputants: one of the parties prevails and subsequently dominates or destroys the other, and both of the parties are usually seriously harmed. Both Jane and Jack suffered from the war between them. Jack was wounded and permanently handicapped; Jane was sent to prison for life. No war between nations occurs without irreparable harm to both.

Conclusion

Struggle can be productive and useful when it is managed and contained. To manage and contain it we must understand it and its potential for good and destruction. The "Struggle Spectrum" is meant to help develop this understanding.

The threat of the destruction of the human race was never more prevalent than it is now. Struggle within and between people and nations is escalating daily in every aspect of our lives. Temporary exhaustion may stop violence for a time, but it will return until we learn more about managing the whole process of struggle.

We need to become more aware of the opportunities for managing struggle that our communication skills can provide. Our interpersonal communication serves as one of our most significant systems for coping with struggle. The more we understand and develop our communication skills and understand their function within the struggle spectrum, the more we can function to manage a peaceful relationship around us.

Peace is not an abstraction that can be dealt with at a distance. It is a concrete reality that can occur only through our ability to understand and track the internal and external pathways of struggle that lead us toward violence and destruction. It can occur only when we follow up this understanding with the application of methods of resolution that allow us to solve our problems and resolve our differences without destroying each other. Understanding the struggle spectrum and using it to aid in plotting the resolution of disputes and conflicts is not an abstract exercise. It is a daily process that challenges all of us to confront our own struggles and their effects on all those around us.

References

Bacharach, Samuel B., and E. J. Lawler. *Bargaining: Power, Tactics, and Outcomes.* San Francisco: Jossey-Bass, 1981.

Greenhalgh, Leonard. "The Case Against Winning in Negotiations." *Negotiation Journal,* Vol. 3, No. 2, April 1987, p. 167 ff.

Fisher, Robert, and William Ury. *Getting to Yes: Negotiating Agreement Without Giving In.* Boston: Houghton Mifflin, 1981.

Keltner, J. W. (Sam). *Mediation: Toward a Civilized System of Dispute Resolution.* Annandale, Va.: Speech Communication Association and ERIC, 1987.

————. *Arbitration in Labor-Management Disputes: Preparation and Presentation. A Guide for Advocates.* Corvallis, Oregon: Consulting Associates, 1988.

Kohn, Alfie. *No Contest: The Case Against Competition: Why We Lose in Our Race to Win.* Boston: Houghton Mifflin, 1986.

Lewicki, Roy J., and J. A. Litterer. *Negotiation.* Homewood, Ill.: Richard D. Irwin, 1985.

Moore, Christopher W. *The Mediation Process: Practical Strategies for Resolving Conflict.* San Francisco: Jossey-Bass, 1986.

Nierenberg, Gerard I. *Fundamentals of Negotiating.* New York: Hawthorne Books, 1973.

Pruit, Dean G. *Negotiation Behavior.* New York: Academic Press, 1981.

Rangarajan, L. N. *The Limitation of Conflict: A Theory of Bargaining and Negotiation.* New York: St. Martins Press, 1985.

Rule, Gordon Wade. *The Art of Negotiation.* Gordon Wade Rule, 1962.

Schatski, Michael. *Negotiation: The Art of Getting What You Want.* New York: New American Library, 1981.

Sherif, Musafer. *In Common Predicament.* Boston: Houghton Mifflin, 1966.

Yarbrough, Elaine. "Intrapersonal Conflict," in A. Goldman (ed.), *Public Communication: Perception, Criticism, Performance,* pp. 361–378. Malabar, Fla.: E. Krieger, 1983.

Zimbardo, Philip G., Craig Haney, W. Curtis Banks, and David Jafre. "The Psychology of Imprisonment: Privation, Power, and Pathology," in David Rosenham and Perry London (eds.), *Theory and Research in Abnormal Psychology,* 2d ed. New York: Holt, Rinehart and Winston, 1975.

Review Questions

1. True or False: The Struggle Spectrum does not only apply to situations like that between Jack and Jane; it can be used to track almost every kind and level of struggle.
2. Trace the changes in "Relationships" (row 3 on the Struggle Spectrum) in the dispute between Jack and Jane. Do the same with "Communication" (row 6).
3. Does Keltner say that every struggle will progress through the Spectrum unless it's resolved or that some struggles naturally fade out at stage 3, 4, or 5? Explain.
4. Keltner discusses seven assumptions about struggle and conflict. What does assumption 4 say about the "win-lose" orientation of much of modern society?
5. Explain the difference between "internal intentional competition" and "external structural competition."
6. What does it mean for people to become "polarized"?
7. At which stages of the Struggle Spectrum can the services of a formal or informal *mediator* be most helpful?
8. Explain what Keltner means when he says that "the most significant difference between the dispute stage and those which precede it are the *goal and orientation* conditions."
9. It's obvious how Stage 4, Campaign, happens in national, state, or even local politics. But what's an example of the Campaign stage in a struggle between roommates or friends?
10. What's the difference between mediation and arbitration?
11. Give examples of *psychological* and *economic violence* as they can occur in a dispute between family members.

Probes

1. One benefit of Keltner's essay is that he reminds us that we don't always have to try to handle struggles alone. Dispute resolution tools and procedures can also be used. What are some examples of dispute resolution processes that you might be able to use to help with struggles you experience?
2. Why is it important to recognize that, as assumption 1 states, "Conflict does not emerge suddenly from a peaceful context"?

3. Do you agree or disagree with Keltner's claim that "The structure of our present society is such that it almost forces us to the dispute level of struggle in many contexts"? Explain.

4. Give an example from your own experience of the movement from "Mild Difference" to "Disagreement."

5. Keltner notes that one feature of the movement to Stage 3 is that "Old unresolved issues get dragged into the dispute and become points of contention." Give an example from your own experience where this happened.

6. Our seemingly natural inclination to adopt a win-lose orientation seems to be at the root of many of our problems. Give an example of a struggle you experienced or witnessed where the parties were actually able to move beyond win-lose. What do you notice about this struggle?

7. At what point in the Spectrum do the parties give up control over their dispute? What happens then?

8. How do you respond to Keltner's final point that peace begins with the individual?

I n the next selection, Jack Gibb shares some insights about how conflict happens and what you can do to promote a supportive rather than a defensive climate for communication.

As Gibb points out, when you anticipate or perceive that you are threatened by a person or a situation, you will usually react defensively and so will the other persons involved. When any combination of the six "defensiveness-producing" elements are present, a spiral usually begins, a spiral that starts with a little discomfort and often escalates into all-out conflict.

But, Gibb notes, you can also start a spiral in the other direction. The more supportive you can be, the less other people are likely to read into the situation distorted reactions created by their own defensiveness. So when you can manifest any combination of the six alternative attitudes and skills, you can help reduce the defensiveness that's present. You don't have to "give up" or "give in." You just have to stop trying so hard to demean, control, and impose your hard-and-fast superiority on the others.

Most of the people I work with find this article very useful. They discover that they can apply Gibb's analysis of the six characteristics of defensive and supportive communication climates to their own experience. They also find that Gibb is right when he says that most people are much more aware of being manipulated or deceived than the manipulators or deceivers think and that such awareness creates defensiveness. They are usually able to perceive quite accurately another's communication strategy or "gimmicks." When they learn that sometimes it's their own transparently manipulative behavior that creates defensiveness in others, they get one step closer to communicating interpersonally.

Defensive Communication

Jack R. Gibb

One way to understand communication is to view it as a people process rather than as a language process. If one is to make fundamental improvement in communication, he must make changes in interpersonal relationships. One possible type of alteration—and the one with which this paper is concerned—is that of reducing the degree of defensiveness.

Definition and Significance

Defensive behavior is defined as that behavior which occurs when an individual perceives threat or anticipates threat in the group. The person who behaves defensively, even though he also gives some attention to the common task, devotes an appreciable portion of his energy to defending himself. Besides talking about the topic, he thinks about how he appears to others, how he may be seen more favorably, how he may win, dominate, impress, or escape punishment, and/or how he may avoid or mitigate a perceived or an anticipated attack.

Such inner feelings and outward acts tend to create similarly defensive postures in others; and, if unchecked, the ensuing circular response becomes increasingly destructive. Defensive behavior, in short, engenders defensive listening, and this in turn produces postural, facial, and verbal cues which raise the defense level of the original communicator.

Defense arousal prevents the listener from concentrating upon the message. Not only do defensive communicators send off multiple value, motive, and affect cues, but also defensive recipients distort what they receive. As a person becomes more and more defensive, he becomes less and less able to perceive accurately the motives, the values, and the emotions of the sender. The writer's analyses of tape recorded discussions revealed that increases in defensive behavior were correlated positively with losses in efficiency in communication.[1] Specifically, distortions became greater when defensive states existed in the groups.

The converse, moreover, also is true. The more "supportive" or defense reductive the climate the less the receiver reads into the communication distorted loadings which arise from projections of his own anxieties, motives, and concerns. As defenses are reduced, the receivers become better able to concentrate upon the structure, the content, and the cognitive meanings of the message.

Categories of Defensive and Supportive Communication

In working over an eight-year period with recordings of discussions occurring in varied settings, the writer developed the six pairs of defensive and sup-

From Jack R. Gibb, "Defensive Communication," *Journal of Communication* 11, no. 3 (September 1961): 141–148. Reprinted by permission of the *Journal of Communication* and the author.

TABLE 1
Categories of Behavior Characteristic of
Supportive and Defensive Climates in
Small Groups

Defensive Climates	*Supportive Climates*
1. Evaluation	1. Description
2. Control	2. Problem orientation
3. Strategy	3. Spontaneity
4. Neutrality	4. Empathy
5. Superiority	5. Equality
6. Certainty	6. Provisionalism

portive categories presented in Table 1. Behavior which a listener perceives as possessing any of the characteristics listed in the left-hand column arouses defensiveness, whereas that which he interprets as having any of the qualities designated as supportive reduces defensive feelings. The degree to which these reactions occur depends upon the personal level of defensiveness and upon the general climate in the group at the time.[2]

Evaluation and Description

Speech or other behavior which appears evaluative increases defensiveness. If by expression, manner of speech, tone of voice, or verbal content the sender seems to be evaluating or judging the listener, then the receiver goes on guard. Of course, other factors may inhibit the reaction. If the listener thought that the speaker regarded him as an equal and was being open and spontaneous, for example, the evaluativeness in a message would be neutralized and perhaps not even perceived. This same principle applies equally to the other five categories of potentially defense-producing climates. The six sets are interactive.

Because our attitudes toward other persons are frequently, and often necessarily, evaluative, expressions which the defensive person will regard as nonjudgmental are hard to frame. Even the simplest question usually conveys the answer that the sender wishes or implies the response that would fit into his value system. A mother, for example, immediately following an earth tremor that shook the house, sought for her small son with the question: "Bobby, where are you?" The timid and plaintive "Mommy, I didn't do it" indicated how Bobby's chronic mild defensiveness predisposed him to react with a projection of his own guilt and in the context of his chronic assumption that questions are full of accusation.

Anyone who has attempted to train professionals to use information-seeking speech with neutral affect appreciates how difficult it is to teach a person to say even the simple "who did that?" without being seen as accusing. Speech is so frequently judgmental that there is a reality base for the defensive interpretations which are so common.

When insecure, group members are particularly likely to place blame, to see others as fitting into categories of good or bad, to make moral judgments of their colleagues, and to question the value, motive, and affect loadings of the speech which they hear. Since value loadings imply a judgment of others, a belief that the standards of the speaker differ from his own causes the listener to become defensive.

Descriptive speech, in contrast to that which is evaluative, tends to arouse a minimum of uneasiness. Speech acts which the listener perceives as genuine requests for information or as material with neutral loadings is descriptive. Specifically, presentations of feelings, events, perceptions, or processes which do not ask or imply that the receiver change behavior or attitude are minimally defense producing. The difficulty in avoiding overtone is illustrated by the problems of news reporters in writing stories about unions, communists, Blacks, and religious activities without tipping off the "party" line of the newspaper. One can often tell from the opening words in a news article which side the newspaper's editorial policy favors.

Control and Problem Orientation

Speech which is used to control the listener evokes resistance. In most of our social intercourse someone is trying to do something to someone else—to change an attitude, to influence behavior, or to restrict the field of activity. The degree to which attempts to control produce defensiveness depends upon the openness of the effort, for a suspicion that hidden motives exist heightens resistance. For this reason attempts of nondirective therapists and progressive educators to refrain from imposing a set of values, a point of view, or a problem solution upon the receivers meet with many barriers. Since the norm is control, noncontrollers must earn the perceptions that their efforts have no hidden motives. A bombardment of persuasive "messages" in the fields of politics, education, special causes, advertising, religion, medicine, industrial relations, and guidance has bred cynical and paranoidal responses in listeners.

Implicit in all attempts to alter another person is the assumption by the change agent that the person to be altered is inadequate. That the speaker secretly views the listener as ignorant, unable to make his own decisions, uninformed, immature, unwise, or possessed of wrong or inadequate attitudes is a subconscious perception which gives the latter a valid base for defensive reactions.

Methods of control are many and varied. Legalistic insistence on detail, restrictive regulations and policies, conformity norms, and all laws are among the methods. Gestures, facial expressions, other forms of nonverbal communication, and even such simple acts as holding a door open in a particular manner are means of imposing one's will upon another and hence are potential sources of resistance.

Problem orientation, on the other hand, is the antithesis of persuasion. When the sender communicates a desire to collaborate in defining a mutual problem and in seeking its solution, he tends to create the same problem orientation in the listener; and, of greater importance, he implies that he has no predetermined solution, attitude, or method to impose. Such behavior is permissive in that it allows the receiver to set his own goals, make his own decisions, and evaluate his own progress—or to share with the sender in doing so. The exact methods of attaining permissiveness are not known, but they must involve a constellation of cues and they certainly go beyond mere verbal assurances that the communicator has no hidden desires to exercise control.

Strategy and Spontaneity

When the sender is perceived as engaged in a stratagem involving ambiguous and multiple motivations, the receiver becomes defensive. No one wishes to be a guinea pig, a role player, or an impressed actor, and no one likes to be the victim of some hidden motivation. That which is concealed, also, may appear larger than it really is with the degree of defensiveness of the listener determining the perceived size of the suppressed element. The intense reaction of the reading audience to the material in *Hidden Persuaders* indicates the prevalence of defensive reactions to multiple motivations behind strategy. Group members who are seen as "taking a role," as feigning emotion, as toying with their colleagues, as withholding information, or as having special sources of data are especially resented. One participant once complained that another was "using a listening technique" on him!

A large part of the adverse reaction to much of the so-called human relations training is a feeling against what are perceived as gimmicks and tricks to fool or to "involve" people, to make a person think he is making his own decision, or to make the listener feel that the sender is genuinely interested in him as a person. Particularly violent reactions occur when it appears that someone is trying to make a stratagem appear spontaneous. One person has reported a boss who incurred resentment by habitually using the gimmick of "spontaneously" looking at his watch and saying, "My gosh, look at the time—I must run to an appointment." The belief was that the boss would create less irritation by honestly asking to be excused.

Similarly, the deliberate assumption of guilelessness and natural simplicity is especially resented. Monitoring the tapes of feedback and evaluation sessions in training groups indicates the surprising extent to which members perceive the strategies of their colleagues. This perceptual clarity may be quite shocking to the strategist, who usually feels that he had cleverly hidden the motivational aura around the "gimmick."

This aversion to deceit may account for one's resistance to politicians who are suspected of behind-the-scenes planning to get his vote, to psychologists whose listening apparently is motivated by more than the manifest or content-level interest in his behavior, or to the sophisticated, smooth, or clever person whose "oneupmanship" is marked with guile. In training groups the role-flexible person frequently is resented because his changes in behavior are perceived as strategic maneuvers.

In contrast, behavior which appears to be spontaneous and free of deception is defense reductive. If the communicator is seen as having a clean id, as having uncomplicated motivations, as being straightforward and honest, and as behaving spontaneously in response to the situation, he is likely to arouse minimal defense.

Neutrality and Empathy

When neutrality in speech appears to the listener to indicate a lack of concern for his welfare, he becomes defensive. Group members usually desire to be perceived as valued persons, as individuals of special worth, and as objects of concern and affection. The clinical, detached, person-is-an-object-of-study attitude on the part of many psychologist-trainers is resented by group members. Speech with low affect that communicates little warmth or caring is in such contrast with the affect-laden speech in social situations that it sometimes communicates rejection.

Communication that conveys empathy for the feelings and respect for the worth of the listener, however, is particularly supportive and defense reductive. Reassurance results when a message indicates that the speaker identifies himself with the listener's problems, shares his feelings, and accepts his emotional reactions at face value. Abortive efforts to deny the legitimacy of the receiver's emotions by assuring the receiver that he need not feel bad, that he should not feel rejected, or that he is overly anxious, though often intended as support giving, may impress the listener as lack of acceptance. The combination of understanding and empathizing with the other person's emotions with no accompanying effort to change him apparently is supportive at a high level.

The importance of gestural behavioral cues in communicating empathy should be mentioned. Apparently spontaneous facial and bodily evidences of concern are often interpreted as especially valid evidence of deep-level acceptance.

Superiority and Equality

When a person communicates to another that he feels superior in position, power, wealth, intellectual ability, physical characteristics, or other ways, he arouses defensiveness. Here, as with the other sources of disturbance, whatever arouses feelings of inadequacy causes the listener to center upon the affect loading of the statement rather than upon the cognitive elements. The receiver then reacts by not hearing the message, by forgetting it, by competing with the sender, or by becoming jealous of him.

The person who is perceived as feeling superior communicates that he is not willing to enter into a shared problem-solving relationship, that he probably does not desire feedback, that he does not require help, and/or that he will be likely to try to reduce the power, the status, or the worth of the receiver.

Many ways exist for creating the atmosphere that the sender feels himself equal to the listener. Defenses are reduced when one perceives the sender as being willing to enter into participative planning with mutual trust and respect. Differences in talent, ability, worth, appearance, status, and power often exist, but the low defense communicator seems to attach little importance to these distinctions.

Certainty and Provisionalism

The effects of dogmatism in producing defensiveness are well known. Those who seem to know the answers, to require no additional data, and to regard themselves as teachers rather than as co-workers tend to put others on guard. Moreover, in the writer's experiment, listeners often perceived manifest expressions of certainty as connoting inward feelings of inferiority. They saw the dogmatic individual as needing to be right, as wanting to win an argument rather than solve a problem, and as seeing his ideas as truths to be defended. This kind of behavior often was associated with acts which others regarded as attempts to exercise control. People who were right seemed to have low tolerance for members who were "wrong"— i.e., who did not agree with the sender.

One reduces the defensiveness of the listener when he communicates that he is willing to experiment with his own behavior, attitudes, and ideas. The person who appears to be taking provisional attitudes, to be investigating issues rather than taking sides on them, to be problem solving rather than debating, and to be willing to experiment and explore tends to communicate that the listener may have some control over the shared quest or the investigation of the ideas. If a person is genuinely searching for information and data, he does not resent help or company along the way.

Conclusion

The implications of the above material for the parent, the teacher, the manager, the administrator, or the therapist are fairly obvious. Arousing defensiveness interferes with communication and thus makes it difficult—and sometimes impossible—for anyone to convey ideas clearly and to move effectively toward the solution of therapeutic, educational, or managerial problems.

References

1. J. R. Gibb, "Defense Level and Influence Potential in Small Groups," *Leadership and Interpersonal Behavior*, ed. L. Petrullo and B. M. Bass (New York: Holt, Rinehart and Winston, 1961), pp. 66–81.
2. J. R. Gibb, "Sociopsychological Processes of Group Instruction," *The Dynamics of Instructional Groups*, ed. N. B. Henry (Fifty-ninth Yearbook of the National Society of the Study of Education, Part II, 1960), pp. 115–135.

Review Questions

1. How does Gibb define "defensiveness"?
2. What does "defensiveness" defend? What does "supportiveness" support?
3. How can description accomplish the same purpose as evaluation?
4. Based on what you've already read about empathy, how is neutrality the opposite of empathy?

Probes

1. Does Gibb see defensiveness as a relational thing—something that's created *between* persons—or does he see it as something one person or group creates and forces on another person or a group?
2. Gibb cautions us about the negative effects of evaluation. But is it possible actually to be nonevaluative? Or is that what Gibb is asking us to do?
3. Although most of Gibb's examples use verbal cues, each of the categories of defensiveness and supportiveness is also communicated nonverbally. Can you identify how you nonverbally communicate Evaluation? Control? Strategy? Superiority? Spontaneity? Empathy? Equality?
4. Self-disclosing is one way to communicate spontaneity. Can you identify communication behaviors that help create the other kinds of supportive climate?
5. Which categories of defensive behavior are most present in your relationship with your lover or spouse? Your employer? Your parents? Which categories of supportive behavior characterize those relationships?

There's probably no greater interpersonal communication challenge than what to do with your anger. On the one hand, anger seems to be a pervasive emotion; we all feel it at one time or another almost every day. On the other hand, it seems like any expression of anger drives a wedge between us and the other person. So what are we supposed to do? Suppress our anger all the time? Or just give up and expect to go around making other people mad at us?

In this next reading, John and Kris Amodeo apply some of what they've learned about anger in their work as family counselors. They begin by admitting that it's a powerful but little-understood emotion. Then they suggest that we begin working with anger by recognizing that it is natural and not necessarily bad. Bottled-up anger often *is* bad, as is anger that is destructively expressed. In fact, unexpressed anger often surfaces in what's called "passive-aggressive" behavior such as arriving late, withhholding affection, or forgetting appointments. It can also contribute to such stress-related physical symptoms as backache, headaches, and hypertension.

But effectively expressed anger can actually increase, not decrease, both your own sense of well-being and your intimacy with someone else. The first step is to accept anger as normal and natural. Most anger is not evidence of some deep psychological maladjustment or childhood trauma. It's simply one of our natural responses to things not going our way.

Then the key to dealing with it is, in their words, to learn to express "clean" anger. When you express clean anger, you reveal your own feelings and unmet needs in ways that are uncontaminated by blame or guilt-producing statements. This communication skill can be a difficult one both to practice and to hear. When you're angry, you need to learn to substitute "I don't like those dishes in the sink!" for statements like, "How many times have I told you not to leave your dirty dishes in the sink?" or "Why do you always leave such a mess in the sink?" The difference between these two kinds of statements may sound subtle, but it's enormously important. In the first case you're forcefully expressing your *own* anger—which is an accurate reflection of what you're feeling. In the second two cases you're blaming the other person, attributing your own anger to his or her actions. The first is much cleaner than the second two.

Even "clean" expressions of anger, though, are often interpreted as blaming statements. Naturally enough—as we learned above in Chapter 4—people respond to the nonverbal aspects of volume and tone of voice. So even though you might have *said,* "I'm angry!" they *hear,* "You screwed up!" There is no easy solution to this problem, but in this essay the Amodeos make several suggestions about how to cope with it.

For example, they emphasize the importance of both people involved learning that others do not cause our feelings. It also helps to learn to express and to hear anger as an emphatic "I don't like this!" or "No!" rather than an attack on someone else. The way anger is expressed often reveals a great deal about how power is distributed in a relationship. And it can also echo what we learned from watching and listening to our parents and other family members.

The Amodeos conclude this reading by sketching some of the benefits that you can experience when you learn to express anger cleanly. One of the most obvious is catharsis, the feeling of release, that you don't have to carry around a bottled-up emotion any more. But it can also help you discover important insights about yourself. If you can learn simply to notice anger rather than judging it good or bad, you can sometimes discover what's under the surface of your own everyday emotions. For example, as they say, "we may realize that just below the surface of our anger about the dishes not being washed lies a deeper concern about whether we are really loved."

Another important benefit of the "clean" expression of anger is that it can increase intimacy. When you express anger directly and nondefensively, you place yourself in a vulnerable position. You've given the other person an insight into how you really feel about something important. If both of you can deal with this anger as a clean expression, your vulnerability can get translated into enhanced intimacy. Obviously it won't work that way every time. But there is the genuine potential in work, friend, family, and intimate relationships that, as the Amodeos conclude, "The mutual sharing of anger in clean, self-revealing ways can lead to a process of communication that can help two individuals feel closer to one another."

Working with Anger

John and Kris Amodeo

Anger is a powerful, yet little understood human emotion. Our inability to deal with it effectively is a frequent cause of problems in our relationships. A major factor that contributes to this difficulty is the common misconception that anger is somehow "bad," destructive, or inappropriate. It is true that the way in which resentments are expressed can lead to a great deal of hurt in relationships and violence in the world. However, it would be a grave error to conclude that anger, in itself, is responsible for the destructiveness, and should therefore be avoided.

Rather than maintain a simplistic good/bad perception of anger, it is more useful to adopt a non-judgmental attitude toward it. If it is true that growth involves learning to love ourselves, then it follows that we must learn to fully accept ourselves, including our anger. The unfortunate alternative is to turn the anger inward against ourselves. In other words, unacknowledged and unexpressed anger gets held in the body, creating tension that may be experienced as frustration or anxiety. Or, when resentments have no healthy outlet, our bodily held anger may be felt as a chronic fatigue or depression—the anger turns against us, suppressing our energy and vitality. Internalized anger may also be partially responsible for those times when we feel confused—resentments fuse with other emotions and unproductive thoughts that then overwhelm us.

Bottled-up anger can also lead to physical symptoms such as headaches, ulcers, and an array of other illnesses whose causes we are only beginning to understand. In the years ahead, we may recognize that an accumulation of unacknowledged anger coupled with an inability to deal with it responsibly contributes significantly to the origin of many common diseases.

A key to our physical as well as emotional well-being involves allowing the experience of anger to simply be, without either judging it or trying to get rid of it due to our fear or aversion. Opening to our anger can then become a way to unlock suppressed energy and vitality. Dealing with it responsibly can enliven our relationships and rejuvenate those that have become stagnant or boringly comfortable.

Once we accept anger as a neutral energy, rather than morally judge it, we are in a position to differentiate between its responsible expression, and the impulse to vent it in destructive, hurtful ways. The need to communicate it in healthy ways becomes particularly obvious once we realize that we cannot *not* express our anger. There is some kind of inner intelligence within our organism that wants to express it. This healthy urge manifests in unhealthy, indirect ways when our belief system does not permit a direct experience of the anger.

It is the indirect expression of anger that has harmful, insidious effects upon relationships. Psychologists call this "passive-aggressive" behavior because, instead of expressing the anger or communicating about it, we act it out in passive ways. For example, if we fear the consequences of sharing our resentment directly, we may express anger indirectly by missing appointments, arriving late, withholding affection, or acting in a variety of spiteful ways. One client, for instance, stated that she took great satisfaction in running up her husband's charge accounts. At the time, she was not even aware of her anger, but upon closer exploration of her motives, she realized what she was actually feeling. She had experienced some relief (a re-emergence of her sense of power) by "getting back" at her husband for not giving her the caring and affection she wanted. But the relationship suffered because the anger did not have a chance to be expressed openly and explored in terms of its deeper meaning. Once the wisdom of the anger was understood, some resolution occurred as she became more willing to express her need for affection.

While some people disguise their anger through its passive expression, others vent it in an exaggerated fashion through unpredictable explosions. We sometimes read stories about the "nice guy" on the block who kills his wife and children. While the neighbors are left puzzled, it is no wonder to those who know that when resentments are repressed, they go underground and amass greater force for a future eruption. This pattern is familiar in relationships where one has a self-image of not being an angry person. For example, one individual who was deeply involved with spiritual practices had a strong conviction that it was wrong to get angry. One day, however, she exploded in a fierce rage. Being uncomfortable with her anger, she tried to cover it up by being sweet and forgiving. But, as inevitably occurs when anger is submerged, her fury erupted despite her best efforts to keep it under control.

Once we can acknowledge and feel our anger, we can begin to differentiate between its responsible expression and the impulse to vent it in destructive ways. It is not the anger that hurts others, but rather the blaming, judgmental ways in which it is often communicated. Gaining greater control over our anger does not mean suppressing it, but rather learning how to channel it in a way that can lead to greater intimacy and communication.

Learning to Express "Clean" Anger

The expression of anger can be distinguished by whether it is "clean" or "destructive." Destructive anger is very hurtful because it is tinged with personality attacks or judgmental criticisms. For example, through choice of words, tone of voice, or movements of the body, we may convey a message such as "You're pretty stupid," or "You're really selfish," or "You're wrong, don't you know anything!?" These and similar invalidating communications constitute an attack on the other person. They say, in effect, "You are not a worthwhile human being; you do not deserve love and respect." Such messages are especially hurtful because they rein-force the bad feelings we may already have about ourselves.

Receiving hurtful communications from another, we instinctively protect ourselves by either attacking or withdrawing. We may withdraw in a number of ways, such as by watching television, compulsively eating, drinking, going to sleep, refusing to talk, or threatening to end the relationship. Or, rather than withdraw-ing, we may retaliate by blaming or verbally attacking the other—becoming self-righteous and mentally deciding that the other person is wrong, bad, selfish, or immature. This leads to a spiraling escalation of tensions. Whether we withdraw or attack, the relationship suffers because one or both parties are left feeling hurt, defensive, or isolated. Surprisingly, this toxic pattern can continue indefinitely, leading to a painful negativity toward relationships and bitterness toward life.

Clean anger, on the other hand, does not focus on making the other person wrong for their behavior, feelings, or opinions. Instead of blaming or analyzing the other person ("you're too needy" or "you're so depressed!"), or assuming to know their motives ("you're just trying to get back at me," or "you only care about your-self!"), a clean communication reveals one's own feelings and unmet needs, uncon-taminated by blame or guilt-producing statements. For example, clean anger could be expressed in the following manner: "I'm angry about these dishes in the sink!" Included in this communication may be an emotional intensity in one's voice, but it is clean because the individual is merely expressing his or her feeling without implying (through words, tone of voice, or gestures) that the other person is wrong or suspect in some way. In contrast, a destructive communication would involve saying something like, "How many times do I have to tell you not to leave your dirty dishes in the sink!" At first, the distinction may appear to be a subtle one, but there is a crucial difference. Receiving the clean expression of anger, we hear, "This person is angry about dishes in the sink." Since we do not feel attacked, we may feel inclined to respond in an accommodating way. In the destructive com-munication, we feel nagged at and hear, "I'm bad for doing something wrong." As a result, we may withdraw in order to remove ourselves from a hurtful situation. Or we may give voice to our anger through an ineffectual, sarcastic remark such as, "Yes, dear," or "There you go complaining again...."

Feeling entitled to experience anger and express it in a clean, self-revealing way provides a direct, psychologically healthy outlet for it. As a result, there is less of a tendency for it to leap out later in irrational, hurtful ways (whether passively or actively). Our anger, plus other issues surrounding it, have a greater chance of being resolved through a simple, guiltless expression in the moment. Daniel Wile, a couples therapist, describes this clearly:

> An angry feeling or impulse, experienced and expressed in a direct and straightfor-ward manner, often has a clarifying and beneficial effect ... when anger is warded off, it reappears in regressive forms, as sudden rage, sadistic fantasies, or chronic irritability. If fear or self-criticism (guilt) prevent people from being assertive, the impulse goes underground and re-emerges in sudden blatant expressions (aggression) or subdued, inhibited ones (nonassertion).[1]

In addition, by releasing anger, our genuine love for the other can continue to grow, rather than be smothered by ever-increasing layers of resentment.

A clean expression of anger reflects the understanding that others do not cause our feelings. The common statement, "You make me so angry," depicts how anger is often blamed on the one toward whom we feel it. While another's words or actions can certainly bring up our anger, the other person cannot be held fully responsible for it. Our present upset is often the result of many factors, such as our unmet need for love, a re-stimulation of unresolved past hurts, feelings of unworthiness, fears of rejection, as well as the present anger-provoking situation. Our present feeling cannot be reduced simply to past causes or only to the present circumstance. Rather, our feeling is usually created by both. Growth comes through honoring our emotion as it arises, expressing it cleanly, and exploring it further internally if it seems particularly charged or out of proportion to the current situation.

The expression of anger need not be seen as threatening when expressed responsibly. In effect, it states, "I do not like this!" or "I won't accept that!" Anger sends a big "No!" message to the other: "No! I won't stand for this!" Through our anger, we stand up for ourselves, recover our self-esteem, and express our unwillingness to be abused, ignored, or depreciated by another. Even if we feel powerless to change the actual circumstances, expressing our anger enables us to release bodily held frustrations and energies, which can lead to a welcome change of attitude toward the situation. And, perhaps surprisingly, the situation itself may change once we have dealt with our feelings about it.

While it is important to be mindful of our felt experience, we are not suggesting that anger be expressed without regard for another's feelings or needs. As we grow more intimate with ourselves—becoming better acquainted with our true feelings and discovering patterns that no longer serve us—it becomes more possible to express ourselves while having an awareness of another's experience and a sensitivity to his or her feelings and well-being. Once the anger has subsided, we can demonstrate concern about the impact that our anger may have had by asking how the other person is feeling as a result of our communication. We can then be available to receive their response in a caring way.

One of the most difficult and challenging aspects of skillful communication is to integrate a sense of personal power with compassion—developing an ability to assert our own feelings and needs while maintaining a genuine caring for others. If we attend only to our own feelings, we become narcissistic. Preoccupied with ourselves, out of touch with the world around us, we feel disconnected from intimacy and therefore undernourished in our very being. It is one of the great paradoxes of life that when we are focused only upon our own needs, they cannot possibly be fully met. On the other hand, if we pay exclusive attention to other people's feelings and reactions, we abandon our own genuine needs. This pattern may be reinforced by becoming identified with the self-image of being a compassionate or loving person. Seeing ourselves as more "evolved" than others and obliged to care for them regardless of personal needs, we will again be left undernourished and disconnected from the interdependence that is natural to human existence. Eventually we may experience an angry outrage resulting from an accumulated sense of deprivation and self-neglect.

We grow up in a society that teaches us to conceal our anger. As a result, we hold it back, and may justify this through statements such as, "I don't want to hurt him," or "I don't want her to feel badly." What seems like a noble concern for protecting others is frequently a hidden fear of being disliked. The fear of rejection, and subsequent fear of feeling isolated and alone, is a major reason for withholding our anger and failing to be completely honest with one another. However, taking the risk to be authentic in this way can often lead to the growth of trust when we are relating to a person who appreciates such honesty.

Taking care of ourselves by expressing clean anger can be done in a variety of ways. "Getting angry" without blame is the most intense way, as in shouting, "I want to have a say in what movie we see tonight!" This vocal anger may be especially appropriate in situations where we have stifled resentments and felt unheard for a long time.

As we work with our anger and release some of the charge that may have been accumulating, we can eventually learn to stand up for ourselves without becoming irate. Becoming comfortable with our right to say "no," or to stand up for what we want, we can begin to embody an assertiveness that appropriately matches the situation. Doing so, we learn to simply state how we feel, what is bothering us, or what we want, untinged by leftover anger that we may still be carrying from the past.

Experiencing anger and learning to express it cleanly can lead to other important insights about ourselves. For instance, we may discover a sense of hurt or fear beneath a more obvious layer of resentment. For example, we may realize that just below the surface of our anger about the dishes not being washed lies a deeper concern about whether we are really loved. In this case, our reactive anger is precariously sitting atop a storehouse of hurt of which we may only be vaguely aware. However, if anger is our most distinct feeling, then that is where we must begin to access our deeper level of experience. If we avoid the anger entirely (for example, by believing that we should just forgive and forget), then we may rob ourselves of a vital opportunity to follow the wisdom of our felt process to its natural outcome. As a result, we bypass a chance to learn more about ourselves and become more intimate with another person.

Expressing anger cleanly and non-defensively can place us in a vulnerable position in relation to the person with whom we are angry. In order to help us feel safer in beginning new patterns of behavior in a relationship, we may wish to agree to the basic ground rule that each person has permission to cleanly express anger. This implies a willingness to make clearer discrimination between clean and destructive anger. Perceiving this distinction is not always easy. Individuals with a commitment to their own growth and to one another's well-being can sensitively explore how to communicate their anger in ways that lead to a resolution of conflicts.

Another factor that can support productive communication concerns how we relate to others' anger. Can we simply receive it? Can we hear how they are feeling without counter-attacking or defending ourselves? We certainly have a right to respond, but can we first hear their feelings and point of view? Responding differs from reacting. Reactions tend to be automatic and habitual, and are often triggered by underlying fears, such as feeling unloved. Responding occurs after we have received their communication, allowed it to touch us in some way, and taken time to notice the fresh feelings and meanings that then arise within us. Can we hear them without assuming that it means something negative about ourselves, or that the person no longer loves us simply because they are feeling angry? The simple act of hearing others' resentments can go a long way toward resolving it. People feel better when they sense that their anger is heard rather than avoided, received rather than judged as being wrong or inappropriate. The process of receiving others' anger and opening to the meaning it holds for them can lead to a precious moment of interpersonal contact.

A relationship that has love and trust as its context can become stronger through its ability to accommodate a wide range of human emotions. If trust is tenuous or uncertain, a wave of anger can jeopardize it. However, as trust grows, then, instead of being a threat, anger can be seen as conveying a crucial message that is calling for attention. If we really care about another, then we want to hear his or her anger and understand what it is really all about. Perhaps, for example, we gradually discover that they are feeling misunderstood, unappreciated, or unloved.

Learning to acknowledge our anger and hold a healthy respect for the wisdom it contains is an important step toward the development of meaningful intimacy. The mutual sharing of anger in clean, self-revealing ways can lead to a process of communication that can help two individuals feel closer to one another. As normally suppressed energies are released and we more intimately touch one another, our relationships can flourish in unexpected ways.

Note

1. D. Wile, *Couples Therapy—a Nontraditional Approach* (New York: John Wiley, 1981), p. 12.

Review Questions

1. True or false: The Amodeos believe that anger is good for relationships. Discuss.
2. What is "passive-aggressive behavior"?
3. What is the primary difference between "clean" and "destructive" expressions of anger?
4. Explain what the Amodeos mean when they say that "others do not cause our feelings."
5. What do the Amodeos say about power and the expression of anger?
6. Paraphrase what the Amodeos say in the third from the last paragraph in the article, where they talk about how we *hear* anger.

Probes

1. Have you ever experienced a physical symptom—headache, backache, etc.—that you later discovered was due to anger? What did you discover from that experience?
2. It's one thing to urge people, as the Amodeos do, not to "judge" anger but just to notice it when it occurs. It's quite another thing to follow that advice, especially when your anger is intense. Create two or three practical, helpful suggestions for people who want to learn to stop evaluating their own anger.
3. Try illustrating the differences between "clean" and "destructive" anger by making a column of five or six different "destructive" expressions of anger. For example, throwing dishes or spitting in someone's face. Put as much variety in this column as you can. Then write out clean expressions to correspond with each different destructive one. What characteristics of clean expressions emerge from your lists?
4. The Amodeos claim that our society teaches us not to express anger. Has that been true in your experience? How has that proscription affected you?
5. What do you hear the Amodeos saying about what other authors have called the difference between "assertiveness" and "aggressiveness"?
6. I believe that anger is clean or destructive not because of what one person does but because of what happens *between* persons. Like all other aspects of communication, I believe anger is a relational phenomenon. As a result, I don't think the Amodeos pay enough attention to how anger is *heard*. What is your opinion on this issue?

This reading offers a fairly complete outline of how to think about and prepare for a productive, rather than a destructive conflict. The authors have a long connection with *Bridges Not Walls.* In 1972, when I was working on the first edition of this book, I wrote Hugh Prather asking for permission to reprint excerpts from his book *Notes to Myself.* I was struck by how his brief, journallike notations captured several of the central points I wanted this book to make. He generously agreed to let me use some of his material, and his selections have appeared prominently in this book ever since. Now Hugh and his wife Gayle have written *A Book for Couples,* and I believe their discussion of conflict is among the best I've ever read.

They begin with an example of a typical everyday conflict that reveals how many issues are often buried in an argument between friends or intimates. It starts as an argument about the cat window and only lasts a couple of minutes, but the Prathers identify seventeen separate issues that get raised. No wonder arguments like this create more problems than they solve!

The next important point that's made in this reading is that discussions like the one about the cat window "create the relationship's terrain." In other words, the way these discussions are carried out defines the quality of the couple's relationship. This means that *process* is vital. *How* an argument happens is more important than the outcome that emerges. Process is literally more important than product.

With their tongues firmly planted in their cheeks, the Prathers then offer seven "magic rules for ruining any discussion." You can probably recognize some of your favorite fighting moves in this list—I know I do. The point of the list is to contrast the main features of productive and destructive conflict.

Then the authors explicitly highlight the point about process that they introduced earlier. They urge you to recognize that when you are in a conflict with a person you're close to, "to agree is not the purpose." Rather, "The only allowable purpose" for this kind of discussion "is to bring you and your partner closer." This, it seems to me, is a profoundly simple but important idea. It challenges one primary assumption most of us carry into our conflicts with people we care about: that the point is to get my way, be sure the other knows how I feel, or make the other feel bad. What might happen if couples could actually internalize this idea: that the real point of our argument is to get closer?

The rest of this reading builds on this foundation. The Prathers offer five steps for preparing to argue. All these guidelines make good sense and, taken together, as I mentioned earlier, they provide a fairly comprehensive outline of how to prepare to "do" conflict well. I won't repeat what they say here, but I do want to highlight some points.

Preparation step 2 is to "try to let go" of the issue you're thinking of raising. Although I don't think it's good to suppress genuinely felt emotions, I do believe that couples could frequently profit from applying this suggestion. I've found that it can frequently be relaxing, freeing, and empowering simply to let an irritation go.

Preparation steps 4 and 5 operationalize the Prathers' point about the only allowable purpose for a conflict. It's revealing to ask about a conflict whether "communication is your aim" rather than winning or venting. It is also helpful for me to try to be clear that "the problem is the relationship's and not your partner's."

As I read some sections of their essay I am a little frustrated by what can sound like oversimplification and rose-colored naivete. The real tough arguments are much more intense and difficult than these two authors seem to realize. But when I look again at their advice, I recognize that they understand well enough how gut-wrenching a fight with a loved one can be. They are simply convinced, as have been a great many wise people over the ages, that returning anger for anger doesn't help. Ultimately love, which in this case means the often unromantic commitment to a relationship, is stronger than defensiveness and bitterness.

How to Resolve Issues Unmemorably

Hugh and Gayle Prather

Unfinished Arguments Accumulate

It's not that issues don't get resolved. Indeed they are settled but settled like ketchup settles into a carpet. An uncleaned carpet can triple in weight within five years, and most relationships get so laden with undigested arguments that they collapse into a dull, angry stupor and cease to move toward their original goal.

"Albert, you've just got to install the cat window. I woke up again at 3 A.M. with Runnymede standing on my chest staring at me. I'm not getting enough alpha sleep."

"Sorry about that, Paula. I'll get to it this weekend."

"But Albert, you've been saying that for a month."

"Well, you know, honey, we could just put the cat out at night like everyone else."

"Oh, sure, and then what if he needed to get in? What if something was after him? What then?"

"What difference will the cat window make? He can still stay out all night if he wants to."

"Yes, Albert, but he can *also* get in if he *needs* to. You know, if you're not going to be a responsible pet owner, you shouldn't have a pet."

"Now there's a thought."

"I see. And I guess you don't mind breaking Gigi's heart."

"That's another thing, Paula, her name is Virginia, not Gigi. Why do we have to have a cat named Runnymede and a daughter named Gigi? Besides, I'll buy her a nice stuffed Garfield after the cat is comfortably settled in at the animal shelter."

"You know, Albert, this conversation is opening my eyes to something I've felt for a very long time."

"What's that, Paula?"

"You only care about mixed soccer. Since joining that team with the silly name you haven't been playing horsey with Gigi and you haven't been scratching

Runnymede under the chin where he can't lick. You certainly pretended to like Runnymede well enough when we were dating."

"You were the one who insisted I join the team. You were the one who said it would be good for me to 'get out of the house for a change.' I like the cat. I love my daughter. But I don't want to spend my Saturdays ruining a window with a perfectly good view."

"I guess you don't really care about me either, Albert. And you can stand there calmly peeling your Snickers while wanting Runnymede to be gassed. If I didn't know how much emotion you devote to *mixed* soccer I would say you have become psychotically insensitive and unfeeling. Perhaps you should seek help."

Here Albert, proving that he is neither insensitive nor unfeeling, flings his Snickers at the window in question, grabs his soccer gear, and storms from the house, where in an afternoon match playing goalie for the Yuma Yuccas he fractures the middle three phalanges in his right hand, thus ending the question of installing anything.

Each New Issue Resurrects the Old

We wish we could say that this dialogue was a transcript but it is a composite. If we reprinted verbatim some of the typical arguments we have heard during counseling, they would be dismissed as overwrought fiction. The large number of digressions seen here is actually commonplace and illustrates the typical residue of unsettled questions found in most long-term relationships. The difference between this and the average disagreement is that some of these words might have been thought but left unspoken. Yet the feeling of estrangement by the end of the argument would have been the same.

On this Saturday morning Paula is upset because her sleep continues to be interrupted by the cat asking to be put out. That is the sum of the issue. If the couple had sat down together instead of using the problem as a means of separating still further, they could easily have solved this one difficulty in any of a hundred different mutually acceptable ways. But a hive of older discord lies just beneath their awareness, and therefore settling just one problem in peace is harder than it would seem.

The cry of unresolved issues is strong and persistent. Any couple will feel their failure to have joined. They yearn to bridge the old gaps and fear the potential of further separation more than they welcome the opportunity to reverse the process. To bring up former differences during a discussion is not blameworthy, it is in fact a call for help, but it is mistimed.

Without realizing it—because most arguments are conducted with no deep awareness—Albert and Paula allude to seventeen other issues, none of which had to be brought up to solve *this* problem. In the order they appear, here are the questions they have left unanswered in the past, a small fraction of the total residue if you consider all the others that will be mentioned in future arguments: (1) Why has Albert's promise gone unfulfilled for a month? (2) Should the cat be left out overnight? (3) Is Albert irresponsible? (4) Should the family continue having this pet? (5) Is Albert insensitive to his daughter? (6) Should Paula continue calling Virginia "Gigi"? (7) Should the cat be renamed? (8) Would a stuffed animal sufficiently compensate? (9) Is mixed soccer affecting Albert's attitude toward his daughter and pet? (10) Does the team have a silly name? (11) Is Albert being sufficiently attentive to Paula or has he changed in some fundamental way? (12) Does Paula want Albert around the house? (13) How important is the window view to Albert's happiness? (14) Does Albert still love Paula? (15) Should Albert eat Snickers? (16) Is Albert's contact with other women on Saturdays the root cause of his, in Paula's view, wavering commitment to his family? (17) Does Albert have serious psychological problems?

As can be seen here, it is not easy for most couples to concentrate on a single issue. Nevertheless it is certainly possible and, in itself, to practice doing so will begin giving them a new kind of evidence: that within this relationship there are still grounds for unity and happiness. If one of the partners deviates from this guideline, the other should not make still another issue of this or get caught up in the irrelevant point raised, but should see instead the real desire behind the digression and treat it gently and answer it with love.

Discussions Create the Relationship's Terrain

... To resolve issues in the usual way is as damaging to a relationship as not resolving them at all, because the gap is not truly bridged and the unsuccessful attempt merely adds more weight to the couple's doubts about each other. In the argument over the cat window, Paula's concern about the health of her marriage surfaces, a question of far greater importance to her than how she will manage to get more sleep, and yet without fully realizing it she exacerbates this larger problem and works against her own interests. By arguing in the manner they did, this couple, as do most, merely manufactured new issues between them. Albert probably did not mean to take that hard a stand on getting rid of the cat—he may actually have wanted to keep it. And Paula did not have real doubts about Albert's mental health.

The past that drives so many relationships into the ground is built piece by piece, smallness fitted to smallness, selfishness answered with selfishness. Yet the process is largely unconscious. Each couple quickly settles into a few sad methods of conducting arguments, but seldom is the means they use thought through or the results closely examined. One person nags, the other relents. One person reasons, the other becomes silent. One person flares, the other backs down. One person cajoles, the other gives in. But where are the joy and grandeur, where is the friendship that was supposed to flourish, the companionship that through the years was to fuse an invulnerable bond, a solace and a blessing at the close of life? Instead there is a bitter and widening wedge between the two, and even the briefest of discussions contains a hundred dark echoes from the past.

No matter how entrenched are our patterns of problem solving, they can be stepped away from easily once we see that they do not serve our interests. The only interest served in most discussions is to be right. But, truly, how deep is this? Do we actually want to make our partner wrong, to defeat a friend, and slowly to defeat a friendship? It certainly may feel that way. Caught up once again in the emotions of a disagreement, we stride doggedly toward our usual means of concluding every argument: adamant silence, crushing logic, patronizing practicality, collapsed crying, quelling anger, martyred acquiescence, loveless humor, sulking retreat.

These postures and a thousand more are attempts to prove a point other than love, and as with all endeavors to show up one's partner, the friendship itself is the victim, because the friendship becomes a mere tool, a means of making the other person feel guilty. The love our partner has for us is now seen as leverage, and in our quiet or noisy way we set about making the relationship a shambles, not realizing that we ourselves are part of the wreckage.

The Magic Rules for Ruining Any Discussion

... The dialogue with which we began this chapter incorporates a few of but not all the rules for disastrous communication—yet only one or two are needed to neutralize the best of intentions. Follow these guidelines, even a little sloppily, and you are guaranteed a miserable time.

1. *Bring the matter up when at least one of you is angry.*

    Variations: Bring it up when nothing can be done about it (in the middle of the night; right before guests are due; when one of you is in the shower). Bring it up when concentration is impossible (while driving to a meeting with the IRS; while watching the one TV program you both agree on; while your spouse is balancing the checkbook).

2. *Be as personal as possible when setting forth the problem.*

    Variations: Know the answer before you ask the question.
    While describing the issue, use an accusatory tone. Begin by implying who, as usual, is to blame.

3. *Concentrate on getting what you want.*

    Variations: Overwhelm your partner's position before he or she can muster a defense (be very emotional; call in past favors; be impeccably reasonable).
    Impress on your partner what you need and what he or she must do without.
    If you begin losing ground, jockey for position.

4. *Instead of listening, think only of what you will say next.*

    Variations: Do other things while your partner is talking. Forget where your partner left off.
    In other words, listen with all the interest you would give a bathroom exhaust fan.

5. *Correct anything your partner says about you.*

    Variations: Each time your partner gives an example of your behavior, cite a worse example of his or hers.
    Repeat "That's not what I said" often.
    Do not accept anything your partner says at face value (point out exceptions; point out inaccuracies in facts and in grammar).

6. *Mention anything from the past that has a chance of making your partner defensive.*

    Variations: Make allusions to your partner's sexual performance.
    Remind your husband of his mother's faults.
    Compare what your wife does to what other women do, and after she complains, say, "I didn't mean it that way."

7. *End by saying something that will never be forgotten.*

Variations: Do something that proves you are a madman.
Let your parting display proclaim that no exposure of your partner could be amply revealing, no characterization too profane, no consequence sufficiently wretched.
At least leave the impression you are a little put out.

To Agree Is Not the Purpose

All couples believe they know how to hold a discussion, and yet it is not an exaggeration to say that in most long-term relationships there has rarely been one wholly successful argument. Obviously they are filled with disagreements that end in agreements, but when these are examined, it can be seen that at least a small patch of reservation had to be overlooked in order for accord to be reached.

We believe this is simply how differences are settled, and so even though we sense that our partner is still in conflict, we barge ahead with our newly won concession, thinking the bad moment will pass. Later it becomes painfully clear that it has not and we judge our partner irresolute. Or if we are the one who complied, we count our little sacrifice dear and wait for reparation—which never comes or is never quite adequate, and we cannot understand why our partner feels such little gratitude.

The aim of most arguments is to reach outward agreement. Until that is replaced with a desire for friendship, varying degress of alienation will be the only lasting outcome. Couples quickly develop a sense of helplessness over the pattern that their discussions have fallen into. They believe they are sincerely attempting to break out of it and are simply failing. They try different responses, going from shouting to silence, from interminable talking to walking out of the room, from considering each point raised to sticking tenaciously to one point, but nothing they do seems to alter the usual unhappy ending.

There is no behavioral formula to reversing the habitual course of an argument. It requires a shift in attitude, not in actions, even though actions will modify in the process. No more is needed than one partner's absolute clarity about the purpose of the argument. This is not easy but it is simple. Therefore let us look again at what the aim should be....

The only allowable purpose for a discussion is to bring you and your partner closer. Minds must come together to decide instead of backing away in order to apply pressure. How is this possible, given the fact that you and your partner are deeply selfish? Fortunately, the selfishness is compartmentalized and your hearts remain unaffected. You need not eliminate it; merely bypass it because you recognize that it is not in your interests to be selfish. To the ego, this concept is insane because it sees no value in love. But love is in your interests because you *are* love, or at least part of you is, and thus each discussion is a way of moving into your real self.

A little time is obviously needed to see one's true interests. If you rush into a discussion you will operate from your insensitivity by habit and aim for a prize your heart cares nothing about. Do not kid yourself. You *do* know whether the discussion is ending with the two of you feeling closer. The selfish part of your mind will tell you that the little sadness and sense of distance you may now feel was a small price to pay for the concession you won or the point you made. Or it will argue that it was all unavoidable. This may happen many times before you begin reversing your ordinary way of participating. This transition is an important stage of growth and entails looking more and more carefully at selfish impulses and their aftermath. Is how you feel really worth it? Was the way it went truly unavoidable?

Thus you will come to see the result you want, and this deeper recognition will begin to eclipse your pettiness in the midst of an argument. Gradually you will catch the mistakes sooner, and eventually you will learn to avoid them from the start. For you *do* want these times of deciding to warm your hearts and lighten your steps. So persist in the guidelines we will give, and these little defeats to your relationship will slowly give way to friendship.

We are so used to thinking of a discussion as a symbol of separation that it can often be helpful to change its form enough that something new will appear to be happening and thus the old mind set is undercut. To take the usual process, break it into steps and put them in order is usually all that is needed to accomplish this.

An issue could be said to pass through five stages in reaching resolution. First, it must be thought of by at least one of the partners as an issue. Second, a moment is chosen to bring the matter up. Third, a decision is made as to the manner in which it will be presented. Fourth, there is an exchange of thoughts and feelings. And fifth, the discussion is concluded.

Most couples give very little thought to the first three stages. They simply find themselves in the thick of a so-called spontaneous argument and no one is certain at what point it began. Obviously you must become more conscious of the subjects you bring up so carelessly. Any sign of fear over what you are about to say is a very useful indicator. If you see you have a question about whether to say it, let this be your cue to break these preliminary choices into conscious steps. Do not begrudge the time; remember instead how strongly you want to begin building a real friendship.

Five Steps in Preparing to Argue

First, you might ask yourself if the issue you are thinking of is actually a present issue or merely one you have been reminded of. In other words, be certain this is currently a problem and not one the relationship may already be on its way to solving. Many people habitually rake over their marriage for signs of imperfection and naturally they find a great many, but it can be far more disrupting to friendship to be constantly questioning and comparing than to wait to see if the problem continues in any severe way. Meanwhile, enjoy what is already between you without telling yourself what this is....

If the issue is unquestionably a present one, the second step you might try is to let go of it. Letting go is not "better," but it is an option that current values tend to underrate. However, it must be accomplished thoroughly and honestly or the issue will grow like mold in a dark unseen place. If it is done consciously dismissal is not denial. Essentially it entails examining in detail what you do not like and then making a deliberate effort to identify with another part of you that never "takes issue" with any living thing, that is still and at ease, that acts only from peace....

If a couple espouses world energy consciousness or is on a tight budget, for one of the partners to habitually leave the hot water running, not turn off lights, or keep the refrigerator door open may be grating or even shocking to the other partner. Yet the spectacle of someone wasting energy and money is *not* grating or shocking. The interpretation we assign it, and not the act itself, determines the emotions we feel. Jordan, age two, is "shockingly irresponsible." He has even been known (yesterday, in fact) to flush a toilet five times in a row and then run to tell his big brother about the accomplishment. "John, I flush, I flush!" "That's nice," said John, blatantly contributing to the delinquency of a minor. The reason Jordan didn't tell his father (who is the family's conscience in these matters) was that he was the very one who kept showing him how it was done, thereby encouraging him to waste over fifteen gallons of water (plus six more his father used researching that figure)....

So here we have four reactions issuing from four interpretations: pride from the father, support from the seven-year-old, excitement from the two-year-old and, having no originality, curiosity from the cat. Clearly no uniform effect was produced by an external and unreachable cause. How then might you let go of your reaction to your spouse's wasteful habits in lieu of bringing it up one more time? Certainly you would not try dishonestly to convince yourself that the practice was not costing money or energy. Or that it did not really matter to you. Neither would you attempt to assign some motive to your partner's acts that you did not believe, such as not knowing any better or really trying hard but being unable to stop. Dishonesty does not end an unhappy line of thought. That is why reinterpretation is generally not effective....

If in your moment of consideration you are able to see these facts deeply enough, you may open your eyes to your partner's innocence and no longer feel compelled to *understand* why he or she does these things. But if after making the attempt to free your mind you see that you have not let the issue go, then perhaps to bring it up would be the preferable course, for undoubtedly that is better than storing anger or fear....

The third step is to consider if this is the time. If you feel an urge to bring it up quickly, be very alert to anger. Your heart is willing to wait but your ego is not, especially if it senses an opportunity to strike back. The ego is merely our love of misery, of withdrawal and loneliness, and it can feel like our own deep impulse even though it exists on the most superficial level of the mind.

For too long now our relationships have been jerked around by our own lack of awareness. There is more to your mind than selfishness. So be still a moment and let peace arise from you. Is this the time? A simple question. There need not be great soul-searching and hand-wringing over it. If your partner has just done something and this is the issue, clearly he or she is likely to be more defensive if instantly called on it. If your partner is not in a particularly happy frame of mind, is hostile, worried or depressed, a more receptive state will surely come and nothing is lost by waiting. Is this the time? Merely look and know the answer. The urge to attack when you are angry is very strong, but if you will allow yourself time to reflect on your genuine feelings, this will do more to relieve your frustration.

The fourth step is to be certain that communication is your aim. Trying to get someone to change is not communication because you have already decided what change is needed. Your partner is therefore left with nothing to say and will definitely feel your unwillingness to consider, to listen, to appreciate. So before you speak take time to hear your heart.

You are not two advocates arguing a case. You are interested in joining, not in prevailing. You are like the directors of a business you both love coming together to help it over a difficult situation. You don't care from whose lips the solution comes. You welcome the *answer*. To this end what are you willing to do if your partner becomes defensive? Are you prepared, and have you prepared, to carry through your love of the relationship? ...

The final point to consider is whether you are clear that the problem is the relationship's and not your partner's. In our example the problem was not Paula's, because her lack of sleep was affecting Albert also. One person's jealousy, appetite, hypersensitivity, frigidity, phobia or any other characteristic that has become an issue cannot successfully be viewed as more one's responsibility than the other's because friendship is always a mutual sharing of all burdens....

You must understand that unless you make a specific effort to see through the fallacy, you *will* go into a discussion thinking one of you is more to blame than the other, and this will make it very hard to listen and be open. Learn to treat every issue as an impersonal and neutral enemy and to close ranks against it. An addiction, for example, can be viewed as you would a hurricane or a deluge—you need each other's help to survive the storm. Our dog, Sunny Sunshine Pumpkin Prather (whose very name is a masterpiece of family compromise), gets sprayed by a skunk about once a month and the smell is everyone's problem. What good would it do to blame the dog? And yet we have seen other families get angry at their dog "for being so stupid." ...

These preliminary steps, which should only take an instant or two to complete, will at least make it possible for a discussion to begin with some chance of success. Now you are ready for a *real* argument, one in which your minds can join rather than separate.

Review Questions

1. What point are the Prathers making by listing seventeen issues that were brought up in the argument between Albert and Paula?
2. What do the authors mean when they say that discussions "create the relationship's terrain"?
3. Paraphrase this statement: "The only allowable purpose for a discussion is to bring you and your partner closer." Do you agree or disagree with it? Explain.
4. What do the authors mean when they say that you should "Learn to treat every issue as an impersonal and neutral enemy and to close ranks against it"?
5. What keeps the "protect your gains" step from being selfish?

Probes

1. What alternative do the authors offer to "being right" in a conflict?
2. What general principle or principles are violated by the seven "Magic Rules for Ruining any Discussion"? In other words, what general attitudes makes these moves destructive?
3. Which of the five steps for preparing to argue do you *least* often follow? What does that fact tell you about your way of "doing" conflict?
4. A fundamental, perhaps even a radically different perspective or point of view is behind just about everything the Prathers say about "resolving issues unmemorably." By "different," I mean different from the attitude we normally carry into a conflict. How would you describe this alternative point or view or perspective?

Chapter 12

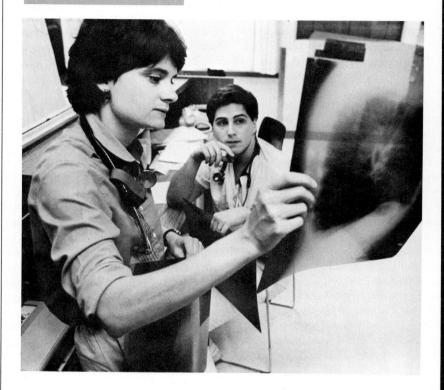

Communication Between Women and Men

I do not want to insist that equality between the sexes depends on women's meanings predominating; I do want to insist that women's meanings should be allowed to coexist, that they should be accorded equal validity. In other words, I am seeking a radical solution: I want a woman's word to count as much as a man's, no more and no less.

DALE SPENDER

T hese are excerpts from a recently published book called *Gender and Communication*. Its author is a speech communication professor who has familiarized herself with just about all the research on female–male communication. That was a major task; the bibliography at the end of Pearson's book includes over 1200 references to books and articles written by anthropologists, psychologists, sociologists, linguists, and communication researchers and teachers.

The first section of this reading makes a case for studying gender and communication. Pearson points out that in the United States, and to some extent in at least the rest of the Western world, we are undergoing a "paradigm shift" in our attitudes about masculinity and femininity. The controversy over the Equal Rights Amendment, Geraldine Ferraro's historic vice presidential candidacy, the growing presence of women in traditionally male professions such as law and medicine, and the growing presence of men in historically female professions such as nursing and elementary education are relatively obvious features of this paradigm shift. Less obvious, more indirect evidences of the shift also abound in, for example, changing family patterns and parenting practices, arguments over abortion, and disputes about the roles of women in religious institutions.

Whatever its general features, the paradigm shift touches each of us individually as we communicate with same- and opposite-sex persons affected by it. We can cope with the shift most gracefully as we learn more about the characteristics of male and female communication. That is why the bulk of this reading reproduces Pearson's discussion of male–female language differences. I don't mean by my selection to imply that nonverbal differences are unimportant. Verbal differences, however, may be more subtle and less well known. In any case, this overview should work as an introduction to the topic.

Pearson identifies three kinds of language differences: substantive ones, "substantive differences merging into structural differences," and differences of structure. Substantive differences include variations in word choice, structural differences include how long or often a person talks, and the borderline category includes such features of a conversation as questioning and offering compound requests.

As you may have expected, there are significant differences in male and female vocabularies. Terms for colors, for genitalia and intercourse, and the use of profanity and expletives all differ, according to the research Pearson cites. In addition, women appear to engage more than men in what Pearson calls "hypercorrection" and to use more intensifiers, hedges, fillers, and qualifiers. At the same time, Pearson notes, the differences appear to be shrinking rather than growing; "Men and women appear to be using more similar forms."

The research Pearson reviews also indicates that women make more "compound requests" than men and use more tag questions. The difference between "Come here" and "Would you please come here" is the difference between a simple and a compound request. A tag question softens a declarative statement by adding, for example, an "isn't it?" or a "can't we?" Pearson points out that both forms of talk are considered nonassertive and that at least one study suggests that they significantly weaken the impact of the women who use them.

Pearson next discusses general questioning patterns, and in that discussion, as in others, she makes some suggestions about what you might do with your knowledge of the differences. For example, she suggests that if you are a woman you "consider the questions you are asked before responding freely, then try to determine the purpose of prefacing comments with a question." If you are a man you "consider the appropriateness of the questions which you would like to ask and your own sensitivity in responding to the questions asked of you."

Pearson's discussion of structural differences reviews talk time, interruptions, overlaps, and silence. Briefly, men and high-status persons talk more, interrupt more, and overlap the talk of women more, and women "fall silent more often when they are interacting with men than do women or men in same-sex dyads, or than men do in mixed-sex dyads."

In the final section of the reading, Pearson suggests some "corrective action." Despite some research findings to the contrary, Pearson does not advise women to adopt a male style. A feminine linguistic style has some positive attributes, but the wisest course of action is for both women and men to broaden their language repertoire. In the final paragraph of this section Pearson offers some specific suggestions about how we might do that.

The primary value of this information is that it teaches both women and men about the actual, as contrasted with the assumed, differences that characterize male and female communicating. Knowledge of the differences can alert us to efforts by others to stereotype us and it can alert us to our own stereotyping, too. That can be one step toward the goal of contacting persons as *persons,* not ignoring the differences but also not exacerbating or unnecessarily emphasizing them.

Language Usage of Women and Men

Judy Cornelia Pearson

Introduction

A judge in Wisconsin claims that a 5-year-old girl involved in a sexual assault case was "promiscuous," and the case receives national attention as local citizens demand the recall of the judge. In 1977 a Massachusetts father is the first male to win child custody in that state, and the movie *Kramer vs. Kramer* shows a father in the role of single parent for his son. Betty Friedan authors a new book in 1981, *The Second Stage,* in which she implies that her first book, published in 1963, *The Feminine Mystique,* is out of date. In *The Second Stage* she puts forth a new challenge for women, overcoming the "feminist mystique."

The changing roles of women and men are inescapable. The contemporary women's movement, which had its auspices in Betty Friedan's *The Feminine Mystique,* has obscured the clear perceptions of women and men which once prevailed in our culture. New definitions of "male" and "female" in the psychological literature call into question traditional masculine and feminine sex roles. Consistent with this new approach, the changing sociological nature of the family requires flexibility and demonstrates that the "nuclear family" is obsolete.

The topic of "gender and communication" is relevant today because of the vast sociological and psychological changes which are part of our culture in the 1980's. Whether we choose to entertain ourselves with the movies, television, or the radio, we encounter this topic. In the best-selling books we select, the magazines or newspapers we read, we are confronted with the importance of "gender and communication." And, whether we focus on legal decision-making, governmental action, or religious tracts, we see the central, but often hidden, role of this newly emerging topic of consideration.

Why are we concerned with the issue of gender and communication *today?* Why are research studies that focus on the communication of women and men, nonexistent twenty years ago, now filling traditional journals and necessitating the creation of new journals which are devoted solely to this topic? Why are courses on sex differences in communication, female/male communication, and sex and communication being introduced on campuses throughout the country?

Thomas Kuhn, in *The Structure of Scientific Revolutions,* offers some theoretical explanation for the prevalence of the topic of gender and communication. Describing the stages through which people perceive knowledge, Kuhn suggests that when we believe a set of "facts," we have what is known as a *paradigm.* A paradigm may be thought of as a set of beliefs which are internally consistent and which are derived from an over-riding belief or "fact." For instance, at one time people thought that the world was flat and developed theories based on that central belief. Later, people believed that the world was round and replaced their outdated theories with contemporary views that were in line with their new paradigm. The time span between the two paradigms, when some people hold to one point of view and others maintain the other perspective, is known as a *paradigm shift.*

In the same way that scientific knowledge moves through differing paradigms, our belief systems also change. At one time, we believed that women and men had specific roles to play and that deviation from these roles was suspect. For instance, women have been viewed to be nurturers of children, while men have been perceived to be hunters, or providers of food. Today, these perceptions appear to a number of people to be unusual and impractical.

We are now undergoing a paradigm shift concerning women and men in our culture. In the United States the sharp divisiveness over the Equal Rights Amendment demonstrates the positions of the two bodies of belief. On the one hand, there are persons who support the traditional perspective in which men and women are viewed as more different than alike; on the other, there are those who propose a more contemporary view in which men and women are viewed as more alike than different. The traditionalists do not maintain that men and women are completely different, and persons with the contemporary perspective do not hold that men and women are completely alike. Nonetheless, a considerable gap exists between the perceived proportions of similarity and dissimilarity which are ascribed to persons who are labeled "female," and "male." . . .

The association of gender and communication is an important topic for you because of the frequency with which you communicate with members of the opposite and same sex and the difficulty of explaining and predicting successful communication interactions. Without a knowledge of the contrasting and similar communication styles of women and men, you are likely to encounter defeat in your interactions with others. It is less probable that you will have satisfying personal relationships, and your chances for success in your career are reduced. To the extent that you are able to understand the information in this text and to apply it to your interactions with others, you will be more likely to understand, predict, and have successful interactions with others....

General Language Differences

In order to organize the language differences that appear to occur between women and men in a useful way, we have categorized them into substantive differences, structural differences, and a category of differences which appear to be hybrids of these two. We will call this third category substantive differences merging into structural differences and will consider it between the other two categories for proper placement. Substantive differences are those modifications or variations that occur within messages; they may be thought of as the differing words or vocabularies used by men and women. Structural differences include the frequency of times that someone talks, how long each person talks, how willing an individual is to yield the floor, and how each person was able to secure his or her turn to talk. When we refer to substantive differences merging into structural differences, we include such features of a conversation as questioning, controlling the topic of the conversation, and offering compound requests. Let us first consider substantive differences.

Vocabularies

Women and men appear to have different working vocabularies as they make distinctive lexical choices. A recent study added behavioral verification to Lakoff's (1975) hypothesis that men and women make differing lexical choices (Crosby & Nyquist, 1977). Men use more colloquial or nonstandard forms than do women (cf. Graves & Price, 1980).

Another difference in the language of women and men concerns color terms. Before you continue reading this chapter, ask a friend of the opposite sex to name the colors of ten items in the room. At the same time, when she or he is writing down her or his perceptions, write down your own color descriptors for the same items. Compare your lists. You may find that they conform to the research findings in this area. Lakoff (1975) noticed that women appear to have a far more discriminating set of names for colors than do men. Words like "puce," "chartreuse," "mauve," "ecru," and "teal" are more likely to show up in a conversation among women than among men. Specific career lines make great use of color, however, and it would not be surprising for a person in interior design, painting, or other creative fields to be sharply aware of these colors, regardless of this individual's sex. We may also see an alteration in the awareness of colors by men in the future. While women use more exotic or "fancy" words for colors than do men, younger men tend to use more discriminating or elegant words than do older men (Rich, 1977). In other words, younger men who at this time do not have the same vocabulary for colors as do women are making strides in learning and becoming aware of far more than were their predecessors.

Men and women do not discuss male and female body parts nor intercourse in similar language. Two researchers asked respondents to identify the terms that they would use to describe male genitals, female genitals, and copulation in each of four contexts—in informal conversation in a mixed-sex group, in informal conversation in a same-sex group, in private conversations with their parents, and in private conversations with a lover or spouse. They found that norms concerning sexual terminology did differ according to the context, with the most limited, most "clinical," terminology being used by both sexes in the "parent" context. Female subjects used a more limited vocabulary in all contexts than male subjects. Both sexes were more hesitant to name female than male genitals. Males used more "power slang" in discussing genitals and copulation, such as "my weapon," "my pistol," and "bolt action;" they were more verbal and employed greater variety in terms. Females used more clinical terms and more often manifested vagueness or made no response. The researchers speculate that the differences in terms between the two sexes may lead to confusion. In addition, women may feel more discomfort about their own sexuality and that of others than do men (Sanders & Robinson, 1979).

A more recent study replicated this investigation and provided more information. Simkins (1982) asked undergraduate students the terms they would use to describe female genitalia, male genitalia, and sexual intercourse in the same four settings used by Sanders and Robinson. Simpkins found that men and women tended to use formal terminology in mixed company and with parents. With same-sexed friends, males used colloquial terms for all three concepts, while females retained more formal terminology. In discussion with a spouse or lover, both males and females used formal terminology for the female genitalia; females retained a preference for formal terminology for male genitalia while men used more colloquial terms; both males and females used colloquial terminology for sexual intercourse.

A useful sidenote to this research is provided by Otto Jespersen, who wrote a classic text on language in 1922. Jespersen included a chapter on sex differences in language. Excerpts from the chapter are quoted, sometimes out of context, to illustrate how far we have come in eradicating language differences between women and men, or how little distance we have traveled in altering linguistic patterns between the sexes. Jespersen contends that men are the innovators of language and that they have far more words than do women. Although we can only speculate on the number of words which men and women each "possess," it is apparent that the two sexes tend to use different words.

Hostility, Profanity, and Expletives

Men appear more likely than women to use hostile words, profanity, and expletives. In 1975, Lakoff speculated that women are less likely to use profanity than are men. More recently Staley tested Lakoff's assertion and found significant results. She asked students who were ages 18–47 to respond to a questionnaire listing a series of emotional situations. For each situation, the respondents were to report the expletive they would use, the expletive which they predicted a member of the opposite sex would use, and to define each expletive they provided. Males and females averaged about the same number of expletives per questionnaire. A great difference in predicted response was observed; however, men predicted fewer expletives for women and women predicted more expletives for men. In addition, men predicted weaker expletive use by women. Both sexes judged female expletive use as weaker than male expletive use, even when the terms were identical. Both sexes viewed the expletives as devoid of literal meaning (Staley, 1978).

In the case of expletives, our stereotypes are not keeping pace with our behavioral practices. Men and women engage in similar behavior, yet they are judged to behave differently. The same situation may be true for modifications in hostile language since the most recent study was done in the early 1970's. At that time, females were found to use fewer hostile verbs than males. The researchers concluded that males are less inhibited in expressing hostility, although group pressure or social context may also influence the use of hostile verbs by men (Gilley & Summers, 1970). In the intervening 15 years since this study was completed, females may have increased their use of hostile language.

At the same time that Jespersen (1922) was describing male language as consisting of more vocabulary than female language, he was describing female language as that which included the most "decent words" and frequently included euphemisms. The notion that women would use more *euphemisms,* inoffensive words which are substituted for offensive terms, than men is parallel to the idea that men use more *dysphemisms,* offensive words which are substituted for inoffensive words. Although this conclusion is consistent with men using more expletives, more slang terms, and perhaps more hostile verbs, these findings are not stable. Instead, language may be changing in these areas for both men and women; in any case, we have little empirical verification for concluding that women do indeed use more euphemisms than do men.

Hypercorrection

Lakoff (1975) also hypothesized that women engage in *hypercorrection,* or reminding people of correct forms when they make errors. For instance, hypercorrection would occur if a person asked another, "You mean 'lie' instead of 'lay,' don't you?" "Do you mean *set* the glass on the table?" or "When are *she* and *he* coming?" Crosby and Nyquist (1977) demonstrated that women do tend to engage in hypercorrection more than men.... This correctness in pronunciation is parallel to women's greater likelihood to correct others; men's incorrectness in pronunciation makes them more likely candidates for correction.

Intensifiers, Hedges, Fillers, and Qualifiers

Women appear to use more intensifiers, hedges, fillers, and qualifiers than do men. Adverbs like "so," "such," "quite," and "awfully" are examples of *intensifiers* which women appear to use more than men (Key, 1972; Lakoff, 1975; Jespersen, 1922). One behavioral study which employed small groups of five to seven people found that women in all-female groups used six times more intensifiers than did men. In mixed sex groups, women used fewer intensifiers than women in same sex groups; however, in mixed sex groups, women used five times as many intensifiers than men in the mixed sex groups (McMillan, Clifton, McGrath, & Gale, 1977).

Hedges, or *qualifiers,* are words which modify, soften, or weaken other words or phrases. Hewitt and Stokes (1975) explain that hedges indicate the tentative nature of a statement or indicate some measure of uncertainty about the other person's response to it. Examples of such words and phrases are "maybe," "perhaps," "somewhat," "you know," "in my opinion," "it seems to me," and "let's see." When qualifiers or hedges are added to otherwise direct statements, such assertions become weakened and sound more tentative. For instance, imagine a parent scolding a child, "You should never touch a hot stove," compared to "Possibly you should never touch a hot stove." Or, contrast the woman who tells her date, "It's time to go," with her friend who states, "I guess it's time to go." Would you respond differently to your supervisor if she or he directed you to "Come into my office," than if the message was "Perhaps you could come into my office"? Crosby and Nyquist (1977) found that adult women use more hedges or qualifiers than do men, but Staley (1982) did not find any gender differences in the use of hedges by children aged 4, 8, 12, and 16. Staley observes that language behavior in society may be in the process of change and that linguistic sex role stereotyping may not be as predictable as it has been.

Disclaimers are a special class of hedges. Disclaimers are words or phrases which weaken or disparage the speaker's request or statement. The disclaimer suggests that the speaker is not serious, sincere, or very interested in his or her request. For instance, a person might say, "If you don't mind, could we ...," "I know this will sound unreasonable, but would you ...," "I hope you don't think I'm being unreasonable, but would you ...," or "Of course I don't know anything about politics, but I think...." Persons who use disclaimers put the other person in an awkward position. The respondent does not know how he or she is to respond to the request or the information. If one acts upon it, he or she may be told later that the speaker said that it was unimportant or that one was being unreasonable; if the listener fail to act upon it, the speaker might say that he or she had made a request. Disclaimers confuse communication between two people and weaken the messages we send to others.

Verbal fillers and *vocal fluencies* frequently occur in our communication with others. Verbal fillers are those words or phrases that we use to fill in silences such as "like," "right," "okay," "well," and "you know." Vocal fluencies include uncodified sounds like "mmh," "ahh," and "eh" which are used for the same purpose. We are sometimes afraid of allowing a silence to occur when we are talking, so that we fill in the blanks with fillers or fluencies. Hirschman (1975) found that when women talk to men in two-person interactions, women use more fillers than do men. Women used fewest fillers when they were engaged in conversations with other women, although even here they used more fillers than did males in same-sex pairs.

Let us summarize the substantive language differences between women and men. First, they make different lexical choices or use different vocabularies. Women tend to use more formal terms, while men use more colloquial forms. Men use more hostile words, profanity, and expletives. Women engage in more hypercorrection than men. Women use more intensifying modifiers than do men, as well as more verbal fillers. In general, women appear to be more precise, more proper, and more polite than men. Although men and women exhibit substantive language differences, we may be perceiving far greater differences than those which actually occur. Our usage of language is constantly in flux, and men and women appear to be using more similar forms; at the same time, our perceptions of those forms tend to be somewhat outdated and stereotypical. Thus, our perceptions of language differences do not appear to be keeping pace with actual practice.

Substantive Differences Merging into Structural Differences

When we discuss structural differences in conversations, we are referring to a number of different components. Zimmerman and West (1975), for example, thought that the basic structure in a conversation must include the assumptions that usually one person speaks at a time and that generally people alternate as speaker and listener. We can thus discuss conversations from the point of view of "taking turns": how many turns each person took, how long each one's turn lasted, how willing each individual was to allow another to have a turn, and how each was able to secure his or her turn.

The notion of turns and taking turns is neither complex nor difficult to understand. At a noisy dinner table it is not unusual for children as young as two or three to tell others to be quiet because it is their turn. One of our children remarked to his garrulous grandmother that she had taken two turns when she had spoken and now was required to listen to him for two turns before she could again proceed. Although the notion of dividing conversations into turns is elementary, it is very useful.

When we examine taking turns in conversations, we find that all people do not take the same number of turns, that some tend to take far longer turns than others, that people challenge each other for turns, and that some people have definite ideas about who has the right to take a turn. Turns alternate very quickly. Anyone who has been associated with the theatre, radio, or television knows that silences generally do not occur after one person has spoken and before the next person begins to speak. When we are engaged in a conversation, we are typically ready to speak the moment the other person stops. Speakers generally provide us with transition cues which indicate that they are about to conclude their message and we can begin ours. Sometimes those cues are not present, however, or we do not notice them, so that two people are speaking at once, or no one is speaking.

When we examine language differences between women and men, we find that some variations are easily categorized as substantive differences while others are as readily classified as structural differences. At the same time, some differences appear to fall between these two categories. Substantive differences appear to merge into structural differences. For example, when sex differences are found on questioning-asking, are we considering structural or substantive differences? The substance of a comment is changed if it is phrased as a question rather than as a declarative statement; but the structure of the interaction is also affected as it calls for a comment from the other communicator. In this section ... we will consider a number of such sex differences in communication, including compound requests, tag questions, the use of questions, the final word, and the control of the topic of conversation.

Compound Requests

When we make a request of another person, we may do so in a direct manner or we may add qualifiers and other terms to soften the request. If you wish to have someone come closer to you, you may simply say, "Come here." On the other hand, you may add, "Please come here," or "Would you please come here," or "If you don't mind, would you please come here." In each case, you are adding words and phrases which soften the request. If you use the command, "Come here," you are making a direct request or giving a direct order; if you use any of the other longer forms, you are making a *compound request*.

What are the effects of compound requests? They tend to sound more polite and less demanding than direct requests. At the same time, they sound tentative. If you ask someone to behave in a certain way, "If you do not mind," "If you would," or "If it would not inconvenience you," you appear to be asking them a question in which a choice is possible, rather than making a request of some action that you wish to have accomplished. Propriety and politeness are acquired at the expense of being misunderstood or not achieving your goal.

Compound requests are viewed as less assertive than direct requests or orders, and they are viewed as feminine linguistic forms (Newcombe & Arnkoff, 1979). Apparently women use compound requests more frequently than do men (Thorne & Henley, 1975; Zimmerman & West, 1975). Women are more likely to ask others to do things for them with more words than their male counterparts would use. Though women may be viewed as more polite in their requests, they may find that they do not always obtain the action or response which they are seeking.

Tag Questions

Tag questions occur when we make a declarative statement, then follow it with a question relating to the same statement. For example, "It's really hot in here, isn't it?" "This is a good movie, don't you think?" and "They are all going out to dinner, aren't they?" are all tag questions. We sometimes use tag questions when we are not sure of information. If someone has told you something that you did not hear completely, or if you have reason to believe that a situation has changed, you might inquire, "You're going to attend U.S.C. this fall, aren't you?" We also use tag questions when we are trying to elicit information from another person, when we are attempting to obtain an answer to a question, or when we are trying to strike up a conversation. We might ask, "Texas is really lovely at this time of the year, isn't it?" "The game between Michigan State and Iowa was interesting, wasn't it?" or "This party is pretty dull, don't you think?" Finally, we use tag questions when we are attempting to persuade someone to accept or share a belief which we hold. You might suggest to your spouse, "Playing cards with the Millers tonight sounds like fun, doesn't it?" You might ask one of your parents, "The tuition at Georgetown is really expensive compared to Princeton, where I want to go, isn't it?" To a friend you might say, "I can borrow your brown suit for my job interview tomorrow, can't I?"

Tag questions are clearly less assertive than declarative statements; moreover, tag questions are viewed as being part of the female's linguistic repertoire rather than the male's language usage (Newcombe & Arnkoff, 1979). Early research in this area indicates that women make more frequent use of tag questions than do men (Zimmerman & West, 1975). In actual communication situations, women use twice as many tag questions as do men. In mixed sex groups, women use three times as many tag questions as men. Women in mixed sex groups also used three times as many tag questions as women in all-female groups (McMillan, Clifton, McGrath, & Gale, 1977).

Men in a professional meeting used far more tag questions than did the women who were in attendance. The context in which such questions are used should be considered in order to determine whether they are more likely to be used by men or by women. Tag questions do not necessarily indicate condescension; they may indicate simple requests, be used to forestall opposition to the speaker's statement, or function as requests for agreement or confirmation (Dubois & Crouch, 1975). Thorne (1981) also views tag questions as a contextual variable. She suggests that women may use tag questions in conversations with men in order to draw men out. Men are somewhat uncommunicative so that women may feel obligated to do the "embroidery" or "dirty work" in conversations. In other words, tag questions may not be a sign of uncertainty, but rather may indicate an interest in continuing a conversation. Women may ask tag questions in order to engage the other person in talking to them and give them an opportunity to look at the other person, listen actively, and contribute feedback.

A recent examination of tag questions yielded some disturbing results. In this investigation, tag questions were detrimental only when they were used by women. In general, women who used certain devices, including tag questions and disclaimers, were perceived to have little knowledge, little intelligence, and little influence. The same negative effect was not produced by men who used tag questions and disclaimers (Bradley, 1981). This study implies that the linguistic devices which women have traditionally used may not be the significant elements in the devaluation of women's language; rather, the lower status of the women may be the relevant factor. Women who use tag questions are underestimated because of their biological sex rather than because of their linguistic style.

Tag questions may place the speaker in a subservient position or they may be functional in a conversation. Sometimes women appear to use tag questions to demonstrate concern for another person, and not because they perceive themselves as subservient. Nonetheless, others may perceive them to be subservient, even though this is not their intent.

Another linguistic style which is sometimes an appropriate, effective substitute for the tag question is the statement followed by a question relating to the other person's perceptions. Instead of using the tag question, "The University of Kansas really has a great number of courses in interpersonal communication, doesn't it?" a person may say, "The University of Kansas really has a great number of courses in interpersonal communication. Were you aware of that?" Instead of stating, "This is delicious lasagna, isn't it?" you might assert, "I think this lasagna is delicious. What's your opinion?" In each case, you clarify your own perceptions and still invite the opinion of the other person. At the same time, you are not compromising your own point of view; in other words, your perception of the university or of food may be different from that of your partners. The use of the statement followed by a question may be considered a useful addition to your behavioral repertoire. It is especially helpful when you are actually using tag questions to express your own opinions or feelings.

Questioning

Do women or men ask each other more questions? Sometimes men ask women more questions than women ask men. For instance, in a study of interaction among male-male dyads and female-female dyads, a greater proportion of the women's comments consisted of answers to questions than did the men's comments (Rosenfeld, 1966). In an analysis of the conversations of three middle-class couples between the ages of twenty-five and thirty-five, the women used three times more questions than did the men (Fishman, 1978). Thus, it is not clear which sex asks the other more questions.

Perhaps more useful than merely trying to determine whether questions are asked more frequently by one sex than the other is consideration of the rationale for asking questions. Eakins and Eakins (1978) state that asking questions and interrogating people are associated with behavior of the superior, while acquiescing or replying is often considered to be the behavior of a subordinate. We know that sharing personal information about ourselves, self-disclosure, which was discussed in Chapter 8, can be perceived as the loss of a resource, when viewed negatively.

In other words, when we tell others about ourselves, we are providing them with information which they can use.... Women tend to provide more information about themselves than do men. The idea that women disclose more than men is related to the fact that they are asked more questions.

In those instances in which we determine that men ask more questions, we may hypothesize that this is done to gain information, and in a sense, to acquire power. On the other hand, men may be asking questions because they are interested in the other person. Similarly, either consciously or subconsciously women may answer questions in order to demonstrate subservience, or they may reply to questions because they enjoy interacting with others. Question asking and answering can be part of a power struggle in conversational interaction, or it may be a functional method of communicating, as in the interviewing process.

How can we explain the large number of questions women ask in established relationships compared to men? Fishman (1978) theorizes that women ask questions in order to elicit verbal responses from men. Frequently women preface their comments with phrases such as "Do you know what?" in order to gain a response from men. In these instances, they may be attempting to gain a "What?" or similar response which serves, in effect, as permission to speak.

The inconsistent findings on questioning and the alternative explanations for these differences disallow clear prescriptions regarding the use of questions in interactions. Nonetheless, to the extent that differences occur between men and women, we need to be cautious about behaving in traditional, stereotyped ways. If you are a woman, consider the questions you are asked before responding freely, then try to determine the purpose of prefacing comments with a question. If you are a man, consider the appropriateness of the questions which you would like to ask, and your own sensitivity in responding to the questions asked of you.

Control of the Topic

In *Through the Looking Glass,* this conversation between Alice and Humpty Dumpty occurs:

> "I don't know what you mean by 'glory'," Alice said.
>
> Humpty Dumpty smiled contemptuously. "Of course you don't—till I tell you. I meant there's a nice knockdown argument for you!"
>
> "But 'glory' doesn't mean 'a nice knockdown argument'," Alice objected.
>
> "When I use a word," Humpty Dumpty said, in a rather scornful tone, "it means just what I choose it to mean—neither more nor less."
>
> "The question is," said Alice, "whether you can make words mean so many different things."
>
> "The question is," said Humpty Dumpty, "which is to be master—that's all" [Carroll, 1965].

Although Humpty Dumpty was referring to the definition of words, his point is useful as we consider topic selection in conversations. Thorne (1981) asserts that the real power in controlling the topic of a conversation is the power to define reality.

Male–male, female–female, and male–female dyads have been investigated to determine patterns of topic change. Males, in male–female conversations, appear to assert strongly their claim to control topics (Zimmerman & West, 1975; Fishman, 1977, 1978). Male–female dyads in developing relationships do not talk as long about a topic as do two people of the same sex. In addition, male–female dyads use different strategies to change the topic. They tend to use more abrupt and direct methods, which may indicate that they are attempting to avoid over-commitment. Men, in male–male dyads, tend to use more indirect and gradual methods of topic change, that is, procedures which could be associated with a relational control process. Men may wish to avoid confronting the issue of who is to control the change of topics within conversation in male–male dyads (Ayres, 1980).

Associated with topic changes are the topics to which the conversation is changed. Four-, 8-, and 12-year-old males make more references to sports and specific locations while females of the same ages make more references to school, items they wish for, their needs, and their identity (Haas, 1981). Kelly, Wildman, and Ural (1982) contend that the use of male stereotypical topics may inhibit females from participating in conversations. Thus, both the content and the structure of the interaction encourage male control of the conversation.

Topic control is accomplished in a variety of ways. Among the more common are minimal responses to the other person's comment, silence, and interruptions. Delayed responses are also used to bring a topic to its conclusion, and if a theme is repeated too aggressively, you may decide to stop communicating with the other person: Walk away, say nothing, or look away from the other individual. In any event, keep in mind that in order for another person to control the topic, you must be willing to "relinquish the floor." The other person cannot control the subject of conversation unless you allow it to occur.

We can now summarize the material in this section on substantive differences merging into structural differences. Women make more compound requests than do men. Women tend to use more tag questions than men; although in some contexts, men tend to use this construction to a greater extent. Both women and men ask questions, but they appear to do so for different reasons. Males control the topics of conversations in male–female dyads, and may use abrupt and direct methods to do so. In male–male dyads, men use less abrupt and direct strategies to change the topic.

These linguistic forms tend to weaken or minimize women's statements, but they do not lessen or impair men's statements. At the same time, many of these forms serve necessary functions in the management of conversations. For instance, tag questions result in a woman being viewed as less knowledgable and less influential; however, tag questions may encourage another communicator to continue a conversation. When men use tag questions, they are not perceived as lacking in knowledge or influence. More than in the past, men and women may be using these linguistic forms in a similar way. Nevertheless, women are provided with negative sanctions when they use these forms, but men are not.

Structural Differences

We have considered substantive differences and the hybrid category of substantive distinctions merging into structural differences. In this section of the chapter, we will consider those language differences between men and women which appear to be purely structural. These include who dominates or talks more in a conversation, who interrupts, who overlaps, and how silence is used in conversational interactions.

Talk Time

Who talks more, men or women? If you ask people on the street their opinion on this question, you are more likely to receive consistently incorrect responses to this than to any other question discussed in this book. One of the most popular myths surrounding male/female communication is the notion that women talk more than men. In fact, men talk more than women (Eakins & Eakins, 1976; Wood, 1966; Swacker, 1975). In a summary of the research in this area, Thorne (1981) stated that most studies demonstrate that men either talk more than women, or there are no differences between the amount of talking men and women do. She points out that no studies have demonstrated that women talk more than men. Higher status women tend to talk more than lower status women. Boys are involved in more interactions than are girls. Male students talk more than female students, particularly when the teacher is female. Thorne's summary demonstrates that in a variety of contexts, and at various ages, men talk more than women.

An interesting study of parental interaction shows similiar findings. This study investigated mothers and fathers talking with their children. The parents and their children were placed in a room and told to play with each other. At first they were told to simply interact, but after a period of time a complex toy was introduced to the situation and the parents were told to explain it to the child. Women tended to adjust their speech when talking to the children, reducing their sentence length, making their ideas less complex, including more redundancy, and offering more pauses. When the parents were free to interact with the children, before the toy was introduced, the mothers and fathers talked about the same amount. When the toy was added to the situation, the women allowed the men to talk far more. The men were treated as "experts," even though they had no more information about the toy than did the women (Golinkoff & Ames, 1979). This study implies that one of the reasons that men may be allowed to talk more than women is that they are perceived as more knowledgeable, more competent, or in some way more credible.

Interruptions

Interruptions occur when the person who is listening begins to speak before the last word that could suggest the end of the speaker's statement, question, or comment. For instance, if one person were to state, "I can't wait to tell you what my mother said," and the second person began his or her comment, "Did you talk to Professor Fisher?" on the third word of the first person's statement, "wait," we would call the second person's comment an interruption.

Why do people interrupt each other? Some persons may interrupt because they are unaware of the implicit conversational rules which imply that one person waits for the other to complete expressing his or her thought before beginning to respond. Few people, however, are really unaware of this rule. More often, individuals interrupt because they are enthusiastic about something they have to share and are impatient about "waiting their turn," because they believe that what they have to offer is more important than the first person's message, or because they feel that they are personally more important than the other speaker.

Men interrupt others more than women do, and women are more frequently interrupted by others than men are interrupted by others (Zimmerman & West, 1975; Thorne & Henley, 1975; Baird, 1976; Kramer, 1974; Eakins and Eakins, 1978). Women appear to be less obtrusive and less forceful than men in conversational dominance (Frost & Wilmot, 1978; McMillan, Clifton, McGrath, & Gale, 1977). The pattern of interruptions between men and women might be anticipated, in view of our discussion of topic control. We noted that topic control occurs, to some extent, because people interrupt the speaker. We will see that this pattern is also consistent with overlaps which we will discuss in the next section.

The unequal distribution of interruptions between women and men should immediately cause us to be suspicious. Interruptions are generally perceived as attempts at conversational dominance, since they minimize the communicative role of the person being interrupted (Markel, Long, & Saine, 1976). Whether or not the interruptor is aware of this behavior, this individual is asserting relational dominance over the other person. Less pejoratively, interruptions are sometimes perceived as methods of controlling the interaction. In the same way that people control the topic of a conversation by "breaking in," they maintain control over the structure of the conversation by interrupting. Brandt (1980) demonstrated that the frequency of interruption is often correlated with a person's control over the direction of the conversation. In either case, interruptions serve to manage the interaction.

The same kinds of suggestions that were offered at the end of the section on topic changes apply here. If you are a person who is regularly interrupted, you should consider possible options. You can continue to talk even after you have been interrupted, you can ignore the interruption, or you can increase your volume. You can use the same tactics as the person who has interrupted you and allow him or her to talk but begin a new thought in the middle of his or her discourse. You can decide that you will not communicate with someone who continually interrupts you, say nothing, look away, or walk away from the other person. You can stop in order for the other person to present his or her message, then continue from the same point that you were interrupted, without responding to the interruption. You can describe to the other individual, in a non-evaluative manner what has occurred: "You have interrupted me three times in the last five minutes." Interruptions involve two people: the person who is doing the interrupting and the person whose statement or presentation is being interrupted. You are susceptible to being interrupted by others if you choose, or can indicate clearly that you will not be regularly interrupted by them if you find the practice dissatisfying to you. At the same time, you need to understand that your behavior will have consequences. To the extent that your communicative behavior is altered, the relationship between yourself and the other communicator is changed.

Overlaps

Overlaps occur when the individual who is listening makes a statement before the other person has finished speaking, but about the same time as the speaker's last word is uttered, or a word which could be perceived as his or her last word. For example, if someone states, "I would like to go to the movie at the Varsity tonight," and the second person responds, "Yes, me, too!" while the first person is verbalizing "tonight," the respondent's act would be considered an overlap.

Overlaps may occur for the same reason that interruptions occur: the second person believes what she or he has to add is more important than the message of the first person, or she or he is very enthusiastic about talking. Overlaps can be more easily justified than can interruptions. Often, the second speaker senses that the first speaker has about finished expressing his or her thought, and has simply begun talking a moment too soon. On the other hand, the person who overlaps may be attempting to shorten the first person's statement or to "gain the floor." Dominance and control are also possible reasons why people overlap each other. Whatever the rationale, men overlap women more than women overlap men (Zimmerman & West, 1975).

Silence

A final area in which sex differences occur is in the use of silences. Zimmerman and West (1975) examined the use of silence in female–female, male–male, and male–female dyads. They found that females in female–male conversations were silent more than any other person in the various combinations. In male–male and female–female conversations, the silences were scattered among the comments in a relatively equal manner. These researchers explained their findings by noting that most often the females who fell silent in the female–male dyads did so after one of three occurrences: a delayed minimal response by the male, an overlap by the male, or an interruption by the male. In these instances the female may have been uncertain about her partner's reaction to her comment or about the other person's feeling concerning the conversation. The less-than-positive response from the male partner appeared to affect the female's approval or enthusiasm about communicating.

Let us summarize these research findings. Men and persons of high status talk more than do women and low status persons. Men interrupt others more than women do, and women are the victims of more interruptions than are men. Men overlap women more than women overlap men. Women fall silent more often when they are interacting with men than do women or men in same-sex dyads, or than men do in mixed-sex dyads. The communicative patterns in this area imply that women are less competitive and aggressive in interactions; men appear to compete and win. Men talk, interrupt, and overlap more frequently, while women respond with silence. . . .

Taking Corrective Action

We have determined in this chapter that far more restrictions and limitations are placed on women than on men in language usage, but men, too, have distinct ways of talking. One author writes that women are cautious about their language usage today because of the hold-overs from previous times (Haas, 1979). In other words, the role modeling provided by mothers and other groups or individuals influences our contemporary behavior to some extent. Differing language systems are detrimental to both men and women since they limit their behavioral options. In addition, the divergent language systems are conducive to misunderstandings between women and men.

Should women adopt a male style? Some authors have suggested that women use male structures (Lakoff, 1975). Specific research findings support this suggestion. Wright and Hosman (1983) determined that male or female witnesses in a courtroom setting were both perceived as more credible when they used a lower number of hedges. Stake and Stake (1979) posited that in women, confidence is followed by assertiveness. They imply that assertiveness is a characteristic which women should adopt.

All of the research does not encourage women to adopt male structures. While Wright and Hosman's investigation recommended the use of fewer hedges by both women and men, they also found that women were perceived to be more attractive when they used numerous intensifiers, a traditional form for women.

Another study shows that women who appear to be confident in small group interaction exert influence, but they are not viewed as positively as are confident men (Bradley, 1980). In other words, even when women adopt male strategies and behaviors, they may not succeed. Kramer (1978) notes that women find themselves in a paradoxical situation when they identify men as their oppressors but use a rhetoric which reflects a male-oriented culture that is being challenged. In other words, oppression is viewed as undesirable by women, yet they use the oppressive techniques on others to achieve their goals. Adopting a male style, then, does not appear to be the answer, since it does not necessarily assist women to attain their goals, and indeed tends to call into question the basic assumptions and values of women.

We observed in the last section that the female style has positive attributes. Kramer (1978) determined that many female language characteristics are rated as close to ideal speech. Baird and Bradley (1979) concluded that female managers were perceived as more effective than male managers. McMillan, Clifton, McGrath, & Gale (1977) questioned whether the qualities characterizing female speech are actually perceived negatively by listeners. Mulac and Lundell (1980) demonstrated that female speakers are rated as more pleasant and more attractive in aesthetic quality than males.

Bradac, Hemphill, and Tardy (1981) examined the effects of "powerful" and "powerless" speech on the attribution of blame to a defendant and a plaintiff in an artificial courtroom situation. The "powerless" style was comparable to the female style as it included hedges, intensifiers, polite forms, and hesitation forms. The "powerful" style included short or one-word replies. In one instance, respondents attributed greater fault to the individual who used the "powerful" style. These results imply that the "powerless" female style may be advantageous in eliciting less attribution of blame.

Though feminine linguistic style is not without positive attributes, it is more than questionable to recommend it as the style that should be adopted by all speakers. Earlier in this chapter, we determined that the feminine style may result in being devalued, may be less effective, and that it encourages dominance by others. The female style of communication has both positive *and* negative characteristics, so that it cannot be indiscriminatingly recommended. Men in positions of authority and power who acquired and maintained their status through "man talk" would tend to resist change. Other men may be discouraged from adopting a female style because of ridicule and denigration by others in the culture. Finally, persons who have strong instrumental inclinations, including women, would find that this style of communication was not suitable to their personality and individual style.

Women and men who wish to communicate with each other with minimal misunderstanding and with maximal effectiveness should consider a wide language repertoire, one which incorporated elements of the masculine and the feminine styles that have been outlined in this chapter. We should freely select from a variety of behaviors the appropriate cues for the situation. A woman who is dealing with a man who is attempting to control a conversation by interruptions, overlaps, and delayed responses might adopt a similar aggressive stance rather than submit to domination. A man conversing with a woman who is unusually silent might consider listening more than talking. Adopting a flexible stance and moving in and out of traditionally masculine and feminine behaviors is not a solution that will meet with immediate success. Men who behave in ways which are associated with stereotypical females and women who behave in a manner that is correlated with stereotypical males are still questionable characters in our culture. Nonetheless, this approach appears to hold the most promise for alteration of our language styles. To the extent that we can adapt new behaviors as necessary, we can eradicate the sexism which is harmful to all of us. Our language, as a symbol system, can move us from a social order in which discrimination is codified to a higher level of social organization in which distinctions between males and females are minimized.

References

Ayres, Joe. "Relationship Stages and Sex as Factors in Topic Dwell Time," *Western Journal of Speech Communication* 44 (1980): 253–260.

Baird, John E. "Sex Differences in Group Communication: A Review of Relevant Research," *The Quarterly Journal of Speech* 62 (1976): 179–192.

Baird, John E., and Patricia Hayes Bradley. "Styles of Management and Communication: A Comparative Study of Men and Women," *Communication Monographs* 46 (1979): 101–111.

Bradac, J. J, C. H. Tardy, and L. A Hosman. "Disclosure Styles and a Hint at Their Genesis," *Human Communication Research* 6 (1980): 228–238.

Bradley, Patricia Hayes. "The Folk-Linguistics of Women's Speech: An Empirical Examination," *Communication Monographs* 48 (1981): 73–90.

Bradley, Patricia Hayes. "Sex, Competence and Opinion Deviation: An Expectation States Approach," *Communication Monographs* 47 (1980): 105–110.

Brandt, D. R. "A Systematic Approach to the Measurement of Dominance in Human Face-to-Face Interaction," *Communication Quarterly* 28 (1980): 31–43.

Carroll, Lewis. *Through the Looking Glass.* New York: Random House, 1965.

Crosby, Faye, and Linda Nyquist. "The Female Register: An Empirical Study of Lakoff's Hypotheses," *Language in Society* 6 (1977): 313–322.

Dubois, Betty Lou, and Isabel Crouch. "The Question of Tag Questions in Women's Speech: They Don't Really Use More of Them, Do They?" *Language in Society* 4 (1975): 289–294.

Eakins, Barbara Westbrook, and R. Gene Eakins. *Sex Differences in Human Communication.* Boston, Mass.: Houghton Mifflin Co., 1978.

Eakins, Barbara, and Gene Eakins. "Verbal Turn-Taking and Exchanges in Faculty Dialogue," *Papers in Southwest English IV: Proceedings of the Conference on the Sociology of the Languages of American Women,* ed. Betty Lou Dubois and Isabel Crouch, San Antonio, Tex.: Trinity University, 1976, pp. 53–62.

Fishman, Pamela M. "Interaction: The Work Women Do," *Social Problems* 25 (1978): 397–406.

Fishman, Pamela M. "International Shitwork," *Heresies: A Feminist Publication on Art & Politics* 2 (May 1977): 99–101.

Frost, Joyce Hocker, and William W. Wilmot. *Interpersonal Conflict.* Dubuque, Iowa: William C. Brown, 1978.

Gilley, Hoyt M., and Collier Summers. "Sex Differences in the Use of Hostile Verbs," *Journal of Psychology* 76 (1970): 33–37.

Golinkoff, Roberta Michnick, and Gail Johnson Ames. "A Comparison of Father's Speech to Mother's Speech with their Young Children," *Child Development* 50 (1979): 28–32.

Graves, Richard L., and Gayle B. Price. "Sex Differences in Syntax and Usage in Oral and Written Language," *Research in the Teaching of English* 145 (May 1980): 147–153.

Haas, Adelaide. "Male and Female Spoken Language Differences: Stereotypes and Evidence," *Psychological Bulletin* 86 (1979): 616–626.

Haas, Adelaide. "Partner Influence on Sex-Associated Spoken Language of Children," *Sex Roles* 7 (1981): 225–234.

Haas, L. "Determinants of Role-Sharing Behavior: A Study of Egalitarian Couples," *Sex Roles* 8 (1982): 747–760.

Hewitt, John P., and Randall Stokes. "Disclaimers," *American Sociological Review* 40 (1975): 1–11.

Hirschman, Lynette. "Female–Male Differences in Conversational Interaction," abstracted in *Language and Sex: Difference and Dominance*, ed. Barrie Thorne and Nancy Henley. Rowley, Mass.: Newbury House, 1975, p. 249.

Jespersen, Otto. *Language: Its Nature, Development and Origin.* London: Allen and Unwin, 1922.

Kelly, Jeffrey A., Hal E. Wildman, and Jon K. Ureg. "A Behavioral Analysis of Gender and Sex Role Differences in Group Decision Making and Social Interactions," *Journal of Applied Social Psychology* 12 (1982): 112–127.

Key, Mary Ritchie, *Male/Female Language.* Metuchen, N.J.: The Scarecrow Press, 1975.

Kramer, Cheris R. "Women's Speech: Separate But Unequal?" *Quarterly Journal of Speech* 60 (1974): 14–24.

Kramer, Cheris, Barrie Thorne, and Nancy Henley. "Perspectives on Language and Communication," *Signs* 3 (1978): 638–651.

Lakoff, Robin. "You Are What You Say," *Ms.* 3 (1974): 63–67.

Markel, Norman N., Joseph, F. R. Long, and Thomas J. Saine. "Sex Effects in Conversational Interaction: Another Look at Male Dominance," *Human Communication Research* 2 (1976): 356–364.

McMillan, Julie R., A. Kay Clifton, Diane McGrath, and Wanda S. Gale. "Women's Language: Uncertainty or Interpersonal Sensitivity and Emotionality?" *Sex Roles* 3 (1977): 545–559.

Mulac, Anthony, and Luisa Lundell Torborg. "Differences in Perceptions Created by Syntactic-Semantic Productions of Male and Female Speakers," *Communication Monographs* 47 (1980): 111–118.

Newcombe, Nora, and Diane B. Arnkoff. "Effects of Speech Style and Sex of Speaker on Person Perception," *Journal of Personality and Social Psychology* 37 (1979): 1293–1303.

Rich, Elaine. "Sex-Related Differences in Colour Vocabulary," *Language and Speech* 20 (1977): 404–409.

Rosenfeld, Howard M. "Approval-Seeking and Approval-Inducing Functions of Verbal and Nonverbal Responses in the Dyad," *Journal of Personality and Social Psychology* 4 (1966): 597–605.

Sanders, Janet S., and William L. Robinson. "Talking and Not Talking about Sex: Male and Female Vocabularies," *Journal of Communication* 29 (1979): 22–30.

Simkins, Rinck. "Male and Female Sexual Vocabulary in Different Interpersonal Contexts," *The Journal of Sex Research* 18 (1982): 160–172.

Staley, Constance. "Male–Female Use of Expletives: A Heck of a Difference in Expectations," *Anthropological Linguistics* 20 (1978): 367–380.

Staley, Constance. "Sex Related Differences in the Style of Children's Language," *Journal of Psycholinguistic Research* 11 (1982): 141–152.

Stake, Jayne E., and Michael N. Stake. "Performance—Self-Esteem and Dominance in Mixed Sex Dyads," *Journal of Personality* 47 (1979): 23–26 and 71–84.

Swacker, Marjorie. "The Sex of the Speaker as a Sociolinguistic Variable," in *Language and Sex: Difference and Dominance*, ed. Barrie Thorne and Nancy Henley. Rowley, Mass.: Newbury House Publishers, 1975.

Thorne, Barrie. Public speech at Michigan State University, East Lansing, Michigan, 1981.

Thorne, Barrie, and Nancy Henley. "Difference and Dominance: An Overview of Language, Gender and Society," *Language and Sex: Difference and Dominance*. Rowley, Mass.: Newbury House Publishers, 1975, pp. 5–31.

Thorne, Barrie, and Nancy Henley. "Sex and Language Difference and Dominance," *Language in Society* 6 (1977): 110–113.

Wood, Marion M. "The Influence of Sex and Knowledge of Communication Effectiveness on Spontaneous Speech," *Word* 22 (1966): 117–137.

Wright, J. W., and L. A. Hosman. "Language Style and Sex Bias in the Courtroom: The Effects of Male and Female Use of Hedges and Intensifiers on Impression Information," *The Southern Speech Communication Journal* 48 (1983): 137–152.

Zimmerman, Don H., and Candace West. "Sex Roles, Interruptions and Silences in Conversation," in *Language and Sex: Difference and Dominance*, ed. Barrie Thorne and Nancy Henley. Rowley, Mass.: Newbury House Publishers, 1975.

Review Questions

1. According to Pearson, what "paradigm shift" has led to our current interest in gender and communication?
2. Describe the three kinds of differences Pearson identifies between the language of women and the language of men (substantive, structural, and hybrid).
3. Summarize what Pearson says about male/female vocabulary differences.
4. What is "hypercorrection"?
5. What male/female differences in turn-taking does Pearson describe?
6. What is a "compound request"? A "tag question"?
7. According to the research, who talks more, men or women?
8. Who interrupts more, men or women? Who gets interrupted more?
9. Does Pearson believe women should adopt a male communication style? Explain.

Probes

1. How do you respond to Judy Pearson's rationale for studying gender and communication? Do you agree that because of our "paradigm shift" it's a topic that needs study and discussion today? Or do you think that communication issues and problems are common to all humans and don't need to be narrowly treated as "female–male"?
2. Did you try the experiment about color vocabulary that Pearson suggests? If not, give it a try and see whether your findings support or contradict hers. How might you account for the difference?
3. I believe that there are fewer differences between women's and men's uses of profanity than Pearson suggests. That is, I believe that since 1970, females have, as she puts it, "increased their use of hostile language." What is your experience with this aspect of communication?
4. At several points in this reading (e.g., in the discussion of profanity and expletives) Pearson suggests that *actual* male–female communication differences are less important than our *perceptions* of those differences. For example, even when females use strong expletives, males still perceive their communication as weak. This same phenomenon appears to be true with tag questions. In your opinion, how significant is this part of the problem? Can this difference be changed? How?
5. Which of the substantive differences Pearson discusses has the most impact? Which does the most to weaken women's communication?
6. How do you generally interpret tag questions? Do you usually hear them as welcome efforts to continue the conversation or as signs of weakness and uncertainty?
7. To what extent do you think that a discussion like this one contributes to our sexual stereotypes? Is this effort helpful or harmful?

his reading is a chapter from a small book that's been widely read and even positively reviewed in at least one scholarly journal. The author, Deborah Tannen, was trained in linguistics, but the insights and skills she developed fit right into what I'd call interpersonal communication. As you'll notice, she has a keen ability to develop social science research results into clear and practical suggestions for effective communication.

Tannen begins by arguing that "male-female conversation is cross-cultural communication." At first I didn't agree with that claim, but after reading the chapter I became convinced that that's a very useful way to look at it.

The one technical term Tannen applies in this chapter is a real mouthful: *complementary schismogenesis.* This is communication theorist Gregory Bateson's term for a process by which people exhibit more and more extreme forms of the behaviors that trigger in the other person increasing manifestations of a destructive behavior. Bateson's daughter gives this example:

> The situation he depicted is something like the practical joke that can be played using a dual-control electric blanket. If you reverse the controls, the first attempt by either person to make an adjustment will set off a cycle of worsening maladjustment—I am cold, I set the controls beside me higher, you get too hot and turn your controls down, so I get colder, and so on. The attempt to correct actually increases the error.*

One of Tannen's basic points is that differences in male-female communication style often create complementary schismogenesis. One style rubs the other one in such a wrong way that efforts to make things better end up making them worse. When this happens, the result is a negative spiral.

The notion of the *metamessage* is another key concept Tannen uses. As you probably remember, metamessages are messages about messages, indirect messages that tell someone how to take what's said. Tannen argues that some male-female communication problems are created by the different ways men and women listen for and respond to metamessages. Her examples from Jules Feiffer's play *Grown Ups* illustrate clearly what she means.

Tannen also analyzes difference in male-female communication by reflecting on what boys and girls learn from observing their parents. She reviews some of the results of research by anthropologists Daniel Maltz and Ruth Borker on boys' and girls' playing and talking patterns. One of Tannen's basic themes is that males typically have significantly different expectations about how much to "talk things out" than do females.

Listening patterns, says Tannen, also differ between women and men. Maltz and Borker report, for example, that males and females have characteristically different ways of showing that they're listening. Listening can also be complicated by different attitudes about what kind of content is important. Males typically emphasize details about politics, history, or how things work, while women include more details about relationships—tone of voice, timing, intonation, and wording.

Tannen concludes that becoming aware of the characteristics of male and female conversational style won't dissolve the differences, but it can make them easier to live

*Mary Catherine Bateson, *With a Daughter's Eye: A Memoir of Margaret Mead and Gregory Bateson* (New York: William Morrow, 1984), quoted in Tannen, pp. 121–122.

with. As she says, "You may not always correctly interpret your partner's intentions, but you will know that if you get a negative impression, it may not be what was intended—and neither are your responses unfounded."

I am not comfortable with all of the generalizations that Tannen seems to make about males and females. I notice some "typically female" behaviors in my own communication, for example, and some "typically male" ones in my attorney-wife Kris's. But I think that the concept of complementary schismogenesis is a powerful one, and I like what Tannen says about communication always balancing conflicting needs for involvement and independence. I also believe that it can be helpful to view male-female contact as a kind of intercultural communication, and I think that the overall thrust of Tannen's analysis and advice is very helpful.

Talk in the Intimate Relationship: His and Hers

Deborah Tannen

Male-female conversation is cross-cultural communication.[1] Culture is simply a network of habits and patterns gleaned from past experience, and women and men have different past experiences. From the time they're born, they're treated differently, talked to differently, and talk differently as a result. Boys and girls grow up in different worlds, even if they grow up in the same house. And as adults they travel in different worlds, reinforcing patterns established in childhood. These cultural differences include different expectations about the role of talk in relationships and how it fulfills that role.

{Earlier I discussed} how complementary schismogenesis—a mutually aggravating spiral—can intensify style differences in ongoing relationships. To see how male-female differences in conversational style can cause misunderstandings that lead to complementary schismogenesis in close relationships, let's start by seeing what some of those differences are.

He Said/She Said: His and Her Conversational Styles

Everyone knows that as a relationship becomes long-term, its terms change. But women and men often differ in how they expect them to change. Many women feel, "After all this time, you should know what I want without my telling you."

Excerpt from pp. 125–144 of *That's Not What I Meant!* by Deborah Tannen, Ph.D. Copyright © 1986 by Deborah Tannen, Ph.D. By permission of William Morrow and Company, Inc.

Many men feel, "After all this time, we should be able to tell each other what we want."

These incongruent expectations capture one of the key differences between men and women. Communication is always a matter of balancing conflicting needs for involvement and independence. Though everyone has both these needs, women often have a relatively greater need for involvement, and men a relatively greater need for independence. Being understood without saying what you mean gives a payoff in involvement, and that is why women value it so highly.

If you want to be understood without saying what you mean explicitly in words, you must convey meaning somewhere else—in how words are spoken, or by metamessages. Thus it stands to reason that women are often more attuned than men to the metamessages of talk. When women surmise meaning in this way, it seems mysterious to men, who call it "women's intuition" (if they think it's right) or "reading things in" (if they think it's wrong). Indeed, it could be wrong, since metamessages are not on record. And even if it is right, there is still the question of scale: How significant are the metamessages that are there?

Metamessages are a form of indirectness. Women are more likely to be indirect, and to try to reach agreement by negotiation. Another way to understand this preference is that negotiation allows a display of solidarity, which women prefer to the display of power. Unfortunately, power and solidarity are bought with the same currency: Ways of talking intended to create solidarity have the simultaneous effect of framing power differences. When they think they're being nice, women often end up appearing deferential and unsure of themselves or of what they want.

When styles differ, misunderstandings are always rife. As their differing styles create misunderstandings, women and men try to clear them up by talking things out. These pitfalls are compounded in talks between men and women because they have different ways of going about talking things out, and different assumptions about the significance of going about it.

The rest of this chapter illustrates these differences, explains their origins in children's patterns of play, and shows the effects when women and men talk to each other in the context of intimate relationships in our culture.

Women Listen for Metamessages

Sylvia and Harry celebrated their fiftieth wedding anniversary at a mountain resort. Some of the guests were at the resort for the whole weekend, others just for the evening of the celebration: a cocktail party followed by a sitdown dinner. The manager of the dining room approached Sylvia during dinner. "Since there's so much food tonight," he said "and the hotel prepared a fancy dessert and everyone already ate at the cocktail party anyway, how about cutting and serving the anniversary cake at lunch tomorrow?" Sylvia asked the advice of the others at her table. All the men agreed: "Sure, that makes sense. Save the cake for tomorrow." All the women disagreed: "No, the party is tonight. Serve the cake tonight." The men were focusing on the message: the cake as food. The women were thinking of the metamessage: Serving a special cake frames an occasion as a celebration.

Why are women more attuned to metamessages? Because they are more focused on involvement, that is, on relationships among people, and it is through metamessages that relationships among people are established and maintained. If you want to take the temperature and check the vital signs of a relationship, the barometers to check are its metamessages: what is said and how.

Everyone can see these signals, but whether or not we pay attention to them is another matter—a matter of being sensitized. Once you are sensitized, you can't roll your antennae back in; they're stuck in the extended position.

When interpreting meaning, it is possible to pick up signals that weren't intentionally sent out, like an innocent flock of birds on a radar screen. The birds are there—and the signals women pick up are there—but they may not mean what the interpreter thinks they mean. For example, Maryellen looks at Larry and asks, "What's wrong?" because his brow is furrowed. Since he was only thinking about lunch, her expression of concern makes him feel under scrutiny.

The difference in focus on messages and metamessages can give men and women different points of view on almost any comment. Harriet complains to Morton, "Why don't you ask me how my day was?" He replies, "If you have something to tell me, tell me. Why do you have to be invited?" The reason is that she wants the metamessage of interest: evidence that he cares how her day was, regardless of whether or not she has something to tell.

A lot of trouble is caused between women and men by, of all things, pronouns. Women often feel hurt when their partners use "I" or "me" in a situation in which they would use "we" or "us." When Morton announces, "I think I'll go for a walk," Harriet feels specifically uninvited, though Morton later claims she would have been welcome to join him. She felt locked out by his use of "I" and his omission of an invitation: "Would you like to come?" Metamessages can be seen in what is not said as well as what is said.

It's difficult to straighten out such misunderstandings because each one feels convinced of the logic of his or her position and the illogic—or irresponsibility—of the other's. Harriet knows that she always asks Morton how his day was, and that she'd never announce, "I'm going for a walk," without inviting him to join her. If he talks differently to her, it must be that he feels differently. But Morton wouldn't feel unloved if Harriet didn't ask about his day, and he would feel free to ask, "Can I come along?," if she announced she was taking a walk. So he can't believe she is justified in feeling responses he knows he wouldn't have.

Messages and Metamessages in Talk Between . . . Grown Ups?

These processes are dramatized with chilling yet absurdly amusing authenticity in Jules Feiffer's play *Grown Ups*. To get a closer look at what happens when men and women focus on different levels of talk in talking things out, let's look at what happens in this play.

Jake criticizes Louise for not responding when their daughter, Edie, called her. His comment leads to a fight even though they're both aware that this one incident is not in itself important.

JAKE: Look, I don't care if it's important or not, when a kid calls its mother the mother should answer.
LOUISE: Now I'm a bad mother.
JAKE: I didn't say that.

LOUISE: It's in your stare.
JAKE: Is that another thing you know? My stare?

Louise ignores Jake's message—the question of whether or not she responded when Edie called—and goes for the metamessage: his implication that she's a bad mother, which Jake insistently disclaims. When Louise explains the signals she's reacting to, Jake not only discounts them but is angered at being held accountable not for what he said but for how he looked—his stare.

As the play goes on, Jake and Louise replay and intensify these patterns:

LOUISE: If I'm such a terrible mother, do you want a divorce?
JAKE: I do not think you're a terrible mother and no, thank you, I do not want a divorce. Why is it that whenever I bring up any difference between us you ask me if I want a divorce?

The more he denies any meaning beyond the message, the more she blows it up, the more adamantly he denies it, and so on:

JAKE: I have brought up one thing that you do with Edie that I don't think you notice that I have noticed for some time but which I have deliberately not brought up before because I had hoped you would notice it for yourself and stop doing it and also—frankly, baby, I have to say this—I knew if I brought it up we'd get into exactly the kind of circular argument we're in right now. And I wanted to avoid it. But I haven't and we're in it, so now, with your permission, I'd like to talk about it.
LOUISE: You don't see how that puts me down?
JAKE: What?
LOUISE: If you think I'm so stupid why do you go on living with me?
JAKE: *Dammit! Why can't anything ever be simple around here?!*

It can't be simple because Louise and Jake are responding to different levels of communication. As in Bateson's example of the dual-control electric blanket with crossed wires, each one intensifies the energy going to a different aspect of the problem. Jake tries to clarify his point by overelaborating it, which gives Louise further evidence that he's condescending to her, making it even less likely that she will address his point rather than his condescension.

What pushes Jake and Louise beyond anger to rage is their different perspectives on metamessages. His refusal to admit that his statements have implications and overtones denies her authority over her own feelings. Her attempts to interpret what he didn't say and put the metamessage into the message makes him feel she's putting words into his mouth—denying his authority over his own meaning.

The same thing happens when Louise tells Jake that he is being manipulated by Edie:

LOUISE: Why don't you ever make her come to see you? Why do you always go to her?
JAKE: You want me to play power games with a nine year old? I want her to know I'm interested in her. Someone around here has to show interest in her.
LOUISE: You love her more than I do.

JAKE: I didn't say that.

LOUISE: Yes, you did.

JAKE: You don't know how to listen. You have never learned how to listen. It's as if listening to you is a foreign language.

Again, Louise responds to his implication—this time, that he loves Edie more because he runs when she calls. And yet again, Jake cries literal meaning, denying he meant any more than he said.

Throughout their argument, the point to Louise is her feelings—that Jake makes her feel put down—but to him the point is her actions—that she doesn't always respond when Edie calls:

LOUISE: You talk about what I do to Edie, what do you think you do to me?

JAKE: This is not the time to go into what we do to each other.

Since she will talk only about the metamessage, and he will talk only about the message, neither can get satisfaction from their talk, and they end up where they started—only angrier:

JAKE: That's not the point!

LOUISE: It's *my* point.

JAKE: It's hopeless!

LOUISE: Then get a divorce.

American conventional wisdom (and many of our parents and English teachers) tell us that meaning is conveyed by words, so men who tend to be literal about words are supported by conventional wisdom. They may not simply deny but actually miss the cues that are sent by how words are spoken. If they sense something about it, they may nonetheless discount what they sense. After all, it wasn't said. Sometimes that's a dodge—a plausible defense rather than a gut feeling. But sometimes it is a sincere conviction. Women are also likely to doubt the reality of what they sense. If they don't doubt it in their guts, they nonetheless may lack the arguments to support their position and thus are reduced to repeating, "You said it. You did so." Knowing that metamessages are a real and fundamental part of communication makes it easier to understand and justify what they feel.

"Talk to Me"

An article in a popular newspaper reports that one of the five most common complaints of wives about their husbands is "He doesn't listen to me anymore." Another is "He doesn't talk to me anymore." Political scientist Andrew Hacker noted that lack of communication, while high on women's lists of reasons for divorce, is much less often mentioned by men.[2] Since couples are parties to the same conversations, why are women more dissatisfied with them than men? Because what they expect is different, as well as what they see as the significance of talk itself.

First, let's consider the complaint "He doesn't talk to me."

The Strong Silent Type

One of the most common stereotypes of American men is the strong silent type.... The image of a silent father is common and is often the model for the lover or husband. But what attracts us can become flypaper to which we are unhappily stuck. Many women find the strong silent type to be a lure as a lover but a lug as a husband. Nancy Schoenberger begins a poem with the lines "It was your silence that hooked me,/ so like my father's." Adrienne Rich refers in a poem to the "husband who is frustratingly mute." Despite the initial attraction of such quintessentially male silence, it may begin to feel, to a woman in a long-term relationship, like a brick wall against which she is banging her head.

In addition to these images of male and female behavior—both the result and the cause of them—are differences in how women and men view the role of talk in relationships as well as how talk accomplishes its purpose. These differences have their roots in the settings in which men and women learn to have conversations: among their peers, growing up.

Growing Up Male and Female[3]

Children whose parents have foreign accents don't speak with accents. They learn to talk like their peers. Little girls and little boys learn how to have conversations as they learn how to pronounce words: from their playmates. Between the ages of five and fifteen, when children are learning to have conversations, they play mostly with friends of their own sex. So it's not surprising that they learn different ways of having and using conversations.

Anthropologists Daniel Maltz and Ruth Borker point out that boys and girls socialize differently. Little girls tend to play in small groups or, even more common, in pairs. Their social life usually centers around a best friend, and friendships are made, maintained, and broken by talk—especially "secrets." If a little girl tells her friend's secret to another little girl, she may find herself with a new best friend. The secrets themselves may or may not be important, but the fact of telling them is all-important. It's hard for newcomers to get into these tight groups, but anyone who is admitted is treated as an equal. Girls like to play cooperatively; if they can't cooperate, the group breaks up.

Little boys tend to play in larger groups, often outdoors, and they spend more time doing things than talking. It's easy for boys to get into the group, but not everyone is accepted as an equal. Once in the group, boys must jockey for their status in it. One of the most important ways they do this is through talk: verbal display such as telling stories and jokes, challenging and sidetracking the verbal displays of other boys, and withstanding other boys' challenges in order to maintain their own story—and status. Their talk is often competitive talk about who is best at what.

From Children to Grown Ups

Feiffer's play is ironically named *Grown Ups* because adult men and women struggling to communicate often sound like children: "You said so!" "I did not!"

The reason is that when they grow up, women and men keep the divergent attitudes and habits they learned as children—which they don't recognize as attitudes and habits but simply take for granted as ways of talking.

Women want their partners to be a new and improved version of a best friend. This gives them a soft spot for men who tell them secrets. As Jack Nicholson once advised a guy in a movie: "Tell her about your troubled childhood—that always gets 'em." Men expect to *do* things together and don't feel anything is missing if they don't have heart-to-heart talks all the time.

If they do have heart-to-heart talks, the meaning of those talks may be opposite for men and women. To many women, the relationship is working as long as they can talk things out. To many men, the relationship isn't working out if they have to keep working it over. If she keeps trying to get talks going to save the relationship, and he keeps trying to avoid them because he sees them as weakening it, then each one's efforts to preserve the relationship appear to the other as reckless endangerment.

How to Talk Things Out

If talks (of any kind) do get going, men's and women's ideas about how to conduct them may be very different. For example, Dora is feeling comfortable and close to Tom. She settles into a chair after dinner and begins to tell him about a problem at work. She expects him to ask questions to show he's interested; reassure her that he understands and that what she feels is normal; and return the intimacy by telling her a problem of his. Instead, Tom sidetracks her story, cracks jokes about it, questions her interpretation of the problem, and gives her advice about how to solve it and avoid such problems in the future.

All of these responses, natural to men, are unexpected to women, who interpret them in terms of their own habits—negatively. When Tom comments on side issues or cracks jokes, Dora thinks he doesn't care about what she's saying and isn't really listening. If he challenges her reading of what went on, she feels he is criticizing her and telling her she's crazy, when what she wants is to be reassured that she's not. If he tells her how to solve the problem, it makes her feel as if she's the patient to his doctor—a metamessage of condescension, echoing male one-upmanship compared to the female etiquette of equality. Because he doesn't volunteer information about his problems, she feels he's implying he doesn't have any.

Complementary schismogenesis can easily set in: His way of responding to her bid for intimacy makes her feel distant from him. She tries harder to regain intimacy the only way she knows how—by revealing more and more about herself. He tries harder by giving more insistent advice. The more problems she exposes, the more incompetent she feels, until they both see her as emotionally draining and problem-ridden. When his efforts to help aren't appreciated, he wonders why she asks for his advice if she doesn't want to take it.

"You're Not Listening to Me"

The other complaint wives make about their husbands is "He doesn't listen to me anymore." The wives may be right that their husbands aren't listening, if they don't value the telling of problems and secrets to establish rapport. But some of the time men feel unjustly accused: "I *was* listening." And some of the time, they're right. They were.

Whether or not someone is listening only that person can really know. But we judge whether or not we think others are listening by signals we can see—not only their verbal responses but also their eye contact and little listening noises like "mhm," "uh-huh," and "yeah." These listening noises give the go-ahead for talk; if they are misplaced along the track, they can quickly derail a chugging conversation.

Maltz and Borker also report that women and men have different ways of showing that they're listening. In the listening role, women make—and expect—more of these noises. So when men are listening to women, they are likely to make too few such noises for the women to feel the men are really listening. And when women are listening to men, making more such listening noises than men expect may give the impression they're impatient or exaggerating their show of interest.

Even worst, what women and men mean by such noises may be different. Does "uh-huh" or "mhm" mean you agree with what you heard, or just that you heard and you're following? Maltz and Borker contend that women tend to use these noises just to show they're listening and understanding. Men tend to use them to show they agree. So one reason women make more listening noises may be that women are listening more than men are agreeing with what they hear.

In addition to problems caused by differences in how many signals are given, there is bound to be trouble as a result of the difference in how they're used. If a woman cheers a man on in his talk by saying "mhm" and "yeah" and "uh-huh" all over the place, and it later comes out that she disagrees with what he said, he may feel she misled him (thereby reinforcing his stereotype of women as unreliable). Conversely, if a man sits through a woman's talk and follows all she says but doesn't agree, he's not going to shower her with "uh-huh's"—and she's going to think he's not paying attention.

Notice that the difference in how women and men use listening noises is in keeping with their focus in communication. Using the noises to show "I'm listening; go on" serves the relationship level of talk. Using them to show what one thinks of what is being said is a response to the content of talk. So men and women are being stylistically consistent in their interactive inconsistency.

"Why Don't You Talk About Something Interesting?"

Sometimes when men and women feel the other isn't paying attention, they're right. And this may be because their assumptions about what's interesting are different. Muriel gets bored when Daniel goes on and on about the stock market or the world soccer match. He gets bored when she goes on and on about details of her daily life or the lives of people he doesn't even know.

It seems natural to women to tell and hear about what happened today, who turned up at the bus stop, who called and what she said, not because these details are important in themselves but because the telling of them proves involvement—that you care about each other, that you have a best friend. Knowing you will be able to tell these things later makes you feel less alone as you go along the lone path of a day. And if you don't tell, you are sending a metamessage about the relationship—curtailing it, clipping its wings.

Since it is not natural to men to use talk in this way, they focus on the inherent insignificance of the details. What they find worth telling are facts about such topics as sports, politics, history, or how things work. Women often perceive the telling of facts as lecturing, which not only does not carry (for them) a metamessage of rapport, but carries instead a metamessage of condescension: I'm the teacher, you're the student. I'm knowledgeable, you're ignorant.

A *New Yorker* cartoon shows a scene—probably the source of a thousand cartoons (and a million conversations)—of a breakfast table, with a husband reading a newspaper while the wife is trying to talk to him. The husband says, "You want to talk? Get a newspaper. We'll talk about what's in the newspaper." It's funny because everyone knows that what's in the newspaper is not what the wife wants to talk about.

Conversations About Conversations

When women talk about what seems obviously interesting to them, their conversations often include reports of conversations. Tone of voice, timing, intonation, and wording are all re-created in the telling in order to explain—dramatize, really—the experience that is being reported. If men tell about an incident and give a brief summary instead of recreating what was said and how, the women often feel that the essence of the experience is being omitted. If the woman asks, "What exactly did he say?," and "How did he say it?," the man probably can't remember. If she continues to press him, he may feel as if he's being grilled.

All these different habits have repercussions when the man and the woman are talking about their relationship. He feels out of his element, even one down. She claims to recall exactly what he said, and what she said, and in what sequence, and she wants him to account for what he said. He can hardly account for it since he has forgotten exactly what was said—if not the whole conversation. She secretly suspects he's only pretending not to remember, and he secretly suspects that she's making up the details.

One woman reported such a problem as being a matter of her boyfriend's poor memory. It is unlikely, however, that his problem was poor memory in general. The question is what types of material each person remembers or forgets.

Frances was sitting at her kitchen table talking to Edward, when the toaster did something funny. Edward began to explain why it did it. Frances tried to pay attention, but very early in his explanation, she realized she was completely lost. She felt very stupid. And indications were that he thought so too.

Later that day they were taking a walk. He was telling her about a difficult situation in his office that involved a complex network of interrelationships among a large number of people. Suddenly he stopped and said, "I'm sure you can't keep track of all these people." "Of course I can," she said, and she retraced his story with all the characters in place, all the details right. He was genuinely impressed. She felt very smart.

How could Frances be both smart and stupid? Did she have a good memory or a bad one? Frances's and Edward's abilities to follow, remember, and recount depended on the subject—and paralleled her parents' abilities to follow and remember. Whenever Frances told her parents about people in her life, her mother could follow with no problem, but her father got lost as soon as she introduced a second character. "Now who was that?" he'd ask. "Your boss?" "No, my boss is Susan. This was my friend." Often he'd still be in the previous story. But whenever she told them about her work, it was her mother who would get lost as soon as she mentioned a second step: "That was your tech report?" "No, I handed my tech report in last month. This was a special project."

Frances's mother and father, like many other men and women, had honed their listening and remembering skills in different arenas. Their experience talking to other men and other women gave them practice in following different kinds of talk.

Knowing whether and how we are likely to report events later influences whether and how we pay attention when they happen. As women listen to and take part in conversations, knowing they may talk about them later makes them more likely to pay attention to exactly what is said and how. Since most men aren't in the habit of making such reports, they are less likely to pay much attention at the time. On the other hand, many women aren't in the habit of paying attention to scientific explanations and facts because they don't expect to have to perform in public by reciting them—just as those who aren't in the habit of entertaining others by telling jokes "can't" remember jokes they've heard, even though they listened carefully enough to enjoy them.

So women's conversations with their women friends keep them in training for talking about their relationships with men, but many men come to such conversations with no training at all—and an uncomfortable sense that this really isn't their event.

"What Do You Mean, My Dear?"

Most of us place enormous emphasis on the importance of a primary relationship. We regard the ability to maintain such relationships as a sign of mental health—our contemporary metaphor for being a good person.

Yet our expectations of such relationships are nearly—maybe in fact—impossible. When primary relationships are between women and men, male-female differences contribute to the impossibility. We expect partners to be both romantic interests and best friends. Though women and men may have fairly similar expectations for romantic interests, obscuring their differences when relationships begin, they have very different ideas about how to be friends, and these are the differences that mount over time.

In conversations between friends who are not lovers, small misunderstandings can be passed over or diffused by breaks in contact. But in the context of a primary relationship, differences can't be ignored, and the pressure cooker of continued contact keeps both people stewing in the juice of accumulated minor misunderstandings. And stylistic differences are sure to cause misunderstandings—not, ironically, in matters such as sharing values and interests or understanding each other's philosophies of life. These large and significant yet palpable issues can be talked about and agreed on. It is far harder to achieve congruence—and much more surprising and troubling that it is hard—in the simple day-to-day matters of the automatic rhythms and nuances of talk. Nothing in our backgrounds or in the media (the present-day counterpart to religion or grandparents' teachings) prepares us for this failure. If two people share so much in terms of point of view and basic values, how can they continually get into fights about insignificant matters?

If you find yourself in such a situation and you don't know about differences in conversational style, you assume something's wrong with your partner, or you for having chosen your partner. At best, if you are forward thinking and generous minded, you may absolve individuals and blame the relationship. But if you know about differences in conversational style, you can accept that there are differences in habits and assumptions about how to have conversation, show interest, be considerate, and so on. You may not always correctly interpret your partner's intentions, but you will know that if you get a negative impression, it may not be what was intended—and neither are your responses unfounded. If he says he really is interested even though he doesn't seem to be, maybe you should believe what he says and not what you sense.

Sometimes explaining assumptions can help. If a man starts to tell a woman what to do to solve her problem, she may say, "Thanks for the advice but I really don't want to be told what to do. I just want you to listen and say you understand." A man might want to explain, "If I challenge you, it's not to prove you wrong; it's just my way of paying attention to what you're telling me." Both may try either or both to modify their ways of talking and to try to accept what the other does. The important thing is to know that what seem like bad intentions may really be good intentions expressed in a different conversational style. We have to give up our conviction that, as Robin Lakoff put it, "Love means never having to say 'What do you mean?'"

Notes

1. I always feel uneasy when I talk about male/female differences. There are many for whom the suggestion that there are such differences constitutes ideological heresy, and there are others who maintain that even if such differences exist, it is best not to talk about them, because anything that bolsters the idea that women are different from men will be used to denigrate women. (The same can be said of research on racial, ethnic, and class differences.) I see this danger, and I also see the danger of generalizing, especially when not enough research has been done to test intuition and observation. There are always exceptions to general patterns, and describing the patterns seems to slight the individuals who are exceptions. (To such individuals I offer sincere apologies.) But I decided to go ahead and confront these issues because I have found that talking about male/female differences in this way evokes a very strong "aha" response: Many people exclaim that this description fits their experience and that seeing what they previously perceived as their individual problem in terms of a widespread pattern lifts from them a burden of pathology and isolation. Questions will doubtless remain about the generalizability of my observations and the cultural versus biological sources of differences. If the result is to spark questioning and observation by both researchers and individuals in their lives, it will be all to the good.
2. Hacker makes this point in "Divorce à la Mode," *The New York Review of Books,* May 3, 1979, p. 24.
3. Information in the section "Growing Up Male and Female" is based on Daniel N. Maltz and Ruth A. Borker, "A Cultural Approach to Male-Female Miscommunication," in John J. Gumperz, ed., *Language and Social Identity* (Cambridge, England: Cambridge University Press, 1982), pp. 196–216.

Review Questions

1. What's "complementary schismogenesis"? Give an example of it from your own communication experience.
2. What does Tannen mean when she says, "Communication is always a matter of balancing conflicting needs for involvement and independence"?
3. How would you describe the metamessages that Tannen says women typically listen for?
4. What does Tannen say are the most important patterns little girls learn that are different from what's learned by little boys?
5. Tannen gives an example of the communication between Frances and Edward in which Frances seems to be "both smart and stupid." What point is she making with this example?
6. According to this reading, what is the primary *benefit* of viewing male-female communication as a kind of intercultural contact?

Probes

1. Draw a spiral with three or four complete turns in it. Review what Tannen says about the spiral called "complementary schismogenesis," and label the "3 o'clock," "6 o'clock," "9 o'clock," and "12 o'clock" spots on one of the turns of the spiral. (You might want to refer to the example Tannen quotes from the play *Grown Ups.* on pages 379–381. So, for example, "Is that another thing you know? My stare?" from page 380 might go at the "6 o'clock" spot on your spiral.) Continue labeling the quadrants of one more turn. This process will produce a detailed model of one example of this complex interpersonal phenomenon.
2. Do you believe that women typically listen for metamessages and men typically don't, *or* that the two sexes listen for different kinds of metamessage? Explain.
3. Identify two specific aspects of your own communication style that you inherited—probably unconsciously—from your immediate family (parents or siblings). What does it do to this part of your communication style to notice that you inherited it?
4. To what degree does Tannen's discussion of male-female listening behaviors accurately describe your listening? What does this tell you about your own communication style?
5. In the final paragraphs, Tannen suggests that sometimes "explaining assumptions" can help. From your own experience, what are the advantages and disadvantages of explaining assumptions to someone?

Chapter 13

Communicating Across Cultures

I t's possible to view this chapter on intercultural communication as something that's "tacked on" to a book that doesn't really deal with this topic. But I don't think that's accurate. I believe there's a strong link between interpersonal and intercultural communication. For one thing, intercultural communication situations confront all of us on an almost daily basis, regardless of whether we are at home or in some other country, state, city, or neighborhood. That's because, as the author of this next essay points out, intercultural communication is not defined by national boundaries. As we saw in Chapter 12, male-female communication can usefully be viewed as intercultural. In addition, communication between a young person and an old person is often intercultural, as are contacts between a homosexual and a heterosexual, a born-again Christian and a Jew, or two residents of Atlanta, one from Cambodia and the other a child of U.S. citizens born in Japan. The "prime discriminator," as Sarbaugh puts it, is heterogeneity, or how dissimilar the persons are. Homogeneous or similar participants engage in *intra*cultural communication and heterogeneous participants communicate *inter*culturally.

Another reason I believe this chapter belongs in this book is that it emphasizes how effective communication attitudes and actions can be solidly grounded in what we know about the nature of persons, *all* persons. There are obviously significant differences among cultures, differences that can create a great deal of awkwardness and misunderstanding. But there are even more fundamental similarities, and the way to communicate well in intercultural contexts is to notice and build on the similarities. The authors of the second reading in this chapter emphasize this point.

So the purpose of these two essays is to provide an overview of intercultural communication in general terms. Then the third reading in this chapter explores specific examples of interpersonal communication between people of a variety of different cultures.

Some Boundaries for Intercultural Communication

L. E. Sarbaugh

... There appears to be a temptation among scholars and practitioners of communication to approach *intercultural* communication as though it were a different process than *intracultural* communication. As one begins to identify the variables that operate in the communication being studied, however, it becomes apparent that they are the same for both intercultural and intracultural settings. In all communication analysis, we are concerned with the characteristics of the partici-

Excerpt from *Intercultural Communication* by L. E. Sarbaugh, © 1979. Reprinted by permission of L. E. Sarbaugh, professor emeritus, Michigan State University.

pants, the relationships among them, their encoding and decoding behaviors, the channels by which they relay symbols to one another, the social and physical contexts within which they operate, and their intentions in the communicative act.

Intercultural and International Compared

... There are two aspects of international communication which must be considered. One aspect is the communication which occurs between or among any two or more individuals of differing nationalities. The second aspect is that official communication, in which governmental representatives acting on behalf of their national government exchange messages with governmental representatives of another nation, who also are authorized to act on behalf of their nation.

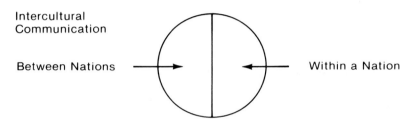

Intercultural
Communication

Between Nations ⟶   ⟵ Within a Nation

The level of interculturalness in any of these international transactions will depend on the kind and amount of expertise the participants have had with life in the other nation. It will be claimed here that some international transactions may well be categorized as intracultural, while others would be definitely intercultural. This could be true for either non-official or official communication.

Let's take an example in which international communication is not entirely subsumed within the intercultural. There are two school teachers from two different countries. Both have studied the same subjects under the same teachers in a third country; and both are now teaching agricultural irrigation in rural villages. Their cultural similarity has been further increased by extensive and intensive interaction as students so that they developed similar world views and beliefs while studying together. It is expected that their communication with one another will have higher fidelity and require less energy than will the communication of either of them with unschooled and unskilled workers in their respective countries.

The tendency to equate intercultural with international communication likely stems from the greater ease of identifying national boundaries. National boundaries somehow become more tangible than cultural boundaries; and, of course, there are noticeable differences in many aspects of behavior as one passes from one nation to another. There are noticeable differences also as one goes from a remote rural village in a country to metropolitan centers of that country. It's the differences between and among people, irrespective of geographical boundaries, that this text focuses on.

Heterogeneity—the Prime Discriminator

A useful discriminator between intercultural and intracultural communication is the heterogeneity of the participants. The notion of "ideal types" in regard to homogeneity-heterogeneity is helpful in developing this basis of distinguishing between intercultural and intracultural communication.

With the concept of ideal type, it is recognized that we would not expect to find two persons who were different on every characteristic; nor would we expect to find two persons who are alike on every characteristic. Yet it is useful to establish a continuum with the assumption of a pure homogeneous pair at one end and a pure heterogeneous pair at the other end.

This view of intercultural and intracultural communication emphasizes that some communication events may rather easily be categorized as intercultural or intracultural. Others may be almost impossible to clearly classify as one or the other, i.e., those near the mid-point of the continuum. A perspective which classifies communication as either inter- or intracultural presumably does so using boundary criteria, either implicit or explicit.

The study and practice of communication can be approached with more precision if we classify it by level of interculturalness rather than as two dichotomous categories of intra- and intercultural. The initial difficulty will be to identify the critical dimensions of difference and to be able to specify the level among those dimensions a given transaction occurs at.

Another way of visualizing the inter-intracultural distinction (rather than the continuum) is to let two circles represent the life experiences of two persons (or groups). If the circles have minimal overlap (representing minimal similarity of experience), the two persons would be near the heterogeneous end of the continuum.

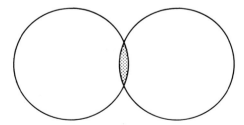

If the circles have maximum overlap, the two persons would be near the homogeneous end of the continuum, i.e., the intracultural communication end.

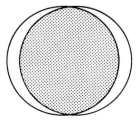

The homogeneity–heterogeneity distinction may lead to classifying communication across generations within the same village or town as highly intercultural communication. In societies where sex roles are quite distinct and clearly defined, there are aspects of intercultural communication in the communication between male and female. What is suggested here is that age or sex differences may or may not be intercultural. The classification of the communication as inter- or intracultural in this case will depend on what degree of homogeneity or heterogeneity of experiences the transactions of these persons have produced.

Review Questions

1. What is the difference between the prefixes "inter" and "intra"?
2. Sarbaugh says some international transactions may be categorized as intracultural. Give an example of one.
3. Define the terms "homogeneous" and "heterogeneous."
4. What does the overlapping part of Sarbaugh's circle diagram represent? In other words, specifically what "overlaps"?

Probes

1. Catalog the intercultural communication contacts you have experienced in the last forty-eight hours. Try not to overlook the less obvious ones. In this time period, virtually everyone has had at least half a dozen contacts with "heterogeneous" others.
2. What misunderstandings might be minimized by Sarbaugh's distinction between intra- and intercultural communication? In other words, what are the benefits of this way of defining intercultural communication?

This reading consists of substantial excerpts from the final chapter of a book called *Understanding Intercultural Communication*. Earlier in the book the authors have talked about culture and communication, American cultural patterns, non-American cultural patterns, intercultural perception, and verbal/nonverbal communication differences. In this chapter they describe six potential problems in intercultural communication and six ways you can respond to these potential problems.

One of the main reasons I selected this essay was because the authors directly discuss *ethnocentrism,* the tendency to evaluate other groups exclusively on the basis of your own group's values. Clearly ethnocentrism is one primary cause of intercultural misunderstanding, whether it occurs between blacks and whites in the United States, Québecois and British Columbia residents in Canada, or between United States and Soviet or British and Iranian governments.

Larry Samovar and his coauthors also discuss how different communication purposes, lack of trust, and lack of empathy can contribute to intercultural misunderstanding. Their comments about the problem of stereotyping make some obvious points, but they're worth repeating in this context. It is also useful, I think, to reflect as they do on the impact of power in intercultural contacts. In fact, if you define politics — as do many political scientists — as the study and practice of the exercise of power, it becomes obvious that political science and intercultural communication have much in common.

When they turn to offering solutions, these authors are similarly straightforward and helpful. They don't couch their advice in behavioral science jargon; they simply suggest that you should "know yourself," "use a shared code," "take time," "encourage feedback," "develop empathy," and "seek the commonalities among diverse cultures."

Their first suggestion parallels what was discussed in Chapter 5 of *Bridges Not Walls*. Their point about "using a shared code" is important and it only hints at the tip of the iceberg. It can takes years of cultural immersion to develop a shared code in any depth. But it is at least helpful to recognize what's needed—both verbally and nonverbally.

Their advice about taking time is simple but potentially profound. It is helpful to learn both to suspend one's own judgments and to give the other person time to accomplish his or her purpose. Moreover, time and timing constitute one of the message systems that differentiate one culture from another. So it's important not to apply your own calendar and clock-time assumptions to a situation in a culture other than your own. This discussion and the authors' comments about encouraging feedback reflect the considerable practical experience that they have had with communication in intercultural contexts.

The authors' discussion of developing empathy is as incomplete as their treatment of using a shared code. They outline six steps for increasing your own empathic response, but in the space they're given, all they can do is highlight a topic that could be expanded almost indefinitely. It would be nice to have a fuller treatment here, but even this brief, necessarily unfinished account is helpful.

Their final suggestion makes a point that I believe is not made often enough in this context. It is important, I think, to emphasize the reality of uniqueness, both of individuals and of cultures. But it is also important to acknowledge the ways in which we are similar. For example, as I mentioned regarding the final reading in Chapter 9, confirmation is communicated differently in different cultures, but all cultures value it and communicate it in one way or another. Respect, trust, and a sense of humor are three other messages that are valued in every human culture. Our communication with people of other cultures ought to acknowledge both that individuals and cultures are unique and that, *as persons,* we have a great deal in common.

Intercultural Communication Problems and Guidelines

Larry A. Samovar, Richard E. Porter, and Nemi C. Jain

Diversity of Communication Purposes

Communication problems often occur because we all have different reasons and motivations that prompt us to interact with other people. These reasons range from the simple to the complex, covering purposes as diverse as seeking the time of day to receiving emotional catharsis. In the intercultural setting this diversity of purposes often can be a potential problem. For example, our communication purpose might be misunderstood if, while traveling in Turkey, we were to approach an elderly female and ask her to recommend a hotel or restaurant. Such an advance, by a male stranger, would be highly inappropriate in Turkey. Our innocent reason for making contact could be misconstrued.

There are countless other instances when communication purposes and goals are at such variance that they create a climate for potential problems. Visualize a situation in which a member of one culture believes that a religious ceremony is a time for joyous behavior and humorous stories, while a person from another culture sees the purpose of such ceremonies as sacred and serious. A lack of understanding regarding this diversity can create ill feelings as well as some embarrassment. An American, while traveling in Japan, stopped to take pictures of a Buddhist wedding. For him, weddings were occasions of great merriment and hence picture taking seemed a natural activity. To the Buddhists, however, weddings had a different purpose, and hence they were greatly offended by the picture taking. People use communication for a variety of purposes, and although this diversity is normal, it can be a source of misunderstanding.

Ethnocentrism

This book has stressed the notion of individual differences and the uniqueness of each person. Yet there also have been corollary themes that emphasized the role of culture in our perceptions and our attitudes. Contained in each of those discussions was the role individual differences play in our perception of ourselves and the world. This position grows out of a number of assumptions. If we accept the belief that our past influences our view of reality and the corresponding tenet that each of us may have similar but not identical personal past histories, then it should follow that another person's picture of the universe will not be exactly like ours. Yet most of us act as if our way of perceiving things is the correct and only way. We often overlook perceptual differences and conclude that if the other person doesn't see that Pablo Picasso is the greatest artist that ever lived, he simply does not know art. Actually, it may well be that he has a different past history and what is great art for him may not match our perception of art.

The problem of perceptual differences is often far deeper than the evaluation of art. In our daily activities these differences appear between different groups and subgroups. Various generations, minorities, occupations, and cultures have conflicting values and goals that will influence their orientation and interpretation of reality. We know from our own experiences that if we were to see a man with long hair hitchhiking, we most likely would stop and offer him a ride. On the other hand, people from a different generation that associated long hair with "those freaky types" might well drive right past the hitchhiker because their background causes them to view the world differently than we do. The difficulty, as we mentioned, grows out of the fact that we usually behave as if the view of the world that we hold is the right one, the correct one, and the only one.

Our culture is a major factor in perceptual discrepancies. Culture helps supply us with our perspective of reality. It therefore plays a dominant role in intercultural communication. For example, if our culture admires thin women, then we would tend to have negative reactions (at least concerning appearance) to cultures that venerate the stout female. If we perceive openness as a positive trait while another culture fosters silence, we again have perceptual differences. These differences and countless others are learned at an early age and can influence the type of communication that takes place.

When our perceptions and our subsequent communication behavior are characterized by this narrow and rigid orientation, we are guilty of ethnocentrism. Ethnocentrism, which is "the tendency to interpret or to judge all other groups, their environments, and their communication according to the categories and values of our own culture,"[1] is one of those communication problems that seems to cut across nearly all cultures. There are very few instances of cultures that are free of this negative characteristic. Many serious students of intercultural communication believe that ethnocentrism is not only common among most cultures, but it also is a major barrier to intercultural understanding.

Because ethnocentrism usually is learned at the unconscious level, and manifested at the conscious level, it is hard to trace its origins. Ethnocentric biases seem, in most instances, to be part of our cultural package. But regardless of who or what is the culprit, ethnocentrism is a potential communication problem that plagues most intercultural encounters. . . .

Lack of Trust

When we trust other persons they usually are sending both verbal and nonverbal messages that inform us that they are the type of persons we wish to take into our confidence—the type of persons who, because we can trust them, make us feel comfortable and at ease. As we reflect upon the people we have met, a long list of traits that encourage and discourage trust becomes apparent. For example, how often do we trust someone who is critical of whatever we do or say? Do we confide in the individuals who, by words or deeds, create a partition between themselves and us? And what about the person who seldom smiles? In all three of these instances we are faced with someone who makes trusting rather difficult. On the other hand, notice how we tend to trust the person who makes us feel comfortable and manifests concern for us and our ideas. In short, we reveal more and are freer when our partner allows us the opportunity to be honest and open instead of inhibited and restrained.

The intercultural setting, because of its unique characteristics, is often a communication exchange that is marked by a lack of trust. Most of us are reluctant to take personal risks with strangers. We tend to perceive differences in color and culture to be far greater than they really are. Individual differences often are more profound than are cultural variations. Yet even knowing this fact, in most inter-cultural situations we let the differences inhibit communication. Instead of finding enjoyment and stimulation from cultural contact, we develop feelings that make trusting extremely complicated. In the United States this lack of trust is perhaps most evident in those situations involving a black person or a Hispanic who is interacting with a white person. Most of this mistrust centers on intent and back-ground. When this happens there is very little opportunity for meaningful com-munication. "... It is so easy for people who bear suspicion or hostility toward each other to miss the basic assumptions upon which a message rests. ... If this occurs, then the communicators are talking at different levels."[2]

Lack of Empathy

As producers and consumers of messages it behooves us to understand how to send our messages and also what to make of the messages we receive from others. One important factor in making decisions about what to say, and in comprehend-ing what other people intended to say, centers on the issue of empathy, which is the "ability to feel like another or to place oneself in another's shoes."[3] To com-municate effectively with other people, we must be able to create inner images that give us some insight into their feelings and characteristics. This sharing of experi-ences is a difficult task, for empathy hinges on the assumption that we are able to understand and in some way share the internal states of those whom we resemble. Yet the fact remains, that however similar we may appear to be, there is something distinctive and unique about each of us. Our internal states are elusive, fleeting, and only known to us in forms and shapes resembling distorted shadows. Hence, knowing the other person, predicting their reactions, and anticipating their needs, is a troublesome assignment.

Our inability to understand completely, to appreciate, accept, and even take pleasure in these individual and cultural differences is but one problem we face in trying to develop empathy. In addition, there appears to be a number of behaviors we often employ that keep us from understanding the feelings, thoughts, and motives of another person. Perhaps the most common of all barriers to empathy is *a constant self-focus*. It is difficult to concentrate on another person if we are con-sumed by thoughts of ourselves. If the main focus of our attention is directed toward thoughts of how much the other person likes our boots or hair style, we certainly are not in a position to expend much energy in the direction of devel-oping empathy.

The tendency to note only some features at the exclusion of others often causes us to misuse the data we gather about another person. If, for example, we notice only a person's skin color or surname, and from this limited information assume we know all there is to know about that person, we are apt to do a poor job of empa-thizing with that person. Admittedly color and names offer us some information about the person in front of us, but this type of data must be considered along with a whole host of other behaviors being generated by the person. Although it is an obvious analogy, we should remember that most outward features only rep-resent the tip of the iceberg.

The stereotyped notions concerning race and culture that we carry around in our heads also serve as potential inhibiters to empathy. If we have the idea that "all English people dislike the Irish," we might allow this stereotype to influence our view of an English person who happens to hold no ill feelings toward the Irish. Stereotyped notions are part of our personalities, so we must be careful not to allow these generalizations to serve as our models of other people.

Lack of previous knowledge about a certain group, class, or person also impedes the development of empathy. If we have never been around Mexicans nor had an opportunity to share in their culture, it might be quite easy for us to misread some of their behavior associated with their concept of time (a somewhat laissez faire attitude toward the clock). This lack of knowledge could cause us to draw a conclusion from some specific action that is not at all related to the real motivation behind the behavior....

Stereotyping

Our propensity for stereotyping is perhaps one of the most serious problems in intercultural communication.... Recall that, in general terms, stereotyping involves our beliefs about groups of individuals based on previously formed opinions, perceptions, and attitudes. Stereotyping is very common in intercultural settings. The widespread nature of stereotyping can best be pointed out by asking ourselves this question: "How often am I guilty of jumping to conclusions and treating a specific individual as if he or she were just like the preconceived model I carry around in my head?" Most of us would have to conclude that our behavior toward others is often characterized by some degree of stereotyping.

As just noted, the pervasive nature of stereotyping is most evident in the intercultural setting. It is in this context that we tend to stereotype people and groups based on very little knowledge or contact. It is both effortless and comfortable to be able to quickly say "All Jews are ..." or "He is a Mexican, therefore he must ..." Such conclusions take little energy, and also exonerate the individual from any other reflection or observation. He is able, often without ever knowing a Jew or a Mexican, to act as if he knows all about the person who stands before him. It is, in short, a lazy method of interaction.

Not only is stereotyping an indolent way of perceiving and communicating with other people, but for many it is a defense mechanism and a device for reducing anxiety. To depend on preconceptions and stereotypes is a common defense technique for reducing culture shock.[4] And as we all realize, culture shock is that overwhelming and disturbing feeling we experience when we are thrust into a situation or environment that contains very few familiar symbols or behaviors. What happens is that we become frustrated and simply do not know how to act. In these instances, stereotyping often takes over. Stereotyping is not necessary, but it is often easier than suspending conclusions and coping with ambiguity. Because many of us are lazy, and reluctant to expend the energy necessary to know others in alien situations, we are willing to reduce our confusion by accepting misleading information. The problem, however, is that stereotypes, as pictures in our head, are usually rigid, resistant to change, used as defense mechanisms, incorrect, and often highly unfavorable. This type of list, as we surely must realize, is not conducive to successful intercultural communication. In fact, this sort of fixation on negative traits keeps both parties from ever experiencing the joy of knowing about another person and his culture. In summary, to be negative and to overgeneralize (sterotyping) can only serve to hinder communication.

Power

Our concern with power begins with these two assertions: (1) In every communication relationship there is some degree of power. (2) It is not power that represents the potential communication problem, but the misuse of power. Let us now examine these two statements and relate them to intercultural communication.

In most instances power so permeates the encounter that most of us just assume its presence. From parent-child relationships to world power politics, we learn about power. The methods of power are as diverse as they are widespread. People and cultures have employed guns, bombs, language, space, money, and even history as devices for controlling others. Cries of black, brown, gray, red, and gay power only serve to attest to the importance of power in the intercultural context. Understanding power and its effect on communication, therefore, is an important part of understanding intercultural communication.

Our degree of power is contingent upon the person(s) we are interacting with and the resources that we control. In intercultural communication these two factors take on added significance, for the sources of power are culturally based, and what one culture deems as a source of power another culture may not even consider a power variable. For example, in England one's language is often a sign of potential power. It signals one's class and station in that culture. There are countless cultures, however, where language is not a consideration. There also are instances when one culture believes that power is derived from simply being a member of that particular culture. The whites' relationship with the blacks in the United States is often an example of this assumed power, and, for over a century whites in the United States have been hesitant to relinquish this power. It is easy to see how this use, or misuse, of power, when employed to control and to determine another's behavior, can restrict openness and communication. "To allow customary subservience or power a place in human interaction is to introduce an inevitable obstruction."[5] Adherence to the following philosophy could help us avoid that obstruction.

> The ideal power relationship ... is not concerned with the idea of control.... Rather, the desire is to attribute to all ... groups the credibility that allows them positive influence in communication situations.[6]

Perhaps the most appropriate way to end this section on potential problems is to try to place all {six} propositions under one heading. Looking for just such a phrase or summary we recall the words of a famous modern philosopher who was searching for a cause behind much of man's failure. His plight is analogous to ours. For where do we look for dragons to slay or metaphors to explain? We believe that Pogo, our modern sage, gave us the answer when he said, "We have met the enemy, and he is us." So be it with communication problems. If problems occur, we must not look to someone else as a means of locating and placing blame—we must look to ourselves. We are the enemy.

Improving Intercultural Communication

Sincere and conscientious attempts to improve intercultural communication are neither new nor original with this book. Since World War II we have had to learn to deal with an entire new series of relationships. During the fifties and sixties, travel and new and advanced technology brought about more and closer intercultural contact. During the 1970s these earlier trends accelerated and were added to by problems of shortages of natural resources, forced integration, nuclear proliferation, and an ever-increasing distance between the world's have's and have-not's. As the issues become more acute, so does the need for improved intercultural communication. What those who offer suggestions rely on are the observations of people who have had experience dealing with intercultural communication. We have tried, thus far, to share with you some of the benefits of their experience.

... The same attitudes and skills that we need to develop to communicate in general apply to intercultural communication, only more so. To be communicative is to be open, responsive, and nonjudgmental. It may be difficult to achieve these attitudes, especially in intercultural interactions, but it is not impossible. ...

Know Yourself

Perhaps the first thing we can do to improve our intercultural communication and resolve many of our problems is to know ourselves. By knowing ourself we are not referring to any mystical notions or deep psychological soul searching, but rather to the simple act of identifying those attitudes, opinions, and biases that we all carry around. These attributes help determine not only what we say but what we hear others say. If we hold a certain attitude toward homosexuals, and a man who is a homosexual talks to us, our response to what he says will be colored by our precommunication attitude. Knowing our likes, dislikes, and degrees of personal ethnocentrism enables us to place them out in the open so that we can identify them and deal with them. This is essential for successful intercultural communication. Hidden personal premises, be they directed at ideas, people, or entire cultures, are often a cause of many of our problems.

The second step in knowing ourself is somewhat more difficult than simply identifying our prejudices and predispositions. It involves discovering the kind of image we portray to the rest of the world. That is to say, how do we communicate? The importance of this type of introspection cannot be stressed enough. We all have heard stories regarding how foreigners view Americans who travel abroad. The "Ugly American" example might be trite, but often it is true. Therefore, if we are to improve our communication and understand the reaction of others toward us, we must have some ideas of how other people perceive us. If, for instance, we see ourself as serious and austere, while in reality we present a different image to people, we will have a hard time trying to determine why people react to us as they do. We must, therefore, take stock of our actions, both verbal and nonverbal, if we are to understand why people behave around us as they do. ...

We must learn to ask ourselves questions such as the following: Do I give people my undivided attention? Do I seem at ease or tense? Do I often change the subject after people finish a sentence? Do I deprecate the statements of others? Do I smile often? Do I interrupt repeatedly? And do I show sympathy when someone has a problem? In addition to these questions, we can gain insight into ourselves by observing the topics we select to talk about when the choice is ours. We also can gain some personal knowledge by noting the type of people toward whom we gravitate. Our tone of voice, our expressions, our apparent receptiveness to the responses of others, and literally hundreds of other factors all have an impact on those we wish to reach. Frequently overlooked, these subtleties of communication often affect a person's reaction to us and our message.

Use a Shared Code

... There are countless subcodes contained within the English language, and to improve our communication we must know the specific code being used by the other person. If he uses a jargon that is indigenous to a certain group, we must know that jargon as part of the code. If he uses a black argot and says "Am I right Leroy, you was cribbin' over there then," we also must attempt to share that symbol system if communication is going to take place.

As the last example indicates, the ambiguity of our language is compounded when we attempt to share our ideas with someone considerably removed from our specific background and frame of reference. Although it is a stereotyped illustration, try to imagine the difficulty of sharing a code if one person uses street argot from the "hip" culture ("Man, that's cool") and the other person is from a small rural community that has developed yet another form of slang. Admitting the exaggerated nature of our example, it nevertheless underscores the necessity for sharing a common code.

The importance of a shared code is greatly compounded when a foreign language is being spoken. The issue of translation has already been discussed elsewhere in the book, so our purpose here is to remember that vocabulary, syntax, and dialects represent only a small portion of the variables of the spoken code. We must always work toward trying to break the code—to understand the picture in the head of the other person. That picture will tell us more about what is being discussed than will the sound of the word. Nonverbal behavior also shifts from culture to culture. For example, in Japan a female may cover her mouth as a sign of shyness, while in America that same activity is apt to be stimulated by fear.

Because nonverbal differences are often subtle they tend to be overlooked. Yet nonverbal actions usually offer insight into what is being communicated and at the same time they also are offering a glimpse into the deep structure of the culture. Hence, we must be aware of these nonverbal elements as we begin our intercultural training.

Take Time

The notion of taking time when communicating actually includes two separate observations. The first relates to our common tendency to jump to conclusions. We all know how hard it is to suspend judgment and hold off on our evaluations. Think of those occasions when we decided we did not like a particular class even before we gave it an opportunity to get started and yet ultimately enjoyed the experience. In communication we often end up doing much the same thing. We finish the thought or idea for the other person before he has finished talking, and in many instances it is only our conception of what he would have said. There is no positive compensation for a quick decision, particularly if that decision was made without sufficient evidence. In fact, we most likely will discover that by suspending our conclusions, and taking time to communicate, we might be learning things we did not know. In this way we reap the rewards that accompany increased understanding.

When the parties are from different cultures the need to defer conclusions becomes even more manifest. If we do not know the world view, value structure, family orientation, nonverbal codes, and the like, of the other culture we might rush to a false conclusion regarding their communicative behavior. For example, if in our head we do not allow a Jewish person to finish a story, we may well miss the point of the entire transaction, for story telling, and the embellishing of a simple tale, is an important aspect of the Jewish culture. By taking time, therefore, we not only discover the person's main idea, but we also might enjoy the story.

The second way we must learn to take time involves not ourselves but the other person. We must allow the other person the time necessary to accomplish his purpose. We have repeatedly seen that each person and culture has a communication style that is unique. Some cultural nonverbal styles call for periods of silence and long pauses. We must learn to respect these phases in the encounter and allow the other person enough time to utilize those periods. We should try to cultivate the necessary patience that will offer us and the other person the time needed to think through and explore ideas and feelings....

Being aware of *timing* often can make the difference between a successful engagement and one that is characterized by ill feelings and antagonism. What are the circumstances under which someone should tell his or her parents that they plan to drop out of college? Have they rendered their decision at the same time their father has lost his job? Or try to picture attempting to talk over some important business transaction during a period that our communication partner believed to be a solemn occasion. In short, the time we select to communicate might well be as important as the message itself. Few professors will sympathize with the student who waits until the last week of the semester to announce "I would like to come to your office and talk about the midterm examination I missed a few months ago." This is poor timing....

Encourage Feedback

The importance of feedback to human communication has already been stressed. So, in this final section we will examine feedback from still another perspective. This time our orientation will focus on how to use and encourage feedback effectively.

Recall that we have seen that feedback enables us to adapt future messages because we are aware of the response produced by earlier messages. Feedback "enables communicators to correct and adjust messages so that they say what the communicators want them to say, and so that requests for responses are understood accurately by the receiver. Without feedback there is no way to monitor the communication process, no way to seek integration and agreement."[7]

Granting that feedback is important, we must learn to create an atmosphere whereby other people are encouraged to offer us feedback. Therefore, let us examine a number of ways we can create situations that encourage others to give us information about ourselves and our messages.

Perhaps there will be occasions when silence instead of words will inspire feedback. If we want the other person to speak up or respond in some nonverbal way, we may want to remain silent and wait. We all probably remember a professor who had the habit of ending each sentence or idea with the phrase "Are there any questions?" The only problem with this technique was that he never paused long enough to allow anyone to respond but would immediately move on to a new idea. His lack of pause and silence did not encourage feedback, and instead forfeited an important method of checking on the success of his communication.

Nonverbal feedback often is as useful as verbal. When we examined nonverbal communication we saw that our nonverbal responses often were harder to control and censor than our verbal. To improve our use of feedback we must, there-fore, be tuned in to all aspects of the situation. We must not only recognize the obvious nonverbal signs, like an entire group of people standing up and walking out of the hall during our presentation, but also the more subtle and elusive responses we make with our eyes, fingers, and the like.

We also can encourage feedback by using ourselves as a model of an efficient feedback system. If we offer feedback to others it is likely that this example will become contagious, and people around us will do the same.

Asking questions is also an excellent method of gathering information. We can ask specific questions such as "What do you mean when you say John is lazy?" Or we can ask questions with simple words and phrases such as "What?" or "How come?" In either instance we gather additional data.

Finally, the quality and quantity of available feedback cues shifts from culture to culture. In cultures that are very amicable and animated, such as the Italian and Jewish cultures, there is usually an abundance of data to be evaluated. In most ori-ental cultures, however, outward displays of emotions and feelings, either by words or actions, often are lacking. Hence, in these instances the communicator must take great care when reading the responses produced by his messages.

Develop Empathy

A lack of empathy nearly always represents a potential communication prob-lem. Our inability to understand and appreciate the point of view and life orien-tation of others often keeps us from effectively communicating with them. The greater the difference between ourselves and others, the harder it is to empathize. For not only do we lack a common background, but most of us have very little tolerance for people who do not share our particular world view and value system. Our ability to empathize can be greatly enhanced by avoiding some of the pitfalls mentioned earlier in this chapter.

In addition, there are six steps we can follow to improve our skill in devel-oping empathy....

The first step in developing empathy is to *assume there are differences* among individuals and cultures. The philosophical assumption necessary for empathy is a multiple-reality theory, which holds that not all people see the same view of the world. The second step is to *know ourselves.* This has already been discussed but we mention it here because it is necessary for the steps that follow. In the third step, the self-identity that was part of stage two is temporarily set aside for what is called *suspended-self.* "One way of thinking about this procedure is to imagine that the self, or identity, is an arbitrary boundary that we draw between ourselves and the rest of the world, including other people. The suspension of self is the temporary expansion of this boundary—the elimination of separation between self and envi-ronment."[8] In the fourth step we *imaginatively put ourselves in the other person's place.* Once we let our imagination inside the other person we are ready for the fifth step—*the empathic experience.* While this experience is still imaginative, it neverthe-less comes close to our experience and feelings. Finally, we must *reestablish self.* Granting the excitement and exhilaration of sharing another's experience, we must, however, be able to return to ourselves. To be able to see ourselves and our culture once again.[9]

By learning how to use these six steps we all might be able to overcome our ethnocentric tendencies while becoming more sensitive to the needs, values, and goals of other people.

Seek the Commonalities among Diverse Cultures

Although there has been an attempt to avoid it, this type of book tends to overemphasize the differences existing between people and cultures. Admittedly some of these differences are important; however, in many ways it is our likenesses that enable us to find common ground and establish rapport. It might be interesting to know that "an American child sticks out his tongue to show defiance, a Tibetan to show courtesy to a stranger, and a Chinese to express wonderment,"[10] but it is more important to know that they also share a series of more crucial characteristics that link them together. These likenesses are as obvious as the fact that we all share the same planet, and as subtle as our desire to be free from external restraint. The effective intercultural communicator is aware of these likenesses and seeks to develop them as a means of establishing a bond between himself and the rest of humanity. To know our commonalities, and to be able to deal with them, is not a philosophical issue, but rather a practical matter. For example, there is nothing religious or metaphysical in appreciating and utilizing the notion that all people seek to avoid stress and try to locate some degree of happiness. It is knowing this kind of general information, combined with the important specifics of a particular culture, that marks the person who is successful in traveling in and out of various intercultural settings.

Notes

1. Sharon Ruhly, *Orientations to Intercultural Communication* (Chicago: Science Research Associates, 1976), p. 22.
2. Arthur L. Smith, *Transracial Communication* (Englewood Cliffs, N.J.: Prentice-Hall, 1973), p. 71.
3. Arthur Combs and Donald Snygg, *Indidivual Behavior: A Perceptual Approach to Behavior* (New York: Harper & Row, 1959), pp. 234–36.
4. La Ray M. Barna, "How Culture Shock Affects Communication" (Paper presented in the Distinguished Scholars Program at the 1976 Communication Association of the Pacific Annual Convention, Koke, Japan, June, 1976), p. 14.
5. Smith, p. 119.
6. Jon A. Blubaugh and Dorthy L. Pennington, *Crossing Differences: Interracial Communication* (Columbus, Ohio: Charles E. Merrill, 1976), p. 39.
7. William D. Brooks and Phillip Emmert, *Interpersonal Communication* (Dubuque, Iowa: Wm. C. Brown, 1976), pp. 147–48.
8. Milton J. Bennett, "Overcoming the Golden Rule: Sympathy and Empathy" (Paper delivered at the 29th Annual Conference of the International Communication Association, Philadelphia, May, 1979), p. 31.
9. Bennett, pp. 29–34.
10. Yu-Kuang Chu, "Six Suggestions for Learning about Peoples and Cultures" in Seymour Fersh, ed., *Learning About People and Cultures* (Evanston, Ill.: McDougal & Littell, 1974), p. 52.

Review Questions

1. Define ethnocentrism. Give an example of it from your own communication experience.
2. What is the relationship in an intercultural situation between ethnocentrism and trust?
3. Paraphrase the three reasons for a lack of empathy that Samovar and his colleagues discuss.
4. According to these authors, how do some people use stereotyping to deal with culture shock?

5. The authors say that it is not power itself that creates problems in intercultural communication, but the _____ of power. Explain.
6. What are the two steps for coming to "know yourself" that these authors advise?
7. You can probably think of various kinds of "feedback." Which kinds do you think the authors have in mind when they suggest that you "encourage feedback" as a way of coping with an intercultural situation?
8. What are the six steps the authors offer for developing empathy?

Probes

1. The problem of ethnocentrism is so pervasive that it seems like it might be inherent. Perhaps our tendency to judge other groups only by the standards of our own is "hard-wired" into the human psyche. What do you think? Do you know anyone who is naturally and habitually *not* ethnocentric? What does it take to overcome this problem?
2. How do you think Samovar and his coauthors would respond to the criticisms of the concept of empathy that Milt Thomas and I outline in Chapter 7?
3. You knew something about stereotyping before you read this essay. What did these authors add to your knowledge of stereotyping in an intercultural communication situation?
4. Do you agree with Samovar and his colleagues that there is some degree of power in *every* communication relationship? Discuss.
5. How effectively do you believe Pogo's aphorism captures the essence of the communication problems these authors discuss? (Pogo's aphorism is, "We have met the enemy, and he is us.")
6. Which of the other six suggestions will help you respond to suggestion 2, "Use a shared code"?
7. Give an example of how time communicates in your own life. What does this example tell you about the function of time and timing in intercultural contacts?
8. How might your recognition of *similarities* between "different" cultures affect your attitude toward intercultural communication?

I n 1987 Letty Cottin Pogrebin published an exhaustive book on friendship based on two very thorough friendship surveys, many additional published research reports, and interviews with almost 150 people ranging in age from early adolescence to eighty-two years and representing most of the spectrum of cultures and subcultures in the United States. The following reading consists of excerpts from Chapter 11 of her sixteen-chapter book. As the title indicates, the chapter deals with friendship across a variety of cultural boundaries including color, culture, sexual preference, disability, and age. As with other readings, I chose this one because it blends sound research and straightforward writing, credible theory, and solid practice.

This rigorous but accessible flavor of Pogrebin's work emerges in the section right after the introduction. She begins with the obvious but important point that if you're going to cross a boundary, you'll find yourself doing a lot of explaining—to yourself, to each other, and to your respective communities. Then she takes a couple of pages to elaborate on what that "explaining" will probably consist of.

The next major section develops another potentially profound theme: intercultural relationships consistently have to deal with the reality that the two persons might be "the same," but that they're also "never quite the same." She illustrates the point with examples from black/redneck white, Jewish/Irish-Catholic, Puerto Rican/white, and Spanish/Jewish relationships. Pogrebin's discussion of "moving in one another's world" extends the notion of "the same but never quite the same" to include challenges introduced by second and third languages and fundamental cultural values. She also discusses several "hazards of crossing" that emerge when fundamental differences in cultural values meet.

Under the heading "The Problem with 'Them' Is 'Us,' " Pogrebin discusses gay/ straight, disabled/nondisabled, and young/aged relationships. All three topics became current only in the past decade as the minority rights movement spread to include gays and lesbians, the disabled, and "senior citizens," and government regulations made these groups increasingly visible. As the author notes, these groups warrant separate discussions in part because, "To a large degree, our society still wants to keep them out of sight—the gays and lesbians for 'flaunting their alternative life-styles,' the disabled for not 'getting better,' and the old for reminding us of our eventual fate."

Pogrebin's outline of the kinds of "explaining" one has to do about his or her gay/ straight relationships accurately captures the last ten years or so of my experience communicating with gays and lesbians. The strong relationship Kris and I have with Bill and John Paul, our "married" next-door neighbors, is one example of some of the problems and much of the potential Pogrebin discusses. I also appreciate her summary of the contrasts between gay and straight views on homophobia, AIDS, lesbian politics, and acceptance.

Until recently, disabled persons in the United States made up perhaps an even more invisible subculture than gays. Thanks in part to major changes in building codes affecting all public construction, wheelchair-bound, deaf, and blind persons are becoming increasingly visible. Pogrebin explains some of the unique problems the nondisabled can have establishing and maintaining relationships with these persons. As one quadriplegic succinctly puts it, "We need friends who won't treat us as weirdo asexual second-class children or expect us to be 'Supercrips'—miracle cripples who work like crazy to make themselves whole again. . . . We want to be accepted the way we are." Many nondisabled persons are guilty of exactly these charges and can be shocked to hear them expressed so bluntly.

In the final section of this reading, Pogrebin discusses cross-age friendships. She cites some studies that indicate that three-year-olds already have developed "ageist" perceptions of the elderly—believing that old people are sick, tired, and ugly. Other studies reveal the stereotypes older people have of children and teenagers. She discusses some of the typical reasons for cross-age miscommunication and then suggests some reasons why age can be immaterial to developing friendships. As the average age of the U.S. populace continues to increase, Pogrebin's comments will become more and more applicable and important.

I like the way this reading extends the general theoretical ideas in the pieces by Sarbaugh and Samovar et al. I also appreciate the breadth of application that's here. I believe that Pogrebin is writing about some "cutting-edge" aspects of interpersonal communication and that her ideas are going to become increasingly important between now and the turn of the century.

The Same and Different: Crossing Boundaries of Color, Culture, Sexual Preference, Disability, and Age

Letty Cottin Pogrebin

On August 21, 1985, as they had done several times before, twenty-one men from a work unit at a factory in Mount Vernon, New York, each chipped in a dollar, signed a handwritten contract agreeing to "share the money equaly {sic} & fairly to each other," and bought a ticket in the New York State Lottery. The next day, their ticket was picked as one of three winners of the largest jackpot in history: $41 million.

The story of the Mount Vernon 21 captivated millions not just because of the size of the pot of gold but because of the rainbow of people who won it. Black, white, yellow, and brown had scribbled their names on that contract—Mariano Martinez, Chi Wah Tse, Jaroslaw Siwy, and Peter Lee—all immigrants from countries ranging from Paraguay to Poland, from Trinidad to Thailand.

"We're like a big family here," said Peter Lee. "We thought by pooling our efforts we would increase our luck—and we were right."[1]

The men's good fortune is a metaphor for the possibility that friendships across ethnic and racial boundaries may be the winning ticket for everyone. This is not to say that crossing boundaries is a snap. It isn't. There are checkpoints along the way where psychic border guards put up a fuss and credentials must be reviewed. We look at a prospective friend and ask, "Do they want something from me?" Is this someone who sees personal advantage in having a friend of another race at his school, in her company, at this moment in history? Is it Brotherhood Week? Does this person understand that "crossing friendships" require more care and feeding than in-group friendship, that it takes extra work?

Explaining

Most of the extra work can be summed up in one word: *explaining*. Whatever the boundary being crossed—race, ethnicity, or any other social category—both partners in a crossing friendship usually find they have to do a lot of explaining—to themselves, to each other, and to their respective communities.

Explaining to Yourself

One way or another, you ask yourself, "What is the meaning of my being friends with someone not like me?"

In his classic study, *The Nature of Prejudice*, Gordon Allport distinguishes between the in-group, which is the group to which you factually belong, and the reference group, which is the group to which you relate or aspire.[2] Allport gives the example of Blacks who so wish to partake of white skin privilege that they seek only white friends, disdain their own group, and become self-hating. One could as easily cite Jews who assume a WASP identity or "Anglicized Chicanos" who gain education and facility in English and then sever their ties of kinship and friendship with other Mexican-Americans.[3]

When you have a friend from another racial or ethnic group, you ask yourself whether you are sincerely fond of this person or might be using him or her as an entrée into a group that is your unconscious reference group. The explaining you do to yourself helps you understand your own motivations. It helps you ascertain whether the friend complements or denies your identity, and whether your crossing friendships are in reasonable balance with your in-group relationships.

Explaining to Each Other

Ongoing mutual clarification is one of the healthiest characteristics of crossing friendships. The Black friend explains why your saying "going ape" offends him, and the Jewish friend reminds you she can't eat your famous barbecued pork. Both of you try to be honest about your cultural sore points and to forgive the other person's initial ignorance or insensitivities. You give one another the benefit of the doubt. Step by step, you discover which aspects of the other person's "in-groupness" you can share and where you must accept exclusion with grace.

David Osborne, a white, describes his close and treasured friendship with an American Indian from Montana: "Steve was tall and athletic—the classic image of the noble full-blooded Indian chief. We were in the same dorm in my freshman year at Stanford at a time when there were only one or two other Native Americans in the whole university. He had no choice but to live in a white world. Our friendship began when our English professor gave an assignment to write about race. Steve and I got together to talk about it. We explored stuff people don't usually discuss openly. After that, we started spending a lot of time together. We played intramural sports. We were amazingly honest with each other, but we were also comfortable being silent.

"When I drove him home for spring vacation, we stopped off at a battlefield that had seen a major war between Chief Joseph's tribe and the U.S. Cavalry. Suddenly it hit me that, had we lived then, Steve and I would have been fighting on opposite sides, and we talked about the past. Another time, an owl flew onto our windowsill and Steve was very frightened. He told me the owl was a symbol of bad luck to Indians. I took it very seriously. We were so in touch, so in sync, that I felt the plausibility of his superstitions. I was open to his mysticism."

Mutual respect, acceptance, tolerance for the faux pas and the occasional closed door, open discussion and patient mutual education, all this gives crossing friendships—when they work at all—a special kind of depth.

Explaining to Your Community of Origin

Accountability to one's own group can present the most difficult challenge to the maintenance of crossing friendships. In 1950 the authors of *The Lonely Crowd* said that interracial contact runs risks not only from whites but from Blacks who may "interpret friendliness as Uncle Tomism."[4] The intervening years have not eliminated such group censure.

In her article "Friendship in Black and White," Bebe Moore Campbell wrote:

"For whites, the phrase 'nigger lover' and for Blacks, the accusation of 'trying to be white' are the pressure the group applies to discourage social interaction."[5] Even without overt attacks, people's worry about group reaction inspires self-censorship. Henry, a Black man with a fair complexion, told me he dropped a white friendship that became a touchy subject during the Black Power years. "We'd just come out of a period when many light-skinned Negroes tried to pass for white and I wasn't about to be mistaken for one of them," he explains. "My racial identity mattered more to me than any white friend."

Black-white friendships are "'conducted underground,'" says Campbell, quoting a Black social worker, who chooses to limit her intimacy with whites rather than fight the system. "'I'd feel comfortable at my white friend's parties because everybody there would be a liberal, but I'd never invite her to mine because I have some friends who just don't like white people and I didn't want anybody to be embarrassed.'"

If a white friend of mine said she hated Blacks, I would not just keep my Black friends away from her, I would find it impossible to maintain the friendship. However, the converse is not comparable. Most Blacks have at some point been wounded by racism, while whites have not been victimized from the other direction. Understanding the experiences *behind* the reaction allows decent Black people to remain friends with anti-white Blacks. That these Blacks may have reason to hate certain whites does not excuse their hating all whites, but it does explain it....

Historically, of course, the biggest enemies of boundary-crossing friendships have not been Blacks or ethnic minorities but majority whites. Because whites gain the most from social inequality, they have the most to lose from crossing friendships, which, by their existence, deny the relevance of ethnic and racial hierarchies. More important, the empowered whites can put muscle behind their disapproval by restricting access to clubs, schools, and businesses.

If you sense that your community of origin condemns one of your crossing friendships, the amount of explaining or justifying you do will depend on how conformist you are and whether you feel entitled to a happiness of your own making....

The Same but Never Quite the Same

"I go coon hunting with Tobe Spencer," said former police officer L. C. Albritton about his Black friend in Camden, Alabama. "We're good friends. We stay in town during the day for all the hullabaloo and at night we go home and load up the truck with three dogs and go way down into the swamps. We let the dogs go and sit on a log, take out our knives and a big chew of tobacco ... and just let the rest of the world go by."

Looking at a picture of himself and Spencer taken in 1966, Albritton mused: "It's funny that a police officer like me is standing up there smiling and talking to a nigger because we were having marches and trouble at that time.... Old Tobe Spencer—ain't nothing wrong with that nigger. He's always neat and clean as a pin. He'll help you too. Call him at midnight and he'll come running just like that."[6]

Two friends with the same leisure-time pleasures, two men at ease together in the lonely night of the swamps. Yet race makes a difference. Not only does the white man use the derogatory "nigger," but he differentiates his friend Tobe from the rest of "them" who, presumably, are not neat and clean and helpful. *The same but never quite the same.*

Leonard Fein, the editor of *Moment,* a magazine of progressive Jewish opinion, gave me "the controlling vignette" of his cross-ethnic friendships: "An Irish-Catholic couple was among our dearest friends, but on that morning in 1967 when we first heard that Israel was being bombed, my wife said, 'Who can we huddle with tonight to get through this ordeal,' and we picked three Jewish couples. Our Irish friends were deeply offended. 'Don't you think we would have felt for you?' they asked. 'Yes,' we said, 'but it wasn't sympathy we wanted, it was people with whom, if necessary, we could have mourned the death of Israel—and that could only be other Jews.'

"The following week, when the war was over, my wife and I went to Israel. The people who came to live in our house and take care of our children were our Irish friends. They had understood they were our closest friends yet they could never be exactly like us." ...

For Raoul, a phenomenally successful advertising man, crossing friendships have been just about the only game in town. He reminisced with me about growing up in a Puerto Rican family in a Manhattan neighborhood populated mostly by Irish, Italians, and Jews:

"In the fifties I hung out with all kinds of guys. I sang on street corners—do-wopping in the night—played kick the can, and belonged to six different basketball clubs, from the Police Athletic League to the YMCA. My high school had 6000 kids in it—street kids who hung out in gangs like The Beacons, The Fanwoods, The Guinea Dukes, The Irish Lords, and The Diablos from Spanish Harlem and Jewish kids who never hung out because they were home studying. The gang members were bullies and punks who protected their own two-block area. They wore leather jackets and some of them carried zip guns and knives. I managed to be acceptable to all of them just because I was good at sports. I was the best athlete in the school and president of the class. So I was protected by the gangs and admired by the Jewish kids and I had a lot of friends."

Raoul's athletic prowess won him a scholarship to a large midwestern university where he was the first Puerto Rican to be encountered by some people. "They wanted me to sing the whole sound track of *West Side Story.* They asked to see my switchblade. And I was as amazed by the midwesterners as they were by me. My first hayride was a real shock. Same with hearing people saying 'Good morning' to each other. Every one of my friends—my roommate, teammates, and fraternity brothers, Blacks from Chicago and Detroit and whites from the farms—they were all gentle and nice. And gigantic and strong. Boy, if one of them had moved into my neighborhood back home, he'd have owned the block.

"After graduation, a college friend went to work in a New York City ad agency that played in a Central Park league and needed a softball pitcher. He had me brought in for an interview. Even though I knew nothing about advertising, I was a helluva pitcher, and the owner of the agency took sports seriously. So he hired me. I always say I had the only athletic scholarship in the history of advertising. I pitched for the agency, I played basketball with the owner, and I learned the business. So I found my friends and my career through sports. Even though I may have been a Spic to most everyone, sports opened all the doors."

The same but never quite the same. . . .

"At the beginning, because of difficulties of adaptation, we immigrants pro-tect ourselves by getting together with people from the same culture who speak the same language," says Luis Marcos, a psychiatrist, who came to the United States from Seville, Spain. "Next, when we feel more comfortable, we reach out to people who do the same work we do, mostly those who help us or those we help in some way. Then we have a basis for friendship. My mentor, the director of psychiatry at Bellevue, is a native-born American and a Jew. He helped me in my area of research and now he's one of my best friends. I also began to teach and to make friends with my medical students as they grew and advanced."

That Marcos and his friends have the health profession in common has not prevented misunderstandings. "When we first went out for meals together, my impulse was to pay for both of us," he says of another doctor, a Black woman who taught him not to leave his own behavior unexamined. "It wasn't that I thought she couldn't afford to pay; we were equally able to pick up the check. It was just that the cultural habit of paying for a woman was ingrained in my personality. But she misconstrued it. She felt I was trying to take care of her and put her down as a Black, a professional, and a woman. In order for our friendship to survive, she had to explain how she experiences things that I don't even think about."

Moving in One Another's World

Ethnotherapist Judith Klein revels in her crossing friendships. "My interest in people who are different from me may be explained by the fact that I'm a twin. Many people look to be mirrored in friendship; I've had mirroring through my sister, so I can use friendship for other things. One thing I use it for is to extend my own life. People who aren't exactly like me enhance my knowledge and expe-rience. They let me be a vicarious voyager in their world."

As much as friends try to explain one another's world, certain differences remain particular barriers to intimacy.

Luis Marcos mentions the language barrier. "No matter how well I speak, I can never overcome my accent," he says. "And some people mistake the way I talk for lack of comprehension. They are afraid I won't understand an American joke, or if I choose to use aggressive words, they don't think I mean it, they blame my 'language problem.' "

While many Americans assume people with an accent are ignorant, many ethnics assume, just as incorrectly, that someone *without* an accent is smart. Some Americans have a habit of blaming the other person for doing or saying whatever is not understandable to Americans. Ethnics also have been known to blame their own culture—to use their "foreignness" as an excuse for behavior for which an American would have to take personal responsibility. "I can't help it if we Latins are hot-tempered" is a way of generalizing one's culpability.

Of course, the strongest barrier to friendship is outright resistance. After two years of off-and-on living in Tokyo, Angie Smith came to terms with the fact that "the Japanese do not socialize the way we do." She found, as many have, that in Japan friendship is considered an obligation more than a pleasure and is almost always associated with business.[7]

"Three times I invited two couples for dinner—the men were my husband's business associates—and three times the men came and the women didn't," Smith recalls. "They sent charming little notes with flowers, but they would not have been comfortable in our house for an evening of social conversation. Yet these same Japanese women would go out to lunch with me and tell me more intimate things than they tell each other. While we were in Japan, I just had to get used to sex-divided socializing and not having any couple friendships."

When people's differences are grounded in racism rather than alien styles of socializing, it can be especially painful to move in the other person's world.

"I felt myself a slave and the idea of speaking to white people weighed me down," wrote Frederick Douglass a century ago.[8] Today, most Blacks refuse to be weighed down by whites. They do not "need" white friends. Some doubt that true friendship is possible between the races until institutional racism is destroyed. Feminists of every shade have debated the question "Is Sisterhood Possible?" Despite the issues that affect *all* women, such as sexual violence, many Black women resist working together for social change or organizing with white women because they believe most whites don't care enough about welfare reform, housing, teen pregnancies, or school dropouts—issues that are of primary concern to Blacks.

Bell Hooks, a writer and a professor of Alfro-American studies, wrote: "All too frequently in the women's movement it was assumed one could be free of sexist thinking by simply adopting the appropriate feminist rhetoric; it was further assumed that identifying oneself as oppressed freed one from being an oppressor. To a very great extent, such thinking prevented white feminists from understanding and overcoming their own sexist-racist attitudes toward black women. They could pay lip service to the idea of sisterhood and solidarity between women but at the same time dismiss black women."[9]

Phyllis Marynick Palmer, a historian, says white women are confounded by Black women's strong family role and work experience, which challenge the white stereotype of female incapacity. White women also criticize Black women for making solidarity with their brothers a priority rather than confronting Black men's sexism. In turn, Black women get angry at white women who ignore "their own history of racism and the benefits that white women have gained at the expense of black women."[10] With all this, how could sisterhood be possible? How can friendship be possible?

"I would argue for the abandonment of the concept of sisterhood as a global construct based on unexamined assumptions about our similarities," answers Dill, "and I would substitute a more pluralistic approach that recognizes and accepts the objective differences between women."

Again the word "pluralistic" is associated with friendship. An emphasis on double consciousness, not a denial of differences. The importance of feeling both the same and different, of acknowledging "the essence of me," of understanding that friends need not *transcend* race or ethnicity but can embrace differences and be enriched by them. The people who have managed to incorporate these precepts say that they are pretty reliable guidelines for good crossing friendships. But sometimes it's harder than it looks. Sometimes, the "vicarious voyage" into another world can be a bad trip.

The Hazards of Crossing

"Anglo wannabes" are a particular peeve of David Hayes Bautista. "These are Anglos who wanna be so at home with us that they try too hard to go native. For instance, Mexicans have a certain way that we yell along with the music of a mariachi band. When someone brought along an Anglo friend and he yelled 'Yahoo, Yahoo' all night, every Chicano in the place squirmed."

Maxine Baca Zinn gives the reverse perspective: of a Chicano in an Anglo environment. "Once, when I was to speak at the University of California, a Chicana friend who was there told me that the minute I walked into that white academic world my spine straightened up. I carried myself differently. I talked differently around them and I didn't even know it." Was Zinn just nervous about giving her speech or did she tighten up in anticipation of the tensions Chicanos feel in non-Hispanic settings? She's not certain.

When Charlie Chin, a bartender, started work in a new place, a white coworker quipped, "One thing you have to watch out for, Charlie, are all the Chinks around here." I winced when Chin said this, but he told me, "I just smiled at the guy. I'm used to those jokes. That's the way whites break the ice with Asians. That's the American idea of being friendly." ...

For another pair of friends, having different sensitivities did not destroy the relationship but did create a temporary misunderstanding. Yvonne, a Black woman, was offended when her white friend, Fran, came to visit, took off her shoes, and put her feet up on the couch. "I felt it showed her disregard for me and I blamed it on race," says Yvonne. "Black people believe the way you behave in someone's home indicates the respect you have for that person. Also, furniture means a lot to us because we buy it with such hard-won wages." Weeks later, Yvonne saw one of Fran's white friends do the same thing while sitting on Fran's couch. Yvonne realized that the behavior had nothing to do with lack of respect for Blacks. "For all I know millions of whites all over America put their feet up when they relax—I'd just never seen that part of their world before."

What Bill Tatum discovered about a couple of his white friends was not so easy to explain away. When the couple asked Tatum to take some food to Helen, their Black housekeeper who was sick, he asked her name and address. They knew her only as "Helen" but were able to get her address from their 6-year-old who had spent a week at her apartment when they had been on vacation.

"I arrived to find a filthy, urine-smelling building, with addicts hanging out on the front stoop. Rags were stuffed in the broken windows in Helen's apartment. She was wearing a bag of asafetida around her neck, a concoction made by southern Blacks to ward off bad luck and colds. She was old, sick, and feverish. She said she'd never been sick before and her employers—my friends—had provided her with no health insurance. Obviously, they'd never imagined where or how this poor woman might live—or else they wouldn't have left their little girl with her. They treated their Black housekeeper with none of the respect and concern they showed me, their Black *friend* and a member of their economic class."

Until that experience, if anyone had ever accused the couple of racism, Tatum says he'd have gone to the mat defending them. Now he has to square what he's seen with his old love for them and he is finding it very, very difficult.

He makes another point about moving in the world of white friends. "Some whites make me feel completely comfortable because they say exactly what they think even if it contradicts whatever I've said. But other whites never disagree with me on anything. They act as if Blacks can't defend their positions, or they're afraid it would look like a put-down to challenge what I say even though they would challenge a white person's opinion in a minute."

While Tatum resents whites' misguided protectiveness, he also finds fault with "many Blacks who are climbing socially and are too damned careful of what *they* say. They won't advance an opinion until they have a sense of what the white friend is thinking." Not only is that not good conversation, he says, "that's not good friendship."

The Problem with "Them" Is "Us"

If you're a young, heterosexual, nondisabled person and you do not have one friend who is either gay, old, or disabled, there might be something wrong with *you*. If you're gay, old, or disabled and all your friends are just like you, it may not be because you prefer it that way.

Gay people, the elderly, and disabled people get the same pleasure from companionship and intimacy and have the same problems with friendship as does anyone else. They merit a separate discussion in this book for the same reason that class, race, and ethnicity required special discussion: because on top of the usual friendship concerns, they experience additional barriers.

In essence, the barriers exist because we don't *know* each other. Many people—some of whom are homophobic (have a fear of homosexuality)—reach adulthood without ever to their knowledge meeting a homosexual or a lesbian. Many have neither known someone who is blind or deaf or who uses a wheelchair nor spent time with an old person other than their grandparents. That there are such things as Gay Pride marches, disability rights organizations, and the Gray Panthers does not mean that these groups have achieved equal treatment under the law or full humanity in the eyes of the world. To a large degree, our society still wants to keep them out of sight—the gays for "flaunting their alternative life-styles," the disabled for not "getting better," and the old for reminding us of our eventual fate.

As a result of our hang-ups, these populations may be even more segregated than racial or ethnic minorities. When these groups are segregated, "we" don't have to think about "them." Out of sight, out of mind, out of friendship. People told me they had no gay, elderly, or disabled friends because "we live in two different worlds" or because "they" are so different—meaning threatening, unsettling, or strange. Closer analysis reveals, however, that we *keep* them different by making this world so hard for them to live in and by defining human norms so narrowly. It is our world—the homophobic, youth-worshipping, disability-fearing world— that is threatening, unsettling, and strange to them. In other words, their biggest problem is us.

To make friends, we have to cross our self-made boundaries and grant to other people the right to be both distinctive and equal.

Gay-Straight Friendship

Forming relationships across gay-straight boundaries can be as challenging as crossing racial and ethnic lines because it too requires the extra work of "explaining":

- Explaining to yourself why, if you're gay, you need this straight friend ("Am I unconsciously trying to keep my heterosexual credentials in order?"), or why, if you're straight, you need this gay friend ("Am I a latent homosexual?")

- Explaining to each other what your lives are like—telling the straight friend what's behind the words "heavy leather" or explaining to the gay friend just why he *cannot* bring his transvestite lover to a Bar Mitzvah
- Explaining to your respective communities why you have such a close relationship with one of "them"

Gay-straight friendship is a challenge not only beacuse the heterosexual world stigmatizes gays but because homosexual society is a culture unto itself. Straights who relate comfortably with their gay friends say they get along so well because they respect the distinctive qualities of gay culture—almost as if it were an ethnic group. Interestingly enough, a Toronto sociologist has determined that gay men have the same institutions, "sense of peoplehood," and friendship networks as an ethnic community; all that gays lack is the emphasis on family.[11] And in places where lesbians congregate, such as San Francisco, there are women's bars, music, bookstores, publications, folklore, and dress styles—an elaborate self-contained culture.[12]

Since gay men and lesbians have to function in a straight world during most of their lives, it's not too much to ask a straight friend to occasionally accommodate to an environment defined by homosexuals. But even when both friends accommodate, gay-straight relations can be strained by disagreements over provocative issues.

Gay-Straight Debate

The Gay's View	*The Straight's View*
	On Homophobia
You're not relaxed with me. You think gayness rubs off or friendship might lead to sex. You act like every gay person wants to seduce you. You fear others will think you're gay. You are repulsed by gay sex though you try to hide it. You bear some responsibility for the discrimination against gays and if you're my friend, you'll fight it with me.	I am the product of a traditional upbringing. I cannot help being afraid or ignorant of homosexuality. My religion taught me that homosexuality is a sin. I'm trying to overcome these biases and still be honest with you about my feelings. I support gay rights, but I cannot be responsible for everyone else's homophobia.
	On AIDS
Ever since the AIDS epidemic, you have not touched me or drunk from a glass in my house. I resent your paranoia. I shouldn't have to watch my gay friends die and at the same time feel that my straight friends are treating me like a leper. If I did get AIDS, I'm afraid you would blame the victim and abandon me. Can I trust a friend like that?	I *am* afraid. I don't know how contagious the AIDS virus is or how it's transmitted. From what I read, no one does. All I know is that AIDS is fatal, homosexuals are the primary victims, and you are a homosexual. I'm caught between my affection for you and my terror of the disease. I don't know what's right and you're in no position to tell me.

On Lesbian Politics

Lesbianism is not just sexual, it's political. Every woman should call herself a lesbian, become woman-identified, and reject everything masculinist. Women who love men and live in the nuclear family contribute to the entrenchment of patriarchal power and the oppression of women. Authentic female friendship can only exist in lesbian communities. If you don't accept "lesbian" as a positive identity, it will be used to condemn all women who are not dependent on men.

I support lesbian rights and even lesbian separatism if lesbians choose it. I believe lesbian mothers must be permitted to keep their children. I oppose all discrimination and defamation of lesbians. I believe that lesbian feminists and straight women can work together and be friends, *but* I resent lesbian coercion and political strong-arming. I also resent your more-radical-than-thou attitude toward heterosexuals. Like you, what I do with my body is my business.

On Acceptance

You want me to act straight whenever having a gay friend might embarrass you. I'm not going to tone down my speech or dress to please your friends or family. I do not enjoy being treated as a second-class couple when my lover and I go out with you and your spouse. If you can kiss and hold hands, we should be able to show affection in public. If straights ask each other how they met or how long they have been married, they should ask us how we met and how long we've been together.

You refuse to understand how difficult it is to explain gay life-styles to a child or an 80-year-old. You make me feel like a square in comparison with your flashy gay friends. You treat married people like Mr. and Mrs. Tepid, as if the only true passion is gay passion. Your friends make me feel unwanted on gay turf and at political events when I'm there to support gay rights. You put down all straights before you know them. It's hard to be your friend if I can't introduce you to other people without your feeling hostile or judging their every word.....

Disabled and Nondisabled Friendship

About 36 million Americans have a disabling limitation in their hearing, seeing, speaking, walking, moving, or thinking. Few nondisabled people are as sensitive to the experiences of this population as are those with close friends who are disabled.

"Last week," recalls Barbara Spring, "I went to have a drink at a midtown hotel with a friend who uses a wheelchair. Obviously it's not important to this hotel to have disabled patrons because we had to wait for the so-called accessible elevator for thirty minutes. Anyone who waits with the disabled is amazed at how long the disabled have to wait for everything."

"In graduate school, one of my friends was a young man with cerebral palsy," says Rena Gropper. "Because he articulated slowly and with great difficulty, everyone thought he was dumb and always interrupted him, but if you let him finish, you heard how bright and original his thinking was."

Terry Keegan, an interpreter for the deaf, has become friends with many deaf people and roomed for two years with a coworker who is deaf. "If they don't understand what we're saying it's not because they're stupid but because we aren't speaking front face or we can't sign." Keegan believes all hearing people should learn 100 basic words in Ameslan, American Sign Language. "Historically, this wonderful language has been suppressed. Deaf people were forced to use speech, lipreading, and hearing aids so they would not look handicapped and would 'fit in' with the rest of us. Their hands were slapped when they tried to sign. This deprived them of a superior communication method. Deafness is not a pathology, it's a difference. When we deny deaf people their deafness, we deny them their identity."

Many nondisabled people have become sensitized to idioms that sound like racial epithets to the disabled, such as "the blind leading the blind" or "that's a lame excuse." Some find "handicapped" demeaning because it derives from "cap in hand." A man who wears leg braces says the issue is accuracy. "*I'm* not handicapped, people's attitudes about me handicap me." Merle Froschl, a nondisabled member of the Women and Disability Awareness Project, points out that the opposite of "disabled" is "*not* disabled"; thus, "nondisabled" is the most neutral term. Disabled people are infuriated by being contrasted with "normal" people—it implies that the disabled are "abnormal" and everyone else is perfect. And the term "able-bodied" inspires the question, Able to do what: Run a marathon? See without glasses? Isn't it all relative?

"Differently abled" and "physically challenged" had a brief vogue, but, says Harilyn Rousso, those terms "made me feel I really had something to hide." Rousso, a psychotherapist who has cerebral palsy, emphasizes, "Friends who care the most sometimes think they're doing you a favor by using euphemisms or saying 'I never think of you as disabled.' The reason they don't want to acknowledge my disability is that they think it's so negative. Meanwhile, I'm trying to recognize it as a valid part of me. I'm more complex than my disability and I don't want my friends to be obessed by it. But it's clearly there, like my eye color, and I want my friends to appreciate and accept me with it."

The point is not that there is a "right way" to talk to people who are disabled but that friendship carries with it the obligation to *know thy friends*, their sore points and their preferences. That includes knowing what words hurt their feelings as well as when and how to help them do what they cannot do for themselves.

"Each disabled person sends out messages about what they need," says Froschl. "One friend who is blind makes me feel comfortable about taking her arm crossing the street, another dislikes physical contact and wants to negotiate by cane. I've learned not to automatically do things for disabled people since they often experience help as patronizing."

"I need someone to pour cream in my coffee, but in this culture, it's not acceptable to ask for help," says Rousso, adding that women's ordinary problems with dependency are intensified by disability. "I have to feel very comfortable with my friends before I can explain my needs openly and trust that their reaction will not humiliate both of us. For some people it raises too many anxieties."

Anxieties that surround the unknown are dissipated by familiarity. Maybe that explains why so many disabled-nondisabled friendships are composed of classmates or coworkers who spend a lot of time together.

"There are those who can deal with disability and those who can't," says Phil Draper, a quadriplegic whose spinal cord was injured in a car accident. "If they can't—if they get quiet or talk nervously or avoid our eyes—the work of the relationship falls entirely on us. We need friends who won't treat us as weirdo asexual second-class children or expect us to be 'Supercrips'—miracle cripples who work like crazy to make themselves whole again. Ninety-nine percent of us aren't going to be whole no matter what we do. We want to be accepted the way we are."

To accept friends like Phil Draper, the nondisabled have to confront their unconscious fears of vulnerability and death. In one study, 80 percent of nondisabled people said they would be comfortable having someone in a wheelchair as their friend. But "being in a wheelchair" came immediately after "blind" and "deaf-mute" as the affliction they themselves would least want to have.[13] If we fear being what our friend *is*, that feeling is somewhere in the friendship.

Nondisabled people also have to disavow the cult of perfectability. Disabled people are not going to "get better" because they are not "sick"; they are generally healthy people who are not allowed to function fully in this society—as friends or as anything else.

"Friendship is based on people's ability to communicate," says Judy Heumann, the first postpolio person to get a teacher's license in New York City and now a leader of the disability rights movement. "But barriers such as inaccessible homes make it hard for disabled people to just drop in. Spontaneity is something disabled people enjoy infrequently and the nondisabled take for granted.

"While more public places have ramps and bathrooms that accommodate wheelchairs, many parties still occur in inaccessible spaces. If I have to be carried upstairs or if I can't have a drink because I know I won't be able to use the bathroom later, I'll probably decide not to go at all. One way I measure my friends is by whether they have put in the effort and money to make their houses wheelchair-accessible. It shows their sensitivity to me as a person.

"Good friends are conscious of the fact that a movie theater or concert hall has to be accessible before I can join them; they share my anger and frustration if it's not. They understand why I'm not crazy about big parties where all the non-disabled are standing up and I'm at ass-level. It makes me able to function more as an equal within the group if people sit down to talk to me. I can't pretend I'm part of things if I can't hear anyone. I don't want to *not* be invited to large parties—I just want people to be sensitive to my needs.

"I always need help cooking, cleaning, driving, going to the bathroom, getting dressed. I pay an attendant to do most of those things for me but sometimes I have to ask a friend for help, which presents a lot of opportunities for rejection. Often, the friends who come through best are other disabled people whose disabilities complement mine. I can help a blind woman with her reading, child care, and traveling around town; she can do the physical things I need. And we don't have to appreciate each other's help, we can just accept it." ...

Cross-Age Friendship

I am now 46, my husband is 51. Among our good friends are two couples who are old enough to be our parents. One woman, a poet, can be counted on for the latest word on political protests and promising writers. She and I once spent a month together at a writers' colony. The other woman—as energetic and as well-read as anyone I know—is also involved in progressive causes. Although the men of both couples have each had a life-threatening illness, the one with a heart condition is a brilliant civil liberties lawyer and the one who had a stroke is a prize-winning novelist with stunning imaginative powers. The lawyer taught our son to play chess when he was 5. The novelist has encouraged our daughters to write stories ever since they could read. The men have been fine surrogate grandfathers.

When I described these couples to somone my own age, he said, "Ah, it's easy to be friends with *interesting* old people, but what about the dull ones?" The answer is, I am not friends with dull young or middle-aged people so why should I want to be friends with dull old people? And why does he immediately think in terms of old people *not* being interesting? Perhaps the crux of the problem with cross-generational friendship is this *double* double standard. First, to think we "ought" to be friends with the elderly—as a class—denies old people the dignity of individuality and devalues their friendship through condescension. But second, to assume that those who are young or in mid-life will necessarily be more interesting and attractive than those over 65 maintains a double standard of expectation that cheats younger people of friends like ours.

Ageism hurts all ages. And it begins early: Studies show that 3-year-olds already see old people as sick, tired, and ugly and don't want to associate with them.[14] Older people also have their biases about youthful behavior. Some 70-year-olds think children are undependable, unappreciative, ask too many questions, and must be told what to do. They believe teenagers are callow, impatient, and unseasoned.[15]

The authors of *Grandparents/Grandchildren* write, "We shouldn't blame adolescents for not being adults. To become adults, the young need to be around adults."[16] But age segregation keeps us apart. Without benefit of mutual acquaintance, stereotypes mount, brick by brick, until there is a wall high enough to conceal the real human beings on either side.

Another big problem is miscommunication. Conversations between young and old often founder because "sensory, physical, or cognitive differences" cause "distortion, message failure, and social discomfort."[17] That's a fancy way of saying they can't understand each other. And anyone who has ever talked with a young person whose span of concentration is the length of a TV commercial or with an old person whose mind wanders to the blizzard of '48 when asked how to dress for today's weather will understand how each generation's communication style can be a problem for the other.

But stereotypes and miscommunication do not entirely account for the gulf between young and old. Homophily—the attraction to the similar self—is the missing link. Those who are going through the same thing at the same time find it comforting to have friends who mirror their problems and meet their needs, and, usually, people of similar chronological age are going through parallel experiences with wage-earning, setting up house, child-rearing, and other life-cycle events.

Age-mates also tend to have in common the same angle of vision on history and culture. Two 65-year-olds watching a film about the Depression or World War II can exchange memories and emotional responses that are unavailable to a 30-year-old who did not live through those cataclysms. And while a person of 18 and one of 75 might both love Vivaldi, their simultaneous appreciation for Bruce Springsteen is unlikely.

Claude Fischer's studies reveal that more than half of all friend-partners are fewer than five years apart. But the span is reduced to two years if their relationship dates back to their youth when age gradations matter the most and the places where youngsters meet—school, camp, military service, and entry-level jobs—are more age-segregated. Contrary to popular wisdom, elderly people, like the rest of us, prefer friends of their own age. The more old people there are in a given community, the more likely it is that each one will have a preponderance of same-age friends. And, believe it or not, a majority of old people say they think it's more important for them to have age-mates than family as their intimates.

Given this overwhelming preference for homophily at every age, why am I on the bandwagon for cross-generational friendship? Because when it's good, it's very, very good—both for friends of different ages who are undergoing similar experiences at the same time and for friends of different ages who are enjoying their differences.

- A 38-year-old woman meets 22-year-olds in her contracts class at law school.
- A couple in their early forties enrolled in a natural childbirth course make friends with parents-to-be who are twenty years younger.
- Three fathers commiserate about the high cost of college; two are in their forties, the third is a 60-year-old educating his second family.

Age-crossing friendships become less unusual as Americans follow more idiosyncratic schedules for marrying, having children, and making career decisions.

But there are other reasons for feeling that age is immaterial to friendship. Marie Wilson, a 45-year-old foundation executive who has five children of high school age or older, told me, "My friends are in their early thirties, and they have kids under 8. But these women are where I am in my head. We became close working together on organizing self-help for the poor. Most women my age are more involved in suburban life or planning their own career moves."

Sharing important interests can be as strong a basis for friendship as is experiencing the same life-cycle events. However, without either of those links, the age difference can sit between the young and the old like a stranger. I'm not asking that we deny that difference but that we free ourselves from what Victoria Secunda calls "the tyranny of age assumptions"[18] and that we entertain the possibility of enriching ourselves through our differences. ...

As we cross all these lines and meet at many points along the life cycle, people of diverse ages, like people of every class and condition, are discovering that we who are in so many ways "the same and different" can also be friends.

Notes

1. L. Rohter, "Immigrant Factory Workers Share Dream, Luck and a Lotto Jackpot," *New York Times*, August 23, 1985.
2. G. Allport, *The Nature of Prejudice*, Doubleday, Anchor Press, 1958.
3. J. Provinzano, "Settling Out and Settling In." Papers presented at annual meeting of the American Anthropological Association, November 1974.
4. D. Riesman, R. Denney, and N. Glazer, *The Lonely Crowd: A Study of the Changing American Character*, Yale University Press, 1950.
5. B. M. Campbell, "Friendship in Black and White," *Ms.*, August 1983.
6. B. Adelman, *Down Home: Camden, Alabama*, Times Books, Quadrangle, 1972.
7. R. Atsumi, "Tsukiai—Obligatory Personal Relationships of Japanese White Collar Employees," *Human Organization*, vol. 38, no. 1 (1979).
8. F. Douglass, *Narrative of the Life of Frederick Douglass, an American Slave*, New American Library, Signet, 1968.
9. B. Hooks, *Ain't I a Woman: Black Women and Feminism*, South End Press, 1981.
10. P. M. Palmer, "White Women/Black Women: The Dualism of Female Identity and Experience in the United States," *Feminist Studies*, Spring 1983.

11. S. O. Murray, "The Institutional Elaboration of a Quasi-Ethnic Community," *International Review of Modern Sociology*, vol. 9, no. 2 (1979).
12. J. C. Albro and C. Tully, "A Study of Lesbian Lifestyles in the Homosexual Micro-Culture and the Heterosexual Macro-Culture," *Journal of Homosexuality,* vol. 4, no. 4 (1979).
13. L. M. Shears and C. J. Jensema, "Social Acceptability of Anomalous Persons," *Exceptional Children*, October 1969.
14. R. K. Jantz et al., *Children's Attitudes Toward the Elderly,* University of Maryland Press, 1976.
15. A. G. Cryns and A. Monk, "Attitudes of the Aged Toward the Young," *Journal of Gerontology,* vol. 1 (1972); see also, C. Seefeld et al., "Elderly Persons' Attitude Toward Children," *Educational Gerontology,* vol. 8, no. 4 (1982).
16. K. L. Woodward and A. Kornhaber, *Grandparents, Grandchildren: The Vital Connection* (Doubleday, Anchor Press, 1981), quoted in "Youth Is Maturing Later," *New York Times,* May 10, 1985.
17. L. J. Hess and R. Hess, "Inclusion, Affection, Control: The Pragmatics of Intergenerational Communication." Paper presented at the Conference on Communication and Gerontology of the Speech Communication Association, July 1981.
18. V. Secunda, *By Youth Possessed: The Denial of Age in America,* Bobbs-Merrill, 1984.

Review Questions

1. According to the author, when we engage in a cross-cultural relationship, what do we typically need to "explain" about it to ourselves? To each other? To our friends?
2. What is meant by Pogrebin's label, "the same but never quite the same"?
3. In the paragraph before the heading "The Hazards of Crossing," the author distinguishes "double consciousness" from "a denial of differences." What do those two terms mean?
4. The essay includes a story about a white couple asking their black friend, Bill Tatum, to take some food to their black housekeeper who lived in Harlem and was sick. Tatum was shocked to discover the housekeeper living in a filthy slum. What was racist about the white couple's "generosity"?
5. How accurate is Pogrebin's summary of each side's views in the section titled "Gay-Straight Debate"?
6. What is the point of the author's discussion of the words we use to label disabled persons?
7. Paraphrase the following comment by Pogrebin: "If we fear being what our friend *is,* that feeling is somewhere in the friendship."

Probes

1. Which of the three kinds of "explaining" that Pogrebin describes has been most difficult for you?
2. The author claims that "many Americans assume people with an accent are ignorant" and that "many ethnics assume, just as incorrectly, that someone *without* an accent is smart." How is this distorted value mirrored in the major television networks' choices of news anchors and reporters?
3. You may be surprised to read a discussion of gay/straight relationships here. What might justify putting a discussion of this topic in this book?
4. Do you commonly think about relationships with disabled persons as examples of "intercultural communication"? What happens when you do?
5. What problems have you encountered in your relationships with older persons? What is the most helpful thing Pogrebin says about these relationships?

Part

5

Approaches to Interpersonal Communication

Chapter 14

Leo Buscaglia's Approach

I 've never met Leo Buscaglia, but I've liked him ever since I heard a tape recording of one of his speeches in the early 1970s. The speech was about love, and Buscaglia was just beginning to be widely known as the professor from the University of Southern California who actually taught a course on the subject. It was obvious from the tape that Buscaglia was passionately involved with his subject matter and with the chance to share his ideas with others. He was an enthusiastic, dynamic presenter, and the applause and laughter on the tape told how much the audience loved him.

It's easy for some people to dismiss Buscaglia as a crazy Italian, some kind of unreconstructed flower child, or an example of all that's unstable in southern California. I have to admit I've even felt that way about him from time to time, and I *like* him. But I've also discovered that it's just about impossible to read his best-selling book *Living, Loving and Learning* without getting caught up in his enthusiasm and his love of life. Things may not be as simple as he sometimes makes them sound, but when you get right down to it, your attitude toward life *is* the foundation of everything else, and in a sense that is simple: It's either generally positive, ho-hum, or negative.

I chose this excerpt because it's about "togetherness." Buscaglia does not present an approach to interpersonal communication that you can logically outline or reduce to formal propositions. But his major ideas are pretty clear. The first one has to do with how we define the situations we find ourselves in: We can either see the positive or the negative side, and our choice helps determine the quality of life we experience. There are even advantages to being seen as a "crazy kook"; Buscaglia claims that when he's dancing in the leaves, "I'm having a ball and the sane ones are bored to death."

It's also important to have models and to model for others. Buscaglia tells how Tulio and Rosa, his mom and dad, didn't tell him how to enjoy life, they *showed* him. "Tactility" was one thing he was shown; Buscaglia loves hugging and, as he puts it, "I have never had an existential problem as to whether I exist or not. If I can touch you and you can touch me, I exist."

Another lesson he learned from his mother is that nondirective permissiveness is not the only way to love. His mama would say, "Shut up!" and as he puts it, "We always knew what that meant. It was a beautiful kind of interaction in the family. Not too amazing, none of us has ever had a mental problem."

Buscaglia's central theme is that "loving relationships, togetherness, away from 'I' and 'me' and to 'us' and 'we,' is where the joy really lies." How do you move toward togetherness? By risking, for one thing. "We need to reach out, we need to bring in, we need not to be afraid." We also need to reexamine our myth of romantic love. And to stay open to change. And to learn from our pain. And to exploit the therapeutic value of hugging and touching. And to live in the present.

In short, "Your relationships will be as vital and alive as *you* are. If you're dead, your relationship is dead. And if your relationships are boring and inadequate it's because *you* are boring and inadequate. Liven yourself up!"

Together with Leo Buscaglia

Leo Buscaglia

I'd like to talk to you about a concept that means a great deal to me, and that is the concept of togetherness. I really am concerned about how separated we all are. Everybody seems to be involved in what Schweitzer talked about so many years ago when he said we're all so much together in crowds and yet all of us are dying of loneliness. It's as if we don't know how to reach out to each other any more, to hold each other, to call to each other, to build bridges. And so I'd like to talk about togetherness, you and I, and some crazy ideas I have about building some of those bridges so that we can get a little bit closer.

I think it's personified, that separateness, loneliness, and despair, by what happened to me recently while I was traveling across country. So many things happen on airplanes. I just love airplanes. You meet old friends you've never seen, you make new friends because people know they may never see you again; it's like true confessions. They tell you about their wives and their husbands. I'm a real people person as you know, and I love to hear about wives, husbands, children, triumph, tears—all the wonderful things that make us human.

In a 747 jet another man and I were lucky to have the area with just two seats. At least *I* thought it was very lucky. He was at the window and as I walked to him I said, "Hello," which I always do, thinking we could start things going. If you're going to be together for five hours, you might as well say "hello," even though some people won't answer. I said, "Hello," and he said, "Oh, damn, I thought this seat next to me was going to be left empty so I could stretch out." And I said, "Oh I promise you that as soon as we get in the air, if there's an empty seat, I'll take it and let you have this one."

I sat next to him and got the seat belt tightened and a woman came on with a little baby. I couldn't help thinking, "Isn't it lucky to have airplane travel for women who have to travel with babies?" I think of Mama when she had little Vincenzo in her arms traveling across the country when she first came from Italy. It took seven days! And here this woman would make it to New York in just about five or six hours. I was thinking this positive thing when he said, "Oh damn. Look, there's a woman with a baby. The baby is going to squawk all the way to New York." That was number two. We hadn't even taken off yet! Number three occurred when the stewardess announced that there was a "no-smoking section" and he said, "Smokers should be shot!" I said, "All of them? I know some very nice smokers. I don't happen to be one, but I wouldn't want them all to be shot." Then we received the menu. Isn't it amazing that you can fly across the country and not only do they feed you, but they give you a menu with a choice of three entrées? That's phenomenal! He looked at everything and said, "Oh God, they never have anything good on these damn planes." Imagine, we still hadn't taken off yet. And then the stewardess got up and started pointing to the two exits in the rear, two exits in the front, you know how they do? They *have* to do that. He said, "Look at

Excerpt from pages 225-242 of *Living, Loving, and Learning* by Leo Buscaglia, © 1982 by Leo F. Buscaglia, Inc. Reprinted by permission.

those stupid dames. You know, they don't do anything. They're only there to meet wealthy men. They don't work, they're just glorified waitresses." On and on he went. It was amazing me—all of this before the plane even left the ground.

When we were in the air (I couldn't move; I was stuck there; but I was determined he would be a lover before we arrived in New York), he turned to me and said, "What do you do?" I replied, "I'm a professor at a university." He said, "What do you teach?" And I said, "Courses in counseling and in loving people and relationships." He said, "Thank God, there's someone else who feels about people the way I do." Everybody thinks they are lovers! Before we got to New York I found out his wife had left him and he defined his children as "thankless bums." Isn't that amazing?

Reach out. Learn to reach out. Listen to yourself and hear how many times you say, "I am a lover." My question is, how many times a day do you hear yourself say, "I love," as opposed to "I hate, I hate, I hate." Very interesting phenomenon. I am sick of this kind of an approach to life, that's so centered on "I" and "me." I'm tired of hearing people say "I" and "me." I would love to hear people using "us" and "we" for a change. Isn't that nice? "us" and "we"? "I" is important, but my goodness, the strength comes from "us" and "we"! You and I together are much stronger than you or I alone, and I like to think that when we get together, I'm not only giving, I'm getting. I will now have four arms, two of yours and two of mine, two heads—that means we've got all kinds of new creative ideas—and two different worlds, your world and my world. And so I want you to come in.

I have learned some very interesting things that I believe are a result of people getting trapped in the concept of "I" and "me." This is from a book called *On an Average Day in America*. Get this: On an average day in America, 9,077 babies are born, and that's wonderful; 1,282 are illegitimate and not wanted. About 2,740 kids run away from home on an average day in America. About 1,986 couples divorce on an average day in America. An estimated 69 beautiful, incredible people will commit suicide on an average day in America. Someone is raped every 8 minutes, murdered every 27 minutes and robbed every 76 seconds. A burglar strikes every 10 seconds, a car is stolen every 33 seconds, and the average relationship in America today lasts three months. Now if that doesn't freak you out! And that's the world we're creating for ourselves! That's the world of I and me. Well, I don't want to be a part of that world, I want to create a different kind of world—and we can do it together. That's the wondrous thing.

I really have nothing to sell; I have a lot to share. And I'm positive that if we could relate, you could give me some ideas of how we can reverse this trend by recognizing that we can't survive alone and that aloneness and ego involvement leads to death and destruction.

Also we're learning a great deal about learning. I'm a teacher and I've been a teacher all my life and I love being a teacher, but I've only just recently found out that I teach nothing to no one. That's an ego trip if you believe that you can teach anything to anybody. All that I can be, at best, is an excited, wondrous, magical facilitator of knowledge. I can lay it out, but if you don't want to eat it, I can do nothing about it. But I also find that if I can make it attractive and exciting, that maybe a few people get hooked and wonder, "What is that kook talking about? Maybe if he's so crazy about life, maybe life is worth living." When I dance in the leaves, and I do it often, I find that other people get enough courage to go and dance in their leaves, too. And that's good. If I can teach someone to dance in the leaves, I'll run the risk of being called crazy. I love being called crazy because, as I said before, when you're called crazy it gives you a lot of leeway for behavior. You can do damn near anything and everybody says, "Oh, that's crazy Buscaglia dancing in the leaves." And I'm having a ball and all the sane ones are bored to death.

You see, what we really need, the behavior modifiers tell us, are good *models*. We need models of love, people who can show us. Those of you who know my book *Love* know that I dedicated it to my parents, Tulio and Rosa Buscaglia, because they didn't teach me to love, they *showed* me how to love. And they had no idea about behavior modification. But people like Bandura at Stanford are showing us that the best way to teach is by modeling. Without telling anybody anything, without teaching anybody anything, you *be* what you want your children to be and watch them grow.

Many of you know that I grew up in a wonderful, great big, fantastic, loving Italian family and grew healthy and happy and wonderful on bagna calda and pasta fasule and polenta and all those marvelous dishes. But I also learned a lot of other things from these models, most of which was taught without my knowing. One thing they taught me is that we need to be touched and we need to be loved. And so I've been touching and loving all my life and I've been having a ball, touching and loving. It's been so nice and I didn't know that in "the outside world" you don't touch and you don't love—not without reservations. The first note I ever received from a teacher in America was a note written to Mama. You can imagine how sensitive this lady was if she wrote the following to a poor Italian immigrant woman who could barely speak English. "Dear Mrs. Buscaglia. Your son Felice is too *tactile*." Can you believe that? I brought the note home to my mama who looked and said, "Hey what's this a-tactile? Felice, if you did something wrong, I'll smack your head in." I said, "I don't know what tactile is Mama, honest. I don't know what I did." So we went to the dictionary, which we did a lot of, and flipped to the word "tactile." It says, to feel, to touch. Mama says, "So what's wrong with that? That's a-nice. You gotta crazy teacher." I have never had an existential problem as to whether I exist or not. If I can touch you and you can touch me, I exist. So many people are dying of loneliness because they are not touched.

Also, they taught me how to share. We had a tiny house and a big family and boy, do you learn to share! Now we have enormous houses; everybody could get lost. Then we had lots of people and one toilet. Oh, do I remember! That was the center of the house. Everybody was in and out of the toilet all the time and the minute you'd get in there and sit down and relax for 30 seconds, "Get out of there, it's my turn." So you learned to give and you learned to share, you learned to get out and you learned to speed up and you learned to use the same sink and sleep in the same rooms. It's a wonderful thing to learn. I'm convinced that the family that goes to the toilet together, stays together. But now we have a toilet for Mary and a toilet for Sally and a toilet for Papa and a dressing room for Mama. That's too bad—we don't need all that space. It's so funny, but we build enormous houses and we work our fingers to the bone and we say it's for our children. But if you think about it, we bring them into these beautiful houses with lovely furniture and we don't let them live in them. "Don't touch this!" "Don't touch that!" "You're going to break that." For goodness sakes, who's the house for, the neighbors? Not in our house! The house was there for us to live in.

So I learned to share and I learned a wonderful sense of responsibility from Mama, who was a rugged lady. When she said something, it went. This always amused me when I got into the university and I studied theories of counseling and all this permissive stuff. Mama was the most magnificent nondirective, permissive counselor. She'd say, "Shut up!" We always knew what that meant. It was a beautiful kind of interaction with the family. Not too amazing, none of us have ever had a mental problem.

I remember as a kid, I wanted to go to Paris. She said, "Felice, you're too young for traveling." "But, Mama, I want to go." At that time, Jean Paul Sartre and Simone de Beauvoir were all involved in the wonderful concept of existentialism; and Felice wanted to go there because he heard that everybody was in misery and he wanted to go there and be miserable, too. I wanted to try everything. Mama says, "OK, you go, but if you do, you're declaring yourself an adult and don't ask me for anything after that. You're an adult. You're free, go." Oh, was it fantastic! I didn't have a lot of money, but I had a little bit and I went there and I lived everybody's dream. I had a tiny apartment. I could see from my skylight all the rooftops of Paris. I sat at the feet of people like Sartre and de Beauvoir—didn't understand a damn word they said—loved every minute of it. Suffered! Oh, did I suffer! And it was wonderful, on Camembert cheese and French wine. Pretty soon there was no money. I had no real concept of money. I was sharing with everybody, I was the last of the big spenders. I always had the bottle of wine, everyone came to my place to share it. This had been the way I grew up, the modeling I had learned. At our house the postman would come and Papa would pour him a glass of wine. "Eh, poor man, he's working all day. He needs a good glass of wine." We would say, "Papa, don't give him wine!" It would kill us when the teacher came to visit and Papa offered her wine. "The teacher won't drink wine." Then we were shocked when the teacher drank wine. She was no kook. It was good wine! But I remember getting to the point where I really had very little money—almost none. I thought I'd just wire home, that's all. I went to the telegraph office in Paris, and, to save money, just wrote, "Starving. Felice." One word but significant. Twenty-four hours later I had a telegram from Mama and *it* said, "Starve! Mama." The moment of truth! At long last I was an adult. What was I going to do now?

I'm going to tell you what that taught me. It taught me about hunger, it taught me about how cold a place can be, not only physically, but when you don't have the bottles of wine to share, the people who called themselves your "friends" don't come around anymore. It taught me a lot and I never would have learned it if Mama had relented and sent me a check. And I stayed there and stayed there, just to show her I could do it. When I went home many months later, she said to me one evening, "That was the hardest thing I ever had to do, but if I hadn't done it, you would never have grown to be Felice." And it was true. So through modeling, they taught me so much about living and loving together.

I'm often asked to be on talk shows. It always interests me that every other call, if not every single call, has to do with loneliness. "What do I do? I was married, I had kids and now I'm alone. I'm in an old apartment house, by myself. What happened? I would love to make friends with my neighbors, but I'm scared to knock at the door." "I walk down the street and I see attractive people and I try smiling at them, but I'm scared." We're teaching everybody everything there is except what is essential, and that is how to live in joy, how to live in happiness, how to have a sense of personal worth and personal dignity. Those things are taught, and they're learned. We need more people who teach that sort of thing by doing it, by risking, by saying hello, by sitting next to this man, by trying to show him that the stewardesses are people just like him, that this woman does have a baby and it's wonderful.

Recently on a talk show I heard a woman make an incredible statement. She said, "You know, I've spent the last 20 years trying to change my husband and I'm very disappointed in him. He's no longer the man I married." Isn't that marvelous?

I don't know how many of you know Rodney Dangerfield, but he says the craziest things. This is the zenith of what I'm talking about. He says, "We sleep in separate rooms, we have dinner apart, we take separate vacations, we're doing everything we can to keep our marriage together." Isn't that outrageous? And yet it's almost come to that.

Loving relationships, togetherness, away from "I" and "me" and to "us" and "we," is where the joy really lies. Eating a good dinner by yourself is fine, but sharing it with five or six people whom you love is heaven. Going in the park and looking at the trees by yourself can be lovely, but having someone on your arm who says "Look at the purple ones" while you're looking at the blue ones, and you don't miss the purple or the blue ones, is fantastic! Don't miss togetherness, because it's yours and it's available to you. Erich Fromm, who has written so many beautiful things about togetherness and love, said "The deepest need of man is to overcome his separateness. To leave the prison of his aloneness. The absolute failure to achieve this aim means insanity." And, he's a psychiatrist.

If you think about people who are mentally ill, they're the ones who have moved the farthest away from other people. The healthy ones dive right in the middle, no matter what it means. In love class we talked about risking and going out and I would say, "Why don't you do it?" "Oh, I'm afraid to be hurt." Good grief. What a crazy attitude. Being hurt occasionally can spice up your life. When you're crying, you're at least alive. Pain is better than nothing. We need to reach out, we need to bring in, we need not to be afraid. The biological sciences tell us this. I read something really interesting by Ashley Montague. He said, "Without interdependence, no living group of organisms could ever survive." Imagine—that's *all* forms of life! "And in so far as any group of organisms depart from their functioning, from their requirement of interdependence, to that extent does it then become malfunctional and inoperative." But, he adds, "Whenever organisms are interacting in a related manner, they are conferring *survival* benefits upon each other, giving each other *life.*" So, I'm involved in the process of *giving life*. It's the most incredible gift and it's yours to take.

Since all of these things are *learned*, what are some of the things that can bring us together, some of the things we need to know about togetherness, about relationships, about caring, about love? The first is so essential, because we have a very crazy concept in our culture called romantic love. That's why so many of us are disappointed! We really still believe what they tell us in musical comedies, that we look across a crowded room and there we see those special eyeballs that have been waiting for 20 years. You are drawn together, you embrace and walk out into the sunset and never have a problem. What a shame! And what about that wonderful courtship, when you are on your best behavior, she is on her best behavior? She always looks glorious every time you go to the door. You are always gallant. You even bring flowers and chocolates. You tell her how nice she looks and then you get married and the next day you say, "Who are you?" All of a sudden she appears in rollers. You say, "My God! I married someone from outer space!" "Wouldn't it be nice just once during courtship to answer the door and say, "Look, I wear rollers. So if that freaks you out, it's going to have to be." Why not? Presenting ourselves as we are, you recognize that if you are expecting a relationship to be a continual honeymoon of perfection you're going to be so disappointed.

But there are many kinds of honeymoons. I just love to talk to old people because they can tell you about the honeymoon transitions. Looking back, in order to learn. We don't do that, we're always looking ahead. But in looking back, they can tell you so many things. There was certainly a honeymoon of getting acquainted. Then there was a honeymoon of the first apartment and all that used furniture, maybe even boxes for bookcases, but in those times who the hell cared? You were so happy in that honeymoon. And then there was the honeymoon of the first kid coming. The honeymoon of watching everybody grow up, much to your amazement those 12, 15 years pass so fast and all of a sudden there you are, honeymoon after honeymoon after honeymoon. Elisabeth Kübler Ross tells us even that last honeymoon called "death" can be a glorious experience if we embrace it as we do all the other honeymoons, with no expectations. It's there, it's mine to experience and I want to know it when my time comes. I would like to live that way.

I don't want to harp on Mama and Papa, but since it's so close to me ... do you know that my mother used to tell us the story that she had never seen my father until five days after they were married? It was an arranged marriage and in Italy when you arrange a marriage, the man comes over to the home and, of course, all the women there were waiting on the table, with him sitting at the table, but she would never dare look at him. She would ask her sisters, "What does he look like?" They'd say "Oooh, he's so handsome. You're really going to freak out on this one." She said she didn't dare look at him. At the wedding her eyes were always down, and that marvelous day about five days into the marriage where she actually turned around and faced him, she said, "I did good!" He already knew it. But isn't it amazing these two people who supposedly didn't go through this period of having to fall madly in love, managed to survive in a beautiful relationship that was constantly growing for over 55 years? If you had seen how close they were when they parted. You just had a feeling that death wasn't going to break them apart, there was some way that it would just be a transitional period and eventually they would be reunited, there's no question about it. So remember always, the most essential thing about a relationship is that one and one together always make two, and if you want to survive the relationship, you must always maintain who you are and continue to grow through change. You are two wonderful, magical individuals. You have your life, he has his life and you build bridges to each other; but you always maintain your integrity and your dignity because all relationships, no matter how magnificent they are, even if they last for 60 years, are temporary, and eventually you are going to be faced again with you. One of the saddest things is the person who has invested everything in a relationship and when the relationship ends they must ask, "What do I do now?"

If you love someone, your goal is to want them to be all that they are and you will encourage them every inch of the way. Everytime they do something that helps them to grow or learn something to help them to become more, you dance and celebrate the occasion. You're not growing apart, you are growing together, but hand in hand, not melting one into the other. You are a unique person, it's impossible to melt into somebody else.

Some of you know the beautiful poem by Gibran about relationships. I'm just going to quote a couple of sentences. It's so lovely. He says, "Sing and dance together and be joyous, but let each one also be alone. Even as the strings of a lute are alone, though they quiver to the same music." Isn't that nice? Go to someone and say, "I want to quiver with you." "Give your hearts, but not into each other's keeping, for only the hand of Life can contain your hearts. Stand together and yet not too near together for the pillars of the temple, in order to hold the temple up, stand apart. The oak tree and the cypress do not grow in each other's shadow." Don't ever grow in anybody's shadow, you cannot *grow* in someone else's shadow. You find your own sunlight and you get as big and wonderful and as glorious as possible. And you share, telling them, "Let's communicate, let's talk, let's let it happen." But it doesn't happen in someone else's shadow. There you wilt, you forget who you are, you lose you and if you've lost you, you've lost the most essential thing you have. So you're one and one but you're two and you're together. You're an "I." He's an "I" and you are together an "us."

Secondly, I think loving relationships and togetherness are made in heaven, but it has to be *practiced* on earth, and sometimes that is very difficult. In fact, I know of nothing that is more difficult. I'm preparing a book now on loving relationships and I've done an enormous amount of research on what I consider to be the most dynamic aspect of human behavior—and I can't find much. If you want to learn about loving relationships, you're hard pressed to do it. Sure, loving relationships may bring pain. Coming together and having to give some of yourself up may bring pain. But you can also learn from pain. It really annoys me when, in our society, nobody wants any suffering at all. The minute you begin to suffer, you start popping pills or drowning yourself in alcohol, not knowing that some of the greatest learning can take place in a state of pain and despair. The difference is, you experience it and you don't *cling* to it. It's sick to *cling* to despair. You experience it and you *let it go.* There are great moments in all of our lives that were despairing. If you think back and you used them well, they helped you to grow and become a far greater person.

I mentioned earlier about how estranged we are from each other. In this culture we learn that the way to meet people is to stand erect and say, "How do you do?" Talk about a distancing phenomenon! If you're really lucky, somebody will give their hand and say "How do you do?" It's usually very quick. It's no wonder that though we all crave each other, we don't have each other, we don't touch each other. In our culture, at the age of five and six, a boy child is told "No more of this hugging nonsense, you're a *man* now and men don't do these things." I'm glad I was in a home where people said, "Who said?" Nobody in my house said, "How do you do?" When the door opened and someone arrived, everybody kissed. Everybody! Nobody was ignored, everybody was touched. What a wondrous experience to be touched in love. And there are many ways of touching. Do you know the wonder of walking into a room and having people happy because you are there? That's the greatest thing. Instead of an expression on their faces saying "Oh my God, there he is again," a joyous smile appears because you've walked in. An aura comes with you that lights up the whole house. Know that feeling? Don't miss it!

What amuses me, is that now we're finding out that scientifically touching does make a difference in our lives, physiologically and psychologically. There is a Doctor Bresler at the UCLA pain clinic. He isn't writing regular prescriptions any more, he's writing a prescription that says, "four hugs a day." People will say the man is crazy. "Oh no," he says, "hug once in the morning, once at lunch, once in the evening and once before bed and you'll get well." Dr. Harold Falk, senior psychiatrist at the Menninger Foundation, said this: "Hugging can lift depression, enabling the body's immunization system to become tuned up. Hugging breathes fresh life into tired bodies and makes you feel younger and more vibrant. In the home, hugging can strengthen relationships and significantly reduce tensions." Helen Colton in her book, *Joy of Touching,* said that the hemoglobin in the blood increases significantly when you are touched, fondled and hugged. Hemoglobin is that part of the blood that carries the vital supplies of oxygen to the heart and to the brain—and she says that if you want to be healthy, you must touch each other, you must love each other, you must hold each other. One of the saddest things in our culture is that we stress the sexual aspect of a relationship way out of proportion. What a pity, because in those things we are often missing the tenderness, the warmth. The kiss when it's not expected, the touch on the shoulder when you really need it most—that's "sensual" gratification. Jim Sanderson, a syndicated columnist who writes for the *L.A. Times,* recently had a letter I just loved. It came from a woman who just gave her name as Margaret. She was 71 years old. Her son came to see her one night and burst into the house without knocking. What nerve! He burst into the house and there was Margaret on the couch really having a blast with one of her boyfriends from the Senior Citizens. Do you know that this man was so horrified to see his mother kissing a man on the couch that he turned on his heels, said, "That's disgusting," and left. What an ass! So poor Margaret writes, "Did I do wrong?" And you know what Sanderson answered her? I've got to read this because it's so beautiful. He said,

> The best things in life, Margaret, go on forever. Every human being requires conversation and friendship. Why do we assume that the needs of older people stop there? The body may creak a little but there is no arteriosclerosis of emotions. Older people literally hunger for caring and affection and physical touching, just like anybody. Adult children and other family members seldom provide anything more than starvation rations—an occasional kiss. We know that sex is perfectly feasible at any age, given good health, but even when this does not seem appropriate for various reasons, why should there not be a little latter day romance, a little love, a little innocent contact, a stolen kiss, a gentle massage, a caress on the cheek, one hand fondling another? Many women of your age, Margaret, often feel strange and alarming stirrings within themselves, feelings that may not have surfaced for years. This is the life force coming to your rescue to remind you that you are a male or a female, not just an all-purpose senior citizen. Rejoice in this, Margaret, you've had enough bad news.

You never cease needing to be recognized in a hundred different ways. Relationships and togetherness must be lived in the *present.* You have to live *now,* you have to enjoy it *now,* you have to do for people *now.* One of the saddest things I heard in the last year was a colleague of mine whose wife died suddenly, very young. Because death is an amazingly democratic thing, it never tells you when it's going to come. We just all know, believe it or not, someday it will come to *us.* And by living every moment you are ready for it. The only people who scream and yell at the moment of death are those people who have never lived at all. If you live now, when death comes you say, "C'mon, who's afraid of you?" But my colleague told me his wife had always wanted a red satin dress. He said, "I always thought that was really stupid and in bad taste." Then he said to me, with tears in his eyes, "Do you think it would be all right if I buried her in a red satin dress?" I felt like doing a Mama and saying, "Stupido!"

If your wife wants a red satin dress, get it now! Don't wait to decorate her casket with roses. Come in one day while she's sitting there alive and inundate her in roses. Throw them at her. We're always putting things off for tomorrow, especially, with people whom we love. Who cares what "people will say"? In reality they don't really care. "It's foolish for me to tell her I love her. She knows it." Are you sure? And do you ever get tired of having somebody say, "I love you"? Do you ever get tired of picking up your coffee cup and finding a little note underneath it that says, "You're incredible"? Do you ever tire of getting a card, not when it's your birthday or Valentine's Day, but a card that says, "My life is so much richer because you're in it"? The time to buy the dress is *now*. The time to give the flowers is *now*. The time to make the phone call is *now*. The time to write the note is *now*. The time to reach over and touch is *now*. The time to say "You're important to me, sometimes I seem to forget, but I don't. My life would be pretty empty without you," with no strings attached, is *now*. Losing a loved one is a hard way to learn that love is lived in the now. It's a hard way to learn that you buy the dress now, or write the note now. But *we* have another chance. That husband *doesn't*.

Loving relationships depend upon open, honest, beautiful communication. Never have a short argument. Never! The worst kind of argument in the world is when you walk in and say, "What's the matter honey?" "Nothing." "Oh, c'mon, there's something." "No, there's nothing." I've found a wonderful way to make the next argument a forever argument; you say "Oh, I'm so glad, it really seemed to me like there was something, and I'm glad to know that there is nothing. Bye." Next time you say, "What's the matter?" they're going to tell you. We don't listen to ourselves and the things that we say.

We need to listen to the way we say things because we've learned them from others. It's like teachers who say to kids, "I'm waiting for Sally!" It's no wonder Sally says, "Wait you old...." But we say things that are just as obnoxious. You hear yourself saying, for instance, "The trouble with you is...." Usually the trouble with me is *you*. "One of these days, you'll be sorry." Oh, *no* I won't. "If I've told you once, I've told you a thousand times." Then what the hell are you telling me *again* for? "I've given you the best years of my life." If these are the best years, what do I have to look forward to? "Do as you please, it's your life." Well, you know, if it is, will you let ME *live* it?

Togetherness. From "I" and "me" to "us" and "we." Your relationships will be as vital and alive as *you* are. If you're dead, your relationship is dead. And if your relationships are boring and inadequate, it's because *you* are boring and inadequate. Liven yourself up! Be aware that the world and the people in it are not created solely for *you*. Try making *someone else* comfortable. Assume that people are good until you *actually* and *specifically* learn differently. And even then, know that they have potential for change and that you can help them out. Practice using and thinking "us" and "we" rather than "I" and "me." Love *many* things intensely because the measure of you as a lover is how deeply you love how much. Remember that all things *change,* especially human relationships, and to maintain them, *we* must change with them. Make the change in growth. Make sure that you're constantly growing *together* but *separately*. Seek *healthy* people in your life who still remember how to laugh, how to love and how to cry. Remember that misery doesn't only love company, it *demands* it. Have none of it.

And lastly, I heard the Dalai Lama of Tibet last year. One of the things that he said was so poignant. He said, "We live very close together. So, our prime purpose in life is to *help* others." Then he sort of smiled and said, "And if you can't *help* them at least don't *hurt* them." If each of us promised ourselves that in terms of our human relationships and our togetherness, we were dedicated to the process of helping each other to grow, and that if we couldn't do that, we were at least not going to hurt each other, what a magical thing that would be. An Italian poet, Quasimodo, who won the Nobel prize for poetry, wrote a little poem that says: "Each of us stands alone in this vast world, momentarily bathed in a ray of sunlight. And suddenly it's night." The poem is called "Ed e' Subito Sera"—And Suddenly It's Night. If you stand together with me, we can share the sunlight, and believe me, the night won't seem so frightening.

Review Questions

1. What does Leo Buscaglia apparently believe about the relationship between your language and your attitudes?
2. What does Buscaglia mean when he says "I teach nothing to no one"?
3. What is Buscaglia's belief about the role of models in learning?
4. What role does risk-taking play in Buscaglia's philosophy?
5. Describe the "honeymoon" phenomenon Buscaglia discusses. Does it only apply to romantic relationships? Explain.
6. What substantive point is Leo making with his extreme example of "throwing roses at your wife"?

Probes

1. In a group of five to seven, share examples from your own experience of how your definition of the situation directly affected the quality of your life experience.
2. What do you think Buscaglia means by "getting trapped in the concept of 'I' and 'me'"?
3. How is the relationship Buscaglia discusses between "telling" and "showing" similar to the relationship between verbal codes (Chapter 3) and nonverbal cues (Chapter 4)?
4. What made Rosa Buscaglia's "Shut up!" a loving communication?
5. Buscaglia claims that mentally ill people are the "ones who have moved the farthest away from other people," whereas the "healthy ones dive right in the middle, no matter what it means." Do you agree or disagree? How so?
6. Buscaglia emphasizes, with the help of some lines from a book by Kahlil Gibran, the importance of separateness in a loving relationship. What implications does this point have for your communication with the people you love?
7. How do you respond to Buscaglia's references to the medical doctors who "prescribed" hugs? Could there be something to that? Or is this just another example of Leo's "craziness?"

Chapter 15

Carl R. Rogers's Approach

Carl Rogers was a psychotherapist and communication theorist who influenced many of the authors represented in this book. I highly recommend that you read at least one of his books—for example, *On Becoming a Person, Person to Person: The Process of Becoming Human,* or his most recent book, *A Way of Being.* In the 1950s Rogers was one of the half-dozen persons responsible for moving psychology away from an exclusive focus on Freudian psychodynamics and quantifiable variables to a concern with the whole person and communication relationships. By the time of his death in the late 1980s, he was known all over the world as a psychotherapist, group facilitator, and teacher.

This reading is made up of excerpts from a chapter in *A Way of Being.* Like many of his writings, this one was originally a talk he gave, in this case an invited speech at the California Institute of Technology. Rogers reports that as he prepared for the occasion, he became frustrated at his own efforts to describe what he believed about communication. So he decided to demonstrate rather than simply discuss, to endeavor, as he put it, "to *communicate,* rather than just to speak *about* the subject of communication."

In another place, Rogers wrote that over his lifetime he had discovered that "What is most personal is most general." This talk is evidence of this same insight. Rogers tries to stick close to his personal experiences with communication, and as he describes them he finds himself talking about my experience—and probably yours, too. So this essay demonstrates how "what is most personal is most general."

One of the reasons I like much of what Rogers says is that he begins discussing communication by focusing not on talk but on listening. He describes what it means really to hear someone and to be heard, to be listened to by another. Over his forty years as a psychotherapist, Rogers learned that complete hearing—listening, clarifying, and responding to all the levels at which the other is communicating—is one key to a therapeutic, growth-promoting relationship. The therapist, he argues, doesn't need to be able to administer psychometric tests or interpret dreams. The most important thing is that he or she needs to make contact, to communicate interpersonally. As he summarizes, "a creative, active, sensitive, accurate, empathic, nonjudgmental listening is for me terribly important in a relationship."

The second of Rogers's three main points involves what he calls "congruence." This is his label for the state where "my experiencing of this moment is present in my awareness and when what is present in my awareness is present in my communication." As he explains in other writings, this does not mean that you impulsively blurt out every thought that enters your mind. Especially when you're experiencing mixed feelings, it's important to reflect on the dimensions of experience that deserve communicating. Rogers also believes that incongruence is often an outgrowth of fear.

The flip side of congruence, of course, is allowing and encouraging the other to be congruent too. As Rogers says, this is often the ultimate test for the leader, teacher, and parent. But when at least some measure of congruence characterizes both sides of a relationship, the communication is enriched by it.

Rogers's third learning is that what he's called unconditional positive regard or nonpossessive warmth is also vital to effective communication. People typically experience so much evaluation and criticism that when they feel accepted for who they are, they often blossom. As he notes, people can be appreciated just as we appreciate a sunset.

In other writings, Rogers has also clarified that he doesn't mean we should go around in a naive pink fog, loving every terrorist, rapist, and sociopath who makes the front page. He worked extensively with "sick" persons, and he knew what it was like to apply the principle of unconditional positive regard to his communication with them. Often the key is to separate the person and the behavior so that you can accept the former while rejecting the latter. It is also important to remember that persons act in ways that make the most sense to them at the time they act. Observers may not be able to fathom the sense that some actions make, but if we want to communicate with these persons—without necessarily condoning what they do—positive regard helps.

When Rogers gave this talk it was remarkable to hear a person being so open and straightforward in such a relatively "formal" situation. Rogers was often disarmingly direct in just that way. I hope his directness enables you to hear what he has to say. Carl Rogers had an approach to interpersonal communication that is very much worth getting to know.

Experiences in Communication

Carl R. Rogers

... What I would like to do is very simple indeed. I would like to share with you some of the things I have learned for myself in regard to communication. These are personal learnings growing out of my own experience. I am not attempting at all to say that you should learn or do these same things but I feel that if I can report my own experience honestly enough, perhaps you can check what I say against your own experience and decide as to its truth or falsity for you.... Another way of putting this is that some of my experiences in communicating with others have made me feel expanded, larger, enriched, and have accelerated my own growth. Very often in these experiences I feel that the other person has had similar reactions and that he too has been enriched, that his development and his functioning have moved forward. Then there have been other occasions in which the growth or development of each of us has been diminished or stopped or even reversed....

The first simple feeling I want to share with you is my enjoyment when I can really *hear* someone. I think perhaps this has been a long-standing characteristic of mine. I can remember this in my early grammar school days. A child would ask the teacher a question and the teacher would give a perfectly good answer to a completely different question. A feeling of pain and distress would always strike me. My reaction was, "But you didn't hear him!" I felt a sort of childish despair at the lack of communication which was (and is) so common.

I believe I know why it is satisfying to me to hear someone. When I can really hear someone, it puts me in touch with him; it enriches my life. It is through hearing people that I have learned all that I know about individuals, about personality, about interpersonal relationships....

When I say that I enjoy hearing someone, I mean, of course, hearing deeply. I mean that I hear the words, the thoughts, the feeling tones, the personal meaning, even the meaning that is below the conscious intent of the speaker. Sometimes too, in a message which superficially is not very important, I hear a deep human cry that lies buried and unknown far below the surface of the person.

So I have learned to ask myself, can I hear the sounds and sense the shape of this other person's inner world? Can I resonate to what he is saying so deeply that I sense the meanings he is afraid of yet would like to communicate, as well as those he knows?

I think, for example, of an interview I had with an adolescent boy. Like many an adolescent today he was saying at the outset of the interview that he had no goals. When I questioned him on this, he insisted even more strongly that he had no goals whatsoever, not even one. I said, "There isn't anything you want to do?" "*Nothing*.... Well, yeah, I want to keep on living." I remember distinctly my feeling at that moment. I resonated very deeply to this phrase. He might simply be telling me that, like everyone else, he wanted to live. On the other hand, he might be telling me—and this seemed to be a definite possibility—that at some point the question of whether or not to live had been a real issue with him. So I tried to resonate to him at all levels. I didn't know for certain what the message was. I simply wanted to be open to any of the meanings that this statement might have, including the possibility that he might at one time have considered suicide. My being willing and able to listen to him at all levels is perhaps one of the things that made it possible for him to tell me, before the end of the interview, that not long before he had been on the point of blowing his brains out. This little episode is an example of what I mean by wanting to really hear someone at all the levels at which he is endeavoring to communicate....

I find, both in therapeutic interviews and in the intensive group experiences which have meant a great deal to me, that hearing has consequences. When I truly hear a person and the meanings that are important to him at that moment, hearing not simply his words, but him, and when I let him know that I have heard his own private personal meanings, many things happen. There is first of all a grateful look. He feels released. He wants to tell me more about his world. He surges forth in a new sense of freedom. He becomes more open to the process of change....

Let me move on to a second learning that I would like to share with you. I like to *be heard*. A number of times in my life I have felt myself bursting with insoluble problems, or going round and round in tormented circles or, during one period, overcome by feelings of worthlessness and despair. I think I have been more fortunate than most in finding at these times individuals who have been able to hear me and thus to rescue me from the chaos of my feelings, individuals who have been able to hear my meanings a little more deeply than I have known them. These persons have heard me without judging me, diagnosing me, appraising me, evaluating me. They have just listened and clarified and responded to me at all the levels at which I was communicating. I can testify that when you are in psychological distress and someone really hears you without passing judgment on you, without trying to take responsibility for you, without trying to mold you, it feels damn good! At these times it has relaxed the tension in me. It has permitted me to bring out the frightening feelings, the guilts, the despair, the confusions that have been a part of my experience. When I have been listened to and when I have been heard, I am able to reperceive my world in a new way and to go on. It is astonishing how elements that seem insoluble become soluble when someone listens, how confusions that seem irremediable turn into relatively clear flowing streams when one is heard. I have deeply appreciated the times that I have experienced this sensitive, empathic, concentrated listening.

I dislike it myself when I can't hear another, when I do not understand him. If it is only a simple failure of comprehension or a failure to focus my attention on what he is saying or a difficulty in undersanding his words, then I feel only a very mild dissatisfaction with myself. But what I really dislike in myself is not being able to hear the other person because I am so sure in advance of what he is about to say that I don't listen. It is only afterward that I realize that I have heard what I have already decided he is saying; I have failed really to listen. Or even worse are those times when I catch myself trying to twist his message to make it say what I want him to say, and then only hearing that. This can be a very subtle thing, and it is surprising how skillful I can be in doing it. Just by twisting his words a small amount, by distorting his meaning just a little, I can make it appear that he is not only saying the thing I want to hear, but that he is the person I want him to be. Only when I realize through his protest or through my own gradual recognition that I am subtly manipulating him, do I become disgusted with myself. I know too, from being on the receiving end of this, how frustrating it is to be received for what you are not, to be heard as saying something which you have not said. This creates anger and bafflement and disillusion.

This last statement indeed leads into the next learning that I want to share with you: I am terribly frustrated and shut into myself when I try to express something which is deeply me, which is a part of my own private, inner world, and the other person does not understand. When I take the gamble, the risk, of trying to share something that is very personal with another individual and it is not received and not understood, this is a very deflating and a very lonely experience. I have come to believe that such an experience makes some individuals psychotic. It causes them to give up hoping that anyone can understand them. Once they have lost that hope, then their own inner world, which becomes more and more bizarre, is the only place where they can live. They can no longer live in any shared human experience. I can sympathize with them because I know that when I try to share some feeling aspect of myself which is private, precious, and tentative, and when this communication is met by evaluation, by reassurance, by distortion of my meaning, my very strong reaction is, "Oh, what's the use!" At such a time, one knows what it is to be alone.

So, as you can readily see from what I have said thus far, a creative, active, sensitive, accurate, empathic, nonjudgmental listening is for me terribly important in a relationship. It is important for me to provide it; it has been extremely important, especially at certain times in my life, to receive it. I feel that I have grown within myself when I have provided it; I am very sure that I have grown and been released and enhanced when I have received this kind of listening.

Let me move on to another area of my learnings.

I find it very satisfying when I can be real, when I can be close to whatever it is that is going on within me. I like it when I can listen to myself. To really know what I am experiencing in the moment is by no means an easy thing, but I feel somewhat encouraged because I think that over the years I have been improving at it. I am convinced, however, that it is a lifelong task and that none of us ever is totally able to be comfortably close to all that is going on within our own experience.

In place of the term "realness" I have sometimes used the word "congruence." By this I mean when my experiencing of this moment is present in my awareness and when what is present in my awareness is present in my communication, then each of these three levels matches or is congruent. At such moments I am integrated or whole, I am completely in one piece. Most of the time, of course, I, like everyone else, exhibit some degree of incongruence. I have learned, however, that realness, or genuineness, or congruence—whatever term you wish to give it—is a fundamental basis for the best of communication.

What do I mean by being close to what is going on in me? Let me try to explain what I mean by describing what sometimes occurs in my work as a therapist. Sometimes a feeling "rises up in me" which seems to have no particular relationship to what is going on. Yet I have learned to accept and trust this feeling in my awareness and to try to communicate it to my client. For example, a client is talking to me and I suddenly feel an image of him as a pleading little boy, folding his hands in supplication, saying, "Please let me have this, please let me have this." I have learned that if I can be real in the relationship with him and express this feeling that has occurred in me, it is very likely to strike some deep note in him and to advance our relationship. . . .

I feel a sense of satisfaction when I can dare to communicate the realness in me to another. This is far from easy, partly because what I am experiencing keeps changing every moment. Usually there is a lag, sometimes of moments, sometimes of days, weeks or months, between the experiencing and the communication: I experience something; I feel something, but only later do I dare to communicate it, when it has become cool enough to risk sharing it with another. But when I can communicate what is real in me at the moment that it occurs, I feel genuine, spontaneous, and alive.

I am disappointed when I realize—and of course this realization always comes afterward, after a lag of time—that I have been too frightened or too threatened to let myself get close to what I am experiencing, and that consequently I have not been genuine or congruent. There immediately comes to mind an instance that is somewhat painful to reveal. Some years ago I was invited to be a Fellow at the Center for Advanced Study in the Behavioral Sciences at Stanford. The Fellows are a group of brilliant and well-informed scholars. I suppose it is inevitable that there is a considerable amount of one-upmanship, of showing off one's knowledge and achievements. It seems important for each Fellow to impress the others, to be a little more assured, to be a little more knowledgeable than he really is. I found myself doing this same thing—playing a role of having greater certainty and greater competence than I really possess. I can't tell you how disgusted with myself I felt as I realized what I was doing: I was not being me, I was playing a part.

I regret it when I suppress my feelings too long and they burst forth in ways that are distorted or attacking or hurtful. I have a friend whom I like very much but who has one particular pattern of behavior that thoroughly annoys me. Because of the usual tendency to be nice, polite, and pleasant I kept this annoyance to myself for too long and, when it finally burst its bounds, it came out not only as annoyance but as an attack on him. This was hurtful, and it took us some time to repair the relationship.

I am inwardly pleased when I have the strength to permit another person to be his own realness and to be separate from me. I think that is often a very threatening possibility. In some ways I have found it an ultimate test of staff leadership and of parenthood. Can I freely permit this staff member or my son or my daughter to become a separate person with ideas, purpose, and values which may not be identical with my own? I think of one staff member this past year who showed many flashes of brilliance but who clearly held values different from mine and behaved in ways very different from the ways in which I would behave. It was a real struggle, in which I feel I was only partially successful, to let him be himself, to let him develop as a person entirely separate from me and my ideas and my values. Yet to the extent that I was successful, I was pleased with myself, because I think this permission to be a separate person is what makes for the autonomous development of another individual.

I am angry with myself when I discover that I have been subtly controlling and molding another person in my own image. This has been a very painful part of my professional experience. I hate to have "disciples," students who have molded themselves meticulously into the pattern that they feel I wish. Some of the responsibility I place with them, but I cannot avoid the uncomfortable probability that in unknown ways I have subtly controlled such individuals and made them into carbon copies of myself, instead of the separate professional persons they have every right to become.

From what I have been saying, I trust it is clear that when I can permit realness in myself or sense it or permit it in another, I am very satisfied. When I cannot permit it in myself or fail to permit it in another, I am very distressed. When I am able to let myself be congruent and genuine, I often help the other person. When the other person is transparently real and congruent, he often helps me. In those rare moments when a deep realness in one meets a realness in the other, a memorable "I-thou relationship," as Martin Buber would call it, occurs. Such a deep and mutual personal encounter does not happen often, but I am convinced that unless it happens occasionally, we are not living as human beings.

I want to move on to another area of my learning in interpersonal relationships—one that has been slow and painful for me.

I feel warmed and fulfilled when I can let in the fact, or permit myself to feel, that someone cares for, accepts, admires, or prizes me. Because of elements in my past history, I suppose, it has been very difficult for me to do this. For a long time I tended almost automatically to brush aside any positive feelings aimed in my direction. My reaction was, "Who, me? You couldn't possibly care for me. You might like what I have done, or my achievements, but not me." This is one respect in which my own therapy helped me very much. I am not always able even now to let in such warm and loving feelings from others, but I find it very releasing when I can do so. I know that some people flatter me in order to gain something for themselves; some people praise me because they are afraid to be hostile. But I have come to recognize the fact that some people genuinely appreciate me, like me, love me, and I want to sense that fact and let it in. I think I have become less aloof as I have been able to take in and soak up those loving feelings.

I feel enriched when I can truly prize or care for or love another person and when I can let that feeling flow out to that person. Like many others, I used to fear being trapped by letting my feelings show. "If I care for him, he can control me." "If I love her, I am trying to control her." I think that I have moved a long way toward being less fearful in this respect. Like my clients, I too have slowly learned that tender, positive feelings are not dangerous either to give or to receive....

I think of one governmental executive in a group in which I participated, a man with high responsibility and excellent technical training as an engineer. At the first meeting of the group he impressed me, and I think others, as being cold, aloof, somewhat bitter, resentful, and cynical. When he spoke of how he ran his office, it appeared that he administered it "by the book," without any warmth or human feeling. In one of the early sessions he was speaking of his wife, and a group member asked him, "Do you love your wife?" He paused for a long time and the questioner said, "O.K. That's answer enough." The executive said, "No. Wait a minute. The reason I didn't respond was that I was wondering, 'Have I ever loved anyone?' I don't really think I have ever *loved* anyone."

A few days later, he listened with great intensity as one member of the group revealed many personal feelings of isolation and loneliness and spoke of the extent to which he had been living behind a facade. The next morning the engineer said, "Last night I thought and thought about what he told us. I even wept quite a bit myself. I can't remember how long it has been since I have cried, and I really felt something. I think perhaps what I felt was love."

It is not surprising that before the week was over, he had thought through different ways of handling his growing son, on whom he had been placing very rigorous demands. He had also begun to really appreciate the love his wife had extended to him—love that he now felt he could in some measure reciprocate.

Because of having less fear of giving or receiving positive feelings, I have become more able to appreciate individuals. I have come to believe that this ability is rather rare; so often, even with our children, we love them to control them rather than loving them because we appreciate them. One of the most satisfying feelings I know—and also one of the most growth-promoting experiences for the other person—comes from my appreciating this individual in the same way that I appreciate a sunset. People are just as wonderful as sunsets if I can let them *be*. In fact, perhaps the reason we can truly appreciate a sunset is that we cannot control it. When I look at a sunset as I did the other evening, I don't find myself saying, "Soften the orange a little on the right hand corner, and put a bit more purple along the base, and use a little more pink in the cloud color." I don't do that. I don't *try* to control a sunset. I watch it with awe as it unfolds. I like myself best when I can appreciate my staff member, my son, my daughter, my grandchildren, in this same way. I believe this is a somewhat Oriental attitude; for me it is a most satisfying one.

Another learning I would like to mention briefly is one of which I am not proud but which seems to be a fact. When I am not prized and appreciated, I not only *feel* very much diminished, but my behavior is actually affected by my feelings. When I am prized, I blossom and expand, I am an interesting individual. In a hostile or unappreciative group, I am just not much of anything. People wonder, with very good reason, how did he ever get a reputation? I wish I had the strength to be more similar in both kinds of groups, but actually the person I am in a warm and interested group is different from the person I am in a hostile or cold group.

Thus, prizing or loving and being prized or loved is experienced as very growth enhancing. A person who is loved appreciatively, not possessively, blooms and develops his own unique self. The person who loves nonpossessively is himself enriched. This, at least, has been my experience.

I could give you some of the research evidence which shows that these qualities I have mentioned—an ability to listen empathically, a congruence or genuineness an acceptance or prizing of the other—when they are present in a relationship make for good communication and for constructive change in personality. But I feel that, somehow, research evidence is out of place in a talk such as I have been giving.

Review Questions

1. What does Rogers mean by "hearing deeply"?
2. According to Rogers, what is the primary outcome of someone being fully or deeply heard?
3. What does "congruence" mean? What does it *not* mean?
4. How does the fact that I am changing from moment to moment affect my being congruent?
5. At what points in his talk does Rogers suggest that the communication he is discussing is appropriate in nonintimate—that is, business or professional—settings?

Probes

1. Which discussion of listening in Chapter 7 is closest to Rogers's description of hearing another and being heard?
2. How is Rogers's concept of congruence related to what the Amodeos say about self-revealing communication in Chapter 8?
3. Do you think congruence helps create a defensive or a supportive communication climate (see Chapter 11)?
4. What is the relationship between what Rogers says about suppressing feelings and the discussion of anger in Chapter 11?
5. Did you ever feel uncomfortable as you read Rogers's words? What do those feelings tell you about the topic of Chapter 8, self-disclosure?
6. How do you think Neil Postman, the author of "The Communication Panacea" in Chapter 8, would respond to what Rogers says here?

Chapter 16

Martin Buber's Approach

artin Buber, a Jewish philosopher, teacher, and theologian, was born and raised in what is now part of the Soviet Union, and died in 1965 in Israel. Throughout his life, Buber was both a "scholar" or "intellectual" and an intensely practical person interested in everyday life experiences. As an intellectual, he was hungry to learn and to write all he could about how humans relate with one another. As a practical person, he was determined to keep all of his theorizing and scholarship firmly based on the concrete events he experienced every day. Because he was raised by his grandparents in Europe during the late nineteenth and early twentieth centuries (Buber's parents were separated), lived through both world wars, was active in several political movements, and was a well-known, even famous, citizen of Israel, his life experiences are different in many ways from yours and mine. But for me, Buber's peculiar genius is that he can sense that part of his experience that is universal and can project that universal knowledge about human meetings through his European heritage and his "foreign" native language in such a way that he talks to me directly. In other words, even though he is in many ways very different from me, he says, "this is my experience; reflect on it a little and you might find that it's your experience too." Sometimes I stumble over Buber's language, the way he puts things. For example, like some other older authors in this book, Buber uses "man" when he means "human." But when I listen to him and do what he asks, I discover that he's right. It *is* my experience, only now I understand it better than I did before.

I don't know whether this one excerpt from Buber's writing will work that way for you. But the possibility is there if you will open yourself to hear him.* That's one thing about Buber's writings. Although he's a philosopher, he has been criticized because he doesn't state philosophical propositions and then try to verify and validate them with "proof." Instead, Buber insists that his reader try to meet him in a *conversation*, a dialogue. The main thing is for the reader to see whether his or her life experiences resonate with Buber's. This resonance is the only "proof" of the validity of Buber's ideas that the reader will receive. So far, millions of persons have experienced that resonance. Books by and about Buber, especially his *I and Thou*, have been translated into over twenty languages and are read around the world.

In almost all his writing, Buber begins by observing that each of us lives a twofold reality. He describes the two "folds" in the section of *I and Thou* I paraphrased in my essay in Chapter 2. One "fold" is made up of our interaction with objects—human and otherwise—in the world. In this mode of living, we merely need to develop and maintain our ability to be "objective," to explain ourselves and the world with accurate theories and valid cause-and-effect formulations. But the other "fold" occurs when we become fully human *persons* in genuine relationships with others, when we meet another and "make the other present as a whole and as a unique being, as the person that he is."

This genuine relationship Buber talks about is the "highest form" of what I've been calling interpersonal communication. You've probably heard of Buber's term for

*You might also be interested in other things written by or about Buber. For starters I recommend Aubrey Hodes, *Martin Buber: An Intimate Portrait* (New York: Viking, 1971); or Hilary Evans Bender, *Monarch Notes: The Philosophy of Martin Buber* (New York: Monarch, 1974). Maurice Friedman has written the definitive Buber biography, and I'd especially recommend the third volume, *Martin Buber's Life and Work: The Later Years, 1945–1965* (New York: Dutton, 1983). Buber's most important and influential book is *I and Thou*, trans. Walter Kaufmann (New York: Scribner, 1970).

it—an "*I-Thou* relationship."* According to Buber, the individual lives always in the world of *I-It;* the *person* can enter the world of *I-Thou.* Both worlds are necessary. You can't expect to communicate interpersonally with everyone in every situation. But you can only become a fully human person by sharing genuine interpersonal relationships with others. As Buber puts it, without *It* the person cannot live. But he who lives with *It* alone is not a person.

This article is taken from a talk Buber gave when he visited the United States in 1957. It's especially useful because it is a kind of summary of much of what he had written in the first seventy-nine years of his life (he died when he was eighty-seven).

I've outlined the article to simplify it some and to show how clearly organized it actually is. As you can see from the outline, Buber's subject is interpersonal relationships, which he calls "man's personal dealings with one another," or "the interhuman." Like the rest of this book, Buber's article doesn't deal with some mystical spirit world in which we all become one. Rather, he's writing about communication between today's teachers and students, politicians and voters, preachers and parishioners, and between you and me. First, he explains some attitudes and actions that keep people from achieving "genuine dialogue." Then he describes the characteristics of this dialogue, or *I-Thou* relationship. In the outline I've paraphrased each point that he makes.

When you read the essay, you'll probably be able to see where several of the other writers in this book got some of their ideas. For example, compare Carl Rogers's explanation of "congruence" with what Buber says about "being and seeming." Or note Buber's way of talking about the six "persons" in a one-to-one conversation—my me, your you, and so on—which were also identified by Dean Barnlund in Chapter 2.

Whether or not you note that kind of thing, however, read this article as thoughtfully as you can. It sums up everything in this book. And I know from the experience I have lived that it's worth understanding.

Outline of Martin Buber's "Elements of the Interhuman"

    I. Interhuman relationships are not the same as "Social Relationships."

        A. Social relationships can be very close, but no *existential* or person-to-person relation is necessarily involved.

        B. That's because the collective or social suppresses individual persons.

        C. But in the interhuman, person meets person. In other words, "the only thing that matters is that for each of the two men the other happens as the particular other, that each becomes aware of the other and is thus related to him in such a way that he does not regard and use him as his object, but as his partner in a living event, even if it is no more than a boxing match."

---

*As I noted in Chapter 2, Buber's translators always point out that this "thou" is not the religious term of formal address. It is a translation of the German *Du,* the familiar form of the pronoun "you." As Walter Kaufmann, one of Buber's translators, explains, "German lovers say *Du* to one another and so do friends. *Du* is spontaneous and unpretentious, remote from formality, pomp, and dignity."

D. In short, "the sphere of the interhuman is one in which a person is confronted by the other. We [i.e., Buber] call its unfolding the dialogical."

II. There are three problems that get in the way of dialogue.

  A. The first problem is the duality of *being* and *seeming*. Dialogue won't happen if the people involved are only "seeming." They need to try to practice "being."

    1. "Seeming" in a relationship involves being concerned with your image or front—with how you wish to appear.

    2. "Being" involves the spontaneous and unreserved presentation of what you really are in your personal dealings with the other.

    3. These two are generally found mixed together. The most we can do is to distinguish between persons in whose essential attitude one or the other (being or seeming) predominates.

    4. When seeming reigns, real interpersonal communication is impossible: "Whatever the meaning of the word 'truth' may be in other realms, in the interhuman realm it means that men communicate themselves to one another as what they are."

    5. The tendency toward seeming, however, is understandable.

      a. We *essentially* need personal confirmation, i.e., we can't live without being confirmed by other people.

      b. Seeming often appears to help us get the confirmation we need.

      c. Consequently, "to yield to seeming is man's essential cowardice, to resist it is his essential courage."

    6. This view indicates that there is no such thing as "bad being," but rather people who are habitually content to "seem" and afraid to "be." "I have never known a young person who seemed to me irretrievably bad."

  B. The second problem involves the way we perceive others.

    1. Many modern fatalists, such as Jean-Paul Sartre, believe that we can ultimately know *only* ourselves, that "man has directly to do only with himself and his own affairs."

    2. But the main prerequisite for dialogue is that you get in direct touch with the other, "that each person should regard his partner as the very one he is."

      a. This means becoming aware of the other person as an essentially unique being. "To be aware of a man . . . means in particular to perceive his wholeness as a person determined by the spirit: it means to perceive the dynamic centre which stamps his every utterance, action, and attitude with the recognizable sign of uniqueness."

      b. But this kind of awareness is impossible so long as I objectify the other.

    3. Perceiving the other in this way is contrary to everything in our world that is scientifically analytic or reductive.

      a. This is not to say that the sciences are wrong, only that they are severely limited.

      b. What's dangerous is the extension of the scientific, analytic method to all of life, because it is very difficult for science to remain aware of the essential uniqueness of persons.

4. This kind of perception is called "personal making present." What enables us to do it is our capacity for "imagining the real" of the other.

   a. Imagining the real "is not a looking at the other but a bold swinging—demanding the most intensive stirring of one's being—into the life of the other."

   b. When I *imagine* what the other person is *really* thinking and feeling, I can make direct contact with him or her.

C. The third problem which impedes the growth of dialogue is the tendency toward imposition instead of unfolding.

   1. One way to affect a person is to impose yourself on him or her.

   2. Another way is to "find and further in the soul of the other the disposition toward" that which you have recognized in yourself as right.

      a. Unfolding is not simply "teaching," but rather *meeting*.

      b. It requires believing in the other person.

      c. It means working as a helper of the growth processes already going on in the other.

   3. The propagandist is the typical "imposer"; the teacher *can* be the correspondingly typical "unfolder."

   4. The ethic implied here is similar to Immanuel Kant's, i.e., persons should never be treated as means to an end, but only as ends in themselves.

      a. The only difference is that Buber stresses that persons exist not in isolation but in the interhuman, and

      b. for the interhuman to occur, there must be:

         (1) as little seeming as possible.

         (2) genuine perceiving ("personal making present") of the other, and

         (3) as little imposing as possible.

III. Summary of the characteristics of genuine dialogue:

   A. Each person must turn toward and be open to the other, a "turning of the being."

   B. Each must make present the other by imagining the real.

   C. Each confirms the other's being; however, confirmation does not necessarily mean approval.

   D. Each must be authentically himself or herself.

      1. Each must say whatever she or he "has to say."

      2. Each cannot be ruled by thoughts of his or her own effect or effectiveness as a speaker.

   E. Where dialogue becomes genuine, "there is brought into being a memorable common fruitfulness which is to be found nowhere else."

   F. Speaking is not always essential; silence can be very important.

   G. Finally, all participants must be committed to dialogue; otherwise, it will fail.

Again, Buber's language sometimes can get in the way of understanding him. But if you listen carefully to him, I think you will be able to resonate with at least some of what he says.

Elements of the Interhuman

Martin Buber

The Social and the Interhuman

It is usual to ascribe what takes place between men to the social realm, thereby blurring a basically important line of division between two essentially different areas of human life. I myself, when I began nearly fifty years ago to find my own bearings in the knowledge of society, making use of the then unknown concept of the interhuman, made the same error. From that time it became increasingly clear to me that we have to do here with a separate category of our existence, even a separate dimension, to use a mathematical term, and one with which we are so familiar that its peculiarity has hitherto almost escaped us. Yet insight into its peculiarity is extremely important not only for our thinking but also for our living.

We may speak of social phenomena wherever the life of a number of men, lived with one another, bound up together, brings in its train shared experiences and reactions. But to be thus bound up together means only that each individual existence is enclosed and contained in a group existence. It does not mean that between one member and another of the group there exists any kind of personal relation. They do feel that they belong together in a way that is, so to speak, fundamentally different from every possible belonging together with someone outside the group. And there do arise, especially in the life of smaller groups, contacts which frequently favour the birth of individual relations, but, on the other hand, frequently make it more difficult. In no case, however, does membership in a group necessarily involve an existential relation between one member and another. It is true that there have been groups in history which included highly sensitive and intimate relations between two of their members—as, for instance, in the homosexual relations among the Japanese samurai or among Doric warriors—and these were countenanced for the sake of the stricter cohesion of the group. But in general it must be said that the leading elements in groups, especially in the later course of human history, have rather been inclined to suppress the personal relation in favour of the purely collective element. Where this latter element reigns alone or is predominant, men feel themselves to be carried by the collectivity, which lifts them out of loneliness and fear of the world and lostness. When this happens—and for modern man it is an essential happening—the life between person and person seems to retreat more and more before the advance of the collective. The collective aims at holding in check the inclination to personal life. It is as though those who are bound together in groups should in the main be concerned only with the work of the group and should turn to the personal partners, who are tolerated by the group, only in secondary meetings.

The difference between the two realms became very palpable to me on one occasion when I had joined the procession through a large town of a movement to which I did not belong. I did it out of sympathy for the tragic development which I sensed was at hand in the destiny of a friend who was one of the leaders of the movement. While the procession was forming, I conversed with him and with another, a good-hearted "wild man," who also had the mark of death upon him. At that moment I still felt that the two men really were there, over against me, each of them a man near to me, near even in what was most remote from me; so different from me that my soul continually suffered from this difference, yet by virtue of this very difference confronting me with authentic being. Then the formations started off, and after a short time I was lifted out of all confrontation, drawn into the procession, falling in with its aimless step; and it was obviously the very same for the two with whom I had just exchanged human words. After a while we passed a café where I had been sitting the previous day with a musician whom I knew only slightly. The very moment we passed it the door opened, the musician stood on the threshold, saw me, apparently saw me alone, and waved to me. Straightway it seemed to me as though I were taken out of the procession and of the presence of my marching friends, and set there, confronting the musician. I forgot that I was walking along with the same step; I felt that I was standing over there by the man who had called out to me, and without a word, with a smile of understanding, was answering him. When consciousness of the facts returned to me, the procession, with my companions and myself at its head, had left the café behind.

The realm of the interhuman goes far beyond that of sympathy. Such simple happenings can be part of it as, for instance, when two strangers exchange glances in a crowded streetcar, at once to sink back again into the convenient state of wishing to know nothing about each other. But also every casual encounter between opponents belong to this realm, when it affects the opponent's attitude— that is, when something, however imperceptible, happens between the two, no matter whether it is marked at the time by any feeling or not. The only thing that matters is that for each of the two men the other happens as the particular other, that each becomes aware of the other and is thus related to him in such a way that he does not regard and use him as his object, but as his partner in a living event, even if it is no more than a boxing match. It is well known that some existentialists assert that the basic factor between men is that one is an object for the other. But so far as this is actually the case, the special reality of the interhuman, the fact of the contact, has been largely eliminated. It cannot indeed be entirely eliminated. As a crude example, take two men who are observing one another. The essential thing is not that the one makes the other his object, but the fact that he is not fully able to do so and the reason for his failure. We have in common with all existing things that we can be made objects of observation. But it is my privilege as man that by the hidden activity of my being I can establish an impassable barrier to objectification. Only in partnership can my being be perceived as an existing whole.

The sociologist may object to any separation of the social and the interhuman on the ground that society is actually built upon human relations, and the theory of these relations is therefore to be regarded as the very foundation of sociology. But here an ambiguity in the concept "relation" becomes evident. We speak, for instance, of a comradely relation between two men in their work, and do not merely mean what happens between them as comrades, but also a lasting disposition which is actualized in those happenings and which even includes purely psychological events such as the recollection of the absent comrade. But by the sphere of the interhuman I mean solely actual happenings between men, whether wholly mutual or tending to grow into mutual relations. For the participation of both partners is in principle indispensable. The sphere of the interhuman is one in which a person is confronted by the other. We call its unfolding the dialogical.

In accordance with this, it is basically erroneous to try to understand the interhuman phenomena as psychological. When two men converse together, the psychological is certainly an important part of the situation, as each listens and each prepares to speak. Yet this is only the hidden accompaniment to the conversation itself, the phonetic event fraught with meaning, whose meaning is to be found neither in one of the two partners nor in both together, but only in their dialogue itself, in this "between" which they live together.

Being and Seeming

The essential problem of the sphere of the interhuman is the duality of being and seeming. Although it is a familiar fact that men are often troubled about the impression they make on others, this has been much more discussed in moral philosophy than in anthropology. Yet this is one of the most important subjects for anthropological study.

We may distinguish between two different types of human existence. The one proceeds from what one really is, the other from what one wishes to seem. In general, the two are found mixed together. There have probably been few men who were entirely independent of the impression they made on others, while there has scarcely existed one who was exclusively determined by the impression made by him. We must be content to distinguish between men in whose essential attitude the one or the other predominates.

This distinction is most powerfully at work, as its nature indicates, in the interhuman realm—that is, in men's personal dealings with one another.

Take as the simplest and yet quite clear example the situation in which two persons look at one another—the first belonging to the first type, the second to the second. The one who lives from his being looks at the other just as one looks at someone with whom he has personal dealings. His look is "spontaneous," "without reserve"; of course he is not uninfluenced by the desire to make himself understood by the other, but he is uninfluenced by any thought of the idea of himself which he can or should awaken in the person whom he is looking at. His opposite is different. Since he is concerned with the image which his appearance, and especially his look or glance, produces in the other, he "makes" this look. With the help of the capacity, in greater or lesser degree peculiar to man, to make a definite element of his being appear in his look, he produces a look which is meant to have, and often enough does have, the effect of a spontaneous utterance—not only the utterance of a physical event supposed to be taking place at that very moment, but also, as it were, the reflection of a personal life of such-and-such a kind.

This must, however, be carefully distinguished from another area of seeming whose ontological legitimacy cannot be doubted. I mean the realm of "genuine seeming," where a lad, for instance, imitates his heroic model and while he is doing so is seized by the actuality of heroism, or a man plays the part of a destiny and conjures up authentic destiny. In this situation there is nothing false; the imitation is genuine imitation and the part played is genuine; the mask, too, is a mask and no deceit. But where the semblance originates from the lie and is permeated by it, the interhuman is threatened in its very existence. It is not that someone utters a lie, falsifies some account. The lie I mean does not take place in relation to particular facts, but in relation to existence itself, and it attacks interhuman existence as such. There are times when a man, to satisy some stale conceit, forfeits the great chance of a true happening between I and Thou.

Let us now imagine two men, whose life is dominated by appearance, sitting and talking together. Call them Peter and Paul. Let us list the different configurations which are involved. First, there is Peter as he wishes to appear to Paul, and Paul as he wishes to appear to Peter. Then there is Peter as he really appears to Paul, that is, Paul's image of Peter, which in general does not in the least coincide with what Peter wishes Paul to see; and similarly there is the reverse situation. Further, there is Peter as he appears to himself, and Paul as he appears to himself. Lastly, there are the bodily Peter and the bodily Paul. Two living beings and six ghostly appearances, which mingle in many ways in the conversation between the two. Where is there room for any genuine interhuman life?

Whatever the meaning of the word "truth" may be in other realms, in the interhuman realm it means that men communicate themselves to one another as what they are. It does not depend on one saying to the other everything that occurs to him, but only on his letting no seeming creep in between himself and the other. It does not depend on one letting himself go before another, but on his granting to the man to whom he communicates himself a share in his being. This is a question of the authenticity of the interhuman, and where this is not to be found, neither is the human element itself authentic.

Therefore, as we begin to recognize the crisis of man as the crisis of what is between man and man, we must free the concept of uprightness from the thin moralistic tones which cling to it, and let it take its tone from the concept of bodily uprightness. If a presupposition of human life in primeval times is given in man's walking upright, the fulfillment of human life can only come through the soul's walking upright, through the great uprightness which is not tempted by any seeming because it has conquered all semblance.

But, one may ask, what if a man by his nature makes his life subservient to the images which he produces in others? Can he, in such a case, still become a man living from his being, can he escape from his nature?

The widespread tendency to live from the recurrent impression one makes instead of from the steadiness of one's being is not a "nature." It originates, in fact, on the other side of interhuman life itself, in men's dependence upon one another. It is no light thing to be confirmed in one's being by others, and seeming deceptively offers itself as a help in this. To yield to seeming is man's essential cowardice, to resist it is his essential courage. But this is not an inexorable state of affairs which is as it is and must so remain. One can struggle to come to oneself—that is, to come to confidence in being. One struggles, now more successfully, now less, but never in vain, even when one thinks he is defeated. One must at times pay dearly for life lived from the being; but it is never too dear. Yet is there not bad being, do weeds not grow everywhere? I have never known a young person who seemed to me irretrievably bad. Later indeed it becomes more and more difficult to penetrate the increasingly tough layer which has settled down on a man's being. Thus there arises the false perspective of the seemingly fixed "nature" which cannot be overcome. It is false; the foreground is deceitful; man as man can be redeemed.

Again we see Peter and Paul before us surrounded by the ghosts of the semblances. A ghost can be exorcized. Let us imagine that these two find it more and more repellent to be represented by ghosts. In each of them the will is stirred and strengthened to be confirmed in their being as what they really are and nothing else. We see the forces of real life at work as they drive out the ghosts, till the semblance vanishes and the depths of personal life call to one another.

Personal Making Present

By far the greater part of what is today called conversation among men would be more properly and precisely described as speechifying. In general, people do not really speak to one another, but each, although turned to the other, really speaks to a fictitious court of appeal whose life consists of nothing but listening to him. Chekhov has given poetic expression to this state of affairs in *The Cherry Orchard*, where the only use the members of a family make of their being together is to talk past one another. But it is Sartre who has raised to a principle of existence what in Chekhov still appears as the deficiency of a person who is shut up in himself. Sartre regards the walls between the partners in a conversation as simply impassable. For him it is inevitable human destiny that a man has directly to do only with himself and his own affairs. The inner existence of the other is his own concern, not mine; there is no direct relation with the other, nor can there be. This is perhaps the clearest expression of the wretched fatalism of modern man, which regards degeneration as the unchangeable nature of *Homo sapiens* and the misfortune of having run into a blind alley as his primal fate, and which brands every thought of a breakthrough as reactionary romanticism. He who really knows how far our generation has lost the way of true freedom, of free giving between I and Thou, must himself, by virtue of the demand implicit in every great knowledge of this kind, practice directness—even if he were the only man on earth who did it—and not depart from it until scoffers are struck with fear and hear in his voice the voice of their own suppressed longing.

The chief presupposition for the rise of genuine dialogue is that each should regard his partner as the very one he is. I become aware of him, aware that he is different, essentially different from myself, in the definite, unique way which is peculiar to him, and I accept whom I thus see, so that in full earnestness I can direct what I say to him as the person he is. Perhaps from time to time I must offer strict opposition to his view about the subject of our conversation. But I accept this person, the personal bearer of a conviction, in his definite being out of which his conviction has grown—even though I must try to show, bit by bit, the wrongness of this very conviction. I affirm the person I struggle with: I struggle with him as his partner, I confirm him as creature and as creation, I confirm him who is opposed to me as him who is over against me. It is true that it now depends on the other whether genuine dialogue, mutuality in speech arises between us. But if I thus give to the other who confronts me his legitimate standing as a man with whom I am ready to enter into dialogue, then I may trust him and suppose him to be also ready to deal with me as his partner.

But what does it mean to be "aware" of a man in the exact sense in which I use the word? To be aware of a thing or a being means, in quite general terms, to experience it as a whole and yet at the same time without reduction or abstraction, in all its concreteness. But a man, although he exists as a living being among living beings and even as a thing among things, is nevertheless something categorically different from all things and all beings. A man cannot really be grasped except on the basis of the gift of the spirit which belongs to man alone among all things, the spirit as sharing decisively in the personal life of the living man, that is, the spirit which determines the person. To be aware of a man, therefore, means in particular to perceive his wholeness as a person determined by the spirit; it means to perceive the dynamic centre which stamps his every utterance, action, and attitude with the recognizable sign of uniqueness. Such an awareness is impossible, however, if and so long as the other is the separated object of my contemplation or even observation, for this wholeness and its centre do not let themselves be known to contemplation or observation. It is only possible when I step into an elemental relation with the other, that is, when he becomes present to me. Hence I designate awareness in this special sense as "personal making present."

The perception of one's fellow man as a whole, as a unity, and as unique—even if his wholeness, unity, and uniqueness are only partly developed, as is usually the case—is opposed in our time by almost everything that is commonly understood as specifically modern. In our time there predominates an analytical, reductive, and deriving look between man and man. This look is analytical, or rather pseudo analytical, since it treats the whole being as put together and therefore able to be taken apart—not only the so-called unconscious which is accessible to relative objectification, but also the psychic stream itself, which can never, in fact, be grasped as an object. This look is a reductive one because it tries to contract the manifold person, who is nourished by the microcosmic richness of the possible, to some schematically surveyable and recurrent structures. And this look is a deriving one because it supposes it can grasp what a man has become, or even is becoming, in genetic formulae, and it thinks that even the dynamic central principle of the individual in this becoming can be represented by a general concept. An effort is being made today radically to destroy the mystery between man and man. The personal life, the ever-near mystery, once the source of the stillest enthusiasms, is levelled down.

What I have just said is not an attack on the analytical method of the human sciences, a method which is indispensable wherever it furthers knowledge of a phenomenon without impairing the essentially different knowledge of its uniqueness that transcends the valid circle of the method. The science of man that makes use of the analytical method must accordingly always keep in view the boundary of such a contemplation, which stretches like a horizon around it. This duty makes the transportation of the method into life dubious; for it is excessively difficult to see where the boundary is in life.

If we want to do today's work and prepare tomorrow's with clear sight, then we must develop in ourselves and in the next generation a gift which lives in man's inwardness as a Cinderella, one day to be a princess. Some call it intuition, but that is not a wholly unambiguous concept. I prefer the name "imagining the real," for in its essential being this gift is not a looking at the other, but a bold swinging—

demanding the most intensive stirring of one's being—into the life of the other. This is the nature of all genuine imagining, only that here the realm of my action is not the all-possible, but the particular real person who confronts me, whom I can attempt to make present to myself just in this way, and not otherwise, in his wholeness, unity, and uniqueness, and with his dynamic centre which realizes all these things ever anew.

Let it be said again that all this can only take place in a living partnership, that is, when I stand in a common situation with the other and expose myself vitally to his share in the situation as really his share. It is true that my basic attitude can remain unanswered, and the dialogue can die in seed. But if mutuality stirs, then the interhuman blossoms into genuine dialogue.

Imposition and Unfolding

I have referred to two things which impede the growth of life between men: the invasion of seeming, and the inadequacy of perception. We are now faced with a third, plainer than the others, and in this critical hour more powerful and more dangerous than ever.

There are two basic ways of affecting men in their views and their attitude to life. In the first a man tries to impose himself, his opinion and his attitude, on the other in such a way that the latter feels the psychical result of the action to be his own insight, which has only been freed by the influence. In the second basic way of affecting others, a man wishes to find and to further in the soul of the other the disposition toward what he has recognized in himself as the right. Because it is the right, it must also be alive in the microcosm of the other, as one possibility. The other need only be opened out in this potentiality of his; moreover, this opening out takes place not essentially by teaching, but by meeting, by existential communication between someone that is in actual being and someone that is in a process of becoming. The first way has been most powerfully developed in the realm of propaganda, the second in that of education.

The propagandist I have in mind, who imposes himself, is not in the least concerned with the person whom he desires to influence, as a person; various individual qualities are of importance only in so far as he can exploit them to win the other and must get to know them for this purpose. In his indifference to everything personal the propagandist goes a substantial distance beyond the party for which he works. For the party, persons in their difference are of significance because each can be used according to his special qualities in a particular function. It is true that the personal is considered only in respect of the specific use to which it can be put, but within these limits it is recognized in practice. To propaganda as such, on the other hand, individual qualities are rather looked on as a burden, for propaganda is concerned simply with *more*—more members, more adherents, an increasing extent of support. Political methods, where they rule in an extreme form, as here, simply mean winning power over the other by depersonalizing him. This kind of propaganda enters upon different relations with force; it supplements it or replaces it, according to the need or the prospects, but it is in the last analysis nothing but sublimated violence, which has become imperceptible as such. It places men's souls under a pressure which allows the illusion of autonomy. Political methods at their height mean the effective abolition of the human factor.

The educator whom I have in mind lives in a world of individuals, a certain number of whom are always at any one time committed to his care. He sees each of these individuals as in a position to become a unique, single person, and thus the bearer of a special task of existence which can be fulfilled through him and through him alone. He sees every personal life as engaged in such a process of actualization, and he knows from his own experience that the forces making for actualization are all the time involved in a microcosmic struggle with counterforces. He has come to see himself as a helper of the actualizing forces. He knows these forces; they have shaped and they still shape him. Now he puts this person shaped by them at their disposal for a new struggle and a new work. He cannot wish to impose himself, for he believes in the effect of the actualizing forces, that is, he believes that in every man what is right is established in a single and uniquely personal way. No other way may be imposed on a man, but another way, that of the educator, may and must unfold what is right, as in this case it struggles for achievement, and help it to develop.

The propagandist, who imposes himself, does not really believe in his own cause, for he does not trust it to attain its effect of its own power without his special methods, whose symbols are the loudspeaker and the television advertisement. The educator who unfolds what is there believes in the primal power which has scattered itself, and still scatters itself, in all human beings in order that it may grow up in each man in the special form of that man. He is confident that this growth needs at each moment only that help which is given in meeting and that he is called to supply that help.

I have illustrated the character of the two basic attitudes and their relation to one another by means of two extremely antithetical examples. But wherever men have dealings with one another, one or the other attitude is to be found to be in more or less degree.

These two principles of imposing oneself on someone and helping someone to unfold should not be confused with concepts such as arrogance and humility. A man can be arrogant without wishing to impose himself on others, and it is not enough to be humble in order to help another unfold. Arrogance and humility are dispositions of the soul, psychological fact with a moral accent, while imposition and helping to unfold are events between men, anthropological facts which point to an ontology, the ontology of the interhuman.

In the moral realm Kant expressed the essential principle that one's fellow man must never be thought of and treated merely as a means, but always at the same time as an independent end. The principle is expressed as an "ought" which is sustained by the idea of human dignity. My point of view, which is near to Kant's in its essential features, has another source and goal. It is concerned with the presuppositions of the interhuman. Man exists anthropologically not in his isolation, but in the completeness of the relation between man and man; what humanity is can be properly grasped only in vital reciprocity. For the proper existence of the interhuman it is necessary, as I have shown, that the semblance does not intervene to spoil the relation of personal being to personal being. It is further necessary, as I have also shown, that each one means and makes present the other in his personal being. That neither should wish to impose himself on the other is the third basic presupposition of the interhuman. These presuppositions do not include the demand that one should influence the other in his unfolding; that is, however, an element that is suited to lead to a higher stage of the interhuman.

That there resides in every man the possibility of attaining authentic human existence in the special way peculiar to him can be grasped in the Aristotelian image of entelechy, innate self-realization; but one must note that it is an entelechy of the work of creation. It would be mistaken to speak here of individuation alone. Individuation is only the indispensable personal stamp of all realization of human existence. The self as such is not ultimately the essential, but the meaning of human existence given in creation again and again fulfills itself as self. The help that men give each other in becoming a self leads the life between men to its height. The dynamic glory of the being of man is first bodily present in the relation between two men each of whom in meaning the other also means the highest to which this person is called, and serves the self-realization of this human life as one true to creation without wishing to impose on the other anything of his own realization.

Genuine Dialogue

We must now summarize and clarify the marks of genuine dialogue.

In genuine dialogue the turning to the partner takes place in all truth, that is, it is a turning of the being. Every speaker "means" the partner of partners to whom he turns as this personal existence. To "mean" someone in this connection is at the same time to exercise that degree of making present which is possible to the speaker at that moment. The experiencing senses and the imagining of the real which completes the findings of the senses work together to make the other present as a whole and as a unique being, as the person that he is. But the speaker does not merely perceive the one who is present to him in this way; he receives him as his partner, and that means that he confirms this other being, so far as it is for him to confirm. The true turning of his person to the other includes this confirmation, this acceptance. Of course, such a confirmation does not mean approval; but no matter in what I am against the other, by accepting him as my partner in genuine dialogue I have affirmed him as a person.

Further, if genuine dialogue is to arise, everyone who takes part in it must bring himself into it. And that also means that he must be willing on each occasion to say what is really in his mind about the subject of the conversation. And that means further that on each occasion he makes the contribution of his spirit without reduction and without shifting his ground. Even men of great integrity are under the illusion that they are not bound to say everything "they have to say." But in the great faithfulness which is the climate of genuine dialogue, what I have to say at any one time already has in me the character of something that wishes to be uttered, and I must not keep it back, keep it in myself. It bears for me the unmistakable sign which indicates that it belongs to the common life of the word. Where the dialogical word genuinely exists, it must be given its right by keeping nothing back. To keep nothing back is the exact opposite of unreserved speech. Everything depends on the legitimacy of "what I have to say." And of course I must also be intent to raise into an inner word and then into a spoken word what I have to say at this moment but do not yet possess as speech. To speak is both nature and work, something that grows and something that is made, and where it appears dialogically, in the climate of great faithfulness, it has to fulfill ever anew the unity of the two.

Associated with this is that overcoming of semblance to which I have referred. In the atmosphere of genuine dialogue, he who is ruled by the thought of his own effect as the speaker of what he has to speak has a destructive effect. If, instead of what has to be said, I try to bring attention to my I, I have irrevocably miscarried what I had to say; it enters the dialogue as a failure and the dialogue is a failure. Because genuine dialogue is an ontological sphere which is constituted by the authenticity of being, every invasion of semblance must damage it.

But where the dialogue is fulfilled in its being, between partners who have turned to one another in truth, who express themselves without reserve and are free of the desire for semblance, there is brought into being a memorable common fruitfulness which is to be found nowhere else. At such times, at each such time, the word arises in a substantial way between men who have been seized in their depths and opened out by the dynamic of an elemental togetherness. The inter-human opens out what otherwise remains unopened.

This phenomenon is indeed well known in dialogue between two persons; but I have also sometimes experienced it in a dialogue in which several have taken part.

About Easter of 1914 there met a group consisting of representatives of sev-eral European nations for a three-day discussion that was intended to be prelimi-nary to further talks. We wanted to discuss together how the catastrophe, which we all believed was imminent, could be avoided. Without our having agreed before-hand on any sort of modalities for our talk, all the presuppositions of genuine dialogue were fulfilled. From the first hour immediacy reigned between all of us, some of whom had just got to know one another; everyone spoke with an unheard-of unreserve, and clearly not a single one of the participants was in bondage to semblance. In respect of its purpose the meeting must be described as a failure (though even now in my heart it is still not a certainty that it had to be a failure); the irony of the situation was that we arranged the final discussion for the middle of August, and in the course of events the group was soon broken up. Nevertheless, in the time that followed, not one of the participants doubted that he shared in a triumph of the interhuman.

One more point must be noted. Of course it is not necessary for all who are joined in a genuine dialogue actually to speak; those who keep silent can on occa-sion be especially important. But each must be determined not to withdraw when the course of the conversation makes it proper for him to say what he has to say. No one, of course, can know in advance what it is that he has to say; genuine dialogue cannot be arranged beforehand. It has indeed its basic order in itself from the beginning, but nothing can be determined, the course is of the spirit, and some discover what they have to say only when they catch the call of the spirit.

But it is also a matter of course that all the participants, without exception, must be of such nature that they are capable of satisfying the presuppositions of genuine dialogue and are ready to do so. The genuineness of the dialogue is called in question as soon as even a small number of those present are felt by themselves and by the others as not being expected to take any active part. Such a state of affairs can lead to very serious problems.

I had a friend whom I account one of the most considerable men of our age. He was a master of conversation, and he loved it: his genuineness as a speaker was evident. But once it happened that he was sitting with two friends and with the three wives, and a conversation arose in which by its nature the women were clearly not joining, although their presence in fact had a great influence. The conversation among the men soon developed into a duel between two of them (I was the third). The other "duelist," also a friend of mine, was of a noble nature; he too was a man of true conversation, but given more to objective fairness than to the play of the intellect, and a stranger to any controversy. The friend whom I have called a master of conversation did not speak with his usual composure and strength, but he scintillated, he fought, he triumphed. The dialogue was destroyed.

Review Questions

1. What distinction does Buber make between the "social" and the "interhuman"?
2. What feature of interpersonal contact does Buber say can characterize even "a boxing match"?
3. What does Buber mean when he says that "it is basically erroneous to try to understand the interhuman phenomena as psychological"?
4. Does Buber say that a person can practice "being" consistently, all the time? Explain.
5. Paraphrase the last sentence in the first paragraph under the heading, "Personal Making Present." What is Buber challenging his reader to do here?
6. Identify three possible things that a person who is "imposing" could impose on his or her conversational partner. In other words, what is (are) imposed when a person is "imposing"? What is "unfolded" when a person is "unfolding"?
7. What does Buber mean when he says that "To keep nothing back is the exact opposite of unreserved speech"?

Probes

1. What does it mean to you when Buber says that social contacts don't involve an *existential* relation, but that interhuman contacts do?
2. How is Buber's discussion of "being" and "seeming" similar to and different from Rogers's discussion of "congruence" (Chapter 15)?
3. For Buber, does "being" mean total honesty? Is "seeming" lying?
4. What circumstances make it difficult for you to "be"? How can you best help others to "be" instead of "seem"?
5. How do Buber's comments about the way we perceive others relate to the discussion of person perception in Chapter 6?
6. It sounds as if Buber is saying that science *cannot* be used to study human life. Is he saying that? Do you agree with him? Why or why not?
7. How is Buber's discussion of "imagining the real" related to what Bolton (Chapter 7) and Rogers (Chapter 15) say about empathy? How does it fit what Milt and I say about sculpting mutual meanings (Chapter 7)?
8. Which teacher that you've had has functioned most as an "imposer"? Which teacher has been most consistently an "unfolder"?
9. What does "personal making present" mean to you? What do you need to do in order to perceive someone that way?
10. Have you ever experienced a silent "dialogue" of the kind Buber mentions here? What happened?

Ideas are clean. They soar in the serene supernal. I can take them out and look at them, they fit in books, they lead me down that narrow way. And in the morning they are there. Ideas are straight—
But the world is round, and a
messy mortal is my friend.
Come walk with me in the mud. . . .

HUGH PRATHER

Index